Global Issues in Antitrust and Competition Law

Second Edition

Eleanor M. Fox

Walter J. Derenberg Professor of Trade Regulation
New York University School of Law

Daniel A. Crane

Frederick Paul Furth Sr. Professor of Law
University of Michigan Law School

GLOBAL ISSUES SERIES®

WEST
ACADEMIC
PUBLISHING

Global Issues Series is a trademark registered in the U.S. Patent and Trademark Office.

© 2010 Thomson Reuters
© 2017 LEG, Inc. d/b/a West Academic
    444 Cedar Street, Suite 700
    St. Paul, MN 55101
    1-877-888-1330

Printed in the United States of America

ISBN: 978-1-63460-526-7

Acknowledgments

The authors thank Hiroaki Matsunaga, Gabriel Orazi, Kurt Rajpal, Felipe Serrano Pinilla, Holden A. Steinhauer, Yusuke Takamiya and Michael Watts for excellent research assistance and Cheri Fidh, Brendan L. Heldenfels and Linda Smalls for excellent assistance in preparing the manuscript. The Filomen D'Agostino and Max E. Greenberg Foundation provided generous research support to Eleanor Fox.

Foreword to the First Edition

Eleanor Fox has frequently reminded us that while markets are global, antitrust laws—the rules that undergird effectively functioning markets—are national. She would be first to recognise that each of the key elements of this insight require a degree of qualification. In fact, surprisingly few markets are seamlessly global. And increasingly the practice of antitrust law is already in the process of becoming international, although it is certainly true that the instruments of antitrust enforcement and merger regulation are overwhelmingly national, notwithstanding their extraterritorial reach.

This monumental volume is focused on the critical interplay between the national and the global elements of antitrust. It does so through the medium of national jurisprudence, through the reproduction of key speeches, through an analysis of commissions and treaties and the efforts of antitrust enforcers to align their practice, or, at the very least, to understand the bases of divergent national practices.

Few are better qualified to undertake this task than the two authors. Eleanor Fox is the scholar most closely associated with describing, understanding and analysing international antitrust, as evidenced by her truly massive output in this area alone, and by no means her only area of contribution to antitrust scholarship. But even more than her scholarship, for those of us whose work in antitrust started at its geographical margins—that is to say, beyond the borders of the United States and the European Union—Eleanor is distinguished by her empathy with and her deep interest in these efforts. She has been a voice of the new antitrust authorities and as they have grown in stature and importance, so has she expanded her already vast horizons by incorporating the work of these new agencies into the corpus of international antitrust law and practice. The range of experiences drawn upon to produce this volume is testament not only to the centrality of the international markets/national antitrust insight, but to Eleanor's intellectual curiosity and willingness to embrace the experiences and insights of those who are not used to making an appearance in the scholarly antitrust tomes emanating from the US and Europe.

My introduction to Daniel Crane's work comes by way of his seminal historical accounts of the ups and downs, the ebbs and flows, of US antitrust. Just as I would insist that economic historians, rather than plain and simple economists, are best placed to understand contemporary economic phenomenon and even predict their future paths, so are legal historians best placed to understand the place to which decades of antitrust law has evolved and where it is likely to go. Historians are, per definition, sensitive to the often determinative force and power of context—politics, economics, stages of development, state-business relations, even wars all, as Daniel's work reminds us, influence the character and course of antitrust. This is the canvas of history and Daniel's regard for history permeates this volume.

We are at an important cusp in the development of international antitrust. Effective public international institutions are working precisely in those interstices between global markets and national antitrust that are the concern of this volume. The International Competition Network has brought together the vast majority of the world's national antitrust authorities. The ICN has developed best practices, not only in antitrust rules and approaches, but also in the building of effective antitrust authorities. And at least, as important, it has, largely through the active participation of precisely those of its members who used to be on the antitrust margins, that the ICN is beginning to appreciate "informed divergence", essentially an appreciation of why historical and other contexts may necessitate divergence rather than convergence. The OECD continues to produce applied scholarship of high quality and to embrace participation from way beyond its membership. UNCTAD continues to support those antitrust authorities from nations whose resource endowment and history most constrains their ability to develop into effective members of the international community of national antitrust authorities. And if the WTO is the avowed and self-proclaimed agent of a globalised world, for how long can antitrust remain on the periphery of its agenda.

Forewords traditionally extol the timeliness of the volumes that they are introducing. This volume is a majestic survey of an issue whose time has truly come. It will not only be a building block in the enterprise of aligning global markets and national antitrust, it is a veritable world tour of the rules and practices that already propel that world further and map out its future direction.

In their introduction to the volume the authors note that this volume on global antitrust issues may be used "to supplement domestic antitrust casebooks". They then immediately identify the oddity implicit in treating a volume on global antitrust as a supplement to national antitrust scholarship precisely because markets—the very stuff of antitrust—are global. As markets become ever more global—and even that inexorable development will experience ebbs and flows—so will this volume come to occupy a central place on the bookshelves of antitrust scholars and in the reading lists of their students.

DAVID LEWIS
GORDON INSTITUTE OF BUSINESS SCIENCE
JOHANNESBURG, SOUTH AFRICA
IMMEDIATE PAST CHAIRPERSON, SOUTH AFRICA COMPETITION TRIBUNAL

March 2010

Summary of Contents

Table of Contents

Table of Cases

The principal cases are in bold type.

Global Issues in Antitrust and Competition Law

Second Edition

INTRODUCTION

This volume is a global reader. It is the second edition of materials and cases on the global issues of antitrust and competition policy. It may be used on its own or to supplement domestic antitrust casebooks.

It might seem strange to consider the treatment of global issues as a *supplement* to antitrust casebooks, for, in an important sense, antitrust *is* global. Markets commonly cross national boundaries. Mergers are as likely as not to combine firms from different nations and in any event to affect markets in many nations. Acts and conspiracies in New York, Washington, Tokyo, Zurich, Frankfurt, Johannesburg, Beijing, Delhi, or Sao Paulo may affect people around the world. Nonetheless, the great body of antitrust law is national. Two mature—although always changing—bodies of antitrust law, European and American, are the most visible models. Other jurisdictions, including developing countries, lend their own voices. Most antitrust casebooks are devoted to national law. This volume puts the global dimension at center stage.

More than 130 jurisdictions have antitrust (or competition) laws. Most of these were enacted after the Berlin Wall fell in late 1989. The antitrust nations span the world, from US, Canada and Mexico to Brazil, Argentina and Chile; the EU and the nations of Europe; to most nations in Africa, Asia and the Middle East, Australia, and New Zealand. Recent entries into the family of antitrust prominently include China and India, and it is sometimes said that the newer entrants may eventually shift the balance of influence in antitrust.

Global issues are themselves diverse. They include:

1. Analysis: How to think about analysis of any conduct or transaction that has transnational dimensions. For example, how to define the market; what foreign production to include within it; how to analyze effects of conduct or transactions in view of foreign competition or potential competition; whether non-competition criteria are admissible and possibly influential

2. Jurisdiction and reach of the law: What principles define the reach of the law to control conduct or transactions that take place abroad or whose direct effects are abroad?

3. Coherence: In view of international markets, international transactions, and international effects, what have antitrust

1

authorities done to coordinate their efforts and minimize conflicts? What institutions have been developed to consider international problems? Is there a need for greater coherence, and should it be orchestrated at a higher level; for example, through an international competition law or framework?

4.   Globalization, antitrust and trade: Globalization has shrunk the world. Freer trade, combined with Internet and other communication technologies, has made distant markets quicker and easier to access. It has increased opportunities for firms to find low-cost sources of labor and supply, and has increased opportunities for firms to find markets. It has made firms more mobile. Globalization has revealed the strong links between trade and competition. Historically, state restraints have been the domain of trade law and private or business restraints have been the domain of antitrust law. Are the lines blurring? If foreign markets are closed to imports, are they closed by state or private restraints? by private acts supported by state restraints, or vice versa? Do we need coherence between rules of trade and rules of competition? Should we have a global trade-and-competition regime?

5.   Comparative antitrust: For US and EU, it is now generally accepted that antitrust/competition law should be designed and enforced to remove impediments and help make markets work, for the benefit of consumers and the efficient and potentially efficient and innovative firms that are trying to serve them. There is room also to protect suppliers from boycotts and exploitation (e.g., buying cartels); but there is no room in US or EU antitrust law to promote nationalism and to sanction protectionist industrial policies at the expense of consumers. The non-protectionist, non-discriminatory* stance of US and EU competition laws helps to undergird the effective functioning of world markets and as well to link the hundred-plus national and regional antitrust regimes. But not all antitrust jurisdictions are committed to this view of antitrust. Moreover, jurisdictions may disagree on key perspectives and modes, such as to how best to realize or preserve efficiency. In addition, differences in degrees of economic development and differences in economic and political environment and institutions can result in different rules, standards, or emphases. This global reader will engage with these issues and give comparative examples.

The plan of this book is as follows. In order to track, more or less, traditional antitrust casebooks, we organize our discussion under the usual topics of antitrust: cartels, monopoly and abuse of dominance,

---

*   Non-discrimination means no discrimination based on nationality.

agreements other than cartels—horizontal and vertical, and mergers. We then treat the critical subject of restraints by the state— an area in which antitrust regimes are increasingly active. Finally, we cover enforcement systems, jurisdictional issues, and the ultimate over-arching issue, global governance.

Logistical details of the book

We want to introduce you to a few conventions of the book.

In the case edits, deletions of paragraphs are shown by three asterisks. Deletions of words less than a full paragraph are shown by three dots. We have omitted many case citations, internal references to recitals, paragraph numbers, and footnotes without designating an omission. Brackets at the beginning and sometimes within the text of cases indicates the editors' summary.

ELEANOR M. FOX
DANIEL A. CRANE

New York and Michigan
June 2017

Chapter 1

CARTELS

___

A. INTRODUCTION

Cartels are a logical starting point for this global reader, for five reasons. First, while 50 years ago there was basic divergence in attitudes towards cartels as a form of business activity, today there is enormous agreement around the world; cartels are bad; they undermine the market. Second, even so, there is constant pressure to allow some exceptions from the rules against cartels. Export cartels are largely exempted or not covered, usually on grounds that the nation's jurisdiction does not extend so far. Crisis cartels are a different matter. Arguments are made for crisis cartel exemptions, especially in times of financial crisis. This is a subject on which nations disagree; thus, a fruitful basis to explore comparative treatment. Third, a large percentage of contemporary cartels are international; as a result cartels have become a laboratory for enforcement cooperation among national competition authorities as well as for sharing methodologies for detection and punishment. Fourth, since many cartel conspiracies take place off the shores of victim nations, cartels have become the main subject for development of the principles of extraterritorial jurisdiction. Fifth, given the shared condemnation of cartels, the high degree of harm they inflict, and the frequency with which they occur, cartels have become the centerpiece for considering a world competition law regime, possibly in the World Trade Organization. Although such a development is not currently foreseeable, the study of an international competition law necessarily includes contours of a world framework.

Indeed, enforcement against world cartels continues to occupy the spotlight of antitrust. World fines in 2016 increased by 20% over the previous year and totaled $6.7 billion. More countries ordered behavioral restrictions, such as bans on cartel leaders' future board memberships, as imposed in the UK, Australia, and Sweden. In 2016, the European Commission imposed Europe's highest-ever cartel fine—2.93 billion euros—on five truck makers who had, by agreement, passed on the costs of environmental compliance to their customers. In 2016 and 2017, the European Commission imposed large fines in the financial services industry attributable to rigging the LIBOR (London interbank) exchange rate.

In 2016 the EU posted record fines of US $4.1 billion. The United States had an unusually low figure of $386.8 million. Mexico imposed $11 million in fines, including actions against sugar producers, automotive air condition compressors, and ferry operators. Brazil is in the throes of the Petrobas corruption scandal, which involved numerous bid-rigging cartels that are being prosecuted under the rubric Operation Car Wash by Brazil's CADE. Chile and other nations raised permissible fine levels for cartel activity.

In Asia, Korea is monitoring cartel-related activity in intermediary goods, commodities, and public sectors. In 2016, Korea's fines increased 550% over 2015, and in this year Korea imposed the largest fines of any Asia-Pacific enforcer—$764.81 million. Japan imposed $84 million in fines in 2016, more than double the amount from 2015, including $60 million in fines for a price-fixing violation in the capacitors industry. Japan also assessed fines against communications equipment and construction firms for bid-rigging violations. Elsewhere in the world, South Africa levied the largest cartel fine in the history of the South Africa Competition Commission, which was against a steel manufacturer. Australia imposed $39 million in fines in 2016, the largest of which was against a cement firm. Also in 2016, the Australian Competition and Consumer Commission brought its first two criminal cartel cases.

B. LAW AND ATTITUDE TOWARDS CARTELS

Hard core cartels—agreements of competitors to lessen the competition among them—are generally illegal on their face or presumptively illegal under national law, except when they are subject to a specific exemption. In the United States, cartels are illegal per se under Section 1 of the Sherman Act. No justification is allowed, as you will have seen, for example, in *Socony Vacuum*, 310 U.S. 150 (1940).

In the European Union, agreements are treated under the competition law as set forth in the Treaty on the Functioning of the European Union ("TFEU"), Article 101. This revised version of the Treaty of Rome establishing the European Communities ("Treaty of Rome" or "EC Treaty") became effective December 1, 2009. Article 101 TFEU (formerly Article 81 EC Treaty) prohibits agreements "which have as their object or effect the prevention, restriction or distortion of competition within the common market." It singles out in particular agreements that (among other things) fix buying or selling prices or other trading conditions, limit production, or share markets. As to any particular agreement that prevents, restricts or distorts competition, the prohibition of Article 101 may be declared inapplicable if the agreement improves production, distribution or technical or economic progress, allows a fair share of the benefits to consumers, contains no unnecessary restrictions on competition, and does not create the possibility of eliminating competition in a substantial part of the market. See the text of Article 101 in Appendix 1. Under the case law interpreting Article 101, cartels by definition have as their object distortion of competition.

In 1980 the United Nations Conference on Trade and Development (UNCTAD), which caters particularly to developing nations, promulgated a set of principles and rules for the control of restrictive business practices. These principles were adopted as a voluntary code by members of the United Nations. The UNCTAD Set states, in Part D (see Chapter 9), that enterprises "should refrain from practices such as the following" when they unduly restrain competition and harm international trade, particularly harming economic development of developing countries:

"(a) Agreements fixing prices, including as to exports and imports;

(b) Collusive tendering;

(c) Market or customer allocation agreements;

(d) Allocation by quota as to sales and production . . . ."

UNCTAD has also published a model law on competition, and a commentary on the Model Law. The commentary describes the above quoted section as a "prohibition in principle." This means that, in general, for cartel agreements, purpose and effect need not be shown.

Some countries do not have a per se or presumptive approach to cartels. Cartel agreements may be illegal only if it is shown that, for example, they restrict or substantially restrict competition. The competition law of Chile, Decree Law No. 211/1973 as amended, forbids agreements attempting to restrain free competition. Article 1. The Chilean law has been interpreted to require proof of market power. In Brazil, Law No. 8884/94, Article 21, prohibits agreements for fixing prices or sales conditions. In the opinion of officials of CADE—the Administrative Council for Economic Defense—the offense requires that the cartel cause or may cause harm to the market. Similarly, Japan does not recognize the existence of "per se" antitrust offenses; hence greater proof may be necessary to hold a cartel illegal than would be required in jurisdictions with a categorical approach to cartel illegality.

The generally accepted rule against cartels is embedded in the 1998 Recommendation of the Organization for Economic Cooperation and Development ("OECD") Against Hard Core Cartels, which we examine further in Chapter 9, Global Governance.

Although many jurisdictions have had laws prohibiting cartel activity on their books for some time, many of these jurisdictions have only begun to impose serious fines on cartels relatively recently. A recent study by Professor John Connor, a leading authority on anti-cartel enforcement, identifies the following dates for the first major cartel fine in the following significant jurisdictions: India (1996), Mexico (1998), Australia (1998), South Korea (1999), Japan (1999), Taiwan (2000), Israel (2003), Kazakhstan (2005), Argentina (2005), New Zealand (2006), Brazil (2007), Colombia (2007), Indonesia (2007), Egypt (2008), Pakistan (2008), Russia (2008), Saudi Arabia (2010), Vietnam (2010), Nigeria (2012), Turkey (2012), Singapore (2013), China (2014). Vigorous anti-cartel enforcement remains in its early stages in much of the world.

Several questions recur, across jurisdictions. First, proof of agreement: Has the plaintiff presented sufficient evidence to allow the fact finder to infer that the defendants agreed with one another? Second, characterization: Is this agreement a cartel, or is it a joint venture or other presumptively efficient agreement? Third, effects: Is it necessary that the plaintiff prove the agreement's effect in harming competition? Fourth, public interest: Is crisis a defense (are crisis cartels permitted)? Is there any other "public interest" justification? Fifth, state blessing: When is encouragement by the state, act of state, foreign sovereign compulsion, or political question a defense? Does comity ever require or justify deference to a home jurisdiction's permissive law?

We present two European cases on proof of agreement, *Quinine* and *Wood pulp*. Students of US antitrust law can compare these cases with *Interstate Circuit* (306 U.S. 208, 1939) and *Matsushita* (475 U.S. 574, 1986). For characterization, we refer you to *Appalachian Coals* (288 U.S. 344, 1933)—the American depression era case that looks very much like a cartel but was characterized as a joint sales arrangement. Regarding need to prove effect, we refer back to *Quinine*, and also note the US case of *Nippon*, an offshore cartel. Next, we look at justifications and defenses, including public interests—an inquiry that takes us to a recent European case involving the financially-troubled Irish beef industry. Then we turn to the state and the significance of its support for and involvement in cartels. We include an excerpt from the US international enforcement guidelines, an opinion dismissing a suit against four Chinese vitamin cartelists in which the Chinese government argued that the cartel was ordered by the government, and court opinions on legality under US law of the OPEC oil cartel. Finally, the materials note the high degree of cooperation among antitrust authorities. We leave the details about cooperation and the debate about a possible world regime for the last chapter.

C. PROOF OF A CARTEL AGREEMENT

Many cartel cases are lost for lack of proof admissible in court or attainable at trial. This is especially so when the case is prosecuted criminally, as the United States does in the case of hard core cartels. Famously, the United States lost its case against General Electric/De Beers for an industrial diamond cartel for failure to procure a key witness and obtain evidence from abroad. See Anne K. Bingman, U.S. International Antitrust Enforcement: The Past Three Years and the Future, Chap. 2 in 1996 Fordham Corporate Law Institute, INTERNATIONAL ANTITRUST LAW & POLICY (B. Hawk ed. 1977).

Since the United States and then many other nations adopted leniency policies to induce cartel members to defect and to be the first to reveal all details (see speech of Scott Hammond below), enforcement against cartels has reached new heights. The authorities now typically receive much valuable direct evidence of particular cartels. The process usually results in guilty pleas, imprisonments, and settlements. But direct evidence is not always available. A cartel might be proved, also, by circumstantial evidence; but circumstantial evidence might not satisfy the fact-finder, especially for criminal conviction.

At the time of the adoption of the Treaty of Rome establishing the European Economic Community (EC Treaty) in 1957, there were high trade barriers isolating each of the European countries. Predictably, monopolies and oligopolies developed within each. A major motivation of the EC Treaty was to break down the border barriers and to integrate Europe—in order to anchor peace in Europe. Thus, the Treaty required its Member States (six at the start) to remove their trade barriers in the internal market. As soon as the Member States complied, firms that had been insulated began to feel competitive pressures from across the borders. They co-opted the competition by entering cross-border agreements. The agreements typically divided markets along country lines, re-cementing the old, insular patterns of trade. Europe did not then have a culture against cartels, but it had a mission of market integration for a higher value—peace. The European Commission detected and enjoined a large number of cartels—including sugar, cement, dyestuffs, and quinine. The quinine cartel may be the earliest example of trans-Atlantic agency cooperation in prosecuting a cross-border cartel, as you will read below.

Consider, as you read the *Quinine* case, what tools the firms used to form a cartel, to make it work, and to make it stable. What characteristics about the market and its structure made it more or less likely for a quinine cartel to work? Consider also: What evidence was the give-away that the cartel continued to operate after 1962, when the European competition enforcement system went into effect and the firms insisted to the Competition Directorate that they had called their cartel to an end.

We include the *Quinine* case to reflect on the questions above and to introduce case law on: What evidence is sufficient to prove "agreement" or "understanding"? Since the time of *Quinine*, courts in general have become more rigorous in requiring evidence that defendants' parallel actions were conspiratorial rather than independent. We follow *Quinine* with the European *Wood Pulp* case and notes on the U.S. *Twombly* case, both examining sufficiency of proof of agreement by circumstantial evidence.

Quinine

ACF CHEMIEFARMA v. COMMISSION (QUININE)
Case 41/69, EU:C:1970:71 (European Court of Justice 1970)

[Nedchem and five other Dutch firms, and Boehringer and Buchler, both German firms, produced quinine and quinidine, ingredients used to manufacture drugs to treat malaria and heart disease. In 1958 they entered into a series of agreements to reserve their home markets for themselves and to fix prices and quotas for exports to all other countries. After the German Federal Cartel Office discovered the cartel, Nedchem and Boehringer concluded a new agreement that excluded deliveries within the EU from the arrangement. In March 1960 Nedchem, the two German firms, and French and British producers of quinine and quinidine concluded a new export cartel agreement. The new agreement excluded sales into EU Member States, set quotas for exports to non-member nations, and reserved certain markets outside of the common market for specified cartel members. It also provided for equalization of quantities to be sold by members if quotas were exceeded or not reached and provided that no cartel member could cooperate in the production or sale of quinine or quinidine outside of the common market with firms not participating in the agreement. Each party agreed to supply the others with information about where, to whom, and how much they sold, on the basis of which Nedchem would equalize the quantities to be sold by each.

In April 1960, two gentlemen's agreements were drawn up among the parties—though never signed—which extended the provisions of the export agreements to sales within the common market and reserved home markets. The French parties agreed not to manufacture synthetic quinidine, and all parties agreed that noncompliance with the gentlemen's agreement would terminate the written export agreement and vice versa. The agreements were supplemented by a pool agreement for bark to make quinine. The parties would jointly purchase this critical raw material through Nedchem. Nedchem would buy stockpile surpluses of bark from the United States' General Services Administration, allocate the bark among the cartel members, and receive a two percent commission from the members.

In 1962, Regulation 17 went into effect, giving the Commission the powers necessary to enforce Article [101].* Also in 1962, a dispute arose regarding the bark pool, and the parties claimed that they abandoned their gentlemen's agreement shortly thereafter.

In 1963–64 the United States, needing quinine to save the lives of sick American soldiers in Viet Nam, became suspicious of the existence of an international quinine cartel as a result of Nedchem's purchases of large quantities of the United States bark stockpile. The Department of Justice conducted extensive investigations (eventually resulting in civil and criminal cases under the US Sherman Act), and in 1967 it shared information with the EC Commission. See 1 W. Fugate, Foreign Commerce and the Antitrust Laws § 4.2 (5th ed. 1996). The Commission and national authorities began investigations into whether and to what extent the gentlemen's agreements were being applied in the common market

---

*   Editors' note: We use the current Treaty number. The Article was then numbered 85, and later 81.

after 1962. The Commission found that violations continued until February 1965, and imposed fines.]

115 The defendant bases its view that the gentlemen's agreement was continued until February 1965 on documents and declarations emanating from the parties to the agreement the tenor of which is indistinct and indeed contradictory so that it is impossible to conclude whether those undertakings intended to terminate the gentlemen's agreement at their meeting on 29 October 1962.

116 The conduct of the undertakings in the Common Market after 29 October 1962 must therefore be considered in relation to the following four points: sharing out of domestic markets, fixing of common prices, determination of sales quotas and prohibition against manufacturing synthetic quinidine.

Protection of the Producers' Domestic Markets

117 The gentlemen's agreement guaranteed protection of each domestic market for the producers in the various Member States.

118 After October 1962 when significant supplies were delivered on one of those markets by producers who were not nationals, as for example in the case of sales of quinine and quinidine in France, there was a substantial alignment of prices conforming to French domestic prices which were higher than the export prices to third countries.

119 It does not appear that there were alterations in the insignificant volume of trade between the other Member States referred to by the clause relating to domestic protection in spite of considerable differences in the prices prevailing in each of those States.

120 The divergences between the domestic legislation of those States cannot by itself explain those differences in price or the substantial absence of trade.

121 Obstacles which might arise in the trade in quinine and quinidine from differences between national legislation governing pharmaceutical products under trademark cannot relevantly be invoked to explain those facts.

122 The correspondence exchanged in October and November 1963 between the parties to the export agreement with regard to the protection of domestic markets merely confirmed the intention of those undertakings to allow this state of affairs to remain unchanged.

[123] This intention was subsequently confirmed by Nedchem during the meeting of the undertakings concerned in Brussels on 14 March 1964.

[124] From those circumstances it is clear that with regard to the restriction on competition arising from the protection of the producers' domestic markets the producers continued after the meeting on 29 October 1962 to abide by the gentlemen's agreement of 1960 and confirmed their common intention to do so.

[125] The applicant maintains that owing in particular to the shortage of raw materials the sharing out of domestic markets, as emerges from the exchange of letters of October and November 1963, had no effect on competition in the Common Market.

[126] Despite the scarcity of raw materials and an increase in the demand for the products in question, as the contested decision finds, a serious threat of shortage nevertheless emerged only in 1964 as a result of the interruption of Nedchem's supplies from the American General Service Administration.

[127] On the other hand such a situation cannot render lawful an agreement the object of which is to restrict competition in the Common Market and which affects trade between the Member States.

[128] The sharing out of domestic markets has as its object the restriction of competition and trade within the Common Market.

[129] The fact that, if there were a threatened shortage of raw materials, such an agreement might in practice have had less influence on competition and on international trade than in a normal period in no way alters the fact that the parties did not terminate their activities.

[130] Furthermore the applicant has furnished no conclusive evidence capable of proving that it had ceased to act in accordance with the agreement before the date of expiry of the export agreement.

[131] Consequently, the submissions concerning that part of the decision relating to the continuation of the agreement on the protection of the producers' domestic markets until the beginning of February 1965 are unfounded.

Joint Fixing of Sales Prices

[132] With regard to the joint fixing of sales prices for the markets which were not shared out, that is to say, the Belgo-Luxembourg

Economic Union and Italy, the gentlemen's agreement provided for the application to such sales of the current prices for exports to third countries fixed by mutual agreement, in accordance with the export agreement. * * *

[134] If, as the defendant maintains, the parties to the export agreement continued until February 1965 to apply their current export prices to supplies to the above-mentioned Member States, it would follow that they continued to abide by that part of the gentlemen's agreement relating to the joint fixing of sales prices.

[135] With regard to the period from November 1962 to April 1964, the figures supplied by the defendant show a substantial and constant identity between the current prices fixed for export within the framework of the agreement and the prices maintained by the undertakings concerned, including the applicant, for their sales in unprotected domestic markets in the Community.

[136] Where such prices deviate from the scale of export prices they do so in terms of rebates or increases corresponding generally to those agreed on under the gentlemen's agreement.

[137] The applicant had supplied no evidence capable of proving that this argument is unfounded.

[138] Moreover the increase in prices of 15%, which was jointly decided upon on 12 March 1964 under the export agreement which led Nedchem to withdraw its opposition, was uniformly applied—although that undertaking would have preferred to continue to fix lower prices—with regard to supplies to Italy, Belgium and Luxembourg also.

[139] These circumstances show that with regard to sales prices the parties to the export agreement continued after October 1962 to act in the Common Market as if the gentlemen's agreement of 1960 were still in force. * * *

[141] It is clear from the oral procedure, taking into account the information supplied by the parties, that during 1964 and in particular from May onwards, a party to the agreement applied prices which in an increasing number of cases deviated from the current export prices, and that the defendant has been unable to give a convincing explanation as to how this might be reconciled with the continuation in force of the agreement in question.

[142] The failure to communicate to the undertakings concerned the results of the investigations carried out in Italy and Belgium, which

excluded any possibility of clarification and discussion at the stage of the administrative procedure, may have contributed to leaving unexplained facts which ought to have been clarified.

[143] In these circumstances proof has not been sufficiently established in law that the applicant by mutual agreement with the other producers maintained uniform prices for its sales in the Belgo-Luxembourg Economic Union and Italy after May 1964.

[144] Consequently the period from May 1964 to February 1965 must be omitted from the infringement. * * *

Restrictions on the Manufacture of Synthetic Quinidine

[154] The gentlemen's agreement prohibited the group of French undertakings from manufacturing synthetic quinidine. * * *

[156] The fact relied upon that, when the gentlemen's agreement was concluded, the French undertakings were not in a position to manufacture synthetic quinidine does not render lawful such a restriction which entirely precluded them from taking up this activity.

[157] That the French undertakings should accede to this restriction of their freedom of action is explicable in terms of their interest—owing to the particularly high prices which they maintained for their products in France—in preserving the territorial protection which they enjoyed on their domestic market.

[158] Taking into account the connexion thus existing between those two restrictions on competition, it may reasonably be concluded that the prohibition on production lasted as long as the territorial protection. * * *

[160] Although it is possible that, owing to the scarcity of raw materials which [w]as established by the contested decision (No 29, last paragraph), in its ultimate period protection of the domestic markets did not have important effects on competition and trade between Member States, this cartel nevertheless lasted until February 1965.

[161] In the absence of any indication to the contrary and having regard to the above-mentioned connexions between the two aspects of the cartel, it must be considered that the agreement restricting the French undertakings' freedom to manufacture was of the same duration.

[162] Consequently the applicant's complaints in this respect are unfounded.

General Appraisal of the Agreement Within the Common Market

163 It is clear from the foregoing that the applicant participated with other producers of quinine and quinidine in an agreement prohibited by Article [101] of the [TFEU].

164 This agreement continued in most of its forms even after the meeting on 29 October 1962.

165 Serious doubts as to the continuation of the agreement after 1962 exist only with regard to the application of sales quotas.

166 Nevertheless, the fact that the undertakings did not continue to apply the system of quotas does not seem perceptibly to have improved the conditions of competition, since they continued jointly to fix prices, to apply uniformly to their deliveries in the Common Market joint price increases arranged in March and October 1964 and decided within the framework of the export agreement and finally to maintain protection of their respective domestic markets and the prohibition on the French undertakings' production of synthetic quinidine.

167 However, the application of uniform prices for deliveries to Italy, Belgium and Luxembourg has only been proved to exist up to April 1964.

* * *

Notes and Questions

1.   In *Quinine*, consider the evidence (esp. paras. 118–124)—which was only circumstantial—from which the Court concluded that the gentlemen's agreements continued after 1962. Did the facts raise an inference that the agreements continued in force? How strong was the alternative inference that, after 1962, the parties had no agreement with respect to sales in the Community; that each one simply chose to follow past patterns of behavior and hoped that its export partners would do so too? Does the latter scenario constitute concerted action under *Quinine*? By implication, under *Twombly*? See Bell Atlantic Corp. v. Twombly, 550 U.S. 544 (2007) (interdependence is not concert).

2.   Note how the quinine export cartel tended to facilitate a domestic (European) cartel. Note also how the parties used various devices that helped to make the cartel work. For example, by pooling raw material purchases in the early years of the agreement and by designating one of their members—Nedchem—to be their purchasing agent and to allocate the raw material in accordance with assigned quotas, the firms could police their own cartel agreement and be sure

that no one cheated by producing too much. Likewise, as a result of sharing extensive information with one another, cheating would become obvious, and cheating was explicitly punishable by expulsion from both cartels. Finally, the agreement not to produce synthetic quinine by the French, who were selling at a particularly high price in France, tended to keep off the market a substitute product that could have undermined the cartel by driving down the cartel price.

3.   Why was the quinine export agreement as such of no interest to the Court? What is the scope of EU law with respect to export cartels selling to destinations outside of the Community? Consult the language of the Treaty on the Functioning of the European Union, Article 101. US antitrust law also excludes from its scope export cartels that hurt foreigners only. See Chapter 8 *infra*.

Wood Pulp

United States, Canadian, Finnish, Swedish and Norwegian firms shipped wood pulp to the European Community. The Commission alleged and found that the US, Canadian and Finnish firms agreed on prices, and it imposed large fines. The companies sought annulment of the Commission decision before the Court of Justice. They asserted lack of jurisdiction by reason of extraterritoriality. Also, they claimed that there was not sufficient evidence from which the Commission could find concert of action. Below are excerpts from the case on proof of agreement. Before this aspect of the case came before the Court of Justice, the Court held that the alleged cartel, while not illegal under US law because it was an export cartel filed under the Webb-Pomerene Act,[1] was properly subject to EU law. We deal with the jurisdictional aspects in Chapter 8.

---

[1]   The Webb-Pomerene Act provides that nothing in the Sherman Act shall be construed as declaring export associations illegal, as long as they do not enhance or depress prices in the United States or restrain the export trade of a domestic competitor, and as long as they are filed with the Federal Trade Commission. 15 US Code § 61–66.

Moreover, export agreements that do not harm US commerce are jurisdictionally beyond reach of the Sherman Act, as codified in the Foreign Trade Antitrust Improvement Act of 1982. See Chapter 8. Finally, for yet further protection from application of US antitrust law, exporters can get an "export trade certificate of review" under the Export Trading Company Act of 1982. For the text of all three statutes, see Appendix 3.

Å. ÅHLŠTRÖM OSAKEYHTIÖ v. COMMISSION
(*WOOD PULP*)
(proof of agreement)
Cases C–89, 104, 114, 116–117, 125–129/85,
EU:C:1993:120 (European Court of Justice 1993)

[The Commission brought proceedings against 40 wood pulp producers from the United States, Canada and Finland and three of their trade associations for concerting on price announcements and on price. The producers made quarterly price announcements sometimes simultaneously and sometimes nearly so. Prices were almost always quoted in dollars, a practice that both increased the transparency of the producers' intentions to one another and assured that shifts in exchange rates in the various Member States would have no impact. Prices and price changes tended to be uniform. The Commission determined that the pulp producers had engaged in concerted conduct in violation of Article [101].

The Court annulled most of the Commission's decision.]

55 The Finnish, US and Canadian applicants have sought the annulment of art. 1(1) of the decision, according to which they, and other Swedish, US and Norwegian producers, concerted "on prices for bleached sulphate wood pulp announced for deliveries to the European Economic Community" during the whole or part of the period from 1975 to 1981.

* * *

A.   *Quarterly price announcements as the infringement*

59 According to the Commission's first hypothesis, it is the system of quarterly price announcements in itself which constitutes the infringement of art. [101] of the Treaty.

60 First, the Commission considers that that system was deliberately introduced by the pulp producers in order to enable them to ascertain the prices that would be charged by their competitors in the following quarters. The disclosure of prices to third parties, especially to the press and agents working for several producers, well before their application at the beginning of a new quarter, gave the other producers sufficient time to announce their own, corresponding, new prices before that quarter and to apply them from the commencement of that quarter.

61 Secondly, the Commission considers that the implementation of that mechanism had the effect of making the market artificially

transparent by enabling producers to obtain a rapid and accurate picture of the prices quoted by their competitors. * * *

[64] In this case, the communications arise from the price announcements made to users. They constitute in themselves market behavior which does not lessen each undertaking's uncertainty as to the future attitude of its competitors. At the time when each undertaking engages in such behavior, it cannot be sure of the future conduct of the others.

[65] Accordingly, the system of quarterly price announcements on the pulp market is not to be regarded as constituting in itself an infringement of art. [101](1) of the Treaty.

B.   Concertation on announced prices as the infringement

[66] In the second hypothesis, the Commission considers that the system of price announcements constitutes evidence of concertation at an earlier stage. . . . [T]he Commission states that, as proof of such concertation, it relied on the parallel conduct of the pulp producers in the period from 1975 to 1981 and on different kinds of direct or indirect exchange of information. * * *

[70] Since the Commission has no documents which directly establish the existence of concertation between the producers concerned, it is necessary to ascertain whether the system of quarterly price announcements, the simultaneity or near-simultaneity of the price announcements and the parallelism of price announcements as found during the period from 1975 to 1981 constitute a firm, precise and consistent body of evidence of prior concertation.

[71] In determining the probative value of those different factors, it must be noted that parallel conduct cannot be regarded as furnishing proof of concertation unless concertation constitutes the only plausible explanation for such conduct. It is necessary to bear in mind that, although art. [101] of the Treaty prohibits any form of collusion which distorts competition, it does not deprive economic operators of the right to adapt themselves intelligently to the existing and anticipated conduct of their competitors.

[72] Accordingly, it is necessary in this case to ascertain whether the parallel conduct alleged by the Commission cannot, taking account of the nature of the products, the size and the number of the undertakings and the volume of the market in question, be explained otherwise than by concertation.

(a) System of price announcements

* * *

[74] In their pleadings, on the other hand, the applicants maintain that the system is ascribable to the particular commercial requirements of the pulp market. * * *

[76] The experts [appointed by the Court] observe first that the system of announcements at issue must be viewed in the context of the long-term relationships which existed between producers and their customers and which were a result both of the method of manufacturing the pulp and of the cyclical nature of the market. In view of the fact that each type of paper was the result of a particular mixture of pulps having their own characteristics and that the mixture was difficult to change, a relationship based on close co-operation was established between the pulp producers and the paper manufacturers. Such relations were all the closer since they also had the advantage of protecting both sides against the uncertainties inherent in the cyclical nature of the market: they guaranteed security of supply to buyers and at the same time security of demand to producers.

[77] The experts point out that it is in the context of those long-term relationships that, after the Second World War, purchasers demanded the introduction of that system of announcements. Since pulp accounts for between 50–75 per cent of the cost of paper, those purchasers wished to ascertain as soon as possible the prices which they might be charged in order to estimate their costs and to fix the prices of their own products. However, as those purchasers did not wish to be bound by a high fixed price in the event of the market weakening, the announced price was regarded as a ceiling price below which the transaction price could always be renegotiated.

[78] The explanation given for the use of a quarterly cycle is that it is the result of a compromise between the paper manufacturers' desire for a degree of foreseeability as regards the price of pulp and the producers' desire not to miss any opportunities to make a profit in the event of a strengthening of the market.

[79] The US dollar was, according to the experts, introduced on the market by the North American producers during the 1960s. That development was generally welcomed by purchasers who regarded it as a means of ensuring that they did not pay a higher price than their competitors.

(b) Simultaneity or near-simultaneity of announcements

80 . . . [T]he Commission claims that the close succession or even simultaneity of price announcements would not have been possible without a constant flow of information between the undertakings concerned.

81 According to the applicants, the simultaneity or near-simultaneity of the announcements—even if it were established—must instead be regarded as a direct result of the very high degree of transparency of the market. Such transparency, far from being artificial, can be explained by the extremely well-developed network of relations which, in view of the nature and the structure of the market, have been established between the various traders. * * *

83 First, . . . a buyer was always in contact with several pulp producers. One reason for that was connected with the paper-making process, but another was that, in order to avoid becoming overdependent on one producer, pulp buyers took the precaution of diversifying their sources of supply. With a view to obtaining the lowest possible prices, they were in the habit, especially in times of falling prices, of disclosing to their suppliers the prices announced by their competitors.

84 Secondly, it should be noted that most of the pulp was sold to a relatively small number of large paper manufacturers. Those few buyers maintained very close links with each other and exchanged information on changes in prices of which they were aware.

85 Thirdly, several producers who made paper themselves purchased pulp from other producers and were thus informed, in times of both rising prices and falling prices, of the prices charged by their competitors. That information was also accessible to producers who did not themselves manufacture paper but were linked to groups that did.

86 Fourthly, that high degree of transparency in the pulp market resulting from the links between traders or groups of traders was further reinforced by the existence of agents established in the Community who worked for several producers and by the existence of a very dynamic trade press. * * *

88 Finally, it is necessary to add that the use of rapid means of communications, such as the telephone and telex, and the very frequent recourse by the paper manufacturers to very well-informed trade buyers meant that, notwithstanding the number of stages involved—producer, agent, buyer, agent, producer—information on

the level of the announced prices spreads within a matter of days, if not within a matter of hours on the pulp market. * * *

Conclusions

[126] Following that analysis, it must be stated that, in this case, concertation is not the only plausible explanation for the parallel conduct. To begin with, the system of price announcements may be regarded as constituting a rational response to the fact that the pulp market constituted a long-term market and to the need felt by both buyers and sellers to limit commercial risks. Further, the similarity in the dates of price announcements may be regarded as a direct result of the high degree of market transparency, which does not have to be described as artificial. Finally, the parallelism of prices and the price trends may be satisfactorily explained by the oligopolistic tendencies of the market and by the specific circumstances prevailing in certain periods. Accordingly, the parallel conduct established by the Commission does not constitute evidence of concertation.

Notes and Questions

1. In paragraph 71 the Court declares that parallel conduct cannot furnish proof of concertation "unless concertation constitutes the only plausible explanation for such conduct." Why such a heavy burden? If agreement was the most probable explanation of the parallel price moves, should the Court have drawn an inference of a concerted practice?

2. The buyers desired advance price information. Does that explain the quarterly price announcements? Does it explain the virtual simultaneity of the price announcements? Does it explain the uniform price rises?

3. Did evidence suggest that the behavior was not competitive but was nonetheless not conspiratorial?

4. In *Wood pulp*, the European Court moved from an elastic definition of "concertation" to a focused and demanding one. In the United States, the Supreme Court similarly moved from a soft test for proof of "combination" or "concert" to a demanding standard. Compare *Interstate Circuit*, 306 U.S. 208, 1939 with *Matsushita,* 475 U.S. 574, 1986. What are the policy reasons for the modern approach?

5. Observe the conundrum of oligopoly behavior. A few firms in a high-barrier market may be able to mimic the effects of a cartel without an explicit agreement or even an understanding. Should this

phenomenon be relevant to a judicial construction of the word "concert"? Should it make proof of concert harder or easier?

6.   "Smoking gun" evidence of an agreement is often lacking, sometimes because it is adroitly concealed and other times because the parties were able to coordinate their behavior without any overt agreement. In a 2003 enforcement decision against Toshiba Corp. and NEC Corp, the Japan Fair Trade Commission found sufficient evidence of coordination on bidding to supply the postal authority's letter-sorting machines, even though there was no explicit evidence of agreement. The JFTC considered the following factors sufficient: (1) a duopoly market structure; (2) a pattern of past business conduct before the postal service opened up for competitive bidding; (3) a meeting in which the parties contemplated limiting bidding competition; (4) the continuation of exclusive bidding even after the authority opened up competitive bidding; (5) the absence of competitive bidding was economically irrational absent coordination; and (6) prices fell dramatically once competitive bidding began.

7.   Conspiracy by algorithm. Online booking platforms and algorithms to determine prices can make cartels easier to form and cheating easier to detect and punish. It can also make participants in online booking systems more vulnerable to cartel accusations. In Lithuania, travel agents used a common online booking system. The system administrator asked the travel agents, by email, for a vote on whether to cap discounts for online bookings at 3%. After an affirmative vote of those who voted, the administrator declared the 3% maximum and set the system for an automatic 3% maximum, although individual agents were not blocked from offering a higher discount if they took the trouble to maneuver around the setting. When the Lithuanian Competition Council opened proceedings, some of the agents claimed not to have received the relevant emails. The Competition Council found infringements by all of the agents who were members of the system. The national court to which the allegedly innocent agents appealed posed a question to the Court of Justice. The Court answered:

"Article 101(1) TFEU must be interpreted as meaning that, where the administrator of an information system, intended to enable travel agencies to sell travel packages on their websites using a uniform booking method, sends to those economic operators, via a personal electronic mailbox, a message informing them that the discounts on products sold through that system will henceforth be capped and, following the dissemination of that message, the system in question undergoes the technical modifications necessary to implement that measure, those economic operators may—if they were aware of that message—be presumed to have participated in a concerted practice within the meaning of that provision, unless they publicly distanced themselves from that practice, reported it to the administrative authorities or adduced other evidence to rebut that presumption, such as evidence of a systematic application of a discount exceeding the cap in question.

It is for the referring court to examine—on the basis of the national rules governing the assessment of evidence and the standard of proof— whether, in view of all the circumstances before it, the dispatch of a message, such as that at issue in the main proceedings, may constitute sufficient evidence to establish that the addressees of that message were aware of its content. The presumption of innocence precludes the referring court from considering that the mere dispatch of that message constitutes sufficient evidence to establish that its addressees ought to have been aware of its content." Eturas, Case C–74/14, EU:C:2016:42.

EU Competition Commissioner Margrethe Vestager cited *Eturas* in cautioning that algorithms and other automated systems can make cartels more effective, and noting the opening of investigations in consumer electronics markets.

8.   When does competitors' exchange of sensitive information spill over into a price-fixing cartel? In China, exchange of sensitive information, plus, for example, meetings followed by a similar price rise, can be interpreted as a concerted practice. In 2016 the NDRC, the agency in charge of price conduct, found a price cartel compromising two pharmaceutical companies. A third firm, Chang Zhou No. 4 Pharmaceutical Ltd., was not a party to this cartel but had communicated with the two cartelists and raised its prices in rhythm with them. It was fined for a concerted practice. Estazolam Raw Materials and Pills Case, July 27, 2016. *https://www.nysba.org/ Sections/Antitrust_Law/Resources/Resource_PDFs/2017/Antitrust_ Complicance_-2017-03-02_pdf.html.*

The European Union, too, is more likely than the United States to draw an inference of a cartel from exchange of confidential information and surrounding circumstances. It did so in the case of smart card chips, where it determined that the exchange was aimed at slowing down price decreases. 758/14, Infineon Technologies v. Commission, EU:T:2016:737.

9.   An important threshold question in jurisdictions that allow private anti-cartel enforcement is what evidence a private plaintiff must have of cartel behavior at the time of filing the complaint. In *Bell Atlantic Corp. v. Twombly,* 550 U.S. 544 (2007), the telephone companies had been regulated; they had legal monopolies, each for its own territory. When the regulation was lifted, each one still stayed in its historical territory and did not go across the border to compete. Plaintiff thought

this must mean that they had an agreement to divide territories, and so alleged.

The US Supreme Court dismissed the complaint. Not going across the border was entirely consistent with independent, and interdependent, action. Each one liked it the way it was; they did not want competition to break out and were not going to trigger it; they hoped that each other telecom firm would do the same thing (not compete). The Court dismissed the complaint. It held that a plaintiff must allege concrete facts plausibly evidencing a conspiracy before it can proceed to discovery. This holding arguably creates a chicken-and-egg problem, since plaintiffs may need access to discovery in order to uncover the facts evidencing the alleged conspiracy. Nonetheless, some plaintiff's' lawyers report that *Twombly* has not significantly deterred the filing of private antitrust cases—only made them more careful in their pleading.

D. ARE EFFECTS NECESSARY?

In the United States, *Socony-Vacuum* (310 U.S. 150, 1940) established in dictum in famous footnote 59 that a cartel agreement is illegal on its face. A plea of "We tried to raise prices but could not do it because the market overwhelmed us" does not work.

The quinine producers tried the same tack. They argued: We tried to run a cartel but our agreement had no effect because quinine bark became scarce. What did the Court of Justice say about this defense? In what paragraph?

In the 1990s, the US authorities sued Nippon Paper Industries for a conspiracy with other Japanese manufacturers for fixing the price of thermal fax paper for export into the United States. Nippon argued that, for the time period not blocked by the statute of limitations, the conditions of supply and demand had so changed that the agreement had no effect, and also that it had already withdrawn from the conspiracy. The court held that, for purposes of subject matter jurisdiction, the United States had to prove intended and substantial effects in the US market within the statute of limitations period. The government had failed to carry this burden. United States v. Nippon Paper Indus., 62 F.Supp.2d 173 (D. Mass. 1999).

E. CRISIS CARTELS

Are all cartels legal? Are "good" cartels exempted? Some jurisdictions allow public interest defenses (but not the United States). Some jurisdictions allow a crisis cartel defense. Also, not the United States. Whole industries may fall into crises of overcapacity.

Should they be allowed to combine, in order to lift themselves out of the crisis?

The Irish beef industry faced such a crisis. The Irish government requested the industry to agree to a plan of rationalization, and, in response, all of the principal Irish beef processors, accounting for 93% of the Irish industry, formed an association and entered into a rationalization agreement. The Irish Competition Authority challenged the agreement. The Irish court sided with the Irish government and the industry, finding that the industry was in survival mode and it needed to be rationalized; the rationalization would save costs and help to restore the industry to efficiency and competitiveness; and that no credible evidence had been adduced to show that the agreement would restrict or distort competition or hurt consumers.

The Irish court made a reference to the European Court of Justice for a ruling on the interpretation of the Treaty of Rome.

COMPETITION AUTHORITY v. BEEF INDUSTRY DEVELOPMENT SOCIETY LTD.

Case C–209/07, EU:C:2008:643 (European Court of Justice 2008)

[1] This reference for a preliminary ruling concerns the interpretation of Article 81(1) EC [now 101(1) TFEU].

[2] The reference was made in proceedings between the Competition Authority, on the one hand, and Beef Industry Development Society Ltd ('BIDS') and Barry Brothers (Carrigmore) Meats Ltd ('Barry Brothers'), on the other, in respect of decisions of BIDS rationalizing the beef and veal sector in Ireland.

The main proceedings and the question referred for a preliminary ruling

[3] It is apparent from the decision making the reference that the dispute before the Supreme Court arises in the context of overcapacity in the beef industry in Ireland and, more particularly, in the processing sector (slaughter and de-boning of meat).

[4] A study carried out in 1998 at the joint request of the Irish Government and representatives of the beef industry concluded that it was necessary to reduce the number of processors from 20 to a figure between 4 and 6. The report also recommended that the undertakings which were to remain in the sector ('the stayers') should compensate those forced to withdraw ('the goers').

⁵ In 1999, a task force set up by the Minister for Agriculture and Food came to similar conclusions and recommended that the processors should create a compensation fund.

⁶ In accordance with those conclusions, the 10 principal processors formed BIDS on May 2002. BIDS prepared a draft rationalization plan which provided, inter alia, for a reduction in processing capacity of about 25%, the equivalent of an annual volume of about 420 000 head of cattle.

⁷ BIDS planned to implement that objective by means of agreements between the stayers and the goers, in the terms of a standard form of contract, the principal features of which are summarized in the following paragraph.

⁸ That standard form of contract provides that the stayers are to compensate the goers, the amount of that compensation to be determined by the parties. BIDS is to pay the compensation to the goers. The stayers are to repay BIDS by means of a levy of EUR 2 per head of cattle up to their traditional cattle kill volume and EUR 11 above that volume. In return, the goers undertake:

   —to decommission or put beyond use their processing plants or sell them only to persons established outside the island of Ireland, or, if necessary, to the stayers on condition that they be used as back-up equipment or spare parts;

   —not to use the land on which those plants were situated for the purposes of beef or veal processing for a period of five years;

   —not to compete with the stayers in the beef and veal processing market in Ireland for two years.

⁹ Barry Brothers is a beef and veal processing company. It made an agreement with BIDS complying with the features described in the previous paragraph.

¹⁰ BIDS notified the Competition Authority of that agreement and the standard form of contract ('the BIDS arrangements').

¹¹ Having informed BIDS, on 5 and 26 June 2003, that it considered the BIDS arrangements contrary to Article [101(1) TFEU], the Competition Authority applied to the High Court, on 30 June 2003, for an order restraining BIDS and Barry Brothers from giving effect to them.

[12] By judgment of 27 July 2006, the High Court dismissed that application. It held that the agreement between BIDS and Barry Brothers did not fall under the prohibition laid down in Article [101(1) TFEU] but nor did it satisfy the requirements for exemption laid down in Article [101(3) TFEU].

[13] The Competition Authority appealed against that decision to the Supreme Court, which decided to stay the proceedings and to refer the following question to the Court of Justice for a preliminary ruling:

'Where it is established to the satisfaction of the court that:

(a) there is overcapacity in the industry for the processing of beef which, calculated at peak throughput, would be approximately 32%;

(b) the effect of this excess capacity will have very serious consequences for the profitability of the industry as a whole over the medium term;

(c) while . . . the effects of surplus requirements have not been felt to any significant degree as yet, independent consultants have advised that, in the near term, the overcapacity is unlikely to be eliminated by normal market measures, but over time the overcapacity will lead to very significant losses and ultimately to processors and plants leaving the industry;

(d) processors of beef representing approximately 93% of the market for the supply of beef of that industry have agreed to take steps to eliminate the overcapacity and are willing to pay a levy in order to fund payments to processors willing to cease production, and

the said processors, comprising 10 companies, form a corporate body ("the society") for the purpose of implementing an arrangement with the following features:

—[goers] killing and processing 420 000 animals per annum, representing approximately 25% of active capacity would enter into an agreement with [stayers] to leave the industry and to abide by the following terms;

—goers would sign a two year non-compete clause in relation to the processing of cattle on the entire island of Ireland;

—the plants of goers would be decommissioned;

—land associated with the decommissioned plants would not be used for the purposes of beef processing for a period of five years;

—compensation would be paid to goers in staged payments by means of loans made by the stayers to the society;

—a voluntary levy would be paid to the society by all stayers at the rate of EUR 2 per head of the traditional percentage kill and EUR 11 per head on cattle kill above that figure;

—the levy would be used to repay the stayers' loans; levies would cease on repayment of the loans;

—the equipment of goers used for primary beef processing would be sold only to stayers for use as back-up equipment or spare parts or sold outside the island of Ireland;

—the freedom of the stayers in matters of production, pricing, conditions of sale, imports and exports, increase in capacity and otherwise would not be affected, and that it is agreed that such an agreement is liable, for the purpose of application of Article [101(1) TFEU], to have an appreciable effect on trade between Member States, is such arrangement to be regarded as having as its object, as distinct from effect, the prevention, restriction or distortion of competition within the common market and therefore, incompatible with Article [101](1) of the Treaty [on the Functioning of the European Union]?'

The question referred for a preliminary ruling

[14] By its question, the national court asks, in essence, whether agreements with features such as those of the BIDS arrangements are to be regarded, by reason of their object alone, as being anti-competitive and prohibited by Article [101(1) TFEU] EC or whether, on the other hand, it is necessary, in order to reach such a conclusion, first to demonstrate that such agreements have had anti-competitive effects.

[15] It must be recalled that, to come within the prohibition laid down in Article [101(1) TFEU], an agreement must have 'as [its] object or effect the prevention, restriction or distortion of competition within the common market'. It has, since the judgment in Case 56/65 *LTM* [1966] ECR 235, 249, been settled case-law that the alternative

nature of that requirement, indicated by the conjunction 'or', leads, first, to the need to consider the precise purpose of the agreement, in the economic context in which it is to be applied. Where, however, an analysis of the clauses of that agreement does not reveal the effect on competition to be sufficiently deleterious, its consequences should then be considered and for it to be caught by the prohibition it is necessary to find that those factors are present which show that competition has in fact been prevented or restricted or distorted to an appreciable extent.

16 In deciding whether an agreement is prohibited by Article [101(1) TFEU], there is therefore no need to take account of its actual effects once it appears that its object is to prevent, restrict or distort competition within the common market. . . .

17 The distinction between 'infringements by object' and 'infringements by effect' arises from the fact that certain forms of collusion between undertakings can be regarded, by their very nature, as being injurious to the proper functioning of normal competition.

18 In their written observations submitted to the Court, the Competition Authority, the Belgian Government and the Commission of the European Communities all submit that the object of the BIDS arrangements is obviously anti-competitive so that there is no need to analyses their actual effects and that those arrangements were concluded in breach of the prohibition laid down in Article [101(1) TFEU].

19 On the other hand, BIDS submits that those arrangements do not come within the category of infringements by object, but should, on the contrary, be analyzed in the light of their actual effects on the market. It argues that the BIDS arrangements, first, are not anti-competitive in purpose and, second, do not entail injurious consequences for consumers or, more generally, for competition. It states that the purpose of those arrangements is not adversely to affect competition or the welfare of consumers, but to rationalize the beef industry in order to make it more competitive by reducing, but not eliminating, production overcapacity.

20 That argument cannot be accepted.

21 In fact, to determine whether an agreement comes within the prohibition laid down in Article [101(1) TFEU], close regard must be paid to the wording of its provisions and to the objectives which it is intended to attain. In that regard, even supposing it to be established

that the parties to an agreement acted without any subjective intention of restricting competition, but with the object of remedying the effects of a crisis in their sector, such considerations are irrelevant for the purposes of applying that provision. Indeed, an agreement may be regarded as having a restrictive object even if it does not have the restriction of competition as its sole aim but also pursues other legitimate objectives. It is only in connection with Article [101(3) TFEU] that matters such as those relied upon by BIDS may, if appropriate, be taken into consideration for the purposes of obtaining an exemption from the prohibition laid down in Article [101(1) TFEU].

22 BIDS argues, in addition, that the concept of infringement by object should be interpreted narrowly. Only agreements as to horizontal price-fixing, or to limit output or share markets, agreements whose anti-competitive effects are so obvious as not to require an economic analysis come within that category. The BIDS arrangements cannot be assimilated to that type of agreement or to other forms of complex cartels. BIDS maintains that an agreement on the reduction of excess capacity in a sector cannot be assimilated to an agreement to 'limit production' within the meaning of Article [101(1)(b) TFEU]. That concept must be understood as referring to a limitation of total market output rather than a limitation of the output of certain operators who voluntarily withdraw from the market, without causing a lowering of output.

23 However, as the Advocate General pointed out in point 48 of her Opinion, the types of agreements covered by Article [101(1)(a) to (c) TFEU] do not constitute an exhaustive list of prohibited collusion.

24 Therefore, it must be examined whether agreements with features such as those described by the national court have as their object the restriction of competition.

25 In BIDS' submission, if an agreement does not affect the total output on a market or obstruct operators' freedom to act independently, any anti-competitive effect can be excluded. In the main proceedings, the withdrawal of certain operators from the market is irrelevant, because the stayers are in a position to satisfy demand.

26 BIDS adds that the structure of the market does not allow the processors to influence it, since up to 90% of demand is from outside Ireland. On the Irish market, the power of the processors is largely counteracted by the purchasing power of the four major retailers.

Account must also be taken of the competition which new operators entering the market concerned could bring about.

[27] BIDS observes that the cases in which a limitation on output has been held to be infringement by object concerned agreements supplemental to horizontal price or production-fixing agreements . . ., to which the BIDS arrangements are not comparable.

[28] BIDS submits that the Commission's decision-making practice and the case-law do not permit the conclusion that there is a restriction by object. . . . * * *

[30] . . . [T]he BIDS arrangements provide for neither the freezing nor the non-use of capacity, nor exchange of information, nor quotas or other measures intended to preserve the stayers' market shares.

[31] In that regard, it is apparent from the documents before the Court and from the information provided by the national court that the object of the BIDS arrangements is to change, appreciably, the structure of the market through a mechanism intended to encourage the withdrawal of competitors.

[32] The matters brought to the Court's attention show that the BIDS arrangements are intended to improve the overall profitability of undertakings supplying more than 90% of the beef and veal processing services on the Irish market by enabling them to approach, or even attain, their minimum efficient scale. In order to do so, those arrangements pursue two main objectives: first, to increase the degree of concentration in the sector concerned by reducing significantly the number of undertakings supplying processing services and, second, to eliminate almost 75% of excess production capacity.

[33] The BIDS arrangements are intended therefore, essentially, to enable several undertakings to implement a common policy which has as its object the encouragement of some of them to withdraw from the market and the reduction, as a consequence, of the overcapacity which affects their profitability by preventing them from achieving economies of scale.

[34] That type of arrangement conflicts patently with the concept inherent in the . . . Treaty provisions relating to competition, according to which each economic operator must determine independently the policy which it intends to adopt on the common market. Article [101(1) TFEU] is intended to prohibit any form of coordination which deliberately substitutes practical cooperation between undertakings for the risks of competition.

[35] In the context of competition, the undertakings which signed the BIDS arrangements would have, without such arrangements, no means of improving their profitability other than by intensifying their commercial rivalry or resorting to concentrations. With the BIDS arrangements it would be possible for them to avoid such a process and to share a large part of the costs involved in increasing the degree of market concentration as a result, in particular, of the levy of EUR 2 per head processed by each of the stayers.

[36] In addition, the means put in place to attain the objective of the BIDS arrangements include restrictions whose object is anti-competitive.

[37] As regards, in the first place, the levy of EUR 11 per head of cattle slaughtered beyond the usual volume of production of each of the stayers, it is, as BIDS submits, the price to be paid by the stayers to acquire the goers' clientele. However, it must be observed, as did the Advocate General . . ., that such a measure also constitutes an obstacle to the natural development of market shares as regards some of the stayers who, because of the dissuasive nature of that levy, are deterred from exceeding their usual volume of production. That measure is likely therefore to lead to certain operators freezing their production.

[38] As regards, secondly, restrictions imposed on the goers as regards the disposal and use of their processing plants, the BIDS arrangements also contain, by their very object, restrictions on competition since they seek to avoid the possible use of those plants by new operators entering the market in order to compete with the stayers. As the Competition Authority pointed out in its written observations, since the investment necessary for the construction of a new processing plant is much greater than the costs of taking over an existing plant, those restrictions are obviously intended to dissuade any new entry of competitors throughout the island of Ireland.

[39] Finally, the fact that those restrictions, as well as the non-competition clause imposed on the goers, are limited in time is not such as to put in doubt the finding as to the anti-competitive nature of the object of the BIDS arrangements. As the Advocate General observed in point 86 of her Opinion, such matters may, at the most, be relevant for the purposes of the examination of the four requirements which have to be met under Article [101(3) TFEU] in order to escape the prohibition laid down in Article [101(1) TFEU].

[40] In the light of the foregoing considerations, the reply to the question referred must be that an agreement with features such as those of the standard form of contract concluded between the 10 principal beef and veal processors in Ireland, who are members of BIDS, and requiring, among other things, a reduction of the order of 25% in processing capacity, has as its object the prevention, restriction or distortion of competition within the meaning of Article [101(1) TFEU]. . . . * * *

Notes and Questions

1.   What was really the purpose of the agreement? Was BIDS' purpose to address the crisis of overproduction of beef in Ireland by reducing overcapacity, thereby resuscitating the industry and making it more competitive? Assume that BIDS and the Irish government thought there was a good chance that the plan would succeed. Is such an agreement caught by Article 101(1) as a restraint by object? Should it be?

2.   BIDS maintained in the Irish court that, if caught by Article 101(1), the agreement should be exempted under Article 101(3). This issue came before the Irish High Court in 2010. The European Commission submitted an *amicus curiae* brief, advising the High Court on its views of how the Article 101(3) analysis should proceed. Among other points, the Commission asserted: (1) an industry rationalization plan should ensure that the factory capacity left on the market is the most efficient and that surviving firms have the practical ability to increase output following implementation of the rationalization plan; (2) "so-called 'crisis cartels' which aim to reduce industry capacity cannot be justified by economic downturns and recession-induced freefalls. As a general rule in a free market economy, market forces should reduce unnecessary capacity from a market;" spontaneous market restructuring is likely to be impeded only where (a) giving up capacity is costly for all firms, and (b) the market is structurally stable, transparent, and symmetric; and (3) consumers typically receive a fair share of the resulting benefits only when the industry rationalization results in marginal cost savings, which is not generally characteristic of the elimination of fixed capacity such as factories or entire firms.

How much room do these standards leave for a lawful crisis cartel? Under these standards, was BIDS likely to get an exemption?

3.   In *Dutch brickmakers*, the European Commission exempted, under Article 101(3), a rationalization agreement by brickmakers who were plagued by overcapacity. The brickmakers agreed to reduce surplus capacity over a limited period time, while not making any agreement on prices. Stichting Baksteen, Case IV/34.456, O.J. L 131/15 (May 26, 1994).

This case is exceptional, and may be the last crisis cartel ever to be approved by the Commission.

The wisdom of allowing judicial or administrative authorization of crisis or restructuring cartels is much debated. United States law makes no allowance for crises, on the theory that market solutions are better than private solutions, and a crisis justification for cartels would weaken the clear rule of law. Germany and the UK once allowed authorization of crisis cartels in the public interest. They have revised their laws to mirror Article 101. Until 1999, Japanese law allowed authorization of depression and rationalization cartels. This authorization was repealed. Anti-Monopoly Law of Japan, § 24(3), Law No. 54, 1947 (amended). However the Anti-Monopoly Act of Japan prohibits "unreasonable restraint of trade" when it is "contrary to the public interest." AMA Article 2(6). In the *Oil Cartel* case, which arose under conditions of crisis, the Supreme Court of Japan condemned the cartel but nonetheless stated that " 'public interest' may, in 'exceptional circumstances,' override the direct objective of preservation of free competition under the AMA, from the viewpoint of the ultimate objective of consumer interests and development of the national economy." Oil Cartel, 38(4) Keishu 1287, 1311 (Sup. Ct. Feb. 24, 1984), as summarized by Toshiaki Takigawa in Competition law and policy of Japan, 54 Antitrust Bulletin 435, 440–41 (2009). The relatively new Chinese Anti-Monopoly Law allows for the exemption of an agreement made "for the purpose of mitigating a severe decrease of sales volume or excessive oversupply during economic recessions." AML Art. 15(v). To obtain an exemption the undertakings must prove that their agreement "will not substantially restrict competition . . . and can enable consumers to share the benefits." These burdens suggest that "it would be difficult for crisis cartels to be exempted in practice." Wang Xiaoye, The new Chinese Anti-Monopoly Law: A survey of a work in progress, 54 Antitrust Bul. 579, 600 (fall 2009).

In nations that do not allow a crisis cartel justification, are jurists sometimes "clever" in recasting the problem as not a cartel, or as state action or a political question? See *Appalachian Coals* (288 U.S. 344 (1933)). See also Hammons v. Alcan Aluminum Corp., 1997–1 (CCH) Trade Cas. ¶ 71,714 (C.D. Cal. 1996), aff'd mem., 132 F.3d 39 (9th Cir. 1997), cert. denied, 525 U.S. 948 (1998) (when Russian aluminum flooded the market, US government induced producers to limit their output; they did, but no agreement was proved). Is this flexibility necessary? inevitable?

4.   See Chapter 6 for an account of the role of the European Competition Commissioner and the Competition Directorate-General in responding to the urgent public needs in the financial crisis of 2008–09.

They presented competition as part of the solution, not part of the problem.

We turn now to foreign government action defenses. There are other defenses and immunities that we do not treat here but that are common to most nations. These include the state action defense (action by one's own state that may shield private anticompetitive acts), and various immunities that may be provided by statute, such as for labor collective bargaining, agricultural cooperatives, and aspects of regulated industries.

F. FOREIGN GOVERNMENT ACTION OR INVOLVEMENT: A DEFENSE?

Prosecutors might lose domestic cartel cases because the state has authorized the cartel and actively supervises it—a subject we deal with in Chapter 6, The State. Prosecutors might lose international cartel cases because of foreign government sovereignty and involvement. Should defenses based on foreign government involvement be more or less cogent than defenses based on involvement of the nation's own government?

The United States Department of Justice and Federal Trade Commission have issued international guidelines, relevant parts of which are included below. Ask yourself, as you read these: Do the foreign government defenses put a large or small hole in the purview for antitrust actions against international or transnational cartels?

After we look at the International Guidelines, we study case law addressing foreign sovereign defenses, including the persistent matter of the world oil cartel—OPEC, and the case of the Chinese vitamin C cartel.

1. US Agency Guidelines

ANTITRUST GUIDELINES FOR INTERNATIONAL ENFORCEMENT AND COOPERATION

US DEPARTMENT OF JUSTICE AND FEDERAL TRADE COMMISSION (2017)

(excerpts; footnotes omitted)

4. **Agencies' Consideration of Foreign Jurisdictions**

4.1. Comity

In enforcing the federal antitrust laws, the Agencies consider international comity.   Comity itself reflects the broad concept of respect among co-equal sovereign nations   and plays a role in determining "the recognition which one nation allows within its territory to the legislative, executive or judicial acts of another nation." In determining whether to investigate or bring an action, or to seek particular   remedies in a given case, the Agencies take into account whether significant interests of any foreign sovereign would be affected.

A decision to take an investigative step or to prosecute an antitrust action under the federal antitrust laws represents a determination that the importance of antitrust enforcement outweighs any relevant foreign policy concerns. That determination is entitled to deference. Some courts have undertaken a comity analysis in disputes between private parties.

In performing this comity analysis, the Agencies consider a number of relevant factors. The relative weight given to each factor depends on the facts and circumstances of each case. Among other things, the Agencies weigh: the existence of a purpose to affect or an actual effect on U.S. commerce; the significance and foreseeability of the effects of the anticompetitive conduct on the United States; the degree of conflict with a foreign jurisdiction's law or articulated policy; the extent to which the enforcement activities of another jurisdiction, including remedies resulting from those enforcement activities, may be affected; and the effectiveness of foreign enforcement as compared to U.S. enforcement.

An investigation or enforcement action by a foreign authority will not preclude an investigation or enforcement action by either the Department or the Commission. Rather, the Agency will determine whether, in light of actions by the foreign authority, investigation or enforcement is warranted to address harm or threatened harm to U.S. commerce and consumers from anticompetitive conduct. In cases in which an Agency opens an investigation or brings an enforcement action concerning conduct under investigation by a foreign authority, it may coordinate with that authority.

Several of the comity factors considered by the Agencies warrant further discussion.

First, when considering the degree of conflict with foreign laws, the Agencies review the relevant laws of the interested foreign sovereigns. In the context of the Agencies' enforcement, conflicts of law are rare. As more jurisdictions have adopted and enforce antitrust laws that are compatible with those of the United States, it has become increasingly common that no conflict exists between U.S. antitrust enforcement interests and the laws or policies of a foreign sovereign. Further, no conflict of law exists if a person subject to the laws of two sovereigns can comply with both.108 Moreover, no conflict exists in cases where foreign law is neutral as to particular conduct, because it remains possible for the parties in question to comply with the U.S. antitrust laws without violating foreign law. In situations where a conflict of law exists, however, comity may counsel in favor of declining enforcement.

Second, the Agencies will assess the articulated interests and policies of a foreign sovereign beyond whether there is a conflict with foreign law. In determining whether to investigate or bring an enforcement action regarding an alleged antitrust violation, the Agencies consider the extent to which a foreign sovereign encourages or discourages certain courses of conduct or leaves parties free to choose among different courses of conduct.

Third, the Agencies consider whether the objectives sought to be obtained by U.S. enforcement could be achieved by foreign enforcement. The Agencies may consult with interested foreign authorities with the purpose of working to understand and address harm or threatened harm to U.S. commerce and consumers from anticompetitive conduct.

4.2. Consideration of Foreign Government Involvement

In some instances, a foreign government may be involved in anticompetitive conduct that involves or affects U.S. commerce. In determining whether to conduct an investigation or to file an enforcement action in cases in which foreign government involvement is known or suspected, the Agencies consider four legal doctrines that lie at the intersection of government action and the antitrust laws: (1) foreign sovereign immunity; (2) foreign sovereign compulsion; (3) act of state; and (4) petitioning of sovereigns.

4.2.1 Foreign Sovereign Immunity

In civil cases, the Foreign Sovereign Immunities Act of 1976 ("FSIA")110 provides the "sole basis for obtaining jurisdiction over a foreign state in the courts of this country." The FSIA shields foreign states from the civil jurisdiction of the courts of the United States, subject to certain enumerated exceptions and to treaties in place at the time of the FSIA's enactment.113 Under the FSIA, federal courts have jurisdiction over foreign states in certain cases in which the foreign state has:

a.   waived immunity explicitly or by implication;

b.   engaged in commercial activity;

c.   expropriated property in violation of international law;

d.   acquired rights to property in the United States;

e.   committed certain torts within the United States; or

f.   agreed to arbitration of the dispute.

The "commercial activity" exception is the most relevant exception for antitrust purposes. The FSIA provides that a foreign state is not immune from jurisdiction of U.S. courts when:

> the action is based upon a commercial activity carried on in the United States by the foreign state; or upon an act performed in the United States in connection with a commercial activity of the foreign state elsewhere; or upon an act outside the territory of the United States in connection with a commercial activity of the foreign state elsewhere and that act causes a direct effect in the United States.

"Commercial activity" is defined to include "either a regular course of commercial conduct or a particular commercial transaction or act," and the FSIA provides that "the commercial character of an activity shall be determined by reference to the nature of the course of conduct or particular transaction or act, rather than by reference to its purpose." Commercial activity is distinct from sovereign activity inasmuch as the former is understood to include "those powers that can also be exercised by private citizens," while the latter is understood to include "powers peculiar to sovereigns."118 In other words, the principal question is whether the government is acting "not as a regulator of a market, but in the manner of a private player within it."

To determine whether an action is "based upon" a commercial activity, a court must focus on "the particular conduct on which the plaintiff's action is based," i.e., "those elements that, if proven, would entitle a plaintiff to relief and the gravamen of the complaint."

As a practical matter, most activities of foreign state-owned enterprises operating in the commercial marketplace are "commercial" and, therefore, such enterprises are not immune from the jurisdiction of the U.S. courts in actions to enforce the antitrust laws by virtue of the FSIA. The commercial activities of these enterprises are subject to the U.S. antitrust laws to the same extent as the activities of privately owned foreign firms.

4.2.2 Foreign Sovereign Compulsion

Because U.S. antitrust laws can extend to foreign persons and conduct with a sufficient connection to the United States, some persons may find themselves subject to foreign legal requirements that conflict with the laws of the United States. In these circumstances, courts have recognized a limited defense against application of the U.S. antitrust laws when a foreign sovereign compels the very conduct that the U.S. antitrust law would prohibit. If it is possible, however, for a party to comply with both the foreign law and the U.S. antitrust laws, the existence of the foreign law does not provide any legal excuse for actions that do not comply with U.S. law. Similarly, that conduct may be lawful, approved, or encouraged in a foreign jurisdiction does not, in and of itself, bar application of the U.S. antitrust laws—even when the foreign jurisdiction has a strong policy in favor of the conduct in question.

Two rationales underlie the limited defense of foreign sovereign compulsion. First, Congress enacted the U.S. antitrust laws against the background of well-recognized principles of international law and comity, pursuant to which U.S. authorities give due deference to the official acts of foreign governments. A defense for actions compelled by foreign sovereigns under certain circumstances serves to accommodate equal sovereigns. Second, fairness considerations require a mechanism to provide a predictable rule of decision for those seeking to conform their behavior to all applicable laws.

The Agencies recognize and consider this foreign sovereign compulsion defense when determining whether to bring an enforcement action. Because of the limited scope of the defense, however, the Agencies will refrain from bringing an enforcement action based on considerations of foreign sovereign compulsion only when certain criteria are satisfied.

First, the foreign government must have compelled the anticompetitive conduct under circumstances in which a refusal to comply with the foreign government's command would give rise to the imposition of penal or other severe sanctions. As a general matter, the Agencies regard the foreign government's formal representation that refusal to comply with its command would have such a result as being sufficient to establish that the conduct in question has been compelled. To be sufficient, however, the representation must contain enough detail to enable the Agencies to see precisely how the compulsion would be accomplished under foreign law. Foreign government measures short of compulsion do not suffice for this defense, although they may be a relevant comity consideration if, for example, the measures reflect an articulated policy of the foreign government.

Second, the defense generally applies only when the compelled conduct can be accomplished entirely within the foreign sovereign's own territory. If the compelled conduct occurs in the United States, the Agencies will not recognize the defense. For example, the defense would not apply if a foreign government required the U.S. subsidiaries of several firms to organize a cartel in the United States to fix the price at which products would be sold in the United States.

Third, the order must come from the foreign government acting in its governmental capacity. The defense does not arise from conduct that would fall within the FSIA commercial activity exception.

* * *

Illustrative Example E

Situation:

Increased quantities of Commodity X have flooded the world market over the last several years, including substantial amounts coming into the United States. The officials of Countries Alpha, Beta, and Gamma meet with their respective domestic firms and urge them to "rationalize" production of Commodity X by cooperatively cutting back. Going one step further, the government of Country Gamma orders cutbacks from its domestic firms, subject to substantial penalties for non-compliance. Producers from Countries Alpha and Beta agree among themselves to institute comparable cutbacks, but their governments do not require them to do so. The overseas production cutbacks have sufficient effects on U.S. commerce for the antitrust laws to apply.

Discussion:

The Agencies would not find that foreign sovereign compulsion precludes prosecution of the agreement in restraint of trade entered into by the participants from Countries Alpha and Beta. The Agencies would acknowledge a defense of sovereign compulsion, however, for the participants from Country Gamma.

4.2.3 Act of State Doctrine

The act of state doctrine prevents courts from "declar[ing] invalid the official act of a foreign sovereign performed within its own territory." Applying this doctrine, courts decline to adjudicate claims or issues that would require the court to judge the validity of the sovereign act of a foreign state in its own territory. This doctrine is rooted in considerations of international comity and the separation of powers.

The doctrine does not apply to every act taken by an individual or entity affiliated with a sovereign state. For instance, it does not apply to the acts of individual government officials acting outside their official capacity. Nor does it apply to private actors, even when those acts are approved or condoned by the foreign government in question.

Accordingly, when a restraint on competition arises directly from the act of a foreign sovereign, such as the grant of a license, award of a contract, or expropriation of property, the Agencies may refrain from bringing an enforcement action based on the principles animating the act of state doctrine. More specifically, the Agencies may exercise enforcement discretion and decline to challenge foreign acts of state if the facts and circumstances indicate that: (1) the specific conduct complained of is a public act of the sovereign, (2) the act was taken within the territorial jurisdiction of the sovereign, and (3) the conduct relates to a matter that is governmental, rather than commercial.

4.2.4 Petitioning of Sovereigns

Under the Noerr-Pennington doctrine, a genuine effort to obtain or influence action by governmental entities in the United States falls outside the scope of the Sherman Act, even if the intent or effect of that effort is to restrain or monopolize trade. It is the view of the

Agencies that the principles undergirding this doctrine apply to the petitioning of foreign governments. The Agencies, therefore, will not challenge under the antitrust laws genuine efforts to obtain or influence action by foreign government entities. But as with Noerr-Pennington, the Agencies will not exercise this discretion when faced with "sham" activities, in which petitioning "ostensibly directed toward influencing governmental action, is a mere sham to cover . . . an attempt to interfere directly with the business relationships of a competitor," or when Noerr-Pennington would otherwise not apply.

Illustrative Example F

Situation:

Corporation 1 and Corporation 2 have mines in Country Alpha where they extract Mineral X. Corporation 1 and Corporation 2 use different techniques to extract Mineral X. Corporation 1 launches a campaign designed to foster the adoption and retention of regulations that would effectively outlaw Corporation 2's mining technique. As part of this broader campaign, Corporation 1 files a complaint with Country Alpha's Ministry of Mines alleging severe health and safety concerns stemming from Corporation 2's mining technique and demanding the permanent closure of Corporation 2's mine. If successful, Corporation 1 would have an effective monopoly on the U.S. market for Mineral X. The Country Alpha Ministry of Mines decides to investigate the complaint, leading to the temporary shutdown of Corporation 2's operations.

Discussion:

Had Corporation 1's activities been directed at a U.S. government entity and the Noerr-Pennington doctrine applied, the Agencies would not take action against Corporation 1. Applying like principles here, the Agencies would not institute enforcement action against Corporation 1 for lodging a complaint with the Country Alpha Ministry of Mines.

Notes and Questions

Comment on the Guidelines. Do they include within the purview of US law essentially all acts and agreements of foreign actors that substantially impair competition in the United States? With what exceptions?

2.   US Caselaw

In the 1990s and early 2000s, just before China's modern competition law was adopted and spanning the period of China's entry into the WTO, the Chinese producers of vitamin C agreed to fix their export prices into the U.S. and elsewhere. They raised prices about 28% to 80%. They did so in the context of their trade association, which approved the minimum level of their prices. When the US buyers sued, the Chinese firms defended that the Chinese government ordered them to fix prices, and that the trade association was effectively a government body. The Chinese Ministry MOFCOM supported the Chinese manufacturers; MOFCOM stated in an amicus brief in the case that it ordered the firms to fix export prices. The district court refused to grant the Chinese manufacturers summary judgment. It sent to trial the issue whether MOFCOM had really ordered the Chinese manufacturers to fix the prices of their exports. The jury had evidence that MOFCOM contradicted itself in other fora; it told the WTO that it had made no such order. The jury found that MOFCOM had not ordered the price fix. It returned a verdict for plaintiffs which, after trebling, was $147 million. Defendants appealed.

a.   Act of State, Foreign Sovereign Compulsion, Comity

IN RE VITAMIN C ANTITRUST LITIGATION
837 F.3d 175 (2d Cir. 2016)
petition for certiorari pending

JUDGE HALL: * * *

This case presents the question of what laws and standards control when U.S. antitrust laws are violated by foreign companies that claim to be acting at the express direction or mandate of a foreign government. Specifically, we address how a federal court should respond when a foreign government, through its official agencies, appears before that court and represents that it has compelled an action that resulted in the violation of U.S. antitrust laws. In so doing we balance the interests in adjudicating antitrust violations alleged to have harmed those within our jurisdiction with the official acts and interests of a foreign sovereign in respect to economic regulation within its borders. When, as in this instance, we receive from a foreign government an official statement explicating its own laws and regulations, we are bound to extend that explication the deference long accorded such proffers received from foreign governments.

Here, because the Chinese Government filed a formal statement in the district court asserting that Chinese law required Defendants to set prices and reduce quantities of vitamin C sold abroad, and because Defendants could not simultaneously comply with Chinese law and U.S. antitrust laws, the principles of international comity required the district court to abstain from exercising jurisdiction in this case. Thus, we vacate the judgment, reverse the district court's order denying Defendants' motion to dismiss, and remand with instructions to dismiss Plaintiffs' complaint with prejudice.

Background

For more than half a century, China has been a leading producer and exporter of vitamin C. In the 1970s, as China began to transition from a centralized state-run command economy to a market economy, the Chinese Government began to implement various export controls in order to retain a competitive edge over other producers of vitamin C on the world market. In the intervening years, the Government continued to influence the market and develop policies to retain that competitive edge. . . . By 2001, Chinese suppliers had captured 60% of the worldwide vitamin C market.

In 2005, various vitamin C purchasers in the United States, including Plaintiffs Animal Science Products, Inc. and The Ranis Company, filed numerous suits against Defendants . . . [for] an illegal cartel with the "purpose and effect of fixing prices, controlling the support of vitamin C to be exported to the United States and worldwide . . . . Plaintiffs assert that Defendants colluded with an entity that has been referred to in this litigation as both the "Western Medicine Department of the Association of Importers and Exporters of Medicines and Health Products of China" and the "China Chamber of Commerce of Medicines & Health Products Importers & Exporters," (the "Chamber") and agreed to "restrict their exports of Vitamin C in order to create a shortage of supply in the international market." Plaintiffs allege that, from December 2001 to the time the complaint was filed, Defendants, their representatives, and the Chamber devised and implemented policies to address price cutting by market actors and to limit production levels and increase vitamin C prices with the intent to create a shortage on the world market and maintain China's position as a leading exporter.

Rather than deny the Plaintiffs' allegations, Defendants instead moved to dismiss on the basis that they acted pursuant to Chinese regulations regarding vitamin C export pricing and were, in essence, required by the Chinese Government, specifically the Ministry of

Commerce of the People's Republic of China (the "Ministry"), to coordinate prices and create a supply shortage. Defendants argued that the district court should dismiss the complaint pursuant to the act of state doctrine, the doctrine of foreign sovereign compulsion, and/or principles of international comity. In an historic act, the Ministry filed an amicus curiae brief in support of Defendants' motion to dismiss.[5]

In its brief to the district court, the Ministry represented that it is the highest authority within the Chinese Government authorized to regulate foreign trade. The Ministry explained that the Chamber, which Plaintiffs refer to as an "association," is entirely unlike a "trade association" or the "chamber of commerce" in the United States and, consistent with China's state-run economy, is a "Ministry-supervised entity authorized by the Ministry to regulate vitamin C export prices and output levels." . . .

According to the Ministry, the Chamber was an instrumentality of the State that was required to implement the Ministry's administrative rules and regulations with respect to the vitamin C trade.

In support of Defendants' motion to dismiss, the Ministry also provided evidence of two Ministry-backed efforts by the Chamber to regulate the vitamin C industry: (1) a vitamin C Subcommittee ("the Subcommittee") created in 1997 and (2) a "price verification and chop" policy ("PVC") implemented in 2002. The Chamber created the Subcommittee to address "intense competition and challenges from the international [vitamin C] market." Before 2002, only companies that were members of the Subcommittee were allowed to export vitamin C. Under this regime, a vitamin C manufacturer qualified for the Subcommittee and was granted an "ex port quota license" if its export price and volume was in compliance with the Subcommittee's coordinated export price and export quota. In short, the Ministry explained to the district court that it compelled the Subcommittee and its licensed members to set and coordinate vitamin C prices and export volumes.

In 2002, the Chamber abandoned the "export quota license" regime and implemented the PVC system, which the Ministry

---

[5]   As Judge Trager noted, the Ministry's appearance in this case is historic because it is the first time any entity of the Chinese Government has appeared *amicus curiae* before any U.S. court. On appeal, the Ministry also appears *amicus curiae* before this court.

represented was in place during the time of the antitrust violations alleged in this case. To announce the new regime, the Ministry issued an official notice, a copy of which is attached to the Ministry's brief in support of Defendants' motion to dismiss. This document, hereinafter "the 2002 Notice," explains that the Ministry adopted the PVC regime, among other reasons, "in order to accommodate the new situations since China's entry into [the World Trade Organization], maintain the order of market competition, make active efforts to avoid anti-dumping sanctions imposed by foreign countries on China's exports, promote industry self-discipline and facilitate the healthy development of exports." The 2002 Notice, furthermore, refers to "industry-wide negotiated prices" and states that "PVC procedure shall be convenient for exporters while it is conducive for the chambers to coordinate export price and industry self-discipline." According to the Ministry, under this system, vitamin C manufacturers were required to submit documentation to the Chamber indicating both the amount and price of vitamin C it intended to export. The Chamber would then "verify" the contract price and affix a "chop," i.e., a special seal, to the contract, which signaled that the contract had been reviewed and approved by the Chamber. A contract received a chop only if the price of the contract was "at or above the minimum acceptable price set by coordination through the Chamber." Manufacturers could only export vitamin C if their contracts contained this seal. The Ministry asserted that under the PVC regime, Defendants were required to coordinate with other vitamin C manufacturers and agree on the price that the Chamber would use in the PVC regime. In short, the Ministry represented to the district court that all of the vitamin C that was legally exported during the relevant time was required to be sold at industry-wide coordinated prices.

Defendants moved to dismiss the complaint based on the act of state doctrine, the defense of foreign sovereign compulsion, and the principle of international comity. The district court denied the motion in order to allow for further discovery with respect to whether Defendants' assertion that the actions constituting the basis of the antitrust violations were compelled by the Chinese Government. . . .
* * *

The case ultimately went to trial. In March 2013, a jury found Defendants liable for violations of Section 1 of the Sherman Act. The district court awarded Plaintiffs approximately $147 million in damages and issued a permanent injunction barring Defendants from further violating the Sherman Act. This appeal followed.

Discussion

The central issue that we address is whether principles of international comity required the district court to dismiss the suit. As part of our comity analysis we must determine whether Chinese law required Defendants to engage in anticompetitive conduct that violated U.S. antitrust laws. Within that inquiry, we examine the appropriate level of deference to be afforded a foreign sovereign's interpretation of its own laws. We hold that the district court abused its discretion by not abstaining, on international comity grounds, from asserting jurisdiction because the court erred by concluding that Chinese law did not require Defendants to violate U.S. antitrust law and further erred by not extending adequate deference to the Chinese Government's proffer of the interpretation of its own laws.

A.   *Standard of Review*

* * *

B.   *International Comity*

Defendants argue that the district court erred by not dismissing Plaintiffs' complaint on international comity grounds. Comity is both a principle guiding relations between foreign governments and a legal doctrine by which U.S. courts recognize an individual's acts under foreign law. "Comity, in the legal sense, is neither a matter of absolute obligation, on the one hand, nor of mere courtesy and good will, upon the other." *Hilton v. Guyot*, 159 U.S. 113, 163–64 (1895) (internal quotations omitted). "[I]t is the recognition which one nation allows within its territory to the legislative, executive or judicial acts of another nation, having due regard both to international duty and convenience, and to the rights of its own citizens or of other persons who are under the protection of its laws." *Id.* This doctrine "is not just a vague political concern favoring international cooperation when it is in our interest to do so [but r]ather it is a principle under which judicial decisions reflect the systemic value of reciprocal tolerance and goodwill." *Societe Nationale Industrielle Aerospatiale v. U.S. Dist. Court of S. Dist. of Iowa*, 482 U.S. 522, 555 (1987). While we approach Defendants' international comity defense from the "legal sense," we do not lose sight of the broader principles underlying the doctrine. See JP Morgan 1 Chase Bank, 412 F.3d at 423 ("Whatever its precise contours, international comity is clearly concerned with maintaining amicable working relationships between nations, a shorthand for good neighborliness, common courtesy and mutual respect between those who labor in adjoining judicial vineyards." (internal quotation omitted)). Our analysis reflects an obligation to balance "the interests of the United States, the interests of the foreign state, and those mutual interests the family of nations have in just and efficiently functioning rules of international law." In re *Maxwell Commc'n Corp.*, 93 F.3d [1036], 1048 [2d Cir. 1996]. * * *

To determine whether to abstain from asserting jurisdiction on comity grounds we apply the multi-factor balancing test set out in *Timberlane Lumber Co. v. Bank of Am., N.T. & S.A.*, 549 F.2d 597, 614–15 (9th Cir. 1976) and *Mannington Mills, Inc. v. Congoleum Corp.*, 595 F.2d 1287, 1297–98 (3d Cir. 1979). . . . Both *Timberlane Lumber* and *Mannington Mills* addressed the unique international concerns that are implicated by exercising jurisdiction over antitrust violations that occur abroad and that involve the laws and regulations of a foreign nation. See *Timberlane Lumber Co.*, 549 F.2d at 613 ("[T]here is the additional question which is unique to the international setting of whether the interests of, and links to, the United States including the magnitude of the effect on American foreign commerce are sufficiently strong, vis-a-vis those of other nations, to justify an assertion of extraterritorial authority."); *Mannington Mills, Inc.*, 595 F.2d at 1296 ("When foreign nations are involved, however, it is unwise to ignore the fact that foreign policy, reciprocity, comity, and limitations of judicial power are considerations that should have a bearing on the decision to exercise or decline jurisdiction."). Combined and summarized here, the enumerated factors from *Timberlane Lumber* and *Mannington Mills* (collectively the "comity balancing test") guiding our analysis of whether to dismiss on international comity grounds include: (1) Degree of conflict with foreign law or policy; (2) Nationality of the parties, locations or principal places of business of corporations; (3) Relative importance of the alleged violation of conduct here as compared with conduct abroad; (4) The extent to which enforcement by either state can be expected to achieve compliance, the availability of a remedy abroad and the pendency of litigation there; (5) Existence of intent to harm or affect American commerce and its foreseeability; (6) Possible effect upon foreign relations if the court exercises jurisdiction and grants relief; (7) If relief is granted, whether a party will be placed in the position of being forced to perform an act illegal in either country or be under conflicting requirements by both countries; (8) Whether the court can make its order effective; (9) Whether an order for relief would be acceptable in this country if made by the foreign nation under similar circumstances; and (10) Whether a treaty with the affected nations has addressed the issue.

Mannington Mills, Inc., 595 F.2d at 1297–98; *Timberlane Lumber Co.,* 549 F.2d at 614.

Since our adoption of the comity balancing test, the Supreme Court, in determining whether international comity cautioned against exercising jurisdiction over antitrust claims premised entirely on foreign conduct, relied solely upon the first factor—the degree of conflict between U.S. and foreign law—to decide that abstention was inappropriate. *Hartford Fire,* 509 U.S. at 798 ("The only substantial question in this litigation is whether there is in fact a true conflict between domestic and foreign law."). The Court explained that just because "conduct is lawful in the state in which it took place will not, of itself, bar application of the United States antitrust laws." *Id.* Thus, in that case, the degree of conflict between the laws of the two states had to rise to the level of a true conflict, i.e. "compliance with the laws of both countries [must have been] impossible," to justify the Court's abstention on comity grounds. *Id.* at 799. In other words, "[n]o conflict exists . . . 'where a person subject to regulation by two states can comply with the laws of both.' " *Id.*

We read *Hartford Fire* narrowly. . . . That a true conflict was lacking in *Hartford Fire* does not, in the inverse, lead us to conclude that the presence of such a conflict alone is sufficient to require dismissal and thereby vitiate the need to consider the remaining factors.

Some courts, after *Hartford Fire,* have gone further and do not require a true conflict between laws before applying the remaining factors in the comity balancing test. . . . We need not, however, determine whether absent a true conflict, the district court could have abstained from asserting jurisdiction on comity grounds because, in our view and as explained below, there is a true conflict between U.S. law and Chinese law in this case.

C.   True Conflict Analysis

To determine whether Defendants could have sold and distributed vitamin C while in compliance with both Chinese and U.S. law, and thus whether a "true conflict" exists, we must determine conclusively what the law of each country requires.

* * *

The Ministry, *as amicus,* has proclaimed on behalf of the Chinese Government that Chinese law, specifically the PVC regime during the relevant period, required Defendants, as manufacturers of vitamin C, to fix the price and quantity of vitamin C sold abroad.

The Ministry mainly relies on the reference to "industry-wide negotiated prices" contained in the 2002 Notice to support its position. Plaintiffs, however, argue that the Ministry's statements are not conclusive and that because the 2002 Notice does not explicitly mandate price fixing, adherence to both Chinese law and U.S. antitrust law is possible. Our interpretation of the record as to Chinese law thus hinges on the amount of deference that we extend to the Chinese Government's explanation of its own laws.

1.   Standard of Deference

There is competing authority on the level of deference owed by U.S. courts to a foreign government's official statement regarding its own laws and regulations. . . .

* * *

. . . [W]e reaffirm the principle that when a foreign government, acting through counsel or otherwise, directly participates in U.S. court proceedings by providing a sworn evidentiary proffer regarding the construction and effect of its laws and regulations, which is reasonable under the circumstances presented, a U.S. court is bound to defer to those statements. If deference by any measure is to mean anything, it must mean that a U.S. court not embark on a challenge to a foreign government's official representation to the court regarding its laws or regulations, even if that representation is inconsistent with how those laws might be interpreted under the principles of our legal system. *Cf. Abbott*, 560 U.S. at 20 ("Judges must strive always to avoid a common tendency to prefer their own society and culture, a tendency that ought not interfere with objective consideration . . . ."); *Banco Nacional de Cuba v. Sabbatino*, 376 U.S. 398, 430 (1964) (recognizing, among other things, that the "basic divergence between the national interests of capital importing and capital exporting nations and between the social ideologies of those countries that favor state control of a considerable portion of the means of production and those that adhere to a free enterprise system" creates "disagreements as to [the] relevant international legal standards" such that inquiring into the validity of a foreign sovereign's actions is barred by the state action doctrine). Not extending deference in these circumstances disregards and unravels the tradition of according respect to a foreign government's explication of its own laws, the same respect and treatment that we would expect our government to receive in comparable matters before a foreign court. . .

2. *Applying Deference to the Ministry's Brief*

The official statements of the Ministry should be credited and accorded deference. On that basis, we conclude, as Defendants and the Ministry proffer, that Chinese law required Defendants to engage in activities in China that constituted antitrust violations here in the United States.

The 2002 Notice, *inter alia*, demonstrates that from 2002 to 2005, the relevant time period alleged in the complaint, Chinese law required Defendants to participate in the PVC regime in order to export vitamin C. This regulatory regime allowed vitamin C manufacturers the export only of vitamin C subject to contracts that complied with the "industry-wide negotiated" price. Although the 2002 Notice does not specify how the "industry-wide negotiated" price was set, we defer to the Ministry's reasonable interpretation that the term means what it suggests—that members of the regulated industry were required to negotiate and agree upon a price. It would be nonsensical to incorporate into a government policy the concept of an "industry-wide negotiated" price and require vitamin C manufacturers to comply with that minimum price point if there were no directive to agree upon such a price. Moreover, while on their face the terms "industry self-discipline," "coordination," and "voluntary restraint" may suggest that the Defendants were not required to agree to "industry-wide negotiated" prices, we defer to the Ministry's reasonable explanation that these are terms of art within Chinese law connoting the government's expectation that private actors actively self-regulate to achieve the government's policy goals in order to minimize the need for the government to resort to stronger enforcement methods. In this context, we find it reasonable to view the entire PVC regime as a decentralized means by which the Ministry, through the Chamber, regulated the export of vitamin C by deferring to the manufacturers and adopting their agreed upon price as the minimum export price. In short, by directing vitamin C manufacturers to coordinate export prices and quantities and adopting those standards into the regulatory regime, the Chinese Government required Defendants to violate the Sherman Act. . .

We reiterate that deference in this case is particularly important because of the unique and complex nature of the Chinese legal- and economic-regulatory system and the stark differences between the Chinese system and ours. As the district court recognized, "Chinese law is not as transparent as that of the United States or other constitutional or parliamentary governments." China's legal system is distinct from ours in that "[r]ather than codifying its statutes, the Chinese government [ ] frequently governs by regulations promulgated by various ministries . . . . [and] private citizens or companies may be authorized under Chinese regulations to act in certain circumstances as government agents." Moreover, the danger that "an interpretation suggested by the plain language of a governmental directive may not accurately reflect Chinese law" is all the more plausible where the documents the district court relied upon are translations and use terms of art which are unique to the Chinese system. Deferring to the Ministry's explanation of what is legally required under its system is all the more important where, as here, the record evidence shows a clear disparity between China's economic regulatory regime and our own.

. . . [T]he district court found problematic the possibility that the "defendants [made] their own choices and then ask[ed] for the government's imprimatur."

* * *

Whether Defendants had a hand in the Chinese government's decision to mandate some level of price-fixing is irrelevant to whether Chinese law actually required Defendants to act in a way that violated U.S antitrust laws. Moreover, inquiring into the motives behind the Chinese Government's decision to regulate the vitamin C market in the way it did is barred by the act of state doctrine. . . . Thus, we decline to analyze why China regulated vitamin C in the manner it did and instead focus on what Chinese law required.

* * *

Finally, the district court made a conceptual error about the potential difference between foreign compulsion and a true conflict. The district court credited Plaintiffs' argument that because there was evidence that Defendants routinely agreed to export vitamin C at a price well above the agreed upon price of $3.35/kg, the Defendants alleged anticompetitive conduct was not compelled. But this conclusion misses the mark. Even if Defendants' specific conduct was not compelled by the 2002 Notice, that type of compulsion is not required for us to find a true conflict between the laws of the two sovereigns. . . . * * *

D.   *Applying the Remaining Comity Factors* * * *

. . . [The] remaining factors [also] decidedly weigh in favor of dismissal and counsel against exercising jurisdiction in this case.

All Defendants are Chinese vitamin C manufacturers with their principal places of business in China, and all the relevant conduct at issue took place entirely in China. Although Plaintiffs may be unable to obtain a remedy for Sherman Act violations in another forum, complaints as to China's export policies can adequately be addressed through diplomatic channels and the World Trade Organization's processes. Both the U.S. and China are members of the World Trade Organization and are subject to the same rules on export restrictions. Moreover, there is no evidence that Defendants acted with the express purpose or intent to affect U.S. commerce or harm U.S. businesses in particular. Rather, according to the Ministry, the regulations at issue governing Defendants' conduct were intended to assist China in its transition from a state run command economy to a market-driven economy, and the resulting price fixing was intended to ensure China remained a competitive participant in the global vitamin C market and to prevent harm to China's trade relations. While it was reasonably foreseeable that China's vitamin C policies would generally have a negative effect on Plaintiffs as participants in the international market for vitamin C, as noted above, there is no evidence that Defendants' antitrust activities were specifically directed at Plaintiffs or other U.S. companies.

Furthermore, according to the Ministry, the exercise of jurisdiction by the district court has already negatively affected U.S.-China relations. See U.S. Vitamin Fine "unfair and inappropriate" Says Mofcom, Global Competition Review, Katy Oglethorpe, March 21, 2013 (quoting the Chinese government as stating that the district court's judgment "will cause problems for the international community and international enterprises, and will eventually harm the interests of the United States due to the increase in international disputes"). The Chinese Government has repeatedly made known to the federal courts, as well as to the United States Department of State in an official diplomatic communication relating to this case, that it considers the lack of deference it received in our courts, and the exercise of jurisdiction over this suit, to be disrespectful and that it "has attached great importance to this case.". . .

Currently, the district court's judgment orders Defendants to comply with conflicting legal requirements. This is an untenable outcome. It is unlikely, moreover, that the injunctive relief the Plaintiffs obtained would be enforceable in China. If a similar injunction were issued in China against a U.S. company, prohibiting that company from abiding by U.S. economic regulations, we would undoubtedly decline to enforce that order. . . .

Simply put, the factors weigh in favor of abstention. Recognizing China's strong interest in its protectionist economic policies and given the direct conflict between Chinese policy and our antitrust laws, we conclude that China's "interests outweigh whatever antitrust enforcement interests the United States may have in this case as a matter of law." *O.N.E. Shipping Ltd.*, 830 F.2d at 450. Accordingly, we hold that the district court abused its discretion by failing to abstain on international comity grounds from asserting jurisdiction, and we reverse the district court's order denying Defendants' motion to dismiss.

We further note that while we abstain from adjudicating Plaintiffs' claims with respect to the Defendants' conduct, the Plaintiffs are not without recourse to the executive branch, which is best suited to deal with foreign policy, sanctions, treaties, and bi-lateral negotiations. Because we reverse and remand for dismissal on the basis of international comity, we do not address the act of state, foreign sovereign compulsion, or political question defenses.

* * *

Notes and Questions

1.   The Chinese manufacturers agreed to fix prices, and raised them as much as 80%. There is a soft world norm that price-fixing is illegal, and the strong US anti-cartel law is well known. Should China be able to immunize its firms from US antitrust law by saying in court: I ordered them to do it?

2.   Suppose there were a parallel case wholly within the United States. Suppose that, in the heyday of US car manufacturing, Michigan ordered General Motors, Ford and Chrysler to agree on the prices they would charge for out-of-state sales, and the car companies did so. They would soon discover that their price fixing was illegal, for a state of the United States cannot order its firms to fix prices and free them from application of the federal antitrust laws. California Retail Liquor Dealers Ass'n v. Midcal Aluminum, Inc., 445 U.S. 97 (1980); Schwegmann Bros. v. Calvert Distillers Corp., 341 U.S. 384 (1951). Should a foreign government have more power than the states of the United States to confer immunity?

A somewhat parallel case arose in the European Union. An Italian government official set the price for matches in Italy and an Italian law required the Italian match producers to set quotas. The producers set the quotas, doing so in a way that slighted the Germans and Swedes, who wanted to sell matches in Italy. EU law has a counterpart to the US state action doctrine—if acts of a private party are compelled by the state and thus are not autonomous, the acts are attributable to the state and the private parties do not violate the competition law. But, the court said, in the *Italian matches* case, the Italian match producers did not *have* to set the quotas in so anticompetitive a way. To the extent of this discretion, the quota-setting was an act of the producers and the producers violated the competition law. Consorzio Industrie Fiammiferi v. Autoria Garante della Concorrenza, EU:C:2003:430

What is distinct about the Chinese vitamin cartel as compared with any other private cartel? Does the US antitrust action against the Chinese manufacturers interfere with US foreign relations because China entered the fray and said: "I ordered it"? Is the Second Circuit's deference comity at work: We respect China's word and command, and expect that Chinese courts will similarly respect America's word and command when the facts are reversed? How much does the doctrine of deference depend on American confidence that a Chinese court in some future litigation will do the same thing?

b. OPEC

The big oil producing nations of the world, centered in the Middle East, have had an oil producers' cartel since 1960. OPEC accounts for some three quarters of the world's oil reserves, and has been blamed for several oil crises and about a trillion dollars of oil overcharges to Americans alone.

On several occasions the US government has considered suit against OPEC or its member countries or companies; but—for diplomatic reasons—has not sued. A private action was brought against OPEC in the 1970s in the wake of an oil crisis, but the suit was dismissed as raising a political question and as barred by the Act of State doctrine. *International Association of Machinists v. OPEC*, 649 F.2d 1354 (9th Cir. 1981).

In later years, in the face of rising oil prices, Congress has repeatedly vetted its ire against OPEC. It introduced—but never passed—a bill that would authorize the Justice Department to sue OPEC. The colloquial name of the bill is NOPEC—No Oil Producing and Exporting Cartels.

US judicial opinions have differed on whether OPEC should be liable in US courts even without a federal statute authorizing antitrust actions against the cartel. In *Prewitt Enterprises, Inc. v. OPEC*, 2001 WL 2001 WL 624789; 2001–2 Trade Cas. (CCH) ¶ 73,246 (N.D. Ala. 2001) (opinion vacated and case dismissed for failure of service, 353 F.3d 916 (11th Cir. 2003), the district court would have permitted a class action by oil purchasers to proceed against OPEC. The member states of OPEC (Iraq, Libya, Iran, Saudi Arabia, United Arab Emirates, Qatar, Kuwait, Algeria, Nigeria, Indonesia, and Venezuela) and non-member cooperating states (Norway, Mexico, Russia, and Oman) were not named as defendants, thus avoiding a suit against a sovereign. The court found it "beyond dispute that OPEC was created and exists for the express purpose of coordinating, limiting, stabilizing and otherwise controlling crude oil production and export in order to increase its members' revenues." It further found that "the Sherman Act plainly reaches agreements in restraint of trade entered into by foreign entities such as OPEC acting abroad that have a substantial and adverse impact in the United States." Turning to the sovereign immunity question, the court found that neither OPEC nor the state co-conspirators (non-defendants) could claim immunity given that they were engaging in conduct "plainly commercial in nature," as evidenced by the fact that the illegal acts "can be performed by private persons as well as sovereign states." Finding OPEC's conduct to be a *per se* violation of Section 1 of the Sherman Act, the district court entered a permanent injunction against its continued price fixing. The case was eventually vacated and dismissed for failure of service.

By contrast, in a case against a Venezuelan-based oil company and related corporate entities that allegedly colluded with OPEC to fix oil prices, the Federal Court of Appeals for the 5th Circuit declared that the courts had no subject matter jurisdiction.

The court said:

> ... Appellants, retailers of gasoline products in the United States, have asked the federal courts to adjudicate the merits of their antitrust claims against oil production companies that have allegedly participated in a conspiracy to fix prices. ... Appellants allege a conspiracy that is orchestrated by the sovereign member nations of OPEC. We hold today that Article III courts lack subject matter jurisdiction over Appellants' claims because they present nonjusticiable political questions that are constitutionally committed to the political branches responsible for the conduct of United States foreign relations and national security policy. Any ruling on the merits of this case would, by its core essence, impermissibly interfere with the Executive Branch's longstanding policy of engaging with OPEC nations regarding the global supply of oil through

diplomacy instead of private litigation. The constitutional concerns that inform our declination of jurisdiction under the political question doctrine similarly persuade us that adjudication of Appellants' claims is precluded by the act of state doctrine.

Spectrum Stores Inc. v. Citgo Petroleum Corp., 632 F.3d 938 (5th Cir.), cert. denied (Sup. Ct. 2011).

Congress, meanwhile, at various times, has introduced the NOPEC bill—No Oil Producing and Exporting Cartels. Here is the text of the NOPEC bill introduced in the Senate in 2009.

NOPEC
Senate, 111th CONGRESS, 1st Session, S. 204

To amend the Sherman Act to make oil-producing and exporting cartels illegal.

IN THE SENATE OF THE UNITED STATES
JANUARY 12, 2009
A BILL

To amend the Sherman Act to make oil-producing and exporting cartels illegal.

Be it enacted by the Senate and House of Representatives of the United States of America in Congress assembled,

SECTION 1. SHORT TITLE.

This Act may be cited as the 'No Oil Producing and Exporting Cartels Act of 2009' or 'NOPEC'.

SEC. 2. SHERMAN ACT.

The Sherman Act (15 U.S.C. 1 et seq.) is amended by adding after section 7 the following:

'SEC. 7A. OIL PRODUCING CARTELS.

'(a) In General—It shall be illegal and a violation of this Act for any foreign state, or any instrumentality or agent of any foreign state, to act collectively or in combination with any other foreign state, any instrumentality or agent of any other foreign state, or any other person, whether by cartel or any other association or form of cooperation or joint action—

'(1) to limit the production or distribution of oil, natural gas, or any other petroleum product;

'(2) to set or maintain the price of oil, natural gas, or any petroleum product; or

'(3) to otherwise take any action in restraint of trade for oil, natural gas, or any petroleum product;

when such action, combination, or collective action has a direct, substantial, and reasonably foreseeable effect on the market, supply, price, or distribution of oil, natural gas, or other petroleum product in the United States.

'(b) Sovereign Immunity—A foreign state engaged in conduct in violation of subsection (a) shall not be immune under the doctrine of sovereign immunity from the jurisdiction or judgments of the courts of the United States in any action brought to enforce this section.

'(c) Inapplicability of Act of State Doctrine—No court of the United States shall decline, based on the act of state doctrine, to make a determination on the merits in an action brought under this section.

'(d) Enforcement—The Attorney General of the United States may bring an action to enforce this section in any district court of the United States as provided under the antitrust laws.' * * *

Should Congress pass NOPEC? If it should do so, what are the difficulties in implementation? the benefits? the probable results? How would a court order against OPEC or its members be likely to be formulated? How could it be enforced? If in the future OPEC should be abandoned, what, would you predict, will have been the cause?

G. COOPERATION, CONVERGENCE, AND CROSS-FERTILIZATION IN INTERNATIONAL CARTEL ENFORCEMENT

Cooperation and convergence are a vital part of international cartel enforcement. While US anti-cartel efforts thrive on criminal enforcement and a number of jurisdictions follow the US lead, criminalization remains a lively issue in Europe and Asia. The European Commission has no criminal authority, although an increasing number of nations in Europe and the rest of the world do. Developments from the US point of view are summarized in the following remarks by a US deputy assistant attorney general in charge of antitrust. A counterpart essay on European law appears in Chapter 7, on Enforcement. We give further treatment to extraterritoriality and comity in Chapter 8, and we address issues of cooperation and convergence more fully in Chapter 9.

THE EVOLUTION OF CRIMINAL ANTITRUST ENFORCEMENT OVER THE LAST TWO DECADES

Scott D. Hammond, Deputy Assistant Attorney General for Criminal Enforcement
Antitrust Division, U.S. Department of Justice
February 25, 2010
(footnotes omitted)

I.   Introduction

Over the last two decades the cartel enforcement landscape has dramatically changed in the United States and around the globe. In the early 1990's, the sanctions imposed in criminal cartel cases brought by the Antitrust Division of the U.S. Department of Justice were not sufficiently severe and our original Corporate Leniency Program was simply not producing cases. In the last two decades, the world has seen the proliferation of effective leniency programs, ever-increasing sanctions for cartel offenses, a growing global movement to hold individuals criminally accountable, and increased international cooperation among enforcers in cartel investigations.

The Antitrust Division has spent the last two decades building and implementing a "carrot and stick" enforcement strategy by coupling rewards for voluntary disclosure and timely cooperation pursuant to the Antitrust Division's Corporate Leniency Program with severe sanctions. In addition, the Antitrust Division utilizes all available investigatory tools to create a significant risk and fear of detection and prosecution for violators of U.S. antitrust laws. The seeds of this "carrot and stick" enforcement strategy were planted by the Antitrust Division in the mid-1990s and began to bear fruit over the next decade. Since the mid-1990, the Antitrust Division has uncovered and prosecuted dozens of international cartels, secured convictions and jail sentences against culpable U.S. and foreign executives, and obtained hefty corporate fines. In recent years, competition enforcers around the world have intensified their cartel enforcement efforts and achieved similar results.

This paper will trace the evolution of cartel enforcement over the last two decades, highlighting U.S. milestones and achievements critical to the current success of cartel enforcement programs around the world.

II. The Carrot: Proliferation of Effective Corporate Leniency Programs

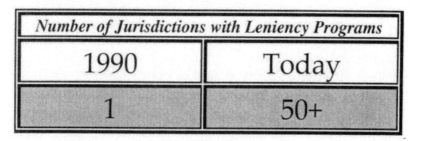

Number of Jurisdictions with Leniency Programs	
1990	Today
1	50+

The single most significant development in cartel enforcement is the proliferation of effective leniency programs. The advent of leniency programs has completely transformed the way competition authorities around the world detect, investigate, and deter cartels. Cartels by their nature are secretive and, therefore, hard to detect. Leniency programs provide enforcers with an investigative tool to uncover cartels that may have otherwise gone undetected and continued to harm consumers. While the notion of letting hard core cartel participants escape punishment was initially unsettling to many prosecutors, the Antitrust Division recognized that the grant of full immunity was necessary to induce cartel participants to turn on each other and self-report, resulting in the discovery and termination of the conduct, the successful prosecution of the remaining cartel participants, and damage recovery for victims. Moreover, the hope was that the benefits of leniency would extend beyond the cartels it directly uncovered and that the very existence of the leniency policy would be viewed by executives as raising the risk of detection and punishment, leading to greater deterrence of cartel activity.

The original version of the U.S. Corporate Leniency Program dates back to 1978. However, the original Corporate Leniency Program was rarely utilized and the Antitrust Division received on average only about one leniency application per year. No leniency application made under the original Corporate Leniency Program resulted in the detection of an international or large domestic cartel. In August 1993, the Antitrust Division revised its Corporate Leniency Program to make it easier and more attractive for companies to come forward and cooperate with the Antitrust Division. Three major revisions were made to the program: (1) leniency is automatic for qualifying companies if there is no pre-existing investigation; (2) leniency may still be available even if cooperation begins after the investigation is underway; and (3) all officers, directors, and employees who come forward with the company and cooperate are protected from criminal prosecution.

These revisions made the program more transparent and raised the incentives for companies to report criminal activity and cooperate with the Antitrust Division. As a result of these changes, the Antitrust Division has seen a nearly twenty-fold increase in the leniency application rate, making the Leniency Program the Antitrust Division's most effective investigative tool. Leniency programs provide unparalleled information from cartel insiders about the origins and inter-workings of secretive cartels. In the United States, companies have been fined more than $5 billion for antitrust crimes since Fiscal Year 1996, with over 90 percent of this total tied to investigations assisted by leniency applicants. The Antitrust Division typically has approximately 50 international cartel investigations open at a time, and more than half of these investigations were initiated, or are being advanced, by information received from a leniency applicant.

The success of the Antitrust Division's revised leniency program led to the adoption of similar voluntary disclosure programs by other jurisdictions. For example, Canada had some form of leniency in place since 1991 and the European Commission's first leniency notice was adopted in 1996. However, these programs, like the Antitrust Division's pre-1993 leniency program, lacked sufficient transparency and predictability to effectively induce self-reporting. When Canada issued its Immunity Bulletin in 2000 and the European Commission issued its revised Leniency Notice in 2002, the corporate leniency programs of the United States, the European Union, and Canada came into substantial convergence. This convergence in leniency programs has made it much easier and far more attractive for companies to simultaneously seek and obtain leniency in the United States, Europe, Canada, and in a growing list of other jurisdictions where the applicants have exposure. In the last decade, many other jurisdictions around the world have implemented leniency programs and today over 50 jurisdictions have leniency programs in place.

Leniency programs have led to the detection and dismantling of the largest global cartels ever prosecuted and resulted in record-breaking fines in Australia, Brazil, Canada, the European Union, Japan, Korea, Poland, the United Kingdom, the United States, and other jurisdictions.

Effective leniency programs create a race among conspirators to disclose their conduct to enforcers, in some instances even before an investigation has begun, and quickly crack cartels that may have otherwise gone undetected. However, simply creating a leniency program does not ensure that it will be *effective*. The business community and the private bar must have confidence in a leniency program or there will be no race to the enforcer's door to take advantage of it. There are three essential cornerstones that must be in place before a jurisdiction can successfully implement a leniency program. First, the jurisdiction's antitrust laws must provide the threat of severe sanctions for those who participate in hard core cartel activity and fail to self-report. Second, organizations must perceive a high risk of detection by antitrust authorities if they do not self-report. Third, there must be transparency and predictability to the greatest extent possible throughout a jurisdiction's cartel enforcement program, so that companies can predict with a high degree of certainty how they will be treated if they seek leniency, and what the consequences will be if they do not. These three major cornerstones—severe sanctions, heightened fear of detection, and transparency in enforcement policies—are the indispensable components of every effective leniency program.

Effective leniency programs destabilize cartels. If cartel members have a significant fear of detection and the consequences of getting caught are too severe, then the rewards of self-reporting become too important to risk losing the race for leniency to another cartel member, or perhaps to its own employee if individual leniency is available. The dynamic literally creates a race to be the first to the prosecutor's office.

Consider the "empty seat at the table" scenario. Five members of a cartel are scheduled to hold an emergency meeting, but when the meeting starts there is an empty seat at the table. One of the conspirators has unexpectedly not arrived at the meeting and is not returning phone calls. The cartel members at the meeting start to get nervous. Has the missing cartel member had a change of heart and abandoned the cartel? Has he already reported the others to the government? Or did he just miss his plane? In this environment, with the risk of detection and resulting sanctions so high, can the conspirators afford to trust one another? Each member of a cartel knows that any one of its co-conspirators can report the others in exchange for total immunity—a decision that will seal their fate. Imagine the vulnerability of cartel members in that position asking, "Can I really trust my competitors to look out for my best interests?" The answer to this question leads them directly to the prosecutor's door.

III. The Stick: Movement Toward Severe Sanctions, Including Individual Accountability

If the potential penalties that can be imposed upon cartel participants are not perceived as outweighing the potential rewards of participating in a cartel, then the fine imposed becomes merely part of the cost of doing business. The Antitrust Division has steadfastly emphasized the importance of individual accountability and stiff corporate fines to induce leniency applications and optimize deterrence of cartel conduct.

Over the last three decades sanctions imposed in cartel cases brought by the Antitrust Division have increased exponentially. This increase is attributable to a number of factors, including increases in maximum penalties for antitrust crimes, the Antitrust Division's reallocation of resources to focus on international cases involving larger volumes of commerce, and the change in perception by judges as to the seriousness of antitrust crimes. These factors came together in the 1990s to produce record fines, and this trend has continued in the 21st Century.

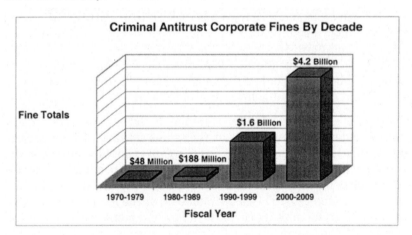

The Antitrust Division's sentencing statistics over the last two decades show a steady trend toward higher corporate fines for cartel offenses and longer jail sentences for individuals. For example, in Fiscal Year 1991 the average corporate fine for an antitrust offense in the United States was a little less than $320,000 and the largest corporate fine ever imposed for a single Sherman Act count was $2 million. In the mid-1990's the amount of corporate fines began to grow steadily, with multimillion dollar fines becoming more commonplace. In 1996, corporate fines reached a new order of magnitude when the Archer Daniels Midland Company ("ADM") paid a $100 million fine for its participation in two international antitrust conspiracies (lysine and citric acid) in the food and feed additives industry. Then-Deputy Assistant Attorney General of the Antitrust Division Gary Spratling predicted that the historic ADM fine was not an aberration, and that we would see more corporate fines in criminal antitrust cases above $100 million. This prediction quickly proved to be accurate. In April 1998, UCAR International agreed to pay a $110 million fine for its participation in the graphite electrodes conspiracy and in 1999, SGL agreed to pay a $135 million for its role in the graphite electrodes conspiracy. These record fines were quickly eclipsed in May 1999 when the worldwide vitamin cartel was exposed and pharmaceutical giant F. Hoffmann-La Roche Ltd agreed to plead guilty and pay a record $500 million criminal fine for leading the conspiracy and BASF AG agreed to pay a $225 million fine for its role.

The ADM fine truly was the tip of the iceberg for large corporate antitrust fines. The Antitrust Division's record of cracking large international cartels affecting huge amounts of commerce and obtaining nine-figure fines has continued in the new millennium with the Antitrust Division's prosecutions of cartels in the air transportation (more than $1.6 billion in criminal fines obtained to date), liquid crystal display (more than $860 million in criminal fines obtained to date), and dynamic random access memory (more than $730 million in criminal fines obtained to date) industries, among others. To date, the Antitrust Division has obtained 18 fines above $100 million and this trend shows no signs of decline, with the Antitrust Division obtaining just over $1 billion in fines in Fiscal Year 2009.

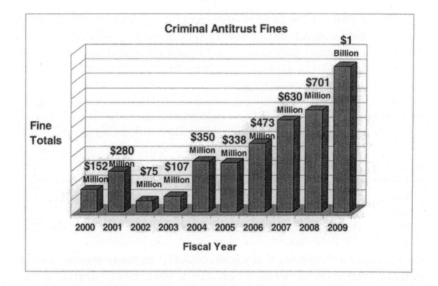

Other jurisdictions, most notably the European Union, have also steadily raised fines over the last two decades and imposed increasingly large fines against cartel participants. Before 1990, the highest cartel fines imposed in Europe were fines totaling 60 million ECU on 23 petrochemical producers for price fixing in the plastic industry. Since 2006, the European Commission has imposed more than 1 billion in cartel fines per year, reaching a high of over 3 billion in 2007. In December 2008, the Commission imposed its largest fines ever, ordering four car glass manufacturers to pay a combined total of more than 1.3 billion for their cartel conduct.

Individual Accountability

The Antitrust Division's detection and prosecution of the worldwide vitamin cartel was important not only because it resulted in record fines, but because for the first time a foreign executive agreed to serve time in U.S. prison for his participation in an international cartel. The historic plea agreement the Antitrust Division entered into in May 1999 with a Swiss vitamin executive was the first that called for the imposition of jail time for a foreign national who had participated in an international cartel. This plea agreement marked a watershed in the Antitrust Division's prosecution of international cartels. Before the filing of this case, foreign defendants prosecuted for their participation in international cartels, such as the lysine and citric acid cartels, had pled guilty but the Division did not seek a jail sentence in return for their admission of guilt, cooperation, and submission to U.S. jurisdiction. When the

Division began prosecuting international cartels, just convincing a foreign national to submit to U.S. jurisdiction and plead guilty was a major achievement. At that time, a no-jail deal was necessary for the Division to secure access to an important foreign witness or key foreign-located documents.

However, by 1999, the Antitrust Division's ability to successfully investigate and prosecute foreign nationals who violate U.S. antitrust laws had significantly advanced, with enhanced investigative tools and increased international cooperation. Thus, "no-jail" deals became a relic of the past. Division practice now is to insist on jail sentences for *all defendants* domestic and foreign. The Division will not agree to a "no-jail" sentence for any defendant, and our practice is not to remain silent at sentencing if a defendant argues for a no-jail sentence.

Since May 1999, more than 40 foreign defendants have served, or are serving, prison sentences in the United States for participating in an international cartel or for obstructing an investigation of an international cartel. Foreign nationals from France, Germany, Japan, Korea, Norway, the Netherlands, Sweden, Switzerland, Taiwan and the United Kingdom are among those defendants. The antitrust bar and business community understand that the Division is serious about its policy of insisting on jail sentences for both U.S. and foreign defendants. This realization provides further incentive for corporations to apply for leniency so that their cooperating executives will receive non-prosecution coverage. And if leniency is no longer available in an investigation, the Division's insistence on jail terms encourages executives to come in early to cooperate to minimize their jail time and companies to come in early to minimize the number of individual carve outs who could be subject to jail sentences.

During the last decade, the Antitrust Division has made increased individual accountability a critical piece of its cartel enforcement program and the Antitrust Division's enforcement statistics demonstrate that individuals who violate U.S. antitrust laws are being sent to jail with increasing frequency and for longer periods of time. Since 2000, the Antitrust Division has seen a steady increase in the percentage of defendants sentenced to jail.

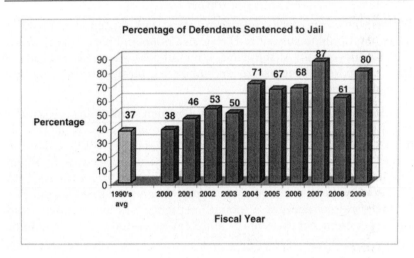

In addition, over the last decade the Antitrust Division has obtained successively greater jail sentences and set new deterrent marks, including the highest number of total jail days imposed in a fiscal year (31,391 in 2007) and the highest average jail sentence for all defendants in a fiscal year (31 months in 2007).

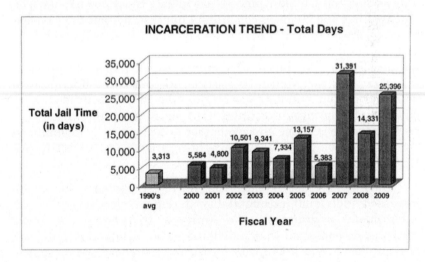

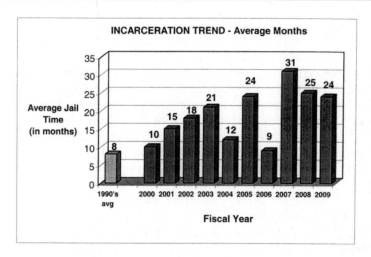

Consistent with the Antitrust Division's emphasis on promoting deterrence through individual accountability, the Antitrust Division also began prosecuting more culpable individuals from each corporate defendant. In the Antitrust Division's prosecutions of international cartels in the mid-1990s, it was typical for the Antitrust Division to prosecute only the single most culpable employee from each foreign company prosecuted. However, beginning in 1999 with the prosecution of six foreign executives from F. Hoffmann-La Roche and BASF for their participation in the vitamin cartel, the Antitrust Division began a policy of greater accountability for culpable executives. During the last decade, the Antitrust Division has routinely prosecuted multiple individuals from each corporate defendant, and over time, the Antitrust Division has tended to prosecute greater numbers of individuals from each corporate defendant.

The prosecution of the vitamin cartel was also important because it helped trigger a rethinking of the adequacy of competition laws around the world. The vitamin cartel was one of the most pervasive and harmful ever prosecuted by the Antitrust Division. The cartel was so sophisticated that its members were able to carve up the world's billion-dollar vitamin market among a few multi-national companies and fix prices on a country-by-country basis around the world for nearly ten years. The vitamin cartel operated with such precision and profit that it was called "Vitamins, Inc." by its members. The cartel impacted products that appeared not only in the cupboards of Americans, but in those of consumers worldwide.

The high-profile nature of the vitamin cartel and the nearly billion dollars in fines imposed against the vitamin cartel members in the United States grabbed the attention of the foreign press, as well as foreign businesses and consumers. Many foreign business and consumer groups then began asking whether their governments would be acting to protect their interests against cartel behavior. The vitamin cases helped fuel a movement to rethink the adequacy of competition laws and law enforcement powers that was already beginning to take place in many governments abroad as a result of the lysine and citric acid conspiracies. These governments began to consider whether they had sufficient penalties in place to deter cartel activity; whether cartel activity should be treated as an administrative or a criminal offense; and whether individuals as well as corporations should be sanctioned for cartel offenses. Twelve individuals, including six European executives, were sentenced to serve time in U.S. prisons for their role in the vitamin conspiracy. Ultimately, other jurisdictions including Canada, the European Union, Australia, and Korea imposed then-record fines against participants in the vitamin cartel, but no cartel member served a single day in jail outside the United States for their participation in the vitamin cartel.

The Antitrust Division has long emphasized that the most effective way to deter and punish cartel activity is to hold culpable individuals accountable by seeking jail sentences. That view is now gathering momentum around the world. In 2008, three executives were sentenced to lengthy jail terms in the United Kingdom for their participation in the marine hose conspiracy, marking the first jail sentences for a cartel offense under the 2002 Enterprise Act. In August 2008, the U.K.'s Office of Fair Trading continued its criminal prosecutions of individuals under the Enterprise Act when it announced charges against four British Airways executives in its investigation of price fixing of passenger fuel surcharges. The Australian Parliament introduced a criminal cartel offence effective July 24, 2009. Other jurisdictions such as Chile, the Czech Republic, Greece, Mexico, the Netherlands, New Zealand, Russia and South Africa have also recently adopted, or are considering, legislation that will criminalize cartel offenses. In addition, there have been major domestic criminal cartel prosecutions in a number of jurisdictions around the world. For instance, since making the prosecution of hard core cartels a top priority in Brazil in 2003, competition enforcers in Brazil have cooperated closely with State and Federal Public Prosecutor's Offices and the Federal Police to combat cartel conduct and to date more than 100 executives are facing criminal proceedings, at least ten executives have been sentenced to serve jail time, and another 19 executives have been sentenced to pay criminal fines for their participation in cartel conduct. Similarly, competition enforcers in Denmark, Ireland, Israel, Japan, and Korea have teamed with public prosecutors to bring criminal charges against cartel offenders.

The criminalization of cartel offenses will certainly be an area of continued evolution in cartel enforcement around the world in the years to come.

IV. The Chase: Creating a Fear of Detection Through the Use of Increased Investigative Tools

If executives perceive little risk of being caught by cartel enforcers, then stiff statutory penalties alone will not be sufficient to deter cartel activity. During the last two decades, cartel enforcers around the world have utilized an increasingly robust arsenal of investigative tools to instill a genuine fear of detection among executives. The covert tape recordings of the lysine cartel that were used to convict cartel participants, and have since been shown by the Antitrust Division around the world as an example of a cartel in action, show the cartel participants brazenly mocking enforcers in the U.S., Europe, and Asia. The lysine cartel members who were caught in the act clearly demonstrated a consciousness of guilt, but continued to meet because they had no fear of detection. Perhaps that is because such a large, global cartel had never before been detected and criminally prosecuted.

The lysine tapes provided a striking visual tour inside an actual cartel. As the Antitrust Division took the tapes around the world, members of the bar and business community witnessed the inner-working of a cartel with their own eyes. Members of this same cartel were sentenced to lengthy jail sentences and then-record fines were imposed against the corporate defendants. The successful detection and prosecution of the lysine cartel led to increased awareness in the international business community of the risks and the consequences of engaging in cartel activity.

The lysine tapes themselves also had a monumental impact on how many foreign governments viewed the efficacy of their investigative powers and sanctions. After the case, the Antitrust Division showed the tapes to enforcers at meetings of the OECD and the inaugural International Cartel Workshop held in Washington D.C. in October 1999, and also met individually with many foreign government officials and played the tapes for them. In many of those jurisdictions, the antitrust officials were already well aware of the harm caused by cartel activity, and they were already pushing for reform in their laws or in their investigative powers. Foreign enforcers arranged for Antitrust Division personnel to meet with key government policy makers such as treasury officials who held the purse strings for additional funding to fight cartels, legislative members who were contemplating changes in the law, and representatives of influential trade or business groups in an effort to help gain their support for increased enforcement. These stakeholders watched the tapes and saw with their own eyes how their businesses and their consumers had been victimized. Simply put, the lysine tapes caused some foreign governments to question, if not rethink, how they investigated and treated cartel offenses. Thereafter, numerous governments around the world began making cartels a top priority, devoting additional resources to cartel enforcement, and utilizing more traditional law enforcement tools such as search warrants and wire taps in cartel investigations. The global utilization of all available law enforcement powers in cartel investigation has helped to ensure that, in a growing number of countries, "crime in the suites" is treated the same as crime in the streets.

In the United States, since the 1990's the Antitrust Division has increased our arsenal of investigative tools in international cartel investigations to include the use of border watches, INTERPOL Red Notices, and extradition requests. In 2001, the Division adopted a policy of placing indicted fugitives on a "Red Notice" list maintained by INTERPOL. A red notice watch is essentially an international "wanted" notice that, in many INTERPOL member nations, serves as a request that the subject be arrested, with a view toward extradition. Multiple fugitive defendants have been apprehended through a Division INTERPOL red notice. The Division has sought, and will continue to seek, the extradition of fugitive defendants apprehended through the INTERPOL red notice watch wherever possible. The Division's use of red notices clearly raises the stakes for foreign executives who hope to avoid prosecution by simply remaining outside of the United States. With the stiffening resolve that foreign governments are taking toward punishing cartel activity and their increased willingness to assist the United States in prosecuting cartel activity, the safe harbors for antitrust offenders are rapidly shrinking. The use of these tools also assists the Antitrust Division in gathering evidence and provides strong incentives for those executives to accept responsibility and cooperate with Antitrust Division investigations.

V. The Global Network of Cartel Enforcement: Increased International Cooperation

In today's global economy, cartels do not stop at national borders, so cartel investigations cannot either. There is a growing worldwide consensus that international cartel activity is harmful, pervasive, and is victimizing businesses and consumers everywhere. The shared commitment of competition enforcers to fighting international cartels has led to the establishment of cooperative relationships among competition law enforcement authorities around the world in order to more effectively investigate and prosecute international cartels.

One of the interesting developments in international cartel cooperation can be found in the work of the International Competition Network's (ICN) Cartel Working Group. Initiated in 2004, this working group is an important forum for agencies to share expertise regarding the challenges of cartel enforcement. Informed by input and experiences of the participating agencies, the working group seeks to identify the best investigative techniques and policy approaches from around the world. A main focus of ICN work in the cartel area is assisting agencies in honing their operational and practical skills. In this vein, the Cartel Working Group organizes the annual ICN Cartel Workshop, a continuation of the successful series of agency-led International Cartel Conferences initiated by the U.S. Department of Justice in 1999. This annual event—hosted in 2009 by the Egyptian Competition Authority—provides a venue for anti-cartel enforcers from around the world to come together, learn from each other, and develop close working relationships that serve as the basis for future cooperation.

The ICN has assisted cartel enforcers in developing cross-border relationships that have resulted in real-time coordination among enforcers conducting parallel investigations of the same cartel. In addition, the proliferation of effective leniency programs has resulted in an increasing number of applicants seeking leniency simultaneously in multiple jurisdictions. Enforcers can then coordinate investigative steps, share—with the applicant's consent—information provided by a mutual leniency applicant, and coordinate searches. Coordinated searches and other investigative steps are becoming more prevalent.

Two recent high-profile examples of successful cooperation and coordination are the air transportation investigation where the United States cooperated with authorities on five continents in order to coordinate the executions of search warrants on multiple subject locations in the United States and abroad. The filing of the Antitrust Division's plea agreement with British Airways calling for a $300 million criminal fine coincided with the announcement by the U.K.'s Office of Fair Trading that the airline also agreed to pay a record fine of 121.5 million British pounds (roughly $250 million) for its role in the passenger fare conspiracy. To date, a total of 15 airlines and four executives have pled guilty in the Antitrust Division's ongoing investigation into price fixing in the air transportation industry. Collectively, the companies have paid or agreed to pay criminal fines totaling more than $1.6 billion and four executives have been sentenced to jail time.

In addition, recent Antitrust Division coordination with the U.K.'s Office of Fair Trading and the European Commission regarding cartel conduct in the marine hose industry is a model of international coordination and the monumental results it can achieve. On the same day that the Antitrust Division and the FBI conducted multiple searches in the United States and arrested eight foreign executives in Houston and San Francisco for their roles in the marine hose conspiracy, the United Kingdom and European antitrust authorities searched locations in Europe. The marine hose investigations also resulted in an international cooperation milestone when the Antitrust Division filed plea agreements with three British nationals in 2007, calling for lengthy jail sentences. For the first time, the Antitrust Division plea agreements anticipated and addressed the criminal prosecution of, and imposition of a jail sentence upon, the defendants for a cartel offense in another jurisdiction. The resulting charges in the United Kingdom against the defendants were the first criminal cartel offenses charged under the U.K.'s Enterprise Act since it came into force in 2003. The unparalleled level of cooperation in the marine hose cases not only made history, but it raised the stakes and provides a strong deterrent message for would-be cartel participants who seek to victimize consumers in multiple jurisdictions.

VI. Conclusion

As we see the next generation of jurisdictions adopt criminal sanctions or leniency programs, join in simultaneous coordinated raids on target companies around the world, or impose a record sanction, it is worth noting that the DNA for these developments dates back to policies and practices that were put in place by the Antitrust Division in the 1990s and proliferated and flourished through the dedicated efforts of global cartel enforcers over the last two decades.

_____

US enforcement against world cartels remains on the same high pitch. In 2015, the United States collected a record $3.6 billion in cartels fines. In the fiscal year 2015, the Department of Justice brought criminal charges against 66 individuals and 20 corporations. The average prison time for the period from 2010 to 2015 was 24 months. In fiscal year 2016, fines dropped to $386.8 million, partly in view of the completion of major investigations the year before.

_____

Notes and Questions

1.   The illegality of hard core cartels is no longer a contested question. But nations have somewhat different exceptions and exemptions, and different remedies. They disagree on whether cartels should be punished criminally, although more and more nations are criminalizing cartels. By the start of 2016, the list of countries that impose criminal penalties for cartel activities includes, in addition to the United States, Australia, Brazil, Canada, Cyprus, Czech Republic, Denmark, Egypt, Estonia, France, Germany, Greece, Hungary, Ireland, Israel, Japan, Kazakhstan, Latvia, Malta, Mexico, Norway, Peru, Romania, Russia, Slovak Republic, Slovenia, South Korea, Taiwan, and the United Kingdom. For criminal punishment, nations disagree on incarceration. The United States is the nation that most commonly uses jail sentences. Other jurisdictions are beginning to prescribe incarceration. Is some of the diversity a function of cultural context? We discuss this point in Chapter 7, on Enforcement.

2.   We have now examined approaches to cartels, which are widely regarded as the most harmful and heinous anticompetitive practice. We have looked at proof, possible defenses of crisis and government involvement, and outlines of world cooperation and coordination. The extraterritorial and comity issues of foreign action defenses are revisited and deepened in Chapter 8, Extraterritoriality and Jurisdiction. World cooperation is revisited and deepened in Chapter 9, Global Governance. We turn now to another most important substantive subject of competition law, monopolies and abuse of dominance. Indeed, for many developing nations whose economic landscape is populated by monopolies, not competitors, hard core abuse of dominance is the most harmful conduct.

Chapter 2

MONOPOLIES AND ABUSE
OF DOMINANCE

A. INTRODUCTION

Virtually all established or developing antitrust regimes prohibit monopolistic or abusive behavior by dominant firms. While cartels harm competition through competitor cooperation, dominant firms may harm competition through exclusionary or exploitative behavior. But despite agreement in principle that competition law should rein in misbehavior by dominant firms, the views on what is misbehavior are widely divergent. For convenience, we can group the issues into two categories.

First, there is a question about the goals of monopolization or abuse of dominance law. In recent years, the US courts have taken a narrow view—essentially holding that monopolization law is solely concerned with harms to consumer welfare usually involving lowering consumer surplus. The narrow view is designed to give freedom to business firms on the theory that freedom to act will produce the most efficient, innovative, and competitive results. In the United States, antitrust is not about business fairness, or ethics, or achieving a level playing field. The US Supreme Court has stated that "even an act of pure malice by one business competitor against another does not, without more, state a claim under the federal antitrust laws." *Brooke Group v. Brown & Williamson*, 509 U.S. 209, 225 (1993). US courts and antitrust agencies often repeat the mantra that antitrust law protects competition, not competitors. US courts have also held that monopolization is not a status offense—a firm cannot be condemned for *being* a monopolist but only for engaging in exclusionary behavior that creates or entrenches monopoly or comes dangerously close to doing so, harming consumers.

In many jurisdictions abuse of dominance is a more copious offense, on both economic and fairness grounds. They may use abuse of dominance law to help create a level playing field for business rivals, ensuring some degree of competitive fairness and business morality, and encouraging economic rivalry to produce more output and innovation without a need to show harm to consumers in every case.

A second difference of perspective concerns "prior beliefs" that antitrust enforcers and courts bring to monopolization or abuse of dominance cases. The US Supreme Court expresses skepticism that anticompetitive exclusionary conduct happens very often or that it will succeed in increasing monopoly power. It also expresses the belief that when exclusionary conduct does occur, markets tend to correct the monopolistic distortions quickly. Finally, US courts have viewed monopolization litigation itself as a potential source of anticompetitive restraint, chilling procompetitive conduct and imposing high costs on business.

Antitrust enforcers and courts in other parts of the world may come to monopolization cases with different perspectives. They may be more likely to believe that abusive conduct by dominant firms is frequent and harmful and that markets are not quick to correct the imperfections. They may be more confident that antitrust agencies and reviewing courts can effectively improve the market. The differences may relate both to different economic conditions (facts about how well the markets work in the jurisdiction) and to different political economy leanings.

In this chapter, we survey some of the leading issues in monopolization and abuse of dominance law. We do not cover market definition or proof of dominance or monopoly power, which are preliminary elements of the case, except for a few sentences below. We suggest that you watch ICN curriculum videos; one for market definition: *http://www.internationalcompetitionnetwork.org/about/steering-group/outreach/icncurriculum/marketdef.aspx* and one for market power (which includes the notion of dominance and monopoly power: *http://www.internationalcompetitionnetwork.org/about/steering-group/outreach/icncurriculum/marketpower.aspx.*

If you read the statutes and case law of various jurisdictions, you will see wide differences in what it takes to prove the threshold question of dominance. Jurisdictions vary in how much weight they give to market share, and indeed how large a market share must be to suggest dominance. The South African statute states that if a firm has 45% or more of a market it is dominant, and at market shares between 35% and 45%, the firm is dominant unless it can show that it does not have market power. The German statute provides that a firm is presumed dominant, subject to rebuttal, if it has a market share of 40% or more. In the United States, the plaintiff must prove monopoly power. Large market share is usually the starting point. Courts generally will infer market power, subject to rebuttal, if the firm has a share of about 70% or more and barriers to entry and expansion are significant.

In our treatment of exclusionary practices we include refusals to deal and discriminatory dealing, predatory pricing, margin squeezes, loyalty rebates, and exclusive dealing, among others. For exploitative practices we cover excessive pricing and the high price prong of discrimination, and certain exploitation of intellectual property.

B. EXCLUSIONARY OFFENSES

This section is about exclusionary practices by dominant firms or firms with monopoly power. In the United States the offense is monopolization under Section 2 of the Sherman Act. In the European Union and the many countries that adopt its language, the offense is abuse of dominance, which in the EU is illegal under Article 102 of the Treaty on the Functioning of the European Union (TFEU). We suggest that you read the European Treaty provisions in context in Appendix 1 hereto.

Exclusionary offenses are practices that exclude competitors by anticompetitive means. What qualifies as "anticompetitive" is the key inquiry. The statutory law and the case law of various jurisdictions differ, both in terms of goals and in terms of how to assess the evidence of market harm. Some jurisdictions, such as the United States, focus on consumer welfare and efficiency and take a narrow view of the offense, preferring to give a wide range of freedom to (even) dominant firms to decide on their business strategies, expecting that this freedom will produce the most competitive and innovative results. Some other jurisdictions, worried that firms without power might get squeezed out or marginalized by strategies of dominant firms, focus on harm to the "competitive process" and take a more copious view of the offense. To some extent, the differences are based on different market facts. Where markets work less well, capital markets are poor, barriers are high, and especially where the market leaders have been privileged by the state, there is a stronger case for more antitrust intervention to help make the market work. To some extent the differences are goal-based and ideological. Some jurisdictions' laws mean to advance small enterprises and ease the way of outsiders into the market; and in some jurisdictions there is more trust in the antitrust intervention than in dominant firms' behavior.

Despite the differences, there is a common core. When a firm uses its power to keep out competitors or push them back by means that have no benefits for consumers, when the acts are against consumer interests, and when they increase or maintain the dominant firms' power, these acts constitute monopolization and abuse of dominance. In Europe a number of port cases paradigmatically fit this description. A state owned or licensed firm runs a port and operates a ferry service. The firm refuses to allow access to a would-be ferry competitor. The refusal is illegal. Port of Rødby, 94/119/EC, Commission Decision 1993, OJ L 0052. A US example may be found in the litigation against AT&T beginning in the 1970s when AT&T was the monopoly supplier of all telecom services, including long distance and local, and all related hardware, including telephones and wires, in the United States. For many years AT&T performed great service for the people and was lovingly called Ma Bell. But when MCI appeared on the horizon with microwave technology for long distance service, AT&T erected all possible roadblocks to keep MCI from connecting to the local service structure. See United States v. American Telephone & Telegraph Co., 524 F. Supp. 1336 (D.D.C. 1981). The case was settled by consent decree breaking up AT&T.

Exclusionary practices come in many forms, and we cover a sampling of them. We start with refusals to deal and proceed to predatory pricing, margin squeezes, rebates including loyalty rebates, and cutting edge issues of abuse of intellectual property and Internet technology. To telescope the cutting edge issues, we mention in advance that competition authorities around the world are challenging acts of Google (search engine dominance and owner of Android smartphone technology) and Qualcomm (owner of essential IP in smartphones). We return to these pending issues after setting the stage for abuse of dominance/monopoly law generally.

1.   Refusals to Deal

In the US antitrust law of monopolization, three areas are rather clear: refusal to deal, low pricing, even targeted low pricing to stave off a competitive threat, and innovation. In these three areas, there is a very strong presumption that can amount almost to a per se legal rule. For refusals to deal, the leading case is Verizon v. Trinko, 540 U.S. 398 (2004). In *Trinko*, the Court characterized the incumbent telecom's acts degrading the service of new competitors (who depended upon the incumbent to provide service from the local loop) as a refusal to give sufficient assistance and thus a refusal to deal. It declared that refusals to deal are lawful unless they fit within one of two exceptions: 1) a profit-sacrifice strategy to enhance market power as in the *Aspen Skiing* case, and possibly 2) a violation of essential facility duties if such duties exist (and they rarely if ever do). The Court stressed the importance of firms' freedom to deal or not as necessary to provide incentives to invest and invent. The Court labeled duties to deal as "forced sharing," which undercuts incentives to invent, leads to the "supreme evil" that antitrust forbids—cartels, and imposes on courts supervision duties that they are ill prepared to bear.

European Union law reflects a different perspective, as you shall see. While it too presumes that firms, even dominant firms, can deal with whom they choose, the presumption is weaker and can be countered by the special responsibility of the dominant firm not to distort competition. The presumption does not apply in "exceptional circumstances," and the category of exceptional circumstances is not narrow.

The following cases—*IMS* and *Microsoft*—lay the groundwork for EU duty-to-deal law. EU law is more likely than US law to require dealing, as we see in the following cases.

IMS HEALTH GmbH & CO. AND NDC HEALTH GmbH
Case C–418/01, EU:C:2004:257 (European Court of Justice 2004)

[IMS Health Inc. was a market research company that provided services to the pharmaceutical industry. It devised a "brick structure" in which it divided Germany into geographic areas that were used to measure and report sales of individual pharmaceutical products. Its efforts culminated in the development of the 1860 brick structure—a format for categorizing and reporting data that was the central feature of its regional and wholesaler data-information services. The format was protected by German copyright law.

National Data Corporation entered the German market to provide marketing data to the pharmaceutical industry, in competition with IMS. The pharmaceutical companies wanted the data only in the 1860 format because that was the one they were using. NDC asked IMS for a license for the 1860 format, but IMS refused. NDC thereupon began selling marketing data to the pharmaceutical industry based on copies of the 1860 brick structure.

IMS brought proceedings in a German court to prohibit NDC from using the IMS brick structure, on grounds that the brick structure was a data base protected by copyright and IMS had the right to refuse to license it. The German court granted the injunction but then stayed the proceedings, observing that IMS could not refuse to license NDC if the refusal constituted an abuse of dominance under EU law. The national court referred to the Court of Justice questions concerning the circumstances under which such a refusal constitutes an abuse. The Court of Justice answered: Only in exceptional circumstances may the exercise of an exclusive (IP) right constitute an abuse of dominance. First, access to the product, service or IP must be indispensable to enable the undertaking to carry on business in a market.]

28 [To determine indispensability,] it must be determined whether there are products or services which constitute alternative solutions, even if they are less advantageous, and whether there are technical, legal or economic obstacles capable of making it impossible or at least unreasonably difficult for any undertaking seeking to operate in the market to create, possibly in cooperation with other operators, the alternative products or services. . . . [I]n order to accept the existence of economic obstacles, it must be established, at the very least, that the creation of those products or services is not economically viable for production on a scale comparable to that of the undertaking which controls the existing product or service. * * *

38 [Where access is indispensable,] it is sufficient that three cumulative conditions be satisfied, namely, that that refusal is preventing the emergence of a new product for which there is a potential consumers demand, that it is unjustified and such as to exclude any competition on a secondary market. * * *

44 . . . [I]t is sufficient that a potential market or even hypothetical market can be identified. Such is the case where the products or services are indispensable in order to carry on a particular business and where there is an actual demand for them on the part of undertakings which seek to carry on the business for which they are indispensable.

45 Accordingly, it is determinative that two different stages of production may be identified and that they are interconnected, the upstream product is indispensable in as much as for supply of the downstream product.

46 Transposed to the facts of the case in the main proceedings, that approach prompts consideration as to whether the 1860 brick structure constitutes, upstream, an indispensable factor in the downstream supply of German regional sales data for pharmaceutical products.

47 It is for the national court to establish whether that is in fact the position, and, if so be the case, to examine whether the refusal by IMS to grant a license to use the structure at issue is capable of excluding all competition on the market for the supply of German regional sales data on pharmaceutical products. * * *

_____

The next important EU case involves practices of *Microsoft*. Microsoft had been sued in the US for anticompetitive practices, which it rather blatantly used in order to defeat new technology that challenged its power, as the court found. *United States v. Microsoft*

Corp., 253 F.3d 34 (D.C. Cir. 2001), cert. denied. But the practices condemned were not refusals to deal. The European cases targeted refusals to deal and bundling.

MICROSOFT CORP. v. COMMISSION

(interoperability) Case T–201/04, EU:T:2007:289 (European General Court 2007)

[The European Commission brought proceedings against Microsoft, a "super-dominant" firm with more than 90% of the PC operating systems market, for abusing its dominant position in violation of Article 102. The Commission found two sets of Microsoft's practices to be illegal: 1) Bundling its media player with its operating system (Windows), which had become the standard in the market. RealNetworks had pioneered the media player and RealNetworks' player was popularly used with Windows. Thereafter Microsoft made its own media player and bundled it with Windows, foreclosing media player rivals from the most efficient channels to the market. 2) Refusal to deal, in the form of refusing to provide workgroup server software rivals with full interoperability information to connect with Windows and with Microsoft's workgroup server software. Workgroup servers are servers used by small enterprises to interconnect file, printing, document-sharing and management functions of all PCs within the enterprise. Novell and others had pioneered workgroup server software. Before Microsoft developed such software of its own, it gave full interoperability information to the workgroup server software providers. Then Microsoft made its own workgroup server software and withheld from its rivals the full information they needed for seamless interoperability. Microsoft noted that it provided a good deal of interoperability information and claiming that it had no legal duty to help its rivals. Belatedly, it also claimed that its interface protocols containing the withheld interoperability information contained intellectual property and that it had a right of absolute exclusivity of its intellectual property.

For remedies, the Commission ordered Microsoft to supply the full interoperability protocols, offer an unbundled version of Windows without the media player, and pay a fine of € 497 million for the two violations. Microsoft provided interoperability protocols, but, according to the monitoring trustee, the information provided was not in a form developers would understand. The Commission imposed a € 280 million fine for noncompliance with the interoperability mandate and an additional fine of € 3 million a day until Microsoft should comply.

Microsoft appealed to the Court of First Instance. In this section, we cover only the interoperability (duty to deal) issue.

Microsoft contended that disclosure of the interface protocols would entail disclosure of intellectual property. The Commission disputed this claim but nonetheless argued that the circumstances satisfied the criteria of *Magill/IMS*: (1) access [here, to the complete interoperability information] must be indispensable, (2) the refusal must exclude any effective competition on a neighboring market, and (3) the refusal must prevent the appearance of a new product for which there is a potential consumer demand. (4) If the criteria are satisfied, it then falls to the dominant firm to prove an objective justification.]

(1) Indispensability

369 ... [T]he Commission adopted a two-stage approach in determining whether the information at issue was indispensable, in that, first of all, it considered what degree of interoperability with the Windows domain architecture non-Microsoft work group server operating systems must achieve in order for its competitors to be able to remain viably on the market and, second, it appraised whether the interoperability that Microsoft refused to disclose was indispensable to the attainment of that degree of interoperability. * * *

[The Commission established, and the Court accepted, that users value interoperability; that a lesser degree of interoperability "will have an impact on the efficiency with which that work group server delivers its services to the users of the networks" (para. 413). As a first example, "if a work group server does not interoperate sufficiently with the 'security architecture' of the Windows work group network, the user might be required to log on twice. . . ." para. 415.] * * * [Other examples omitted, including outsiders' encountering security protocol problems.]

421 It follows from all of the foregoing considerations that Microsoft has not established that the Commission made a manifest error when it considered that non-Microsoft work group server operating systems must be capable of interoperating with the Windows domain architecture on an equal footing with Windows work group server operating systems if they were to be marketed viably on the market.

422 The Court also concludes ... that the absence of such interoperability with the Windows domain architecture has the effect of reinforcing Microsoft's competitive position on the work group server operating systems market, particularly because it induces consumers to use its work group server operating system in preference to its competitors', although its competitors' operating systems offer features to which consumers attach great importance. * * *

The refusal excludes any effective competition

560 In the contested decision, the Commission considered whether the refusal at issue gave rise to a 'risk' of the elimination of competition on the work group server operating systems market. Microsoft contends that that criterion is not sufficiently strict, since according to the case-law on the exercise of an intellectual property right the Commission must demonstrate that the refusal to license an intellectual property right to a third party is 'likely to eliminate all competition', or, in other words, that there is a 'high probability' that the conduct in question will have such a result.

561 The Court finds that Microsoft's complaint is purely one of terminology and is wholly irrelevant. The expressions 'risk of elimination of competition' and 'likely to eliminate competition' are used without distinction by the Community judicature to reflect the same idea, namely that Article [102] does not apply only from the time when there is no more, or practically no more, competition on the market. If the Commission were required to wait until competitors were eliminated from the market, or until their elimination was sufficiently imminent, before being able to take action under Article [102], that would clearly run counter to the objective of that provision, which is to maintain undistorted competition in the common market and, in particular, to safeguard the competition that still exists on the relevant market.

562 In this case, the Commission had all the more reason to apply Article [102] before the elimination of competition on the work group server operating systems market had become a reality because that market is characterized by significant network effects and because the elimination of competition would therefore be difficult to reverse.

563 Nor is it necessary to demonstrate that all competition on the market would be eliminated. What matters, for the purpose of establishing an infringement of Article [102], is that the refusal at issue is liable to, or is likely to, eliminate all effective competition on the market. It must be made clear that the fact that the competitors of the dominant undertaking retain a marginal presence in certain niches on the market cannot suffice to substantiate the existence of such competition.

[The Court then summarized the evidence showing the sharp rise of Microsoft's share of workgroup server software, to more than 60%, and the decline of the competitors' shares, as soon as Microsoft stopped providing full interoperability information. It also gave examples of how Microsoft killed off two of competitors' products, NDS for NT developed by Novell, and PC NetLink developed by Sun

Microsystems, by withholding interoperability information. See facts at para. 654 below]. * * *

(3) The new product * * *

646 In *IMS Health*, the Court of Justice, when assessing the circumstance relating to the appearance of a new product, also placed that circumstance in the context of the damage to the interests of consumers. . . . [T]he Court emphasized . . . that that circumstance related to the consideration that, in the balancing of the interest in protection of the intellectual property right and the economic freedom of its owner against the interest in protection of free competition, the latter can prevail only where refusal to grant a license prevents the development of the secondary market, to the detriment of consumers.

647 The circumstance relating to the appearance of a new product, as envisaged in *Magill* and *IMS Health*, cannot be the only parameter which determines whether a refusal to license an intellectual property right is capable of causing prejudice to consumers within the meaning of Article [102](b). As that provision states, such prejudice may arise where there is a limitation not only of production or markets, but also of technical development.

648 It was on that last hypothesis that the Commission based its finding in the contested decision. . . .

649 The Court finds that the Commission's findings at the recitals referred to in the preceding paragraph are not manifestly incorrect.

650 Thus, in the first place, the Commission was correct to observe that '[owing] to the lack of interoperability that competing work group server operating system products can achieve with the Windows domain architecture, an increasing number of consumers are locked into a homogeneous Windows solution at the level of work group server operating systems'.

651 It must be borne in mind that it has already been stated that Microsoft's refusal prevented its competitors from developing work group server operating systems capable of attaining a sufficient degree of interoperability with the Windows domain architecture, with the consequence that consumers' purchasing decisions in respect of work group server operating systems were channeled towards Microsoft's products. The Court has also already observed that it was apparent from a number of documents in the file that the technologies of the Windows 2000 range, in particular Active Directory, were increasingly being taken up by organizations. As interoperability problems arise more acutely with work group server operating systems in that range of products than with those of the

preceding generation, the increasing uptake of those systems merely reinforces the 'lock-in' effect referred to in the preceding paragraph.

652 The limitation thus placed on consumer choice is all the more damaging to consumers because, as already observed, they consider that non-Microsoft work group server operating systems are better than Windows work group server operating systems with respect to a series of features to which they attach great importance, such as 'reliability/availability of the . . . system' and 'security included with the server operating system'.

653 In the second place, the Commission was correct to consider that the artificial advantage in terms of interoperability that Microsoft retained by its refusal discouraged its competitors from developing and marketing work group server operating systems with innovative features, to the prejudice, notably, of consumers. That refusal has the consequence that those competitors are placed at a disadvantage by comparison with Microsoft so far as the merits of their products are concerned, particularly with regard to parameters such as security, reliability, ease of use or operating performance speed.

654 The Commission's finding that '[i]f Microsoft's competitors had access to the interoperability information that Microsoft refuses to supply, they could use the disclosures to make the advanced features of their own products available in the framework of the web of interoperability relationships that underpin the Windows domain architecture' is corroborated by the conduct which those competitors had adopted in the past, when they had access to certain information concerning Microsoft's products. The two examples which the Commission gives at recital 696 to the contested decision, 'PC NetLink' and 'NDS for NT', speak volumes in that regard. PC NetLink is software developed by Sun on the basis of AS/U, which had been developed by AT&T using source code which Microsoft had licensed to it in the 1990s. A document submitted by Microsoft during the administrative procedure shows that the innovative features and added value that PC NetLink brought to Windows work group networks was used as a selling point for that product. Likewise, in its marketing material, Novell highlighted the new features which NDS for NT—software which it had developed using reverse engineering—brought to the Windows domain architecture (in this instance Windows NT).

655 The Commission was careful to emphasize, in that context, that there was 'ample scope for differentiation and innovation beyond the design of interface specifications'. In other words, the same specification can be implemented in numerous different and innovative ways by software designers.

656 Thus, the contested decision rests on the concept that, once the obstacle represented for Microsoft's competitors by the insufficient degree of interoperability with the Windows domain architecture has been removed, those competitors will be able to offer work group server operating systems which, far from merely reproducing the Windows systems already on the market, will be distinguished from those systems with respect to parameters which consumers consider important.

657 It must be borne in mind, in that regard, that Microsoft's competitors would not be able to clone or reproduce its products solely by having access to the interoperability information covered by the contested decision. . . . * * *

659 Last, Microsoft's argument that it will have less incentive to develop a given technology if it is required to make that technology available to its competitors is of no relevance to the examination of the circumstance relating to the new product, where the issue to be decided is the impact of the refusal to supply on the incentive for Microsoft's competitors to innovate and not on Microsoft's incentives to innovate. That is an issue which will be decided when the Court examines the circumstance relating to the absence of objective justification.

660 In the third place, the Commission is also correct to reject as unfounded Microsoft's assertion during the administrative procedure that it was not demonstrated that its refusal caused prejudice to consumers.

661 First of all, as has already been observed, the results of the third Mercer survey show that, contrary to Microsoft's contention, consumers consider non-Microsoft work group server operating systems to be better than Windows work group server operating systems on a number of features to which they attach great importance.

662 Next, Microsoft cannot rely on the fact that consumers never claimed at any time during the administrative procedure that they had been forced to adopt a Windows work group server operating system as a consequence of its refusal to disclose interoperability information to its competitors. . . . [T]he Commission states '[w]hen confronted with a "choice" between putting up with interoperability problems that render their business processes cumbersome, inefficient and costly, and embracing a homogeneous Windows solution for their work group network, customers will tend to opt for the latter proposition' and that '[o]nce they have standardized on Windows, they are unlikely to report interoperability problems between their client PCs and the work group servers'. * * *

[664] Last, it must be borne in mind that it is settled case-law that Article [102] covers not only practices which may prejudice consumers directly but also those which indirectly prejudice them by impairing an effective competitive structure. In this case, Microsoft impaired the effective competitive structure on the work group server operating systems market by acquiring a significant market share on that market. * * *

(4) The absence of objective justification

[666] In the first place, Microsoft claims that the refusal to supply the information was objectively justified by the intellectual property rights which it holds over the 'technology' concerned. It has made significant investment in designing its communication protocols and the commercial success which its products have achieved represents the just reward. It is generally accepted, moreover, that an undertaking's refusal to communicate a specific technology to its competitors may be justified by the fact that it does not wish them to use that technology to compete with it.

[667] In the reply, Microsoft relies on the fact that the technology which it is required to disclose to its competitors is secret, that it is of great value for licensees and that it contains significant innovation.

[668] In its answer to one of the written questions put by the Court, the applicant adds that it had an objective justification for not licensing the technology 'given the prejudice to incentives to innovate that would have resulted if Sun (or others) had used that technology to build a "functional equivalent" that would compete against Microsoft's products on the same market'. * * *

[670] Microsoft contends that the application of . . . a 'balancing test' will have the consequence that dominant undertakings will have less incentive to invest in research and development, because they will have to share the fruits of their efforts with their competitors. Intellectual property rights give the holder an incentive to continue to innovate and they also encourage competing undertakings to undertake their own innovative activities in order to avoid being 'left behind'. Nor does the Commission make any attempt to 'quantify' the negative impact that the compulsory licensing required by the contested decision will have on the applicant's competitors, who will wait to see what technology they can obtain under a license rather than take the trouble to create their own technology. * * *

[690] The Court considers that, even on the assumption that it is correct, the fact that the communication protocols covered by the contested decision, or the specifications for those protocols, are covered by intellectual property rights cannot constitute objective

justification within the meaning of *Magill* and *IMS Health*.
Microsoft's argument is inconsistent with the *raison d'être* of the
exception which that case-law thus recognizes in favor of free
competition, since if the mere fact of holding intellectual property
rights could in itself constitute objective justification for the refusal
to grant a license, the exception established by the case-law could
never apply. . . .

691 It must be borne in mind that the Community judicature considers
that the fact that the holder of an intellectual property right can
exploit that right solely for his own benefit constitutes the very
substance of his exclusive right. Accordingly, a simple refusal, even
on the part of an undertaking in a dominant position, to grant a
license to a third party cannot in itself constitute an abuse of a
dominant position within the meaning of Article [102]. It is only when
it is accompanied by exceptional circumstances such as those hitherto
envisaged in the case-law that such a refusal can be characterized as
abusive and that, accordingly, it is permissible, in the public interest
in maintaining effective competition on the market, to encroach upon
the exclusive right of the holder of the intellectual property right by
requiring him to grant licenses to third parties seeking to enter or
remain on that market. It must be borne in mind that it has been
established above that such exceptional circumstances were present
in this case. * * *

697 The Court finds that, as the Commission correctly submits,
Microsoft, which bore the initial burden of proof, did not sufficiently
establish that if it were required to disclose the interoperability
information that would have a significant negative impact on its
incentives to innovate.

698 Microsoft merely put forward vague, general and theoretical
arguments on that point. Thus, as the Commission observes, in its
response of 17 October 2003 to the third statement of objections
Microsoft merely stated that '[d]isclosure would . . . eliminate future
incentives to invest in the creation of more intellectual property',
without specifying the technologies or products to which it thus
referred. * * *

701 It follows that it has not been demonstrated that the disclosure of
the information to which that remedy relates will significantly
reduce—still less eliminate—Microsoft's incentives to innovate.

702 In that context, the Court observes that it is normal practice for
operators in the industry to disclose to third parties the information
which will facilitate interoperability with their products and
Microsoft itself had followed that practice until it was sufficiently
established on the work group server operating systems market.

Such disclosure allows the operators concerned to make their own products more attractive and therefore more valuable. In fact, none of the parties has claimed in the present case that such disclosure had had any negative impact on those operators' incentives to innovate. * * *

710 The Commission came to a negative conclusion [Microsoft failed to prove an objective justification] but not by balancing the negative impact which the imposition of a requirement to supply the information at issue might have on Microsoft's incentives to innovate against the positive impact of that obligation on innovation in the industry as a whole, but after refuting Microsoft's arguments relating to the fear that its products might be cloned, establishing that the disclosure of interoperability was widespread in the industry concerned and showing that IBM's commitment to the Commission in 1984 was not substantially different from what Microsoft was ordered to do in the contested decision and that its approach was consistent with Directive 91/250 [on the legal protection of computer programs, which considers disclosure of interoperability information beneficial to innovation].

711 It follows from all of the foregoing considerations that Microsoft has not demonstrated the existence of any objective justification for its refusal to disclose the interoperability at issue. * * *

The European General Court affirmed the Commission order that Microsoft provide the competitors with the full interoperability information.

A very similar issue arose in the US courts some years later—a straggler *Microsoft* case delayed by procedural circumstances. Novell invented WordPerfect, the then popular word processing program. Microsoft's Word became its biggest competitor. Microsoft gave Novell the code it needed to operate seamlessly on the Microsoft operating system, Windows. Then Microsoft was about to release Windows 95. In the months leading up to the release, Microsoft agreed to share its code with WordPerfect and others to help them be prepared for compatibility with Windows 95. WordPerfect, however, had begun developing a new, innovative idea to use the code to harness what became known as "the cloud," which could commoditize operating systems. Microsoft found out about the research, pulled the code from Novell, and introduced Windows 95 with Microsoft Word en suite before Novell could figure out the interconnectivity protocols.

Users accordingly shifted from WordPerfect to Word (despite excellent qualities of WordPerfect) and this was the beginning of the decline of WordPerfect. At trial, the jury would have found a violation, 11 to 1, but the one holdout hung the jury. The district court granted Microsoft's motion to dismiss. The Court of Appeals for the 10th Circuit affirmed, in an opinion written by Judge (now Supreme Court Justice) Neil Gorsuch that reads as a reprise to Justice Scalia's opinion in *Trinko*. Thus:

> If the law were to make a habit of forcing monopolists to help competitors by keeping prices high, sharing their property, or declining to expand their own operations, courts would paradoxically risk encouraging collusion between rivals and dampened price competition— themselves paradigmatic antitrust wrongs, injuries to consumers and the competitive process alike. Forcing firms to help one another would also risk reducing the incentive both sides have to innovate, invest, and expand—again results inconsistent with the goals of antitrust. The monopolist might be deterred from investing, innovating, or expanding (or even entering a market in the first place) with the knowledge anything it creates it could be forced to share; the smaller company might be deterred, too, knowing it could just demand the right to piggyback on its larger rival.

Novell v. Microsoft, 731 F.3d 1064 (10th Cir. 2013).

Notes and Questions

1.   Comment on the European court's treatment of Microsoft's refusal to give its rivals full interoperability information, and the relation of this refusal to Microsoft's IP rights. How does this compare with the US jurisprudence against "forced sharing," as in *Trinko*? How important was, and should have been, the Commission's evidence that Microsoft's cut-off of information squelched rivals' innovations?

2.   In *Novell v. Microsoft*, did the court think Novell should have made its own operating system? Would it have mattered to the outcome if the plaintiff were the US government? While not included in the excerpt above, the court expressed concern that if Novell were successful in establishing antitrust injury from a deception claim, this would "turn private parties into bounty hunters entitled to a windfall every time they can ferret out anti-competitive conduct lurking somewhere in the marketplace." Was this a legitimate fear?

3.   What are the differences in premises and assumptions as between the two cases—*Microsoft* Europe and *Novell*? Can the differences be resolved empirically; that is, can empirical analysis answer which set of rules, in view of the incentives they promote, is better for consumers and robust markets? Or is the choice more fundamentally philosophical?

Korea, too, is active in competition law enforcement, and has fined or is scrutinizing Microsoft, Google and Qualcomm for abuses of dominance.

In the following case, the Korea Fair Trade Commission thought it had detected an illegal refusal to supply, but the would-be buyer's ability to purchase elsewhere and thus the conduct's effect on competition became a pivotal fact. In 2001 the Korea Fair Trade Commission condemned acts by Posco, the dominant supplier of hot rolled coil, which was necessary to the production of cold rolled sheet steel, which Posco also made. Hyundai's subsidiary Hysco was an entrant into the market for cold rolled steel. Several times Hysco requested Posco to supply it with hot rolled steel, but Posco refused. Hysco eventually found a source of supply abroad. The KFTC's order and fine against Posco was overturned by Korea's Supreme Court, which ruled:

> The KFTC, in argument that Posco's refusal to deal fell under an abuse of market-dominating position, must prove that such a refusal tended to raise prices, decrease outputs, deter innovation, reduce the number of prominent competitors, impair the industrial diversity, etc. resulting in restraining competition. Only after the above consequences are proven, it may be presumed that the act in question tended to restrict competition and that such an intention or purpose existed at the time of the act. Otherwise, comprehensive consideration should be exerted on such issues as the circumstances and motivation of the refusal to deal, characteristics of the relevant market, the degree of harm suffered by the refused party, the change of price and output, deterrence to innovation, or reduction of diversity. And then, it should be decided whether the refusal to deal in question tended to cause the above restraint of competition and such an intention or purpose existed. . . .

> Unless Hysco could not purchase hot rolled coil from other suppliers and was actually excluded from the new entry due

to Posco's refusal to deal, the refusal in and of itself is not sufficient to be defined as unreasonable refusal to deal which tended to restrain competition. Rather, in this case, despite the refusal by Posco, Hysco imported its needed hot rolled coil from Japan and carried out its production and sale of cold rolled steel plate and gained net profit. Consequently, the domestic market for cold rolled steel plate has expanded . . . In light of the lack of evidence showing plausible restraint of competition such as decrease in outputs or a hike in prices, Hysco's business difficulties caused by Posco's refusal to deal would not suffice to find that the refusal in question tended to restrict competition at the time of the challenged act. Posco, Case no. 2002 Du 8626 (Nov. 22, 2007 Korean Sup. Ct.)

2.   Note on General Exclusionary Practices

We have just examined refusals to deal, which comprise one of the most commonly alleged offenses by dominant firms. We shall proceed to several other categories. Before we do, we note that there are multiple varieties of unilateral acts, practices and strategies that many be contested as anticompetitive and unlawful. They might fit a category, but they might not. The US government's *Microsoft* case comprised various exclusionary practices held illegal. The case is generally considered a sound case, applying good analysis; and at least with respect to the practices found unlawful, almost all jurisdictions would agree.

Microsoft is an example of applying a standard, not rules, to determine whether conduct is anticompetitive and should be prohibited. The standard is: Is the conduct likely to put costs on competitors and thereby to create, increase, or maintain market power, rather than conduct designed to increase efficiency, responsiveness to consumers, and innovation?

When rules are derived for particular categories of conduct, they are generally meant to be an application of this standard, customized to particular conduct, and customized in a way likely to promote incentives of firms to be more responsive to consumers and the market. Rules that focus on incentives recognize, for example, that freedom to price low and freedom to invent are of the essence of the market system.

Here, then, is a brief selective summary of the acts found illegal in the US government *Microsoft* case.

Microsoft had a monopoly in the desktop computer operating system. The biggest barrier to entry was the applications: Users need applications to do their work on the computer, and applications were written specifically to an operating system. Because of network effects, applications writers would prefer to write to the Microsoft code than to any other operating system. But Microsoft saw a serious challenge looming on the horizon: Netscape, which had invented the browser (Navigator) and was teaming up with Sun Microsystems' Java language to create a new language that would be portable. It would figuratively "sit on top" of Windows as "middleware." Applications makers could write to it, and the middleware could port to any other operating system. Netscape needed a critical mass of Navigator users to make its innovation work, and thus it needed to be visible on Windows. Microsoft adopted a strategy to try to make sure that the Netscape/Java challenge would never happen. The strategy included many acts, some of which were dropped during the government's investigation. These included: If anyone loaded a non-Microsoft browser on Windows, a caution notice would pop up threatening a computer crash. Acts that were litigated and held illegal included blocking all efficient routes for Navigator to get on the Windows screen and thus become popular. Thus, in its contracts with Internet service providers such as AOL, Microsoft imposed the condition that they not distribute Navigator on their service. In its contracts with original equipment manufacturers, Microsoft imposed the condition that they not preinstall any browser other than its own, Internet Explorer (IE). In providing IE on Windows, Microsoft bound IE to Windows code so that IE could not be removed without crippling Windows. (These were the days when it was not easy, or was perceived as not easy, to download another browser, and it was perceived as costly to have more than one browser.) Microsoft took a license from Sun for Java language, which was meant to be cross-platform, and deceptively and against the terms of the license converted Java language to Microsoft-only Java language, effectively destroying its cross-platform properties. Microsoft had research joint ventures with a number of firms including Intel and required the partner as a condition of the joint venture not to participate in creating cross-platform interfaces. United States v. Microsoft Corp., 253 F.3d 34 (D.C. Cir. 2001), cert. denied.

* * *

The European Commission gives general guidance regarding exclusionary practices under (now) TFEU Article 102 in its Guidance Paper: Communication from the Commission—Guidance on the Commission's enforcement priorities in Article 82 of the EC Treaty to abusive exclusionary conduct by dominant undertakings, 2009/C 45/02.

With these anchors in place, we proceed to other selected specific categories.

3.   Predatory Pricing

US antitrust jurisprudence strongly favors low pricing. In a succession of cases since the mid-1980s, the US Supreme Court has expressed reluctance to punish dominant firms for unilateral decisions, particularly those relating to prices. In the relatively simple case of single-product price discounting, the Supreme Court requires, for a violation, a showing that the defendant priced below its cost (although the Supreme Court has yet to decide what is the appropriate measure of cost) and that its below-cost pricing created a dangerous probability that defendant would be able to exclude others from the market and thereafter raise its price and recoup all of the costs of predation. *Brooke Group Ltd. v. Brown & Williamson Tobacco Corp.*, 509 U.S. 209 (1993). The Supreme Court has extended its approach to below-cost pricing to other pricing-related claims, including predatory overbidding and price squeezes. *See Weyerhaeuser Co. v. Ross-Simmons Hardwood Lumber Co., Inc.*, 549 U.S. 312 (2007) (predatory overbidding) and *Pacific Bell Tel. Co. v. LinkLine Commun., Inc.*, 555 U.S. 438 (2009) (price squeezes).

Not all other jurisdictions follow the US in condemning low and below-cost pricing only if recoupment is provable.

AKZO CHEMIE BV v. COMMISSION
Case C–62/86, EU:C:1991:286 (European Court of Justice 1991)

[AKZO, a large Dutch multinational firm, and ECS (Engineering and Chemical Supplies Ltd.), a small UK firm, both manufactured organic peroxides. AKZO had a market share of 50%. Benzoyl peroxide is the most important organic peroxide. Benzoyl peroxide is a bleaching agent for flour and is also used in plastics as an initiator of the polymer production process. ECS was engaged in the flour segment of the market. For a decade, ECS was content with its sales for the flour business, but in 1979 it developed excess capacity and started to sell to plastics makers, soliciting and selling to some of AKZO's customers. An AKZO official told ECS's manager Sullivan "that AKZO would take aggressive commercial action on the milling products unless [Sullivan] refrained from supplying his products to the plastics industry." The AKZO official told Sullivan AKZO would pry away ECS's flour customers at prices far below prevailing prices. When ECS ignored AKZO's threats, AKZO implemented selective, low prices, with the intent to damage the business of ECS.

From the end of 1980 for about four years, AKZO targeted ECS's customers in the flour segment, selling to them at prices that were below its average total cost and that were much lower than the previously prevailing rates. Meanwhile, AKZO charged its own loyal customers (whose business was not at risk) about sixty percent more than the targeted customers of ECS. As part of its strategy, AKZO sold these customers flour milling complements they needed at prices below AKZO's average variable cost, and it sold them some vitamin mixes (which it bought specifically for resale to these customers) below its own purchase price. ECS's business declined by about seventy percent in four years, and its profit margins fell.

The Commission initiated proceedings and obtained an interim order enjoining AKZO's conduct. In its decision on the merits, the Commission noted AKZO's "clear predatory intent" as well as its scheme of price discrimination. However, perhaps because of the interim order, the predatory campaign had little affect on ECS. ECS's share in the flour additive sector went from 35% to 30%, and AKZO's share went from 52% to 55%.

Placing much weight on AKZO's intent to eliminate its competitor, the Commission found an infringement and levied a fine of 10 million ECUs on AKZO.]

A. Dominant position

60 With regard to market shares the Court has held that very large shares are in themselves, and save in exceptional circumstances, evidence of the existence of a dominant position (judgment in Case 85/76 *Hoffmann-La Roche v Commission* [1979] ECR 461, paragraph 41). That is the situation where there is a market share of 50% such as that found to exist in this case.

61 Moreover, the Commission rightly pointed out that other factors confirmed AKZO's predominance in the market. In addition to the fact that AKZO regards itself as the world leader in the peroxides market, it should be observed that, as AKZO itself admits, it has the most highly developed marketing organization, both commercially and technically, and wider knowledge than that of their competitors with regard to safety and toxicology. . . .

62 The pleas put forward by AKZO in order to deny that it had a dominant position within the organic peroxides market as a whole must therefore be rejected.

B. Abuse of a dominant position

63 According to the contested decision (point 75) AKZO had abusively exploited its dominant position by endeavoring to eliminate ECS from the organic peroxides market mainly by massive and prolonged price-cutting in the flour additives sector. * * *

[69] It should be observed that . . . the concept of abuse is an objective concept relating to the behavior of an undertaking in a dominant position which is such as to influence the structure of a market where, as a result of the very presence of the undertaking in question, the degree of competition is weakened and through recourse to methods which, different from those which condition normal competition in products or services on the basis of the transactions of commercial operators, has the effect of hindering the maintenance of the degree of competition still existing in the market or the growth of that competition.

[70] It follows that Article [102] prohibits a dominant undertaking from eliminating a competitor and thereby strengthening its position by using methods other than those which come within the scope of competition on the basis of quality. From that point of view, however, not all competition by means of price can be regarded as legitimate.

[71] Prices below average variable costs (that is to say, those which vary depending on the quantities produced) by means of which a dominant undertaking seeks to eliminate a competitor must be regarded as abusive. A dominant undertaking has no interest in applying such prices except that of eliminating competitors so as to enable it subsequently to raise its prices by taking advantage of its monopolistic position, since each sale generates a loss, namely the total amount of the fixed costs (that is to say, those which remain constant regardless of the quantities produced) and, at least, part of the variable costs relating to the unit produced.

[72] Moreover, prices below average total costs, that is to say, fixed costs plus variable costs, but above average variable costs, must be regarded as abusive if they are determined as part of a plan for eliminating a competitor. Such prices can drive from the market undertakings which are perhaps as efficient as the dominant undertaking but which, because of their smaller financial resources, are incapable of withstanding the competition waged against them.

[73] These are the criteria that must be applied to the situation in the present case. * * *

[114] The prices charged by AKZO to its own customers were above its average total costs, whereas those offered to customers of ECS were below its average total costs.

[115] AKZO is thus able, at least partly, to set off losses resulting from the sales to customers of ECS against profits made on the sales to the 'large independents' which were among its customers. This behavior shows that AKZO's intention was not to pursue a general policy of

favorable prices, but to adopt a strategy that could damage ECS. The complaint is therefore substantiated. * * *

140 By maintaining prices below its average total costs over a prolonged period, without any objective justification, AKZO was thus able to damage ECS by dissuading it from making inroads into its customers. * * *

[The Court concluded that AKZO, at various times, offered customers of ECS prices lower than AKZO's total or average variable costs, and did so as part of its threat to obtain ECS's withdrawal from the plastics sector.

162 . . . [I]t must be observed that the infringement committed by AKZO is particularly serious, since the behavior complained of was intended to prevent a competitor from extending its activity into a market in which AKZO held a dominant position.

[The Court reduced the fine to 7.5 million ECUs—predecessor to the Euro—on grounds that the controlling law had not previously been specified and the infraction did not have a significant effect on market shares.]

High Court of Australia

BORAL BESSER MASONRY LIMITED v. AUSTRALIAN COMPETITION AND CONSUMER COMMISSION
(2003) 215 CLR 374

[In March 1998 the Australian Competition and Consumer Commission (ACCC) instituted proceedings against BBM alleging that it had attempted to drive out a competitor, C & M Brick, from the concrete masonry products market, by pricing below its avoidable costs of production. The First Instance (trial court) judge dismissed the ACCC's case for lack of evidence that BBM had market power. The Full Federal (appellate) Court reversed, finding both market power and below-cost pricing. The High Court reversed and reinstated the trial court's dismissal of the ACCC's case. While agreeing with the Full Federal Court's market definition, it found that BBM did not have market power because it faced strong competitors and entry barriers into the market were low. The case, overruled by legislation on the need for market power, may be more relevant to outside observers for its treatment of the recoupment requirement.]

CHIEF JUDGE GLEESON and JUDGE CALLINAN

[1] This appeal concerns the application of s46 of the *Trade Practices Act 1974* ("the Act") to the conduct of the appellant in relation to the supply of concrete masonry products ("CMP") in Melbourne between April 1994 and October 1996. The central issues are whether the appellant had a substantial degree of power in a market, and whether it took advantage of that power in contravention of s46. * * *

[2] It was pointed out by this Court in *Melway Publishing Pty Ltd v Robert Hicks Pty Ltd* that s46 requires, not merely the co-existence of market power, conduct, and proscribed purpose, but a connection such that the firm whose conduct is in question can be said to be taking advantage of its power. It was also observed that an absence of a substantial degree of market power only requires a sufficient level of competition to deny a substantial degree of power to any competitor in the market.

[3] The essence of power is absence of constraint. Market power in a supplier is absence of constraint from the conduct of competitors or customers. This is reflected in the terms of s46(3). Matters of degree are involved, but when a question of the degree of market power enjoyed by a supplier arises, the statute directs attention to the extent to which the conduct of the firm is constrained by the conduct of its competitors or its customers. The main aspect of the conduct of BBM in question in the present case was its pricing behavior. Therefore, the Federal Court was required by the statute to have regard to the extent to which BBM's pricing behavior was constrained by the conduct of other CMP suppliers, or by purchasers of CMP. The reasoning of Heerey J [the trial court judge] followed that statutory direction.

[4] The purposes proscribed by s46 include the purpose of eliminating or damaging a competitor. Where the conduct that is alleged to contravene s46 is price-cutting, the objective will ordinarily be to take business away from competitors. If the objective is achieved, competitors will necessarily be damaged. If it is achieved to a sufficient extent, one or more of them may be eliminated. That is inherent in the competitive process. The purpose of the statute is to promote competition; and successful competition is bound to cause damage to some competitors.

[5] It follows that, where the conduct alleged to contravene s46 is competitive pricing, it is especially dangerous to proceed too quickly from a finding about purpose to a conclusion about taking advantage of market power. Indeed, in such a case, a process of reasoning that commences with a finding of a purpose of eliminating or damaging a competitor, and then draws the inference that a firm with that objective must have, and be exercising, a substantial degree of power

in a market, is likely to be flawed. Firms do not need market power in order to put their prices down; and firms that engage in price-cutting, with or without market power, cause damage to their competitors. Where, as in the present case, a firm accused of contravening s46 asserts that it is operating in an intensely competitive market, and that its pricing behavior is explained by its response to the competitive environment, including the conduct of its customers, an observation that it intends to damage its competitors, and to do so to such a degree that one or more of them may leave the market, is not helpful in deciding whether the firm has, and is taking advantage of, a substantial degree of market power.

6 Section 46 does not refer specifically to predatory pricing, or recoupment, or selling below variable or avoidable cost. These are concepts that may, or may not, be useful tools of analysis in a particular case where pricing behavior is alleged to contravene s 46. Care needs to be exercised in their importation from different legislative contexts. In the United States, for example, predatory pricing is often discussed in the context of monopolization, or attempts to monopolies, in contravention of the Sherman Act 1890. In Europe, Art [102] of the Treaty of Rome prohibits conduct which amounts to an abuse of a dominant position in a market. We are concerned with the language of s 46. We are principally concerned with whether BBM had a substantial degree of power in a market, and whether, in its pricing behavior, and its upgrading of its production facilities, it took advantage of that power.

7 Predatory pricing is a concept that was examined in the evidence of economists, and in the judgments in the Federal Court. Ultimately, however, it is the language of the Act that must be construed and applied. The expression was used by Dawson J in *Queensland Wire Industries Pty Ltd v Broken Hill Proprietary Co Ltd* as an example of a practice that may manifest market power, but his Honor had no occasion to explain what he meant by it. One of the most important features of the decision in that case was a rejection of the argument that the concept of "taking advantage" in s 46 involves some form of predatory behavior or abuse of power going beyond that which follows from the terms of the statute itself.

8 There is a danger that a term such as predatory pricing may take on a life of its own, independent of the statute, and distract attention from the language of s 46. There is also a danger that principles relevant to the laws of other countries may be adopted uncritically and without regard to the context in which they were developed.

9 Finkelstein J, in his reasons for judgment, pointed out that the context in which predatory pricing has been considered in the United

States is materially different from that of s 46, and that an expectation of recoupment of monopoly prices at the end of a period of illegal pricing behavior is not a statutory requirement for the application of s 46.

[10] It may equally be said that there is nothing in s 46 that, as a matter of law, requires a distinction to be drawn between pricing below or above variable or avoidable costs. As has already been observed, the distinction is in some respects unsatisfactory. Furthermore, in the present case it is of limited utility. For some, but not all, of the relevant period, prices charged by BBM were below BBM's variable costs if no adjustment or allowance is made for the position of the wider Boral group. But we are not in a position to compare BBM's prices with Pioneer's variable costs; and, because C & M were substantially more efficient, it may be inferred that their variable costs were significantly lower than BBM's costs and they may well have been lower than BBM's prices. The process, outlined in the evidence as to pricing on major projects, by which BBM set its prices, clearly involved competitive pressure from Pioneer and C & M, and pressure from customers. In none of those cases is there any evidence that BBM set its prices lower than was necessary to win the business it was seeking. In some cases, BBM refused to reduce its quotes to match its competitors. To observe, as a matter of objective fact, that BBM's prices were often lower than BBM's variable costs is inconclusive if the prices were fixed as a result of competitive market pressure.

[11] If one begins with the fact that a firm is a monopolist, or is in a controlling or dominant position in a market, then, by hypothesis, such a firm has an ability to raise prices without fear of losing business. If such a firm reduces its prices, especially if it reduces them below variable cost, then it may be easy to attribute to the firm an anti-competitive objective, and to characterize its behavior as predatory. But if one finds a firm that is operating in an intensely competitive environment, and a close examination of its pricing behavior shows that it is responding to competitive pressure, then its conduct will bear a different character. That is the present case.

[12] While the possibility of recoupment is not legally essential to a finding of pricing behavior in contravention of s 46, it may be of factual importance. The fact, as found by Heerey J, that BBM had no expectation of being in a position to charge supra-competitive prices even if Rocla and Budget left the market, leaving it facing Pioneer and C & M, was material to an evaluation of its conduct. The inability to raise prices above competitive levels reflected a lack of market strength. A finding that BBM expected to be in a position, at the end of the price war, to recoup its losses by charging prices above a

competitive level may have assisted a conclusion that it had a substantial degree of market power, depending on the other evidence. But no such finding was made.

* * *

Notes and Questions

1.   The *AKZO* court allowed a below-cost price coupled with evidence of predatory intent—intent to eliminate a competitor—to suffice for a violation. Can one reconcile the US insistence on probable recoupment with the *AKZO* test by saying that a dominant firm would not engage in below-cost pricing to eliminate a competitor unless it expected to be able recoup the costs of predation through later supracompetitive pricing? If so, why insist on proof of recoupment? Would a dominant firm ever invest in below-cost pricing to drive out a competitor if it only expected to obtain a greater share of the market at competitive prices?

2.   The *Boral* court's high bar on proof of market power for predatory pricing was controversial. In 2007, the Australian Parliament adopted the Trade Practices Amendment (Predatory Pricing) Bill which entirely eliminated a market power requirement for predatory pricing cases. Until now, the Australian Competition and Consumer Commission ("ACCC") has not enforced the law and there has been considerable discussion about whether it should do so or whether the law should be repealed.

3.   The European Court of Justice decided a major predatory pricing/price discrimination case in 2012: Post Danmark A/S Konkurrenceradet, Case C–209–10, ECLI:EU:C:2012: 172 (also known as Post Danmark I). The dominant firm, a post office with universal service obligations for light mail, charged selectively low prices to the big supermarket customers of its competitor in unaddressed mail, Forbruger-Kontakt. There was no proof that Post Danmark sought to drive Forbruger-Kontakt out of the market. For two of the targeted customers, Post Danmark's prices were above its average total costs and "[i]n those circumstances, it cannot be considered that such prices have anti-competitive effects." In the third instance Post Danmark charged below average total costs but above average incremental costs, and the lower price was worth it because the sale made it possible to achieve considerable economies of scale. The case came before the Court on a preliminary reference from the Danish court, and the European Court responded that the third sale may not be considered an exclusionary abuse just because the selectively low price to one of the customers was below average total costs of the activity while higher than average incremental costs. To assess anticompetitive effects "it is necessary to

consider whether the pricing policy, without objective justification, produces an actual or likely exclusionary effect to the detriment of competition and, thereby, of consumers' interests." The Court noted that, to the extent the price covers the bulk of the costs attributable to the activity, it will generally be possible for an as efficient competitor to compete without unsustainable losses.

The case has been much praised by economically-minded analysts, who have touted the case as adopting a consumer welfare standard and as adopting an "as efficient competitor" litmus test for exclusionary acts; but later judgments, particularly Post Danmark II (loyalty rebates), Case C–23/14, ECLI:EU:C:2015:651, do not bear out the prediction of retrenchment of EU competition law.

4.   Margin Squeezes

In margin squeeze cases, the dominant firm with power over an input prices the input so high and its own integrated product so low that unintegrated downstream rivals cannot profitably sell their product. Typically, the industry involves sector regulation, and the cases may discuss the relationship between antitrust rules and sector regulation. How should antitrust authorities or jurists decide monopolization or abuse of dominance questions where sectoral regulators are also involved in policing the conduct? Should antitrust authorities find it less necessary to police regulated industries since the sectoral regulators are better situated to control abuses of dominance? Or is antitrust enforcement especially needed in heavily regulated sectors where entry barriers are likely to be pervasive, high, and durable and the regulators might be captured by the regulated? We observe a significant divide between the US and the EU on the issue of margin squeezes.

The European Commission accused Deutsche Telekom of violating Article [102 TFEU]. The European Commission eventually found a violation, and imposed a fine. Deutsche Telekom brought suit against the Commission in the General Court—the intermediate appellate court—and later in the Court of Justice to annul the Commission's decision.

DEUTSCHE TELEKOM AG v. COMMISSION
Case C–280/08 P, EU:C:2010:603 (European Court of Justice 2010)

[Deutsche Telekom (DT) was the dominant provider of telecommunications services in Germany and had sole access to the local loop. DT was regulated by the German Regulatory Authority, which imposed price ceilings. DT charged new entrants into the local telecom service market higher fees for wholesale access to the local loop than it charged its customers for services including DSL for fast-speed Internet connection. The competing providers of DSL service complained to the European Commission. The Commission found a margin squeeze in violation of Article 102. The General Court affirmed, and the Court of Justice affirmed. DT had a duty to provide competitors access to the local loop. It therefore had a duty not to create a margin squeeze. DT had sufficient scope to eliminate the margin squeeze on terms consistent with the regulation, and could go back to the German regulator (RegTP) if it needed an adjustment in price. The Court said:]

* * *

[80] According to the case-law of the Court of Justice, it is only if anti-competitive conduct is required of undertakings by national legislation, or if the latter creates a legal framework which itself eliminates any possibility of competitive activity on their part, that Articles [101] and [102] do not apply. In such a situation, the restriction of competition is not attributable, as those provisions implicitly require, to the autonomous conduct of the undertakings. Articles [101] and [102] may apply, however, if it is found that the national legislation leaves open the possibility of competition which may be prevented, restricted or distorted by the autonomous conduct of undertakings.

[81] The possibility of excluding anti-competitive conduct from the scope of Articles [101] and [102] on the ground that it has been required of the undertakings in question by existing national legislation or that the legislation has precluded all scope for any competitive conduct on their part has thus been accepted only to a limited extent by the Court of Justice.

[82] Thus, the Court has held that if a national law merely encourages or makes it easier for undertakings to engage in autonomous anti-competitive conduct, those undertakings remain subject to Articles [101] and [102].

[83] According to the case-law of the Court, dominant undertakings have a special responsibility not to allow their conduct to impair genuine undistorted competition on the common market.

[84] It follows from this that the mere fact that the appellant was encouraged by the intervention of a national regulatory authority such as RegTP to maintain the pricing practices which led to the margin squeeze of competitors who are at least as efficient as the

appellant cannot, as such, in any way absolve the appellant from responsibility under Article [102].*

85 Since, notwithstanding such interventions, the appellant had scope to adjust its retail prices for end-user access services, the General Court was entitled to find, on that ground alone, that the margin squeeze at issue was attributable to the appellant.

86 . . . [A]ppellant does not challenge the General Court's findings . . . that, in essence, the appellant was able to make applications to RegTP for authorization to adjust its retail prices for end-user access services, specifically retail prices for narrowband access services for the period between 1 January 1998 and 31 December 2001, and retail prices for broadband access services for the period from 1 January 2002.

* * *

159 It is clear . . . that, according to the General Court, it is not the level of the wholesale prices for local loop access services—which . . . cannot be challenged in the present appeal—or the level of retail prices for end-user access services which is contrary to Article [102], but the spread between them.

* * *

172 As regards the abusive nature of the appellant's pricing practices, it must be noted that subparagraph (a) of the second paragraph of Article [102] expressly prohibits a dominant undertaking from directly or indirectly imposing unfair prices.

* * *

177 It follows from this [special responsibility] that Article [102] prohibits a dominant undertaking from, inter alia, adopting pricing practices which have an exclusionary effect on its equally efficient actual or potential competitors, that is to say practices which are capable of making market entry very difficult or impossible for such competitors, and of making it more difficult or impossible for its co-contractors to choose between various sources of supply or commercial partners, thereby strengthening its dominant position by using methods other than those which come within the scope of competition on the merits. From that point of view, therefore, not all competition by means of price can be regarded as legitimate.

---

*   Editors' addition: "RegTP took the view in each case that other operators should be able to offer their end users competitive prices by resorting to cross subsidization of access services and call services." General Court, paragraph 267.

[178] In the present case, it must be noted that the appellant does not deny that, even on the assumption that it does not have the scope to adjust its wholesale prices for local loop access services, the spread between those prices and its retail prices for end-user access services is capable of having an exclusionary effect on its equally efficient actual or potential competitors, since their access to the relevant service markets is, at the very least, made more difficult as a result of the margin squeeze which such a spread can entail for them.

[179] At the hearing the appellant submitted, however, that the test applied in the judgment under appeal for the purpose of establishing an abuse within the meaning of Article [102] required it, in the circumstances of the case, to increase its retail prices for end-user access services to the detriment of its own end-users, given the national regulatory authorities' regulation of its wholesale prices for local loop access services.

[180] It is true . . . that Article [102] aims, in particular, to protect consumers by means of undistorted competition.

[181] However, the mere fact that the appellant would have to increase its retail prices for end-user access services in order to avoid the margin squeeze of its competitors who are as efficient as the appellant cannot in any way, in itself, render irrelevant the test which the General Court applied in the present case for the purpose of establishing an abuse under Article [102].

[182] By further reducing the degree of competition existing on a market—the end-user access services market—already weakened precisely because of the presence of the appellant, thereby strengthening its dominant position on that market, the margin squeeze also has the effect that consumers suffer detriment as a result of the limitation of the choices available to them and, therefore, of the prospect of a longer-term reduction of retail prices as a result of competition exerted by competitors who are at least as efficient in that market.

[183] In those circumstances, in so far as the appellant has scope to reduce or end such a margin squeeze . . . by increasing its retail prices for end-user access services, the General Court correctly held . . . that that margin squeeze is capable, in itself, of constituting an abuse within the meaning of Article [102] in view of the exclusionary effect that it can create for competitors who are at least as efficient as the appellant. The General Court was not, therefore, obliged to establish, additionally, that the wholesale prices for local loop access services or retail prices for end-user access services were in themselves abusive on account of their excessive or predatory nature, as the case may be.

(c) i) The complaint concerning the misapplication of the as-efficient-competitor test * * *

[252] The General Court therefore held . . . , without any error of law, that the anti-competitive effect which the Commission is required to demonstrate, as regards pricing practices of a dominant undertaking resulting in a margin squeeze of its equally efficient competitors, relates to the possible barriers which the appellant's pricing practices could have created for the growth of products on the retail market in end-user access services and, therefore, on the degree of competition in that market.

[253] . . . [A] pricing practice such as that at issue in the judgment under appeal that is adopted by a dominant undertaking such as the appellant constitutes an abuse within the meaning of Article [102] if it has an exclusionary effect on competitors who are at least as efficient as the dominant undertaking itself by squeezing their margins and is capable of making market entry more difficult or impossible for those competitors, and thus of strengthening its dominant position on that market to the detriment of consumers' interests.

[254] Admittedly, where a dominant undertaking actually implements a pricing practice resulting in a margin squeeze of its equally efficient competitors, with the purpose of driving them from the relevant market, the fact that the desired result is not ultimately achieved does not alter its categorization as abuse within the meaning of Article [102]. However, in the absence of any effect on the competitive situation of competitors, a pricing practice such as that at issue cannot be classified as exclusionary if it does not make their market penetration any more difficult.

* * *

Note the relationship between EU competition law and Member State sector regulation. Note also that the Court of Justice might find harm to competition and consumers even if prices rise in the short term. See paragraphs 182–183.

The US Supreme Court reached a very different result in *Pacific Bell Tel. Co. v. LinkLine Commun., Inc.*, 555 U.S. 438 (2009). The plaintiffs were four regional digital subscriber line ("DSL") providers who alleged that AT&T (and various corporate affiliates) violated Section 2 of the Sherman Act by selling their telephonic facilities and infrastructure necessary to provide DSL at too high a wholesale price and then charged too low a retail price to AT&T's own customers, thus squeezing plaintiffs out of the market. The Supreme Court held that a price squeeze claim without an allegation of below-cost pricing at retail was not cognizable. The Court found this result required by two of its precedents. In *Verizon v. Trinko*, 540 U.S. 398 (2004), the Court rejected monopolization liability for (almost all) unilateral refusals to deal; hence AT&T could not have had any *antitrust* duty to provide access to its infrastructure at wholesale, much less to provide such access at a reasonable price. In *Brooke Group v. Brown & Williamson*, 509 U.S. 209 (1993), the Court rejected predatory pricing liability absent a showing that defendant priced below cost (and could recoup losses). Hence, AT&T could not be liable for low but above-cost retail prices.

In addition to this fairly formalistic doctrinal analysis, the Court offered policy explanations for its decision.

> Institutional concerns also counsel against recognition of such claims. We have repeatedly emphasized the importance of clear rules in antitrust law. Courts are ill suited "to act as central planners, identifying the proper price, quantity, and other terms of dealing." Trinko, 540 U.S., at 408. " 'No court should impose a duty to deal that it cannot explain or adequately and reasonably supervise. The problem should be deemed irremedia[ble] by antitrust law when compulsory access requires the court to assume the day-to-day controls characteristic of a regulatory agency.' "
> * * *
>
> It is difficult enough for courts to identify and remedy an alleged anticompetitive practice at one level, such as predatory pricing in retail markets or a violation of the duty-to-deal doctrine at the wholesale level. . . . Recognizing price-squeeze claims would require courts simultaneously to police both the wholesale and retail prices to ensure that rival firms are not being squeezed. And courts would be aiming at a moving target, since it is the interaction between these two prices that may result in a squeeze.
>
> Perhaps most troubling, firms that seek to avoid price-squeeze liability will have no safe harbor for their pricing practices. . . . At least in the predatory pricing context, firms know they will not incur liability as long as their retail prices are above cost. No such guidance is available for price-squeeze claims.

Notes and Questions

1.   Compare the US law with the EU law on the relationship between antitrust and sector regulation. What policy and institutional considerations seem to have driven the choice of each jurisdiction?

2.   Compare US and EU law on the notion of what is harm to competition and consumers.

3.   Assuming that neither jurisdiction wants to protect inefficient competitors, is one or the other approach wiser?

5.   Loyalty Rebates and Exclusive Dealing

Dominant firms may reward customers for loyalty or for agreeing not to deal with competitors (in whole or in part). Typically they adopt these strategies when a younger firm is catching up, threatening the incumbent's dominance.

A number of these cases involve Intel, the dominant maker of an essential computer chip. AMD was the weak competitor for a number of years, but when it produced a desirable new chip, Intel took action to forestall its inroads during the crucial first six months of its launch. But the action was based on lower prices. Were Intel's acts anticompetitive?

In 2008, the Korea Fair Trade Commission (KFTC) fined Intel $25 million for offering rebates to the Korean computer makers Samsung and Sambo Computer in exchange for their not doing business with AMD, Intel's chief rival in the computer microprocessor (CPU) market. Among other things, the KFTC found:

- In the fourth quarter of 2001, Intel had a 100% market share at Samsung. In 2002, Samsung began buying CPUs from AMD and Intel's market share fell to about 80%. Intel then offered Samsung rebates in exchange for a commitment to purchase solely from Intel, at which point Intel's market share with Samsung reverted to 100%.

- "Economic analysis on the case showed that with Intel's rebate practice intact, AMD would not be able to viably compete against Intel, even if it supplies its CPUs to OEMs for free."

- Between 2000 and 2006, AMD's market share never exceeded 17%, and was usually no higher than 10%.

- "In the CPU sales agency market where PC consumers' preferences are directly reflected, AMD's [market share] between 2000 and 2006 was continuously on the rise, reaching around 30% at the end of 2005."

Intel's appeal was denied by the Seoul High Court (2013).

The same week that the Korean authority announced its decision, the US FTC announced its own investigation of Intel's rebating practices. (The investigation was settled by consent decree.) Then, in May of 2009, the European Commission announced its own Intel decision and an unprecedented fine of nearly $1.5 billion. The Commission found a violation by object (a category reserved for hard core or near hard core conduct), and found that the conduct was not justified. The General Court affirmed. Intel appealed to the Court of Justice. The appeal called into question whether it was proper to treat Intel's rebates as an abuse by object and thus provable without inquiry into effects; and whether it was proper to declare that, even in the case of an effects inquiry, there was no need for the Commission to prove that AMD was an equally efficient competitor. Case T–286/09 12 June 2014. The European Court of Justice disagreed on both counts.

We reproduce below some selections from the Commission's and later the General Court's press releases. Excerpts from the Court of Justice appear on page 115.

INTEL CORP. v. COMMISSION

[The following excerpt from the Commission's press release summarizes some of the Commission's factual findings.]

Throughout the period October 2002–December 2007, Intel had a dominant position in the worldwide x86 CPU market (at least 70% market share). The Commission found that Intel engaged in two specific forms of illegal practice [when it was challenged by the competitive new chip of its only significant competitor, AMD]. First, Intel gave wholly or partially hidden rebates to computer manufacturers on condition that they bought all, or almost all, their x86 CPUs from Intel. Intel also made direct payments to a major retailer on condition it stock only computers with Intel x86 CPUs. Such rebates and payments effectively prevented customers—and ultimately consumers—from choosing alternative products. Second, Intel made direct payments to computer manufacturers to halt or delay the launch of specific products containing competitors' x86 CPUs and to limit the sales channels available to these products. The Commission found that these practices constituted abuses of Intel's dominant position on the x86 CPU market that harmed consumers throughout the EEA [European Economic Area]. By undermining its competitors' ability to compete on the merits of their products, Intel's actions undermined competition and innovation. . . .

Here is an excerpt from the General Court's press release.

The General Court upholds the fine of €1.06 billion imposed on Intel for having abused its dominant position. . .

General Court of the European Union, Press Release No 82/14 (12 June 2014)

In today's judgment, the General Court dismisses the action and thus upholds the Commission's decision.

The General Court finds, inter alia, that the rebates granted to Dell, HP, NEC and Lenovo are exclusivity rebates. Such rebates are, when applied by an undertaking in a dominant position, incompatible with the objective of undistorted competition within the common market. They are not based—save in exceptional circumstances—on an economic transaction which justifies such a financial advantage, but are designed to remove or restrict the purchaser's freedom to choose his sources of supply and to deny other producers access to the market. That type of rebate constitutes an abuse of a dominant position if there is no objective justification for granting it. Exclusivity rebates granted by an undertaking in a dominant position are, by their very nature, capable of restricting competition and foreclosing competitors from the market. It is thus not necessary to show that they are capable of restricting competition on a case by case basis in the light of the facts of the individual case.

In that regard, the General Court states that, in order to submit an attractive offer, it is not sufficient for a competitor to offer Intel's customer attractive conditions for the units that that competitor can itself supply to the customer; it must also offer that customer compensation for the potential loss of the exclusivity rebate for having switched supplier. In order to submit an attractive offer, the competitor must therefore apportion solely to the share which it is able to offer the customer the rebate granted by Intel in respect of all or almost all of the customer's requirements (including the requirements which Intel alone—as an unavoidable supplier—is able to satisfy).

Given that exclusivity rebates granted by an undertaking in a dominant position are, by their very nature, capable of restricting competition, the Commission was not required, contrary to what Intel claims, to make an assessment of the circumstances of the case in order to show that the rebates actually or potentially had the effect of foreclosing competitors from the market.

The General Court finds, in that context, that it is not necessary to examine, by means of the 'as efficient competitor test', whether the Commission correctly assessed the ability of the rebates to foreclose a competitor as efficient as Intel. . . . Since the exclusivity rebates granted by an undertaking in a dominant position are, by their very nature, capable of restricting competition, the Commission was not required to show, in its analysis of the circumstances of the case, that the rebates granted by Intel were capable of foreclosing AMD from the market. Moreover, even if the competitor were still able to cover its costs in spite of the rebates granted, that would not mean that the foreclosure effect did not exist. The mechanism of the exclusivity rebates is such as to make access to the market more difficult for competitors of the undertaking in a dominant position, even if that access is not economically impossible.* * *

As regards the payments made to HP, Acer and Lenovo for them to postpone, cancel or restrict the marketing of certain products equipped with AMD CPUs, the General Court finds that those payments were capable of making access to the market more difficult for AMD. It also finds that Intel pursued an anti-competitive object, since the only interest that an undertaking in a dominant position may have in preventing in a targeted manner the marketing of products equipped with a product of a specific competitor is to harm that competitor. Such practices clearly fall outside the scope of competition on the merits. Those practices, which the Commission terms 'naked restrictions', amount to an abuse of a dominant position. * * *

INTEL CORP. v. COMMISSION

Case C–413/14P (European Court of Justice, Grand Chamber 6 September 2017)

[The Court of Justice set aside the judgment of the General Court and referred the case back to the General Court for review of whether the rebates were capable of restricting competition. The Court said:]

133 . . . [I]t must be born in mind that it is in no way the purpose of Article 102 TFEU to prevent an undertaking from acquiring, on its own merits, the dominant position on a market. Nor does that provision seek to ensure that competitors less efficient than the undertaking with the dominant position should remain on the market . . . . * * *

137 . . . [T]he Court has already held that an undertaking which is in a dominant position on a market and ties purchasers—even if it does

so at their request—by an obligation or promise on their part to obtain all or most of their requirements exclusively from that undertaking abuses its dominant position within the meaning of Article 102 TFEU . . . .

[138] However, that case-law must be further clarified in the case where the undertaking concerned submits, during the administrative procedure, on the basis of supporting evidence, that its conduct was not capable of restricting competition and, in particular, of producing the alleged foreclosure effects.

[139] In that case, the Commission is not only required to analyse, first, the extent of the undertaking's dominant position on the relevant market and, secondly, the share of the market covered by the challenged practice, as well as the conditions and arrangements for granting the rebates in question, their duration and their amount; it is also [re]quired to assess the possible existence of a strategy aiming to exclude competitors that are at least as efficient as the dominant undertaking from the market . . . .

[140] The analysis of the capacity to foreclose is also relevant in assessing whether a system of rebates which, in principle, falls within the scope of the prohibition laid down in Article 102 TFEU, may be objectively justified. It has to be determined whether the exclusionary effect arising from such a system, which is disadvantageous for competition, may be counterbalanced, or outweighed, by advantages in terms of efficiency which also benefit the consumer . . . .

Notes and Questions

1.   The Court of Justice *Intel* judgment may be read as an important turn-around to put much more weight on actual competitive effects and to weaken prior holdings that adopt formalistic presumptions. Comment on this proposition and consider the judgment's effects on prior EU rulings.

2.   Does the Court of Justice leave standing the analysis of the naked restraints, which it does not mention in the operative portion of its judgment? If so, what is a naked restriction, allowing no defense? When justification is possible, what satisfies an undertaking's burden to justify?

In general, when is it necessary for the plaintiff to prove harm to competition and consumers (competitive effects)? What is anticompetitive foreclosure? When must the plaintiff show that the targeted competitor was actually squeezed out of the market? When must it show that the competitor was as efficient, or potentially so? Is it correct to base foreclosure on the contestable share of the market? How is this share to be calculated?

3.   These questions are difficult ones all over the world. They are not all resolved in the United States, where there is a split of the circuits on the test for loyalty rebates. A principal question in play in the United States is whether, in a loyalty rebate case, the plaintiff must prove that the rebate amounted to a predatory price using the *Brooke Group* test (thus turning on price/cost margins), or whether the question is a more open question of fact as to whether the rebates were unreasonably exclusionary.

4.   Exclusive dealing, tying and bundling by dominant firms reflect all of the same considerations we have discussed. These are leveraging and foreclosure violations, when they are violations. They may be efficiency justified, but they may not be; they may be used to put costs on competitors; to preserve or entrench market power in the main market or to monopolize an adjacent one. Coercive tying by a dominant firm that forecloses a significant share of the market to rivals is often seen as presumptively illegal and in need of justification, as in the European Union. Such tying was once per se illegal in the United States but is now more likely to be examined under a rule of reason, putting plaintiff to the burden of proving probable harm to consumers. In the European Union the Guidance Document gives the Commission's view of how to analyze each of these issues. Communication from the Commission—Guidance on the Commission's enforcement priorities in applying Article 82 of the EC Treaty to abusive exclusionary conduct by dominant undertakings, 2009/C 45/02.

---

6.   Japan

The Japanese Fair Trade Commission (JFTC) promulgated Guidelines for Exclusionary Private Monopolization under the Antimonopoly Act in 2009. They are available in English translation at   *http://www.jftc.go.jp/en/legislation_gls/imonopoly_guidelines. files/guidelines_exclusionary.pdf.*   The Guidelines' "factors for assessing whether conduct falls under exclusionary conduct" appear on the JFTC website on a single page with graphic representations, which we reproduce below.

JFTC: Assessing Exclusionary Conduct

Factors for Assessing Whether Conduct Falls under Exclusionary Conduct

- Exclusionary Conduct refers to various conducts that would cause difficulty for other entrepreneurs to continue their business activities or for new market entrants to commence their business activities, thereby would be likely to cause a substantial restraint of competition in a particular field of trade.
- When the JFTC determines whether the alleged conduct falls under Exclusionary Conduct or not, it will, in general, comprehensively consider the conditions of the entire market of the product, positions of the alleged entrepreneur and its competitors in the market, period of the conduct, conditions of the conduct, etc.

Below-cost Pricing
(X: alleged entrepreneur, Y: competitor, A: trade partner)

Definition	Setting a product price below the cost that would not be generated unless the product was supplied (Average Avoidable Cost)
Required Effect	Causing difficulty in the business activities of an equally or more efficient competitor
Feature	Setting a product price below the cost required for supplying the product (Average Total Cost) and not less than the Average Avoidable Cost is unlikely to fall under Exclusive Conduct, except in extraordinary circumstances.

Below-cost pricing

A purchases only X's product, which is cheaper than Y's.

Exclusive Dealing
(X: entrepreneur concerned, Y: competitor, A: trade partner)

Definition	Dealing with the trade partners on the condition of prohibition or restraint of transactions with the competitors
Required Effect	Causing difficulty in the business activities of competitors who are unable to easily find an alternative trade partner
Feature	Where rebates-giving to the trade partners on the condition for certain amount of purchase from the alleged entrepreneur etc. has effects in restraining the trade partners' dealings of the competitors' products, such conduct (Exclusive Rebate-giving) may have the same effect as Exclusive Dealing.

Prohibiting to trade with Y

A cannot purchase from Y to trade with X.

Tying
(X: alleged entrepreneur, Y: competitor, A: trade partner)

Definition	Supplying one product only on the condition that the trade partners also purchase another product
Required Effect	Causing difficulty in the business activities of competitors who are unable to easily find an alternative trade partner in the market of the tied product
Feature	"Another product" is assessed from the viewpoint of whether or not each of the combined product has a distinctive character and is traded independently.

Tying Product — Tied Product — Tied Product

Supplying in combination

A does not purchase the tied product from Y because A purchases it from X.

Refusal to Supply and Discriminatory Treatment
(X: alleged entrepreneur, Y: competitor, A/B: trading customers, a/b: trade partners)

Definition	Refusing to supply or applying discriminatory treatment beyond reasonable degree, concerning a product necessary for the trading customers to carry out business activities in the downstream market
Required Effect	Causing difficulty in the business activities in the downstream market of the trading customers who are unable to easily find an alternative supplier in the upstream market
Feature	"A product necessary for trading customers" is the product that is unsubstitutable and indispensable for the trading customers to carry out business activities in the downstream market and is impossible for the trading customers to produce.

"Reasonable degree" is assessed from the viewpoint of the details and results of transactions for supply. |

Refusing to supply

B cannot carry out business activities in the downstream market because B cannot purchase from X.

Upstream market

Downstream market

Under the JFTC Guidelines, only exclusionary acts that prevent competition by an equally or more efficient competitor are prohibited. Further, rebates that are conditional on minimum levels of purchases that have the effect of restraining dealing in competitors' products are treated as exclusive dealing agreements. The Guidelines do not provide information on the key issues in *Intel*, such as whether discounts or rebates given in exchange for exclusivity should be assessed across the entire range of output sold by the defendant or only across the contestable share of the market.

Moreover, in two categories—tying and refusal to supply—the harm required for anticompetitive effect is: "Causing difficulties in the business activities of [competitors] [customers] who are unable to easily find an alternative . . . ." This implies a more expansive standard than the standards in the US and EU.

Notes and Questions

1.   The Korean authority took pains to point out the effect that the rebates had on AMD's market share and its viability in the market. The publicly available portions of the European Commission decision contain less concrete detail on the effect on AMD and the effect on competition: "The Commission found that these payments had the potential effect of preventing products for which there was a consumer demand from coming to the market." How much evidence of an exclusionary effect on AMD should be required to find an abuse of dominance or violation of Section 2 of the Sherman Act?

2.   Competition authorities around the world have taken an interest in Intel's activities. In addition to Korean, US FTC, and European decisions mentioned earlier, the Japanese Fair Trade Commission issued a warning to Intel in 2005. Intel subsequently reached a settlement with the JFTC. After a nearly three-year investigation, in December 2009, the US FTC filed an administrative complaint against Intel related to its activities with respect to AMD and also in the separate market for graphics processing units in which Intel competes with Nvidia. As noted, this was settled by consent decree.

3.   The European Commission uses acts capable of excluding an as efficient or potentially as efficient rival as a benchmark for exclusionary conduct, although the Court of Justice (e.g., *Post Danmark II*) has said this test is not always applicable. Some other jurisdictions may apply an equally efficient competitor test as well. See, for example, Japan: *LP Gas Discriminatory Price*, 52 SHINETSHUSHU 818, 826 (Tokyo High Court, May 31, 2005); *Yamato Transp. v. Japan Post*, 2006 (Ne) No. 1078, LEX/DB Legal Database No. 28140088 (Tokyo High Ct., Nov. 28, 2007). However, influential scholars have argued that the test unduly insulates defendants from liability in circumstances where the entry of even a less efficient competitor could benefit consumers. *See,* e.g., Herbert Hovenkamp, *Exclusion and the Sherman Act*, 72 U. Chi. L. Rev. 147, 154–55 (2005). Do you see why?

4.   The Intel/AMD saga led to an important US Supreme Court decision, although not on the substantive merits of the case. After the European Commission opened its investigation, AMD sought an order from the Federal District Court for the Northern District of California requiring Intel to produce certain documents for use in the European proceedings. In 2004, the Supreme Court ruled that AMD could potentially obtain such discovery in the US and that, on remand, the district court should consider four factors: (1) the fact that Intel was a party to the foreign proceedings and therefore could be ordered by the European Commission to produce documents; (2) "the nature of the foreign tribunal, the character of the proceedings underway abroad, and the receptivity of the foreign government or the court or agency abroad to US federal-court judicial assistance;" (3) whether the "request conceals an attempt to circumvent foreign proof-gathering restrictions or other policies of a foreign country or the United States;" and (4) "unduly intrusive or burdensome requests may be rejected or trimmed." *Intel Corp. v. Advanced Micro Devices, Inc.*, 542 U.S. 241 (2004). On remand, the district court found that AMD was not entitled to the discovery. Still, the Supreme Court's decision has opened up the possibility for parties to obtain the help of US courts in obtaining discovery to aid in European and other proceedings.

7.   Intellectual Property and Digital Economy Issues

a.   Introduction

Some of the highest profile cutting-edge issues involve intellectual property, the digital economy, or both. Antitrust actions have been brought, and a number are still pending and evolving, against some of the most successful new-economy companies in the world, including Google, which is dominant in the search engine function in many countries, and Qualcomm, which owns intellectual property essential to smart phones. The law is in flux across nations and even within nations. Different outcomes can be a function of 1) whether the jurisdiction sees dominant firms as having special responsibilities or whether it stresses freedoms to refuse to deal, and 2) the jurisdiction's degree of deference to IP exclusivity at the IP/competition interface. We present below an excerpt on challenges to Google, followed by three IP/antitrust problems: patent ambush, IP holders' right or not to enjoin infringement of essential patents, and antitrust authorities' right or not to limit the terms of licensing crucial patents.

b.   *Challenges Against Google*

MONOPOLIZATION AND ABUSE OF DOMINANCE: WHY EUROPE IS DIFFERENT

Eleanor Fox, 59 Antitrust Bulletin 129 (2014), updated excerpt

* * *

The recent Google investigations on both sides of the Atlantic provide another pair [of divergent US/EU cases] in point . . . . Google occupies about seventy percent of the computer search market in the United States and more than eighty percent in Europe. Competitors, including Microsoft, complained that Google presents search results on vertical searches (such as maps, restaurants and travel) that give Google services a privileged position thereby diverting business from its competitors. The US Federal Trade Commission conducted an investigation for nearly two years and ultimately closed the investigation on grounds that the evidence "did not justify legal action." The European Commission investigated Google's conduct regarding its comparative shopping service. It found that Google gave prominent placement on search results to its own product, demoting competitors' product, causing sudden acceleration of its own traffic and sudden drops in its competitors' traffic. The Commission found a violation and fined Google €2.42 billion. (Commission press release 27 June 2017) Google has appealed.

Why would it be so difficult to prove a monopolization violation against Google's preferences to itself in the United States and not so difficult to prove an abuse violation in the EU? The following factors are relevant. U.S. law is demanding. It requires proof that Google has monopoly power. It also requires a legal conclusion that Google had a duty of fair dealing with its rivals—a hard burden after *Trinko* and *LinkLine*. If Google had a duty, US law would require proof that Google used its monopoly power to obtain additional power by reason of its preferences to itself that diverted business from its rivals in each separate market, such as maps, travel services, and restaurant guides. It would require a showing of harm to consumers. And, finally, a plaintiff would have to blunt the assertions . . . that (1) Google is the epitome of an inventive firm (it invented its search engine and presumptively has the right to use it for its own advantage); (2) intervention by a court will chill Google's incentive to invent, and a rule of law imposing a duty on Google will in general chill firms' incentive to invent; and (3) more pragmatically and immediately, any court order requiring Google to deal equally with rivals would in effect be invoking the essential facilities doctrine (which the U.S. does not have, at least not for this circumstance) and would risk involving the court in duties of supervision beyond its capabilities, as cautioned against in *Trinko* and *LinkLine*.

In the United States, each of these elements presents a high hurdle for a plaintiff. As to each, the bar is lower under European abuse of dominance law. With respect to the conduct element itself (assuming sufficient proof of dominance and acknowledging no *Trinko* problem regarding duty to deal), it is possible that the European Commission would satisfy European Court of Justice standards of prima facie proof by showing that Google's preferences to itself diverted from its rivals substantial business that they would otherwise have won "on the merits," thus distorting competition.

As appears from the cases, the EU perspective on abuse of dominance at the Court of Justice level stresses the *process* of competition, seeking to enable all market actors to compete on their merits, particularly efficient and potentially efficient competitors. The US law of monopolization at the Supreme Court level stresses the costs of antitrust intervention, tending toward per se legality in a number of situations and otherwise imposing considerable burdens on plaintiffs to show how the particular conduct will increase market power and harm consumers and that the finding of a violation would not compromise low prices and incentives to innovate. * * *

c.   FRAND and Patent Ambush

One area of active controversy involves the interaction of high-technology, intellectual property, and the antitrust laws. In order to make sure that all of the companies working on implementations of new technologies—such as DVDs, computer chips, or cell phones—are compatible, the companies often have to get together and agree on the standards that they will follow. Standard Setting Organizations or "SSOs" are the bodies that create these new standards. New technologies often draw upon a slew of different inventions in which many different inventors have intellectual property rights. Thus, as the members of the SSOs are debating what standards to adopt, they have to be cognizant of what and whose patents they may be treading on if they write the standard in a particular way. If the SSO implements a standard that requires all users of the standardized technology to follow Path A and Company A owns a patent that will be infringed by anyone who follows Path A, Company A has the power to force anyone who wants to practice the standard to pay a hefty royalty.

If all of the members of the SSO are aware of the patents that will be infringed by a particular standard, they presumably will consider the royalty rate to be paid to the patentee a cost of choosing any particular standard. Indeed, they may negotiate up front with the patentee on a royalty rate to be charged or require the patentee to commit to license its patent on "Reasonable and Nondiscriminatory" or RAND (also known as "Fair, Reasonable, and Nondiscriminatory" ("FRAND")—although the "Fair" does not seem to add anything) terms.

What if a patentee participates in the SSO, says nothing about its patents, and then starts sending users of the standardized technology royalty demand letters after the standard has been adopted? Is this sort of "patent ambush" an antitrust violation? The European Commission thought it was. It issued a Statement of Objections. Rambus and the Commission reached a commitment decision under which Rambus would offer licenses at specified maximum royalty rates. No fine was imposed. Case COMP/38.636–RAMBUS (9.12.2009)

* * *

The US Federal Trade Commission shared the European Commission's concern. It ruled that Rambus had violated Section 2 of the Sherman Act by deceiving the SSO JEDEC about its patents and patent applications and subsequently charging a monopoly royalty rate for use of the patents after the SSO standard was announced. A divided US FTC imposed a cap on the amount that Rambus could charge for its patents used to practice JEDEC's standards.

Rambus appealed to the US Court of Appeals for the Federal Circuit. *Rambus, Inc. v. FTC*, 522 F.3d 456 (D.C. Cir. 2008). The court explained its holding as follows:

> The Commission held that Rambus engaged in exclusionary conduct consisting of misrepresentations, omissions, and other practices that deceived JEDEC about the nature and scope of its patent interests while the organization standardized technologies covered by those interests. Had Rambus fully disclosed its intellectual property, "JEDEC either would have excluded Rambus's patented technologies from the JEDEC DRAM standards, or would have demanded RAND assurances, with an opportunity for ex ante licensing negotiations." But the Commission did not determine that one or the other of these two possible outcomes was the more likely. The Commission's conclusion that Rambus's conduct was

exclusionary depends, therefore, on a syllogism: Rambus avoided one of two outcomes by not disclosing its patent interests; the avoidance of either of those outcomes was anticompetitive; therefore Rambus's nondisclosure was anticompetitive.

We assume without deciding that avoidance of the first of these possible outcomes was indeed anticompetitive; that is, that if Rambus's more complete disclosure would have caused JEDEC to adopt a different (open, non-proprietary) standard, then its failure to disclose harmed competition and would support a monopolization claim. But while we can assume that Rambus's nondisclosure made the adoption of its technologies somewhat more likely than broad disclosure would have, the Commission made clear in its remedial opinion that there was insufficient evidence that JEDEC would have standardized other technologies had it known the full scope of Rambus's intellectual property. Therefore, for the Commission's syllogism to survive-and for the Commission to have carried its burden of proving that Rambus's conduct had an anticompetitive effect-we must also be convinced that if Rambus's conduct merely enabled it to avoid the other possible outcome, namely JEDEC's obtaining assurances from Rambus of RAND licensing terms, such conduct, alone, could be said to harm competition. We are not convinced.

Deceptive conduct—like any other kind—must have an anticompetitive effect in order to form the basis of a monopolization claim. "Even an act of pure malice by one business competitor against another does not, without more, state a claim under the federal antitrust laws," without proof of "a dangerous probability that [the defendant] would monopolize a particular market." *Brooke Group*, 509 US at 225. Even if deception raises the price secured by a seller, but does so without harming competition, it is beyond the antitrust laws' reach. Cases that recognize deception as exclusionary hinge, therefore, on whether the conduct impaired rivals in a manner tending to bring about or protect a defendant's monopoly power. * * *

[A]n otherwise lawful monopolist's use of deception simply to obtain higher prices normally has no particular tendency to exclude rivals and thus to diminish competition.

Despite vociferous urging from the FTC, industry and consumer groups, and law professors and scholars, the Supreme Court declined to grant a writ of *certiorari* in *Rambus*. The FTC then closed its Rambus file, giving Rambus the last word in the FTC matter.

Notes and Questions

1.   In rejecting the FTC's findings in *Rambus*, the court relied on the Supreme Court's decision in *NYNEX Corp. v. Discon, Inc.*, 525 U.S. 128 (1998), for the proposition that mere deception leading to higher prices is insufficient to state an antitrust claim without a showing that the deception impaired the market's competitive functioning. *NYNEX*, however, was a private lawsuit and not a government enforcement action. Should the FTC be treated differently from private litigants? After all, most of the concerns that have led the courts to be cautious with private antitrust lawsuits—particularly the fear of abusive or frivolous lawsuits and the chilling effect of treble damages—have little relevance to enforcement actions by the FTC. Some commentators believe that rules applicable to public enforcers like the FTC and Department of Justice have become overwhelmed by the "baggage" of private enforcement and that this has constricted the agencies' ability to win cases in the courts. Do enforcement systems that rely entirely or primarily on public enforcement have an advantage in this regard?

2.   In *Rambus,* the European Commission had one advantage over the US FTC, and one disadvantage. The disadvantage was: EU has no attempt to monopolize violation and Rambus was not dominant at the time of its deception. The advantage was: EU has an excessive pricing law and the US doesn't.

d.   Suits to Enjoin Infringement of Essential Patents as Antitrust Violations

A cutting edge issue today in both the United States and the European Union arises in the context of standard-setting organizations where standards are necessary to facilitate technological progress and access by each player in the market to all essential technology is necessary to produce its products. Each of several players, such as Apple, Samsung, and Microsoft, is likely to need to use the intellectual property of the others to make its product, and barring of access would take its entire product (such as the iPhone) off the market. To assure their access to essential technology, and to prevent hold-ups for excessive license fees by IP owners, the firms (all owners of technology) make FRAND commitments: Each agrees that it will disclose its relevant technology during the standard setting process, and that, if the choice of standard makes its IP essential, it will license all of its essential patents on fair, reasonable, and non-discriminatory terms. Does the holder of a standard essential patent (SEP) under FRAND commitments have an *antitrust* duty to license that patent to willing licensees, and an *antitrust* duty not to seek an injunction for infringement against willing licensees (which typically are still bargaining on the terms of the license)?

Google acquired Motorola Mobility, which gave Google a portfolio of more than 24,000 patents. Motorola Mobility had agreed, in the standard setting organization, to license its patents necessary to work the standards on fair, reasonable and non-discriminatory terms. Motorola Mobility sought or was threatening to seek injunctions against infringers such as Apple and Microsoft, who were willing licensees but had not yet made an offer that Motorola Mobility would accept.

In the US, the FTC accused Motorola Mobility and Google of violating Section 5 of the Federal Trade Commission Act by suing for injunctions. It negotiated a consent order in which Google agreed not to seek injunctions on FRAND-encumbered SEPs against willing licensees. If the parties could not reach agreement on license terms, a neutral third party would settle the terms. Motorola Mobility LLC, Docket No. C–4410, Jan. 3, 2013, issued as modified July 23, 2013, reported at 5 CCH Trade Reg. Rep. ¶ 16,876.

Commissioner Maureen Ohlhausen, later Acting Chair of the FTC, dissented from entry of the consent order. She viewed any limitation on Motorola Mobility's right to seek an injunction for infringement of a FRAND-encumbered patent a matter of contract, not an antitrust problem, and she thought an antitrust duty not to seek an injunction would be an impermissible interference with IP rights. She doubted whether the FRAND agreement was properly construed to bar such a suit, and she thought that, if antitrust were implicated, the *Noerr-Pennington* right to petition courts would be a complete defense. There is virtually no litigated US case on point, and any court would have to contend with the Ohlhausen arguments, bolstered by the *Trinko* philosophy of no duty to deal and the difficulties of proving that a patent is a monopoly.

The European view is more developed, for the European Court of Justice has ruled, in *Huawei v. ZTE*.

HUAWEI TECHNOLOGIES CO. LTD v. ZTE CORP.

Case C–170/13, EU:C:2015:477 (European Court of Justice 2015)

* * *

[44] ... [T]he referring court asks, essentially, in what circumstances the bringing of an action for infringement, by an undertaking in a

dominant position and holding an SEP, which has given an undertaking to the standardization body to grant licenses to third parties on FRAND terms, seeking an injunction prohibiting the infringement of that SEP or seeking the recall of products for the manufacture of which the SEP has been used, is to be regarded as constituting an abuse contrary to Article 102 TFEU.

45 First of all, it must be recalled that the concept of an abuse of a dominant position within the meaning of Article 102 TFEU is an objective concept relating to the conduct of a dominant undertaking which, on a market where the degree of competition is already weakened precisely because of the presence of the undertaking concerned, through recourse to methods different from those governing normal competition in products or services on the basis of the transactions of commercial operators, has the effect of hindering the maintenance of the degree of competition still existing in the market or the growth of that competition (judgments in Hoffmann-La Roche, AKZO, and Tomra).

46 It is, in this connection, settled case-law that the exercise of an exclusive right linked to an intellectual-property right—in the case in the main proceedings, namely the right to bring an action for infringement—forms part of the rights of the proprietor of an intellectual-property right, with the result that the exercise of such a right, even if it is the act of an undertaking holding a dominant position, cannot in itself constitute an abuse of a dominant position.

47 However, it is also settled case-law that the exercise of an exclusive right linked to an intellectual-property right by the proprietor may, in exceptional circumstances, involve abusive conduct for the purposes of Article 102 TFEU. * * *

49 [This case] is characterized, first, by the fact that the patent at issue is essential to a standard established by a standardization body, rendering its use indispensable to all competitors which envisage manufacturing products that comply with the standard to which it is linked.

50 That feature distinguishes SEPs from patents that are not essential to a standard and which normally allow third parties to manufacture competing products without recourse to the patent concerned and without compromising the essential functions of the product in question.

51 Secondly, the case in the main proceedings may be distinguished by the fact . . . that the patent at issue obtained SEP status only in return for the proprietor's irrevocable undertaking, given to the

standardization body in question, that it is prepared to grant licenses on FRAND terms.

[52] Although the proprietor of the essential patent at issue has the right to bring an action for a prohibitory injunction or for the recall of products, the fact that that patent has obtained SEP status means that its proprietor can prevent products manufactured by competitors from appearing or remaining on the market and, thereby, reserve to itself the manufacture of the products in question.

[53] In those circumstances, and having regard to the fact that an undertaking to grant licenses on FRAND terms creates legitimate expectations on the part of third parties that the proprietor of the SEP will in fact grant licenses on such terms, a refusal by the proprietor of the SEP to grant a license on those terms may, in principle, constitute an abuse within the meaning of Article 102 TFEU.

[54] It follows that, having regard to the legitimate expectations created, the abusive nature of such a refusal may, in principle, be raised in defense to actions for a prohibitory injunction or for the recall of products. However, under Article 102 TFEU, the proprietor of the patent is obliged only to grant a license on FRAND terms. In the case in the main proceedings, the parties are not in agreement as to what is required by FRAND terms in the circumstances of that case.

[55] In such a situation, in order to prevent an action for a prohibitory injunction or for the recall of products from being regarded as abusive, the proprietor of an SEP must comply with conditions which seek to ensure a fair balance between the interests concerned. * * *

[57] Thus, the need to enforce intellectual-property rights, covered by, inter alia, Directive 2004/48, which—in accordance with Article 17(2) of the Charter [of Fundamental Rights of the European Union]— provides for a range of legal remedies aimed at ensuring a high level of protection for intellectual-property rights in the internal market, and the right to effective judicial protection guaranteed by Article 47 of the Charter, comprising various elements, including the right of access to a tribunal, must be taken into consideration.

[58] This need for a high level of protection for intellectual-property rights means that, in principle, the proprietor may not be deprived of the right to have recourse to legal proceedings to ensure effective enforcement of his exclusive rights, and that, in principle, the user of those rights, if he is not the proprietor, is required to obtain a license prior to any use.

[59] Thus, although the irrevocable undertaking to grant licenses on FRAND terms given to the standardization body by the proprietor of an SEP cannot negate the substance of the rights guaranteed to that proprietor by Article 17(2) and Article 47 of the Charter, it does, none the less, justify the imposition on that proprietor of an obligation to comply with specific requirements when bringing actions against alleged infringers for a prohibitory injunction or for the recall of products.

[60] Accordingly, the proprietor of an SEP which considers that that SEP is the subject of an infringement cannot, without infringing Article 102 TFEU, bring an action for a prohibitory injunction or for the recall of products against the alleged infringer without notice or prior consultation with the alleged infringer, even if the SEP has already been used by the alleged infringer.

[61] Prior to such proceedings, it is thus for the proprietor of the SEP in question, first, to alert the alleged infringer of the infringement complained about by designating that SEP and specifying the way in which it has been infringed.

[62] . . . [I]n view of the large number of SEPs composing a standard such as that at issue in the main proceedings, it is not certain that the infringer of one of those SEPs will necessarily be aware that it is using the teaching of an SEP that is both valid and essential to a standard.

[63] Secondly, after the alleged infringer has expressed its willingness to conclude a licensing agreement on FRAND terms, it is for the proprietor of the SEP to present to that alleged infringer a specific, written offer for a license on FRAND terms, in accordance with the undertaking given to the standardization body, specifying, in particular, the amount of the royalty and the way in which that royalty is to be calculated.

[64] . . . [W]here the proprietor of an SEP has given an undertaking to the standardization body to grant licenses on FRAND terms, it can be expected that it will make such an offer. Furthermore, in the absence of a public standard licensing agreement, and where licensing agreements already concluded with other competitors are not made public, the proprietor of the SEP is better placed to check whether its offer complies with the condition of non-discrimination than is the alleged infringer.

[65] By contrast, it is for the alleged infringer diligently to respond to that offer, in accordance with recognized commercial practices in the field and in good faith, a point which must be established on the basis

of objective factors and which implies, in particular, that there are no delaying tactics.

⁶⁶ Should the alleged infringer not accept the offer made to it, it may rely on the abusive nature of an action for a prohibitory injunction or for the recall of products only if it has submitted to the proprietor of the SEP in question, promptly and in writing, a specific counter-offer that corresponds to FRAND terms.

⁶⁷ Furthermore, where the alleged infringer is using the teachings of the SEP before a licensing agreement has been concluded, it is for that alleged infringer, from the point at which its counter-offer is rejected, to provide appropriate security, in accordance with recognized commercial practices in the field, for example by providing a bank guarantee or by placing the amounts necessary on deposit. The calculation of that security must include, inter alia, the number of the past acts of use of the SEP, and the alleged infringer must be able to render an account in respect of those acts of use.

⁶⁸ In addition, where no agreement is reached on the details of the FRAND terms following the counter-offer by the alleged infringer, the parties may, by common agreement, request that the amount of the royalty be determined by an independent third party, by decision without delay.

⁶⁹ [The alleged infringer retains the right to challenge the validity of the patent and to challenge its essentiality to the standard, which it can do in parallel with negotiations for the license fee.] * * *

⁷¹ It follows ... that Article 102 TFEU must be interpreted as meaning that the proprietor of an SEP, which has given an irrevocable undertaking to a standardization body to grant a license to third parties on FRAND terms, does not abuse its dominant position, within the meaning of Article 102 TFEU, by bringing an action for infringement seeking an injunction prohibiting the infringement of its patent or seeking the recall of products for the manufacture of which that patent has been used, as long as:

  —prior to bringing that action, the proprietor has, first, alerted the alleged infringer of the infringement complained about by designating that patent and specifying the way in which it has been infringed, and, secondly, after the alleged infringer has expressed its willingness to conclude a licensing agreement on FRAND terms, presented to that infringer a specific, written offer for a license on such terms, specifying, in particular, the royalty and the way in which it is to be calculated, and

—where the alleged infringer continues to use the patent in question, the alleged infringer has not diligently responded to that offer, in accordance with recognized commercial practices in the field and in good faith, this being a matter which must be established on the basis of objective factors and which implies, in particular, that there are no delaying tactics. * * *

Notes and Questions

1.   Before the *Huawei* judgment came down, the European Commission found that Motorola Mobility abused its dominant position in violation of EU competition law by seeking and enforcing an injunction against Apple for using Motorola Mobility's standard essential patents in its smart phones without a license, where Motorola Mobility had made a FRAND commitment and Apple was a willing licensee. At the same time, Samsung settled a separate investigation with the Commission committing to discontinue just such conduct. European Commission—IP/14/489 (29 April 2014).

2.   The *Huawei* judgment resolved divergences in approach taken by some national courts.

3.   Describe the *Huawei* judgment and the steps a SEP holder must take in terms of good faith bargaining for the license fee in order to be entitled to seek an injunction. Is the judgment properly respectful of intellectual property rights, which, as it says, are protected by the Charter on Fundamental Rights as well as the Treaty?

4.   Would you expect the US courts to adopt the European approach? to adopt the approach outlined by Commissioner Ohlhausen? Why? What are the relative merits of each?

e.   Unfair Royalties and Other Licensing Terms as Antitrust Violations

Qualcomm is the dominant supplier in the world of baseband processors, which are chips that manage cellular communications in mobile products. It also holds patents essential to cellular connectivity. Firms in China are the principal manufacturers of mobile products that need the technology. After a long investigation in China by the National Development and Resources Commission, in which the NDRC often stressed its claim that the Chinese firms were paying excessive royalties to Qualcomm, Qualcomm accepted the following terms, including a fine of nearly one billion US dollars—the highest fine yet imposed by the Chinese antitrust authorities.

Here is NDRC's statement, as translated by Linklater's Greater China Translation Team.

NDRC ORDERED RECTIFICATION AND FINED QUALCOMM RMB6 BILLION FOR MONOPOLISTIC CONDUCTS

10 February 2015

The National Development and Reform Commission ("**NDRC**") recently sanctioned Qualcomm Incorporated ("**Qualcomm**") according to laws for its abuse of dominant market position to eliminate or restrict competition, ordered Qualcomm to cease the relevant illegal activities and imposed on it a fine equaling to 8% of its sales in China in 2013, i.e. RMB6.088 billion.

In November 2013, NDRC initiated the anti-monopoly investigation on Qualcomm based on complaints received. In the process of the investigation, NDRC conducted in-depth investigation into dozens of domestic and international cell phone manufacturing enterprises and baseband chip manufacturers, acquired evidence on Qualcomm's price monopoly and other monopolistic conducts, fully solicited Qualcomm's statements and defenses, and analyzed and assessed on whether the relevant activities of Qualcomm constitute the abuse of market dominance under the Anti-Monopoly Law of China (the "**AML**").

Based on the investigation and the evidence obtained and through analysis and assessment as described above, it is found that Qualcomm has a dominant position in the markets of standard essential patents ("**SEPs**") licensing in respect of CDMA, WCDMA and LTE wireless communication and the market of baseband chips, and that Qualcomm has engaged in the following conducts in abuse of its dominant market position:

1. **Charged unfairly high patent licensing fees**. Qualcomm refused to provide Chinese enterprises with its patent lists when granting license to them and charged licensing fees for expired patents which are always included in its patent portfolio. In the meantime, Qualcomm requested a free cross-license of the Chinese licensees' own relevant patents, while refused to deduct the value of such cross-licensed patents from its licensing fees or offer another consideration. In addition, for Chinese licensees who have been forced to accept Qualcomm's packaged licensing of non-SEPs, Qualcomm charged royalties on the basis of the net wholesale price of the device while

imposing a relatively high royalty rate. A combination of these factors resulted in the excessively high royalties.

2. **Bundled sales of non-SEPs in relation to the wireless communication without justifications.** Qualcomm did not distinguish or offered separate licenses in respect of its SEPs and non-SEPs in relation to the wireless communication, which are of a different nature; instead, it took advantage of its dominant position in the market of licensing of SEPs in relation to the wireless communication to bundle the licensing of non-SEPs in relation to the wireless communication. Some of Chinese licensees have been forced to obtain the license of non-SEPs in relation to the wireless communication from Qualcomm.

3. **Imposed unreasonable restrictions on the sales of baseband chips.** Qualcomm conditioned its supply of baseband chips to Chinese customers on the signing without challenging a patent-license agreement by such customers. If a potential licensee did not sign the patent-license agreement including the above unreasonable terms, or the licensee disputed such patent-license agreement and brought actions, Qualcomm would refuse to supply baseband chips to it. Since Qualcomm has a dominant position in the market of baseband chips and the Chinese licensees highly relied on its baseband chip products, Qualcomm imposed unreasonable conditions on the sales of baseband chip and forced Chinese licensees to accept unfair or unreasonable patent licensing terms.

Qualcomm's above conducts have eliminated or restricted the market competition, impeded and restrained the technology innovation and development, harmed the interest of consumers, and violated the provisions under the AML in relation to the prohibition on the business operators with a dominant market position from charging unfairly high prices in the sales of products, bundling sales of products without justifications and imposing unreasonable trading conditions.

In the process of the anti-monopoly investigation, Qualcomm was cooperative and voluntarily proposed a package of rectification commitments in respect of Qualcomm's certain SEPs in relation to the wireless communication, which include: (1) to charge royalties at the rate of 65% of the net wholesale price of the cell phones sold for being used within China; (2) to provide patent lists when granting license to Chinese licensees and not to charge licensing fees for expired patents; (3) not to request a free cross-license from Chinese licensees; (4) not to bundle the non-SEPs when licensing the SEPs in relation to the wireless communication without justifications; and (5) not to request Chinese licensees to enter into a patent-license agreement including unreasonable conditions when selling baseband chips, and not to condition the supply of baseband chips to Chinese licensees on no challenging such patent-license agreement. The rectification commitments proposed by Qualcomm meet the requirements of NDRC. Qualcomm also indicated that it will continue to increase the investment and pursue a better development in China. NDRC welcomes Qualcomm's continued investment in China and supports Qualcomm in also indicated that it will continue to increase the investment and pursue a better development in China. NDRC welcomes Qualcomm's continued investment in China and supports Qualcomm in charging reasonable royalties for the use of its patented technologies.

Since Qualcomm's monopolistic conducts in the abuse of market dominance were severe in nature, implemented in a deep degree and persisted for a long time, NDRC, while ordering Qualcomm to cease its illegal activities, also imposed a fine on Qualcomm equaling to 8% of its sales in China in 2013. This instance of anti-monopoly law enforcement deters Qualcomm's monopolistic conducts, maintains the fair competition of the market and protects the interest of consumers.

Notes and Questions

1.   Does the Chinese enforcement appear to be reasonable? Unreasonable? "Normal" antitrust? Discriminatory antitrust?

2.   In the course of the investigation, here is what the Global Competition Review reported (in an article by Ron Knox, A red wave rising, Oct. 14, 2014) about the US perception of the Chinese investigation:

> "Midway through her speech dedicated to issues in the US, [Federal Trade Commission Chairwoman Edith] Ramirez shifted her focus to a recent spate of Chinese antitrust cases. She broached recent media reports that suggested Chinese enforcers were targeting standard-essential patent holders over competition concerns—a topic familiar to Ramirez and other enforcers in the US, Europe and elsewhere. But rather than attacking patent owners for their apparent abuses,

Ramirez said, it appeared for the all the world that the Chinese investigations were fueled instead by unhappiness with the prices charged to Chinese tech companies for access to those patents.

'I am seriously concerned by these reports, which suggest an enforcement policy focused on reducing royalty payments for local implementers as a matter of industrial policy, rather than protecting competition and long-run consumer welfare,' Ramirez told the crowd. The cutlery quietened.

Ramirez's statements—the harshest yet by one of China's international antitrust counterparts—mirror widespread Western backlash against a host of new Chinese competition cases that appear to be aimed squarely at foreign companies and the prices they charge Chinese businesses."

3.   Meanwhile, challenges to practices of Qualcomm have been made by agencies around the world, including by the US FTC in early January 2017. The US FTC complaint alleges that Qualcomm maintains a monopoly by a no-license, no chips policy, by refusing to license standard essential patents, and by extracting chip exclusivity from Apple in exchange for lower royalties. Commissioner Maureen Ohlhausen dissented to the filing of the complaint. She asserts that the FTC complaint fundamentally attacks unreasonably high royalties on FRAND-encumbered patents. *https://www.ftc.gov/news-events/ press-releases/2017/01/ftc-charges-qualcomm-monopolizing-key- semiconductor-device-used.* The debate on the IP/antitrust interface, including how much deference to give intellectual property, and when and how much antitrust intervention is appropriate continues to rage across countries and even within jurisdictions.

C.   EXPLOITATIVE OFFENSES

1.   Excessive Pricing

A quintessential economic evil of monopoly is output limitation, which causes a distortion in the flow of scarce resources. Fewer resources flow to the monopolized market than would be the case if the market were competitive. The corollary to limiting output is raising prices; higher prices means lower output. Excessive pricing would, then, seem to be an essential evil that competition law could address. But matters are complex. Antitrust is normally intended to free up the market; to remove obstructions to meritorious competition, not to control the market. Price is the central nervous system of the competition process, which is built upon freedom of pricing, up and down. Moreover, the antitrust authority is not a price regulator, at least not normally; it does not normally have functions—and corresponding powers—to decide when price is too high, much less to decide the right price level; nor regulatory powers of supervising the prices of a high-price offender.

These cautionary factors have led the United States to reject an excessive pricing violation under US antitrust law. In its 2004 decision in *Verizon v. Trinko*, 540 U.S. 398 (2004), the US Supreme Court even had good words to say about monopoly pricing. Thus:

> The mere possession of monopoly power, and the concomitant charging of monopoly prices, is not only not unlawful; it is an important element of the free-market system. The opportunity to charge monopoly prices—at least for a short period—is what attracts "business acumen" in the first place; it induces risk taking that produces innovation and economic growth. To safeguard the incentive to innovate, the possession of monopoly power will not be found unlawful unless it is accompanied by an element of anticompetitive conduct.

Similarly, in *Pacific Bell Tel. Co. v. LinkLine Commun., Inc.*, 555 U.S. 438 (2009), the Supreme Court strongly reaffirmed that even monopolists "are free to choose the parties with whom they will deal, as well as the prices, terms, and conditions of that dealing." It said that "antitrust law does not forbid lawfully obtained monopolies from charging monopoly prices." In both *LinkLine* and *Trinko*, the Supreme Court justified this refusal to police monopoly prices on institutional grounds. The Court stated that "[c]ourts are ill suited 'to act as central planners, identifying the proper price, quantity, and other terms of dealing.'" Courts should thus refuse to "assume the day-to-day controls characteristic of a regulatory agency," which they could not do without "examining costs and demands" on the monopolist.

The antitrust laws of a number of other jurisdictions prohibit excessive pricing. Especially in nations with a statist background where the economy was marked by powerful state-owned firms, it seemed natural for the competition law to proscribe excessive pricing. The European Union competition law expressly prohibits dominant firms from "imposing unfair purchase or selling prices or other unfair trading conditions." TFEU Article 102 (a). Numerous jurisdictions have copied this provision of the EU law, whether for efficiency or fairness.

Even in the United States the issue resurfaces from time to time, as we see rogue traders finding profit opportunities to raise the price of life-saving drugs hundreds of percentage points, as did Martin Shkreli, who bought up pharma firms in order to raise the price of drugs. The Federal Trade Commission, apparently urged on by

Congress and public outrage, announced it was examining the matter, but no action resulted. Two years later, ironically following through on a complaint by Shkreli, the FTC sued and settled with Mallinckrodt for buying and shutting down its only potential competitor, creating a monopoly and enabling the monopolist to increase the price of a drug used to treat infant spasms by 85,000%. *http://nypost.com/2017/01/18/complaint-from-martin-shkreli-leads-to-ftc-drug-price-suit/* Proposed Stipulated Order for Permanent Injunction and Equitable Monetary Relief, FTC v. Mallinckrodt ARD Inc. and Mallinckrodt plc, No. 1:17–cv–00120 (D.D.C. Jan. 18, 2017). But the Mallinckrodt episode was not a "mere" extraordinary price rise. It was an acquisition with accompanying conduct to shut down the only competing drug.

In some parts of the world, "mere" extraordinary price hikes of essential drugs have been met with antitrust prohibition, although rarely so. The UK Competition Marketing Authority fined Pfizer and its distributor nearly 90 million pounds for a price hike of 2400% immediately after the drug was de-branded (genericized) and thus freed from price regulation. The National Health Service was a main buyer of the drug. *https://www.gov.uk/government/news/cma-fines-pfizer-and-flynn-90-million-for-drug-price-hike-to-nhs.*

Litigation of excessive pricing charges is, however, usually a complex endeavor. In the remainder of this section we discuss the leading EU case, which is now of older vintage, and more recent South African cases. South Africa has been especially plagued by extraordinarily high prices. In the early days of its modern competition law the Competition Commission successfully challenged GlaxoSmithKline and Boehringer Ingelheim for over-pricing an HIV/AIDS cocktail at the height of the AIDS epidemic in South Africa. When the Commission insisted on examining the companies' books, the companies settled, agreeing to license a generic manufacturer. See note on *Hazel Tau* by South Africa on Generic Pharmaceuticals submitted to the OECD 18–19 June 2014, DAF/COMP/WD(2014)68 at 2.1.

In jurisdictions that prohibit excessive pricing, the agencies and courts tend to exercise their powers with caution so as not to interfere with the normal give and take of the market. The challenge is to adopt standards that will allow the authority or court to identify excessive prices with some confidence and to devise relief likely to be effective without excessive supervision.

In the context of a Latvian collecting society's licenses for public performance of musical works, a Latvian national court asked the Court of Justice how to determine when a price is excessive under

EU law. The Court answered that there is no single method of deciding; that the Competition Council may make the determination by reference to a sufficiently representative sample of other national markets, and that the price difference must be significant and appreciable. Latvian collection society, Case C–177/16, EU:C:2017: [page number forthcoming].

We have mentioned the first leading EU case on excessive pricing—Case 27/76, *United Brands Co. v. Commission*, EU:C:1978:22. In that case, the European Court of Justice reversed a finding of the European Commission that United Brands—the purveyor of the Chiquita banana brand—engaged in excessive pricing of bananas in certain EU member states. The evidence showed that United Brands made its European sales to distributors free on rail at Rotterdam or Bremerhaven and that it charged vastly different prices based on the degree of Chiquita brand recognition in each distributor's country. For example, the price charged to the distributor for Ireland—where the brand was not well known—was half of the price charged to the distributor for Denmark—where the brand was well known.

The Court first found that United Brands' pricing practices amounted to unlawful price discrimination; that they were "obstacles to the free movement of goods" within the European Union and that they distorted competition by placing certain distributors at a great competitive advantage over others. The Court then turned to the unfair pricing claim.

> The questions ... to be determined are whether the difference between the costs actually incurred and the price actually charged is excessive, and, if the answer to this question is in the affirmative, whether a price has been imposed which is either unfair in itself or when compared to competing products.
>
> Other ways may be devised—and economic theorists have not failed to think up several—of selecting the rules for determining whether the price of a product is unfair.
>
> The Commission bases its view that prices are excessive on an analysis of the differences—in its view excessive—between the prices charged in different Member States and on the policy of discriminatory prices which has been considered above.
>
> The foundation of its argument has been the applicant's letter of 10 December 1974 which acknowledged that the margin allowed by the sale of bananas to the Irish ripeners

was much smaller than in some other Member States and it concluded from this that the amount by which the actual prices f.o.r. Bremerhaven and Rotterdam exceed the delivered Rotterdam prices for bananas to be sold to Irish customers c.i.f. Dublin must represent a profit of the same order of magnitude.

Having found that the prices charged to ripeners of the other Member States were considerably higher, sometimes by as much as 100%, than the prices charged to customers in Ireland it concluded that UBC was making a very substantial profit.

Nevertheless the Commission has not taken into account in its reasoning . . . a confidential document . . . pointing out that the prices charged in Ireland had produced a loss.

The applicant also states that the prices charged on the relevant market did not allow it to make any profits during the last five years, except in 1975. * * *

However unreliable the particulars supplied by UBC may be (and in particular the document mentioned previously which works out the "losses" on the Irish market in 1974 without supporting evidence), the fact remains that it was for the Commission to prove that the applicant charged unfair prices.

UBC's retraction, which the Commission has not effectively refuted, establishes beyond doubt that the basis for the calculation adopted by the latter to prove that UBC's prices are excessive is open to criticism and on this point in particular there is doubt which must benefit the applicant, especially as for nearly 20 years banana prices, in real terms, have not risen on the relevant market. * * *

In these circumstances it appears that the Commission has not adduced adequate legal proof of the facts and evaluations which formed the foundation of its findings that UBC had infringed Article [102] of the Treaty by directly and indirectly imposing unfair selling prices for bananas.

As we have mentioned, the *United Brands* case was background for South African cases that were to follow. This is because the South African Competition Act tracks language of *United Brands* in defining excessive price; namely: a price that "bears no reasonable relation to the economic value of that good or service . . ." and is higher than the reasonable value. The two cases that follow—*Mittal* and a note on *Sasol*—both involve import parity pricing of a necessary input by a super-dominant firm with a history of privileges conferred by the state, and the high domestic prices compared with the competitively low international prices disadvantaged the domestic business buyers in their international competition. In *Mittal* we include excerpts from the Competition Tribunal's decision as well as from the Court's judgment that reversed it, to highlight the Tribunal's creative attempt to devise a manageable way to identify and correct excessive import parity pricing by a super-dominant firm.

HARMONY GOLD MINING COMPANY LTD v. MITTAL STEEL CORP
The Competition Tribunal of South Africa

Case No. 13/CR/Feb 04 (2007), reversed and remanded, see infra

DAVID LEWIS, CHAIR:

[Mittal Steel, and its various affiliated companies, was the dominant producer of flat steel products in South Africa and formerly a governmental monopoly. Two Mittal customers, Harmony Gold Mining and Durban Roodepoort, filed a complaint against Mittal alleging that it engaged in excessive pricing of flat steel products in South Africa.]

33 The complainants have sought . . . to demonstrate that those South African consumers who are charged the Mittal SA list price pay a price that is relatively excessive in relation to the prices charged to the other purchasers of steel listed above. As may easily be imagined this approach has entailed the presentation of massive quantities of empirical evidence regarding steel prices across the globe and in every conceivable market segment in which flat steel products are consumed. This approach—the use of comparators in other markets—finds echo in a number of decisions of the courts of the European Union and those of its member states. Many of these decisions are referred to below.

34 Mittal SA, for its part, has not engaged much with the approach of its adversaries and, hence, with much of the voluminous evidence presented in support of the price comparison approach. It has taken a quite different approach to the question of excessive pricing. In essence Mittal SA has argued that a charge of excessive pricing can only be sustained if the complainants can demonstrate that this is reflected in excessive profits. This has entailed a detailed excursion into the complex world of profit measurement, a concept which has different meanings for economists, on the one hand, and, on the

other, for the accountants and auditors who are charged with preparing the accounts of companies. We have heard the deeply contending views of a spiraling group of learned academicians and practitioners on, inter alia, the measurement of profit and the cost of capital and on the correct approach to the question of depreciation. This too has entailed the presentation of reams of empirical data. * * *

[37] . . . [I]n our view, the arguments of both the complainants and Mittal SA would effectively have the competition authorities adopt, by virtue of Section 8(a) [prohibiting excessive prices], the methodologies of price regulation. This is not our approach. While, as will be seen, we do not shy away from the responsibility imposed on us by Section 8(a) [prohibiting excessive prices] to pass judgment on the pricing practices of monopolies or, what we have termed, 'super-dominant' firms, we do so using principles and methodologies firmly rooted in the practice of competition law and economics. Although we have found that Mittal SA is indeed charging excessive prices, and is thereby in contravention of Section 8(a), we have not reached this conclusion by assuming the mantle of a price regulator. * * *

Mittal SA's price setting methodology

[41] [I]n the import parity pricing regime Mittal SA sets its base prices for flat steel products in the domestic market by calculating the notional cost of importing those products. It then adds a 5% 'hassle factor', essentially a reflection of the additional costs or 'hassle' entailed in importing over the advantage of utilizing a domestic supplier. The import parity price is determined monthly by Mittal SA and is conveyed to customers as a discount or surcharge off a list price that is published every three months. * * *

[47] The argument that will be developed in this decision holds that a non-excessive price is one that is determined by competitive conditions in the relevant market. The manner in which the IPPD pricing basis works is to determine the price of flat steel products in South Africa by reference to demand and supply conditions that prevail in an arbitrarily selected market abroad (for example, the 'Black Sea price') markets and then to add to that price the notional costs of 'importing' the product to South Africa. . . . As we will show the key competitive conditions in our market are Mittal SA's structural super-dominance plus ancillary conduct aimed at maintaining the segmentation of differently priced markets, the cumulative effect of which is to produce a price that is not influenced by any competition considerations whatsoever and is, because of this, adjudged to be excessive. * * *

The panel's approach to allegations of excessive pricing

[70] There are few practices condemned by the Competition Act in terms as unambiguous as that identified in Section 8(a) which, in language of crystal clarity, provides that

It is prohibited for a dominant firm to—

(a) Charge an excessive price to the detriment of consumers

[72] Although, as shall be elaborated at length, the hurdles, particularly regarding the extent of dominance, that must be cleared by a complainant in order to prove excessive pricing are, in our view, exceptional, the repugnance attached to this offence is reinforced by the fact that an administrative penalty can be levied for a first time contravention.

[73] However, although this is frequently misunderstood by the broad public which, rightly, views excessive prices as the most likely and egregious consequence of monopoly, the theory and practice of competition law and economics is dominated by an equally unambiguous maxim that asserts that the task of a competition regulator does not extend to the determination and fixing of prices.

[74] The reluctance of competition practitioners to assume a price regulating function does not only derive from the truly massive technical difficulties entailed in determining the 'right' or, for that matter, the 'wrong' price, but from the founding principle underpinning the world view of the practice of competition law and economics that holds that price determination is best left to the interplay of independent actors engaging with each other in the market place. The fundamental task of competition regulators is then to promote and defend competitive market structures and to guard against conduct on the part of market participants which seeks to undermine the promise of those competitive structures to deliver quality goods and services at competitive prices.

[75] Core to competition enforcement is the recognition that the promise held out by competitively structured markets may be denied by co-operation between notional competitors. It is additionally recognized that a number of factors ranging from the acquisition of market share by pro-competitive means through to past or present governmental support and subsidy, may result in single firm domination of markets. Faced by single firm domination the principal function of competition enforcers is to guard against 'exclusionary conduct', that is, unilateral conduct of the dominant firm that has as its objective the reproduction of this dominance through the exclusion of actual or would-be competitors from the market.

[76] Price determination is thus not characteristically part of the armory of competition enforcement. And yet Section 8(a)'s proscription of the charging of an excessive price appears, on the face of it, to assign us a role that precisely requires us to determine whether existing price levels are 'right' or 'wrong' (non-excessive or excessive) and, if 'wrong' (excessive) to determine and impose the 'right' (non-excessive) price.

[77] Confronted by these two unambiguous, but manifestly contradictory, requirements—the one which appears to condemn a particular price level and require us to impose another lower price, the other which resists the administrative determination of a price— one might predict that attempts to enforce Section 8(a) would immediately run into serious conceptual difficulties. And this is indeed the case. . . . * * *

[81] The standard approaches and instruments of competition enforcement comprise interventions in the structure of the affected markets and in the conduct of its participants so as to produce outcomes that are, as far as possible, unsullied by the possession or, rather, the abuse, of market power. As already noted, there are compelling conceptual and practical reasons why a competition authority should eschew a price regulation role and if it is possible— and we believe in this instance it is—to prove and remedy excessive pricing without resort to the methodologies of price regulation, then this is the approach that must be favored. * * *

[84] If we are to approach this allegation in the manner of a competition authority, we must first ask ourselves whether the structure of the market in question enables those who participate in it to charge excessive prices. As we will indicate, we believe this to be a significantly higher hurdle than those that must be cleared in order to establish 'mere' dominance. It requires 'super-dominance', a structural condition the characteristics of which are elaborated below. If that higher hurdle is cleared, we must then ask ourselves whether Mittal SA has engaged in conduct designed to take advantage of—to 'abuse'—those structural opportunities by imposing excessive prices on its customers. If the second question is also answered in the affirmative, the excessive pricing must be proscribed by imposing a remedy which addresses the underlying structural basis for the offending conduct and/or any ancillary conduct arising from the structural advantage that enables the firm in question to charge a price in excess of that which would have prevailed in the absence of the anti-competitive structure and/or the ancillary conduct. Only if both forms of these remedies are impossible to devise should an actual price level be specified. In short, we treat excessive pricing as a phenomenon that may arise from a particular structure

and that itself may be the basis for ancillary conduct that is utilized in order to sustain supra-competitive prices, to sustain, as per the definition of the Act . . . . * * *

[The Tribunal found that Mittal was super-dominant. It was the only significant steel producer in South Africa, it had been so for half a century, barriers to establish another efficient steel plant in South Africa were probably impenetrable, and transportation costs of steel from the geographically nearest producers were very high because steel is heavy. As for excessiveness of the domestic price, the Tribunal determined that it need not wade through the extensive documentation of costs and profits produced by Mittal, for it could infer from certain key facts that the price was excessive. The key facts were: The world price of steel was reasonably low compared with a very much higher domestic price, and for years Mittal sold steel in the world market at the world price, presumably profitably. Accordingly, the domestic price bore no relationship to a competitive price. Further, Mittal engaged in "ancillary abusive conduct" by prohibiting its dealers for export from re-selling into the South African market. The Tribunal deferred the question of remedy to a separate hearing. In a separate decision, the Tribunal fined Mittal 5.5% of its annual turnover and ordered structural relief: In order to counter Mittal's market segmentation and price discrimination, the Tribunal ruled that Mittal could no longer impose contractual restrictions limiting customers' rights to resell to other customers. Mittal appealed.]

MITTAL STEEL SOUTH AFRICA v. HARMONY GOLD MINING
In the Competition Appeal Court of South Africa

Case No. 70/CAC/Apr 07 (2009)

JUDGE DENNIS DAVIS:

* * *

30 Analysis of the Judgment

31 The methodology employed by the Tribunal to determine whether a price is 'excessive' for purposes of s 8(a) depends on its criterion of 'super-dominance'. It said that, as a competition authority, it had to first ask whether the market structure enabled those participating in it to charge excessive prices (the 'structural test'). The market share of the firm concerned should be approaching 100 per cent and the market 'uncontested' and 'incontestable'. This 'hurdle' the Tribunal considered was a significant one, requiring not mere dominance but 'super-dominance'. Once that has been established, it

must further be determined whether the firm concerned has engaged in conduct abusing the structural opportunities by imposing excessive prices (the 'conduct test').

32 The Tribunal's idea that a market must be 'uncontested' and 'incontestable' and the firm 'super-dominant' otherwise the price charged cannot be excessive finds no support in the Act. The wording of s 8(a), read with the definition of 'excessive price' in s 1, calls for the making of certain distinct enquiries. First, the determination of the actual price of the good or service in question and which is alleged to be excessive. Secondly, the determination of the 'economic value' of the good or service expressed in monetary terms, as an amount of money. Thirdly, if the actual price is higher than the economic value of the good or service, is the difference unreasonable or, to put it in another way, is there 'no reasonable relation' between the actual price and the economic value of the good or service? Fourthly, is the charging of the excessive price to the detriment of the consumers? The first two enquiries call for factual determinations of the actual price and the economic value and the third for a value judgment. The fourth enquiry also involves, as we will show, a value judgment.

33 As already noted, the Tribunal did not proceed along these lines. Its approach was that, if a 'super-dominant' firm exercises to the full its market power in setting a price, then its price is *ipso facto* excessive as contemplated by s 8(a). It found in so many words that Mittal had contravened s 8: it had, by virtue of its super-dominance, the structural market power to select a target price for its domestic market (the IPP) [import parity price] and supported this price by withholding supply from the domestic market. This, the Tribunal said was 'the most elementary and offensive of monopolistic conduct'. The cumulative impact of its super-dominance and its resultant conduct led to the withholding of supply from the domestic market resulting in a price that is unconstrained by any competitive considerations and hence 'excessive'. There is no support for this approach in the Act.

34 . . . Because s 8(a) contemplates a relation between a *price* and the *economic value*, it follows that the latter expression must, as is ordinarily the case with price, refer to an amount of money. In contrast with [Article 102 of the TFEU], our legislation does not refer to a price that is 'unfair'. . . . * * *

43 It seems to follow that, in determining the economic value of a good or service, the cost savings to the firm resulting from the subsidized loan or the lower than market rental—or indeed any other special advantage, current or historical, that serves to reduce the particular firm's costs below the notional competitive norm ought to be

disregarded. Thus 'economic value' is a notional objective competitive-market standard, and not one derived from circumstances peculiar to the particular firm. If the firm's price is no higher than economic value, no contravention of s 8(a) can arise. If, however, the firm's price is in fact higher than economic value so determined, the test of reasonableness in respect of the difference remains to be applied. The expression 'reasonable profit' when dealing with economic value should be avoided. The test of reasonableness applies to the excess of price over economic value, and thus only to the element of 'pure profit' (over and above 'normal profit') implicit in that price. It is at this stage of the enquiry that circumstances peculiar to the particular dominant firm would rationally come into the reckoning. It would seem sound, when considering whether the higher price bears a reasonable relation to economic value or not, to take into account the benefits flowing to the firm from the subsidized loan, long-term low rental, or other special advantage which may serve to reduce its own long-run average costs below the notional norm. Having regard to all the particular circumstances, it might then be concluded that no addition of 'pure' or 'economic' profit by means of a price higher than economic value could reasonably be justified, or that the extent of the excess which might otherwise be justified would fall to be reduced. By parity of reasoning, accounting costs may reflect an uncompetitive inefficiency. The criterion of economic value, on the other hand, recognizes only the costs that would be recovered in long-run competitive equilibrium. Accordingly, it is possible that a dominant firm's price may be substantially and also unreasonably higher than economic value even when the accounting profit of the firm reveals no such picture.

44 Import parity pricing * * *

46 . . . Knowing the extent of the transport and related costs may . . . provide a basis for a finding of market power—but the premise remains that a notional competitive price (or economic value) shall first have been established. Once economic value has been established, it is the actual amount of the excess in the price charged by the local firm that has to be measured and evaluated for the purposes of s 8(a). All that import parity pricing will indicate is that the firm is pricing fully to the constraining limit. A dominant supplier which is able, and does, simply set its price at import parity without careful reference to costs would do so at its peril, for, if the import parity price is higher than the economic value of the supply, the supplier could well have difficulty defending the excess as having any reasonable relation to economic value. However, if in fact the supplier references its price to prices prevailing in other comparable but

competitive markets, then its price would be likely to approximate to economic value. * * *

50 In this way [empirical inquiry, quantifying by rough estimate where necessary] a *prima facie* case would have been made out, leaving it to a firm in appellant's position to adduce evidence to the contrary, if it is to avoid the case against it becoming conclusive. . . .

51 Prices ordinarily charged locally in other markets by the same firm or by other firms with broadly comparable cost structures at comparable levels of output, may obviously serve as a measure of the 'economic value' of the same good or service in our market—if the other markets are shown to be, or can be assumed to be, characterized by effective competition in the long run. An assumption of effective competition could usually be made in such a case, without any unfairness to the firm accused, if the comparative price ordinarily charged in the other markets is shown to be lower than the actual price, after all appropriate adjustments have been made. In this way, the difficulty of directly measuring profitability may be overcome.

52 However, there may be no alternative to a detailed exercise in comparative costing. If expert evidence has been given concerning costing data, the necessary adjustments to be made for comparative purposes, the appropriate methodology needed to establish the opportunity cost of capital and allow for depreciation and replenishment of plant etc., then findings based on an evaluation of that evidence will have to be made. When a lower price (e.g., a rebated local price or an ex-works export price) is said to be sufficient to 'cover costs', it is important to establish that the price concerned covers not merely the accounting costs but also the relevant opportunity costs of capital. Where a dominant domestic producer maintains price differentiation between export and domestic customers, and embarks on an expansion of its production capacity wholly or mainly in order to increase its export sales, then it would be difficult to avoid the conclusion that its export price would be at or above economic value—at the expanded level of output intended. In any event, the business calculations involved in the expansion could be expected to provide important evidence regarding both the current and future positions.

* * *

74 **Referral back to the Tribunal . . .**

75 As has been demonstrated in this judgment, the approach of the Tribunal, to the question of an excessive price, the care and considerable thought taken in its formulation notwithstanding, is

fundamentally flawed. Both the decision on the merits and the orders made pursuant thereto in the remedies decision should be set aside. This court was urged in argument that, were it [to] arrive at this conclusion, it should decide the matter, given that it had the benefit of all the necessary evidence. The nature of this decision is not a technical legal one. It entails an evaluation of detailed economic and financial evidence. As a specialized administrative body possessed of economic expertise, it follows that the Tribunal's views on what would be 'excessive' in the circumstances of this case and within the parameters of the law as set out in this judgment, are essential for the proper adjudication of the matter, particularly in a case of such importance. The matter should therefore be referred back to the Tribunal.* * *

[77] It is thus helpful to the expedition of further proceedings which must be conducted within the parameters of this judgment to provide further guidance to the Tribunal upon the referral back to it. As we have earlier in this judgment noted, where the price appears from the evidence and more particularly the manner in which the case is pleaded and argued, to bear no reasonable relation to economic value, then it is upon the firm accused of a breach of s 8(a) to adduce contrary evidence. In the present case, the evidence of Mittal's overwhelming dominance was rarely contested. Appellants sought to contest the finding that, with a share of 82 % of the domestic market, Mittal was not 'super-dominant' but they produced little evidence other than arithmetic hermeneutics to gainsay clear evidence of overwhelming dominance in the domestic market. The difficulties of proving excessive pricing notwithstanding, it is precisely in the case of so dominant a firm, that commentators have advocated the application of an excessive pricing provision by the relevant competition authority. In this case Mittal imposes a system of IPP. It accepts that this results in higher prices for the domestic market price over the export market price. Its explanation, briefly summarized, was set out in Mittal's written argument thus:

> 'On Mittal's version (which the Tribunal did not grapple with nor reject), its business in the export market would not on its own be sustainable, nor would its business in both markets be sustainable at the export price. The net realized export price is a low price which Mittal is forced to accept in the export market because of its locational disadvantage. . . .'

* * *

[81] In summary, the dominance of Mittal read together with its case in answer to respondent's case, as pleaded, raised a prima facie

presumption of a contravention of s 8 (a). The Tribunal was therefore required to analyse the evidence to determine whether Mittal's justification rebutted this presumption sufficiently for it to conclude, on the probabilities, that no breach of s 8(a), as alleged, had been committed. That analysis does not require further evidence but rather an examination of the evidence in terms of the statutory framework as set out in this judgment.

* * *

A new excessive pricing case arose in South Africa; namely: Commission v. Sasol Chemical Industries Limited (Case No: 131/CAC/Jun14). The product was feedstock propylene, a by-product of oil and a necessary input into polypropylene. The Tribunal attempted to apply the Court's ruling in *Mittal*, taking as the cost base the costs that would be recovered in competitive equilibrium, which required a notional competitive market standard. The cost calculations were extremely complicated and required extensive evidence on accounting practices. Among other things, the Tribunal found that the transfer price from the Sasol sister corporation to defendant Sasol Chemical should be adjusted downwards because the transfer price was higher than would have prevailed under conditions of competition. The Tribunal found mark-ups between 25% and 51% and found the pricing of the feedstock propylene excessive. Again, the Court reversed the Tribunal, holding this time that defendant's actual economic costs were the proper benchmark, not the notional competitive equilibrium. The Court disagreed with the Tribunal's cost calculations, and in view of the Court's calculations, the markup was between 12% and 14% and not excessive.

The Court said:

[175] A review of the European jurisprudence indicates that the prices charged have to be substantially higher than the defined economic value before an adverse finding will be made. . . . A price which is significantly less than 20% of the figure employed to determine economic value falls short of justifying judicial interference in this complex area. Ancient support can be found for this finding. The TALMUD (Baba Bathra 90a) ruled that if the profit gained was more than 16.67% it was regarded as excessive.

Notes and Questions

1.   In the South African *Mittal* case, who had the better of the argument—the Tribunal, which saw the problem of import parity pricing by super-dominant historically state-owned firms as a serious and pervasive one and devised (or thought it devised) a manageable market-friendly way to control the price? or the Court, which exercised great caution in identifying a price as excessive and felt the problem could not be solved without engagement with costs, accounting costs, and profits?

2.   In China, competition authorities have questioned the excessiveness of royalties charged by owners of essential or highly important patents. Qualcomm makes important technology used in mobile devices including smartphones. Most of the devices are manufactured in China; they are also manufactured in Korea, the US and elsewhere. The Chinese competition authority NDRC accused Qualcomm of charging royalties that were unreasonably high, charging royalties based on a percentage of the whole end product rather than only the part licensed, charging royalties on expired patents, and requiring licensees to grant-back their improvements in technology free to Qualcomm. After a long investigation, Qualcomm agreed to pay an unprecedented fine (nearly $1 billion), to charge royalties based on no more than 65% of the end product, and to pay for grant-backs. See part 1(d) above. Was this essentially an excessive pricing violation?

3.   An excessive pricing violation is usually, as you see, a complicated one. Yet excessive pricing is often perceived as one of the serious social ills emanating from great market power; one that reflects raw exploitation and widening inequality. Are antitrust institutions competent to challenge pricing as excessive? Should they do so only in egregious cases? What is egregious?

2.   Discriminatory Pricing: Exploitative, Exclusionary, and Unfair

Price discrimination is a complex subject, in part because price discrimination may evidence price competition itself (thus, it may be good for competition and efficiency); in other circumstances it may impair competition and efficiency (and economists debate when, whether and to what extent this is so); and in some circumstances, whether efficient or not, price discrimination is perceived as unfair and legislatures may prescribe it.

Price discrimination is by definition compromised of two prongs: a low price to favored customers and a high price to disfavored customers. The high price might under some circumstances be regarded as excessive. Even jurisdictions, such as the US, that do not recognize an excessive pricing antitrust offense do recognize a discriminatory pricing offense. In the US, the Robinson-Patman Act prohibits price discrimination in commodities where the effect of such discrimination is "substantially to lessen competition or tend to create a monopoly or to injure, destroy, or prevent competition with any person who either grants or knowingly receives" the discriminatory price. The Robinson-Patman Act has been widely criticized as protecting small, less efficient competitors from beneficial competition and, in recent years, the Supreme Court has read the statute essentially to require a showing that the discriminatory price harmed competition at either the level of the firm giving the discriminatory price (primary line) or at the level of the firm receiving the discount (secondary line). See, *e.g.*, *Volvo Trucks v. Reeder-Simco*, 546 U.S. 164 (2006) (observing, in secondary line price discrimination case, that the Robinson-Patman Act should be read consistently with the broader policies of the antitrust laws and that the Court "would resist interpretation geared more to the protection of existing *competitors* than to the stimulation of *competition*").

The European Union Treaty, in Article 102, prohibits dominant firms from imposing certain discriminatory terms "placing other trading parties at a competitive disadvantage." The European Union, as a common market intent on market integration, is especially concerned with acts that disfavor actors or goods from other Member States. Thus, United Brands could not lawfully charge its ripener/distributors varying prices for its unripened bananas depending on the Member State to which the bananas were destined. Case 27/76, *United Brands Co. v. Commission*, EU:C:1978:22.

Certain other jurisdictions may prohibit dominant firms from imposing discriminatory prices or terms where by some measure the terms are perceived as unfair. In some cases the competition statute itself may suggest an "unfairness" violation. In India, for example, the Competition Act (2002) says:

> Abuse of Dominant Position: (2) There shall be an abuse of dominant position . . . if an enterprise or group (a) directly or indirectly, imposes unfair or discriminatory (i) condition in purchase or sale of good or services or (ii) price in purchase or sale (including predatory price) of goods or service.

On its face, the Act contains no requirement of competitive injury. The Indian CCI has applied the act to remedy allegedly unfair bargaining by a real estate firm of questionable dominance. The CCI fined DLF Limited INR 630 crore (US $99.2 million) for abusing its dominant position by entering into one-sided agreements and imposing arbitrary, unfair and unreasonable conditions on home buyers. The targeted conditions included DLF's right to make unilateral changes in an apartment buyers' agreement without any corresponding right for the buyers, its right unilaterally to change apartment plans, and arbitrary forfeitures by apartment buyers in certain situations. *http://www.cci.gov.in/sites/default/files/DLF MainOrder110811.pdf*, reversed for redetermination of the market.

The South African law may have a special claim to a market value of fairness, and we present here a case that potentially would draw upon that value. As you read the case you should consider: Where do competition and fairness values coincide? When do the values point in the same direction? What happens when they point in different directions?

South Africa adopted its competition act at the end of the troubled era of apartheid. As its act recites, the law was designed "to open the economy to greater ownership by a greater number of South Africans," to "achieve a more effective and efficient economy" and to do so while ensuring "that small and medium-sized enterprises have an equitable opportunity to participate . . . ." Preamble and Section 2. The South African Act prohibits abuse of dominance generally in Section 8. Section 9 is entitled: "Price discrimination by dominant firm prohibited." Section 9 provides: "(1) An action by a dominant firm . . . is prohibited price discrimination, if—(a) it is likely to have the effect of substantially preventing or lessening competition; [(b) and 2: it relates to goods or services of like grade and quality, and it is not cost justified]."

Nationwide Poles, owned by Mr. James Foot, was a small producer of poles for grape vines, which were weather-proofed by wood preservatives. His supplier of the preservative, creosote, charged him a significantly higher price than it charged the four or five big buyers with whom he competed, and refused to give him the same lower price. The price difference was admittedly not cost-justified. Mr. Foot's business floundered as a result. He sued his supplier, Sasol, for abuse of dominance by reason of price discrimination. The principal question was whether Mr. Foot had proved his prima facie case.

Here is an excerpt from the decision of the Competition Tribunal, which held that he had, but the Appeals Court reversed. We present excerpts, first, from the Tribunal's decision, which is a forceful presentation of the case for a violation. On what grounds: competition? fairness? statutory construction? You decide.

IN THE MATTER BETWEEN NATIONWIDE POLES AND SASOL (OIL) PTY LTD

Competition Tribunal, South Africa, case 72/CR/Dec03
(*reversed* by Court of Appeal; see below)

DAVID LEWIS, CHAIR:

* * *

Price Discrimination—Its place in Antitrust

[75] Much of the argument in this matter centers upon the impact of price discrimination on competition and, in particular, on the nature of the test mandated by Section 9(1)(a) which provides that in order for an action by a dominant firm to constitute prohibited price discrimination, it must be shown that such action 'is likely to have the effect of substantially preventing or lessening competition'. Before turning to a detailed examination of Section 9(1)(a) some prefatory remarks regarding the place of price discrimination in anti-trust are in order.

[76] Whilst some contemporary anti-trust scholars are highly skeptical of the negative impact of price discrimination on competition, lawmakers, on the other hand, have generally held—and still do hold—that price discrimination offends the principles and objectives of anti-trust and so have proscribed certain forms of its practice in terms of anti-trust law. This is because price discrimination is viewed as a threat to the underlying competitive structure of the market in which it is perpetrated, in other words it is viewed as promoting a market structure conducive to anti-competitive conduct. We will show that our Act mandates this broad interpretation of anti-trust's mandate and that this conclusion is powerfully bolstered by the policy context within which the Competition Act is located.

[77] Anti-trust decision makers in other jurisdictions—notably the US and European courts—have generally and, we shall argue, appropriately, taken their lead from the legislation that they are required to uphold. Accordingly, the misgivings of some eminent scholars notwithstanding, the courts and other anti-trust decision makers have continued to uphold the legislative proscription of price discrimination. While the Department of Justice in the US has prosecuted few price discrimination actions, private access to the US courts has ensured a continuing trickle of price discrimination litigation. In those instances where private action has afforded the US courts the opportunity of pronouncing on the legality of price discrimination, they have honored the express wishes of their legislators by continuing to enforce the prohibition on price discrimination.

[78] Significantly, though, in key anti-trust jurisdictions—notably the United States—legislators have carved out a special place for price discrimination in the armory of anti-trust legislation. Hence, as already noted, in the United States price discrimination is not enforced through the Sherman Act, the general anti-trust statute of that country, but rather through the Robinson-Patman Act, a statute dedicated to dealing with price discrimination. Clearly price discrimination is, in US anti-trust history, regarded as a particular species of anti-trust offence, one not adequately accommodated even within the very broad umbrella of the Sherman Act.

[79] In this regard the South African competition statute, the Competition Act, embodies an approach to price discrimination not entirely dissimilar to that of the United States. While our legislature has not created a statute dedicated to dealing with price discrimination alone it has nevertheless chosen to distinguish the treatment of price discrimination from the standard approach adopted in the Act for dealing with conduct contraventions. As noted, the Act treats price discrimination as a species of abuse of dominance, and, as such, accommodates it within Part B ('Abuse of a Dominant Position') of Chapter 2 ('Prohibited Practices'). However, it has not been accommodated within the very broad ambit of Section 8 of the Act, that section of the Act detailing the variety of instances of abuse of dominance. Section 8 manages to provide for the prohibition of a wide-ranging set of practices construed to abuse market dominance, a section that manages to effectively capture both specific practices and general practices, that provides for the adoption of a rule of reason approach to certain conduct while proscribing other forms of conduct *per se*, and that tailors the operation of onuses in an effort to fine-tune the treatment of the multitude of potential offences that arise under the broad rubric of an abuse of a dominant position, or, in US parlance, monopolization. And yet the legislature did not see fit to extend the coverage of this already very broad provision to include reference to price discrimination. It rather chose to create a section of the Act—Section 9—dedicated to dealing with price discrimination.

[80] Why is price discrimination accorded this special treatment? We would venture to suggest, even at the risk of some simplification, that, regardless of the very different conditions underlying the anti-trust legislative histories of each of these divergent economies and societies, the particularity of treatment accorded price discrimination has strikingly similar roots.

[81] It is our view that the proscription of price discrimination reflects the legislature's concern to maintain accessible, competitively structured markets, markets which accommodate new entrants and

which enable them to compete effectively against larger and well-established incumbents. This set of concerns points directly to problems confronting small and medium sized enterprises (SMEs) which, in the absence of a 'level playing field', or, what is the same thing, in the presence of discrimination, may well find it difficult to enter new markets and even more difficult to thrive, to compete effectively 'on the merits'. The influence of SME-related considerations in the legislative history of the Robinson-Patman Act is absolutely clear. Equally clear is our own Act's concern with the development of small business—it is telling that one of the stated purposes of our Act is to ensure the 'equitable' treatment of small and medium-sized enterprises.

[82] There are, to be sure, considerations of 'fairness' that underlie this bid to ensure 'equitable treatment' for small and large business. It is manifestly clear that the drafters of the Robinson-Patman Act also responded to the perceived inequity embodied in the inability of small traders to acquire stock at the same prices as those available to their larger competitors.

[83] While incorporating considerations of equity into anti-trust analysis may be anathema to an anti-trust approach that insists on the sole claim of a 'pure' consumer welfare standard, one that is solely referenced by a reduction in output or an increase in price, the utilization, in selected, though important, instances of a fairness standard is not alien to our Act and practice. Certainly, in merger analysis, considerations of public interest—which are partly, if not entirely, driven by considerations of 'equity'—are explicitly present and the needs of small business find expression in the definition of public interest. Moreover, SMEs are specifically given consideration in exemption proceedings, whereby they are afforded immunity from prosecution under the exemption provisions under Section 10 of the Act. The mere fact that equity considerations sit uncomfortably in competition economics orthodoxy is no warrant for ignoring our legislature's express desire that they play a role in our decisions.

[84] However, the element of equity that underpins certain of the Act's concerns to protect small business—and it is precisely the element of 'protection' that most offends anti-trust orthodoxy—should not detract from the substantive *competition* considerations that accord small business a special place in anti-trust history and in its contemporary practice.

[85] It is the oft-proclaimed mantra 'protect competition, not competitors' that is usually invoked by those seeking to deny small business a special place in anti-trust considerations. As with many frequently repeated pieces of rhetoric, this one contains more than a grain of truth and serves as a valuable cautionary for anti-trust

authorities who are regularly confronted by competitors opportunistically seeking to invoke competition legislation to advance their own narrow interests even when the conduct of their opponents is manifestly pro-competitive or pro-consumers.

[86] It is however often a feature of even good pieces of rhetoric that they camouflage at least as much as they reveal. In this instance, the obvious rejoinder to the 'protect competition, not competitors' mantra, is one that insists 'no competitors, no competition'. And just as those who adhere to the better-known mantra can claim a solid intellectual foundation for their views—one that rests on a narrow, focused view of the meaning of competition—so too can those more anxious to secure the underpinnings for a robust population of SMEs find support in anti-trust history and in its contemporary practice. In short, those who deem anti-trust's mandate to extend to the securing of pro-competitive market *structures,* may be less troubled at using competition enforcement to secure conditions favorable to the entry and strengthening of SMEs, particularly when the practices that disfavor the latter are themselves not practices that promote competition on the merits.

[87] In our view the relevant, that is, the *South African,* legal and political economy context favors competition enforcement that is concerned to protect the market mechanism from conduct that has the effect of undermining it. The expressed concerns of the South African lawmakers and the policy planners support this finding. This is powerfully manifest, inter alia, in an industrial policy that places the development of SMEs at the center of attempts to improve the workings of the market mechanism. This conclusion is grounded not only in an examination of the general industrial policy context in which concern for SME development looms large but also in an examination of the Act itself.

[88] The Competition Act is, itself, punctuated with references to the legislature's desire that the statute should promote market access and equality of opportunity particularly, in this field, where small enterprise is concerned. As noted references to equality of opportunity are to be found in the Preamble to the Act, and the promotion of small business is specifically provided for in Section 2(e), which expresses one of the 'purposes' of the Act, as well as in the consideration of applications for exemption (Section 10(3)(b)(ii)) and the evaluation of mergers (Section 12A(3)(c)). In fact the Explanatory Memorandum which accompanied the publication of the draft Competition Bill explicitly notes the intention of the policy-makers to support SME developments through the instrumentality of the Competition Act. The Department of Trade and Industry has recently released a report surveying SME development in South Africa and it

concludes that while entry barriers for SMEs are relatively low, the long-term success rates of these entrants is markedly low. Even the President's address at the opening of Parliament in 2005 saw fit to record the urgency with which Government viewed support for SME development.

[89] The Act is clearly concerned to promote market access for SMEs and an important mechanism by which it seeks to do so is by ensuring 'equitable treatment'. Price discrimination—conduct that is, per definition, inequitable—is explicitly proscribed by the Act, it is not, in other words part of a general category of exclusionary practices. In short, the legislature proscribed price discrimination perpetrated by dominant firms because of the threat it poses to its victims, these being a competitive and accessible market structure and the small firms that animate it, potentially robust, though still slender, saplings that will not take root in the face of treatment that is manifestly inequitable relative to that accorded their better resourced competitors. This then is why Section 9 has been carved out of the general abuse of dominance provisions: it is uniquely concerned with the structural impact of abuse of dominance and it is recognized that its victims are most likely to be small customers.

[90] However, in the Act's formulation of the prohibition of price discrimination, certain limiting principles are embodied. There is, in other words, no basis to conclude that Section 9 constitutes a blanket prohibition on price differentiation or on the commercially important and widespread practice of discounting even when these pricing practices explicitly favor large firms over small firms. Hence, and in significant contrast with the Robinson-Patman Act, in our Act the offence of price discrimination is limited to dominant firms. Moreover, Section 9(1) specifies certain elements to which any act of price differentiation must conform if it is to constitute prohibited price discrimination. And then a series of defenses, many of which were developed piece-meal over the course of many years of US and European jurisprudence, are explicitly provided for in Section 9(2). Section 9 cannot therefore be read as an omnibus prohibition of the practice of differentiating on price. Rather, proscription of the practice of price differentiation is confined to particular, specified circumstances.

Section 9(1)(a)—A substantial lessening of competition

[91] Sasol's case, as we have already noted, rests heavily on disposing of Nationwide's case on the interpretive hurdle of section 9(1)(a) of the Act. Sasol advances an interpretation of section 9(1)(a) that would require the complainant to prove actual harm to consumer welfare. Granted Sasol does not say so in so many words, but its

critique of this lacuna in the complainant's evidence amounts to exactly this. Because, on this standard, because Nationwide cannot demonstrate that the increased production costs incurred in consequence of Sasol's discrimination harm the market for treated poles, it must fail.

92 Mr. Foot for his part concedes that he has not been able to show that the price discrimination has led to higher prices or lower output in the market for treated poles. But he does not concede Sasol's interpretation of Section 9(1)(a).

* * *

99 Why, though, was it thought necessary to create a special section of the act to deal with price discrimination? There were undoubtedly practical considerations. It is a long and cumbersome section and the elements of the act and the defenses are specified in considerable detail—this was done, we will argue, precisely to limit the instances of price differentiation that are proscribed. But, in our view, the overriding reason for the separation is given by the policy context that accounts for the legislature's concern with price discrimination in the first place and provides further reason for why the legislature could not have intended the complainant to establish the anti-competitive effect of price discrimination. Mr. Foot has clearly articulated this argument and, in so doing, is on all fours with the legislature's concern with the prospects of small business.

100 Mr. Foot argues that a small business is the most likely complainant in a price discrimination case. Foot points out that on a consumer welfare test small business will always fail, precisely because it is not able to correlate harm that is inflicted upon it to harm that is inflicted on the broader market. A small firm will always be met with the response that its troubles are, in relation to the market as a whole, *de minimus*, that is, that they have little, if any, effect on competition in the market as a whole.

101 We agree. It is unlikely that a discriminator will discriminate against a large customer unless that customer is also a competitor. However were such an instance of discrimination to occur it is more likely to be met by a claim based upon section 8(c), one of the category of general restrictive practices where an anti-competitive effect has to be established by the complainant. This is why we have a separate section 9. The legislature indeed contemplated that complainants under section 9—who will generally be small enterprises—would not be able to show the sort of consumer welfare harms that Sasol contends are contemplated as the test, but who nevertheless need to have a remedy against conduct that might exclude them from access

to markets or limit their ability to compete in those markets on the merits. Thus Section 9 was enacted.

102 In short, what the legislature wanted in section 9(1)(a) was to create a threshold, but a low one that related not to competitive *harm* but to competitive *relevance*. The legislature in availing small firms to bring cases and to switch the onus to the dominant firm did not want them faced with an evidential burden they could never meet. It did not want them to become non-suited at the very next hurdle after establishing dominance by the discriminator.

103 Had Section 9(1)(a) been omitted in its entirety, that is if it had not been included as one of the elements of the act of prohibited price discrimination, then Section 9 would have been consumer protection legislation pure and simple. A mere act of discrimination that met the tests in Sections (9)(1)(b) and (c) but not that in Section 9(1)(a) would be unlawful even if the complainant was not itself a player in a market but just an ultimate consumer of the products of the dominant firm. Thus subsection 9(1)(a) invites a complainant to establish a competition relevance to his complaint but does not require proof of some standard of harm as contended for by Sasol. When the legislature asks is it 'likely' it is asking us to situate the complaint as one relevant to competition. When it asks is it 'substantial' it invites us to distinguish the trivial effect from the weightier.

104 Mr. Foot effectively responds by demonstrating that he is not merely an individual consumer of creosote who purchases it to coat his fence on the weekend. If that were the case he would have no basis for approaching the Tribunal, he would found no cause of action under the Competition Act. What distinguishes Foot from that individual consumer is that he is a competing producer of goods, treated poles, in which the subject-matter of the discrimination, creosote, is a crucial input in his production process and thus Sasol's quantitatively substantial discrimination, persisting year after year, places and other small customers at an ongoing disadvantage relative to other competing producers of treated poles. Hence he has established the *relevance* of the act of discrimination to *competition* and meets the element of *likely*. If something is not relevant to competition—as would be the case of the individual consumer cited above—it is for that reason not *likely* to have an effect on it. This lack of 'relevance' is also likely to apply in respect of discrimination between consumers in separate markets.

105 Moreover, the sub-section also requires *substantiality* as an element. Thus if Mr. Foot was being discriminated against by the Post Office in the price of his stamps for his envelopes that

accompany the invoices to his customers this would not be considered a *substantial* input cost, albeit an input cost. In contrast a more significant input cost that might put him at a competitive disadvantage to those of his competitors who benefit from the discrimination may meet the standard of substantiality.

106 Does this interpretation embody the danger that the absence of a harm test may make competitively neutral price discrimination an offence?

107 We say that it does not. In the first place such an argument would ignore the fact that the legislature has required the complainant to clear some still considerable hurdles of proof as provided for in Section 9(1). And it would also ignore the fact that, after all is said and done, Section 9(2) leaves the discriminator with some important defenses, those most commonly invoked in justification of price discrimination, albeit confined, in terms of Section 9(2), to a closed list.

* * *

121 These considerations, apart from dictating a low level of interest on Sasol's part in its smaller customers, also dictate that its focus is on satisfying its larger customers. To some extent this latter purpose is achieved by giving these larger customers a preferential price relative to the smaller players in the pole market. In a market—the poles market—in which entry barriers are, it is common cause, low, the price differential assists in limiting the entry of new and small entrants and their ability to thrive. This is borne out by evidence presented above on the impact of the price differential on the competitiveness of small firms. It is also starkly confirmed by Sasol's treatment of 'twilight treaters'.

122 'Twilight treaters' are very small players who are not able to purchase their creosote requirements by the lorry load, as in the case of the complainant and the larger customers, but rather in drums supplied by retailers who are, in turn, supplied by Sasol. It appears— and this is conceded by Sasol-Sasol's larger customers requested that Sasol increase the price of drum loads in order to limit access and growth on the part of these micro-producers. Sasol readily acceded to this demand. Mr. Van Wyk's evidence in this regard was instructive. Though he averred that the industry association (SAWPA) had advised Sasol to increase prices to the micro treaters to ensure the integrity and safety of the product chain downstream, Sasol's other motives are apparent:

> "VAN WYK:. . . . . So they are trying to get those guys out of the industry, but then the industry came to us and said but

you're promoting the twilight treaters, because you're selling in drums to the co-ops. So the twilight treater can come back and buy from the co-op and treat, if you can call it treat it or dip it or whatever, and sell it against our customers. And they requested us to increase the price drastically so that it doesn't make it economical for that guy to buy creosote. It's too expensive for him to do his twilight treating. So that's one reason the market requirement or they asked us to do it. It is to prevent the twilight treaters to be active in your market."

[123] If Sasol's large customers fear of new entry is sufficiently great for them to have demanded Sasol's assistance in deterring the entry of micro-treaters, we readily infer that their interest in suppressing competition from established small producers such as the complainant, is even greater. This, bolstered by the evidence elaborated above that establishes the competitive harm that accrues to small producers as a result of the price differential, exposes Sasol's interest in maintaining a discriminatory pricing structure.

[124] Our conclusions are underpinned by Sasol's failure to assert a pro-competitive argument in favor of price discrimination. While we concede that Sasol is not required to prove a pro-competitive effect— in fact, as already elaborated, the Act does not admit of a pro-competitive defense—we are certain that had there been a pro-competitive effect we would have been told of this. Certainly the competitive position of the larger poles producers is enhanced but this is done by way of a practice—price discrimination—that is not competition on the merits but rather that excludes small operators from the market or that, at the very least, compromises their ability to compete effectively.

[125] In summary we are satisfied that—

- The discount structures for the sale of creosote exhibit a material differentiation as between the most and least favored customers;

- Creosote is a significant input cost of firms such as the complainant who compete in the treated poles market against rivals who benefit from the price discrimination;

- That it is 'likely' that the complainant and firms similarly situated presently in the market and new entrants, will be less effective competitors as a result of the discrimination;

- This is a market where small firms, absent price discrimination, can be effective competitors to their larger rivals.

[126] It follows that if firms such as the complainant are rendered less effective competitors that this will have an effect on the competitive structure of the market and so it is likely that this will substantially lessen or prevent competition in the market, in the sense understood by the legislature for the purpose of section 9 (1) (a). * * *

The Court of Appeal disagreed. In a lengthy factual and interpretative analysis, it raised the question whether Sasol was dominant, concluded that the pole market was competitive and expressed concern about the effects of a judgment prohibiting price discrimination. It held:

> "On the evidence, the Court is not able to conclude that there is a reasonable possibility that competition has been significantly prevented or lessened. Putting the evidence in the best possible light for respondent, respondent suggests a disadvantage by way of an additional cost of purchases of creosote pursuant to appellant's pricing policy. However, competition law does not protect the competitor, it protects competition. Evidence which goes no further than suggesting that one competitor may be prejudiced is insufficient to bring the impugned conduct with the scope of section 9(1)(a)."

In the matter between Sasol Oil (Pty) Limited and Nationwide Poles CC, 49CACAApril05.

After the judgment was rendered, the Johannesburg press reported: "The tribunal's ruling reflects a generous interpretation of the language in the act in an apparent bid to protect small businesses in line with the preamble to the act. . . . While the court's ruling has left the legal principles vague, or highlighted the vagueness of this section of the act, it is certain to discourage other small players from approaching the competition authorities for relief from discriminatory actions by dominant firms." Ann Crotty, *Nationwide Poles shuts after Sasol wins creosote appeal*, Business Report, April 1, 2005.

What would it have taken for Mr. Foot to have moved from a mere personal harm to a market harm? Would he have won his case if he had shown that his big, favored rivals behaved as oligopolists? Didn't he?

Which offered the better legal interpretation, the Tribunal or the Court? Which result was better for South Africa as a matter of policy?

D. ABUSE OF A SUPERIOR BARGAINING POSITION

The competition laws of a critical mass of jurisdictions include a provision prohibiting abuse of a superior bargaining position or abuse of economic dependence (ASBP). This thread of the law was highlighted at the Kyoto meeting of the International Competition Network in 2008, for which a special task force prepared a Report on Abuse of Superior Bargaining Position. *http://www.international competitionnetwork.org/uploads/library/doc386.pdf*

In its questionnaire seeking information from the competition authorities (Appendix E to the Report), the task force defined the concept:

> ... In jurisdictions that regulate "abuse of superior bargaining position," the concept typically includes, but is not limited to, a situation in which a party makes use of its superior bargaining position relative to another party with whom it maintains a continuous business relationship to take any act such as to unjustly, in light of normal business practices, cause the other party to provide money, service or other economic benefits. ... A party in the superior bargaining position does not necessarily have to be a dominant firm or firm with significant market power.

Seven of 32 responding jurisdictions reported that their competition laws contain provisions against abuse of a superior bargaining position; namely, Austria, France, Germany, Italy, Japan, Korea and the Slovak Republic. Latvia and Indonesia reported that they were in the process of considering or adopting such provisions. Others indicated that their laws on unilateral conduct/abuse of dominance could apply to ASBP. These jurisdictions include Canada, the EU, Russia, Chile, Brazil, Taiwan, Jamaica, Serbia and Norway.

SPECIAL ICN TASK FORCE REPORT ON ABUSE OF SUPERIOR BARGAINING POSITION (EXCERPT, 2008)

* * *

Of the jurisdictions reporting specific provisions [some are and some are not directly in the competition law]:

. . . The German Act against Restraints of Competition (ARC) provides for a prohibition of unfair hindrance, which applies to firms holding a superior bargaining position as well as dominant undertakings. Regarding the superior bargaining position, Germany responded that section 20 (2) of ARC "stipulates that a firm holds superior bargaining position if small or medium-sized enterprises as suppliers or purchasers of certain kinds of goods or commercial services depend on this firm in such a way that sufficient and reasonable possibilities of resorting to other undertakings do not exist." The German authority also noted that "such dependence exists only if besides the undertaking allegedly holding a superior bargaining position in the relevant market no other undertakings exist which would be able and willing to supply the respective small or medium-sized undertaking on reasonable terms. Based on case law, several case groups are distinguished: Dependence on product line, dependence on a specific firm, scarcity dependence and demand-related dependence." It should be noted that "the presumption" of a superior bargaining position "applies only to buyers" although "a supplier as well as buyer may hold a superior bargaining position in relation to another undertaking." According to the law, a supplier of a certain kind of goods or commercial services shall be presumed to depend on a purchaser within the meaning of section 20 (2) of ARC "if this purchaser regularly obtains from this supplier, in addition to discounts customary in the trade or other remuneration, special benefits which are not granted to similar purchasers."

In Japan the relevant act stipulates, in relatively concrete terms, that "[t]aking any act" specified in the statute is prohibited if the act is conducted "unjustly in the light of the normal business practices by making use of one's superior bargaining position over the other party." According to Japanese response, ASBP refers to "a situation in which a party makes use of its superior bargaining position relative to another party to take unjustly in light of normal business practices, any act specified as follows:

a)   Causing the other party to purchase a commodity or service,

b)   Causing the other party to provide economic benefits,

c)   Setting or changing transaction terms in a way disadvantageous to the other party,

d)   In addition to any act above, imposing a disadvantage on the other party regarding terms or execution of transaction,

e)   Interfering with the appointment of officers of the other company.

The definition applies equally to both supplier and buyer sides of the market." Likewise, the Korean authority defines ASBP as "[a]n enterpriser's act of unfairly taking advantage of its superior trade position when dealing with others." The definition applies to "enterprisers" in both supplier and buyer sides of the market with some exceptions.

In Italy, unlawful exploitation of a situation of inequality of market power (ASBP) can be addressed through a private civil action for "injunctive relief and compensation for breach of section 9 of Law n. 192 of 18 June 1998, which prevents firms from exploiting a situation of 'economic dependence' of their customers or suppliers." It should be noted that this provision applies only to business-to-business relations. The Italian Competition Authority has authority to intervene in this field only if the alleged abuse of economic dependence also has an impact on the protection of competition and the market.

In France "[a]buse of superior bargaining position comes under restrictive trade practices governed by civil law." (article L. 442–6 #1 (2 b) of the Code of Commercial Law) Objectionable practices include: a) unfair discrimination; b) abuse of trade dependence (all forms: open list); c) subjecting a partner to unjustified obligations or trading conditions; d) sudden severance of established business relations (or the threat thereof); e) subjecting a partner to manifestly unfair terms of payment; and f) automatic debiting of suppliers by distributors.

The Slovak legal system contains sector-specific regulations, in the Act on Retail Chains, concerning abuse of economic power in connection with retail chains. These provisions are enforced by a state administration body rather than a competition agency. Pursuant to the Act, the abuse of economic power "shall be the conduct of an operator of a retail chain in connection with its supplier in which the retail chain operator abuses a negotiation advantage arising out of its economic power within contract conclusion with the supplier and enforces more advantageous conditions than those it could achieve without such negotiation advantage." It should be noted that this definition applies only to "a purchaser."

In Austria in addition to general competition law, the Federal Law for the Improvement of Local Supplies and the Competitive Conditions ("Nahversorgungs-Gesetz") prohibits a number of practices, e.g., discriminatory practices or demanding payments or services without equivalent. It should be noted that the Law is not primarily geared to protect competition but to protect local supplies in rural areas.

In addition, two jurisdictions are considering or adopting specific provisions falling within the questionnaire's definition of ASBP. For example, Latvia noted in additional comments that on 13 March 2008 Parliament of the Republic of Latvia has adopted Amendments to the Competition Law. One of the main topics is the definition of dominant position with regard to the retail market and the prohibition of its abuse. The definition will apply only to the buyer side, namely to "such market participant or several market participants who, considering its (their) buying power and suppliers' dependence in relevant market, is able to directly or indirectly apply or impose unfair and unjustified provisions, conditions or payments upon suppliers and can significantly hinder, restrict or distort competition in any relevant market in the territory of Latvia during sufficiently long period of time."

Likewise, in Indonesia a regulation on ASBP in the retail industry is under consideration in the Draft of Presidential Decree on modern market.

* * *

Some respondents that did not adopt ASBP provisions expressed concerns with such rules. Belgium thought that adoption of ASBP could create confusion with unilateral conduct laws. The UK and the US feared that such provisions could undermine efficient bargaining between contracting parties. "[C]ontracts between parties at different level of the manufacturing-distribution chain are likely to reflect an efficient allocation of risks and duties among the parties." Singapore pointed out that its competition law is concerned only with exclusionary and not exploitative offenses, as is the case in the United States also.

Notes and Questions

1.   Are ASBP rules a helpful complement to the traditional single-firm conduct rules? Are they particularly important in developing and

transitional economies worried about exploitations by state and other dominant players, or worried about exploitations and exclusions by global value chains? See Ioannis Lianos and Claudio Lombardi, Superior Bargaining Power and the Global Food Value Chain: The Wuthering Heights of Holistic Competition Law?, *https://www.ucl.ac.uk/cles/research-paper-series/research-papers/cles-1-2016*.

2.   Or, are ASBP provisions in tension with antitrust? Do they interfere with efficient bargaining? Should the problems they address be left to the law of contract? See Masako Wakui and Thomas K. Cheng, Regulating abuse of superior bargaining position under the Japanese competition law: an anomaly or a necessity?, 3(2) J. Antitrust Enforcement 302–333 (2015). Might the answer depend on the state of development of the nation and the availability of alternative solutions to problems of severely and persistently one-sided bargains?

E. CONCLUSION

The law of monopolization and abuse of dominance is the most divergent of all segments of antitrust law. The statutes and cases reveal the fault lines. While all systems target exclusionary conduct by firms with substantial market or monopoly power that have no purpose or effect except to entrench or extend the monopoly, jurisdictions diverge on the extent to which they insist on proof of substantial power, whether excessive pricing is ever a violation, whether low pricing can offend if it does not fall below marginal or average variable cost and plaintiff cannot prove probable recoupment, whether loyalty rebate and margin squeeze violations are merely instances of predatory pricing, the extent of primacy of intellectual property over competition law provisions, and whether access and inclusiveness are antitrust values. The fault lines can be explained by different systems, different stages of development, and different judgments and choices on the role of antitrust in society. This comparative study should help the student and the policy maker to appreciate the differences, identify the convergences, and contemplate the room for more convergence.

Chapter 3

COLLABORATIONS OF COMPETITORS OTHER THAN CARTELS

A. INTRODUCTION

In Chapter 1, we studied hard-core cartels, such as price-fixing or market-division agreements, that are usually considered to be illegal without a searching inquiry into their actual economic effects in a particular case. In this chapter, we turn to agreements among competitors—horizontal agreements—that are not so obviously anticompetitive that they merit per se treatment.

Unlike cartel agreements, whose essential characteristics are usually similar from case to case, there is a great deal of variety in non-hard-core competitor collaborations. Indeed, virtually every form of business organization involves some agreement that restricts competition between its members. Think of corporations that set the terms of sale for products created by hundreds of employees or law firm partnerships that set the price for their lawyers' services. In a colloquial sense, all such arrangements among people who might otherwise be competitors "restrain trade" in the words of Section 1 of the Sherman Act or "prevent[ ], restrict[ ], or distort[ ]" competition in the words of Article 101(1) of the Treaty on the Functioning of the European Union ("TFEU") (formerly Article 81 of the Treaty of Rome). But economic activity would come to a standstill—or be relegated to a pre-industrial form of atomistic competition between individual farmers and tradespeople—if every form of agreement among actual or potential competitors were illegal. Thus, the law of non-cartel restraints of trade among competitors must sort through the myriad varieties of horizontal agreements and only scrutinize those most likely to produce net anticompetitive effects.

Different antitrust regimes employ different procedural and substantive frameworks for scrutinizing non-cartel horizontal restraints. The EU approach, reflected in Article 101(1) and (2), is to begin with a broad prohibition of all agreements that affect trade between Member States that "have as their object or effect" the "prevention, restriction or distortion of competition." Article 101(1) then lists five illustrative, but not exhaustive, prohibited kinds of agreements. Article 101(3) then declares that Article 101(1) may be declared inapplicable if the agreement (1) contributes to improving production or distribution or promoting technical or economic progress, (2) allows consumers a fair share of the benefits, (3) does not impose unnecessary restrictions (any restrictions must be "indispensable to the attainment of [the above] objectives), and (4) does not give the firms concerned the possibility eliminate to competition in a substantial part of the market.

Under EU law, the distinction between restrictions on competition "by object" and "by effect" is significant. When an agreement restricts competition by object, the Commission need not prove that it has an anticompetitive effect—that is presumed. *Consten and Grundig v. Commission* (56/64) [1966] E.C.R. 299, p.342. By contrast, agreements that may restrict competition by effect but not object require a showing of such effects as part of the Commission's burden of proof.

US law, by contrast, follows a simple prohibition on "contracts, combinations, or conspiracies . . . in restraint of trade." The statute contains no catalogue of anticompetitive agreements, no broad prohibition and accompanying exemption, no statement or implication as to burdens of proof or presumptions. Nonetheless, the Supreme Court's jurisprudence on what restraints of trade are per se illegal and which come under the more tolerant rule of reason follow a similar analytical approach. Restrictions are per se illegal only when they "facially appear[ ] to be one[s] that would always or almost always tend to restrict competition and decrease output" and would almost never "increase economic efficiency and render markets more, rather than less, competitive." *Broadcast Music, Inc. v. Columbia Broadcasting System, Inc.*, 441 U.S. 1, 19–20 (1979).

China's Anti-Monopoly Law and India's Competition Act are broadly modeled on Article 101, but contain long lists of prohibited and exempted agreements. Consider the inter-play among Articles 13, 14, and 15 of the Chinese Anti-Monopoly Law, which makes a broad set of agreements illegal and then shifts the burden onto the agreeing parties to justify their agreement on efficiencies grounds.

> **Article 13** Any of the following monopoly agreements among the competing business operators shall be prohibited:
>
> (1) fixing or changing prices of commodities;
>
> (2) limiting the output or sales of commodities;
>
> (3) dividing the sales market or the raw material procurement market;

(4) restricting the purchase of new technology or new facilities or the development of new technology or new products;

(5) making boycott transactions; or

(6) other monopoly agreements as determined by the ˙ Anti-monopoly Authority under the State Council.

For the purposes of this Law, "monopoly agreements" refer to agreements, decisions or other concerted actions which eliminate or restrict competition.

Article 14 Any of the following agreements among business operators and their trading parties are prohibited:

(1) fixing the price of commodities for resale to a third party;

(2) restricting the minimum price of commodities for resale to a third party; or

(3) other monopoly agreements as determined by the Anti-monopoly Authority under the State Council.

Article 15 An agreement among business operators shall be exempted from application of articles 13 and 14 if it can be proven to be in any of the following circumstances:

(1) for the purpose of improving technologies, researching and developing new products;

(2) for the purpose of upgrading product quality, reducing cost, improving efficiency, unifying product specifications or standards, or carrying out professional labor division;

(3) for the purpose of enhancing operational efficiency and reinforcing the competitiveness of small and medium-sized business operators;

(4) for the purpose of achieving public interests such as conserving energy, protecting the environment and relieving the victims of a disaster and so on;

(5) for the purpose of mitigating serious decrease in sales volume or obviously excessive production during economic recessions;

(6) for the purpose of safeguarding the justifiable interests in the foreign trade or foreign economic cooperation; or

(7) other circumstances as stipulated by laws and the State Council.

Where a monopoly agreement is in any of the circumstances stipulated in Items 1 through 5 and is exempt from Articles 13 and 14 of this Law, the business operators must additionally prove that the agreement can enable consumers to share the benefits derived from the agreement, and will not severely restrict the competition in relevant market.

As with hard-core cartels studied in Chapter One, there are often important issues—both substantive and evidentiary—about what constitutes an agreement or understanding. For example, various mechanisms by which competitors effectively exchange information—such as through industry associations or algorithms—may be characterized as an agreement and hence covered by concerted action provisions rather than as unilateral and hence not covered.

There are also important procedural differences between jurisdictions. Some jurisdictions use mandatory or voluntary agreement notification systems to enable early regulatory review of certain classes of horizontal agreements. Other jurisdictions rely on less formal means of regulatory policing—such as the use of informal business review letters by agencies and investigation of anticompetitive agreements upon customer complaints. We will address some of these procedural issues at the end of the chapter.

B. CLASSIFYING COMPETITOR COLLABORATIONS AS PER SE ILLEGAL, PRESUMPTIVELY ILLEGAL, OR SUBJECT TO FULLER RULE OF REASON ANALYSIS

As noted in the previous section, a threshold issue as to competitor collaborations is often whether they will be treated as "hard core" offenses like price-fixing cartels subject to some version of per se illegality, or whether instead they will be analyzed under a more expansive rule of reason. Under the TFEU, this distinction turns on whether the restriction on competition is one "by object" or "by effect," with the former receiving something akin to per se treatment and the latter something closer to rule of reason treatment.

For many years, there has been an active controversy among European competition law experts as to what constitutes an agreement by object within the meaning of Article 101 of the TFEU.

As we have seen, an agreement among competitors to limit output is classically an agreement by object, even if the parties could credibly claim that their purpose was to save a collapsing industry for the good of the country. *See BIDS, supra* Chapter 1. Beyond hard core cartels, what agreements are restraints by object? Does intent play a role? Are agreements by object ones that always harm competition, or is it enough that they pose a potential threat to competition?

The Court's 2014 *Cartes Bancaires* decision addressed this question, and significantly narrowed the potential scope of the "restrictions by object" category.

GROUPEMENT DES CARTES BANCAIRES (CB) v. COMMISSION

Case C–67/13 P, EU:C:2014:2204 (European Court of Justice 2014)

[CB was an economic interest group created in 1984 by the principal French banks in order to achieve interoperability of the systems for payment and withdrawal of banking cards. That interoperability enabled a CB-issued card to make payments or automated teller machine ("ATM") withdrawals from any member of the consortium. In 2002, CB adopted three new measures that the Commission challenged as violations of Articles 101 and 102 of the TFEU. They were: (1) a "mechanism for regulating the acquiring function," which effectively imposed a tax on banks that were disproportionately issuers of bank cards rather than acquirers of financial transactions (i.e., banks setting up ATM machines); (2) a supplementary fee per issued card imposed on banks that issued triple or more of the number of CB cards at the end of their sixth year of membership compared to at the end of their third year of membership; and (3) a "dormant member 'wake up' " per card fee imposed on members who were not very active before the implementation of new pricing measures in 2002 and subsequently became significantly more active. The Commission challenged these practices as alleged restrictions of competition by object—deliberate mechanisms to exclude new competition. The European Court of Justice thought otherwise.]

—Examination of whether there is a restriction of competition by 'object' within the meaning of Article 81(1) EC

48 It must be recalled that, to come within the prohibition laid down in Article 81(1) EC, an agreement, a decision by an association of undertakings or a concerted practice must have 'as [its] object or effect' the prevention, restriction or distortion of competition in the internal market.

[49] In that regard, it is apparent from the Court's case-law that certain types of coordination between undertakings reveal a sufficient degree of harm to competition that it may be found that there is no need to examine their effects.

[50] That case-law arises from the fact that certain types of coordination between undertakings can be regarded, by their very nature, as being harmful to the proper functioning of normal competition.

[51] Consequently, it is established that certain collusive behaviour, such as that leading to horizontal price-fixing by cartels, may be considered so likely to have negative effects, in particular on the price, quantity or quality of the goods and services, that it may be considered redundant, for the purposes of applying Article 81(1) EC, to prove that they have actual effects on the market. Experience shows that such behaviour leads to falls in production and price increases, resulting in poor allocation of resources to the detriment, in particular, of consumers.

[52] Where the analysis of a type of coordination between undertakings does not reveal a sufficient degree of harm to competition, the effects of the coordination should, on the other hand, be considered and, for it to be caught by the prohibition, it is necessary to find that factors are present which show that competition has in fact been prevented, restricted or distorted to an appreciable extent.

[53] According to the case-law of the Court, in order to determine whether an agreement between undertakings or a decision by an association of undertakings reveals a sufficient degree of harm to competition that it may be considered a restriction of competition 'by object' within the meaning of Article 81(1) EC, regard must be had to the content of its provisions, its objectives and the economic and legal context of which it forms a part. When determining that context, it is also necessary to take into consideration the nature of the goods or services affected, as well as the real conditions of the functioning and structure of the market or markets in question.

[54] In addition, although the parties' intention is not a necessary factor in determining whether an agreement between undertakings is restrictive, there is nothing prohibiting the competition authorities, the national courts or the Courts of the European Union from taking that factor into account.

[55] In the present case, it must be noted that, when the General Court defined in the judgment under appeal the relevant legal criteria to be taken into account in order to ascertain whether there was, in the

present case, a restriction of competition by 'object' within the meaning of Article 81(1) EC, it reasoned as follows . . .

> According to the case-law, the types of agreement covered by Article 81(1)(a) to (e) EC do not constitute an exhaustive list of prohibited collusion and, accordingly, the concept of infringement by object should not be given a strict interpretation.
>
> In order to assess the anti-competitive nature of an agreement or a decision by an association of undertakings, regard must be had *inter alia* to the content of its provisions, its objectives and the economic and legal context of which it forms a part. In that regard, it is sufficient that the agreement or the decision of an association of undertakings has the potential to have a negative impact on competition. In other words, the agreement or decision must simply be capable in the particular case, having regard to the specific legal and economic context, of preventing, restricting or distorting competition within the common market. It is not necessary for there to be actual prevention, restriction or distortion of competition or a direct link between [that agreement or decision] and consumer prices. In addition, although the parties' intention is not a necessary factor in determining whether an agreement is restrictive, there is nothing prohibiting the Commission or the Community judicature from taking it into account.

56 It must be held that, in so reasoning, the General Court in part failed to have regard to the case-law of the Court of Justice and, therefore, erred in law with regard to the definition of the relevant legal criteria in order to assess whether there was a restriction of competition by 'object' within the meaning of Article 81(1) EC.

57 First, . . . when the General Court defined the concept of the restriction of competition 'by object' within the meaning of that provision, it did not refer to the settled case-law of the Court of Justice mentioned in paragraphs 49 to 52 of the present judgment, thereby failing to have regard to the fact that the essential legal criterion for ascertaining whether coordination between undertakings involves such a restriction of competition 'by object' is the finding that such coordination reveals in itself a sufficient degree of harm to competition.

58 Secondly, in the light of that case-law, the General Court erred in finding . . . that the concept of restriction of competition by 'object' must not be interpreted 'restrictively'. The concept of restriction of

competition 'by object' can be applied only to certain types of coordination between undertakings which reveal a sufficient degree of harm to competition that it may be found that there is no need to examine their effects, otherwise the Commission would be exempted from the obligation to prove the actual effects on the market of agreements which are in no way established to be, by their very nature, harmful to the proper functioning of normal competition. The fact that the types of agreements covered by Article 81(1) EC do not constitute an exhaustive list of prohibited collusion is, in that regard, irrelevant.

[59] It is, however, necessary to examine whether those errors of law were capable of vitiating the General Court's analysis as regards the characterisation of the measures at issue in the light of Article 81(1) EC.

[60] In that regard, it must be noted . . . that the General Court found that the measures at issue have as their object the restriction of competition within the meaning of Article 81(1) EC in that, essentially, they hinder the competition of new entrants on the market for the issue of payment cards in France.

[61] . . . [T]he General Court found, after reproducing . . . the content of several recitals of the decision at issue, that that anti-competitive object stemmed from the very calculation formulas which were provided for the measures at issue.

[62] In those circumstances, the General Court held . . . that the fact that the measures at issue pursue a legitimate objective of combating free-riding of the CB system did not preclude their being considered to have an object restrictive of competition, all the more so since that object, as was apparent form the very formulas provided for the measures at issue, ran counter to the stated objectives of the Grouping.

[63] The General Court also held . . . that the requirements of balance between the issuing and acquisition activities within the CB system did not have to be examined in the context of Article 81(1) EC, since the only market taken into account was the downstream market for the issue of payment cards.

[64] Lastly, the General Court also held . . . that it was only on the basis of 'additional confirmation' that, in the decision at issue, the Commission relied on the Grouping's intention, as evidenced by the documents gathered during the inspections, containing the comments of the main members at the preparatory stage of the measures at issue.

65 Although it is apparent from the judgment under appeal that the General Court took the view that the restrictive object of the measures at issue could be inferred from their wording alone, the fact remains that it did not at any point explain, in the context of its review of the lawfulness of the decision at issue, in what respect that wording could be considered to reveal the existence of a restriction of competition 'by object' within the meaning of Article 81(1) EC.

66 In that regard, the General Court did indeed observe . . . that the Commission found, 'in the light of the formulas provided for the measures at issue and because of the difficulty of developing acquisition activity, that those measures required the members of the Grouping which were subject to them either to limit the issue of cards or to bear costs (linked to issuing) which were not borne by other members of the Grouping, including the main members. Those formulas therefore limited the possibility for the members subject to those measures to compete (on prices), on the issue market, with the members of the Grouping not subject to them'.

67 In addition, the General Court pointed out . . . that the Commission had stated that the function attributed by the Grouping to MERFA, namely an incentive to expand acquisition, 'was inconsistent with the existence of interchange fees which encouraged issue . . . and by the fact that the supplementary membership fee and the [dormant] member fee penalised banks that had not issued a sufficient number of cards in the recent past'.

68 The General Court inferred from this . . . that the object of the measures at issue, like those at issue in the *BIDS* judgment, is to impede the competition of new entrants on the market for the issue of payment cards in France, since they require the banks subject to them either to pay a fee or to limit their issuing activities.

69 However, although the General Court thereby set out the reasons why the measures at issue, in view of their formulas, are capable of restricting competition and, consequently, of falling within the scope of the prohibition laid down in Article 81(1) EC, it in no way explained—contrary to the requirements of the case-law referred to in paragraphs 49 and 50 above—in what respect that restriction of competition reveals a sufficient degree of harm in order to be characterised as a restriction 'by object' within the meaning of that provision, there being no analysis of that point in the judgment under appeal.

70 Although, as the General Court correctly found . . . , the fact that the measures at issue pursue the legitimate objective of combatting free-riding does not preclude their being regarded as having an object

restrictive of competition, the fact remains that that restrictive object must be established.

[71] It follows that the General Court, in its characterisation of the measures at issue, not only vitiated the judgment under appeal by defective reasoning, but also misinterpreted and misapplied Article 81(1) EC.

[72] It is indeed clear . . . that the General Court rejected on several occasions the appellant's claim that it was apparent from formulas prescribed for the measures at issue that the latter sought to develop the acquisition activities of the members in order to achieve an optimal rate of balance between issuing and acquisition activities. On the other hand, it is not disputed . . . that those formulas encouraged the members of the Grouping, in order to avoid the payment of fees introduced by those measures, not to exceed a certain volume of CB card issuing that enabled them to achieve a given ratio between the issuing and acquisition activities of the Grouping.

[73] After stating . . . that the Grouping is active on the 'payment systems market', the General Court found . . . in its assessment of the facts—which is not subject to appeal and is not challenged in these proceedings—that, in the present case, in a card payment system that is by nature two-sided, such as that of the Grouping, the issuing and acquisition activities are 'essential' to one another and to the operation of that system: first, traders would not agree to join the CB card payment system if the number of cardholders was insufficient and, secondly, consumers would not wish to hold a card if it could not be used with a sufficient number of traders.

[74] Having therefore found . . . that there were 'interactions' between the issuing and acquisition activities of a payment system and that those activities produced 'indirect network effects', since the extent of merchants' acceptance of cards and the number of cards in circulation each affects the other, the General Court could not, without erring in law, conclude that the measures at issue had as their object the restriction of competition within the meaning of Article 81(1) EC.

[75] Having acknowledged that the formulas for those measures sought to establish a certain ratio between the issuing and acquisition activities of the members of the Grouping, the General Court was entitled at the most to infer from this that those measures had as their object the imposition of a financial contribution on the members of the Grouping which benefit from the efforts of other members for the purposes of developing the acquisition activities of the system. Such an object cannot be regarded as being, by its very nature, harmful to the proper functioning of normal competition, the General

Court itself moreover having found . . . that combatting free-riding in the CB system was a legitimate objective.

[76] In that regard, as the Advocate General observed . . . , the General Court wrongly held . . . that the analysis of the requirements of balance between issuing and acquisition activities within the payment system could not be carried out in the context of Article 81(1) EC on the ground that the relevant market was not that of payment systems in France but the market, situated downstream for the issue of payment cards in that Member State.

[77] In so doing, the General Court confused the issue of the definition of the relevant market and that of the context which must be taken into account in order to ascertain whether the content of an agreement or a decision by an association of undertakings reveals the existence of a restriction of competition 'by object' within the meaning of Article 81(1) EC.

[78] In order to assess whether coordination between undertakings is by nature harmful to the proper functioning of normal competition, it is necessary, in accordance with the case-law referred to in paragraph 53 above, to take into consideration all relevant aspects— having regard, in particular, to the nature of the services at issue, as well as the real conditions of the functioning and structure of the markets—of the economic or legal context in which that coordination takes place, it being immaterial whether or not such an aspect relates to the relevant market.

[79] That must be the case, in particular, when that aspect is the taking into account of interactions between the relevant market and a different related market and, all the more so, when, as in the present case, there are interactions between the two facets of a two-sided system.

[80] Admittedly, it cannot be ruled out that the measures at issue . . . hinder competition from new entrants—in the light of the difficulty which those measures create for the expansion of their acquisition activity—and even lead to their exclusion from the system, on the basis, as BPCE argued at the hearing, of the level of fees charged pursuant to those measures.

[81] However, . . . such a finding falls within the examination of the effects of those measures on competition and not of their object.

[82] It must therefore be found that, while purporting to examine . . . the 'options' left open to the members of the Grouping by the measures at issue—at the end of which it concluded . . . that 'in practice MERFA left two options open to the banks subject to it: payment of a fee or limiting the issue of CB cards'—the General Court

in fact assessed the potential effects of those measures, analysing the difficulties for the banks of developing acquisition activity on the basis of market data, statements made by certain banks and documents seized during the inspections, and thereby indicating itself that the measures at issue cannot be considered 'by their very nature' harmful to the proper functioning of normal competition.

[83] In that regard, the General Court erred . . . in finding that the measures at issue could be regarded as being analogous to those examined by the Court of Justice in the *BIDS* judgment, in which the Court of Justice held that the arrangements referred to ('the BIDS arrangements'), concluded between the ten principal beef and veal processors in Ireland, members of BIDS [Beef Industry Development Society Ltd], had as their object the restriction of competition within the meaning of Article 81(1) EC.

[84] By providing for a reduction of the order of 25% in processing capacity, the BIDS arrangements were intended, essentially, as their own wording makes clear, to enable several undertakings to implement a common policy which had as its object the encouragement of some of them to withdraw from the market and the reduction, as a consequence, of the overcapacity which affects their profitability by preventing them from achieving economies of scale. The object of the BIDS arrangements was therefore to change, appreciably, the structure of the market through a mechanism intended to encourage the withdrawal of competitors in order, first, to increase the degree of concentration in the sector concerned by reducing significantly the number of undertakings supplying processing services and, secondly, to eliminate almost 75% of excess production capacity.

[85] In the judgment under appeal, the General Court made no such finding, nor indeed was it argued before it that the measures at issue, like the BIDS arrangements, were intended to change appreciably the structure of the market concerned through a mechanism intended to encourage the withdrawal of competitors and, accordingly, that those measures revealed a degree of harm such as that of the BIDS arrangements.

[86] Although the General Court found . . . that the measures at issue encouraged the members of the Grouping not to exceed a certain volume of CB card issuing, the objective of such encouragement was, according to its own findings . . . , not to reduce possible overcapacity on the market for the issue of payment cards in France, but to achieve a given ratio between the issuing and acquisition activities of the members of the Grouping in order to develop the CB system further.

[87] It follows that the General Court could not, without erring in law, characterise the measures at issue as restrictions of competition 'by object' within the meaning of Article 81(1) EC.

[88] Since the intentions of the Grouping could not in themselves, in accordance with the case-law referred to in paragraph 54 above, be sufficient to establish the existence of an anti-competitive object and the General Court moreover itself stated . . . that those intentions had been analysed as additional confirmation only, its findings in that regard . . . cannot justify such a characterisation and there is no need to examine the arguments put forward by the appellant on that point.

[89] Taken together, the errors of law committed by the General Court with regard to (i) the relevant legal criteria in order to assess the existence of a restriction of competition 'by object', (ii) the grounds of the judgment under appeal and (iii) the characterisation of the measures at issue with regard to Article 81(1) EC indicate, in addition, a general failure of analysis by the General Court and therefore reveal the lack of a full and detailed examination of the arguments of the appellant and of the parties which sought the annulment of the decision at issue.

[90] By simply reproducing on a number of occasions . . . the contents of the decision at issue, the General Court failed to review, even though required to do so, whether the evidence used by the Commission in the decision at issue enabled it correctly to conclude that the measures at issue, in the light of their wording, objectives and context, displayed a sufficient degree of harm to competition to be regarded as having as their object a restriction of competition within the meaning of Article 81(1) EC and, consequently, whether that evidence constituted all the relevant data which had to be taken into consideration for that purpose.

[91] In those circumstances, it is apparent that the General Court failed to fulfil its obligation to observe the standard of review required under the case-law, as set out in paragraphs 42 to 46 above.

[92] In the light of all the foregoing, it must be found that, in holding that the measures at issue had as their object a restriction of competition within the meaning of Article 81(1) EC, the General Court erred in law and failed to observe the standard of review required under the case-law.

Notes and Questions

1.   In *Cartes Bancaires*, the CJEU cautioned against over-expanding the category of restrictions by object, holding that the criterion is satisfied only where the restrictions "reveal a sufficient degree of harm to competition that it may be found that there is no need to examine their actual effects." In others words, the category of restrictions by object seems to be limited to those that either are hard core or generally cause significant anticompetitive harm. How does this framework differ in practice from the treatment of restraints of trade under Section 1 of the Sherman Act?

2.   The Court's analysis suggests that arrangements in complex or novel economic settings may not lend themselves to "by object" analysis, since the actual effects on competition may be too unpredictable for categorical treatment. Does this mean that all "new economy" arrangements that are not hard core cartels are not restraints by object?

C. INFORMATION EXCHANGE AND LOOSE COLLABORATIONS

Competitive information exchange and loose competitor collaborations—loose, because they do not involve economic integration between the collaborating parties—are a standard problem in antitrust analysis. You might consider these agreements to fall closer on the spectrum to cartel agreements than do agreements involving significant degrees of economic integration—such as joint venture agreements. Nonetheless, information exchanges and loose collaborations can be efficiency-enhancing, and have not received as hostile a reception as naked price-fixing agreements.

ASNEF-EQUIFAX v. ASOCIACIÓN DE USUARIOS DE SERVICIOS BANCARIOS (AUSBANC)
Case C–238/05, EU:C:2006:734 (European Court of Justice 2006)

[Financial institutions in Spain agreed to exchange information about solvency of customers and lateness of payment. They planned to establish a register for such information. The Spanish competition authority authorized the register for five years on condition that the register be available to all financial institutions on a non-discriminatory basis and that it not disclose the information it contained on lenders. Ausbanc, an association of bank users, sought an annulment in a Spanish court. It alleged that the register would facilitate a boycott against poor credit risks. The Spanish court made an Article [267] reference to the CJEU regarding applicability and treatment under Article [101]. The CJEU identified the various questions of fact regarding economic and legal context that the national court would have to decide, and it gave considerable guidance both as to when Article [101(1)]) would apply and when the Article [101(3)] criteria would be satisfied. See the Article 101(30 criteria at A. above.]

55 . . . [R]egisters such as the one at issue in the main proceedings, by reducing the rate of borrower default, are in principle capable of improving the functioning of the supply of credit. As the Advocate General observed, . . . if, owing to a lack of information on the risk of borrower default, financial institutions are unable to distinguish those borrowers who are more likely to default, the risk thereby borne by such institutions will necessarily be increased and they will tend to factor it in when calculating the cost of credit for all borrowers, including those less likely to default, who will then have to bear a higher cost than they would if the institutions were in a position to evaluate the probability of repayment more precisely. In principle, registers such as that mentioned above are capable of reducing such a tendency.

56 Furthermore, by reducing the significance of the information held by financial institutions regarding their own customers, such registers appear, in principle, to be capable of increasing the mobility of consumers of credit. In addition, those registers are apt to make it easier for new competitors to enter the market.

57 None the less, whether or not there is in the main proceedings a restriction of competition within the meaning of Article [101(1)] EC depends on the economic and legal context in which the register exists, and in particular on the economic conditions of the market as well as the particular characteristics of the register.

58 In that regard, first of all, if supply on a market is highly concentrated, the exchange of certain information may, according in particular to the type of information exchanged, be liable to enable undertakings to be aware of the market position and commercial strategy of their competitors, thus distorting rivalry on the market and increasing the probability of collusion, or even facilitating it. On the other hand, if supply is fragmented, the dissemination and exchange of information between competitors may be neutral, or even positive, for the competitive nature of the market. In the present case, it is common ground, . . . that the referring court premised its reference for a preliminary ruling on the existence of 'a fragmented market', which it is for that court to verify.

59 Secondly, in order that registers such as that at issue in the main proceedings are not capable of revealing the market position or the commercial strategy of competitors, it is important that the identity of lenders is not revealed, directly or indirectly. In the present case,

it is apparent from the decision for referral that the Tribunal de Defensa de la Competencia imposed on Asnef-Equifax, which accepted it, a condition that the information relating to lenders contained in the register not be disclosed.

[60] Thirdly, it is also important that such registers be accessible in a non-discriminatory manner, in law and in fact, to all operators active in the relevant sphere. If such accessibility were not guaranteed, some of those operators would be placed at a disadvantage, since they would have less information for the purpose of risk assessment, which would also not facilitate the entry of new operators on to the market.

[61] It follows that, provided that the relevant market or markets are not highly concentrated, that the system does not permit lenders to be identified and that the conditions of access and use by financial institutions are not discriminatory, an information exchange system such as the register is not, in principle, liable to have the effect of restricting competition within the meaning of Article [101(1)] EC.

[62] While in those conditions such systems are capable of reducing uncertainty as to the risk that applicants for credit will default, they are not, however, liable to reduce uncertainty as to the risks of competition. Thus, each operator could be expected to act independently and autonomously when adopting a given course of conduct, regard being had to the risks presented by applicants. Contrary to Ausbanc's contention, it cannot be inferred solely from the existence of such a credit information exchange that it might lead to collective anti-competitive conduct, such as a boycott of certain potential borrowers.

[63] Furthermore, since, as the Advocate General observed, . . . any possible issues relating to the sensitivity of personal data are not, as such, a matter for competition law, they may be resolved on the basis of the relevant provisions governing data protection. In the main proceedings, it is apparent from the documents before the Court that, under the rules applicable to the register, affected consumers may, in accordance with the Spanish legislation, check the information concerning them and, where necessary, have it corrected, or indeed deleted.

The applicability of Article [101(3)] EC

[64] Only if the referring court finds, in the light of the considerations set out at paragraphs 58 to 62 of this judgment, that there is indeed in the dispute before it a restriction of competition within the meaning of Article [101(1)] EC will it be necessary for that court to

carry out an analysis by reference to Article [101(3)] EC in order to resolve that dispute.

65 The applicability of the exemption provided for in Article [101(3)] EC is subject to the four cumulative conditions laid down in that provision. First, the arrangement concerned must contribute to improving the production or distribution of the goods or services in question, or to promoting technical or economic progress; secondly, consumers must be allowed a fair share of the resulting benefit; thirdly, it must not impose any non-essential restrictions on the participating undertakings; and, fourthly, it must not afford them the possibility of eliminating competition in respect of a substantial part of the products or services in question.

66 It is clear from the documents before the Court, and in particular from the second question referred by the national court, that that court seeks an answer from the Court in respect of, in particular, the second of those conditions, which provides that consumers are to be allowed a fair share of the profit resulting from the agreement, decision or practice in question. The national court asks, in essence, whether, where all consumers do not derive a benefit from the register, the register might none the less benefit from the exemption provided for in Article [101(1)] EC.

67 Apart from the potential effects described at paragraphs 55 and 56 of this judgment, registers such as the one at issue in the main proceedings are capable of helping to prevent situations of overindebtedness for consumers of credit as well as, in principle, of leading to a greater overall availability of credit. In the event that the register restricted competition within the meaning of Article [101(1)] EC, those objective economic advantages might be such as to offset the disadvantages of such a possible restriction. It would be for the national court, if necessary, to verify that.

68 Admittedly, in principle it is not inconceivable that, as Ausbanc suggests, certain applicants for credit will, owing to the existence of such registers, be faced with increased interest rates, or even be refused credit.

69 However, without its being necessary to decide whether such applicants would none the less benefit from a possible credit discipline effect or from protection against overindebtedness, that circumstance cannot in itself prevent the condition that consumers be allowed a fair share of the benefit from being satisfied.

70 Under Article [101(3)] EC, it is the beneficial nature of the effect on all consumers in the relevant markets that must be taken into

consideration, not the effect on each member of that category of consumers.

71 Moreover, as follows from paragraphs 55 and 67 of this judgment, registers such as the one at issue in the main proceedings are, under favourable conditions, capable of leading to a greater overall availability of credit, including for applicants for whom interest rates might be excessive if lenders did not have appropriate knowledge of their personal situation.

DOLE FOOD COMPANY, INC. v. COMMISSION
Case C–286/13 P, EU:C:2015:184 (European Court of Justice 2015)

[A group of banana producers importing into northern Europe, including Dole, Fresh Del Monte, Chiquita, and Weichert, "engaged in bilateral pre-pricing communications during which they discussed banana price-setting factors, that is to say, factors relevant to the setting of quotation prices for the forthcoming week, or discussed or disclosed price trends or gave indications of quotation prices for the forthcoming week." The Commission charged that these communications served as devices to reduce uncertainty about the prices the companies then quoted to the market. Among other things, Dole argued on appeal to the European Court of Justice that the General Court erred in treating this information exchange as a restriction of competition by object in violation of TFEU Article 101 and in failing to require proof of actual effects on banana prices.]

105 By the fifth part of their third ground of appeal, the Dole companies submit that, by finding that the pre-pricing communications constitute a restriction of competition by object, the General Court erred in its legal characterisation of the facts. According to those companies, the exchange of information which took place cannot be regarded as capable of removing uncertainty as to the intended conduct of the participating undertakings as regards the setting of actual prices.

106 First, the pre-pricing communications were carried out by employees who were not responsible for setting quotation prices. Second, as those communications concerned quotation price trends, they were not capable of removing uncertainty as to actual prices. In that regard, all the market participants involved in the Commission's investigation stated that quotation prices were far removed from actual prices. Moreover, the Commission did not find there had been a restriction of competition by object in relation to the same type of information exchange involving two other undertakings.

107 [T]he General Court rejected those arguments, imposing, incorrectly, the burden of proving that the exchange of information was not capable of removing uncertainty as to the development of actual prices on the Dole companies. However, it was for the Commission to prove that the exchange of information was unlawful. According to the Dole companies, it is apparent from case-law that the mere fact that an exchange of information might have a certain influence on prices is not sufficient to establish the existence of a restriction of competition by object. The Commission was unable to put forward such evidence, however, in view of the fact that there is no reliable connection between quotation price movements and those of actual prices.

108 Furthermore, in so far as the General Court dismissed the Dole companies' argument based on statements made by another undertaking by stating . . . that 'the statements of that undertaking must be assessed in the light of their context, namely that of an undertaking which was an addressee of the statement of objections and which contested the anticompetitive conduct alleged', those companies contend that the General Court failed to have regard to the principle of the presumption of innocence and to fact that the burden of proof lies with the Commission.

109 Lastly, the Dole companies maintain that the pre-pricing communications relating to price-setting factors were not capable of removing uncertainty as to the intended conduct of the undertakings concerned. In particular, they point out that the General Court concluded that the exchanges concerning the industry in general were 'innocuous', that the contested decision did not include information on volume as part of the infringement and that the General Court took the view that weather conditions constituted public information that could be obtained from other sources.

110 In so far as the General Court considered that the pre-pricing communications none the less revealed the competitors' views on those factors, the Dole companies submit that, in the light of the relevant case-law, it is not possible to characterise the exchange of views on weather conditions as a restriction of competition by object, as such discussions are so far removed from the setting of actual price that they cannot reduce uncertainty and facilitate coordination of the prices of the products in question.

—*Findings of the Court*

111 It should be noted that, contrary to what is claimed by the Commission, the Dole companies do not merely seek from the Court a fresh assessment of the facts but put forward errors of law which,

they claim, were committed by the General Court. The present part of the third ground of appeal is, therefore, admissible.

112 As regards the substance, it must be recalled that, to come within the prohibition laid down in Article 81(1) EC, an agreement, a decision by an association of undertakings or a concerted practice must have 'as [its] object or effect' the prevention, restriction or distortion of competition in the internal market.

113 In that regard, it is apparent from the Court's case-law that certain types of coordination between undertakings reveal a sufficient degree of harm to competition that it may be found that there is no need to examine their effects.

114 That case-law arises from the fact that certain types of coordination between undertakings can be regarded, by their very nature, as being harmful to the proper functioning of normal competition.

115 Consequently, it is established that certain collusive behaviour, such as that leading to horizontal price-fixing by cartels, may be considered so likely to have negative effects, in particular on the price, quantity or quality of the goods and services, that it may be considered redundant, for the purposes of applying Article 81(1) EC, to prove that they have actual effects on the market. Experience shows that such behaviour leads to falls in production and price increases, resulting in poor allocation of resources to the detriment, in particular, of consumers.

116 Where the analysis of a type of coordination between undertakings does not reveal a sufficient degree of harm to competition, the effects of the coordination should, on the other hand, be considered and, for the purpose of determining whether such conduct is covered by that defined in Article 81(1)) EC, it is necessary to find that factors are present which show that competition has in fact been prevented, restricted or distorted to an appreciable extent.

117 According to the case-law of the Court, in order to determine whether a type of coordination between undertakings reveals a sufficient degree of harm to competition that it may be considered a restriction of competition 'by object' within the meaning of Article 81(1) EC, regard must be had, inter alia, to its objectives and the economic and legal context of which it forms a part. When determining that context, it is also necessary to take into consideration the nature of the goods or services affected, as well as the real conditions of the functioning and structure of the market or markets in question.

118 In addition, although the parties' intention is not a necessary factor in determining whether a type of coordination between undertakings is restrictive, there is nothing prohibiting the competition authorities, the national courts or the Courts of the European Union from taking that factor into account.

119 In so far as concerns, in particular, the exchange of information between competitors, it should be recalled that the criteria of coordination and cooperation necessary for determining the existence of a concerted practice are to be understood in the light of the notion inherent in the Treaty provisions on competition, according to which each economic operator must determine independently the policy which he intends to adopt on the common market.

120 While it is correct to say that this requirement of independence does not deprive economic operators of the right to adapt themselves intelligently to the existing or anticipated conduct of their competitors, it does, none the less, strictly preclude any direct or indirect contact between such operators by which an undertaking may influence the conduct on the market of its actual or potential competitors or disclose to them its decisions or intentions concerning its own conduct on the market where the object or effect of such contact is to create conditions of competition which do not correspond to the normal conditions of the market in question, regard being had to the nature of the products or services offered, the size and number of the undertakings involved and the volume of that market.

121 The Court has therefore held that the exchange of information between competitors is liable to be incompatible with the competition rules if it reduces or removes the degree of uncertainty as to the operation of the market in question, with the result that competition between undertakings is restricted.

122 In particular, an exchange of information which is capable of removing uncertainty between participants as regards the timing, extent and details of the modifications to be adopted by the undertakings concerned in their conduct on the market must be regarded as pursuing an anticompetitive object.

123 Moreover, a concerted practice may have an anticompetitive object even though there is no direct connection between that practice and consumer prices. Indeed, it is not possible on the basis of the wording of Article 81(1) EC to conclude that only concerted practices which have a direct effect on the prices paid by end users are prohibited.

124 On the contrary, it is apparent from Article 81(1)(a) EC that concerted practices may have an anticompetitive object if they

'directly or indirectly fix purchase or selling prices or any other trading conditions'.

125 In any event, Article 81 EC, like the other competition rules of the Treaty, is designed to protect not only the immediate interests of individual competitors or consumers but also to protect the structure of the market and thus competition as such. Therefore, in order to find that a concerted practice has an anticompetitive object, there does not need to be a direct link between that practice and consumer prices.

126 Lastly, it should be pointed out that the concept of a concerted practice, as it derives from the actual terms of Article 81(1) EC, implies, in addition to the participating undertakings concerting with each other, subsequent conduct on the market and a relationship of cause and effect between the two.

127 In that regard, the Court has held that, subject to proof to the contrary, which the economic operators concerned must adduce, it must be presumed that the undertakings taking part in the concerted action and remaining active on the market take account of the information exchanged with their competitors in determining their conduct on that market. In particular, the Court has concluded that such a concerted practice is caught by Article 81(1) EC, even in the absence of anticompetitive effects on the market.

128 In the present case, the General Court examined . . . the Dole companies' arguments concerning the relevance of quotation prices in the banana sector and the responsibility of the Dole Food employees involved in the pre-pricing communications.

129 As observed by the Advocate General . . . it is apparent from the extremely detailed findings of the General Court, first, that bilateral pre-pricing communications were exchanged between the Dole companies and other undertakings in the banana sector and, as part of those communications, the undertakings discussed their own quotation prices and certain price trends. Moreover, the Dole companies do not contest that finding.

130 Second, the General Court found . . . that quotation prices were relevant to the market concerned, since, on the one hand, market signals, market trends or indications as to the intended development of banana prices could be inferred from those quotation prices, which were important for the banana trade and the prices obtained and, on the other, in some transactions the actual prices were directly linked to the quotation prices.

[131] Third, . . . the General Court found that the Dole employees involved in the pre-pricing communications participated in the internal pricing meetings.

[132] Furthermore, those findings of the General Court are to a large extent based on statements made by Dole Food and the Dole companies have not alleged any form of distortion in that regard.

[133] Accordingly, the General Court was entitled to take the view, without erring in law, that the conditions for the application of the presumption referred to at paragraph 127 above were fulfilled in the present case, with the result that the Dole companies' claims that that court infringed the principle governing the burden of proof and the presumption of innocence are unfounded.

[134] It also follows that the General Court was entitled to take the view . . . , without erring in law, that it was permissible for the Commission to conclude that, as they made it possible to reduce uncertainty for each of the participants as to the foreseeable conduct of competitors, the pre-pricing communications had the object of creating conditions of competition that do not correspond to the normal conditions on the market and therefore gave rise to a concerted practice having as its object the restriction of competition within the meaning of Article 81 EC.

A Note on Trade Associations

In *The Wealth of Nations*, Adam Smith wrote that "[p]eople of the same trade seldom meet together, even for merriment and diversion, but the conversation ends in a conspiracy against the public, or in some contrivance to raise prices." Smith's comments have proven prescient time and time again, as trade associations have become fora for collusion. Although trade associations can serve many positive functions, formal or informal information exchange that begins there often spills over into full-blown price fixing.

China's Anti-Monopoly Law suggests some degree of ambivalence around trade associations. Article 16 provides that "[i]ndustry associations shall not organize the business operators in their industry to engage in the monopolistic conducts prohibited by this Chapter." But, as though to counterbalance Article 16, Article 11 provides that "trade associations shall strengthen self-discipline of the industries, provide guidance for enterprises in their industries to compete lawfully, and protect the order of market competition."

Competition authorities around the world closely scrutinize the practices of trade associations. The Competition Commission of India has published a report on its monitoring of trade associations, noting that "[c]ompetition enforcement is getting increasingly focused on trade associations' practices that facilitate collusion among the members." *http://www.cci.gov.in/sites/default/files/Newsletter_document/ Newsletter_Sept.pdf.* In 2015, the UK Competition and Markets Authority ("CMA") fined a real estate trade association for organizing an anticompetitive restriction on fee advertisements and discounts by the members of the association. *https://www.gov.uk/government/news/ companies-fined-over-775000-in-cma-investigation-into-advertising-of-agents-fees.*

Competition authorities have generally been more inclined to police excesses by trade associations than to disband them altogether, but sometimes only a drastic remedy will suffice. In 2015, the Supreme Court of Chile affirmed a 2011 decision of the Chilean National Economic Prosecutor to disband a poultry trade association after the country's three major poultry producers had used the association as a forum for market allocation. See Press Release, Fiscalia Nacional Economica, Chilean Supreme Court Upholds Fines for Collusion Against Agrosuper, Ariztía and Don Pollo and Hardens Sanction Against the Trade Association (2015), available at *http://www.fne.gob.cl/english/2015/ 10/29/chilean-supreme-court-upholds-fines-for-collusion-against-agrosuper-ariztia-and-don-pollo-and-hardens-sanction-against-the-trade-association/.*

Notes and Questions

1.   The EU's 2011 Guidelines on the Applicability of Article 101 TFEU to Horizontal Cooperation Agreements, *http://eur-lex.europa.eu/ legal-content/EN/TXT/PDF/?uri=CELEX:52011XC0114(04)&from= EN,* provides guidance on information exchanges by competitors. It recognizes that information exchange may sometimes benefit consumers, but that in other circumstances, it may serve to cartelize a market. The guidelines also note that information exchange among a select group of competitors may foreclose competition by unaffiliated companies who are denied access to the shared information.

2.   Many cartel cases hinge on evidence that competitors exchanged data about prices, output levels, or other competitively sensitive information. Certainly, information exchange is necessary to keep cartels functioning smoothly. But information exchange need not be anticompetitive or illegal. Indeed, it may have perfectly innocent explanations. Competitors may need good information on what their rivals are doing in order to prevent waste and make efficient planning decisions about production levels. Exchange of information on prices can even lead a seller to lower its price, realizing the market price is somewhat beneath its previously established price.

3. Some relatively early US decisions seemed to condemn information exchanges as per se illegal, while others tolerated what may be been anticompetitive information exchanges. Since the 1970s, however, several fairly consistent principles have emerged from Supreme Coot and lower court decisions. First, an agreement to share information, standing alone, is never per se illegal as a price-fixing agreement. *United States v. U.S. Gypsum Co.*, 438 U.S. 422 (1978). Second, information exchange may in some cases be treated as a "plus factor," evidencing the existence of an illegal price fix (which is per se illegal). Thirdly, to the extent that a plaintiff challenges an agreement to exchange information as an unreasonable restraint of trade under the rule of reason, several factors are relevant. The more that the information shared related to past prices, was presented in aggregate rather than customer-specific form, was made publicly available, and was unaccompanied by meetings or other interactions between the rivals, the less likely it is that a court will condemn it as anticompetitive. Conversely, the more that the information exchange related to present or future prices, provided customer-specific information, was only made available to the competitors, and was accompanied by other meetings, the more likely a court is to conclude that the information exchange unlawfully restrained price competition. *Todd v. Exxon Corp.*, 275 F.3d 191 (2d Cir. 2001).

4. In reading information exchange cases, it is important to ask whether the information exchange is being used as evidence of a cartel agreement or is challenged on its own as an anticompetitive concerted practice. The Seoul High Court (South Korea) had the following to say about the use of information exchanges to prove collusion in its 2012 *Dairy Cartel Case:* "Although collusion may not be conclusively found based merely on the fact of information exchange among competitors, the exchange of pricing and production information among competitors may be used as a means of facilitating collusion through increased transparency in the market which allows observation of, and response to, competitors' strategies. In this regard, such information exchange may serve as strong circumstantial evidence of collusion depending on factors such as the structure and characteristics of the relevant market, subject of the information, nature of the information, timing and method of information exchange, identity of parties exchanging information."

5. In December of 2015, the Mexican Federal Economic Competition Commission ("FECC") issued guidelines on the exchange of information between economic agents that provide some clarity on the sorts of information exchanges that threaten competition and those that are more competitively benign. The guidelines begin by stating that information exchange in the following categories is most likely to trigger concerns: (1) prices and discounts; (2) costs; (3) inputs; (4) production and commercialization strategies; (5) client or supplier lists; (6) market share; and (7) investments for expansion. They further note that

information exchange is most competitively risky in the following contexts: (1) trade associations and chambers of commerce; (2) discussions about mergers; (3) joint ventures and cooperation agreements; and (4) sharing of directories. Finally, the guidelines discuss the importance of the following information attributes: (1) strategic importance; (2) aggregation (the more aggregated, the less concerning); (3) age (historical information is less concerning; present or future information is more concerning); (4) frequency (the more frequent, the more concerning); (5) public availability (the more publicly available, the less concerning); (6) use of protocols on access (strict protocols limiting access may help mitigate the risk); and (7) purpose (is there a legitimate commercial reason for the information exchange?). These state-of-the-art guidelines reflect a broad consensus among competition experts on the sorts of questions to be posed in information exchange cases.

D. LOOSE COLLABORATIONS IN CONSUMER FINANCIAL SERVICES

One area involving loose competitor collaborations that has seen a significant amount of activity in recent years is consumer financial services or payment systems—particular credit or debit card services and retail banking. Banks and other financial service companies often need to collaborate in various ways in order to allow financial transactions between consumers, merchants, and other banks flow freely. These collaborations frequently entail complex competition law questions involving rival access, discrimination, and collusion.

Until their Initial Public Offerings ("IPOs") in the mid-2000s, Visa and MasterCard were joint ventures between competitor banks, and hence classic joint venture organizations. One set of issues was whether the Visa and MasterCard networks could prohibit their member banks from issuing Discover or American Express (or other) credit cards. In 2003, the US Court of Appeals for the Second Circuit held that Visa U.S.A.'s and MasterCard's so-called "exclusionary" or "exclusivity" rules, which prohibited members of their networks from issuing Am Ex and Discover cards, were unlawful restraints of trade under the rule of reason. *United States v. Visa U.S.A., Inc.*, 344 F.3d 229 (2d Cir. 2003). This ruling broke Visa and MasterCard's deadlock on the banks.

The court did not, however, determine what kinds of rules the networks could employ within their respective systems. This has been a fertile subject of controversy on both sides of the Atlantic.

On January 31, 2007, the European Commission issued a report on the financial services. The Commission 'found widespread competition barriers which unnecessarily raise the cost of retail banking services for European firms and consumers," and vowed to "make full use of its powers under competition law to tackle these barriers, in the market for payment cards and elsewhere when they result from anticompetitive behaviour." In particular, the report identified the following conditions as problematic:

- **highly concentrated markets** in many Member States, particularly for payment card acquiring, may enable incumbent banks to restrict new entry and charge high card fees

- **large variations in merchant fees** across the EU. For example, firms in Member States with high fees have to pay banks three or four times more of their revenue from card sales than firms in Member States with low fees

- **large variations in interchange fees** between banks across the EU, which may not be passed on fully in lower fees for cardholders. The Commission is not arguing for zero interchange fees; however, their operation in some payment networks raises concerns

- **high and sustained profitability**—particularly in card issuing—suggests that banks in some Member States enjoy significant market power and could impose high card fees on firms and consumers

- **rules and practises** which weaken competition at the retailer level; for example blending of merchant fees and prohibition of surcharging and

- **divergent technical standards** across the EU prevent many service providers from operating efficiently on a pan-EU scale.

See COMMISSION OF THE EUROPEAN COMMUNITIES, SECTOR INQUIRY UNDER ARTICLE 17 OF REGULATION (EC) NO 1/2003 ON RETAIL BANKING (2007); European Commission Press Release, IP/07/114 (Jan. 31, 2007).

In response to these concerns, the European Commission has been putting pressure on banks to modify their payment card practices. In at least Austria, Finland, and Portugal, the Commission succeeded in persuading (perhaps with some implicit threat of action) banks to modify their practices in a way that satisfied the Commission's concerns.

Although the European Commission's preference has been to persuade banks and other industry participants to alter their competitively questionable practices, not all of the Commission's activities have been in the arena of gentle persuasion. In December 19, 2007, the Commission issued a decision prohibiting MasterCard from establishing intra-European Economic Area ("EEA") Multilateral Interchange Fees ("MIF"). Interchange fees are the charges that a cardholder's bank (the "issuing" bank) charges a merchant's bank (the "acquiring" bank) for each transaction at merchant outlet with a payment card. When a cardholder uses a payment card to make a purchase, the merchant receives from the acquiring bank the retail price less a merchant service charge, a large part of which is determined by the interchange fee. This merchant service charge is the price a merchant pays its bank for accepting payment cards. The issuing bank, in turn, pays the acquiring bank the retail price minus the MIF.

The Commission found that, by establishing the EEA-wide MIF, MasterCard inflated the price for intra-EEA payment transactions, "effectively determin[ing] a floor under the merchant service charge and merchants are unable to negotiate a price." The Commission found that the effect of the MasterCard establishing the MIF, instead of them being bargained over, was that MasterCard determined the minimum price merchants must pay for accepted credit cards. It enjoined MasterCard from continuing to establish MIFs. See European Commission Press Release, IP/07/1959 (Dec. 19, 2007).

Notes and Questions

1.   The *Cartes Bancaires* decision, studied in the previous section, raises a number of difficult questions regarding what economists call "two-sided markets"—platforms that bring together users on two different sides of the platform, such as merchants and customers in the case of credit cards or card holders, and banks in the case of banking cards. Competition law interventions on only one side of the market—for example, lifting the tax on bank card issuers who fail to meet a particular volume level for acquiring bank withdrawals—may destabilize the entire platform by preventing it from achieving equilibrium between the two sides of the market. On the other hand, it is often difficult for competition enforcers or courts to solve competition problems on both sides of the market simultaneously. Does this suggest that antitrust enforcers—who usually have to decide antitrust matters on a case-by-case basis—are not the best regulators to deal with the payment systems industry? Should a financial regulator with a broader regulatory mandate take charge instead? *See* David Evans, *Essays on the Economics of Two-Sided Markets,   https://www.competitionpolicyinternational.com/assets/ Hot-Tubs/Evans-Two-Sided-Market-Essays-Final.pdf.*

2.   In 2010, the United States Department of Justice and 17 States brought an antitrust case under Section 1 of the Sherman Act against MasterCard, Visa, and American Express, alleging that these

companies' "anti-steering rules," rules that prohibited merchants from "steering" customers to particular credit cards, anticompetitively limited competition among credit cards. Visa and MasterCard quickly settled, but American Express fought the case up to the federal court of appeals for the Second Circuit, which ruled in its favor in 2016. The Court found that the government's theory and lower court opinion condemning the anti-steering rule improperly defined the relevant market as only consisting of card network services, and failed to take into account the interdependence between network services and card issuance. *United States v. American Express Co.*, 838 F.3d 179 (2d. Cir. 2016). In other words, the court accepted as essential considering the effects of any restraint on both sides of the market. As of this writing, Supreme Court review remains possible.

E. STANDARD-SETTING ORGANIZATIONS, PATENT POOLS, AND RELATED PATENT PRACTICES

In order for the benefits of technological innovation to reach consumers, it is often necessary for the firms manufacturing the new products to agree on common interoperability or other technological standards. For example, imagine a world in which each DVD manufacturer created a unique product incompatible with its rivals' DVD players. Consumers would have to own many different DVD players in order to watch all of their DVDs.

Inventors and manufacturers in high technology industries often solve their coordination problems by forming standard-setting organizations ("SSOs"), which decide on standards for particular products or industries. While SSOs are often indispensable to technological progress, they also create serious dangers of anticompetitive abuse.

Consider, for example, what happened in *Allied Tube v. Indian Head*, 486 U.S. 492 (1988). Indian Head, a manufacturer of polyvinyl electrical conduit sought approval from the National Fire Protective Association in its National Electrical Code. Allied and other makers of steel electrical conduit perceived the new vinyl conduit as a competitive threat and allegedly packed the SSO's meetings to ensure that Allied's efforts to become part of the standard were voted down.

Often, SSOs not only set a standard, but also attempt to solve "patent thicket" problems—problems occasioned by the fact that practicing a particular standard will often require using many different patented technologies—by providing for the pooling and blanket licensing of patents necessary to practice the standard. To return to the DVD example, in the late 1990s and early 2000s, several different consortia of DVD manufacturers sought and received approval from both the US Justice Department and the European Commission to implement pools to issue a blanket license to use all of their patents necessary to manufacture DVDs. The European Commission's "comfort letter" found that "this patent pool would help promote technical and economic progress by allowing quick and efficient introduction of the DVD technology" and noted that the pool committed to license on a non-exclusive and non-discriminatory basis. See European Commission Press Release, IP/00/1135 (Oct. 9, 2000).

Patent pooling can also have anticompetitive consequences. For example, in the old cracking patents case, three of the Standard Oil Company's successor companies (the regional Standard companies created by the divestiture required by the 1911 Supreme Court decision) were able to cartelize much of the gasoline industry by cross-licensing to one another, and then licensing to 46 gasoline manufacturers, patents for the process of "cracking" gasoline. See George L. Priest, *Cartels and Patent License Arrangements*, 20 J. L. & Econ. 309 (1977). In Chapter 2, we reviewed the US and EU approaches to *Rambus*—a case involving the intersection of SSOs and patent rights in the computer memory business.

Around the globe, many jurisdictions—particularly those whose economies are heavily dependent on technology transfer—are becoming active in policing standard setting and patent pooling. Canada, the EU, Japan, and South Korea have all promulgated new guidelines on concerted patent practices since 2014. (For a useful summary, see Hartmut Schneider, Sarah H. Licht & Nicole Callan, *Antitrust and Intellectual Property Guidelines: The "Common Core" and Beyond*, ABA Section of Antitrust Law May 2016). Principles common to most or all of these guidelines include:

- Rule of reason or similar treatment for patent pooling arrangements;

- Provision of non-discriminatory access to pooled patents or the patent pooling process;

- Allowance, under most circumstances, of cross-licensing and grant-back arrangements;

- Restrictions on participants in standardization activities seeking to enforce their intellectual property rights injunctively against alleged infringers.

On April 7, 2015, the State Administration for Industry and Commerce of the People's Republic of China ("SAIC") released its

Rules on the Prohibition of Abuses of Intellectual Property Rights for the Purposes of Eliminating or Restricting Competition. It has since been adopted as a draft by China's other two competition agencies. Among other things, the Rules contain prohibitions on the following conduct on competitor participation in patent pools:

- Exchanging competitively sensitive information;

- restricting members of the patent pool from independently licensing their patents;

- restricting members or licensees from researching and developing technologies that compete with the pooled patents;

- forcing licensees to grant back on an exclusive basis to the patent pool management organization or a member of the patent pool any technologies that licensees have developed or improved;

- prohibiting licensees from challenging the validity or effectiveness of the pooled patents; and

- treating pool members or licensees differently with respect to licensing terms than similarly-situated pool members or licensees that operate in the same relevant market.

Regulation on the Prohibition of Conduct Eliminating or Restricting Competition by Abusing Intellectual Property Rights (promulgated by the State Admin. for Indus. and Commerce, Apr. 7, 2015, effective Aug. 1 ,2015), Order No. 74 (China).

The general movement in global antitrust law in recent years has been toward facilitation of technological standardization and patent pooling, subject to antitrust vigilance with regard to potential abuses. One might ask whether the pendulum might swing against standardization and patent pooling at some future point. Despite the many obvious benefits of standardization and patent, there is also some benefit in competition over technological standards (think VHS vs. Betamax) and patent licensing. There may also turn out to be important regional differences in perspective as among jurisdictions that are net technology exporters and those that are net technology importers. And, always lurking in the background of these doctrinal and policy questions are the foundational questions regarding dynamic efficiency and static efficiency—should antitrust policy tolerate measures that increase short-run market power but also incentivize long-run innovation? One should not expect uniform answers to such questions around the globe.

F. LEARNED PROFESSIONS

Although we often think of monopoly power arising from large corporations, some of the most pernicious restrictions on competition arise in the so called "learned professions" like medicine, law, and engineering. Consider, for example, an ethical rule promulgated by an engineers' association that prohibits the engineers from engaging in competitive bidding. The ostensible justification for such a prohibition might be that competitive bidding leads to a reduction in the quality of engineering work and ultimately a threat to public safety, since the engineers who have to accept low prices for their services are likely to cut corners. However, allowing such a rule to remain in place would effectively suppress all price competition for engineering services. *See National Society of Professional Engineers v. United States*, 435 U.S. 679 (1978) (invalidating such a restriction).

Antitrust regimes that wish to allow some space for self-regulation by learned professions must make such decisions about how much deference antitrust law should give the professions when they suppress competition.

WOUTERS ET CIE
Case C–309/99, EU:C:2002:98 (European Court of Justice 2002)

[This judgment arises out of the request for a preliminary ruling referred to the Court by the Netherlands Council of State in the framework of proceedings initiated by Wouters and other members of the Bar seeking to set aside the decisions of the Amsterdam and Rotterdam Bar prohibiting them from practicing law in full partnership with accountants. Those decisions were adopted pursuant to the Regulation on Joint Professional Activity adopted by the Bar of the Nederland in 1993 ("the 1993 Regulation"). The 1993 Regulation prohibits members of the Bar to "assume or maintain any obligations which might jeopardize the free and independent exercise of their profession, including . . . the relationship of trust between lawyer and client" and to "enter into or maintain any professional partnership unless the primary purpose of each partner's respective profession is the practice of the law." Wouters and his colleagues claimed that the decisions of the Amsterdam and Rotterdam Bar, as well as the 1993 Regulation, were incompatible with the Treaty provisions on competition, right of establishment and freedom to provide services.]

Question 1(a) * * *

[56] The question to be determined is whether, when it adopts a regulation such as the 1993 Regulation, a professional body is to be

treated as an association of undertakings or, on the contrary, as a public authority.

[The Court answered that the bar is to be treated as an association of undertakings.] * * *

Question 2

[73] By its second question the national court seeks, essentially, to ascertain whether a regulation such as the 1993 Regulation which, in order to guarantee the independence and loyalty to the client of members of the Bar who provide legal assistance in conjunction with members of other liberal professions, adopts universally binding rules governing the formation of multi-disciplinary partnerships, has the object or effect of restricting competition within the common market and is likely to affect trade between Member States. * * *

[84] The prohibition at issue in the main proceedings prohibits all contractual arrangements between members of the Bar and accountants which provide in any way for shared decision-making, profit-sharing or for the use of a common name, and this makes any form of effective partnership difficult. * * *

[86] It appears to the Court that the national legislation in issue in the main proceedings has an adverse effect on competition and may affect trade between Member States.

[87] As regards the adverse effect on competition, the areas of expertise of members of the Bar and of accountants may be complementary. Since legal services, especially in business law, more and more frequently require recourse to an accountant, a multi-disciplinary partnership of members of the Bar and accountants would make it possible to offer a wider range of services, and indeed to propose new ones. Clients would thus be able to turn to a single structure for a large part of the services necessary for the organisation, management and operation of their business (the 'one-stop shop' advantage).

[88] Furthermore, a multi-disciplinary partnership of members of the Bar and accountants would be capable of satisfying the needs created by the increasing interpenetration of national markets and the consequent necessity for continuous adaptation to national and international legislation.

[89] Nor, finally, is it inconceivable that the economies of scale resulting from such multi-disciplinary partnerships might have positive effects on the cost of services.

[90] A prohibition of multi-disciplinary partnerships of members of the Bar and accountants, such as that laid down in the 1993 Regulation,

is therefore liable to limit production and technical development within the meaning of Article [101(1)(b)] of the Treaty. * * *

[97] However, not every agreement between undertakings or every decision of an association of undertakings which restricts the freedom of action of the parties or of one of them necessarily falls within the prohibition laid down in Article [101(1)] of the Treaty. For the purposes of application of that provision to a particular case, account must first of all be taken of the overall context in which the decision of the association of undertakings was taken or produces its effects. More particularly, account must be taken of its objectives, which are here connected with the need to make rules relating to organisation, qualifications, professional ethics, supervision and liability, in order to ensure that the ultimate consumers of legal services and the sound administration of justice are provided with the necessary guarantees in relation to integrity and experience. . . . It has then to be considered whether the consequential effects restrictive of competition are inherent in the pursuit of those objectives.

[98] Account must be taken of the legal framework applicable in the Netherlands, on the one hand, to members of the Bar and to the Bar of the Netherlands, which comprises all the registered members of the Bar in that Member State, and on the other hand, to accountants. * * *

[102] [The members of the Bar] should be in a situation of independence vis-à-vis the public authorities, other operators and third parties, by whom they must never be influenced. They must furnish, in that respect, guarantees that all steps taken in a case are taken in the sole interest of the client.

[103] By contrast, the profession of accountant is not subject, in general, and more particularly, in the Netherlands, to comparable requirements of professional conduct. * * *

[105] . . . The Bar of the Netherlands was entitled to consider that members of the Bar might no longer be in a position to advise and represent their clients independently and in the observance of strict professional secrecy if they belonged to an organisation which is also responsible for producing an account of the financial results of the transactions in respect of which their services were called upon and for certifying those accounts. * * *

[107] A regulation such as the 1993 Regulation could therefore reasonably be considered to be necessary in order to ensure the proper practice of the legal profession, as it is organised in the Member State concerned. * * *

In 2006, the CJEU revisited the issue of fee-setting for legal services in a case that arose in Italy. Judgment of 12 May 2006, *Cipolla*, C–94/04, EU:C:2006:758. A statute dating from 1933 provided that the National Lawyers' Council shall set a fee schedule, to be approved by the Minister of Justice after consultation with the Interministerial Committee on Prices and the Council of State. Any agreement derogating from the minimum fees set by the scale for lawyers' services is legally void.

The CJEU held that the TFEU's antitrust provisions did not apply because the Italian minimum fee system was not the result of an agreement between undertakings. Since the Italian State and not the Bar Association ultimately exercised the power to make decisions on lawyers' minimum fees, the fee-setting could not be considered a private agreement and the Italian State did not require or encourage the adoption of private anticompetitive agreements.

Turning to the Treaty provision relating to the free movement of services, the Court held that the minimum fee arrangement could be caught by Article 49 because it rendered access to the Italian legal services market more difficult for lawyers established outside of Italy. However, the Court held that the system could potentially be justified based on the protection of consumers and the proper administration of justice, a decision ultimately to be made by the national court.

For many years, many US courts and commentators believed that the learned professions were beyond the reach of antitrust law. In 1975, however, the Supreme Court discarded the "learned professions" exception that many lower courts had recognized for self-regulated professions. *Goldfarb v. Virginia State Bar Ass'n*, 421 U.S. 773 (1975). The Court reasoned:

> The County Bar argues that Congress never intended to include the learned professions within the terms "trade or commerce" in [Section] 1 of the Sherman Act, and therefore the sale of professional services is exempt from the Act. No explicit exemption or legislative history is provided to support this contention; rather, the existence of state regulation seems to be its primary basis. Also, the County Bar maintains that competition is inconsistent with the practice of a profession because enhancing profit is not the goal of professional activities; the goal is to provide services necessary to the community. That, indeed, is the classic basis traditionally advanced to distinguish professions from trades, businesses, and other occupations, but it loses some

of its force when used to support the fee control activities involved here.

In arguing that learned professions are not "trade or commerce" the County Bar seeks a total exclusion from antitrust regulation. Whether state regulation is active or dormant, real or theoretical, lawyers would be able to adopt anticompetitive practices with impunity. We cannot find support for the proposition that Congress intended any such sweeping exclusion. The nature of an occupation, standing alone, does not provide sanctuary from the Sherman Act, nor is the public-service aspect of professional practice controlling in determining whether [Section] 1 includes professions. Congress intended to strike as broadly as it could in [Section] 1 of the Sherman Act, and to read into it so wide an exemption as that urged on us would be at odds with that purpose.

The language of [Section] 1 of the Sherman Act, of course, contains no exception. "Language more comprehensive is difficult to conceive." United States v. South-Eastern Underwriters Assn., 322 U.S. 533, 553 (1944). And our cases have repeatedly established that there is a heavy presumption against implicit exemptions. Indeed, our cases have specifically included the sale of services within s 1. Whatever else it may be, the examination of a land title is a service; the exchange of such a service for money is "commerce" in the most common usage of that word. It is no disparagement of the practice of law as a profession to acknowledge that it has this business aspect, and s 1 of the Sherman Act.

The fact that a restraint operates upon a profession as distinguished from a business is, of course, relevant in determining whether that particular restraint violates the Sherman Act. It would be unrealistic to view the practice of professions as interchangeable with other business activities, and automatically to apply to the professions antitrust concepts which originated in other areas. The public service aspect, and other features of the professions, may require that a particular practice, which could properly be viewed as a violation of the Sherman Act in another context, be treated differently. We intimate no view on any other situation than the one with which we are confronted today.

Although the US Court has scrutinized anticompetitive restraints by learned professions, it has granted self-regulated professions some limited deference, usually refusing to apply the rule of per se illegality to their activities but instead scrutinizing them under the rule of reason. *See, e.g., FTC v. Indiana Federation of Dentists*, 476 U.S. 447 (1986). In the last several decades, the FTC has made a high priority of attacking anticompetitive "ethics rules" of doctors, dentists, lawyers, engineers, and other professional groups. Although sometimes rebuffed in the courts, *e.g. California Dental Ass'n v. FTC*, 526 U.S. 756 (1999), the Commission has had some success in ensuring that professional association ethical rules do not suppress competition without some valid ethical or regulatory justification. In its most recent victory, the Commission persuaded the US Supreme Court that a North Carolina statute delegating regulatory power over the practice of dentistry to a Board constituted of interested dental professionals did not qualify for state action immunity. *North Carolina State Board of Dental Examiners v. FTC*, 135 S. Ct. 1101 (2015).

Although the US is often thought to be more permissive in its treatment of competitor collaborations than other antitrust regimes, it may play a more active role in scrutinizing professional associations than many other regimes. Some regimes explicitly allow for self-regulatory exemptions for professional associations. For example, the South African Competition Act authorizes the Competition Commission to exempt professional rules that are reasonably required:

(1) A professional association whose rules contain a restriction that has the effect of substantially preventing or lessening competition in a market may apply in the prescribed manner to the Competition Commission for an exemption in terms of item 2.

(2) The Competition Commission may exempt all or part of the rules of a professional association from the provisions of Part A of Chapter 2 of this Act for a specified period if, having regard to internationally applied norms, any restriction contained in those rules that has the effect of substantially preventing or lessening competition in a market is reasonably required to maintain—

(a) professional standards; or

(b) the ordinary function of the profession.

Parts (3)–(8) of the statute specify the procedures for applying for and obtaining self-regulatory authority from the Commission.

Part B then lists the professions generally eligible for self-regulatory exemption: Accountants and Auditors; Architects; Engineering; Estate Agents; Attorneys and Advocates; Natural sciences; Quantity Surveyors; Surveyors; Town and Regional Planners; Valuers; Medical; Miscellaneous.

G. COLLABORATIONS IN THE NEW ECONOMY

The Internet has fundamentally disrupted economic relationships and traditional economic categories. On the one hand, the Internet radically reduces consumers' search costs, and hence intensifies competition and facilitates retail participation by many smaller businesses. On the other hand, by lowering coordination costs, the Internet also provides new opportunities for sellers of goods and services to restrict competition. As with much technological change, the Internet brings both risks and opportunities from a competition perspective.

For sellers concerned that online sales risk their profit margins by intensifying competition, one strategy is to try to limit online sales and force customers into conventional brick and mortar sales environments. Consider, for example, the *Pierre Fabre* case, involving the sale of pharmaceutical products in France. Case C–439/09 *Pierre Fabre Dermo-Cosmetique SAS v. President de l'Autorite de la Concurrence and Others*, judgment of 13 October 2011. Pierre Fabre sold pharmaceutical products that were not considered "medicines" under French law, and thus were not restricted by law to sales in brick and mortar pharmacies. Nonetheless, Pierre Fabre implemented distribution agreements that effectively limited sales to physical stores in the presence of a qualified pharmacist. The European Court of Justice found that the restriction was susceptible to being justified under TFEU Article 101(3), but that Pierre Fabre had failed to present sufficient evidence to justify the restriction.

Similarly, the German Bundeskartellamt has been active in investigating agreements that restrict or deny Internet competition. In 2015, it investigated agreements between online portals, car dealerships, and car manufacturers that allegedly restricted online sales, only dropping its investigation once the offending restrictions were deleted. Bundeskartellamt Case B9–28/15. It also required the shoe company Asics to remove various restrictions on online sales of its shoes, which could have limited sales on online platforms such as eBay and/or cross-border sales. Bundeskartellamt Case B 2–98/11.

These restrictions on Internet sales were mostly vertical insofar as they operated as between an upstream manufacturer and downstream distributors. But the Internet is also disrupting the traditional "vertical" and "horizontal" categories. A restriction may be nominally vertical insofar as it expresses contractual terms only between an upstream and downstream firm, and yet have the effect of softening competition horizontally by reducing the incentives of competitors to lower prices. The downstream firm may therefore play a role in coordinating role in reducing upstream competition.

Such concerns have been raised particularly with respect to the use of Most Favored Nations ("MFN"), "parity," "best price," or meeting competition clauses by online platforms that aggregate sales of multiple different sellers' products. For example, suppose an online platform requires every vendor listed on its site to make its best price available on that site. While such a restriction sounds nominally pro-consumer insofar as it ostensibly brings lower prices to that platform, its actual effect may be to homogenize prices across all platforms selling that vendor's product and hence to establish a price floor rather than a price ceiling.

In 2015, the International Competition Network issued a Special Project Report on Online Vertical Restraints. ICN2015 Special Project Report on Online Vertical Restraints, available at: *http://www.icn2015.com.au/download/ICN2015-special-project-online-vertical-restraints.pdf*. It found that 47% of national competition authorities considered online MFNs concerning and identified a number of investigations opened by national competition authorities. Reflecting the perspective of these competition authorities, the ICN identified the following potential problems with the use of MFNs in online vertical agreements:

- disincentivising new market entry as potential new entrants are restricted from accessing lower prices with which to grow market share;

- artificially protecting a platform acting as an intermediary from direct selling by the supplier;

- softening competition between platforms, which can lead to higher fees imposed upon retailers and consequently higher prices paid by consumers; and

- facilitating collusion between platforms by reducing incentives to deviate from a collusive agreement on platform fees.

The hotel industry in Europe has been a particular focus of these enforcement actions. In December of 2014, the European Commission announced the launch of market tests in antitrust investigations by the French, Swedish and Italian competition authorities in the online hotel booking sector. The three national competition authorities expressed concerns that so-called "parity clauses" in contracts between the online travel agent Booking.com and hotels had anticompetitive effects. The parity clauses—often referred to as MFN or most favored nation clauses—obliged the hotel to offer Booking.com the same or better room prices as the hotel made available on all other online and offline distribution channels. The national authorities worried that these clauses might restrict competition between Booking.com and other online travel agents ('OTAs') and hinder new booking platforms from entering the market.

To alleviate these concerns, Booking.com offered commitments that were market tested and subsequently approved by the three national competition agencies. The commitments prevented Booking.com from requiring hotels to offer better or equal room prices via Booking.com than they do via competing OTAs. In addition, under the commitments Booking.com cannot prevent hotels from offering discounted room prices provided that these are not marketed or made available to the general public online. The discounted prices can be offered online to members of a hotel's loyalty scheme and/or via offline channels (e g direct emails, telephone and walk-in bookings).

Booking.com was a case in which the European Commission allowed national competition authorities to take the lead in resolving an arguably pan-European competition problem, because of the peculiarity of local effects. Most often, however, issues of competition in cyberspace overlap national boundaries. See European Commission Press Release, MEX/15/4819 (Apr. 21, 2015).

Some national authorities have gone even further in curtailing vertical restrictions in hotel booking. The German Bundeskartellamt has been particularly active in this area. In 2013, it led the way by prohibiting HRS, an OTA competitor of Booking.com, from enforcing any of its MFN clauses. Bundeskartellamt Case B9–66/10 of 20 December 2013. Then, following the European Commission's acceptance of Booking.com's commitments following the French, Swedish, and Italian investigations, the Bundeskartellamt went further and prohibited Booking.com from preventing hotels from offering their own rooms more cheaply on the hotel's own website than on Booking.com. Andreas Mundt, President of the Bundeskartellamt, explained the decision as follows:

> These so-called narrow best price clauses also restrict both competition between the existing portals and competition between the hotels themselves. Firstly they infringe the hotels' freedom to set prices on their own online sales channels. There is little incentive for a hotel to reduce its

prices on a hotel booking portal if at the same time it has to display higher prices for its own online sales. Secondly, it still makes the market entry of new platform providers considerably difficult. The 'best price' clauses barely provide an incentive for the hotels to offer their rooms on a new portal cheaper if they cannot implement these price reductions on their own websites as well. There is no apparent benefit for the consumer.

Narrow "best price" clauses of Booking.com also anticompetitive, *http://www.bundeskartellamt.de/SharedDocs/Meldung/EN/ Pressemitteilungen/2015/23_12_2015_Booking.com.html.*

In May 2016, the Dusseldorf Higher Regional Court rejected Booking.com's application for an interim injunction, thus preserving the Bundeskartellamt's decision pending litigation. As of this writing, the Bundeskartellamt's decision remains subject to appellate review. There is little doubt, however, that European competition authorities will continue to challenge aggressive use of MFNs to limit online competition.

H. PAY-FOR-DELAY SETTLEMENTS IN THE PHARMACEUTICAL INDUSTRY

Many complex issues arise at the intersection of competition law and intellectual property law—patent law in particular, although copyright, trademark, and trade secrecy law are sometimes implicated as well. An important current example, which has received intensive scrutiny in various jurisdictions, involves allegedly collusive "pay-for-delay" agreements between branded and generic pharmaceutical companies that keep the generic off the market for some period of time.

The legal issues are complicated, involving the interaction of patent law, food and drug regulatory law, and antitrust law, but the basic antitrust theory is simple. When a generic enters the market, the branded firm loses large sums of money in two ways. First, it loses many sales to the generic rival. Second, the price of the generic drug will be significantly lower than the price of the branded drug, so the branded firm may have to sell its own drugs at a significantly lower price.[1] The branded firm would obviously rather avoid generic

---

[1] This is a simplification of the actual economics. Upon generic entry, the price of the branded drug may actually increase, since only brand-sensitive buyers, who have less elastic demand, may continue to buy the branded version. So, upon generic entry, many branded firms begin to offer an "authorized generic" that competes with their own branded drug.

competition, so if it could lawfully pay the generic not to enter, it would have a clear incentive to do so. The generic would be happy not to enter if the payment from the branded firm were greater than the profits the generic would make by entering. Since the branded firm would make monopoly profits if it did not face competition and lose those profits if it did, both the branded and generic firm could be better off if the branded firms shared some of its monopoly profits with the generic in exchange for the generic's agreement not to enter. Consumers, of course, would lose.

On the other hand, if the branded company has valid patent rights, the generic arguably should not be in the market and the branded's monopoly profits are the unavoidable cost of stimulating innovation. Also, the law generally wants to encourage settlements and avoid protracted and costly litigation. Finally, there is some literature suggesting that "pay for delay" settlements may actually encourage more generic entry in the long run.

Beginning in 2008, the European Commission began to take an active interest in pay-for-delay agreements, issuing a series of reports on the practice and actively monitoring any pay-for-delay agreements affecting the European market. In 2010, the Commission opened an investigation of the Danish pharmaceutical firm Lundbeck for allegedly paying rival generic companies to delay production of generic versions of the anti-depressant medication Citalopram. In 2012, it issued a Statement of Objections, eventually resulting in a €93.8 million fine on Lundbeck and fines totaling €52.2 million against several generic manufacturers.

While the *Lundbeck* case was being appealed to the General Court, in 2013 and 2014, the Commission fined companies in two other pay-for-delay investigations—one concerning fentanyl, a painkiller and the other concerning perindopril, a cardiovascular medicine. The Fentanyl Decision was not appealed. Several appeals concerning the perindopril decision (*Servier*) are pending before the General Court as of this writing. They are likely to be influenced by the General Court's decision in *Lundbeck*, rendered on September 8, 2016.

H. LUNDBECK A/S

Case T–472/13, EU:T:2016:449 (European General Court 2016)

[Citalopram is a blockbuster antidepressant medicine and was Lundbeck's best-selling product at the relevant time. After Lundbeck's underlying patent for the citalopram molecule expired, it only held a number of related process patents which provided a more limited protection. Producers of cheaper, generic versions of citalopram were preparing for market entry. One of them had actually started selling its own generic version of citalopram and several other producers had made serious preparations to do so. Prices of generic citalopram dropped on average by 90% in the UK compared to Lundbeck's previous price level following wide-spread generic market entry.

In 2002, the generic producers agreed with Lundbeck not to enter the market in return for substantial payments and other inducements from Lundbeck amounting to tens of millions of euros. The Commission found particularly significant internal documents referring to a "club" being formed and "a pile of $$$" to be shared among the participants. It held these pay-for-delay agreements to be restrictions of competition by object within the meaning of Article 101(1) of the TFEU].

Law

[88] *The first plea in law, alleging errors of law and of assessment in that the contested decision considered that the generic undertakings and Lundbeck were at least potential competitors at the time the agreements at issue were concluded.*

[89] The applicants submit that the contested decision misinterprets the relevant case-law on establishing whether an agreement restricts potential competition, which presupposes the existence of real concrete possibilities of entering the market in the absence of the agreement, and they maintain that the Commission disregarded essential facts in that respect. * * *

B   Applicable principles and case-law

1.   The concept of potential competition

[98] It must be noted, first of all, that, having regard to the requirements set out in Article 101(1) TFEU regarding effect on trade between Member States and repercussions on competition, that provision applies only to sectors open to competition.

[99] According to the case-law, the examination of conditions of competition on a given market must be based not only on existing competition between undertakings already present on the relevant market but also on potential competition, in order to ascertain whether, in the light of the structure of the market and the economic and legal context within which it functions, there are real concrete possibilities for the undertakings concerned to compete among themselves or for a new competitor to enter the relevant market and compete with established undertakings.

100   In order to determine whether an undertaking is a potential competitor in a market, the Commission is required to determine whether, if the agreement in question had not been concluded, there would have been real concrete possibilities for it to enter that market and to compete with established undertakings. Such a demonstration must not be based on a mere hypothesis, but must be supported by factual evidence or an analysis of the structures of the relevant market. Accordingly, an undertaking cannot be described as a potential competitor if its entry into a market is not an economically viable strategy.

101 It necessarily follows that, while the intention of an undertaking to enter a market may be of relevance in order to determine whether it can be considered to be a potential competitor in that market, nonetheless the essential factor on which such a description must be based is whether it has the ability to enter that market.

102 It should, in that regard, be recalled that whether potential competition—which may be no more than the existence of an undertaking outside that market—is restricted cannot depend on whether it can be demonstrated that that undertaking intends to enter that market in the near future. The mere fact of its existence may give rise to competitive pressure on the undertakings currently operating in that market, a pressure represented by the likelihood that a new competitor will enter the market if the market becomes more attractive.

103 Moreover, it also follows from the case-law that the very fact that an undertaking already present on the market seeks to conclude agreements or to establish information exchange mechanisms with other undertakings which are not present on the market provides a strong indication that the market in question is not impenetrable.

104 Although it follows from that case-law that the Commission may rely inter alia on the perception of the undertaking present on the market in order to assess whether other undertakings are potential competitors, nevertheless, the purely theoretical possibility of market entry is not sufficient to establish the existence of potential competition. The Commission must therefore demonstrate, by factual evidence or an analysis of the structures of the relevant market, that the market entry could have taken place sufficiently quickly for the threat of a potential entry to influence the conduct of the participants in the market, on the basis of costs which would have been economically viable.* * *

115 The applicants submit that the contested decision is vitiated by an error in law in that it takes the view that the launch of medicinal products that infringe third parties' intellectual property rights is the

expression of potential competition under Article 101 TFEU. Basing the existence of potential competition on the hypothesis of the launch of generic medicinal products on the market, with the risk of facing infringement proceedings on the basis of those third parties' patents, is incompatible with the protection conferred on patents and the exclusive rights to which they give rise. Article 101 TFEU protects only lawful competition, which cannot exist where an exclusive right, like a patent, precludes market entry, in law or in fact.

[117] The Court notes that the specific purpose of industrial property is, inter alia, to ensure that the patentee, in order to reward the creative effort of the inventor, has the exclusive right to use an invention with a view to manufacturing industrial products and putting them into circulation for the first time, either directly or by the grant of licences to third parties, as well as the right to oppose infringements.

[118] However, the case-law in no way excludes the application of Article 101(1) TFEU to settlement agreements that may be concluded in relation to patents. On the contrary, if follows from the case-law that, although the existence of rights recognised under the industrial property legislation of a Member State is not affected by Article 101(1) TFEU, the conditions under which those rights may be exercised may nevertheless fall within the prohibitions contained in that article. This may be the case whenever the exercise of such a right appears to be the object, the means or the consequence of an agreement, decision or concerted practice.

[119] Likewise, according to the case-law, although the Commission is not competent to determine the scope of a patent, it may not refrain from all action when the scope of the patent is relevant for the purposes of determining whether there has been an infringement of Articles 101 TFEU and 102 TFEU. The Court of Justice has also held that the specific subject matter of the patent cannot be interpreted as also affording protection against actions brought in order to challenge the patent's validity, in view of the fact that it is in the public interest to eliminate any obstacle to economic activity which may arise where a patent was granted in error.

[120] In the present case, the applicants' argument is based on the erroneous premiss that, first, the generic undertakings undoubtedly infringed the applicants' patents and, secondly, those patents would certainly have withstood the claims of invalidity that would have been raised by the generic undertakings in infringement actions.

[121] Whilst patents are indeed presumed valid until they are expressly revoked or invalidated by a competent authority or court, that presumption of validity cannot be equated with a presumption of

illegality of generic products validly placed on the market which the patent holder deems to be infringing the patent.

122 As the Commission rightly points out, without this being called into question by the applicants, in the present case it was for the applicants to prove before the national courts, in the event that generics entered the market, that those generics infringed one of their process patents, since an 'at risk' entry is not unlawful in itself. Moreover, in the context of an infringement action brought by Lundbeck against the generic undertakings, those undertakings could have contested the validity of the patent on which Lundbeck relied by raising a counter-claim. Such claims occur frequently in patent litigation and lead, in numerous cases, to a declaration of invalidity of the process patent relied on by the patent holder. Thus, it can be seen from the evidence . . . that Lundbeck itself estimated the probability that its crystallisation patent would be held invalid at 50 to 60%.

123 In addition, it is clear from the contested decision that, in order to establish the existence of potential competition in the present case, the Commission relied on the case-law established in the judgments in *European Night Services and Others* v *Commission* , and *Visa Europe and Visa International Service* v *Commission*, according to which it must be examined whether, given the structure of the market and the economic and legal context within which it functions, there are real concrete possibilities for the undertakings concerned to compete among themselves or for a new competitor to enter the relevant market and compete with established undertakings.

124 In that respect, . . . it must be found that the Commission did not commit an error in considering that Lundbeck's process patents did not necessarily constitute insurmountable barriers for the generic undertakings, which were willing and ready to enter the citalopram market, and which had already made considerable investments to that end at the time the agreements at issue were concluded.

125 It is indeed possible that, in certain cases, the applicants might have been successful before the competent courts and obtained injunctions or damages against the generic undertakings. However, it can be seen from the evidence in the contested decision as regards each of the generic undertakings that that possibility was not perceived at the time as a sufficiently credible threat to them.

126 In addition, it was not at all certain that the applicants would have actually initiated litigation in the event that generics entered the market. The contested decision indeed acknowledges that the applicants had put in place a general strategy consisting in threatening infringement actions or bringing such actions on the

basis of their process patents. Nevertheless, any decision to bring an action depended on the applicants' assessment of the probability that an action would be successful and that a marketed generic product would be held to be infringing.

128 It must therefore be found, as the Commission did. . . , that in general the generic undertakings had several routes—constituting real concrete possibilities—to enter the market at the time the agreements at issue were concluded. Those possible routes included, inter alia, launching the generic product 'at risk', with the possibility of having to face proceedings brought by Lundbeck.

129 That possibility represents the expression of potential competition, in a situation such as that in the present case where Lundbeck's original patents, concerning both the citalopram API and the cyanation and alkylation processes, had expired and where there were other processes allowing the production of generic citalopram that had not been found to infringe other Lundbeck patents, which the applicants themselves acknowledged in their reply to the statement of objections. In addition, the steps taken and investments made by the generic undertakings in order to enter the citalopram market before concluding the agreements at issue, as set out by the Commission in the contested decision as regards each of the generic undertakings the existence of which has not been contested by the applicants—show that they were ready to enter the market and to accept the risks involved in such an entry.

132 [T]he applicants are not correct in their submission that the Commission disregarded the presumption of validity of their patents and the related intellectual property rights by characterising the 'at risk' entry of generic undertakings to the market as the expression of potential competition between Lundbeck and those undertakings in the present case.* * *

[The Court then found that the contested decision sufficiently found that, absent the challenged agreements, the generics could have found ways to manufacture a generic form of citalopram using non-infringing processes and enter the market].

A   Analysis relating to the existence of a restriction of competition 'by object' in the contested decision

332 The Commission considered, in the contested decision, that the agreements at issue constituted a restriction of competition 'by object', for the purpose of Article 101(1) TFEU by relying, in that respect, on a series of factors relating to the content, the context and the purpose of those agreements.

333 It therefore found that the fact that Lundbeck's original patents had expired before the conclusion of the agreements at issue, but that it had obtained—or was about to obtain—several process patents at the time those agreements were concluded, including the crystallisation patent, was a significant element of the economic and legal context in which the agreements at issue were concluded. The Commission took the view, however, that a patent did not grant the right to limit the commercial autonomy of parties by going beyond the rights granted by that patent . . . .

334 It thus considered that although all patent settlements were not necessarily problematic from a competition law perspective, such agreements were problematic where they provided for the exclusion from the market of one of the parties, which was at the very least a potential competitor of the other party, for a certain period, and where they were accompanied by a transfer of value from the patent holder to the generic undertaking liable to infringe that patent ('reverse payments').

335 It can also be seen from the contested decision that, even if the restrictions set out in the agreements at issue fell within the scope of the Lundbeck patents—that is to say that the agreements prevented only the market entry of generic citalopram deemed to potentially infringe those patents by the parties to the agreements and not that of every type of generic citalopram—they would nevertheless constitute restrictions on competition 'by object', since, inter alia, they prevented or rendered pointless any type of challenge to Lundbeck's patents before the national courts, whereas, according to the Commission, that type of challenge is part of normal competition in relation to patents.

336 In other words, according to the Commission, the agreements at issue transformed the uncertainty in relation to the outcome of such litigation into the certainty that the generics would not enter the market, which may also constitute a restriction on competition by object when such limits do not result from an assessment, by the parties, of the merits of the exclusive right at issue, but rather from the size of the reverse payment which, in such a case, overshadows that assessment and induces the generic undertaking not to pursue its independent efforts to enter the market. * * *

349 It must be recalled that the Commission considered, in the contested decision, that the fact that the restrictions contained in the agreements at issue had been obtained through significant reverse payments was decisive for the legal assessment of those agreements . . . .

350 The contested decision nevertheless acknowledges that the existence of a reverse payment in the context of a patent settlement is not always problematic, particularly when (i) that payment is linked to the strength of the patent, as perceived by each of the parties, (ii) it is necessary in order to find an acceptable and legitimate solution in the eyes of the two parties and (iii) it is not accompanied by restrictions intended to delay the market entry of generics. It thus took as an example the company Neolab, with which Lundbeck had also concluded a settlement agreement, which was not considered to be problematic—even though it involved a reverse payment—since that payment to Neolab had been made in exchange for a commitment on Neolab's part not to seek damages before the competent courts and Lundbeck had agreed to not bring any claims under its patents during a certain period. In that case, the actual object of the reverse payment was to settle a dispute between the parties, without, however, delaying the market entry of generics.

352 However, where a reverse payment is combined with an exclusion of competitors from the market or a limitation of the incentives to seek market entry, the Commission rightly took the view that it was possible to consider that such a limitation did not arise exclusively from the parties' assessments of the strength of the patents but rather was obtained by means of that payment, constituting, therefore, a buying-off of competition.

353 The size of a reverse payment may constitute an indicator of the strength or weakness of a patent, as perceived by the parties to the agreements at the time they were concluded, and of the fact that originator undertaking was not initially convinced of its chances of succeeding in the event of litigation. Similarly, the Supreme Court of the United States has also held that the presence of a significant reverse payment in a patent settlement agreement can provide a workable surrogate for the weakness of a patent, without a court having to carry out a detailed analysis of the validity of that patent. Moreover, the applicants . . . seem to acknowledge that, the higher the originator undertaking estimates the chances of its patent being found invalid or not infringed, and the higher the damage to the originator undertaking resulting from successful generic entry, the more money it will be willing to pay the generic undertakings to avoid that risk.

354 It must be noted, in that respect, that the Commission did not find, in the contested decision, that all patent settlement agreements containing reverse payments were contrary to Article 101(1) TFEU; it found only that the disproportionate nature of such payments, combined with several other factors—such as the fact that the amounts of those payments seemed to correspond at least to the

profit anticipated by the generic undertakings if they had entered the market, the absence of provisions allowing the generic undertakings to launch their product on the market upon the expiry of the agreement without having to fear infringement actions brought by Lundbeck, or the presence, in those agreements, of restrictions going beyond the scope of Lundbeck's patents—led to the conclusion that the agreements at issue had as their object the restriction of competition, within the meaning of Article 101(1) TFEU, in the present case.

355 It must be found, therefore, that the Commission did not err in considering, in the contested decision, that the very existence of reverse payments and the disproportionate nature of those payments were relevant factors in establishing whether the agreements at issue constituted restrictions of competition 'by object' for the purpose of Article 101 TFEU in that, by those payments, the originator undertaking provided an incentive to the generic undertakings not to continue their independent efforts to enter the market.

———————

The *Lundbeck* court relied on the US Supreme Court's decision in *FTC v.* Actavis, 133 S. Ct. 2223 (2013), in holding that the structure of a reverse payment settlement—particularly the presence of a large and otherwise unexplained reverse payment—could be instructive in determining whether the reverse payment was intended to quash competition or instead served some legitimate purpose. *Actavis* resolved a longstanding dispute in the US as to the appropriate treatment of reverse payment settlements. A few lower courts viewed such agreements as akin to naked market division agreements and held them *per se* illegal under Section 1 of the Sherman Act. Another line of cases, which before *Actavis* acquired majority status in the lower courts, held pay-for-delay settlements lawful so long as they fell within the exclusionary scope of the patent. In 2013, the US Supreme Court finally weighed into the controversy, rejecting both per se illegality and the scope of the patent test and holding reverse payment settlements subject to rule of reason analysis. The Court held:

> In sum, a reverse payment, where large and unjustified, can bring with it the risk of significant anticompetitive effects; one who makes such a payment may be unable to explain and to justify it; such a firm or individual may well possess market power derived from the patent; a court, by examining the size of the payment, may well be able to assess its likely anticompetitive effects along with its potential justifications without litigating the validity of the

patent; and parties may well find ways to settle patent disputes without the use of reverse payments.

Despite holding rule of reason analysis applicable, the Court provided relatively few signals as to how such analysis should be conducted. For example, although suggesting that courts need not conduct a detailed review of the strength of the branded firm's patent infringement claim that precipitated the settlement, the Court recognized that some direct or indirect inquiry into "the patent's weakness" might be required. In light of *Actavis,* lower courts are sorting through the methodological questions that both per se illegality and the scope of the patent test had avoided.

Notes and Questions

1.   *Lundbeck* and *Actavis* differ insofar as *Lundbeck* treats pay-for-delay settlements as restrictions of competition "by object," whereas *Actavis* holds them subject to rule of reason analysis. Despite these apparent differences in juridical classification, one might ask whether the form of the analysis differs considerably between the two opinions. Further exposition of the legal tests in coming years may tell.

2.   Although certain aspects of "pay-for-delay" are jurisdiction-specific due to differing pharmaceutical regulations and patent laws, the core issue resonates around the world. In 2014, there were media reports that Competition Commission of India had opened an investigation of "pay-for-delay" patent settlements between US and India pharmaceutical companies engaged in litigation in India. Do you think that competition law can provide a general framework for addressing pay-for-delay issues, or are the issues so bound up in other facets of a jurisdiction's regulatory and economic practices that general answers are unavailing?

I.   JOINT VENTURES

1.   Substantive Rules and Analysis

Joint ventures ("JVs"), like mergers, raise important questions of competition law because of their tendency to create efficiencies and market power simultaneously. Imagine, for example, that two competitors create a research and development joint venture that permits the two companies to pool personnel, patents, and economic resources to create a better product. At the same time, however, the fact of the joint venture reduces competition between the two firms, and perhaps even creates market power—the power to charge a higher price. How should competition law assess the joint venture? Ordinarily, competition law analysis of joint ventures asks two sorts of questions: (1) should the joint venture be permitted at all, or should it rather be prohibited because any efficiencies are overshadowed by anticompetitive effects; and (2) assuming that the joint venture is permitted, are any restrictions it places on competition among the joint venturers more restrictive than necessary to allow the JV to function?

a.   Should the JV Be Permitted?

Although regulators often decline to challenge *the fact* of joint ventures, preferring to challenge their structure or bylaws, in some instances joint ventures themselves are unlawful because they unduly restrict competition. In November of 2008, Yahoo! And Google were forced to abandon an advertising joint venture after the Justice Department made clear that it would challenge the joint venture as monopolistic. Then, on July 29, 2009, Yahoo! and Microsoft announced their plan to form a 10-year joint venture. Under the terms of the deal, Yahoo! licensed Microsoft its existing search engine technology but relied on Microsoft for future software development in the search engine business, even while retaining its own distinctive customer basis. Yahoo manages search-related advertising for both companies. Yahoo! keeps 88% of search and ad revenues from its own websites (subject to re-pricing after five years) and Microsoft keeps 100% of corresponding revenues from Microsoft websites.

Microsoft and Yahoo! justified their proposed joint venture as combining the forces of two struggling search engine companies to keep pace with Google, the industry leader. Google had a 65% share of the search-ad market, whereas Yahoo! and Microsoft together had only a combined 28% share. Regulators in Washington and Brussels ultimately chose not to challenge the deal, apparently finding the prospect of a Microsoft-Yahoo alliance a procompetitive counterweight to the growing power of Google.

A proposed 2010 joint venture for iron ore production in Western Australia between BHP Billiton and Rio Tinto's raised big issues around the globe. With an estimated value of approximately $116 billion, the parties estimated that the JV would generated synergies that would have helped cut costs by about $10 billion. But competition authorities in the European Commission, Australian Competition and Consumer Commission, Japan Fair Trade Commission, Korea Fair Trade Commission, and the German Bundeskartellamt all voiced concerns, leading the parties to abandon the deal.

The analysis of the Japan Fair Trade Commission ("JFTC") was typical. The JFTC notified the parties that the JV would substantially restrain competition in the field of the production and sale of lumps and fines of iron ores in the worldwide seaborne market. The JFTC applied Article 10 of the AMA. This article applies to stock acquisition and usually comes into play as to full mergers. However, once Article 10 is applied to a case, the difference between full merger and a JV is not significant because the ultimate standard, in either case, is whether the challenged activity "substantially restrains competition in the field." Like its peer authorities in Asia and Europe, the JFTC found that the joint venture would substantially restrain competition in the market for iron ore production.

Sometimes, authorities around the world differ as to whether a JV should be permitted to operate. In 2014, three of the major shipping companies—MSC, CMA CGM, and Maersk Line—entered into a long-term operational vessel sharing agreement, the so-called "P3 Alliance." The purported aim of the joint venture was to make container shipment more efficient and improve service quality for the shippers due to more frequent and reliable services. The putative joint venturers announced the following expected benefits of the collaboration:

- Operational efficiencies due to improved port productivity, network optimization and cargo consolidation

- More direct services due to more port pair connections

- Increased flexibility due to the combined capacity of P3 making it easier to increase or move capacity to meet short-term, sudden changes in demand

- Cost savings and environmental benefits

Nonetheless, the shipping companies had a history of collusive or collusive-like behavior, including making regular, simultaneous, and close to identical price increase announcements, which led to an investigation by the European Commission. Antitrust: Commission opens proceedings against container liner shipping companies, *http://europa.eu/rapid/press-release_IP-13-1144_en.htm*. Some observers viewed the P3 alliance as little more than a cover for collusive behavior.

After reviewing the JV, the US Maritime Commission and the European Commission decided not to challenge the arrangement. But, on June of 2014, the Chinese Ministry of Commerce ("MOFCOM") surprised many observers by informing the parties that it would oppose the JV based on merger provisions in China's Anti-Monopoly Law. The parties subsequently abandoned plans for the 3P Alliance.

Although some observers criticized MOFCOM's decision as out of step with competition law globally, the shipping trade has remained subject to antitrust concerns even in light of the 3P Alliance's failure. In 2016, the European Commission reached a settlement with the shipping industry in which the companies agreed to discontinue their practice of advance rate publication. And, in March of 2017, the United States Department of Justice announced that it had issued subpoenas to the executives of five leading container lines on apparent suspicion of collusion. Was MOFCOm correct to see the 3P Alliance as another industry measure to facilitate collusion?

b. Are the JV's Restrictions on Competition Excessive?

Even if a JV is lawful in essence, there remains the question of whether its bylaws, terms, and other contractual provisions or understandings unduly restrict competition. Many cases have been brought challenging JV practices as unnecessarily anticompetitive.

An initial juridical question concerns the mode of analysis to be applied. In the US, all activities within the scope of an otherwise lawful joint venture are subject to the rule of reason. *Texaco, Inc. v. Dagher*, 547 U.S. 1 (2006). But, in some cases, that begs the question of what it means for activities to be within scope of a lawful joint venture.

Take, for example, the U.S. FTC's enforcement action against Polygram and Warner Communications concerning the two music labels' agreement to jointly distribute "The Three Tenors III" in 1998. Warner had distributed Three Tenors I in 1994, and Polygram had distributed Three Tenors II in 1990. (The concerts were set to coincide with the World Cup). Warner and Polygram entered into a separate agreement to suspend, for ten weeks, advertising and discounting on the two earlier Three Tenors materials. The FTC challenged this arrangement as something akin to per se illegal. *Polygram Holding, Inc. v. FTC*, 416 F.3d 29 (2005). Polygram and Warner protested that the agreement to discontinue promotion of Three Tenors I and II was not a "naked" price fixing agreement but rather reasonably ancillary to the promotion of Three Tenors III, since absent that restriction, the joint venturers would have faced incentives to free ride on one another's investments in the promotion of Three Tenors III. The US Court of Appeals for the D.C. Circuit found this justification unconvincing, holding that "a restraint cannot be justified solely on the ground that it increases the profitability of the enterprise that introduces the new product, regardless whether that enterprise is a joint venture or a solo undertaking." Id. at 38.

The South African Competition Tribunal took a similar approach in 2015 when it found that two shipping companies in a joint venture, Nison Yupen Kaisha Shipping Logistics and BLG Logistics, had used to the JV to exchange competitively significant information on matters outside the scope of the JV. Acknowledging that it is "difficult to divorce the conduct of the Parties outside the Joint Venture, with their conduct within the Joint Venture," the Tribunal nonetheless found that the parties had colluded on information exchange outside the scope of the joint venture and imposed a fine of 3.5% of the JV's turnover in the prior year.

India's Competition Act approaches the analysis of restraints by joint ventures as follows. Section 3(3) of the Act states that a specified list of horizontal agreements are "presumed to have an appreciable effect on competition." The list includes those "directly or indirectly determin[ing] purchase or sale price," "limit[ing] or control[ing] production, supply, markets, technical development, investment or provision of service," "shar[ing] the market or source of production or provision of services," and "directly or indirectly result[ing] in bid rigging or collusive bidding." These descriptions literally apply to most joint ventures, therefore Section 3(3) adds the following caveat: "Provided that nothing contained in this sub-section shall apply to any agreement entered into by way of joint ventures if such agreement increases efficiency in production, supply, distribution, storage, acquisition or control of goods or provision of services." The effect of the statute is that efficiency-enhancing joint ventures are lawful.

Joint ventures sometimes raise issues of collusion (the joint venture might be a cover for a cartel or induce cartel-like behavior) and sometimes raise issue of exclusion (the joint venture anticompetitively excludes rivals). In the latter set of cases, the joint venture's activities may be analyzed under "abuse of dominance" or "abuse of joint dominance" principles in addition to or instead of restraint of trade principles. Consider, for example, the consent order entered in the Canadian *Interac* case, *The Director of Investigation and Research v. Bank of Montreal*, CT–85/2 (1995). Interac Association was an electronic network created by nine of Canada's leading banks. The association provided financial services to the member banks, such as shared cash dispensing (i.e., ATM) services and electronic funds transfers at point of sale outlet that allowed consumers to make purchases at participating retail outlets using Interac branded debit cards. The Canadian Competition Bureau charged the nine banks and Interac with abuses of a joint dominant position for putting in place a structure and membership criteria that discriminated against non-financial institutions, imposed excessively high fees for new members wanting to join Interac, and unnecessarily limiting the services that could be provided through the network. The Bureau and the defendants entered into a consent order whereby Interac would become available to other market participants on a non-discriminatory basis and would agree to cease engaging in a list of anticompetitive practices.

2. Procedural Rules

Should competition authorities seek to screen the thousands of horizontal agreements that will arise every year to catch those that are anticompetitive? One approach is to require that all parties to horizontal agreements file their agreements with the competition authorities for a determination whether they are anticompetitive or not. There are some obvious downsides to such an approach, illustrated by Europe's history with "block exemptions" under Article 101.

The institutional and federalism issues with the notification system are discussed in greater detail in Chapter 7, so we will provide just a brief sketch here. As previously noted, the structure of Article 101 provides a broad prohibition on competition-limiting horizontal agreements in Articles 101(1), subject to an exemption for competition and efficiency-enhancing agreements in Article 101(3). In 1962, the European Council promulgated Regulation 17, which required that agreements within the scope of now Article 101(1) had to be notified to the Commission; no Article 101(3) exemptions could be granted until notification was filed. Parties to agreements that did not infringe Article 101(1) were entitled to "negative clearance," a statement by the Commission that the agreements did not violate the Treaty.

The obvious problem with such a system is that the filing and individual review of tens of thousands of commercial contracts would clog the system. So the Commission proceeded under a "block exemption" system. The Commission issued "block exemptions" for certain categories of generally benign contractual provisions, and parties that limited themselves to these clauses were automatically exempt from the filing requirement and Article 101 liability.

Still, notification was required as to many rather routine business contracts, and by the late 1990s competition officials were worried that the notification and prior approval system was becoming too cumbersome and time-intensive to manage. The result—described in greater detail in Chapter 7—was Regulation 1/2003, printed in Appendix 2, which radically altered the procedures for regulatory review of competition-restricting agreements and granted a far greater role to the competition authorities and courts of the Member States. In a nutshell, effective May 2004, Regulation 1 abolished the notification requirement and made Article 101(3) directly effective, so that national competition authorities and courts, as well as the Commission, may decide whether agreements fulfill the requirements of Article 101(3).

A number of other jurisdictions have experimented with mandatory notification rules, often having copied the European system. Block exemptions still exist for many transactions; they have been liberalized, so that it is easier to receive their benefits.

Some jurisdictions are experimenting with a form of voluntary notification that may provide some interesting possibilities for orderly review of joint venture agreements. Take, for example, Singapore 2006 Competition Act. In addition to a pre-Regulation 1 EU-style exemption procedure, the Competition Act allows voluntary submission to the Competition Commission by parties who are concerned that their agreement could be deemed to violate Section 34 of the Competition Act, which prohibits agreements prohibiting or distorting competition. The parties may seek either "guidance" under Section 43 or "decision" under Section 44. In either case, the parties are relieved of the possibility of penalties between the date they file their petition with the Commission and the date specified in the Commission's "guidance" or "decision." The difference between guidance and decision is that in guidance cases the Commission merely specifies a view as to whether the agreement probably infringes Section 34 and in a decision case it actually makes a decision with legal effect.

The Commission's first Section 44 decision came on February 13, 2007 on an application from Qantas Airways and British Airways. Notification for Decision by Qantas Airways and British Airways of their Restated Joint Services Agreement, No. CCS 400/002/06 (Feb. 13, 2007). The parties entered into a Joint Services Agreement that provided for coordination of their business activities in relation to routing, fares, frequencies, aircraft types, production specifications, aircraft configurations, connection requirements, and other aspects of operations, sales, and marketing. The parties submitted that their joint venture was necessary for them to remain competitive on the "Kangaroo route" between Australia and Europe, via Asia or the Middle East. After extensive review of the facts, the Commission found that the agreement fell within the ambit of Section 34, as an agreement that potentially prohibited or distorted competition, but nonetheless brought about net economic benefits to Singapore and hence was "excluded from the Act." It therefore stated that it would take no action against the agreement, but cautioned that it might change if its position if the market facts materially changed or it learned that the information on which it had relied was incorrect, false, or misleading.

Both the US and the EU have informal procedures for seeking agency input into the legality of joint venture agreements. In the US, the primary method is through the process of seeking a business review letter from the Antitrust Division. 28 C.F.R. ¶ 50.6. Parties seeking a business review on a joint venture must supply information in a long list of categories, including documents discussing the competitive state of the market and lists of the top ten customers for any products that the joint venture may offer. The Division attempts to answer requests within sixty to ninety days. Its review letters do not offer immunity from suit, "approve" the joint venture, or have any formal effect on the ability of private parties to sue. Still, receipt of a business review letter provides a significant layer of comfort to the joint venturers.

The European Commission follows a more limited procedure in issuing guidance letters in response to request for the Commission's opinion about case-specific application of Articles 101 or 102. Commission Notice on informal guidance relating to novel questions concerning Articles [101 and 102] of the EC Treaty that raise in individual cases. O.J. C 101 (April 27, 2004).

Both the US and the EU have adopted special provisions to encourage research and development joint ventures, which have the potential to encourage quicker, cheaper, and higher quality innovation. In the US, the National Cooperative Research Act ("NCRA") of 1984, amended in 1993, 15 U.S.C. § 4301, states that research and development joint ventures are to be adjudged under the rule of reason and not as per se illegal. That much is not terribly significant in the modern era, since joint ventures are not judged under the per se rule. A provision with perhaps more importance is that any joint venture notified under the Act cannot subject the parties to treble damages liability—but only single damages—even if the agreement is later found anticompetitive. For its part, the European Commission has adopted a block exemption for research and development joint ventures. Commission Regulation 2659/2000, O.J. L 304/7 (Dec. 5, 2000). Article 1 of the Regulation declares exempt joint R&D and joint exploitation of the results of such R&D, and necessary ancillary restraints, as long as the parties market share does not exceed 25% and does not include any blacklisted clauses. Moreover, to qualify for block exemption, several additional conditions must be satisfied: (1) each party must have access to the results in order to further its research; (2) the supplying partner, in the event of specialisation not entailing joint distribution, must fulfill orders for suppliers from other partners; and (3) in the event of joint exploitation the results must be IP-protected and substantially contribute to technical or economic progress and be decisive for the manufacture of the contract products or the application of contract processes.

Notes and Questions

1.   How are the competition authorities likely to address cases like Yahoo/Microsoft in the future? In a market increasingly dominated by one larger player like Google, should any joint venture between the market's smaller firms that has the potential of creating a counterweight to the dominant firm be viewed with approval? Does it matter that the Internet is uniquely dynamic in terms of the development of the relevant technology, social practices, and economic structures (*i.e.*, advertising-driven versus subscription driven models)? In dynamic markets, is it better to insist on technological competition among even the smaller firms, on the theory that technological advances created by the spur of competition may allow even smaller firms to break out quickly and overtake the industry leader?

2.   In view of the fact that a notification system can be cumbersome, what are the advantages of a voluntary notification system that allows parties to seek review of their joint venture agreements on a prospective basis? Should such systems be formal and determinative, as in Singapore's example, or informal and qualified, as with the U.S. example?

Chapter 4

VERTICAL RESTRAINTS

A. INTRODUCTION

Vertical restraints can harm competition by excessive foreclosures that block access to important inputs or outlets, by increasing barriers to entry and facilitating cooperative behavior among competitors at a horizontal level, and by increasing unilateral power to exploit. There are some recurrent differences among jurisdictions. Principal among these are: 1) Goals—Is the jurisdiction concerned about market integration, as is Europe, and therefore worried about restraints that impair the flow of goods across borders? Is the jurisdiction worried about chilling opportunities of firms to compete on the merits or to get a fair deal, as in many Asian and developing countries? 2) Facts, evidence and burdens, including different default presumptions.

The United States law approaches vertical restraints with a permissive stance: If a restraint is vertical it is probably efficient and good for the market (it is assumed); vertical restraints are often explained as attempts by producers to protect them and their distributors from free riding discounters who undermine investments in service.

The European Union, while recognizing possible efficiency properties of vertical restraints, is less permissive. It fears that such restraints may impede free movement or free access and thereby hurt the market (including consumers). It is less confident that inefficient free riding exists to any worrisome extent. In many developing countries, business firms' efficient access to inputs and to final markets is already impaired by corruption, privilege, and the scarcity of capital, and often the authorities are suspicious that vertical restraints will exploit the country's small suppliers or clog the path to mobility and growth.

Vertical restraints can also have a special importance in jurisdictions such as Japan, whose vertical restraint rules include the rhetoric of equality of opportunity and correction of unequal bargaining power. Moreover, developing countries can be particularly concerned with buyer power, exercised along the vertical chain, which is used to exploit powerless farmers and other small producers.

Therefore, as you approach the materials on vertical restraints from various jurisdictions, you should ask yourself: What does this jurisdiction mean by harm to competition? What does it mean when it says that a restraint forecloses the market, or a part of the market, to outsiders? If the restraint is an exclusionary restraint: When is foreclosure significant, and when is it anticompetitive? When does significant foreclosure shift the burden to the firm imposing the restraint, and can that firm argue that the foreclosure was not anticompetitive or only that the restraint was justified, and justified by what? Which jurisdictions pay attention to these questions, and which jurisdictions are likely to apply a very broad brush, quickly concluding, for example, that a restraint forecloses competitors and it anticompetitive?

Exclusionary vertical restraints may also constitute monopolistic abuses. We have studied exclusive dealing by dominant firms in Chapter 2. Conceptually, the same forms of analysis are applicable.

B. EUROPEAN UNION

1.   Introduction

We revert to the structure of the Treaty. Article 101(1) of the Treaty on the Functioning of the European Union (TFEU), ex Article 81(1) of the Treaty of Rome, prohibits restraints that distort competition. Distortion is broadly construed. Under Article 101(2), agreements that distort competition are void. Under Article 101(3), subparagraph (1) can be declared inapplicable if (in inexact summary) the agreement is on balance procompetitive or efficient.

Enforcement of the competition provisions of the Treaty had to await an implementing regulation, which was adopted in 1962. The first implementing regulation (17/62, or Regulation 17) effectively required all agreements within now Article 101(1) to be notified to the European Commission. The Commission would then determine whether indeed the agreement fell within 101(1). If not it would get a negative clearance. If so the Commission would determine whether the agreement was entitled to an "exemption" under 101(3), which would normally be granted, if at all, with conditions and for a period of years.

In the first several years of competition law enforcement, so many thousands of agreements were filed with the European Commission that the workload and backlog became untenable, and the Commission began to adopt "block exemptions" for agreements of certain sorts that were not problematic. If the agreement fell within a block exemption, it would not be necessary for the parties to file; the block exemption regulation gave them their exemption from the date of the agreement. Most of the block exemptions were tailored for common forms of vertical agreement; for example, automobile dealership agreements. The block exemption regulation specified necessary clauses, permissible clauses, and forbidden clauses, and if the agreement incorporated all necessary and permissible clauses, and no impermissible clauses, it was entitled automatically to the benefits of the block exemption. Block exemptions were adopted for exclusive distribution, exclusive purchasing, motor vehicle distribution, and technology licensing agreement, among others. Successive block exemption regulations became more and more regulatory, with more and more mandates as to what the parties must do and must not do to get the benefit of the exemption. If an agreement did not come within a block exemption, the parties could still apply for an individual exemption, but that process was a long one and the benefits of the block exemption were so attractive that parties often simply molded their agreement to fit what became known as "a straight jacket."

In the 1990s, the Competition Directorate of the Commission began to rethink the institutional design. Vertical restraints began to be recognized as less harmful and more helpful to competition and efficiency than originally perceived. Economic learning was pointing the way to a more liberal approach. The Commission embarked on a process of "modernisation" to reduce regulatory burdens and introduce a more economic approach. The process began with vertical restraints. The vertical block exemptions were simplified, with fewer mandatory and prohibitory clauses, and guidelines for analysis were adopted. The requirement for notification in order to obtain an exemption was abolished for vertical agreements in 1999. A new general vertical distribution block exemption and guidelines became effective in 2000, with a term of ten years. The ten years are now expiring, and the Competition Directorate has promulgated a draft successor block exemption and guidelines for vertical distribution restraints. It has also prepared a draft successor regulation for motor vehicle distribution.

Meanwhile, effective in 2004, the Commission adopted even more thorough-going reform, applicable to both agreements and abuse of dominance. It adopted Regulation 1/2003, printed in Appendix 3, which totally abolished the notification and exemption system (for horizontal as well as vertical restraints), and devolved powers to the Member States to apply (now) Article 101 TFEU in its entirety. Pursuant to the reform, national courts and national competition authorities, as well as the Commission, can decide that an agreement fulfills the requirements of Article 101(3) and that therefore the prohibition of 101(1) does not apply.

Given the system of block exemptions and of individual exemptions imposing conditions that were usually consented to, relatively few vertical cases have gone to the courts. But several have done so.

We present here cases on tight territorial restraints, parallel imports and exports and dual pricing across borders, resale price maintenance, tying and other foreclosures, and materials on block exemptions and guidelines. Also referenced are technology transfer agreements, which are the subject of a 2004 block exemption.

2. Territorial Restraints, Parallel Imports and Exports, and Dual Pricing

The first important competition law case to reach the Court of Justice is the case of *Consten and Grundig*, wherein Grundig, a German manufacturer of GINT electronics products, tried unsuccessfully to defend its distribution system. Grundig had appointed a distributor for each Member State. Each distributor was forbidden to sell GINT product outside of its territory, and each was empowered to defend its territory from GINT products coming in from the outside (parallel imports).

Consten and Grundig

Grundig, a manufacturer of radios, television sets, tape recorders, and dictating machines, appointed Consten to be its exclusive distributor in France. Consten and Grundig wanted Consten to be the only distributor of the Grundig products in France; thus, they wanted Consten to be able to exclude from France Grundig products put on the market in other Member States. To achieve this result they relied on the French trademark law as well as the distribution contract. Since French case law held that only the owner of a trademark was entitled to enforce the trademark, the parties agreed that Consten should apply for and own the trademark GINT (Grundig International). Consten and Grundig agreed that if Consten should cease to be the distributor for Grundig in France, Consten would assign the mark to Grundig. Grundig made similar exclusive distribution and trademark arrangements with each of its distributors in the other countries.

Before the EU Treaty was adopted, the Western European nations had high tariffs and low quotas. Quotas would prevent goods from moving across national borders. The EU Treaty required the Member States to remove the quotas and tariffs in the internal market. In the spring of 1961 when French quotas ended, the French discounter UNEF began purchasing GINT television sets, tape recorders, dictaphones and other electronic equipment from German wholesalers (who had also accepted export bans) and selling them in competition with Consten's dealers in France. Consten sued UNEF under French law for unfair competition and trademark infringement, alleging that UNEF knew that the sales to it were in breach of contract and that the sales by UNEF undermined Consten's contract. Thereupon, UNEF petitioned the Commission to declare the agreement between Consten and Grundig void under Article [101](2). Meanwhile, Regulation 17 came into effect, and Grundig filed a notification of its distribution agreement and sought an exemption under Article [101](3). In justification of the territorial division, Grundig argued that German buyers were familiar with its product and French buyers were not, and that the French market demanded a higher level of service and promotion than the German market. Moreover, it noted that Consten was responsible for guarantees, repair, customer service, accepting advance orders, maintaining stocks, and advertising in France. Grundig argued that cheap imports from Germany would undercut Consten's incentives to fulfill these duties, and that Consten's failure to fulfill its duties would undercut the brand's reputation and frustrate sales. Grundig depicted the market for electronics products as highly competitive, with prices dropping steadily even before UNEF's appearance on the French market.

The Commission refused to consider evidence of competition from competitors of Grundig, and denied Grundig's request for an exemption under Article [101](3). It observed that prices for Grundig products in France were substantially higher than prices for Grundig products in Germany. Consten and Grundig sued the Commission, seeking annulment of its decision.

Consten and Grundig appealed to the Court of Justice. (The Court of First Instance had not yet been established.) For all appeals to the Court of Justice, an advocate general is appointed. The advocate general, who has the status of a judge of the Court, reads all submissions, hears the argument, and writes an advisory opinion for the benefit of the Court. Karl Roemer was the advocate general in *Consten and Grundig*.

Advocate General Karl Roemer criticized the Commission for considering only competition among distributors of Grundig's products and not competition from competing brands. He said:

[I]t is not proper if the Commission proceeds in such a manner that from the very outset it considers *exclusively* the last-mentioned internal competition [intraband competition] and completely neglects in its considerations the competition with similar products [interbrand competition]. In fact, it is conceivable that the competition between different products or, to be more precise, between different producers is so severe as not to leave any room worth mentioning for what was called internal competition in a product (possibly with regard to price and service). . . . Rightfully, it was . . . therefore incumbent on the Commission to make a survey of the entire competition situation. . . . Such a survey of the effects on the market would possibly have led to a result favorable for the plaintiffs. . . . Such more favorable result might have been possible in view of the relatively small share of Grundig in the French market for tape recorders and dictating machines (roughly 17 percent)—as far as we know, the Commission has not conducted any investigations concerning other products—or in view of the plaintiffs' allegation that the markets for television sets . . . and for transistor sets showed so severe a competition of various, and sometimes very strong producers of the Community and of third countries that it repeatedly became necessary to reduce the prices of Grundig sets considerably.

Because of the Commission's narrow concept of the term "restraint of competition," no such survey was made, and the Court of Justice in its proceeding cannot be obligated to make the survey itself belatedly. The only thing we can do in this situation is to find that the results which the Commission arrived at in the investigation of the criterion "restraint of competition" must be deemed to lack a sufficient foundation and must for that reason be rejected.

The Court of Justice disagreed. Here are excerpts from its judgment.

CONSTEN AND GRUNDIG v. COMMISSION

Case C–56/64, EU:C:1966:41 (European Court of Justice 1966)

. . . [A]n agreement between producer and distributor which might tend to restore the national divisions in trade between Member States might be such as to frustrate the most fundamental objectives of the Community. The Treaty, whose preamble and content aim at abolishing the barriers between States, and which in several provisions gives evidence of a stern attitude with regard to their reappearance, could not allow undertakings to reconstruct such barriers. Article [101](1) is designed to pursue this aim, even in the case of agreements between undertakings placed at different levels in the economic process. . . .

The applicants and the German Government maintain that since the Commission restricted its examination solely to Grundig products the decision was based upon a false concept of competition and of the rules on prohibition contained in Article [101](1), since this concept applies particularly to competition between similar products of different makes. . . .

The principle of freedom of competition concerns the various stages and manifestations of competition. Although competition between producers is generally more noticeable than that between distributors of products of the same make, it does not thereby follow that an agreement tending to restrict the latter kind of competition should escape the prohibition of Article [101](1) merely because it might increase the former.

Besides, for the purpose of applying Article [101](1), there is no need to take account of the concrete effects of an agreement once it appears that it has as its object the prevention, restriction or distortion of competition.

Therefore the absence in the contested decision of any analysis of the effects of the agreement on competition between similar products of different makes does not, of itself, constitute a defect in the decision.

It thus remains to consider whether the contested decision was right in founding the prohibition of the disputed agreement under Article [101](1) on the restriction on competition created by the agreement in the sphere of the distribution of Grundig products alone. The infringement which was found to exist by the contested decision results from the absolute territorial protection created [by] the said contract in favour of Consten on the basis of French law. The applicants thus wished to eliminate any possibility of competition at the wholesale level in Grundig products in the territory specified in the contract essentially by two methods.

First, Grundig undertook not to deliver even indirectly to third parties products intended for the area covered by the contract. The restrictive nature of that undertaking is obvious if it is considered in the light of the prohibition on exporting which was imposed not only on Consten but also on all the other sole concessionnaires of Grundig, as well as the German wholesalers. Secondly, the registration in France by Consten of the GINT trade mark, which Grundig affixes to all its products, is intended to increase the protection inherent in the disputed agreement, against the risk of parallel imports into France of Grundig products, by adding the protection deriving from the law on industrial property rights. Thus no third party could import Grundig products from other Member States of the Community for resale in France without running serious risks. . . .

The situation as ascertained above results in the isolation of the French market and makes it possible to charge for the products in question prices which are sheltered from all effective competition. In addition, the more producers succeed in their efforts to render their own makes of product individually distinct in the eyes of the consumer, the more the effectiveness of competition between producers tends to diminish. Because of the considerable impact of distribution costs on the aggregate cost price, it seems important that competition between dealers should also be stimulated. The efforts of the dealer are stimulated by competition between distributors of products of the same make. Since the agreement thus aims at isolating the French market for Grundig products and maintaining artificially, for products of a very well-known brand, separate national markets within the Community, it is therefore such as to distort competition in the Common Market.

It was therefore proper for the contested decision to hold that the agreement constitutes an infringement of Article [101](1). No further considerations, whether of economic data (price differences between France and Germany, representative character of the type of appliance considered, level of overheads borne by Consten) or of the corrections of the criteria upon which the Commission relied in its comparisons between the situations of the French and German markets, and no possible favourable effects of the agreement in other respects, can in any way lead, in the face of abovementioned restrictions, to a different solution under Article [101](1). . . .

The applicants maintain more particularly that the criticized effect on competition is due not to the agreement but to the registration of the trade-mark in accordance with French law, which gives rise to an original inherent right of the holder of the trade-mark from which the absolute territorial protection derives under national law.

Consten's right under the contract to the exclusive use in France of the GINT trade-mark, which may be used in a similar manner in other countries, is intended to make it possible to keep under surveillance and to place an obstacle in the way of parallel imports. Thus, the agreement by which Grundig, as the holder of the trade-mark by virtue of an international registration, authorized Consten to register it in France in its own name tends to restrict competition. . . .

That agreement therefore is one which may be caught by the prohibition in Article [101](1). The prohibition would be ineffective if Consten could continue to use the trade-mark to achieve the same object as that pursued by the agreement which has been held to be unlawful.

[The Court did not interfere with the Commission's decision to deny an exemption under Article [101](3). It acknowledged that Consten, as Grundig's distributor in France, was required to perform various obligations such as to accept advance orders and to provide warranty and after-sales service. The Court stated that territorial protection would give the parties to the agreement an advantage in *their* production and distribution activities. But, it said, to qualify for exemption the "improvement must in particular show appreciable objective advantages of such a character as to compensate for the disadvantages which they cause in the field of competition," and must be indispensable. The argument that every "improvement as conceived by the parties to the agreement must be maintained intact" . . . "not only tends to weaken the requirement of indispensability but also among other consequences to confuse solicitude for the specific interests of the parties with the objective improvements contemplated by the Treaty."]

Notes and Questions

1.   In designing the distribution system that became the subject of this case, Grundig appointed an exclusive distributor for each territory. Grundig agreed that it, itself, would not distribute GINT-brand product in the assigned territory; and each distributor agreed with Grundig to sell the GINT product in its territory (and more, as we note below). These obligations are the essence of an exclusive distribution agreement. The producer says to the distributor: I appoint you and you alone to distribute my product in this territory.

The Commission does not regard such an agreement as within Article 101(1). Why?

2.   The additional obligations on both Consten and Grundig are the key obligations in the case. What were these additional obligations and why were they of particular concern? Did they lessen competition? Clearly by definition, they lessened intrabrand competition. Did they lessen interbrand competition?

3.   How does the rule of *Consten and Grundig* increase market integration? Be specific; state more than: More GINT product will move across Member State lines.

4.   Why do you suppose that German prices were lower than French prices for the GINT product? Why might you want to know? Is the answer relevant to (a) whether the restraint is caught by Article 101(1)? (b) whether the restraint is entitled to an exemption under Article 101(3)?

5.   Note the relationship between French trademark law and EU competition law. Which has the upper hand? Is the Court's answer consistent with Article 345 TFEU, ex 295 ECT, preserving for the Member States the right to define property within their states? Did the Court properly resolve the tension between free movement/competition principles, and the right to exclusive control over one's intellectual property?

6.   In the light of *Consten and Grundig,* can an agreement that absolutely eliminates parallel imports ever be justified as essential for improvement of production or distribution?

7.   *Consten and Grundig* may remind you of *United States v. Arnold, Schwinn & Co.*, 388 U.S. 365 (1967) (overruled in 1977). In *Schwinn*, a manufacturer's imposition of absolute territorial restrictions on its distributors was held to be illegal on its face. The Court held that a manufacturer could not lawfully assign an exclusive territory to a distributor, require the distributor to stay within the territory, and agree to keep parallel imports out of the territory. The *Schwinn* decision protected the autonomy of distributors to sell where they wished. The existence of robust interbrand competition was irrelevant. The US Supreme Court overruled *Schwinn* in *Sylvania. Continental T.V., Inc. v. GTE Sylvania Inc.*, 433 U.S. 36 (1977). In *Sylvania* the Supreme Court observed that non-price restraints imposed by a manufacturer on its own distributors can improve the efficiency of the manufacturer and stimulate competition among brands, and it held that improvements in interbrand competition (e.g., competition between Sylvania and Sony TVs) can outweigh harm from the decrease in intrabrand competition (i.e., competition among Sylvania's own distributors). In *Leegin Creative Leather Products v. PSKS*, 551 U.S. 877 (2007), considered in greater detail below, the US Court went further. Overruling the *per se* rule against resale price maintenance agreements, the Court held that protecting interbrand competition is "the primary purpose of the antitrust laws." According to the Court, competition among producers (interbrand competition) is likely to force manufacturers to behave competitively and to assure that vertical restraints on distributors are efficient and procompetitive. Can *Consten and Grundig* be reconciled with this perspective? Is the difference justified by context? Consider that the European judicature might value intrabrand competition more

than the American judicature, and also that market integration is not a goal of US antitrust. We will consider below how *Consten and Grundig* might have been affected by the European program of modernisation.

Volkswagen

In the 1990s, when the Italian lire was depressed, Volkswagen, maker of Volkswagens and Audis, tried to protect the German and Austrian dealers in its network from a shift of buyers to Italy. It entered into agreements with its subsidiaries and Italian dealers, imposing supply quotas and a bonus system designed to induce the Italian dealers to sell at least 85% of their available vehicles in Italy. The Commission severely fined Volkswagen for partitioning national markets. The Commission describes the case as follows, in the 1998 Competition Policy Report:

Opening-up of markets

68 The Commission has always kept a close eye on distribution agreements and their restrictive effects in so far as they hindered intra-Community trade. Some exclusive distribution agreements lead to the setting-up of watertight national distribution networks. In particular, clauses which prohibit distributors from supplying customers based outside the contract territory. In this way, national markets are artificially isolated from one another. The Commission considers that measures should be taken to combat this situation, not just in order to re-establish effective competition between economic operators but also in order to promote market integration. In practice, the compartmentalisation of national markets prevents price convergence within the Union and restricts access by consumers to the markets with the lowest prices. With the creation of the single currency, price differentials will be obvious because they will be expressed in euro. They will be increasingly viewed as unjustified by ordinary people, who will want to derive full benefit from economic and monetary union.

69 In 1998 the Commission clearly demonstrated its determination to promote the opening-up of markets, a prime example of this being the *Volkswagen* case [O.J. L 124, 23/4/98]. Since 1995 the Commission had received numerous complaints from European consumers, particularly from Germany and Austria, who had been confronted with various difficulties when attempting to buy new Volkswagen and Audi cars in Italy. These consumers wanted to benefit from the price differentials between their Member State and Italy, where prices were particularly advantageous. Following a series of inspections at the offices of Volkswagen AG, Audi AG and Autogerma SpA, which is a subsidiary of Volkswagen and the official importer for both makes in Italy, and at the offices of a number of

Italian dealers, the Commission concluded that Europe's largest motor-manufacturing group had been pursuing a market-partitioning policy in the Union for about 10 years. Volkswagen AG had systematically forced its dealers in Italy to refuse to sell Volkswagen and Audi cars to foreign buyers, especially from Germany and Austria. The Commission fined Volkswagen ECU 102 million, the largest fine ever imposed on a single company."

COMMISSION OF THE EUROPEAN COMMUNITIES, XXVIIIST REPORT ON COMPETITION POLICY 1998, ¶¶ 68–69 (1999).

The Court of First Instance confirmed the existence and gravity of the infringements. It reduced the fine to 90 million euros since the Commission had overstated the time period of the infringement; still the fine set a record at the time. *Volkswagen AG v. Commission*, Case T–62/98, EU:T:2000:180.

In what sense did the system of quotas and of bonuses based on sales in Italy "partition markets"? Should Volkswagen have been able to protect its German and Austrian dealers from the siphoning off of sales as a result of a bad exchange rate?

Volkswagen is one of several car brands that continued to be sold at widely varying prices in different Member States even after the introduction of the Euro. Fines have been imposed, also, on Opel, DaimlerChrysler, and Peugeot for employing distribution systems that deprived consumers of their "single-market right" to buy a car wherever the price is lowest.

In the *Peugeot* case (CFI 2009), Peugeot employed two strategies:

"Firstly, part of the remuneration of Peugeot's Dutch dealers was made dependent on the final destination of the vehicle, and discriminated against sales to foreign consumers. In particular, performance bonuses were refused if dealers sold cars to non-Dutch citizens. Secondly, Automobiles Peugeot SA exercised, through Peugeot Nederland N.V, direct pressure on those dealers who were identified as having developed significant export activities, for example by threatening to reduce the number of cars supplied to them." See European Commission Press Release, MEMO/09/328 (July 9, 2009).

The infringement led to a fine of 44.55 million euros.

* * *

Consten and Grundig established that air-tight territorial distribution restraints at Member States borders are prohibited by

Article 101(1). Did it say or imply anything about treatment under Article 101(3)? After *Consten and Grundig,* such tight territorial restraints have been treated as hard core restraints. (But does this mean *per se*?) The successive block exemptions have retained the hard-core treatment, and an agreement cannot get the benefit of a block exemption if it contains a hard core restriction. Also after *Consten and Grundig,* rules were developed to allow manufacturers to assign territories to distributors and to allow the manufacturer to prohibit the distributor's active solicitation outside of its territory, but the manufacturer may not prohibit the distributor from making "passive sales" (accepting unsolicited bids from outside of the territory). See the block exemption and guidelines, discussed below. Are these wise rules? Do they differ from US law? Do they sufficiently recognize the procompetitive and efficiency properties of distribution restraints? Might a manufacturer need to prevent passive Internet sales in order to prevent destructive free riding on services provided by store-based sellers?

There is a companion to the *Consten and Grundig* rule as applied to exclusive territories. This is the rule against restraints on parallel (intrabrand) imports and exports (illustrated in *Volkswagen*). The rule against restraints on parallel imports and exports implies that the seller may not charge more for goods to be resold as exports than for the same product that is sold domestically. This rule against dual pricing poses challenges especially for pharmaceutical companies faced with capped prices in the domestic market and willing buyers at higher prices in neighboring markets. The unwavering rule against restraints on parallel imports was tested by GlaxoSmithKline.

GLAXOSMITHKLINE SERVICES UNLIMITED v. COMMISSION

Case T–168/01, EU:T:2006:265 (European General Court 2006), CFI
appeals dismissed, 6 Oct. 2009 (see CJEU judgment immediately below)

[Spanish legislation capped the price of pharmaceuticals sold to pharmacies and hospitals and covered by Spanish reimbursement rules. GlaxoSmithKline, a major pharmaceutical producer, made agreements with its wholesalers that for all other products (essentially, pharmaceuticals not for the domestic market), GSK would charge a price set by objective economic factors, and that this would be the price that GSK had initially proposed to the Spanish government as the reimbursement price plus a cost-of-living adjustment. These terms were specified in Clause 4 of the General Sales Conditions. The Commission found that the clause fell within Article 101(1) as a restriction by object, and that, despite GSK's efficiency and innovation justifications, the agreement was not entitled to an Article 101(3) exemption. In particular, the Commission discounted GSK's arguments and evidence as to the virtues and advantages of Clause 4. GSK asked the General Court to annul the Commission's decision. The General Court did so, on grounds of the Commission's "lack of serious examination" of GSK's efficiency and innovation arguments. The General Court held also that Clause 4 was not a restriction by object, for it could not be taken for granted, in this unusual market, that parallel trade would reduce prices and increase consumer welfare. Both parties appealed aspects of the judgment to the Court of Justice. We set forth below excerpts from the General Court judgment related to GSK's efficiency and innovation claims, which the Court of Justice upheld, and then we set forth excerpts from the CJEU judgment, largely confined to the CJEU holding that the restraint on parallel imports was a restraint by object even if it did not harm consumers.]

[295] In the light of the structure of GSK's arguments and also of the discussion of that point during the administrative procedure, the Decision could not avoid examining, first of all, whether parallel trade led to a loss in efficiency for the pharmaceutical industry in general, and for GSK in particular. . . .

[296] However, a comparison of the evidence provided by GSK with the other evidence invoked by the Commission in the Decision clearly reveals that in the medicines sector the effect of parallel trade on competition is ambiguous, since the gain in efficiency to which it is likely to give rise for intrabrand competition, the role of which is limited by the applicable regulatory framework, must be compared with the loss in efficiency to which it is likely to give rise for interbrand competition, the role of which is central.

[297] In those circumstances, the Commission could not refrain from examining, second, whether Clause 4 of the General Sales Conditions could enable GSK's capacity for innovation to be reinstated and thus could give rise to a gain in efficiency for interbrand competition.

[298] That, moreover, formed the very core of the prospective analysis which the Commission was under a duty to carry out in order to respond to GSK's request for an exemption. According to the consistent case-law cited . . ., it is necessary to determine whether the agreement prohibited on account of the disadvantage which it represents for competition (Article [101](1) [TFEU] presents an advantage of such a kind as to offset that disadvantage (Article [101](3) [TFEU].

[299] The Commission was therefore still required to examine GSK's arguments relating to the advantages expected of Clause 4 of the

General Sales Conditions. In that regard, recital 156 to the Decision, the only recital susceptible of attesting to an examination on that point, indicates essentially:

> '[I]t is a matter of discretion for pharmaceutical companies to decide how much they wish to invest in R & D. Any savings they might hypothetically make by preventing parallel trade would therefore not automatically lead to higher R & D investments. It is conceivable that these savings might merely be added to the companies' profits. Obviously, the generation of extra profits alone cannot justify an exemption. In this regard, GSK's argument would mean that the first condition for [the application of Article 101(3) TFEU] would be fulfilled for every agreement that could be said to contribute to an increase in the revenues of a firm engaged in R & D. The condition would in any case be meaningless, since it is in the nature of any agreement restricting competition to be likely to increase a firm's earnings.'

300 However, GSK did not claim that the creation of additional profits would in itself justify an exemption. On the contrary, it maintained that parallel trade prevented it from making the profits necessary for the optimum financing of its R & D, that Clause 4 of the General Sales Conditions would enable it to increase its revenues and that it would have every interest, in the light of the fierce interbrand competition, of the central role played by innovation in that competition and of the methods of financing R & D, in investing a part of this surplus in R & D in order to overtake its competitors or to ensure that it would not be overtaken by them. In other words, it claimed that its General Sales Conditions should be exempted because they would have not merely the immediate effect of increasing its revenues, but above all the secondary effect of increasing its capacity for innovation. Furthermore, it maintained that that advantage must be compared with the fact that, when it was obtained by parallel traders, that surplus did not constitute an advantage, because, not being obliged to engage in genuine competition among themselves, the parallel traders reduced prices only to the extent necessary to attract retailers and therefore kept most of that surplus for themselves, as GSK again submitted at the hearing.

301 The Commission could not merely reject those arguments outright on the ground that the advantage described by GSK would not necessarily be achieved, as it did at recital 156 to the Decision, but was required, in accordance with the case-law, also to examine, as specifically as possible, in the context of a prospective analysis,

whether, in the particular circumstances of the case and in the light of the evidence submitted to it, it seemed more likely that the advantages described by GSK would be achieved or, on the contrary, that they would not. It was not entitled to consider, in a peremptory manner and without providing proper arguments, that the factual arguments and the evidence submitted by GSK must be regarded as hypothetical, as it maintained most recently at the hearing. * * *

303 It follows from the foregoing that the Decision is vitiated by a failure to carry out a proper examination, as the Commission did not validly take into account all the factual arguments and the evidence pertinently submitted by GSK, did not refute certain of those arguments even though they were sufficiently relevant and substantiated to require a response, and did not substantiate to the requisite legal standard its conclusion that it was not proved, first, that parallel trade was apt to lead to a loss in efficiency by appreciably altering GSK's capacity for innovation and, second, that Clause 4 of the General Sales Conditions was apt to enable a gain in efficiency to be achieved by improving innovation.

The balancing exercise * * *

306 . . . [T]he Commission's finding that Clause 4 of the General Sales Conditions restricts competition is well founded only in so far as it finds that Clause 4 has the effect of depriving final consumers of medicines reimbursed by a national sickness insurance scheme of the advantage which they would have derived, in regard to prices and costs, from the participation of the Spanish wholesalers in intrabrand competition on the markets of destination of the parallel trade from Spain.

307 Consequently, the Commission's conclusion that there is no need to carry out a balancing exercise, which would show in any event that the advantage associated with Clause 4 does not offset the disadvantage which it represents for competition, cannot be upheld. The Commission was required, first, to conduct an appropriate examination of GSK's factual arguments and evidence, in order to be in a position to carry out, second, the complex assessment necessary in order to weigh up the disadvantage and the advantage associated with Clause 4 of the General Sales Conditions.

Conclusion

308 It follows from the foregoing that the Commission could not lawfully conclude that, as regards the existence of a contribution to the promotion of technical progress, GSK had not demonstrated that the first condition for the application of Article [101](3) [TFEU] was satisfied. In those circumstances, there is no need to examine GSK's

arguments relating to a contribution to the improvement of the distribution of medicines.

c) Evidence of the advantage being passed on to the consumer, of the indispensability of Clause 4 of the General Sales Conditions and of the absence of the elimination of competition

309 As stated previously, it follows from the Decision and from the oral argument presented at the hearing that the summary conclusions which the Commission reached concerning the existence of a passing-on to consumers, the indispensability of Clause 4 of the General Sales Conditions and the absence of elimination of competition rest on the conclusion relating to the existence of a gain in efficiency.

310 In so far as that conclusion is vitiated by illegality, in that it concerns the existence of a contribution towards the promotion of technical progress, those conclusions are themselves invalid.

311 In so far as, when it examined whether Clause 4 of the General Sales Conditions would or would not eliminate competition for a substantial part of the products, the Commission further stated . . . that, in any event, for several of the leading products affected by the General Sales Conditions, GSK held substantial market shares (for example, for Zofran, Flixonase, Zovirax and Imigran) in one or more Member States, it remains necessary to review that assessment.

312 In that regard, it must be observed that the Commission acknowledged at the hearing that it had not really resolved the question of GSK's market power and further stated that it would have had to continue with the analysis in order to determine that point.

313 In fact, owing to the particular legal and economic context of the sector under consideration, the fact of holding substantial market shares, which, moreover, is limited to certain of the relevant products, of which the Commission provided only four examples, clearly does not in itself make it possible to conclude, in a convincing manner, that competition would be eliminated for a substantial part of the relevant products.

314 In effect, irrespective of the question of the definition of the relevant products market, which has been debated by the parties, a number of elements relied on by GSK during the administrative procedure, and then in its written submissions, prevent such a conclusion from being reached automatically.

315 In particular, GSK's argument . . .was not so irrelevant that the Commission could refrain from making it the subject of a specific

assessment under the fourth condition for the application of Article [101](3) [TFEU]. In effect, the fact that Clause 4 of the General Sales Conditions prevents the limited pressure which might exist, owing to parallel trade from Spain, on the price and the cost of medicines in the geographic markets of destination must be related to the facts, put forward by GSK and not disputed by the Commission, that competition by innovation is very fierce in the sector and that competition on price exists in another form, although by law it emerges only when, upon expiry of the patent, manufacturers of generic medicines are able to enter the market. In those circumstances, it was still necessary . . . to assess what form of competition must be given priority with a view to ensuring the maintenance of effective competition sought by Article 3(1)(g) EU [removed from Treaty to become Protocol 27] and Article [101 TFEU].

4.   Conclusion * * *

[317] Accordingly, the Decision must be annulled in so far as, in Article 2, it rejects GSK's request for an exemption.

GLAXOSMITHKLINE SERVICES UNLIMITED v. COMMISSION

Cases C–501/06 P, C–513/06 P, C–515/06 P, C–519/06 P, EU:C:2009:610
(European Court of Justice 2009)

* * *

[46] . . . [T]he Court of First Instance . . . ruled that the principal conclusion reached by the Commission, namely that Clause 4 of the agreement must be considered to be prohibited by Article [101(1) TFEU] in so far it has as its object the restriction of parallel trade, cannot be upheld. As the prices of the medicines concerned are to a large extent shielded from the free play of supply and demand owing to the applicable regulations and are set or controlled by the public authorities, it cannot be taken for granted at the outset that parallel trade tends to reduce those prices and thus to increase the welfare of final consumers. An analysis of the terms of Clause 4 of the agreement, carried out in that context, therefore does not permit the presumption that that provision, which seeks to limit parallel trade, thus tends to diminish the welfare of final consumers. In this largely unprecedented situation, it cannot be inferred merely from a reading of the terms of that agreement, in its context, that the agreement is restrictive of competition, and it is necessary to consider the effects of the agreement, if only to ascertain what the regulatory authority was able to apprehend on the basis of such a reading. * * *

[55] First of all, it must be borne in mind that the anti-competitive object and effect of an agreement are not cumulative but alternative conditions for assessing whether such an agreement comes within the scope of the prohibition laid down in Article [101(1) TFEU]. According to settled case-law . . ., the alternative nature of that condition, indicated by the conjunction 'or', leads first to the need to consider the precise purpose of the agreement, in the economic context in which it is to be applied. Where, however, the analysis of the content of the agreement does not reveal a sufficient degree of harm to competition, the consequences of the agreement should then be considered and for it to be caught by the prohibition it is necessary to find that those factors are present which show that competition has in fact been prevented, restricted or distorted to an appreciable extent. It is also apparent from the case-law that it is not necessary to examine the effects of an agreement once its anti-competitive object has been established. . . .* * *

[58] According to settled case-law, in order to assess the anti-competitive nature of an agreement, regard must be had inter alia to the content of its provisions, the objectives it seeks to attain and the economic and legal context of which it forms a part. . . . In addition, although the parties' intention is not a necessary factor in determining whether an agreement is restrictive, there is nothing prohibiting the Commission or the Community judicature from taking that aspect into account.

[59] With respect to parallel trade, the Court has already held that, in principle, agreements aimed at prohibiting or limiting parallel trade have as their object the prevention of competition. * * *

[61] The Court has, moreover, held in that regard, in relation to the application of Article [101 TFEU] and in a case involving the pharmaceuticals sector, that an agreement between producer and distributor which might tend to restore the national divisions in trade between Member States might be such as to frustrate the Treaty's objective of achieving the integration of national markets through the establishment of a single market. Thus on a number of occasions the Court has held agreements aimed at partitioning national markets according to national borders or making the interpenetration of national markets more difficult, in particular those aimed at preventing or restricting parallel exports, to be agreements whose object is to restrict competition within the meaning of that article of the Treaty.

[62] With respect to the Court of First Instance's statement that, while it is accepted that an agreement intended to limit parallel trade must in principle be considered to have as its object the restriction of

competition, that applies in so far as it may be presumed to deprive final consumers of the advantages of effective competition in terms of supply or price, the Court notes that neither the wording of Article [101(1) TFEU] nor the case-law lend support to such a position.

[63] First of all, there is nothing in that provision to indicate that only those agreements which deprive consumers of certain advantages may have an anti-competitive object. Secondly, it must be borne in mind that the Court has held that, like other competition rules laid down in the Treaty, Article [101 TFEU] aims to protect not only the interests of competitors or of consumers, but also the structure of the market and, in so doing, competition as such. Consequently, for a finding that an agreement has an anti-competitive object, it is not necessary that final consumers be deprived of the advantages of effective competition in terms of supply or price.

[64] It follows that, by requiring proof that the agreement entails disadvantages for final consumers as a prerequisite for a finding of anti-competitive object and by not finding that that agreement had such an object, the Court of First Instance committed an error of law.

[The Court proceeded to find that the CFI's error was harmless, since the CFI had found that the agreement fell within Article 101(1), albeit by reason of its effect. The Court of Justice then reviewed the Commission's claims of CFI error regarding the Article 101(3) analysis, and found them unfounded. The Commission had examined the inefficiency from loss of parallel trade "without deeming it necessary to examine whether it had also been demonstrated that Clause 4 of the agreement entailed a gain in efficiency." para. 156.]

Notes and Questions

1.   Explain why and how Clause 4 was a restriction by object even if it did not harm consumers. Does your answer reflect a major difference between US and EU competition law?

2.   When the Commission reconsiders the matter, what must GSK establish to entitle it to an exemption? What evidence should and must GSK introduce to show that it will be more inventive if it has the freedom to obtain higher prices on sales for export? In response, how can and should the Commission quantify the harm to competition that must be balanced against the gains in innovation? Is the Commission well placed to conduct the balancing exercise?

3.   Resale Price Maintenance

United States antitrust law long took a skeptical stance towards vertical restraints for many years. The case law was based on the premise that vertical restraints impair the give-and-take of the competition process and harm powerless market actors and consumers. US antitrust law condemned, *per se*, agreements between a manufacturer and a distributor as to the price, customers or territories at which, to whom, or where the distributor must sell.

But perspectives changed. Beginning in the 1970s, the Chicago School of economic analysis was ascendant in the courts. Chicago School scholars generally argued that RPM was often procompetitive and efficient. By 2007, the Supreme Court came around to this point of view, but over the strong dissent of four Justices.

LEEGIN CREATIVE LEATHER PRODUCTS, INC. v. PSKS, INC.

551 U.S. 877 (2007)

KENNEDY, J.:

* * *

A

Though each side of the debate can find sources to support its position, it suffices to say here that economics literature is replete with procompetitive justifications for a manufacturer's use of resale price maintenance. Even those more skeptical of resale price maintenance acknowledge it can have procompetitive effects.

The few recent studies documenting the competitive effects of resale price maintenance also cast doubt on the conclusion that the practice meets the criteria for a *per se* rule.

The justifications for vertical price restraints are similar to those for other vertical restraints. Minimum resale price maintenance can stimulate interbrand competition—the competition among manufacturers selling different brands of the same type of product— by reducing intrabrand competition—the competition among retailers selling the same brand. The promotion of interbrand competition is important because "the primary purpose of the antitrust laws is to protect [this type of] competition." A single manufacturer's use of vertical price restraints tends to eliminate intrabrand price competition; this in turn encourages retailers to invest in tangible or intangible services or promotional efforts that aid the manufacturer's position as against rival manufacturers. Resale price maintenance also has the potential to give consumers more options so that they can choose among low-price, low-service brands; high-price, high-service brands; and brands that fall in between.

Absent vertical price restraints, the retail services that enhance interbrand competition might be underprovided. This is because discounting retailers can free ride on retailers who furnish services and then capture some of the increased demand those services generate. Consumers might learn, for example, about the benefits of a manufacturer's product from a retailer that invests in fine showrooms, offers product demonstrations, or hires and trains knowledgeable employees. Or consumers might decide to buy the product because they see it in a retail establishment that has a reputation for selling high-quality merchandise. If the consumer can then buy the product from a retailer that discounts because it has not spent capital providing services or developing a quality reputation, the high-service retailer will lose sales to the discounter, forcing it to cut back its services to a level lower than consumers would otherwise prefer. Minimum resale price maintenance alleviates the problem because it prevents the discounter from undercutting the service provider. With price competition decreased, the manufacturer's retailers compete among themselves over services.

Resale price maintenance, in addition, can increase interbrand competition by facilitating market entry for new firms and brands. "[N]ew manufacturers and manufacturers entering new markets can use the restrictions in order to induce competent and aggressive retailers to make the kind of investment of capital and labor that is often required in the distribution of products unknown to the consumer." New products and new brands are essential to a dynamic economy, and if markets can be penetrated by using resale price maintenance there is a procompetitive effect.

Resale price maintenance can also increase interbrand competition by encouraging retailer services that would not be provided even absent free riding. It may be difficult and inefficient for a manufacturer to make and enforce a contract with a retailer specifying the different services the retailer must perform. Offering the retailer a guaranteed margin and threatening termination if it does not live up to expectations may be the most efficient way to expand the manufacturer's market share by inducing the retailer's performance and allowing it to use its own initiative and experience in providing valuable services.

B

While vertical agreements setting minimum resale prices can have procompetitive justifications, they may have anticompetitive effects in other cases; and unlawful price fixing, designed solely to obtain monopoly profits, is an ever-present temptation. Resale price maintenance may, for example, facilitate a manufacturer cartel. An unlawful cartel will seek to discover if some manufacturers are undercutting the cartel's fixed prices. Resale price maintenance could assist the cartel in identifying price-cutting manufacturers who benefit from the lower prices they offer. Resale price maintenance, furthermore, could discourage a manufacturer from cutting prices to retailers with the concomitant benefit of cheaper prices to consumers.

Vertical price restraints also "might be used to organize cartels at the retailer level." A group of retailers might collude to fix prices to consumers and then compel a manufacturer to aid the unlawful arrangement with resale price maintenance. In that instance the manufacturer does not establish the practice to stimulate services or to promote its brand but to give inefficient retailers higher profits. Retailers with better distribution systems and lower cost structures would be prevented from charging lower prices by the agreement

A horizontal cartel among competing manufacturers or competing retailers that decreases output or reduces competition in order to increase price is, and ought to be, *per se* unlawful. To the extent a vertical agreement setting minimum resale prices is entered upon to facilitate either type of cartel, it, too, would need to be held unlawful under the rule of reason. This type of agreement may also be useful evidence for a plaintiff attempting to prove the existence of a horizontal cartel.

Resale price maintenance, furthermore, can be abused by a powerful manufacturer or retailer. A dominant retailer, for example, might request resale price maintenance to forestall innovation in distribution that decreases costs. A manufacturer might consider it has little choice but to accommodate the retailer's demands for vertical price restraints if the manufacturer believes it needs access to the retailer's distribution network A manufacturer with market power, by comparison, might use resale price maintenance to give retailers an incentive not to sell the products of smaller rivals or new entrants. As should be evident, the potential anticompetitive consequences of vertical price restraints must not be ignored or underestimated.

[Having found both procompetitive and anticompetitive explanations for RPM, the Court concluded that rule of reason analysis was warranted. In an opinion by Justice Breyer, four Justices dissented. They argued *stare decisis*, the tendency of RPM to increase consumer prices, and judicial administrability counselled in favor of maintaining per se illegality for RPM].

Meanwhile, Europe condemned RPM agreements. In Europe, resale price maintenance agreements were held to fall categorically into Article 101(1) because they have the object to restrict competition (albeit intrabrand competition). RPM agreements are designated as a hard core violation by the vertical block exemption regulation and vertical guidelines. They may be entitled to an Article 101(3) exemption only in rare instances, as in the case of newspaper and periodical distribution where RPM constitutes "the sole means of supporting the financial burden resulting from the taking back of unsold copies . . . if the latter practice constitutes the sole method by which a wide selection of newspapers and periodicals can be made available to readers. . . ." The decision-maker "must take account of those factors. . . ." *SA Binon & Cie v. SA Agence et Messageries de la Presse*, Case 243/83, EU:C:1985:284, paras. 44–46.

Coincidentally with the decision in *Leegin*, the European Commission embarked on a process to reexamine its legislation on vertical restraints, which expired in May 2010. The legislation takes the form of a regulation adopting a block exemption, and accompanying guidelines. The block exemption exempts (automatically unless the exemption is withdrawn) vertical agreements where the parties have 30% or less of the market, subject to certain other conditions, unless the agreement contains a "hard core restriction." Minimum RPM is a hard core restriction. Commission Regulation 330/2010, art. 4(a), 2010 O.J. (L 102), *http:// eur-lex.europa.eu/legal-content/EN/TXT/PDF/?uri=CELEX:320 10R0330&from=EN*. An agreement containing a hard core restriction does not get the benefit of a block exemption. Until recently, a hard core restriction was very close to meaning illegal *per se*. The vertical guidelines accompanying the draft block exemption would now give the following guidance on resale price restrictions, minimum and maximum.

EUROPEAN COMMISSION NOTICE GUIDELINES ON VERTICAL RESTRAINTS (2010)
available at *http://ec.europa.eu/competition/antitrust/legislation/vertical.html*
(resale price maintenance)

* * *

2.10. Resale price restrictions

[223] As explained in section III.3, resale price maintenance (RPM), that is agreements or concerted practices having as their direct or indirect object the establishment of a fixed or minimum resale price or a fixed or minimum price level to be observed by the buyer, are treated as a hardcore restriction. Including RPM in an agreement

gives rise to the presumption that the agreement restricts competition and thus falls within Article 101(1). It also gives rise to the presumption that the agreement is unlikely to fulfil the conditions of Article 101(3), for which reason the block exemption does not apply. However, undertakings have the possibility to plead an efficiency defence under Article 101(3) in an individual case. It is incumbent on the parties to substantiate that likely efficiencies result from including RPM in their agreement and demonstrate that all the conditions of Article 101(3) are fulfilled. It then falls to the Commission to effectively assess the likely negative effects on competition and consumers before deciding whether the conditions of Article 101(3) are fulfilled.

[224] RPM may restrict competition in a number of ways. Firstly, RPM may facilitate collusion between suppliers by enhancing price transparency in the market, thereby making it easier to detect whether a supplier deviates from the collusive equilibrium by cutting its price. RPM also undermines the incentive for the supplier to cut its price to its distributors, as the fixed resale price will prevent it from benefiting from expanded sales. This negative effect is in particular plausible if the market is prone to collusive outcomes, for instance if the manufacturers form a tight oligopoly, and a significant part of the market is covered by RPM agreements. Secondly, by eliminating intra-brand price competition, RPM may also facilitate collusion between the buyers, i.e. at the distribution level. Strong or well organised distributors may be able to force/convince one or more suppliers to fix their resale price above the competitive level and thereby help them to reach or stabilise a collusive equilibrium. This loss of price competition seems especially problematic when the RPM is inspired by the buyers, whose collective horizontal interests can be expected to work out negatively for consumers. Thirdly, RPM may more in general soften competition between manufacturers and/or between retailers, in particular when manufacturers use the same distributors to distribute their products and RPM is applied by all or many of them. Fourthly, the immediate effect of RPM will be that all or certain distributors are prevented from lowering their sales price for that particular brand. In other words, the direct effect of RPM is a price increase. Fifthly, RPM may lower the pressure on the margin of the manufacturer, in particular where the manufacturer has a commitment problem, i.e. where he has an interest in lowering the price charged to subsequent distributors. In such a situation, the manufacturer may prefer to agree to RPM, so as to help it to commit not to lower the price for subsequent distributors and to reduce the pressure on its own margin. Sixthly, RPM may be implemented by a manufacturer with market power to foreclose smaller rivals. The increased margin that RPM may offer distributors, may entice the

latter to favour the particular brand over rival brands when advising customers, even where such advice is not in the interest of these customers, or not to sell these rival brands at all. Lastly, RPM may reduce dynamism and innovation at the distribution level. By preventing price competition between different distributors, RPM may prevent more efficient retailers from entering the market and/or acquiring sufficient scale with low prices. It also may prevent or hinder the entry and expansion of distribution formats based on low prices, such as price discounters.

225 However, RPM may not only restrict competition but may also, in particular where it is supplier driven, lead to efficiencies, which will be assessed under Article 101(3). Most notably, where a manufacturer introduces a new product, RPM may be helpful during the introductory period of expanding demand to induce distributors to better take into account the manufacturer's interest to promote the product. RPM may provide the distributors with the means to increase sales efforts and if the distributors in this market are under competitive pressure this may induce them to expand overall demand for the product and make the launch of the product a success, also for the benefit of consumers.* Similarly, fixed resale prices, and not just maximum resale prices, may be necessary to organise in a franchise system or similar distribution system applying a uniform distribution format a coordinated short term low price campaign (2 to 6 weeks in most cases) which will also benefit the consumers. In some situations, the extra margin provided by RPM may allow retailers to provide (additional) pre-sales services, in particular in case of experience or complex products. If enough customers take advantage from such services to make their choice but then purchase at a lower price with retailers that do not provide such services (and hence do not incur these costs), high-service retailers may reduce or eliminate these services that enhance the demand for the supplier's product. RPM may help to prevent such free-riding at the distribution level. The parties will have to convincingly demonstrate that the RPM agreement can be expected to not only provide the means but also the incentive to overcome possible free riding between retailers on these services and that the pre-sales services overall benefit consumers as part of the demonstration that all the conditions of Article 101(3) are fulfilled.

226 The practice of recommending a resale price to a reseller or requiring the reseller to respect a maximum resale price is covered

---

* This assumes that it is not practical for the supplier to impose on all buyers by contract effective promotion requirements. . . .

by the Block Exemption Regulation when the market share of each of the parties to the agreement does not exceed the 30% threshold, provided it does not amount to a minimum or fixed sale price as a result of pressure from, or incentives offered by, any of the parties. For cases above the market share threshold and for cases of withdrawal of the block exemption the following guidance is provided.

[227] The possible competition risk of maximum and recommended prices is that they will work as a focal point for the resellers and might be followed by most or all of them and/or that maximum or recommended prices may soften competition or facilitate collusion between suppliers.

[228] An important factor for assessing possible anti-competitive effects of maximum or recommended resale prices is the market position of the supplier. The stronger the market position of the supplier, the higher the risk that a maximum resale price or a recommended resale price leads to a more or less uniform application of that price level by the resellers, because they may use it as a focal point. They may find it difficult to deviate from what they perceive to be the preferred resale price proposed by such an important supplier on the market.

[229] Where appreciable anti-competitive effects are established for maximum or recommended resale prices, the question of a possible exemption under Article 101(3) arises. For maximum resale prices, the efficiency described in paragraph 107, point 6 (avoiding double marginalisation), may be particularly relevant. A maximum resale price may also help to ensure that the brand in question competes more forcefully with other brands, including own label products, distributed by the same distributor.

Notes and Questions

1.   Compare the European block exemption and guidelines with the US *Leegin* case. What different perceptions do you observe about the possible harms and possible benefits of RPM? Is the structure of analysis, including burdens of proof, likely to lead to different results? What would be the outcome of the *Leegin* case (agreement not to discount a minor brand of five belts) in each jurisdiction? Is one approach more likely to benefit consumers than the others?

2.   Although some commentators believe that *Leegin* killed off the possibility of a successful challenge to RPM in the US, a few post-*Leegin* challenges have been successful. In 2015, the retailer Cosco brought a challenge to Johnson & Johnson's RPM policies with respect to contact lenses. The case was voluntarily dismissed in 2016, but only after J&J agreed to abandon the practice.

3.   *Leegin* creates a natural experiment for economists: Does RPM in fact increase consumer prices? One of the first large scale post-*Leegin* empirical studies—undertaken, perhaps ironically, by economists at the University of Chicago, found that RPM increased consumer prices and reduced sales output. Alexander MacKay & David Aron Smith, *The Empirical Effects of Resale Price Maintenance, https://papers.ssrn.com/ sol3/papers.cfm?abstract_id=2513533.* Should findings like these motivate courts, agencies, or legislatures to prohibit RPM categorically? Or are such results consistent with RPM incentivizing greater quality, including more service, and hence not necessarily anti-consumer?

4.   Although *Leegin* articulates the federal antitrust standard making RPM subject to rule of reason rather than *per se* treatment, not all US states follow that precedent under their state antitrust laws. The Attorneys General of New York, Illinois, and Michigan have taken the view that RPM remains illegal in those states, and precedent in Maryland and California suggests that it may be unlawful per se in those states as well. The Kansas Supreme Court applied per se illegality to RPM, *O'Brien v. Leegin Creative Leather Products,* Inc., 294 Kan. 318 (2012), but that result was subsequently overturned by Kansas legislation. K.S.A. § 50–163. Does it make sense for states to experiment with a different rule than *Leegin,* or is a uniform national rule important?

5.   On August 1, 2013, the Shanghai High People's Court delivered a much-anticipated decision concerning RPM in the case of *Rainbow v. Johnson & Johnson (J&J).* J&J sells medical equipment, including suture threads for surgeries, in China. Beijing Ruibang Yonghe Science & Technology Company ("Rainbow") distributed J&J's sutures for 15 years. In 2008, however, Rainbow sold below the minimum distribution price stipulated in the parties' distribution agreement, and J&J thereafter terminated Rainbow as a distributor. Article 14 of the Chinese Anti-Monopoly Law prohibits undertakings from fixing the prices of products resold to third parties, and hence appeared to prohibit RPM categorically. Nonetheless, the High Court held that RPM agreements are not categorically illegal but subject to rule of reason analysis including inquiry into: (1) the competitiveness of the relevant market; (2) the defendant's market power; (3) the defendant's purpose in implementing the RPM; and (4) the competitive effect of the RPM. Applying this test, the High Court found the RPM unlawful. For a helpful analysis of the case, see Fei Deng, Edgeworth Economics, and Su Sun, *Rainbow v. Johnson & Johnson: RPM Litigation in China, http://awa 2015.concurrences.com/IMG/pdf/rainbow-_feng_-_su.pdf.*

6.   Outside of the US and EU, RPM is often prohibited, either categorically or with limited exceptions Section 76 of Canada's competition statute prohibits RPM where it is likely to have "an adverse effect on competition." Under 2014 Guidelines by the Canadian

Competition Bureau, suppliers should not engage in behavior that discourages price cutting by retailers. In 2013, the Brazilian *Conselho Administrativo de Defesa Econômica* ("CADE") ruled in the SKF case that RPM is presumptively unlawful; defendants may attempt to rebut the presumption by proving efficiencies. No. 08012.001271/2001–44. By contrast, the Indian statute treats RPM as subject to the rule of reason. In 2015, the Indian Competition Commission launched investigations into RPM in the e-commerce and automotive sectors.

4.   Tying and Exclusive Dealing

The reader will be familiar with US law, which for many years focused on negative aspects of tying: competitors were fenced out of segments of the market to which they could no longer sell their products on the merits. US law also focused on negative aspects of exclusive dealing, which meant that the firm saddled with the exclusive dealing obligation could not deal with competitors of its supplier, even if they offered a better or cheaper product. The inefficiencies and the unfairness of the fencing out led to enactment of Clayton Act Section 3 in 1914. Ultimately, however, it was recognized that these practices may have procompetitive aspects. In general, the presumptions are reversed in the US today. Exclusive dealing is recognized as normally efficient, and it is usually lawful; but it can be illegal if it is a device to keep rivals from needed access to scarce inputs or outlets, is not justified by efficiencies, and is likely to increase or maintain economic power. Tying—although technically still subject to a rule of modified per se illegality with need to prove market power, two products and forcing but no need to prove anticompetitive effects—is now regarded as often efficient or competitively neutral. The fencing out effect in itself is no longer considered a competitive harm. The modified per se rule may be en route to elimination.

Some jurisdictions still have concerns with the fencing-out effect, especially where it results from tying and especially where the share of the market foreclosed is significant. These concerns are underscored where tying is (still) regarded as most likely to be undertaken in order to exploit leverage and not to serve consumers. See, for example, the law of Japan, at C below.

The United Nations Set of Multilaterally Agreed Equitable Principles and Rules singles out, as conduct to be avoided by dominant firms, exclusive dealing and tying. The Set, D(f)(ii) and (iv). The UNCTAD Model Law on Competition sums up one view of the usual motivation for tying:

Tying arrangements are normally imposed in order to promote the sale of slower moving products and in particular those subject to greater competition from substitute products. para. 90.

The Set allows as a justification "ensuring the achievement of legitimate business purposes, such as quality, safety, adequate distribution or service".

In Europe, most tying and other foreclosing restraints are treated under Article 102 as possible abuses of dominance. Tying and exclusive dealing by a dominant firm that forecloses significant parts of an adjoining market are treated as suspect and illegal unless justified. E.g., *Hoffmann-La Roche*, Case 85/76, EU:C:1979:36; *Tetra Pak*, Case C–333/94 P, EU:C:1996:436; *Hilti*, Case C–53/92 P, EU:C:1994:77. See Chapter 2. For proof of tying, it is necessary that there be two separate products. Objective justifications may include efficiencies but not safety. When Hilti, dominant in the market for nail guns, defended its tying of nails to the cartridge strips on grounds that its competitors' products might be dangerous, the court replied that safety is a matter for regulation; it is not the job of the dominant firm.

As with several areas of EU law, the case law on tying has not kept step with the increasing sophistication of analysis within the Competition Directorate and evidenced in case selection and Commission decisions. Since approximately 2003, the Commission has followed a welfare economics approach, essentially asking whether the business practice increases or maintains market power. Meanwhile, the European case law asks also whether the firm with substantial market power is using its power or leverage to obtain competitive advantages over rivals. *E.g.*, *British Airways PLC v. Commission*, Case C–95/04 P, EU:C:2007:166.

We present a small selection of EU cases below, and then reflect the analysis used by the Commission as reflected in the draft vertical guidelines.

The next case, *Delimitis*, delineates when tying is sufficiently significant to be caught by Article 101(1); and the following case, *Schöller Lebensmittal*, delineates when exclusive dealing significantly blocks access and the undertaking cannot prove appreciable objective advantages that compensate for the disadvantages.

STERGIOS DELIMITIS v. HENNINGER BRÄU AG

Case C–234/89, EU:C:1991:91 (European Court of Justice 1991)

[Stergios Delimitis rented a pub from Henninger Bräu, agreeing to sell only Henninger Bräu beer in the pub. Asserting that the contract violated Article 101 and was void, Delimitis failed to pay rent, and Henninger deducted the rent from Delimitis' rental deposit. Delimitis sued for return of the rent. Henninger relied on the contract, which presumably was not intended to harm competition but reflected the brewery's desire for an assured outlet for its beer and Delimitis' desire for the premises and an assured supply.

The national court sought a preliminary ruling on whether the contract was caught by Article 101(1) and if so whether it fell within the then block exemption on exclusive purchasing. The Court of Justice set forth the following framework for determining whether exclusive contracts that are part of a network of similar contracts have the effect, if not the object, of "preventing, restricting or distorting competition":]

[15] . . . [I]t is necessary to analyse the effects of a beer supply agreement, taken together with other contracts of the same type, on the opportunities of national competitors or those from other Member States, to gain access to the market for beer consumption or to increase their market share and, accordingly, the effects on the range of products offered to consumers. * * *

[18] [The relevant market is] the national market for beer distribution in premises for the sale and consumption of drinks.

[19] In order to assess whether the existence of several beer supply agreements impedes access to the market as so defined, it is further necessary to examine the nature and extent of those agreements in their totality, comprising all similar contracts tying a large number of points of sale to several national producers. The effect of those networks of contracts on access to the market depends specifically on the number of outlets thus tied to national producers in relation to the number of public houses which are not so tied, the duration of the commitments entered into, the quantities of beer to which those commitments relate, and on the proportion between those quantities and the quantities sold by free distributors.

[20] The existence of a bundle of similar contracts, even if it has a considerable effect on the opportunities for gaining access to the market, is not, however, sufficient in itself to support a finding that the relevant market is inaccessible, inasmuch as it is only one factor, amongst others, pertaining to the economic and legal context in which an agreement must be appraised. The other factors to be taken into account are, in the first instance, those also relating to opportunities for access.

[21] In that connection it is necessary to examine whether there are real concrete possibilities for a new competitor to penetrate the bundle of

contracts by acquiring a brewery already established on the market together with its network of sales outlets, or to circumvent the bundle of contracts by opening new public houses. For that purpose it is necessary to have regard to the legal rules and agreements on the acquisition of companies and the establishment of outlets, and to the minimum number of outlets necessary for the economic operation of a distribution system. The presence of beer wholesalers not tied to producers who are active on the market is also a factor capable of facilitating a new producer's access to that market since he can make use of those wholesaler's sales networks to distribute his own beer.

[22] Secondly, account must be taken of the conditions under which competitive forces operate on the relevant market. In that connection it is necessary to know not only the number and the size of producers present on the market, but also the degree of saturation of that market and customer fidelity to existing brands, for it is generally more difficult to penetrate a saturated market in which customers are loyal to a small number of large producers than a market in full expansion in which a large number of small producers are operating without any strong brand names. . . .

[23] If an examination of all similar contracts entered into on the relevant market and the other factors relevant to the economic and legal context in which the contract must be examined shows that those agreements do not have the cumulative effect of denying access to that market to new national and foreign competitors, the individual agreements comprising the bundle of agreements cannot be held to restrict competition within the meaning of Article [101](1) of the Treaty. They do not, therefore, fall under the prohibition laid down in that provision.

[24] If, on the other hand, such examination reveals that it is difficult to gain access to the relevant market, it is necessary to assess the extent to which the agreements entered into by the brewery in question contribute to the cumulative effect produced in that respect by the totality of the similar contracts found on that market. Under the Community rules on competition, responsibility for such an effect of closing off the market must be attributed to the breweries which make an appreciable contribution thereto. Beer supply agreements entered into by breweries whose contribution to the cumulative effect is insignificant do not therefore fall under the prohibition under Article [101](1). * * *

[27] The reply to be given to the first three questions is therefore that a beer supply agreement is prohibited by Article [101](1) of the [ ] Treaty, if two cumulative conditions are met. The first is that, having regard to the economic and legal context of the agreement at issue, it

is difficult for competitors who could enter the market or increase their market share to gain access to the national market for the distribution of beer in premises for the sale and consumption of drinks. The fact that, in that market, the agreement in issue is one of a number of similar agreements having a cumulative effect on competition constitutes only one factor amongst others in assessing whether access to that market is indeed difficult. The second condition is that the agreement in question must make a significant contribution to the sealing-off effect brought about by the totality of those agreements in their economic and legal context. The extent of the contribution made by the individual agreement depends on the position of the contracting parties in the relevant market and on the duration of the agreement.

Notes and Questions

1. *Delimitis* was considered a break-through judgment. Prior to *Delimitis* single-branding contracts ("I will sell only your brand") with significant producers were deemed almost automatically caught by Article 101(1) and thus were illegal unless justified.

2. What would have been Delimitis' theory of antitrust harm?

3. Duration of exclusive contracts is a factor to be considered. Long duration, the Court has said, can contribute to the "sealing off effect." In *Neste Markkinointi Oy*, Neste, the leading petrol supplier in Finland, sued former service station proprietors for abandoning their service stations without giving the contractually required one-year notice. The proprietors defended that the contract was void because it contained an exclusivity clause (for one year), that Neste's network of agreements, or its network combined with those of other suppliers, significantly foreclosed access of new oil companies, and that the network ran afoul of Article 101(1). The national court posed to the Court of Justice the question whether the contracts allowing termination on short notice could be separated from contracts of long duration in considering compatibility of the plaintiffs' contracts with the Treaty. The Court noted that all gas stations carry only one brand of motor fuels; the supplier must invest in adapting the sales point to the brand image, so that exclusivity as such was not in question; rather "duration is the decisive factor in the market-sealing effect." (para. 32) A one-year period is reasonably necessary to protect the interests of the parties. The one-year contracts in effect at any given time represented a very small portion of the exclusive purchasing agreements of any particular supplier; therefore they made no significant contribution to any cumulative effect; therefore they were not caught by Article 101(1). Case C–214/99, EU:C:2000:679.

4. Why did the gas station proprietors in *Neste* (who breached their agreement to give proper notice) and the beer house tenant in

Delimitis (who owed rent) have standing to claim that their commitment to purchase goods only from their supplier, combined with a network of similar contracts, amounted to an anticompetitive sealing off of the market for those goods?

Note that European cases are seldom dismissed for lack of standing. Under the Treaty, persons directly and individually concerned have a right to sue. Art. 263 TFEU, ex 230 ECT.

SCHÖLLER LEBENSMITTEL v. COMMISSION

Case T–9/93, EU:T:1995:99 (European General Court 1995)

[Langnese-Iglo, a subsidiary of Unilever, and Schöller Lebensmittel were the leading firms in Germany in the sale of ice cream; particularly impulse-buying ice cream. Each, separately, had a network of agreements with the sellers requiring that the retailers purchase ice cream only from it, or supplying freezers "free" and requiring that the retailer use the freezer only for the supplier's ice cream and not for the ice cream of competitors.

Mars, a French manufacturer of ice cream bars, was trying to pierce the German impulse ice cream market. Finding the two firms' supply contracts to be road blocks to market access, Mars complained to the Commission. The Commission brought proceedings against each. The Commission withdrew a comfort letter that it had previously given to Schöller and decided both the question of applicability of Article 81(1) and the question of entitlement of the applicants to an individual exemption.

In *Schöller*, the court first examined whether the contested supply agreements had an appreciable effect on competition. It found "that the applicant holds a strong position in the relevant market"; it held "more than 25 per cent" in the traditional trade, and, by its agreements, tied more than 10% of the sales outlets. Combined with Langnese's contracts, the tied portion of the market exceeded 30%.]

[83] With respect to [other] factors, the Commission has drawn attention to the existence of additional substantial barriers to access to the market, both in the grocery trade and in the traditional trade. . . . [A]ccess to the market for new competitors is made more difficult by the existence of a system under which a large number of freezer cabinets are lent by the applicant to retailers both in the grocery trade and in the traditional trade . . ., the retailers being obliged to use them exclusively for the applicant's products.

[84] The Court considers that the Commission was right to treat that factor as contributing to making access to the market more difficult. The necessary consequence of that situation is that any new competitor entering the market must either persuade the retailer to

exchange the freezer cabinet installed by the applicant for another, which involves giving up the turnover in the products from the previous supplier, or to persuade the retailer to install an additional freezer cabinet, which may prove impossible, particularly because of lack of space in small sales outlets. Moreover, if the new competitor is able to offer only a limited range of products, as in the case of the intervener, it may prove difficult for it to persuade the retailer to terminate its agreement with the previous supplier.

85 It is also apparent from the documents before the Court that, in the traditional trade, there are numerous individual retailers whose average turnover is rather low. The establishment of a profitable distribution system therefore presupposes that a new competitor must have a large number of retailers concentrated within a specified geographical area which can be supplied through regional or central warehouses. The fact that there are no independent intermediaries means that this fragmentation of demand constitutes an additional barrier to access to the market. Finally, the Commission rightly took into account the fact that the applicant's product brands are very well known.

86 In those circumstances, the Court considers that examination of all the similar agreements concluded on the market and of other aspects of the economic and legal context in which they operate . . . shows that the exclusive purchasing agreements concluded by the applicant are liable appreciably to affect competition within the meaning of Article [101](1) of the Treaty.

87 In view of the strong position occupied by the applicant in the relevant market and, in particular, its market share, the Court considers that the agreements contribute significantly to the closing-off of the market.

88 In view of all the foregoing, the Court considers that the Commission was right to conclude that the contested agreements give rise to an appreciable restriction of competition in the relevant market. * * *

139 In considering whether the Commission was right to refuse to grant an individual exemption, it must first be borne in mind that an individual exemption decision may be granted only if, in particular, the four conditions laid down by Article [81](3) of the Treaty are all met by the agreement in question, with the result that an exemption must be refused if any of the four conditions is not met. * * *

142 As regards the first of the four conditions laid down by Article [101](3) of the Treaty, the Court points out that, according to that provision, the agreements capable of being exempted are those which

contribute "to improving the production or distribution of goods or to promoting technical or economic progress". It is settled law that the improvement cannot be identified with all the advantages which the parties obtain from the agreement in their production or distribution activities. The improvement must in particular display appreciable objective advantages of such a character as to compensate for the disadvantages which they cause in the field of competition.

[143] ... Although it is apparent ... that exclusive purchasing agreements lead in general to an improvement in distribution, in that they enable the supplier to plan the sale of his goods with greater precision and for a longer period and ensure that the reseller's requirements will be met on a regular basis for the duration of the agreement, and even if it is assumed that it would be necessary for the applicant, for reasons of cost, to terminate supplies to certain small sales outlets if it were obliged to give up supplies to them on an exclusive basis, the Commission considers nevertheless that the contested agreements do not give rise to objective and specific advantages for the public interest such as to compensate for the disadvantages which they cause in the field of competition.

[144] In support of that argument, the Commission states, first, that, in view of the strong position on the market held by the applicant, the contested agreements do not ... have the effect of intensifying competition between different brands of products. The Commission rightly took the view that the network of agreements at issue constitutes a major barrier to access to the market, with the result that competition is restricted.

[145] ... [It is clear] that the Commission considered that supplies to any small sales outlets abandoned by the applicant, for reasons of costs, would be taken over either by other suppliers, for example small local producers, or by independent dealers selling several ranges of products. Moreover, the Commission points out that the applicant itself recognised that it continues to supply even very small sales outlets, whose annual turnover hovers around 300 German marks, in those cases where their geographical situation is favourable.

[146] Against that background, it must be borne in mind that the intervener, Mars, stated that it is wholly exceptional for impulse products to be distributed using a transport system owned by the producers. The parties agree that it is only in Germany, Denmark and Italy that undertakings in the Unilever group, including Langnese, have concluded exclusive agreements covering sales outlets.

[147] Although the applicant claims that it would be obliged, for reasons of cost, to cease supplying a number of small sales outlets if it had to give up its exclusive purchasing agreements, the Court considers that it has not provided any evidence to show that such a situation would be liable to jeopardise regular supplies of impulse ice-cream to the territory as a whole and, in particular, that the small sales outlets concerned would not subsequently be supplied by other suppliers or wholesalers, simply as a consequence of the unrestricted competition which would then prevail. Nor has the applicant produced any convincing evidence of the special conditions in Germany which made it necessary to create an ice-cream distribution system belonging to the producers. The Court therefore considers that the applicant has not shown that the Commission committed a manifest error of assessment in considering that the contested agreements did not fulfil the first condition laid down by Article [101](3) of the Treaty. . . . * * *

Notes and Questions

1.   Did Schöller have market power? Is market power a necessary condition for a violation? Should it be?

2.   What were the effects of the exclusivity and freezer clauses on competitors? on potential competitors? on consumers? Which effects are most important?

3.   What were the efficiencies of the exclusive supply contracts? of the "free" freezer arrangements? How would you balance the efficiencies against the anticompetitive aspects of the agreements? Did the court agree?

4.   What was the strongest case for granting the exemption? Was the Commission right to deny it? Note that the case arose before modernisation measures abolished the notification/exemption process. Still, given the Treaty language, agreements caught by Article 101(1) must fulfill the four conditions of 101(3).

5.   If you were Mars and if you could not expect the European Commission to grant you relief from your competitors' exclusivity and freezer clauses, what strategies would you adopt?

6.   If Schöller and Langnese withdrew the exclusivity obligation and offered retailers the choice of a) freezers for sale at market price, b) freezers for rent at market price, or c) freezers "free" with an obligation to use only the supplier's ice cream in the freezer, would the new arrangement be permissible? What if virtually all of the retailers chose option (c)? See *Van den Bergh Foods Ltd.* (subsidiary of Unilever), Cases

IV/34.073, 34.395, 35.436, Commission Decision 98/531, O.J. L 246/1 (Sept. 4, 1998). *Langnese-Iglo GmbH v. Commission*, Case T–7/93, the companion case to *Schöller*, is reported at EU:T:1995:98, aff'd, Case C–279/95 P, EU:C:1998:447.

7.   The Irish court took an entirely different view of the freezer arrangement and its effects, even when the freezer clause was imposed by a dominant firm. Masterfoods (Mars) had been enlisting numerous retailers in Ireland to stock and display Mars bars in their freezers. HB Ice-cream (of the Unilever family), the dominant impulse ice cream seller in Ireland, sought to enforce its exclusive contracts with the retailers. In 1992 it persuaded an Irish court to permanently restrain Masterfoods from inducing breach of HB's contracts. The Irish court, by Judge Lynch, analyzed the contracts as follows:

> I think that a breach of paragraph (e) [distorting competition by imposing unrelated obligations] does not arise at all in this case. The contracts in question are bailments of freezers whether they be on loan or hire. The terms objected to relate to the very basis of the contract of bailment, namely, the purpose for which the goods (the freezers) are bailed to the bailee (the retailer). The freezers are bailed to the bailees for the purpose of storing, selling and advertising HB ice cream products only. Those terms are not supplementary obligations nor by their nature or according to commercial usage do they not have an essential connection with the contracts of bailment. They do. It would seem that none of the particular breaches set out in paragraphs (a) to (e) of Article [101](1) apply: certainly, none clearly apply to the facts of Article [101] if it was reasonably clear that there was a contravention of the general intention of the article. Is it reasonably likely that these contracts of bailment of freezers may affect trade between member states of the European Community and may prevent, restrict or distort competition within the common market? I am not satisfied that Mars has made out a sufficient prima facie or serious case to that effect.

H.B. Ice-cream Ltd. v. Masterfoods Ltd. (trading as Mars Ireland), [1990] 2 IR 463.

Masterfoods complained to the European Commission about the exclusivity clauses and the Irish court injunction. The Commission, after finding that 40% of sales outlets in Ireland were tied up by the exclusivity clause, held:

> [T]he exclusivity provision in the freezer-cabinet agreement concluded between HB and retailers in Ireland, for the placement of cabinets in retail outlets which have only one or more freezer cabinets supplied by HB for the stocking of single-

wrapped items of impulse ice cream, and not having a freezer cabinet either procured by themselves or provided by another ice-cream manufacturer constitutes an infringement of Article [101](1) of the Treaty. * * *

HB's inducement to retailers in Ireland to enter into freezer-cabinet agreements subject to a condition of exclusivity by offering to supply them with one or more freezer cabinets for the stocking of single-wrapped items of impulse ice cream and to maintain the cabinets, free of any direct charge, constitutes an infringement of Article [102] of the Treaty.

Van den Bergh Foods Ltd., Cases IV/34.073, IV/34.395 and IV/35.436, Commission Decision 98/531 of 11 March 1998, O.J. L 246/1 (Sept. 4, 1998), Arts. 1, 3.

Meanwhile, the Irish Supreme Court stayed the Irish appeal and asked the European Court of Justice whether its obligation of sincere cooperation (Art. 4 Treaty on European Union (TEU), ex 10 ECT) required it to stay the Irish case pending the disposition of Van den Bergh's appeal. The Court of Justice responded in the affirmative, holding that Ireland could not maintain a judgment inconsistent with the Community disposition of the same issue. *Masterfoods Ltd.* (Mars Ireland), Case C–344/98, EU:C:2000:689.

On its appeal from the Commission decision, Van den Bergh stressed that the retailers were free to terminate their contract with HB or to install freezers not belonging to HB; and it argued that their freedom to do so meant that there was no foreclosure. The Court of First Instance responded that the retailers had little incentive to exercise this freedom, and seldom did. It noted also the unique circumstances of the market, including the limited space in the retail stores and the popularity of HB's ice cream, and concluded that the Commission did not err in finding that the clause produced a sufficiently high degree of foreclosure to constitute an infringement. *Van den Bergh Foods v. Commission*, Case T–65/98, EU:T:2003:281.

8. US law tends to examine more skeptically, first, the market power of the seller, and second, the practical ability of outsiders to reach the market efficiently notwithstanding exclusivity clauses. Also, US courts would take account of the fact that a "free" freezer is a good deal for the retailer. But if the undertaking had significant market power and if its exclusive contract requirements excluded efficient outsiders, causing the price of impulse ice cream to rise, would the clause be likely to offend US law also? See, e.g., *United States v. Dentsply Int'l Inc.*, 399 F.3d 181 (3d Cir. 2005), cert. denied, 546 U.S. 1089 (2006).

5.   Block Exemptions and Guidelines

In early days of operations, under its system requiring parties to notify potentially anticompetitive agreements and requiring the Commission to clear or exempt the notified agreements, the Commission was flooded with more notifications than it could handle. The largest part of these notifications were vertical distribution agreements. The Commission began the practice of adopting block exemption regulations. Agreements that fell within the block exemptions would get the benefit of an automatic Article 101(3) exemption. The block exemption regulations specified clauses that must be in the agreement, clauses that could not be in the agreement, and clauses that might be in the agreement (white, black, and grey clauses). These block exemption regulations were at first highly detailed. Moreover, firms were induced to bring their deals within the terms of the exemption, for comfort and certainty. Eventually, the block exemption regulations were recognized as straight-jacketing business. Some were withdrawn. The remaining ones were liberalized and modernized and published with guidelines, to announce policy and to give business a degree of certainty.

The most important set of block exemption regulations and guidelines are the general set on distribution. Also adopted are important vertical block exemption regulations and guidelines for the motor vehicle sector and for technology licensing.

Below we include the most important vertical block exemption regulation. We then provide excerpts from the accompanying guidelines.

a.   *Vertical (Distribution and Supply) Block Exemption and Guidelines*

The European Commission has a block exemption and guidelines for the regulation of distribution and supply arrangements. In general, the scheme of the block exemption and guidelines is to provide a safe harbor for vertical agreements involving a seller and a buyer both of whom have market shares not exceeding 30%. The buyer's market share is assessed on the upstream market, to take account of buyer power. In addition, to get advantage of the safe harbor (block exemption), there must be no "hard core" restriction—a category that includes resale price maintenance, tight territorial agreements, and certain Internet restrictions such as terminating Internet customers' transactions if their credit card reveals an address outside of the territory. For agreements not accorded a block exemption, an analysis is performed to consider the net economic effect. Guidelines provide general principles for analysis and then specify the analysis appropriate to various kinds of restraints, such as exclusive supplying, selective distribution and tying. Hard core restraints are presumed illegal and will seldom be allowed, but still, it is possible for the parties to bring forward evidence to show that efficiencies outweigh negative effects.

The block exemption follows.

COMMISSION REGULATION ON THE APPLICATION OF ARTICLE 101(3) OF THE TREATY ON THE FUNCTIONING OF THE EUROPEAN UNION TO CATEGORIES OF VERTICAL AGREEMENTS AND CONCERTED PRACTICES (2010)

available at *http://ec.europa.eu/competition/antitrust/legislation/vertical.html*

(1) Regulation No 19/65/EEC empowers the Commission to apply Article 101(3) of the Treaty on the Functioning of the European Union* by regulation to certain categories of vertical agreements and corresponding concerted practices falling within Article 101(1) of the Treaty.

(2) Commission Regulation (EC) No 2790/1999 of 22 December 1999 on the application of Article 81(3) of the Treaty to categories of vertical agreements and concerted practices[1] defines a category of vertical agreements which the Commission regarded as normally satisfying the conditions laid down in Article 101(3) of the Treaty. In view of the overall positive experience with the application of that Regulation, which expires on 31 May 2010, and taking into account further experience acquired since its adoption, it is appropriate to adopt a new block exemption regulation.

(3) The category of agreements which can be regarded as normally satisfying the conditions laid down in Article 101(3) of the Treaty includes vertical agreements for the purchase or sale of goods or services where those agreements are conclude between non-competing undertakings, between certain competitors or by certain associations of retailers of goods. It also includes vertical agreements containing ancillary provisions on the assignment or use of intellectual property rights. The term "vertical

---

*   With effect from 1 December 2009, Article 8 of the EC Treaty has become Article 101 of the Treaty on the Functioning of the European Union. The two Articles are, in substance, identical. For the purposes of this Regulation, references to Article 101 of the Treaty on the Functioning of the European Union should be understood as references to Article 81 of the EC Treaty where appropriate.

[1]   OJ L 336, 29.12.1999, p. 21.

agreements" should include the corresponding concerted practices.

(4) For the application of Article 101(3) of the Treaty by regulation, it is not necessary to define those vertical agreements which are capable of falling within Article 101(1) of the Treaty. In the individual assessment of agreements under Article 101(1) of the Treaty, account has to be taken of several factors, and in particular the market structure on the supply and purchase side.

(5) The benefit of the block exemption established by this Regulation should be limited to vertical agreements for which it can be assumed with sufficient certainty that they satisfy the conditions of Article 101(3) of the Treaty.

(6) Certain types of vertical agreements can improve economic efficiency within a chain of production or distribution by facilitating better coordination between the participating undertakings. In particular, they can lead to a reduction in the transaction and distribution costs of the parties and to an optimisation of their sales and investment levels.

(7) The likelihood that such efficiency-enhancing effects will outweigh any anticompetitive effects due to restrictions contained in vertical agreements depends on the degree of market power of the parties to the agreement and, therefore, on the extent to which those undertakings face competition from other suppliers of goods or services regarded by their customers as interchangeable or substitutable for one another, by reason of the products' characteristics, their prices and their intended use.

(8) It can be presumed that, where the market share held by each of the undertakings party to the agreement on the relevant market does not exceed 30%, vertical agreements which do not contain certain types of severe restrictions of competition generally lead to an improvement in production or distribution and allow consumers a fair share of the resulting benefits.

(9) Above the market share threshold of 30%, there can be no presumption that vertical agreements falling within the scope of Article 101(1) of the Treaty will usually give rise to objective advantages of such a character and size as to compensate for the disadvantages which they create for competition. At the same time, there is no presumption that those vertical agreements are either caught by Article 101(1) of the Treaty or that they fail to satisfy the conditions of Article 101(3) of the Treaty.

(10) This Regulation should not exempt vertical agreements containing restrictions which are likely to restrict competition and harm consumers or which are not indispensable to the attainment of the efficiency-enhancing effects. In particular, vertical agreements containing certain types of severe restrictions of competition such as minimum and fixed resale-prices, as well as certain types of territorial protection, should be excluded from the benefit of the block exemption established by this Regulation irrespective of the market share of the undertakings concerned.

(11) In order to ensure access to or to prevent collusion on the relevant market, certain conditions should be attached to the block exemption. To this end, the exemption of non-compete obligations should be limited to obligations which do not exceed a defined duration. For the same reasons, any direct or indirect obligation causing the members of a selective distribution system not to sell the brands of particular competing suppliers should be excluded from the benefit of this Regulation.

(12) The market-share limitation, the non-exemption of certain vertical agreements and the conditions provided for in this Regulation normally ensure that the agreements to which the block exemption applies do not enable the participating undertakings to eliminate competition in respect of a substantial part of the products in question.

(13) The Commission may withdraw the benefit of this Regulation, pursuant to Article 29(1) of Council Regulation (EC) No 1/2003 of 16 December 2002 on the implementation of the rules on competition laid down in Articles 81 and 82 of the Treaty[2], where it finds in a particular case that an agreement to which the exemption provided for in this Regulation applies nevertheless has effects which are incompatible with Article 101(3) of the Treaty.

(14) The competition authority of a Member State may withdraw the benefit of this Regulation pursuant to Article 29(2) of Regulation (EC) No 1/2003 in respect of the territory of that Member State, or a part thereof where, in a particular case, an agreement to which the exemption provided for in this Regulation applies nevertheless has effects which are incompatible with Article 101(3) of the Treaty in the territory of that Member State, or in

---

[2]   OJ L 1, 4.1.2003, p. 1.

a part thereof, and where such territory has all the characteristics of a distinct geographic market.

(15) In determining whether the benefit of this Regulation should be withdrawn pursuant to Article 29 of Regulation (EC) No 1/2003, the anti-competitive effects that may derive from the existence of parallel networks of vertical agreements that have similar effects which significantly restrict access to a relevant market or competition therein are of particular importance. Such cumulative effects may for example arise in the case of selective distribution or non-compete obligations.

(16) In order to strengthen supervision of parallel networks of vertical agreements which have similar anti-competitive effects and which cover more than 50% of a given market, the Commission may by regulation declare this Regulation inapplicable to vertical agreements containing specific restraints relating to the market concerned, thereby restoring the full application of Article 101 of the Treaty to such agreements.

HAS ADOPTED THIS REGULATION:

Article 1

Definitions [Omitted]

Article 2

Exemption

1.   Pursuant to Article 101(3) of the Treaty and subject to the provisions of this Regulation, it is hereby declared that Article 101(1) of the Treaty shall not apply to vertical agreements.

This exemption shall apply to the extent that such agreements contain vertical restraints.

2.   The exemption provided for in paragraph 1 shall apply to vertical agreements entered into between an association of undertakings and its members, or between such an association and its suppliers, only if all its members are retailers of goods and if no individual member of the association, together with its connected undertakings, has a total annual turnover exceeding EUR 50 million. Vertical agreements entered into by such associations shall be covered by this Regulation without prejudice to the application of Article 101 of the Treaty to horizontal agreements concluded between the members of the association or decisions adopted by the association.

3.   The exemption provided for in paragraph 1 shall apply to vertical agreements containing provisions which relate to the assignment to the buyer or use by the buyer of intellectual property rights, provided that those provisions do not constitute the primary object of such agreements and are directly related to the use, sale or resale of goods or services by the buyer or its customers. The exemption applies on condition that, in relation to the contract goods or services, those provisions do not contain restrictions of competition having the same object as vertical restraints which are not exempted under this Regulation.

4.   The exemption provided for in paragraph 1 shall not apply to vertical agreements entered into between competing undertakings. However, it shall apply where competing undertakings enter into a non-reciprocal vertical agreement and:

   (a)   the supplier is a manufacturer and a distributor of goods, while the buyer is a distributor and not a competing undertaking at the manufacturing level; or

   (b)   the supplier is a provider of services at several levels of trade, while the buyer provides its goods or services at the retail level and is not a competing undertaking at the level of trade where it purchases the contract services.

5.   This Regulation shall not apply to vertical agreements the subject matter of which falls within the scope of any other block exemption regulation, unless otherwise provided for in such a regulation.

Article 3

Market share threshold

1.   The exemption provided for in Article 2 shall apply on condition that the market share held by the supplier does not exceed 30% of the relevant market on which it sells the contract goods or services and the market share held by the buyer does not exceed 30% of the relevant market on which it purchases the contract goods or services.

2.   For the purposes of paragraph 1, where in a multi party agreement an undertaking buys the contract goods or services from one undertaking party to the agreement and sells the contract goods or services to another undertaking party to the agreement, the market share of the first undertaking must respect the market share threshold provided for in that

paragraph both as a buyer and a supplier in order for the exemption provided for in Article 2 to apply.

Article 4

Restrictions that remove the benefit of the block exemption—hardcore restrictions

The exemption provided for in Article 2 shall not apply to vertical agreements which, directly or indirectly, in isolation or in combination with other factors under the control of the parties, have as their object:

(a)   the restriction of the buyer's ability to determine its sale price, without prejudice to the possibility of the supplier to impose a maximum sale price or recommend a sale price, provided that they do not amount to a fixed or minimum sale price as a result of pressure from, or incentives offered by, any of the parties;

(b)   the restriction of the territory into which, or of the customers to whom, a buyer party to the agreement, without prejudice to a restriction on its place of establishment, may sell the contract goods or services, except:

    (i)   the restriction of active sales into the exclusive territory or to an exclusive customer group reserved to the supplier or allocated by the supplier to another buyer, where such a restriction does not limit sales by the customers of the buyer,

    (ii)   the restriction of sales to end users by a buyer operating at the wholesale level of trade,

    (iii) the restriction of sales by the members of a selective distribution system to unauthorised distributors within the territory reserved by the supplier to operate that system, and

    (iv) the restriction of the buyer's ability to sell components, supplied for the purposes of incorporation, to customers who would use them to manufacture the same type of goods as those produced by the supplier;

(c)   the restriction of active or passive sales to end users by members of a selective distribution system operating at the retail level of trade, without prejudice to the possibility of prohibiting a member of the system from operating out of an unauthorised place of establishment;

(d) the restriction of cross-supplies between distributors within a selective distribution system, including between distributors operating at different level of trade;

(e) the restriction, agreed between a supplier of components and a buyer who incorporates those components, of the supplier's ability to sell the components as spare parts to end-users or to repairers or other service providers not entrusted by the buyer with the repair or servicing of its goods.

Article 5

Excluded restrictions

1. The exemption provided for in Article 2 shall not apply to the following obligations contained in vertical agreements:

    (a) any direct or indirect non-compete obligation, the duration of which is indefinite or exceeds five years;

    (b) any direct or indirect obligation causing the buyer, after termination of the agreement, not to manufacture, purchase, sell or resell goods or services;

    (c) any direct or indirect obligation causing the members of a selective distribution system not to sell the brands of particular competing suppliers.

For the purposes of point (a) of the first subparagraph, a non-compete obligation which is tacitly renewable beyond a period of five years shall be deemed to have been concluded for an indefinite duration.

2. By way of derogation from paragraph 1(a), the time limitation of five years shall not apply where the contract goods or services are sold by the buyer from premises and land owned by the supplier or leased by the supplier from third parties not connected with the buyer, provided that the duration of the non-compete obligation does not exceed the period of occupancy of the premises and land by the buyer.

3. By way of derogation from paragraph 1(b), the exemption provided for in Article 2 shall apply to any direct or indirect obligation causing the buyer, after termination of the agreement, not to manufacture, purchase, sell or resell goods or services where the following conditions are fulfilled:

    (a) the obligation relates to goods or services which compete with the contract goods or services;

    (b) the obligation is limited to the premises and land from which the buyer has operated during the contract period;

(c)   the obligation is indispensable to protect know-how transferred by the supplier to the buyer;

(d)   the duration of the obligation is limited to a period of one year after termination of the agreement.

Paragraph 1(b) is without prejudice to the possibility of imposing a restriction which is unlimited in time on the use and disclosure of know-how which has not entered the public domain.

Article 6

Non-application of this Regulation

Pursuant to Article 1a of Regulation No 19/65/EEC, the Commission may by regulation declare that, where parallel networks of similar vertical restraints cover more than 50% of a relevant market, this Regulation shall not apply to vertical agreements containing specific restraints relating to that market.

Article 7

Application of the market share threshold

For the purposes of applying the market share thresholds provided for in Article 3 the following rules shall apply:

(a)   the market share of the supplier shall be calculated on the basis of market sales value data and the market share of the buyer shall be calculated on the basis of market purchase value data. If market sales value or market purchase value data are not available, estimates based on other reliable market information, including market sales and purchase volumes, may be used to establish the market share of the undertaking concerned;

(b)   the market shares shall be calculated on the basis of data relating to the preceding calendar year;

(c)   the market share of the supplier shall include any goods or services supplied to vertically integrated distributors for the purposes of sale;

(d)   if a market share is initially not more than 30% but subsequently rises above that level without exceeding 35%, the exemption provided for in Article 2 shall continue to apply for a period of two consecutive calendar years following the year in which the 30% market share threshold was first exceeded;

(e)   if a market share is initially not more than 30% but subsequently rises above 35%, the exemption provided for in Article 2 shall continue to apply for one calendar year following the year in which the level of 35% was first exceeded;

(f) the benefit of points (d) and (e) may not be combined so as to exceed a period of two calendar years;

(g) the market share held by the undertakings referred to in point (e) of the second subparagraph of Article 1(2) shall be apportioned equally to each undertaking having the rights or the powers listed in point (a) of the second subparagraph of Article 1(2).

Article 8

Application of the turnover threshold

1. For the purpose of calculating total annual turnover within the meaning of Article 2(2), the turnover achieved during the previous financial year by the relevant party to the vertical agreement and the turnover achieved by its connected undertakings in respect of all goods and services, excluding all taxes and other duties, shall be added together. For this purpose, no account shall be taken of dealings between the party to the vertical agreement and its connected undertakings or between its connected undertakings.

2. The exemption provided for in Article 2 shall remain applicable where, for any period of two consecutive financial years, the total annual turnover threshold is exceeded by no more than 10%.

The block exemption regulation is accompanied by guidelines. The guidelines describe vertical agreements that fall outside of Article 101(1), comment on application of the block exemption regulation, state the principles concerning withdrawal of the block exemption, treat market definition and market share calculations, and describe the framework for analysis of individual cases under Article 101(3).

The guidelines section devoted to analysis in individual cases describes the general framework for analysis and then the framework for analyzing specific restraints. Individual analysis is applied to cases that fall outside of the block exemption. These are largely cases in which either the seller's or buyer's share of the market is more than 30%. It may also include agreements that contain a hard core restriction—such as resale price maintenance— where the undertaking might possibly have a justification under Article 101(3).

The framework for analysis in general and for single-branding, exclusive distribution, exclusive supply, and tying follows.

EUROPEAN COMMISSION NOTICE GUIDELINES ON VERTICAL RESTRAINTS (2010)

(excerpts)

available at *http://ec.europa.eu/competition*

* * *

VI. ENFORCEMENT POLICY IN INDIVIDUAL CASES

1. The framework of analysis

[93] Outside the scope of the block exemption it is relevant to examine whether in the individual case the agreement is caught by Article 101(1) and if so whether the conditions of Article 101(3) are satisfied. Provided that they do not contain restrictions of competition by object and in particular hardcore restrictions of competition, there is no presumption that vertical agreements falling outside the block exemption because the market share threshold is exceeded are caught by Article 101(1) or fail to satisfy the conditions of Article 101(3). Individual assessment of the likely effects of the agreement is required. Companies are encouraged to do their own assessment. Agreements that either do not restrict competition within the meaning of Article 101(1) or which fulfil the conditions of Article 101(3) are valid and enforceable. Pursuant to Article 1(2) of Regulation 1/2003 no notification needs to be made to benefit from an individual exemption under Article 101(3). In the case of an individual examination by the Commission, the latter will bear the burden of proof that the agreement in question infringes Article 101(1). The undertakings claiming the benefit of Article 101(3) bear the burden of proving that the conditions of that paragraph are fulfilled. When likely anti-competitive effects are demonstrated, undertakings may substantiate efficiency claims and explain why a certain distribution system is indispensable to bring likely benefits to consumers without eliminating competition, before the Commission decides whether the agreement satisfies the conditions of Article 101(3).

[97] The assessment of whether a vertical agreement has the effect of restricting competition will be made by comparing the actual or likely future situation in the relevant market with the vertical restraints in place with the situation that would prevail in the absence of the vertical restraints in the agreement. In the assessment of individual cases, the Commission will take, as appropriate, both actual and likely effects into account. For vertical agreements to be restrictive of competition by effect they must affect actual or potential competition to such an extent that on the relevant market negative effects on prices, output, innovation, or the variety or quality of goods and

services can be expected with a reasonable degree of probability. The likely negative effects on competition must be appreciable. Appreciable anticompetitive effects are likely to occur when at least one of the parties has or obtains some degree of market power and the agreement contributes to the creation, maintenance or strengthening of that market power or allows the parties to exploit such market power. Market power is the ability to maintain prices above competitive levels or to maintain output in terms of product quantities, product quality and variety or innovation below competitive levels for a not insignificant period of time. The degree of market power normally required for a finding of an infringement under Article 101(1) is less than the degree of market power required for a finding of dominance under Article 102.

[98] Vertical restraints are generally less harmful than horizontal restraints. The main reason for being less concerned about a vertical restraint than a horizontal restraint lies in the fact that the latter may concern an agreement between competitors producing identical or substitutable goods or services. In such horizontal relationships the exercise of market power by one company (higher price of its product) may benefit its competitors. This may provide an incentive to competitors to induce each other to behave anti-competitively. In vertical relationships the product of the one is the input for the other, in other words the activities of the parties to the agreement are complementary to each other. This means that the exercise of market power by either the upstream or downstream company would normally hurt the demand for the product of the other. The companies involved in the agreement therefore usually have an incentive to prevent the exercise of market power by the other.

[99] However, this self-restraining character should not be over-estimated. When a company has no market power it can only try to increase its profits by optimising its manufacturing and distribution processes, with or without the help of vertical restraints. More in general, because of the complementary role of the parties to a vertical agreement in getting a product to the market, vertical restraints may provide substantial scope for efficiencies. However, when an undertaking does have market power it can also try to increase its profits at the expense of its direct competitors by raising their costs and at the expense of its buyers and ultimately consumers by trying to appropriate some of their surplus. This can happen when the upstream and downstream company share the extra profits or when one of the two uses vertical restraints to appropriate all the extra profits.

1.1. Negative effects of vertical restraints

100 The negative effects on the market that may result from vertical restraints which EU competition law aims at preventing are the following:

(1) anticompetitive foreclosure of other suppliers or other buyers by raising barriers to entry or expansion;

(2) softening of competition between the supplier and its competitors and/or facilitation of collusion amongst these suppliers, often referred to as reduction of inter-brand competition;

(3) softening of competition between the buyer and its competitors and/or facilitation of collusion amongst these competitors, often referred to as reduction of intra-brand competition if it concerns distributors' competition on the basis of the brand or product of the same supplier;

(4) the creation of obstacles to market integration, including, above all, limitations on the possibilities for consumers to purchase goods or services in any Member State they may choose.

101 Foreclosure, softening of competition and collusion at the manufacturers' level may harm consumers in particular by increasing the wholesale prices of the products, limiting the choice of products, lowering their quality or reducing the level of product innovation. Foreclosure, softening of competition and collusion at the distributors' level may harm consumers in particular by increasing the retail prices of the products, limiting the choice of price-service combinations and distribution formats, lowering the availability and quality of retail services and reducing the level of innovation of distribution.

102 In a market where individual distributors distribute the brand(s) of only one supplier, a reduction of competition between the distributors of the same brand will lead to a reduction of intra-brand competition between these distributors, but may not have a negative effect on competition between distributors in general. In such a case, if inter-brand competition is fierce, it is unlikely that a reduction of intra-brand competition will have negative effects for consumers.

103 Exclusive arrangements are generally worse for competition than non-exclusive arrangements. Exclusive dealing makes, by the express language of the contract or its practical effects, one party fulfil all or practically all its requirements from another party. For

instance, under a non-compete obligation the buyer purchases only one brand. Quantity forcing, on the other hand, leaves the buyer some scope to purchase competing goods. The degree of foreclosure may therefore be less with quantity forcing.

104 Vertical restraints agreed for non-branded goods and services are in general less harmful than restraints affecting the distribution of branded goods and services. Branding tends to increase product differentiation and reduce substitutability of the product, leading to a reduced elasticity of demand and an increased possibility to raise price. The distinction between branded and non-branded goods or services will often coincide with the distinction between intermediate goods and services and final goods and services.

105 In general, a combination of vertical restraints aggravates their negative effects. However, certain combinations of vertical restraints are better for competition than their use in isolation from each other. For instance, in an exclusive distribution system, the distributor may be tempted to increase the price of the products as intra-brand competition has been reduced. The use of quantity forcing or the setting of a maximum resale price may limit such price increases. Possible negative effects of vertical restraints are reinforced when several suppliers and their buyers organise their trade in a similar way, leading to so-called cumulative effects.

1.2. Positive effects of vertical restraints

106 It is important to recognise that vertical restraints may have positive effects by, in particular, promoting non-price competition and improved quality of services. When a company has no market power, it can only try to increase its profits by optimising its manufacturing or distribution processes. In a number of situations vertical restraints may be helpful in this respect since the usual arm's length dealings between supplier and buyer, determining only price and quantity of a certain transaction, can lead to a sub-optimal level of investments and sales.

107 While trying to give a fair overview of the various justifications for vertical restraints, these Guidelines do not claim to be complete or exhaustive. The following reasons may justify the application of certain vertical restraints:

    (1)   To "solve a 'free-rider' problem". One distributor may free-ride on the promotion efforts of another distributor. This type of problem is most common at the wholesale and retail level. Exclusive distribution or similar restrictions may be helpful in avoiding such free-riding. Free-riding can also occur between

suppliers, for instance where one invests in promotion at the buyer's premises, in general at the retail level, that may also attract customers for its competitors. Non-compete type restraints can help to overcome this situation of free-riding.

For there to be a problem, there needs to be a real free-rider issue. Free-riding between buyers can only occur on pre-sales services and other promotional activities, but not on after-sales services for which the distributor can charge its customers individually. The product will usually need to be relatively new or technically complex or the reputation of the product must be a major determinant of its demand, as the customer may otherwise very well know what he or she wants, based on past purchases. And the product must be of a reasonably high value as it is otherwise not attractive for a customer to go to one shop for information and to another to buy. Lastly, it must not be practical for the supplier to impose on all buyers, by contract, effective promotion or service requirements.

Free-riding between suppliers is also restricted to specific situations, namely to cases where the promotion takes place at the buyer's premises and is generic, not brand specific.

(2)   To "open up or enter new markets". Where a manufacturer wants to enter a new geographic market, for instance by exporting to another country for the first time, this may involve special "first time investments" by the distributor to establish the brand in the market. In order to persuade a local distributor to make these investments it may be necessary to provide territorial protection to the distributor so that he can recoup these investments by temporarily charging a higher price. Distributors based in other markets should then be restrained for a limited period from selling in the new market. . . . This is a special case of the free-rider problem described under point (1).

(3)   The "certification free-rider issue". In some sectors, certain retailers have a reputation for stocking only "quality" products. In such a case, selling through these retailers may be vital for the introduction of a new product. If the manufacturer cannot initially limit

his sales to the premium stores, he runs the risk of being delisted and the product introduction may fail. This means that there may be a reason for allowing for a limited duration a restriction such as exclusive distribution or selective distribution. It must be enough to guarantee introduction of the new product but not so long as to hinder large-scale dissemination. Such benefits are more likely with "experience" goods or complex goods that represent a relatively large purchase for the final consumer.

(4) The so-called "hold-up problem". Sometimes there are client-specific investments to be made by either the supplier or the buyer, such as in special equipment or training. For instance, a component manufacturer that has to build new machines and tools in order to satisfy a particular requirement of one of his customers. The investor may not commit the necessary investments before particular supply arrangements are fixed.

(5) However, as in the other free-riding examples, there are a number of conditions that have to be met before the risk of under-investment is real or significant. Firstly, the investment must be relationship-specific. An investment made by the supplier is considered to be relationship-specific when, after termination of the contract, it cannot be used by the supplier to supply other customers and can only be sold at a significant loss. An investment made by the buyer is considered to be relationship-specific when, after termination of the contract, it cannot be used by the buyer to purchase and/or use products supplied by other suppliers and can only be sold at a significant loss. An investment is thus relationship-specific because for instance it can only be used to produce a brand-specific component or to store a particular brand and thus cannot be used profitably to produce or resell alternatives. Secondly, it must be a long-term investment that is not recouped in the short run. And thirdly, the investment must be asymmetric i.e. one party to the contract invests more than the other party. When these conditions are met, there is usually a good reason to have a vertical restraint for the duration it takes to depreciate the investment. The appropriate vertical restraint will be of the non-compete type or quantity-forcing type when the investment is made by the supplier and of the

exclusive distribution, exclusive customer allocation or exclusive supply type when the investment is made by the buyer.

(6) The "specific hold-up problem that may arise in the case of transfer of substantial know-how". The know-how, once provided, cannot be taken back and the provider of the know-how may not want it to be used for or by his competitors. In as far as the know-how was not readily available to the buyer, is substantial and indispensable for the operation of the agreement, such a transfer may justify a non-compete type of restriction. This would normally fall outside Article 101(1).

(7) The "vertical externality issue". A retailer may not gain all the benefits of its action taken to improve sales; some may go to the manufacturer. For every extra unit a retailer sells by lowering its resale price or by increasing its sales effort, the manufacturer benefits if its wholesale price exceeds its marginal production costs. Thus, there may be a positive externality bestowed on the manufacturer by such retailer's actions and from the manufacturer's perspective the retailer may be pricing too high and/or making too little sales efforts. The negative externality of too high pricing by the retailer is sometimes called the "double marginalisation problem" and it can be avoided by imposing a maximum resale price on the retailer. To increase the retailer's sales efforts selective distribution, exclusive distribution or similar restrictions may be helpful.

(8) "Economies of scale in distribution". In order to have scale economies exploited and thereby see a lower retail price for his product, the manufacturer may want to concentrate the resale of his products on a limited number of distributors. For this he could use exclusive distribution, quantity forcing in the form of a minimum purchasing requirement, selective distribution containing such a requirement or exclusive sourcing.

(9) "Capital market imperfections". The usual providers of capital (banks, equity markets) may provide capital sub-optimally when they have imperfect information on the quality of the borrower or there is an inadequate

basis to secure the loan. The buyer or supplier may have better information and be able, through an exclusive relationship, to obtain extra security for his investment. Where the supplier provides the loan to the buyer this may lead to non-compete or quantity forcing on the buyer. Where the buyer provides the loan to the supplier this may be the reason for having exclusive supply or quantity forcing on the supplier.

(10) "Uniformity and quality standardisation". A vertical restraint may help to create a brand image by imposing a certain measure of uniformity and quality standardisation on the distributors, thereby increasing the attractiveness of the product to the final consumer and increasing its sales. This can for instance be found in selective distribution and franchising.

108 The nine situations mentioned in paragraph 107 make clear that under certain conditions vertical agreements are likely to help realise efficiencies and the development of new markets and that this may offset possible negative effects. The case is in general strongest for vertical restraints of a limited duration which help the introduction of new complex products or protect relationship-specific investments. A vertical restraint is sometimes necessary for as long as the supplier sells his product to the buyer (see in particular the situations described in paragraph 107, points (1), (6), (7), (8) and (10)).

109 There is a large measure of substitutability between the different vertical restraints. This means that the same inefficiency problem can be solved by different vertical restraints. For instance, economies of scale in distribution may possibly be achieved by using exclusive distribution, selective distribution, quantity forcing or exclusive sourcing. This is important as the negative effects on competition may differ between the various vertical restraints. This plays a role when indispensability is discussed under Article 101(3).

1.3. Methodology of analysis

110 The assessment of a vertical restraint involves in general the following four steps:

(1) First, the undertakings involved need to establish the market shares of the supplier and the buyer on the market where they respectively sell and purchase the contract products.

(2) If the relevant market share of the supplier and the buyer each do not exceed the 30% threshold, the vertical agreement is covered by the Block Exemption

Regulation, subject to the hardcore restrictions and conditions set out in that regulation.

(3) If the relevant market share is above the 30% threshold for supplier and/or buyer, it is necessary to assess whether the vertical agreement falls within Article 101(1).

(4) If the vertical agreement falls within Article 101(1), it is necessary to examine whether it fulfils the conditions for exemption under Article 101(3).

1.3.1.   Relevant factors for the assessment under Article 101(1) [Omitted]

1.3.2.   Relevant factors for the assessment under Article 101(3) [Omitted]

2.   Analysis of specific vertical restraints

[128] The most common vertical restraints and combinations of vertical restraints are analysed below following the framework of analysis developed in paragraphs 96 to 127. There are other restraints and combinations for which no direct guidance is provided here. They will however be treated according to the same principles and with the same emphasis on the effect on the market.

2.1. Single branding

[129] Under the heading of "single branding" come those agreements which have as their main element that the buyer is obliged or induced to concentrate his orders for a particular type of product with one supplier. This component can be found amongst others in non-compete and quantity-forcing on the buyer. A non-compete arrangement is based on an obligation or incentive scheme which makes the buyer purchase more than 80% of his requirements on a particular market from only one supplier. It does not mean that the buyer can only buy directly from the supplier, but that the buyer will not buy and resell or incorporate competing goods or services. Quantity-forcing on the buyer is a weaker form of non-compete, where incentives or obligations agreed between the supplier and the buyer make the latter concentrate his purchases to a large extent with one supplier. Quantity-forcing may for example take the form of minimum purchase requirements, stocking requirements or nonlinear pricing, such as conditional rebate schemes or a two-part tariff (fixed fee plus a price per unit). A so-called "English clause", requiring the buyer to report any better offer and allowing him only to accept such an offer when the supplier does not match it, can be

expected to have the same effect as a single branding obligation, especially when the buyer has to reveal who makes the better offer.

130 The possible competition risks of single branding are foreclosure of the market to competing suppliers and potential suppliers, softening of competition and facilitation of collusion between suppliers in case of cumulative use and, where the buyer is a retailer selling to final consumers, a loss of in-store inter-brand competition. All these restrictive effects have a direct impact on inter-brand competition.

131 Single branding is exempted by the Block Exemption Regulation when the supplier's and buyer's market share each do not exceed 30% and subject to a limitation in time of five years for the non-compete obligation. Above the market share threshold or beyond the time limit of five years, the following guidance is provided for the assessment of individual cases.

132 The capacity for single branding obligations of one specific supplier to result in anticompetitive foreclosure arises in particular where, without the obligations, an important competitive constraint is exercised by competitors who either are not yet present in the market at the time the obligations are concluded, or who are not in a position to compete for the full supply of the customers. Competitors may not be able to compete for an individual customer's entire demand because the supplier in question is an unavoidable trading partner at least for part of the demand on the market, for instance because its brand is a "must stock item" preferred by many final consumers or because the capacity constraints on the other suppliers are such that a part of demand can only be provided for by the supplier in question. The "market position of the supplier" is thus of main importance to assess possible anticompetitive effects of single branding obligations.

133 If competitors can compete on equal terms for each individual customer's entire demand, single branding obligations of one specific supplier are generally unlikely to hamper effective competition unless the switching of supplier by customers is rendered difficult due to the duration and market coverage of the single branding obligations. The higher his tied market share, i.e. the part of his market share sold under a single branding obligation, the more significant foreclosure is likely to be. Similarly, the longer the duration of the single branding obligations, the more significant foreclosure is likely to be. Single branding obligations shorter than one year entered into by non-dominant companies are in general not considered to give rise to appreciable anti-competitive effects or net negative effects. Single branding obligations between one and five

years entered into by non-dominant companies usually require a proper balancing of pro-and anti-competitive effects, while single branding obligations exceeding five years are for most types of investments not considered necessary to achieve the claimed efficiencies or the efficiencies are 'not sufficient to outweigh their foreclosure effect. Single branding obligations are more likely to result in anti-competitive foreclosure when entered into by dominant companies.

[134] In assessing the supplier's market power, the "market position of his competitors" is important. As long as the competitors are sufficiently numerous and strong, no appreciable anti-competitive effects can be expected. Foreclosure of competitors is not very likely where they have similar market positions and can offer similarly attractive products. In such a case foreclosure may however occur for potential entrants when a number of major suppliers enter into single branding contracts with a significant number of buyers on the relevant market (cumulative effect situation). This is also a situation where single branding agreements may facilitate collusion between competing suppliers. If individually these suppliers are covered by the Block Exemption Regulation, a withdrawal of the block exemption may be necessary to deal with such a negative cumulative effect. A tied market share of less than 5% is not considered in general to contribute significantly to a cumulative foreclosure effect.

[135] In cases where the market share of the largest supplier is below 30% and the market share of the five largest suppliers is below 50%, there is unlikely to be a single or a cumulative anti-competitive effect situation. If a potential entrant cannot penetrate the market profitably, this is likely to be due to factors other than single branding obligations, such as consumer preferences.

[136] "Entry barriers" are important to establish whether there is anticompetitive foreclosure. Wherever it is relatively easy for competing suppliers to create new buyers or find alternative buyers for their product, foreclosure is unlikely to be a real problem. However, there are often entry barriers, both at the manufacturing and at the distribution level.

[137] "Countervailing power" is relevant, as powerful buyers will not easily allow themselves to be cut off from the supply of competing goods or services. . . . But it would be wrong to conclude automatically from this that all single branding obligations, taken together, are overall beneficial for customers in that market and for the final consumers. It is in particular unlikely that consumers as a whole will benefit if there are many customers and the single

branding obligations, taken together, have the effect of preventing the entry or expansion of competing undertakings.

138 Lastly, "the level of trade" is relevant. Anticompetitive foreclosure is less likely in case of an intermediate product. When the supplier of an intermediate product is not dominant, the competing suppliers still have a substantial part of demand that is "free". Below the level of dominance an anticompetitive foreclosure effect may however arise in a cumulative effect situation. A cumulative anticompetitive effect is unlikely to arise as long as less than 50% of the market is tied.

* * *

2.2. Exclusive distribution

151 In an exclusive distribution agreement the supplier agrees to sell his products only to one distributor for resale in a particular territory. At the same time the distributor is usually limited in his active selling into other (exclusively allocated) territories. The possible competition risks are mainly reduced intra-brand competition and market partitioning, which may in particular facilitate price discrimination. When most or all of the suppliers apply exclusive distribution this may soften competition and facilitate collusion, both at the suppliers' and distributors' level. Lastly, exclusive distribution may lead to foreclosure of other distributors and therewith reduce competition at that level.

152 Exclusive distribution is exempted by the Block Exemption Regulation when both the supplier's and buyer's market share each do not exceed 30%, even if combined with other non-hardcore vertical restraints, such as a non-compete obligation limited to five years, quantity forcing or exclusive purchasing. A combination of exclusive distribution and selective distribution is only exempted by the Block Exemption Regulation if active selling in other territories is not restricted. Above the 30% market share threshold, the following guidance is provided for the assessment of exclusive distribution in individual cases. [The Guidelines then discuss various factors as significant, including the market position of the supplier, the position of competitors, entry barriers, conditions of foreclosure, buyer power, maturity of trade, level of the market].

* * *

2.6. Exclusive supply

192 Under the heading of exclusive supply come those agreements that have as their main element that the supplier is obliged or induced to sell the contract products only or mainly to one buyer, in general or for a particular use. This may take the form of an exclusive

supply obligation, restricting the supplier to sell to only one buyer for the purposes of resale or a particular use, but may for instance also take the form of quantity forcing on the supplier, where incentives are agreed between the supplier and buyer which make the former concentrate its sales mainly with one buyer. For intermediate goods or services, exclusive supply is often referred to as industrial supply.

[193] Exclusive supply is exempted by the Block Exemption Regulation when both the supplier's and buyer's market share does not exceed 30%, even if combined with other nonhardcore vertical restraints such as non-compete. Above the market share threshold the following guidance is provided for the assessment of exclusive supply in individual cases.

[194] The main competition risk of exclusive supply is anticompetitive foreclosure of other buyers. There is a similarity with the possible effects of exclusive distribution, in particular when the exclusive distributor becomes the exclusive buyer for a whole market. . . . The market share of the buyer on the upstream purchase market is obviously important for assessing the ability of the buyer to "impose" exclusive supply which forecloses other buyers from access to supplies. The importance of the buyer on the downstream market is however the factor which determines whether a competition problem may arise. If the buyer has no market power downstream, then no appreciable negative effects for consumers can be expected. Negative effects may arise when the market share of the buyer on the downstream supply market as well as the upstream purchase market exceeds 30%. Where the market share of the buyer on the upstream market does not exceed 30%, significant foreclosure effects may still result, especially when the market share of the buyer on his downstream market exceeds 30% and the exclusive supply relates to a particular use of the contract products. Where a company is dominant on the downstream market, any obligation to supply the products only or mainly to the dominant buyer may easily have significant anti-competitive effects.

* * *

2.9. Tying

[214] Tying refers to situations where customers that purchase one product (the tying product) are required also to purchase another distinct product (the tied product) from the same supplier or someone designated by the latter. Tying may constitute an abuse within the meaning of Article 102. Tying may also constitute a vertical restraint falling under Article 101 where it results in a single branding type of obligation . . . for the tied product. Only the latter situation is dealt with in these Guidelines.

215 Whether products will be considered to be distinct depends on customer demand. Two products are distinct if, in the absence of the tying, a substantial number of customers would purchase or would have purchased the tying product without also buying the tied product from the same supplier, thereby allowing stand-alone production for both the tying and the tied product. Evidence that two products are distinct could include direct evidence that, when given a choice, customers purchase the tying and the tied products separately from different sources of supply, or indirect evidence, such as the presence on the market of undertakings specialised in the manufacture or sale of the tied product without the tying product, or evidence indicating that undertakings with little market power, particularly in competitive markets, tend not to tie or not to bundle such products. For instance, since customers want to buy shoes with laces and it is not practicable for distributors to lace new shoes with the laces of their choice, it has become commercial usage for shoe manufacturers to supply shoes with laces. Therefore, the sale of shoes with laces is not a tying practice.

216 Tying may lead to anticompetitive foreclosure effects in the tied market, the tying market, or both at the same time. The foreclosure effect depends on the tied percentage of total sales on the market of the tied product. On the question of what can be considered appreciable foreclosure under Article 101(1), the analysis for single branding can be applied. Tying means that there is at least a form of quantity-forcing on the buyer in respect of the tied product. Where in addition a non-compete obligation is agreed in respect of the tied product, this increases the possible foreclosure effect on the market of the tied product. The tying may lead to less competition for customers interested in buying the tied product, but not the tying product. If there is not a sufficient number of customers who will buy the tied product alone to sustain competitors of the supplier in the tied market, the tying can lead to those customers facing higher prices. If the tied product is an important complementary product for customers of the tying product, a reduction of alternative suppliers of the tied product and hence a reduced availability of that product can make entry to the tying market alone more difficult.

217 Tying may also directly lead to supra-competitive prices, especially in three situations. Firstly, if the tying and the tied product can be used in variable proportions as inputs to a production process, customers may react to an increase in price for the tying product by increasing their demand for the tied product while decreasing their demand for the tying product. By tying the two products the supplier may seek to avoid this substitution and as a result be able to raise its prices. Secondly, when the tying allows price discrimination

according to the use the customer makes of the tying product, for example the tying of ink cartridges to the sale of photocopying machines (metering). Thirdly, when in the case of longterm contracts or in the case of after-markets with original equipment with a long replacement time, it becomes difficult for the customers to calculate the consequences of the tying.

[218] Tying is block exempted when the market share of the supplier, on both the market of the tied product and the market of the tying product, and the market share of the buyer, on the relevant upstream markets, do not exceed 30%. It may be combined with other non-hardcore vertical restraints such as non-compete or quantity forcing in respect of the tying product, or exclusive sourcing. Above the market share threshold the following guidance is provided for the assessment of tying in individual cases.

[219] The market position of the supplier on the market of the tying product is obviously of main importance to assess possible anti-competitive effects. In general this type of agreement is imposed by the supplier. The importance of the supplier on the market of the tying product is the main reason why a buyer may find it difficult to refuse a tying obligation.

[220] To assess the supplier's market power, the market position of his competitors on the market of the tying product is important. As long as his competitors are sufficiently numerous and strong, no anti-competitive effects can be expected, as buyers have sufficient alternatives to purchase the tying product without the tied product, unless other suppliers are applying similar tying. In addition, entry barriers on the market of the tying product are relevant to establish the market position of the supplier. When tying is combined with a non-compete obligation in respect of the tying product, this considerably strengthens the position of the supplier.

[221] Buying power is relevant, as important buyers will not easily be forced to accept tying without obtaining at least part of the possible efficiencies. Tying not based on efficiency is therefore mainly a risk where buyers do not have significant buying power.

[222] Where appreciable anti-competitive effects are established, the question whether the conditions of Article 101(3) are fulfilled arises. Tying obligations may help to produce efficiencies arising from joint production or joint distribution. Where the tied product is not produced by the supplier, an efficiency may also arise from the supplier buying large quantities of the tied product. For tying to fulfil the conditions of Article 101(3), it must, however, be shown that at least part of these cost reductions are passed on to the consumer, which is normally not the case when the retailer is able to obtain, on

a regular basis, supplies of the same or equivalent products on the same or better conditions than those offered by the supplier which applies the tying practice. Another efficiency may exist where tying helps to ensure a certain uniformity and quality standardisation (see efficiency in point 9 of paragraph 107). However, it needs to be demonstrated that the positive effects cannot be realised equally efficiently by requiring the buyer to use or resell products satisfying minimum quality standards, without requiring the buyer to purchase these from the supplier or someone designated by the latter. The requirements concerning minimum quality standards would not normally fall within Article 101(1). Where the supplier of the tying product imposes on the buyer the suppliers from which the buyer must purchase the tied product, for instance because the formulation of minimum quality standards is not possible, this may also fall outside Article 101(1), especially where the supplier of the tying product does not derive a direct (financial) benefit from designating the suppliers of the tied product. * * *

Notes and Questions

1.   The block exemption and guidelines make few changes from the legislation in effect for the previous 10 years. The biggest changes include: 1) Market share safe harbor: The previous block exemption specified only the seller's market share (no more than 30% to get the benefit of the block exemption). Now, concerned about growing frequency of retailer buying power, the block exemption is available only if neither the seller nor the buyer has more than 30% of the market. 2) Internet sales: In the last decade, Internet sales are much more significant. The guidelines address this phenomenon, especially in the context of what is a passive sale (a producer may not restrict its exclusive distributor from making merely passive sales that come in from outside of the territory) and what is an active sale (the producer may restrict its exclusive distributor from making active sales outside of its territory).

Is the addition of the buyer market share threshold justified?

Take a look at the guidelines' treatment of Internet freedoms and restrictions. See Guidelines paragraphs 51–54 and 64 (not included in the printed excerpt). Are the lines drawn in the appropriate place? Consider, for example, that sending unsolicited e-mails to specified customers outside of the territory is an active sale. The agreement may prohibit such a practice and still qualify for the block exemption. Requiring exclusive distributors to reroute web customers to the distributor in their territory would involve a lost opportunity for a passive sale, and would be prohibited. But sellers (often brand owners) can restrict sales to distributors with brick-and-mortar outlets (who then can sell on the Internet), and the brand sellers can block on-line sales of their goods by distributors without brick-and-mortar outlets. Are the Internet provisions appropriately protective of brand owners' needs to guard against free riders? or too restrictive of the freedom of eBay and its ilk to give good deals to consumers?

2. What is your assessment of both the form and the substance of the block exemption? Has the Commission succeeded in moving away from rigid forms to effects-based analysis? Does the block exemption give sufficient guidance? How well does it maneuver between the goals of giving more certainty to business and elucidating the line between clauses that are procompetitive and those that are anticompetitive?

3. Where the relevant market shares are 30% or below, which system—US or EU—fulfills these goals better?

Note that no firm is forced to come within the strictures of a block exemption, but that firms tend to do so if it is possible and not too inconvenient, for simplicity and business certainty. Moreover, clauses that are singled out as disqualifying are likely to fare badly at the stage of individual scrutiny.

4. How helpful is the guidance for individual assessments? In terms of predictors of anticompetitive effects, how accurate and sound is the guidance for exclusive purchasing? exclusive selling? tying? Are the guidelines sufficiently clear to give guidance on what is anticompetitive foreclosure? If not, what more should be stated?

5. Compare the guidelines' analysis with US case law. Is it essentially the same? Are there important respects in which the analysis is different—either in substance or burdens?

6. Describe the major differences in approach between US and EU law on vertical restraints. Are the differences formalistic or substantive? Are they driven by different values and goals, or the same ones? How significant is the goal of achieving EU market integration in explaining the differences?

The current Block Exemption Regulation and Guidelines are available on the Europa website at *http://ec.europa.eu/competition/ antitrust/legislation/legislation.html*.

b. Technology Transfer Licensing Block Exemption and Guidelines

Agreements for the licensing of technology have been the subject of a block exemption for many years. This regulation, too, has been liberalized.

A revised technology transfer block exemption became effective May 1, 2004. The regulation covers patents, knowhow, design rights, and software copyrights. The regulation contains a list of hardcore prohibitions. For example, prohibited clauses in licensing between competitors include price fixing and limitation of output where the restriction is reciprocal; allocation of markets or customers, with exceptions where the restriction is not reciprocal; and restriction on the licensee's using its own technology.

The block exemption regulation imposes a cap of 20% market share for licensing between competitors and a 30% market share for licensing between non-competitors. Outside of the exemption, a rule of reason applies, as explained in accompanying guidelines. The ceilings are low for firms that are significant players in technology-based markets, and for that reason alone licenses may not be able to get the benefit of the block exemption.

The block exemption regulation and guidelines are available at *http://ec.europa.eu/competition/antitrust/legislation/transfer. html.*

The European regime might be compared with the US Department of Justice and Federal Trade Commission Antitrust Guidelines for the Licensing of Intellectual Property, April 1995, updated January 2017, available at *https://www.justice.gov/atr/ guidelines-and-policy-statements-0/2017-update-antitrust- guidelines-licensing-intellectual-property* and the draft Chinese guidelines, discussed in Chapter 3.

APPLE, AMAZON, AND E-BOOKS: A CASE STUDY

In Chapter 3, we saw that restraints sometimes can be characterized as either horizontal or vertical, and that the characterization can be legally significant. The growing market for distribution of e-books has raised many such questions in recent years, with technology giants like Apple and Amazon in alternatively friendly and antagonistic arrangements with book publishers that have led to important antitrust actions in the US and EU.

The immediate history of this story began with the introduction of Amazon's Kindle in 2007. From then until the introduction of Barnes & Noble's Nook in 2009 and Apple's iPad in 2010, Amazon was the juggernaut in the e-book and e-reader market. In the US, Amazon strategically priced premium e-books at $9.99 to stimulate demand for the Kindle and, in the view of some industry players, to entrench its market position in advance of competitive technologies reaching the market.

The book publishers felt that Amazon was devaluing the e-book market in order to promote its proprietary systems and technology. They feared that Amazon's low e-book pricing would condition consumers to expect low e-book prices forever for premium books. Because Amazon was initially the only game in town for e-book distribution, the publishers had little power to resist Amazon's demands. The advent of the iPad and the Nook emboldened the publishers to demand different terms of dealing.

According to the Justice Department and European Commission, in late 2008 the publishers began to conspire with one another, and eventually with Apple, to force Amazon's hand. The conspiracy allegedly began as a deal between Apple and the publishers. Under the terms of the deal, the publishers would set the ultimate retail price, which would be capped in several tiers based on the hard-copy list price. Further, the publishers would agree to a most-favored nation (MFN) contract with Apple, providing that the publisher would guarantee to lower the retail price of each e-book in Apple's iBookstore to match the lowest price offered by any other retailer.

Having agreed to these terms with Apple, the publishers were allegedly able to force Amazon into the same type of arrangement. Because allowing Amazon to continue to undercut prices in iBookstore would quickly erode the whole deal, the publishers collectively forced Amazon to adhere to the new e-book pricing plan and agency model.

Following a Justice Department antitrust lawsuit in 2012, the publishers quickly accepted consent decrees terminating the allegedly offensive practices. The publishers and Apple also quickly offered commitments to settled the EU investigation, terminating on-going agency agreements and excluding certain clauses in their agency agreements during the next five years. The publishers also offered to give retailers freedom to discount e-books, subject to certain conditions, during a two-year period. *Commission accepts legally binding commitments from Simon & Schuster, Harper Collins, Hachette, Holtzbrinck and Apple for sale of e-books* (December 13, 2012), *http://europa.eu/rapid/press-release_IP-12-1367_en.htm.*

Apple, however, decided to take its chances with a trial in the US, where the law on vertical restraints is generally more lenient than in the EU. As the sole defendant at trial, Apple argued that its contracts with the book publishers were all vertical not horizontal, that the shift from the wholesale to agency model was procompetitive, and that it had resulted in new entry, expanded output, and average lower prices. After trial, however, the district court found that Apple had joined the conspiracy among the book publishers and hence that it had committed a per se violation of Section 1 of the Sherman Act. In 2–1 opinion, the US Court of Appeals for the Second Circuit affirmed the district court opinion, finding that district court's decision that "Apple orchestrated a horizontal conspiracy among the Publisher Defendants to raise e-book prices is amply supported and well-reasoned, and that the agreement unreasonably restrained trade in violation of § 1 of the Sherman Act." *United States v. Apple, Inc.*, 791 F.3d 290, 297 (2d 2015). A dissenting judge identified Amazon as the true villain of the story.

Although getting some vindication out of Apple's upbraiding, Amazon faced troubles of its own on the e-book front. On June 11, 2015, the European Commission announced that it had opened a formal antitrust investigation into certain business practices by Amazon in the distribution of electronic books ("e-books"). The Commission investigated contractual clauses requiring publishers to inform Amazon about more favorable or alternative terms offered to Amazon's competitors and/or offer Amazon similar terms and conditions than to its competitors, or through other means ensure that Amazon is offered terms at least as good as those for its competitors. The Commission stated concerns that such clauses might make it more difficult for other e-book distributors to compete with Amazon by developing new and innovative products and services. *Antitrust: Commission Opens Formal Investigation into Amazon's E-Book Distribution Arrangements,* (June 11, 2015) *http://europa.eu/rapid/press-release_IP-15-5166_en.htm.* In May of 2017, Amazon agreed to abandon its MFN clauses for a five-year period in order to settle the EU case.

As of this writing, the US Justice Department has not publicly opened an investigation into Amazon. Should it?

C. JAPAN AND SOUTH KOREA

Japan

Japan's Antimonopoly Law prohibits conduct in three categories: private monopolization, unreasonable restraints of trade (both within Section 3), and unfair trade practices (Section 19). Section 19 provides: "No entrepreneur shall employ unfair trade practices." Market power is not a necessary element of the violation, and the market need not be defined. Section 3 violations may be punished criminally by large fines and even jail. For Section 19 violations, cease and desist orders are common, and 2009 amendments introduced fines for certain categories of conduct.

The Japan Fair Trade Commission (JFTC) is charged with designating the acts that constitute unfair trade practices, but sometimes the Japanese Parliament updates the list of prohibitions in the statute itself. For example, the JFTC has designated resale price maintenance an unfair trade practice, but after 2009 statutory amendments, RPM is directly covered in the Act. Minimum RPM is treated as virtually per se illegal. Suggested resale prices are not caught if they are merely reference prices.

Another JFTC designation prohibits "[u]njustly dealing with the another party on condition that said party shall not trade with a competitor, thereby tending to reduce trading opportunities for the said competitor." (Section 11) Exclusive dealing comes within this section.

Section 12 of the JFTC's General Designations identify as an unfair trade practice "trading with the another party on conditions which unjustly restrict any transaction between said party and its other transacting party or other business activities of said party." Vertical territory and customer restrictions fall within this section. Most vertical territorial, customer, and exclusive dealing restrictions that have been held illegal under these sections have been restrictions in support of resale price maintenance such as restrictions regarding price advertisement.

Other unfair practices include abuse of a dominant bargaining position and tying. The JFTC published "Guidelines Concerning Abuse of Superior Bargaining Position under the Antimonopoly Act" on November 30, 2010, and has since evidenced the will to enforce the regulation. On June 22, 2011, the JFTC imposed an administrative fine of 222,160,000 yen (about $2 million) on a supermarket that allegedly forced its distributors provide employees to help with supermarket renovations without any compensation. The case received wide attention in the Japanese business community and signaled a more aggressive enforcement attitude by the Commission.

Tying is illegal when it amounts to "unjust coercion" or "robs purchasers of the right to choose products, impeding fair competition based on merit, and thus is unreasonable." *Toshiba Elevator*, 40 Shinketsushu 651, 660 (Osaka High Ct., July 30, 1993). Safety is a defense, but is not easily established. Thus, Toshiba Elevator was liable for tying elevator maintenance with supply parts; there was no need to find a relevant market or prove market power. *Id.* See Toshiaki Takigawa, *Competition law and policy of Japan*, 54 Antitrust Bulletin 435, 477–78 (2009).

The JFTC also may examine whether a tie unreasonably reduces opportunities for competitors, although the law does not require this inquiry. The JFTC did so in its *Microsoft* case involving the tying of Word to Excel. Microsoft refused to license Excel to PC manufacturers unless they also licensed Word (for word processing). The JFTC found that the tie unreasonably reduced opportunities for competitors; in particular, it reduced the opportunities of Icharito, which had been the market leader in word processing in Japan. *Microsoft I*, 45 Shinketsushu 153, 155–58 (FTC, Dec. 14, 1998). See generally Toshiaki Takigawa, supra.

In the 1980s, the US and Japan held talks on "structural impediments" to trade and competition. This was called the Structural Impediments Initiative, or SII. During these talks, the United States alleged that Fuji Film, enabled by Japanese law, used distribution restraints to marginalize Kodak in Japan's consumer film market. In 1991, following the conclusion of the SII, Japan adopted Distribution Guidelines, which may be found at *http://www.jftc.go.jp/e-page/legislation/ama/distribution.pdf.*   These guidelines are not binding on the courts. They have been revised at various times since their initial promulgation. Selected excerpts follow.

GUIDELINES CONCERNING DISTRIBUTION SYSTEMS AND BUSINESS PRACTICES UNDER THE ANTIMONOPOLY ACT
Secretary General, Fair Trade Commission

Issued: July 11, 1991
revised: November 1, 2005,
January 1, 2010,
June 23, 2011,
March 30, 2015
March 27, 2016

Table of Contents

Introduction

Introduction

1. Practices regarding distribution systems and business transactions have been formed with various historical and social backgrounds, and they differ from one country to another. And there is the need to review them from time to time in order to change them for the better. In accordance with the increasing globalization of economic activity and the enhancement of Japan's international status, and under increased need to enrich national life, Japanese distribution systems and business practices, too, are called on to change in the direction of further protecting consumers' interests and making the Japanese market more open internationally. For this purpose, it is essential to promote free and fair competition and enable the market mechanism to fully perform its functions: more specifically, to make sure that a, firms be not prevented from freely entering a market, b, each firm can freely and independently select its customers or suppliers, c, price and other transaction terms can be set via each firm's free and independent business judgment, and competition be engaged in by fair means on the basis of price, quality and service.

    This set of the Guidelines is intended to contribute to preventing firms and trade associations from violating the Antimonopoly

Act and helping in the pursuit of their appropriate activities, by specifically describing, with respect to Japanese distribution systems and business practices, the types of conduct which may impede free and fair competition and violate the Antimonopoly Act.

2.   Part I of these Guidelines sets forth guidance under the Antimonopoly Act concerning the continuity and exclusiveness of transactions among firms, mainly keeping in mind transactions of producer goods and capital goods between producers and users, and Part II states guidance under the said Act concerning transactions in distribution, mainly keeping in mind transactions in distribution process in which consumer goods reach their consumers.

However, there is no difference in guidance under the Antimonopoly Act between transactions of producer goods and capital goods and those of consumer goods. That is, if there are business practices regarding transactions of consumer goods which are not described in Part II but in Part I, the guidance provided in Part I shall apply to them. And if there are business practices regarding transactions of producer goods and capital goods which are not described in Part I but in Part II, the guidance provided in Part II shall apply to them.

Furthermore, Part III provides guidance under the Antimonopoly Act concerning sole distributorship for the entire domestic market, regardless of the nature of goods. If there are business practices which are not described in Part III but in Part I or II, the guidance provided in Part I or II shall apply to them. In addition, although these Guidelines provided guidance mainly with respect to goods, the same guidance shall fundamentally apply to service trade.

3.   Among the types of conduct described in these Guidelines, "Customer Allocation" and "Boycotts" in Part I, and "Resale Price Maintenance" and so forth in Part II, in principle constitute violations of the Antimonopoly Act. On the other hand, regarding other types of conduct, whether or not each conduct constitutes a violation of the Antimonopoly Act is to be judged on a case-by-case basis, analyzing its effect on competition in a market.

These Guidelines provide guidance on major types of business practices which may present a problem under the Antimonopoly Act, with respect to distribution systems and business practices. The Guidelines, however, do not cover all types of practices which may present a problem. For example, price-fixing cartels, purchasing volume cartels, and bid riggings, which are not covered in the Guidelines, in principle constitute violations of the Antimonopoly Act. Accordingly, it is to be judged on a case-by-case basis whether other types of business practices not provided in these Guidelines may present a problem under the Antimonopoly Act.

PART I ANTIMONOPOLY ACT GUIDELINES CONCERNING THE CONTINUITY AND EXCLUSIVENESS OF BUSINESS PRACTICES AMONG FIRMS

1. There sometimes could be seen continuous transaction relationships with specific customers or suppliers, mainly in transactions between firms of producer goods and capital goods.

   However, if business relationships between firms continue over a long period of time due to each firm's choice of trading partners on its own independent judgment based on price, quality, service, and other transaction terms, there would be no problem from the viewpoint of the Antimonopoly Act.

   Furthermore, there may be a case where a firm, in selecting its trading partners, takes account of such overall business capability of suppliers as steady supply, technical resources, and flexibility in response to the firm's requests, in addition to price, quality, service, and other transaction terms in individual transactions. If total evaluation by the firm from the viewpoint mentioned above, or transaction terms of goods or services to be purchased from the suppliers, results in continuous transaction relationships, there would be no problem under the Antimonopoly Act.

   If, however, any firm consults with another firm on mutual respect of and priority to the existing business relations to ensure the continuation of such relations, or engages in such conduct as concertedly with another firm excluding competitors, competition to win customers in a market is to be restrained and entries of new competitors hindered, which result in restraining competition in the market. Moreover, if any firm does business with its trading partners on condition that the latter shall not deal with the former's competitors, or the former applies pressure on the latter to prevent it from doing business with the former's competitors, adverse effects on competition in a market is to be produced, including prevention of new entrants from entering the market.

2. [Omitted]

3.   [Omitted].

Chapter 1   Customer Allocation

1.   Viewpoint

Such conduct of a firm in concert with any other firm or firms, or of a trade association as mutually respecting existing business relations without contending for customers or agreeing not to enter a market where another firm has already engaged in business activities, is sometimes employed for the purpose of securing the continuation of existing business relations in a situation where many firms are engaged in continuous transactions. Such conduct is most likely to lead to an attempt to exclude new entrants from the market for the purpose of ensuring the effectiveness of that conduct. Such conduct, which restricts competition for customers, is in principle illegal.

2.   Concerned Restrictions by Firms on Competition for Customers

In cases where a firm, concertedly with any other firm or firms, engages in the following types of conduct, for instance, and if competition for customers is thereby restricted and competition in a market becomes substantially restrained, such conduct constitutes unreasonable restraint of trade and violates Article 3 of the Antimonopoly Act:

(1)   Customer Restrictions

    a.   Manufactures concerted arrangement mutually not to deal with customers of other firms;

    b.   Distributors concertedly restrain each other from winning over customers from other firms by offering lower prices;

    c.   Distributors concertedly arrange to require payment of a rectification charge when one of the distributors deals with any customers of the other firms;

    d.   Manufacturers concertedly arrange to require each other than those registered; or

    e.   Distributors concertedly restrict customers which each of distributors deals with

(2)   Market Allocation

    a.   Manufacturers concertedly restrict each other's sales territory:

> b. Distributors concertedly arrange not to start sales activities in any area where other firm or firms have already engaged in sales activities;
>
> c. Manufacturers concertedly restrict standards and kinds of products to be manufactured by each firm; or
>
> d. Manufacturers concertedly arrange not to start manufacturing any kind of products already being manufactured by other firm or firms.

3. Restrictions by Trade Associations on Competition for Customers [Omitted]

Chapter 2   Boycotts

1. [Omitted]

2. Refusals to Deal in Concert with Competitors [Omitted]

3   Refusals to Deal in Concert with Customers, Suppliers, etc.

> (1) In case where a firms concertedly with their customers, suppliers, etc., engaged in, for instance, the following types of conduct, and if the conduct makes it very difficult for any firm refused to deal with to enter a market, or its effect is to exclude the refused firm from the market, such conduct constitutes unreasonable restraint of trade (Note 3) and violates Article 3 of the Antimonopoly Act.
>
>> a. Distributors and manufacturers concertedly, in an attempt to exclude price-cutting distributors, undertake such conduct that the latter refuses or restricts the supply of products to such distributors and that the former refuses to deal in the products of those manufacturers which have supplied their products of those manufacturers which have supplied their products to such distributors;
>>
>> b. A manufacturer and its distributors concertedly, in an attempt to exclude imported products, undertake such conduct that the latter does not deal in the imported products and that the former refuses to supply products to those distributors selling the imported products;
>>
>> c. Distributors and a manufacturer concertedly, in an attempt to prevent other distributors from

entering a market, undertake such conduct that the latter refuses to supply products to new entrants and that the former refuses to deal in the products to such new entrants and that the former refuses to deal in the products of those manufacturers which have supplied their products to such new entrants: or

d.   Material manufacturers and a finished product manufacturer concertedly, in an attempt to exclude imported materials, and that the former refuses to supply materials to those finished product manufacturers which have purchased the imported materials.

(2)   Any type of conduct described in (1)a, through d, above, undertaken by any firm concertedly with its customers, suppliers, etc., even if the conduct does not cause substantial restraint of competition in a market, is in principle illegal as unfair trade practices (Article 2(9)(i) of the Antimonopoly Act or Paragraph 1 (Concerted Refusal to Deal) or 2 (Other Refusal to Deal) of the General Designation).

1.   Refusal to Deal Arranged by Trade Associations [Omitted]

Chapter 3   Primary Refusals to Deal by a Single Firm

1.   Viewpoint

Basically speaking, it is a matter of freedom of choice of trading partners for a firm to decide which firm it does business with. Even if a firm, considering such factors as price, quality and service, decides not to deal with a certain firm at its own judgment, there would be fundamentally no problem under the Antimonopoly Act.

However, exceptionally, even a refusal to deal by a single firm is illegal in cases where the firm refuses to deal as a means to secure the effectiveness of its illegal conduct under the Antimonopoly Act. A refusal to deal by a single firm may also present a problem in cases where the firm refuses to deal as a means to achieve to achieve such unjust purposes under the Antimonopoly Act as excluding its competitors from a market.

2.   Primary Refusals to Deal by A Single Firm

In cases where a firm engages in such conduct as a, below as a means to secure the effectiveness of its illegal practice under the Antimonopoly Act, such conduct is illegal as unfair trade practices (Paragraph 2 (Other refusal to deal) of the General Designation).

Moreover, in cases where an influential firm in a market engages in such conduct as b, or c, below as a means to achieve such unjust purposes under the Antimonopoly Act as excluding its competitors from a market, and if such conduct may make it difficult for the refused firm to carry on normal business activities, such conduct is illegal as unfair trade practices (Paragraph 2 (Other Refusal to Deal) of the General Designation):

a.   A manufacturer influential in a market (Note 5), by causing its distributors not to deal with its competitors, and prevents them from easily finding alternative trading partners, and, with a view to ensuring the effectiveness of such conduct, refuses to deal with distributors not yielding to this request (Paragraph 11 (Dealing on Exclusive Terms) of the General Designation shall also apply to such conduct);

b.   A material manufacturer influential in a market, in an attempt to prevent its customers (finished product manufacturer), stops the supply of main materials which have been supplied to finished product manufacturers; or

c.   A material manufacturer influential in a market, in an attempt to exclude competitors of its customers (finished product manufacturers) which have close relations with in (Note 6) from the said finished product market, stops the supply of the materials which have been supplied to these competitors.

Chapter 4   Restrictions on Trading Partners of Dealing with Competitors

1.   Viewpoint

If a firm deals with its customers or suppliers on condition that the latter does not deal with the former's competitors, the latter is to be able to deal with other firms, and this may also reduce the business opportunities of the competitors. Moreover, there is the concern that, where firms are doing business with one maintaining the existing business relations, to put pressure on their customers or supplier not to deal with their competitors.

Such conduct infringes on the freedom of choice of trading partners, and at the same time tends to reduce business opportunities of competitors, and, therefore, may pose a problem under the Antimonopoly Act.

* * *

Chapter 5   Unjust Reciprocal Dealings [Omitted]

Chapter 6   Other Anticompetitive Practices on Strength of Continuous Transaction Relationship [Omitted]

Chapter 7   Acquisition or Possession of Stocks of Trading Partners and Anticompetitive Effect [Omitted]

PART II   ANTIMONOPOLY ACT GUIDELINES CONCERNING TRANSACTIONS IN DISTRIBUTION

1.   Scope of the Guidelines

In order to sell its products, a manufacturer tends to conduct a variety of marketing activities, not only in a connection with direct transactions with customers but also extending to the level of retailers and consumers. In cases where as a part of those marketing activities a manufacturer interferes in, or influences in, or influences, sales prices of distributors, kind of products they sell, their sales territories, their customers, etc., it may impede competition among distributors and among manufacturers.

On the other hand, it is most likely to have anticompetitive effect if a large scale retailer seeks to utilize its dominant bargaining positions over its suppliers, on the strength buying power.

This part, mainly keeping in mind transactions in the distribution process in which consumer goods reach their consumers, provides guidance under the Antimonopoly Act on the following types of conduct, from the view point of regulation of unfair trade practices: conduct by manufacturers (Note 1) vis-à-vis their distributors regarding restrictions of sales price, products handled, sales territories, customers, etc., provision of rebates and allowances, and interference in management and interference in management.

2.   Basic principles concerning the criteria for judging the legality and illegality with respect to effects of vertical restraints on competition

The purpose of the AMA is, by prohibiting unfair trade practices, to promote fair and free competition, and thereby to promote the democratic and wholesome development of the national economy as well as to assure the interests of general consumers.

Promoting free and fair competition in the distribution sector will be attained through assuring free and fair competition in each level of distribution; it cannot be accomplished simply by securing either competition among distributors or manufacturers as long as the other one is eliminated.

Manufacturer's business activities which restrain sales price, sales territory, customers, etc. of distributors such as wholesalers and retailers dealing in the manufacture's products (hereinafter, referred to as "vertical restraints") have various effects on competition depending on their degree, shapes and forms etc. Also, even if vertical restraints give effects to competition, such effects may include pro-competitive effects as well as anti-competitive effects.

3.   Criteria for judging the legality and illegality of vertical restraints

    (1) Viewpoint on the criteria for judging the legality and illegality for vertical restraints

        The AMA prohibits business activities which are likely to impede competition as unfair trade practices.

        Whether vertical restraints are likely to impede fair competition or not will be examined by considering the following factors comprehensively. In this examination, not only anticompetitive effects but also procompetitive effects that would be resulted from the vertical restraints will be taken into consideration.

        Also, the effects on potential competitors in each distribution level will be taken into consideration as well.

        a.   Actual conditions of so-called inter-brand competition (competition among manufacturers and competition among distributors carrying the different brand of products) (market concentration, characteristics of the product, degree of product differentiation, distribution channels, difficulty of new market entry, etc.);

        b.   Actual conditions of so-called intra-brand competition (competition among distributors carrying the same brand of products) (degree of dispersion in price, business types of distributors dealing in the product, etc.);

c.   Position in the market of the manufacturer that imposes the restrictions (in terms of market share, rank of brand name, etc.);

d.   Impact of the restrictions on the business activities of the distributors (degree, shapes and forms of the restriction etc.);

e.   Numbers of distributors affected by the restrictions, and their position in the market.

(2) Pro-competitive effects which may result from vertical restraints

In the case where vertical restraints actually promote sales of new products, ease new entrants, improve quality and services and so on, pro-competitive effects can be recognized. The followings are typical and non-exhaustive examples:

a.   Distributors may sell manufacturer's products without their own promotional activities when other distributors implement such promotional activities as pre-sales services to consumers, which thus actually boost demand for the products.

In such a case, either distributor may eventually refrain from actively implementing voluntary promotional activities, and such situations may come where consumers who would have purchased the products, may not purchase them.

This type of situation is called the "free-rider" problem. One situation in which the free-rider problem is likely to occur is when consumers have limited information on the products. For example, in case of relatively new or technically complex products for consumers, consumers tend to have insufficient information so distributors may have to provide enough information or implement through promotional activities.

In addition, consumers must have a sufficient cost-saving effect on purchasing products when purchasing the products from a distributor that does not implement such promotional activities instead of purchasing from one which actually does so. Generally, consumers will have a profound effect when the price of products is relatively high.

When these conditions are met and therefore the free-rider problem occurs, making it highly likely that distributors will not provide consumers with sufficient information of the product hereby the product will not be supplied, allocating one sales area to one distributor may be one of efficient restrictions to avoid such free-riding.

Provided, however, that pro-competitive effects are recognized, for one thing, only if such promotional activities can benefit many new customers who do not yet have enough information and therefore increase of amount of purchase can be expected and so on. Also, such promotional activities may be unique for the product, and the cost of the promotional activities cannot be recouped (so-called "sunk-cost").

b.   In some cases, it may be vital for manufacturer's marketing strategy to sell its products through retailers which establish a reputation for stocking high-quality products, in order to build a reputation for high quality of their new products.

In such a case, limiting retailers to whom dealers selling their products to such exclusive retailers may be one of helpful restriction for such manufacturers in order to acquire reputation for high quality of their new products.

c.   Where a manufacturer sells a new product, the manufacturer may ask its distributors to make special investments such as establishing special facilities. In such a case, the distributors may not recoup these investments if other distributors which do not make such investments sell the same product. As a result, all distributors may refrain from making such investments.

In such a case, providing a certain territorial protection to the distributor may be one of helpful restrictions for a manufacture to encourage them to make special investments.

d.   A manufacturer may try to create uniform sales services and standardize the quality of sales services to build a reputation among customers (so-called "brand image") for its products. In such a case, limiting the distributor's customers to those who can meet certain criteria or restraining retailers' sales methods might be helpful for a manufacturer in order to build a reputation among consumers.

(4)   The marketing activities which involve restrictions of products handled by distributor, distributors' sales territories or customers, etc. (hereinafter referred to as "vertical non-price restraints"), one of vertical restraints, are generally not illegal unless such restrictions "result in making it difficult for new entrants or competitors to easily ensure alternative distribution channels" (Note 2) or "the price level of the product covered by the restriction is likely to be maintained" (Note 3). On the other hand, price restrictions generally have significant anticompetitive effects and are likely to impede fair and free competition in principle.

4.   Unjust Low-price Sales and Discriminatory Pricing

As an issue under the Antimonopoly Act in relation to distribution, in addition to this type of conduct, there is the matter of unjust low-price sales and discriminatory pricing.

Unjust low-price sales and discriminatory pricing as defined below are prohibited under the Antimonopoly Act as unfair trade practices:

(1)   Unjust low price sales

a.   Without justifiable grounds, continuously supplying goods or services at a price far below the cost incurred to supply them, thereby tending to cause difficulties to the business activities of other enterprises. (Article 2(9)(iii) of the Antimonopoly Act)

b.   In addition to any conduct that falls under the provisions of Article 2, paragraph (9), item (iii) of the Act, unjustly supplying goods or services at a low price, thereby tending to cause difficulties in the business activities of other enterprises.

(Article 6 (Unjust Low-price Sales) of the General Designation)

(2) Discriminatory pricing

a. Unjustly and continually supplying goods or services at a price applied differentially between regions or between parties, thereby tending to cause difficulties to the business activities of other enterprises. (Article 2(9)(ii) of the Antimonopoly Act)

b. In addition to any conduct that falls under the provisions of Article 2, paragraph (9), item (ii) of the Act on Prohibition of Private Monopolization and Maintenance of Fair Trade (Act No. 54 of 1947; hereinafter referred to as "the Act"), unjustly supplying or accepting goods or services whose prices are differentiated by region or by counterparty. (Article 3 (Discriminatory pricing) of the General Designation)

As to unjust low-price sales and discriminatory pricing relating to them, the Fair Trade Commission has already provided guidance on them in the Guideline Concerning Unjust low-price Sales under the Antimonopoly Act Published in December 18, 2009, and will address these practices properly in accordance with these Guidelines.

Chapter 1 Resale Price Maintenance

1. Viewpoint

(1) It is one of the most basic matters in a firm's business activities that it independently determines its own sales price, in keeping with conditions in a market, and moreover this secures competition among firms and consumer choice.

In cases where, as one aspect of marketing activities, or as requested by distributors, a manufacture restricts sales price of distributors, it is in principle illegal as unfair trade practices, because it reduces or eliminates price competition among distributors.

(2) In cases where a manufacturer's suggested retail price or quotation is indicated to distributors as a reference price, such conduct itself is not a problem (Note 5). In

cases where the price, such conduct itself is not merely given as a reference price, however, and the manufacturer seeks to restrict resale price of the distributors by causing them to keep the reference price, such conduct falls under the conduct described (1) above, and is in principle illegal.

2. Restriction of Resale Price

   (1) Restrictions by a manufacture of sales price of distributors (resale price) are in principle illegal as unfair trade practices (Article 12 (Resale Price Restriction) of the General Designation). That is to say, since resale price maintenance (RPM) reduces or eliminates price competition among distributors on the products, generally RPM will have a serious anti-competitive effect and so is likely to impede fair and free competition in principle. Therefore, the Antimonopoly Act stipulates that RPM without "justifiable grounds" is illegal as unfair trade practice. In other words, RPM is not illegal as an exception on the condition that it has "justifiable grounds."

   (2) "Justifiable grounds" might be granted within reasonable scope and reasonable term, in the case where such RPM by a manufacturer will result in actual pro-competitive effects and will promote inter-brand competition, will get demand for the product increased thus benefiting consumers, and pro-competitive effects will not result from less restrictive alternatives other than the RPM.

   For example, when a manufacturer performs RPM, such RPM will be granted to have "justifiable grounds" in the case where such RPM actually results in pro-competitive effects through avoiding the "free-rider" problem mentioned in Part 2, 3(2) a., will promote inter-brand competition, will get the demand of the product increased, thus benefiting consumers, and pro-competitive effects will not result from less restrictive alternatives other than the RPM.

   (3) Whether resale prices have been restricted is to be judged based on the determination of whether any artificial means is taken to secure the effectiveness in attaining sales at the price indicated by the manufacturer.

In the following cases, it shall be judged that the effectiveness in attaining sales at the price indicated by the manufacturer is secured:

a. In case where a written or oral agreement between a manufacturer and its distributors causes the distributors to sell at the price indicated by the manufacturer, examples are as follows:

   (a) In case whether a written or oral contact provides that sales are made at the price indicated by a manufacturer;

   (b) In case where distributors are required to pledge in writing to sell at the indicted by manufacturer:

   (c) In case where a manufacturer only starts dealing with such distributors that accept such condition that they sell at the price indicted by the manufacturer; and

   (d) In case where a manufacturer deals with distributors on conditions that the distributors sell at the price indicated by the manufacturer and that unsold goods are not to be discounted but to be repurchased by the manufacturer.

b. In case where any artificial means, such as imposing or suggesting to impose economic disadvantage if sales are not made at a manufacturer's indicated price, causes distributors to sell at the indicated price. Examples are as follows:

   (a) In case where curtailment of shipments or any other economic disadvantage (including reduction of quantities shipped, raising of shipment price, reduction of rebates, refusal to supply other products: hereinafter the same) is imposed in the event that sales are not made at a manufacturer's indicated price or in case where a notification or suggestion to that effect is made to distributors;

   (b) In case where rebates or other economic rewards (including lowering of shipment price, supplying of the products; hereinafter the same) are provided in the event that sales are made at a manufacturer's indicated price, or in case where a notification or suggestion to that effect is made to distributors; and

(c) In case where a manufacturer cases distributors to sell at the manufacturer's indicated price by the following means:

    i. Collecting sales price reports, patrolling retail establishments, conducting price, supervision by salespersons dispatched to shops, examining ledgers or records of retailers, and so forth in order to ascertain whether sales are being made at the manufacturer's indicated price;

    ii. Identifying price-cutting distributors by making use of secret marks and requesting wholesalers who supplied them to buy the goods to such distributors not to sell to them;

    iii. Buying goods from price-cutting distributors and requesting such distributors or wholesalers who supplied them to buy the goods or pay the cost of their purchases; and

    iv. Transmitting complaints to price cutting distributors from nearby distributors with regard to low-price sales, and requesting the price-cutting distributors to end such sales.

(4) In cases where discriminatory treatment in the form of refusals to deal or provision of rebates, and so on, has been used to secure the effectiveness of restrictions on resale price, such conduct itself is illegal as unfair trade practices (Article 2 (Other Refusal to Deal) or 4 (Discriminatory Treatment on Transaction Terms, etc.) of the General Designation).

(5) In (3) above, the price indicated by a manufacturer to distributors includes both a specific price and any of the following types of price level:

a.   Price to be within x% discount from the manufacturer's suggested retail price;

b.   Price to be in a specific range;

c.   Price to be approved in advance by the manufacturer;

d.   Price to be not less than that charged by nearby stores; or

e.   Price to be suggested by the manufacturer to the distributors as the lowest limit by such means as warning the distributors against discount.

(6)   The guidance regarding restrictions on resale price described in (3), (4) and (5) above shall apply not only to conduct by a manufacturer vis-à-vis direct customers but also to conduct vis-à-vis secondary wholesalers or retailers which are indirect customers, either directly or indirectly via wholesalers (Article 12, 2, or 4 of the General Designation).

(7)   In cases where in the following kinds of transactions, a direct purchaser from a manufacturer only functions as a commission agent, and if it is recognized that in substance the sale is being done between the manufacturer and its ultimate purchasers, even if the manufacturer instructs resale price to the direct purchaser, it is usually not illegal:

a.   In case of consignment sales, and if the transaction is made with a consignor on its own risks and account so that a consignee bears no risk beyond that associated with its obligation to exercise the care of a good manager in shortage and handling of goods, collection of payments, and so on, i.e., is not liable for loss of goods, damage to them, or for unsold goods; or

b.   In case of transactions where a supply price is negotiated and decided directly between a manufacturer and a retailer (or user), and the manufacturer instructs a wholesaler to deliver goods to the retailer (or the user), and if the manufacturer is deemed, in substance, to sell the goods to the retailers (or the user), under such circumstances that the wholesaler is charged only with responsibility for physical delivery of the goods and collection of payment, and a fee is paid for such work.

3. "Distribution Research"

When a manufacturer research actual sales prices, actual customers, etc. of distributors handling the manufacturer's products ("distribution research"), such research itself is generally not illegal, unless the research is accompanied by restrictions of sales prices of distributors such as imposing, notifying or suggesting imposition of curtailment of shipments or other economic disadvantage (including reduction of quantity shipped, raising of shipment price, reduction of rebate, refusal to supply other products) in the event that sales are not made at the manufacturer's indicated price.

Chapter 2 Vertical Non-Price Restraints

1. Viewpoint

(1) A manufacturer tends to conduct a variety of marketing activities directed to distributors handling the manufacturer's products, not only at direct consumers but extending as far as the retail stage. A number of managerial advantages are identified with such marketing activities to distributor, but in cases of vertical non-price restraints, the following problems may arise.

    a. Interference in business activities conducted by distributors through creative efforts;

    b. Maintenance of final sales prices as a result of dependence of distributors on a manufacturer, and cooperative behavior by the manufacturer and the distributors together;

    c. Restriction or elimination of inter-brand competition or intra-brand competition;

    d. Higher barriers to entry by other manufacturers and distributors; and

    e. Reduced consumer choice.

(2) Generally speaking, the effect of vertical non-price restraints on competition in a market differs according to the types of restrictions and specifics of each case. Vertical non-price restraints include the following two categories: a, those which shall not be considered

illegal based on types of restraint, but examined on a case-by-case basis, to analyze their effects on competition in a market, from such viewpoints of whether competitors such as new entrants would be excluded and whether price competition of the product covered by the restriction would be impeded, taking account of various factors, including the position of a manufacturer in a market; and b, those which usually tend to impede price competition and are considered in principle illegal, regardless of the position of a manufacturer in market.

(3) As to whether or not vertical non-price restraints have been imposed by a manufacturer, as is the case of restrictions on resale price described in 2 of Chapter 1 above, it shall be found that restrictions have been imposed not only in cases where a contract or other means of arrangement between the manufacturer and distributors can be found, but also in cases where any artificial means, such as imposing economic disadvantage on distributors who do not comply with the request of the manufacturer, is taken to secure the effectiveness of the restrictions.

2. Restriction on Distributors' Handling of Competing Products

(1) Restrictions on distributors' handling of competing products include the following types of restraint imposed by a manufacturer:

a. Making it mandatory for distributors to handle only the manufacturer's products;

b. Restricting distributors from handling competitors' products;

c. Prohibiting or restricting distributors from handling specific products, or f from handling products from a specific firm; and

d. Restricting distributors from handling competing products by means of requiring the distributors to sell such a large volume of its products as is close to their capacity.

(2) In cases where a restriction on handling of competing products is imposed by an influential manufacturer in a market (Note 7), and if the restriction may result in making it difficult for new entrants or competitors to

easily secure alternative distribution channels, such restriction is illegal as unfair trade practices (Article 11 (Dealing on Exclusive Terms) or 12 (Dealing on Restrictive Terms) of the General Designation).

Note 7:   Whether "a manufacturer is influential in a market" is in the first instance judged by a market share of the manufacturer, that is, whether it has a share exceeding 20% in the market (meaning a product market which consists of a group of products with the same or similar function and utility as the product covered by restriction, and competing each other judging from geographical conditions, relations to customers, and other factors, and which is determined, in principle, in terms of substitutability for users and 42 (Tentative Translation: Only Japanese version is authentic) also, when necessary, substitutability for suppliers). Nevertheless, even if a firm falls under this criterion, the restriction by the manufacturer is not always illegal. In cases, where the restriction "may result in making it difficult for new entrants or competitors to easily secure alternative distribution channels," such restriction is illegal. In cases where a restriction on handling of competing products is imposed by a newly-entered firm or a firm which has a market share of 20% or less, the restriction usually would not result in making it difficult for new entrants or competitors to easily secure alternative distribution channels, and such restriction is not illegal. The same shall apply in the remainder of Part II with regard to whether a firm is "influential in a market."

(3)   The guidance given in (2) immediately above shall also apply to cases where a manufacturer causes wholesalers to restrict retailers' handling of competing products (Article 12 (Dealing on Restrictive Terms) of the General Designation).

3.   Restrictions on Distributors' Sales Territory

  (1)   Restrictions on distributors' sales territory include the following types of restraint imposed by a manufacturer:

      a.   Assigning a specific territory to each distributor as the area of primary responsibility and requiring the distributor to carry out active sales activities within each territory (establishing the area of primary responsibility, without restriction on sales outside the area and not falling under c, or d, below; hereinafter referred to as "area of responsibility system");

      b.   Restricting the area where a distributor may establish business premises such as stores, or designating the plane where such premises are to be established (restricting the location of business premises, and not falling under c, or d, below; hereinafter referred to as "location system");

      c.   Assigning a specific area to each distributor and restricting the distributor from selling outside each area (hereinafter referred to as "exclusive territory");

      d.   Assigning a specific area to each distributor and restricting the distributor from selling to customers outside each area upon request (hereinafter referred to as "restriction of sales to outside customers"); and

  (2)   Area of responsibility system and location system

It is not illegal for a manufacturer to adopt the area of responsibility system or location system, for the purpose of developing an effective network for sales or securing a better system for after-sales service, except where such restriction falls under exclusive territory or restriction on sales to outside customers.

  (3)   Exclusive territory

In cases where an influential manufacturer in market assigns exclusive territory to distributors and if price level of the product covered by the restriction is likely to be maintained, such restriction is illegal as unfair trade practices (Article 12 (Dealing on Restrictive Terms) of the General Designation).

(4) Restriction of sales to customers

In cases where a manufacturer imposes restriction of sales to outside customers, and if price level of the product is likely to be maintained, such restriction is illegal as unfair trade practices (Article 12 of the General Designation).

The guidance given in (2), (3), and (4) immediately above shall also apply to cases where a manufacturer causes wholesalers to restrict retailers' sales territory (Article 12 of the General Designation).

4. Restrictions on Distributors' Customers

(1) Restrictions on distributors' customers include the following types of restraint imposed by a manufacturer.

    a. Requiring each wholesaler to supply only to certain retailers, so that the retailers may buy only to certain retailers, so that the retailers may buy only from that wholesaler (hereinafter referred to as "requirement of designated accounts");

    b. Preventing distributors from buying and selling products among themselves (hereinafter referred to as "prohibition of sales among distributors"); and

    c. Prohibiting wholesalers to sell to price-cutting retailers.

(2) Requirement of designated accounts on wholesalers, and if price level of the product covered by the restriction is illegal as unfair trade practices (Article 12 (Dealing on Restrictive Terms) of the General Designation).

(3) Prohibition of sales among distributors

In cases where a manufacturer prohibits sales among distributors for the purpose of preventing its products from being sold to price-cutting distributors, and if price level of the product is likely to be maintained, such restriction is illegal as unfair trade practices.

(4) Prohibition of sales to price-cutters

In cases where a manufacturer causes wholesalers not to sell to a retailer on account of the retailer's price-cutting (Note9), price level of the product is likely to be maintained, and such restriction is in principle illegal as unfair trade practices (Article 2 (Other Refusal to Deal) or 12 of the General Designation).

Moreover, in cases where a manufacturer stops shipments to a distributor that has been its direct customer, on account of the distributor's price-cutting, price level of the product is likely to be maintained, and such conduct is in principle illegal as unfair trade practices (Article 2 of the General Designation).

5. So-called "selective distribution"

A manufacturer may set up a certain criteria to limit the distributors who handle its product to ones who meet the criteria. In such a case, such a manufacturer may prohibit distributors from reselling its product to other distributors who do not meet the criteria. This is called "selective distribution" and may result in such pro-competitive effects as mentioned in 2(3).

It is generally not illegal in itself, even if such criteria of the selective distribution were to result in preventing certain incompetent price-cutters etc., from handling the product, provided that such criteria are recognized to have plausibly rational reasons from the viewpoint of the consumers' interests such as related to preservation of its qualities, assuring appropriate use, etc., and, that such criteria are equally applied to other distributors who want to deal in the product.

6. Restrictions on Retailers' Sales Methods [Omitted]

Chapter 3 Provision of Rebates and Allowances

1. Viewpoint

The nature of rebates and allowances provided by a manufacturer to its distributors (in general, meaning money paid on a systematic or case-by-case basis, separately from the billing price for goods; hereinafter referred to as "rebates") is diverse, including those that that have the nature of adjusting the nature of adjusting the billing price, and those that have the purpose of promoting sales Thus, rebates are paid for a variety of purposes, and rebates as one element of price also have the aspect of promoting price formation in keeping with actual conditions in a market. Accordingly, the provision of rebates in itself does not necessarily present a problem under the Antimonopoly Act.

There are cases, however, where depending on the ways that rebates are provided, they may restrict business activities of distributors and present a problem under the Antimonopoly Act.

2.   Cases Where There Is a Problem under the Act

   (1)   Rebates used as a means of restrictions on distributors' sales price, handling of competing products, sales territory, or customers, etc. (for example, in such cases that rebates are reduced if the distributors do not sell products at the price indicated by the manufacturer), their illegality is to be judged in accordance with the guidance described in Chapter 1 and 2 above (Article 2(9)(iv) of the Antimonopoly Act (Resale Price Restriction), Article 11 (Dealing on Exclusive Terms) or 12 (Dealing on Restrictive Terms) of the General Designation).

   Furthermore, the conduct of discriminating in the provision of rebates depending on the price, handling of competing products, or the like, if it has the same or similar function as the imposition of illegal restrictions on distributors, such conduct itself is illegal as unfair trade practices (Article 4 (Discriminatory Treatment on Transaction Terms, etc.) of the General Designation). The same shall also apply to (2), (3), and (4) below.

   Also, the same shall apply to cases where a "repayment system" (under which a manufacturer collects all or a part of the margin from the distributors and pays it back after a certain period is used as has the same and similar function as the imposition illegal restriction on the distributors.

   (2)   Coverage rebates

   A manufacturer sometimes provided rebates to its distributors according to the percentage of sales of the manufacturer's products in the total business of each distributor during a specific period, or according to the share that the manufacturer's products have in the display of all goods at the distributor's store.

In cases where the provision of rebates of these kinds (coverage rebates) has the function of restricting the handling of competing products, its illegality is to be judged in accordance with the guidance described in 2 (2) of Chapter 2 (Restriction on Distributors' Handling of Competing Products) above.

That is, in cases where an influential manufacturer provides coverage rebates, and if the provision has the function of restricting distributors' handling of competing products and may result in making it difficult for new entrants or competitors to easily secure alternative distribution channels, such provision is illegal as unfair trade practices (Article 4, 11, or 12 of the General Designation).

(3) Remarkably progressive rebates

At times a manufacturer in providing volume rebates, may set a rebate rate progressively, according to a ranking of distributors based on criteria such as quantity of products supplied to each distributor during a certain period. While progressive rebates have the aspect of promoting price formation in keeping with actual conditions in a market, if the rate is remarkable progressive, they have been the function of encouraging the preferential handling of that manufacturer's products over those of others.

In cases where the provision of remarkably progressive rebates has the function of restricting the handling of competing products, its illegality is to be judged in accordance with the guidance described in 2 (2) of Chapter 2 (Restrictions on Distributors' Handling of Competing Products) above.

That is, in cases where an influential manufacturer provides such rebates, and if the provision has the function of restricting distributors' handling of competing products and may result in making it difficult for new entrants or competitors to easily secure alternative distribution channels, such provision is illegal as b unfair trade practices (Article 4, 11, or 12 of the General Designation).

(4) Rebates that have the function of requiring designated accounts. At times a manufacturer may provide rebates directly or through wholesalers even to retailers who are indirect customers of the manufacturer, in accordance with the purchases by each retailer of the manufacturer's products. In cases where the manufacturer provides such rebates, and if the amount of rebates to each retailer is calculated solely on the purchase amount of the manufacturer's products purchased from a specific wholesaler by each retailer, it is most likely to have the function of requiring designated accounts.

In cases where the provision of such rebates has the function of requiring designated accounts, its illegality is to be judged in accordance with the guidance described in 4 (2) of Chapter 2 (Requiring of designated accounts) above.

That is, in cases where price level of the product is likely to be maintained by the provision of rebates that have such function, such provision of the rebates is illegal as unfair trade practices (Article 4 or 12 of the General Designation).

Chapter 4 Interference in Distributors' Management [Omitted]

* * *

South Korea

South Korea's law on vertical restraints is similar to Japan's. Like Japan, minimum resale prices are illegal per se. Explaining the unfairness content of the Korean competition law, Meong-Cho Yang writes:

It may seem surprising to regulate the unfair content of a transaction in a competition law whose original purpose might be thought to be promotion of competition in a relevant market. Nevertheless, surpassing the role of "pure" competition laws, the MRFT [Monopoly, Regulation and Fair Trade] Act has assumed a role of preserving transactional fairness through allowing small enterprises the freedom to exercise their business judgment. It is fair to say that the KFTC has been vigorous in enforcing the provisions regulating vertical restraints to achieve this objective.

Meong-Cho Yang, Competition Law and Policy of the Republic of Korea, 54 Antitrust Bulletin 621, 635 (2009).

Notes and Questions

1.   Note the center of gravity of harms to be prevented by the Guidelines: reducing business opportunities of competitors and making it difficult for them to find alternative trading partners, and harm to consumers. Comment on these objectives. To what extent is the business opportunity goal consistent or inconsistent with consumer goals?

2.   Part 2, on vertical non-price restraints, contains a safe harbor for manufacturers with a market share less than 20%. This figure was increased in 2016 from the prior figure of 10%, suggesting some liberalization in the treatment of non-price restraints by smaller manufacturers.

3.   Consistent with US law, the JFTC Guidelines recognize that prevention of free-riding may be a procompetitive reason for certain vertical restraints. Some US critics of the Supreme Court's Chicago School era jurisprudence have argued that the free-rider justification for vertical restraints has been unrealistically and uncritically expanded to justify anticompetitive restraints that could not plausibly serve to prevent free-riding. *See generally* HOW THE CHICAGO SCHOOL OVERSHOT THE MARK: THE EFFECT OF CONSERVATIVE ECONOMIC ANALYSIS ON U.S. ANTITRUST (Robert Pitofsky, ed. 2008) (especially essays in Part 5). If the US has gone too far in accepting a free rider explanation, do the JFTC Guidelines provide a more realistic and balanced approach to assessing free-rider justifications?

4.   Part 6 of the JFTC Guidelines, on provision of rebates and allowances, is concerned with discount or rebate structures that disincentivize a distributor from dealing in products made by the manufacturers' rivals. In Chapter 2, we noted abuse of dominance actions against Intel in South Korea, the EU, and the US concerning Intel's allegedly exclusionary loyalty rebates. In 2005, the JFTC also challenged Intel's rebating practices with respect to five Japanese personal computer manufacturers. Japan Fair Trade Commission Press Release (Mar. 8, 2005), The JFTC Rendered a Recommendation to Intel K.K., *http://www.jftc.go.jp/en/pressreleases/yearly_2005/mar/2005_ mar_8.html*.

5.   Compare the Japanese distribution guidelines with the law and guidelines of the EU and the law of the US in form, goals, and substance. What are the main divergences? Comment on the wisdom of each approach, given its context.

D.   DEVELOPING COUNTRIES: SPECIAL CONCERNS

Developing countries have special concerns, given extreme poverty, high concentration, often high barriers to entry, often a culture of statism and special privilege, and characteristics of their economies including the importance of farming and commodities for a source of livelihood and large, informal economies.

These factors may produce rules for vertical restraints that differ from the rules in the developed world in two regards. First, vertical restraints in the form of backward integration or tie-ups may create buying power that squeezes farmers and transfers a larger and larger part of the value chain to multinational firms. The story is told graphically about cocoa bean growing in Ivory Coast, Africa, and the value added chain from cocoa bean to dark chocolate bars, by Bruno Dorin, *From Ivorian Cocoa Bean to French Dark Chocolate Tablet*, in THE EFFECTS OF ANTI-COMPETITIVE BUSINESS PRACTICES ON DEVELOPING COUNTRIES AND THEIR DEVELOPMENT PROSPECTS (H. Qaqaya and G. Lipimile, eds., UNCTAD 2008), 237.

Second, one or a few large firms often dominate the most important markets. The dominant firms establish strong distribution systems, from production to the ultimate consumer. Beer is an example. The dominant beer company "gives" refrigerators to the small retailer establishments, all of which need to carry the dominant firm's beer, need a refrigerator, and have no room for a second one. If the dominant firm's agents find other brands in the refrigerator, they may toss them out. Entry is difficult. You have read the European *Schöller Lebensmittel* case and the reference to the *Van den Bergh (Unilever)* case, in which the European Court ordered that rivals' brands must have access to the ice cream freezers. The European cases have been criticized for insufficient analysis of harm to competition, and US law is even more reluctant than EU law to impose a duty to give access. In poor developing countries, the foreclosure effects are likely to be magnified. Should these factors affect the choice of legal rule?

Consider the following excerpt from the article by Bruno Dorin, preceded by an excerpt from the editors' introductory essay. Dorin's analysis includes and goes beyond vertical restraints. It has implications for abuse of dominance and mergers.

For a different, more market-trusting point of view, see Ignacio De Leon, *A Neo-Institutional Analysis of Vertical Integration and its Implications for Antitrust Enforcement in Developing Countries*, 26 Brooklyn J. Int'l L. 251 (2000).

QAQAYA AND LIPIMILE, IN THE EFFECTS OF ANTI-COMPETITIVE BUSINESS PRACTICES ON DEVELOPING COUNTRIES AND THEIR DEVELOPMENT PROSPECTS (UNCTAD 2008)

(Executive Summary, v, xiii–xiv)

. . . [D]evelopments in commodity sectors have implications for poverty reduction.

There are certain competition problems in commodity markets, which are usually characterized by a high degree of concentration as well as vertical integration between various stages of the value chain. [The Dorin article] provides the developments and problems encountered in the cocoa market in the Ivory Coast, which supplies 40 per cent of the world demand for cocoa. The analysis of the value chain from Ivorian farm gate to a bar of dark chocolate on the shelves of French supermarkets reveals that chocolate makers and/or distributors have been gaining more and more from a bar of dark chocolate between 1992 and 2001. . . .

The trend following the liberalization of cocoa markets has been the elimination of small local traders through tough competition with large multinational firms. Over time, the remaining local exporting and processing companies became subsidiaries of large multinational firms. On the other hand, cocoa markets have been experiencing increased horizontal concentration through mergers of large multinational companies, such as those between large chocolate companies and cocoa processing firms, or through takeovers by large international companies of smaller companies operating at the national market. As a result of these developments, small local cocoa producers have to contend with a strong purchasing power held by several large multinational companies.

The existence of an oligopolistic market structure with high concentration and market power points to competition law enforcement as a potential instrument to curb anti-competitive practices. Nonetheless, it is difficult to gather evidence on anti-competitive behaviour, such as collusive agreements and other concerted practices, in oligopolistic markets. Another policy option is merger control, which ensures that mergers and acquisitions likely to increase market concentration and reduce potential competition are either prevented or approved with conditions. As for abuse of market power in commodity markets local farmers do not have enough bargaining power and are in a disadvantaged position to negotiate fair prices for their products *vis-à-vis* large international cocoa traders. The approach to competition law implementation in commodity markets should be on how to protect producers from the purchasing power of international traders and processors rather than how to protect consumers from market power. . . .

Bruno Dorin, on the Ivorian cocoa bean market[1]

More and more agricultural producers are currently being held by a few major firms in a pincer movement (Marette et Raynaud, 2003), with the major world seed and agrochemical suppliers upstream (AstraZeneca/Norvatis, Bayer-Aventis, Monsanto, etc.) and, downstream, the emergence of major distributors operating over vast consumer zones, such as the French Carrefour or American Wal-Mart (the world's leading company in terms of turnover for 2001 according to *Fortune* magazine). In both cases, competition policies— at least in Europe and the USA—are not failing to monitor the phenomenon, which is amplified in the distribution field by purchasing platforms set up by the major distributors to ensure collective supplies. However, this last point has not received all the attention it deserves, insofar as—more generally and in slightly overstating things—the aim of such checking of concentrations is to protect consumers from market powers, and not producers from purchasing powers. Yet, as already clearly pointed out in the report by the Conseil d'Analyse Economique (Rey et Tirole, 2000), producers also need to be protected, notably in cases where they are led to make specific investments[16] which they would ultimately be unable to amortize if distributors subsequently imposed inadequate prices on them[17]. . . .

Why such pronounced concern for consumers? Probably because competition policies are based on an economic theory presenting the same bias. As indeed suggested by Alain and Chambolle (2003), traditional microeconomic analysis tends to neglect upstream oligopsony powers since it automatically models producer-distributor

---

[1]   From Bruno Darin, From Ivorian Cocoa Bean To French Dark Chocolate Tablet: Price Transmission, Value Sharing and North/South Competition Policy, in Qaqaya and Lipimile, eds., supra, pp. 237, 309–311.

[16]   Like setting up a cocoa plantation.

[17]   To solve this problem, the solution would then consist, according to the authors, in rebalancing contracts, and stepping up sanctions in cases of violation of the commitments. This is perfectly realistic for the particular case of French fruit and vegetable producers, but barely so for the more universal case we are examining: agricultural producers far from major distributors, not only vertically (numerous processes and numerous middlemen before the end product) but also horizontally (production in developing countries of foodstuffs consumed in industrialized countries), i.e. a case in which the possibilities of contractualization, and applying sanctions are severely limited, or even ruled out.

relations by a principal-agent relation in which the dominant role is assigned to the producer (i.e. power to impose his conditions on distributors). Likewise, since Spengler revealed the inefficiency of double marginalization in 1950, that same literature has focused on the effect of vertical contracts on efficiency and total profit of vertical structures, but virtually ignores its impact on profit sharing within those structures. Yet an imbalance in profit sharing can be harmful to long-term social well-being, by threatening the survival of certain producers and reducing the variety or quality of products available to consumers.... Some ... recent work seems to corroborate theoretically what we observe empirically in the cocoa-chocolate commodity chain. But as Allain and Chambolle (2003) concluded, whilst several questions omitted from the vertical analysis are at last starting to be explored today, the work still required remains considerable.

Once this work has made some headway, competition policies may then perhaps speak more of producers than consumers, of monopsonies and oligopsonies than monopolies and oligopolies, of a "hypothetical monopsonist test" rather than a "hypothetical monopolist test".

Notes and Questions

1. From Dorin's formulation, what implications do you draw regarding competition rules that advance efficient development? Does Dorin want to protect competitors? Or does he suggest that analysis focused on efficient *development* may differ from an analytical framework designed to serve consumers in developed economies?

2. In the developed world, it is easy to take for granted the availability of certain basic services, such as financial transactions, that are that vital to the welfare of low-income people in developing countries. Competition law can play an important role in increasing access to such services. In 2014, the Competition Authority of Kenya launched an investigation into potentially anticompetitive vertical restrictions imposed by Safaricom, a leading mobile network operator in Kenya. In 2007, Safaricom launched the M-Pesa mobile money system that allows users to pay for goods and services, access loans, and exchange money on a cash-free basis. The service has become a huge success, with over 30 million users in ten African countries, and plans to expand throughout the African continent. However, the Kenyan Competition Authority became concerned about exclusivity clauses in Safaricom's contracts with financial agents that restricted those agents' ability to work for rival mobile money providers. The Authority and Safaricom reached an official settlement in 2014, with Safaricom agreeing to expunge the exclusivity clauses from its agency contracts. If you were the head of competition

agency in the developing world, how would you prioritize your scarce agency resources? What industry sectors or practices deserve the most attention?

Chapter 5

MERGERS

A. INTRODUCTION

Global issues with respect to mergers can be divided into three parts: First, with respect to domestic mergers, how do we define markets that have a transborder dimension? Should effects on competition be seen through a wider lens—i.e., one that captures the whole market, even beyond the nation's borders? Second, comparatively, are issues framed and resolved in the same way in all parts of the world? Is the standard of prohibition the same? We know that US law does not allow for defenses based on public interest or industrial policy. How do other nations treat these concerns? Third, cooperation and conflict. Almost 100 jurisdictions have premerger notification regimes. Fifty nations or so might claim jurisdiction over the same merger. What is the state of convergence on premerger notification processes and procedures? When jurisdictions vet the same merger and reach different assessments as to anticompetitiveness or appropriate relief, how is the conflict resolved? How might it be resolved? Is there room for transnational cooperation in the process of investigating and analyzing mergers that are of interest to more than one jurisdiction?

B. DOMESTIC ISSUES IN ANALYSIS OF TRANSBORDER MERGERS

1. Market Definition, and Deciding What Sales and What Firms Are in the Market

The problem of defining the market and determining what sales or capacity to include in the market is the most straightforward of the issues. The question that the analyst wants to answer is the same as with any other merger. The analyst wants to include in the market all good constraints on pricing power. This means inclusion of all constraints that would tend to keep the post-merger price down to the premerger price. If outsiders are already selling the relevant product into the geographic market, their product is included in the geographic market. If higher domestic prices would induce an increased flow of the foreign product, this larger quantity should be included. If suppliers not already selling in the market would enter in response to a non-transitory price increase, their expected effect on the market should be assessed.

Thus in *United States v. Baker Hughes*, 908 F.2d 981 (D.C. Cir. 1990), a Finnish company's subsidiary, Tamrock, sought to buy the French subsidiary of a Texas firm, Secoma. Both merger partners manufactured and sold hydraulic underground drilling rigs in the highly concentrated United States and world markets. Judge (now Justice) Thomas said: "[A] number of firms competing in Canada and other countries had not penetrated the United States market, but could be expected to do so if Tamrock's acquisition of Secoma led to higher prices." "[E]ntry in the United States HHUDR market would likely avert anticompetitive effects from Tamrock's acquisition of Secoma."

In some cases markets are global. Sellers seek buyers and buyers seek sellers without regard to borders. Transportation costs are low in proportion to the size of transaction. Such was the case in the jet aircraft market, as in *Boeing/McDonnell Douglas*, which we discuss below. While in that case the United States and Europe was each concerned about its own citizens, both recognized that the market was global.

2.   Effects Beyond Borders

Most jurisdictions are directed by their laws to consider only effects within their borders.

Canada has a total-Canadian-welfare standard. Competition Act, Canada, R.S.C. 1985, C–34, as revised, Sec. 96 (1) (stating the efficiency exception), and Canada's Merger Enforcement Guidelines, Sept. 1, 2004, available at *http://www.competitionbureau.gc.ca/eic/site/cb-bc.nsf/eng/03420.html* , and Bulletin on Efficiencies in Merger Review, March 2, 2009, available at *http://www.competition bureau.gc.ca/eic/site/cb-bc.nsf/eng/02989.html*. Thus, if Canadian producers profit at the expense of foreign buyers, and the producers gain more than the Canadian consumers lose, the law recognizes a welfare gain.

However, a merger approved in Canada on total welfare grounds may run into resistance elsewhere, as two Canadian chemical manufacturers discovered in the summer of 2016. Toronto-based Superior Plus Corp., and Canexus Corp., headquartered in Alberta, are two of the three major North American producers of sodium chlorate—a commodity chemical used to bleach wood pulp that is then processed into paper, tissue, diaper liners, and other products. Their proposed merger would have left the new company and rival

AkzoNobel controlling approximately 80 percent of the total sodium chlorate production capacity in North America.

The Canadian Competition Bureau and the US FTC ran parallel and collaborative investigations, both concluding on June 27, 2016, but with different results. The Competition Bureau issued a No Action Letter, thus allowing the transaction to proceed. It acknowledged that "customers of Superior and Canexus could face materially higher prices for these chemical inputs and would have limited options for alternative supply as a result of the merger." However, it then applied the efficiency defense, finding that the merger would create significant efficiencies from the "elimination of overhead costs, freight optimization, and the elimination of duplicate corporate services." On balance, it found that the efficiencies outweighed the anticompetitive effects:

> The Bureau retained an external economic expert to model the likely effects of the proposed merger and, in particular, to estimate the deadweight loss (allocative inefficiency) that would likely result from the merger, as well as an external efficiencies expert to evaluate Superior's claims. The Bureau concluded that the anti-competitive effects of the merger would be clearly outweighed by the efficiency gains from the transaction.

Competition Bureau Statement Regarding Superior's Proposed Acquisition of Canexus, *http://www.competitionbureau.gc.ca/eic/ site/cb-bc.nsf/eng/04111.html.*

By contrast, the FTC brought an administrative challenge against the merger, alleging that it would lead to anticompetitive reductions in output and higher prices, and that by removing Canexus as an independent sodium chlorate producer, with its large scale and low-costs, the acquisition would increase the likelihood of coordination in an already vulnerable market (Under the Justice Department and FTC's 2010 Horizontal Merger Guidelines, efficiencies must be passed onto consumers in order to offset any competitive concerns). Faced with the FTC's opposition, the parties abandoned the transaction.

Jurisdictions generally consider benefits and harms beyond their borders as not their problem. An exception is *Italimpiante*, a merger of an Italian and a German firm that created a monopoly of oil pipeline technology that was becoming obsolete in the Western world but was very much in use in China. The German cartel office declined to address the problem since no harms would fall within Germany, but the Italian Antitrust Authority recognized the harm and ordered the merged firm to grant licenses upon request to any firm within the European Union that sought to make the monopolized technology. Fiatimpresit-Mannesmann Demagtechint/ Italimpianti, Case No. 3622 (C2227), Italian Antitrust Authority (1996).

Mature jurisdictions whose citizens are hurt by an off-shore merger can normally fend for themselves and perhaps even prohibit a harmful off-shore merger. The authorities in small jurisdictions and developing economies are not so fortunate. They can usually do little to prevent world mergers that hurt them or to impose effective conditions. For example, the merger may create buying power that exploits African farmers. Should such negative effects be part of the merger calculus by American or European authorities? Would a broader view encompassing effects wherever they fall require legislative change? Would a national legislature ever vote to increase the scope of domestic law to recognize harms by their nationals to foreigners? We return to some of these issues when we treat cooperation and related global issues below.

C. COMPARATIVE ISSUES

1. Substantive Analysis

a. *Market Definition*

Context dictates the confines of markets. The importance of context is illustrated by the proposed merger of two South African department stores that catered to the poorest consumers.

In the large merger between JD Group Ltd. and Ellerine Holdings Ltd., Competition Tribunal, Republic of South Africa, case 78/LM/Jul00. Two of South Africa's best-known department stores proposed to merge. One of these enterprises had pioneered a marketing approach that offered generous credit to "some of South Africa's poorest consumers, many of whom do not even have access to a bank account." Because no credit had been available to black South Africans, many of these individuals had not previously been able to buy furniture and appliances. In discussing whether the market was limited to credit purchases of furniture and appliances and also whether it included more upscale sellers, the Tribunal said:

> In this case . . . the parties to the transaction are the final link with the consumers, and, at that, the poorest, least powerful of South African consumers. In other words, the interests directly affected by this merger are represented by millions of atomized, disorganized individuals incapable of defending their economic interests except to the extent that they are able to exercise a preference for one retail outlet

over another. This evaluation will seek to assess whether the transaction has the potential to increase the power of the parties over the consumers that they serve and who are the source of their prosperity.

Rejecting defendants' argument that the market included higher end stores, the Tribunal said:

> The distinction [based on Living Standard categories] informs advertising strategy in very subtle ways as an amusing example alluded to during our proceedings shows. Ellerines in the LSM [Living Standard Measure] 3–5 market offer a free sheep worth R300 if goods above a specified amount are purchased. A graphic of a sheep is depicted in the advert. Bradlow's, the high end JD brand, also offers a free gift for customers purchasing above a specific amount. The gift, however, underlines the difference in social status of the LSM categories—Bradlow's offers not a free sheep, but a coffee table book on 101 ways to cook lamb!

The Tribunal found that the relevant market was the sale of furniture and appliances on credit to consumers in a low-end LSM category through national chains of furniture shops. It enjoined the merger.

A second issue concerns the informal economy. In many developing countries, including many in Africa and South America, there is a large informal economy. This means there are many enterprises—often unable to fulfill dense, expensive, and time-consuming licensing requirements—that operate outside of the legal system. They do not pay taxes, they risk being raided, and they cannot enforce contracts in court, but they may impose competitive pressures. Reliable data on the informal economy are hard to obtain. How should the informal economy be counted in defining markets and assessing competitive effects of firms merging in the formal economy? *See* OECD Policy Roundtable, Competition Policy and the Informal Economy 2009, available at *https://www.oecd.org/daf/competition/44547855.pdf.*

b.   *Standard of Violation*

Mergers violate US law when their "effect may be substantially to lessen competition." This is sometimes referred to as the SLC standard. In fact, the modern US standard is whether the merger is likely to create, enhance or entrench market power or facilitate its exercise. See Horizontal Merger Guidelines for Public Comment, released April 20, 2010, US department of Justice and Federal Trade

Commission. For shorthand, this standard is called "enhancing market power." A merger that enhances market power is virtually always illegal. It is possible, however, that such a merger might create efficiencies that are greater than the consumer loss and that would otherwise be unattainable. If the authorities are convinced that this is the case (they seldom are), they might withhold enforcement.

Merger control in the European Union was late in coming. Concentration of business by merger was not an issue in the early days of the European Community. Markets had been bounded by national borders, business was usually smaller than efficient scale, and cross-border mergers were welcomed both to increase efficiency and to integrate the common market. Moreover, various European Member States were skeptical about centralized merger control. Germany was afraid that European standards would be too weak; France did not want to lose control over the structure of its economy; Britain generally opposed more regulation from Brussels. Eventually, however, economic power-creating mergers did become a recognized problem in Europe, and the Member States agreed to a regime of centralized control for mergers (or other concentrations) of community dimension; that is, having cross-border effects and not centrally of interest to one Member State. In 1989, effective in 1990, a European merger control regime was established. It entailed notification, as in the United States, and a one-stop-shop, unlike the United States. That is, if the merger is subject to European jurisdiction, it cannot also be enjoined or conditioned by a Member State.

The standard for violation in the original merger control regulation was: Did the merger "create[ ] or strengthen[ ] a dominant position as a result of which effective competition would be significantly impeded." This "dominance" standard predictably proved too limiting. Many mergers were anticompetitive not because they created nascent monopolies but because they entrenched oligopolies. The European courts addressed the problem by giving a flexible interpretation to "dominance," construing the word to cover "collective dominance"—which meant, essentially, coordinated effects among oligopolists. *Kali und Salz*, [1998] ECR I–1375.

Still, there was a gap. The prohibitory language could not be stretched further to cover unilateral effects where the merger would not create dominance. Moreover, the "collective dominance" stretch was recognized as instrumental, to cover oligopolistic mergers. Because of these limits, the merger regulation was revised. The revised merger regulation, effective in 2004, proscribes mergers "which would significantly impede effective competition, . . . in particular as a result of the creation or strengthening of a dominant position . . . ." This is called the SIEC standard.

Most jurisdictions adopt either a form of SCL (substantial lessening of competition) or a form of SIEC. Some have a dominance standard (i.e., they prohibit mergers that create or entrench dominance), and some (like Germany) have a dominance standard that covers oligopolistic dominance. Act Against Restraints of Competition, § 36, which incorporates in its merger law its definition of dominance. (§ 19). Japan not only prohibits mergers and acquisitions that may result in a "substantial restraint of competition in a particular field of trade"; it also prohibits certain mergers that create "excessive concentration of economic power" (Anti-Monopoly Act, Article 9) and it prohibits financial institutions from holding more than 5% of joint stock in a non-financial institution, with a 10% limit for holdings in insurance companies. AMA Art. 11.

There is a very significant degree of substantive convergence in merger law throughout the world. This is particularly true for horizontal mergers. The US horizontal merger guidelines and the European horizontal merger guidelines are very similar. The formulation for analysis of horizontal mergers is essentially the same. The International Competition Network has produced a very useful merger workbook. See *http://www.internationalcompetition network.org/uploads/library/doc321.pdf*. The content of the workbook confirms the high degree of similarity.

Consider the following European Commission press release explaining its decision to block a merger between two telephone companies operating in the UK market. The Commission's explanation does not sound materially different from the US Justice Department's explanation for challenging the merger between AT&T and T-Mobile in 2011.

MERGERS: COMMISSION PROHIBITS HUTCHISON'S PROPOSED ACQUISITION OF TELEFÓNICA UK

Brussels, 11 May 2016

The Commission has blocked the proposed acquisition of O2 by Hutchison under the EU Merger Regulation. It had strong concerns that UK mobile customers would have had less choice and paid higher prices as a result of the takeover, and that the deal would have harmed innovation in the mobile sector.

Today's decision follows an in-depth investigation by the Commission of the deal, which would have combined Telefónica UK's "O2" and Hutchison 3G UK's "Three", creating a new market leader in the UK mobile market. The takeover would have removed an important competitor, leaving only two mobile network operators, Vodafone and BT's Everything Everywhere (EE), to challenge the merged entity. The significantly reduced competition in the market would likely have resulted in higher prices for mobile services in the UK and less choice for consumers than without the deal. The takeover would also likely have had a negative impact on quality of service for UK consumers by hampering the development of mobile network infrastructure in the UK. Finally, the takeover would have reduced the number of mobile network operators willing to host other mobile operators on their networks.

The remedies proposed by Hutchison failed to adequately address the serious concerns raised by the takeover.

Commissioner Margrethe **Vestager**, in charge of competition policy, said: *"We want the mobile telecoms sector to be competitive, so that consumers can enjoy innovative mobile services at fair prices and high network quality. The goal of EU merger control is to ensure that tie-ups do not weaken competition at the expense of consumers and businesses.*

Allowing Hutchison to takeover O2 at the terms they proposed would have been bad for UK consumers and bad for the UK mobile sector. We had strong concerns that consumers would have had less choice finding a mobile package that suits their needs and paid more than without the deal. It would also have hampered innovation and the development of network infrastructure in the UK, which is a serious concern especially for fast moving markets. The remedies offered by Hutchison were not sufficient to prevent this."

The UK mobile market

The UK mobile market is currently competitive—retail mobile prices are among the lowest in the entire EU. The UK is also one of the most advanced countries in the EU in terms of roll-out of 4G technology and take-up of 4G services.

There are currently four mobile network operators in the UK—BT's mobile business EE, Telefónica's O2, Vodafone and Hutchison's Three.

EE and Three have combined their networks as "Mobile Broadband Network Limited"—MBNL. Similarly, Vodafone and O2 combined their networks to set up Beacon. This allows EE / Three, and Vodafone / O2 respectively, to share the costs of rolling out their networks but they continue to compete with each other for retail customers.

In addition to the four mobile network operators, there are a number of mobile "virtual" operators active in the UK retail mobile market, such as Virgin Media, Talk Talk and Dixons Carphone's iD. These mobile virtual operators do not own the networks they use to provide mobile services to UK consumers. Instead, they entered agreements with one of the mobile network operators to access their network at wholesale rates.

The Commission's competition concerns

The Commission had serious concerns that the takeover would have reduced competition in the market, hampered the development of the UK mobile network infrastructure as well as the ability of mobile virtual operators to compete.

1. **Less competition leads to higher prices and reduced choice and quality for consumers:** The takeover would have eliminated competition between two strong players in the UK mobile market. Three is the latest market entrant and has been an important driver of competition in the UK mobile market. O2 has a strong position with high brand value and reputation. It is the second largest mobile operator by revenues and the largest in terms of subscribers (if its share in the Tesco Mobile joint venture is included). Combined, Three and O2 would have been the market leader with a share of more than 40%. They would have had much less incentive to compete with Vodafone and EE. This would have **reduced choice and quality of service for UK consumers**. The Commission's analysis also showed that with the takeover **retail mobile prices would have been higher** for all UK operators than without.

2. **Future development of entire UK mobile network infrastructure hampered:** The merged entity would have been part of both network sharing arrangements, MBNL and Beacon. It would have had a full overview of the network plans of both remaining competitors, Vodafone and EE. Its role in both networks would have **weakened EE and Vodafone** and **hampered the future development of mobile infrastructure** in the UK, for example with respect to the roll-out of next generation technology (5G), to the detriment of UK consumers and businesses.

3. **Reduced number of mobile network operators effectively willing to host virtual operators:** The transaction would have reduced the number of mobile network operators willing to

host other mobile operators on their networks. Mobile virtual operators rely on access to the infrastructure to provide mobile services to consumers. The reduced number of host mobile networks would have left prospective and existing mobile virtual operators in a **weaker negotiating position to obtain favourable wholesale access terms**.

* * *

We have noted that relatively little substantive divergence appears in horizontal cases. More divergence appears in the analysis of vertical and conglomerate mergers. The divergence is illustrated in the different treatment by the United States and the European Union of the merger of General Electric and Honeywell. General Electric was the dominant producer of engines for jet aircraft and Honeywell was the leading producer of avionic and non-avionic products (such as steering equipment) for jet aircraft. The European Commission was concerned that the combined firm would bundle its products and marginalize competitors, especially Honeywell's competitors, who would find it harder to beat Honeywell and would decrease their investments in those products. These were "conglomerate" issues. The case also raised some horizontal and vertical issues. The European Court of First Instance affirmed the Commission's prohibition of the merger, but only on horizontal issues (both companies made jet engines, albeit at different ends of the value spectrum). The court held that the Commission had not proved that the merged firm would bundle its products. [2005] ECR II–5575. See Eleanor Fox, *GE/Honeywell: The U.S. Merger that Europe Stopped—A Story of the Politics of Convergence*, in ANTITRUST STORIES, Chapter 12 E. Fox and D. Crane, eds. (2007).

The US and the EU (and other jurisdictions) may apply different default presumptions in analyzing conglomerate mergers, especially in matters involving foreclosing effects. The European Commission and European courts are more likely than US courts to find that a merger creates significant foreclosing effects that block the market, undermine rivals' ability to contest the market, and ultimately harm consumers. See the European non-horizontal merger guidelines. *http://eurlex.europa.eu/LexUriServ/LexUriServ.do?uri=CELEX: 52008XC1018(03):EN:NOT*. The US Courts, on the other hand, are more likely to find a merged firm's potentially exclusionary conduct, such as bundling, a stimulus to rivals to compete harder. See *GE/Honeywell* at D. 3 below.

Developing countries often have an additional concern: buyer power. Hassan Qaqaya and George Lipimile note in the Executive Summary of their book, THE EFFECTS OF ANTI-COMPETITIVE

BUSINESS PRACTICES ON DEVELOPING COUNTRIES AND THEIR DEVELOPMENT PROSPECTS (UNCTAD 2008), referencing an article by Bruce Dorin:

> ... [C]ocoa markets have been experiencing increased horizontal concentration through mergers of large multinational companies, such as those between large chocolate companies and cocoa processing firms, or through takeovers by large international companies of smaller companies operating at the national market. As a result of these developments, small local cocoa producers have to contend with a strong purchasing power held by several large multinational companies. *Id.*, xiii.

c.   *Treatment of Efficiencies*

Differences among jurisdictions may appear in the treatment of efficiencies. The United States and the EU both consider efficiencies in connection with the competition analysis; not largely as a defense to anticompetitive mergers but as an important factor in determining whether the merger might be procompetitive. For example, in affirming a district court injunction against a merger between the Anthem and Cigna health insurance groups, the D.C. Circuit noted that the current legal status of the efficiencies defense remains unsettled, but that any cognizable efficiencies defense would need to be merger-specific, verifiable, and sufficient to offset any anticompetitive effects of the merger. *U.S. v. Anthem, Inc.*, ___ F.3d ___, 2017 WL 1521578, at *7 (D.C. Cir. April 28, 2017).

Some jurisdictions, however, allow an efficiencies defense to an anticompetitive merger. As noted above with respect to the Superior Plus/Canexus merger, Canada has a total welfare standard, and if the producers gain more in efficiencies than consumers lose in high prices, the merger is allowed. Also in Canada, increased exports may be a factor justifying a price-raising merger. Competition Act, Section 96. See Commissioner of Competition v. Superior Propane Inc., CT 1998/002, Aug. 30, 2000.

In *Tervita Corp. v. Commissioner of Competition*, CT 2015/3, March 27, 2015, the Supreme Court of Canada explained the efficiencies defense as follows in overruling a Tribunal decision to prohibit a merger between hazardous waste disposal companies operating in Northeastern British Columbia:

> As s. 92 of the Act is engaged [based on a finding that merger is prima facie anticompetitive], it is necessary to determine whether the s. 96 efficiencies defence applies to prevent the making of an order under s. 92. The defence

requires an analysis of whether the efficiency gains of the merger, which result from the integration of resources, outweigh the anti-competitive effects, which result from the decrease in or absence of competition in the relevant geographic and product market. The Commissioner has the burden of proving the anti-competitive effects, and the merging parties bear the onus of proving the remaining elements of the defence. There are different possible methodologies for the comparative exercise under s. 96, two of which have been the subject of judicial consideration in Canada: the "total surplus standard" which involves quantifying the deadweight loss which will result from a merger, and the "balancing weights standard" under which the Tribunal weighs the effects of the merger on consumers against the effects of the merger on the shareholders of the merged entity. Because the Act does not set out which methodology should be used, the Tribunal has the flexibility to make the ultimate choice of methodology in view of the particular circumstances of each merger.

The test may be framed as a two-step inquiry. First, the quantitative efficiencies of the merger should be compared against the quantitative anti-competitive effects. Where the quantitative anti-competitive effects outweigh the quantitative efficiencies, this step will in most cases be dispositive, and the defence will not apply. Under the second step, the qualitative efficiencies should be balanced against the qualitative anticompetitive effects, and a final determination must be made as to whether the total efficiencies offset the total anti-competitive effects of the merger at issue.

In small and developing economies, nations might face a trade-off. A merger might increase prices at home, but the merged firm might be more efficient and thus more competitive in world markets. (Theoretically, this can happen also in the United States and the EU, but given the size of our markets it is much less likely.) The nation might choose to sacrifice its own consumers' welfare in order to get more traction in international markets. See Michal Gal, COMPETITION POLICY FOR SMALL MARKET ECONOMIES (2003).

d.   ICN Recommended Practices for Merger Analysis

The International Competition Network, a network of more than 100 antitrust/competition authorities, has adopted recommended practices for merger analysis. The ICN is open to all competition authorities in the world, and its working groups are open to all members, who are assisted by non-governmental advisors (NGAs). The ICN published recommended best practices guidelines for merger analysis in 2008, with comments by the network's merger working group in 2009. In 2017, the ICN added new sections based on subsequent learning by its members:

ICN RECOMMENDED PRACTICES FOR MERGER ANALYSIS

(International Competition Network, 2008, with revisions as of 2017)
available at *http://www.internationalcompetition network.org/uploads/library/doc1107.pdf.*

These recommendations on substantive merger analysis are derived from the ICN Merger Guidelines Workbook and common practices across member jurisdictions. They are intended to complement the detailed descriptions of merger analysis in the Workbook. [The workbook is available at *http://www.internationalcompetition network.org/uploads/library/doc321.pdf.*] For a description of effective investigative techniques to develop evidence to account for particular facts presented in merger investigations, see the ICN Investigative Techniques Handbook for Merger Review.

The ICN Recommended Practices for Merger Notification and Review Procedures address the procedural aspects of notification and review. Several topics covered in those recommended practices relate to the legal framework for substantive merger analysis. In particular, the practices that address transparency, agency powers, confidentiality, and the conduct of a merger investigation are relevant to the legal framework for substantive merger review.

I.   The Legal Framework for Competition Merger Analysis

    A.   **The purpose of competition law merger analysis is to identify and prevent or remedy only those mergers that are likely to harm competition significantly.**

WORKING GROUP COMMENTS
Original Comments (April 2008)

Comment 1: The legal framework for competition law merger review ("merger review law") should focus exclusively on identifying and preventing or remedying anticompetitive mergers. A merger review law should not be used to pursue other goals.

Comment 2: Most mergers do not harm competition. Many mergers enable the merged firm to reduce costs and become more efficient, leading to lower prices, higher quality products, or increased investments in innovation. Some mergers, however, may harm competition by creating or enhancing the merged firm's ability or incentives to exercise market power—either unilaterally or through coordination with rivals—resulting in price increases above competitive levels for a significant period of time, reductions in quality or a slowing of innovation.

Comment 3: Merger review laws and policies should provide competition agencies with the ability to differentiate mergers that are unlikely to have significant anticompetitive effects from those that require more analysis. The identification of those mergers that potentially threaten to harm competition and expeditious clearance of non-problematic mergers can lead to more efficient use of agency resources and more effective analysis of critical legal and economic issues.

Comment 4: A competition authority's decision to take enforcement action against a merger should not be based on expected anticompetitive effects that are insignificant or transient in duration.

Comment 5: Agencies should only intervene to prohibit or remedy a merger when it is necessary to prevent anticompetitive effects that may be caused by that merger. The appropriate goal of agency intervention to prohibit or remedy a merger is to restore or maintain competition affected by the merger, not to enhance premerger competition.

B. A jurisdiction's merger review law and policy should provide a comprehensive framework for effectively addressing mergers that are likely to harm competition significantly.

WORKING GROUP COMMENTS
Original Comments (April 2008)

Comment 1: A jurisdiction's merger law and policies should enable the competition agency to perform its competition analysis and to take appropriate and effective enforcement action.

Comment 2: A merger review law should have broad application to transactions[1] that may raise significant competitive concerns, regardless of how the transaction is structured. The legal authority to analyze a merger should not be based on the form or technicalities of a merger agreement.

---

[1] A detailed discussion of the types of transactions that merger review laws cover is contained in the ICN report, "Defining 'Merger' Transactions for Purposes of Merger Review."

Comment 3: Specific sector exceptions or exemptions to generally applicable merger review provisions, if any, should be narrowly drawn, clearly delineated, and reviewed periodically.

Comment 4: The substantive legal standard for mergers and any analytical guidelines should be based on sound and robust economic principles. Merger review laws and policies should establish a framework for analysis that can address the likely anticompetitive effects of a merger while retaining sufficient flexibility to adapt to developments in economic learning. Clear, comprehensive, and transparent legal and analytical standards, that include identifying the range of mergers subject to the law and the substantive standard for assessing whether a merger is likely to harm competition significantly, improve the predictability of enforcement actions.

Comment 5: A determination of whether a merger is likely to harm competition significantly should take place within established legal procedures, including an appropriate and transparent standard of proof.

C. An agency's merger analysis should be comprehensive in its assessment of factors affecting the determination of whether a merger is likely to harm competition significantly.

WORKING GROUP COMMENTS
Original Comments (April 2008)

Comment 1: An agency's merger analysis should not be a mechanical application of a legal standard based on rigid presumptions, structural criteria, or formulaic concentration numbers. An agency should apply its merger analysis reasonably and flexibly on a case-by-case basis, recognizing the broad range of possible factual contexts and the specific competitive effects that may arise in different transactions.

Comment 2: The substantive legal standard in a merger review law should permit intervention only where it can be established to the requisite standard of proof that any likely future anticompetitive effects are attributable to the merger itself and not to any other factor. Central to the analysis, therefore, should be a comparison of competition in the relevant market with and without the merger. In most cases, the starting point for such analysis will be an assessment of the competitive conditions existing before the merger, but account should also be taken of any changes in those conditions likely to take place irrespective of the merger.

Comment 3: Merger analysis requires an agency to predict a merger's competitive impact to prevent any competitive problems before they materialize. Agencies should recognize that the further in the future the predicted effects (both harmful and beneficial) are projected to occur, the more difficult it is to predict confidently that they will occur.

Comment 4: The objective application of competition law standards in merger analysis promotes consistency and predictability. An agency's merger analysis practice should also include a commitment to transparency (subject to appropriate confidentiality protections) in order to achieve consistency and predictability and allow merging parties and the public to understand better how the merger laws are enforced. An agency should clearly articulate the analytical factors it uses for merger analysis.

II. Market Definition

A. Agencies generally should assess the competitive effects of a merger within economically meaningful markets. A relevant market consists of a product or group of products and a geographic area in which it is produced or sold that could be subject to an exercise of market power.

[The remaining discussion is omitted. The Recommendations generally advocate the use of the Small but Significant and Nontransitory ("SSNIP") test for defining relevant markets.]

III. Use of Market Shares: Thresholds & Presumptions

A. Market shares and measures of market concentration play an important role in merger analysis but are not determinative of possible competition concerns. Agencies should give careful consideration to market definition and the calculation of market shares and market concentration.

WORKING GROUP COMMENTS
Original Comments (April 2008)

Comment 1: Market shares are an indication of the competitive significance of each merging firm in the relevant market. They provide an indication of a firm's incentives to coordinate its actions with rivals and its ability unilaterally to exercise market power. The significance of market shares and measures of market concentration is specific to the analytical context presented in each investigation. They are not determinative of possible competition concerns in themselves, as they may, for instance, either underestimate or overestimate the future competitive significance of a firm or the impact of a merger.

Comment 2: In general, agencies should pay greater attention to a merger that significantly increases market concentration than to one that does not, or does so only marginally. Whatever the existing level of concentration, the change in concentration caused by a merger is a useful, although imperfect, indicator of the loss of direct competition between the parties and of the potential for competitive harm.

Comment 3: Market shares and measures of concentration are useful in merger analysis only when they are based on properly defined product and geographic markets. Particular caution is needed in markets involving differentiated products, as market definition itself is more complex in these cases. Market share calculations should be based on reliable data and sources and sound assumptions.

Comment 4: Market shares should be based on a measure of economic strength (e.g., sales, production, or capacity) that is appropriate to the circumstances of the market. Market share and concentration estimates used for a merger analysis should reflect the best available indication of the firms' future competitive significance. Market characteristics and changes in market conditions should be considered in interpreting market shares and market concentration data. Before drawing any conclusions from market share and concentration data, agencies should consider imminent or reasonably certain changes to the market, such as the entry or exit of a firm or the introduction of additional capacity. To gain a better insight into the competitive dynamics of some markets, it may also be relevant to analyze changes in market shares and concentration over time.

B. Market shares and measures of market concentration can provide useful initial guidance to help identify mergers that may raise competitive concerns requiring further analysis.

WORKING GROUP COMMENTS
Original Comments (April 2008)

Comment 1: The purpose of initial guidance based upon market shares or measures of concentration is to help differentiate mergers that are unlikely to have anticompetitive consequences from those that require more detailed analysis. Such guidance can enhance predictability and allow for a better allocation of agency resources.

Comment 2: The absence of high market shares or post-merger concentration ordinarily supports a conclusion that a given transaction requires no further analysis. Similarly, a transaction that does not significantly increase post-merger market shares or concentration ordinarily requires no further analysis, as the premerger competitive conditions are unlikely to be significantly altered by the merger. However, there may be exceptions. For example, when at least one party to the merger has substantial market power, even small increases in market share may be indicative of possible competition concerns. Evidence that the merged firm would have a high market share or that the market is highly concentrated can be significant to a decision to initiate an in-depth investigation.

Comment 3: Many agencies identify thresholds based on market shares and levels of concentration to give initial guidance as to the likely need for an in-depth investigation. An agency can set threshold levels of market shares and measures of concentration under which it commits itself not to, or is generally unlikely to, challenge a merger or over which it is likely to continue an in-depth analysis of the merger's effects on competition.

C. High market concentration and significant increases in market shares brought about by a merger are useful, but generally are not conclusive indicators that a merger is likely to harm competition significantly. Jurisdictions that use market concentration and/or market shares to presume competitive harm should ensure that any such presumption may be overcome or confirmed by a detailed review of market conditions.

WORKING GROUP COMMENTS
Original Comments (April 2008)

Comment 1: Mergers that lead to high market share for the merging firms and that result in significant increases to concentration levels are in general the mergers most likely to raise competition concerns.

Comment 2: In some jurisdictions, high market share or market concentration gives rise to a presumption of competitive harm, whereas in others they do not. When agencies use presumptions of competitive harm based on market shares or market concentration, the investigatory process should take into account evidence that may overcome or confirm the presumption. Agencies should be transparent about the meaning and use of any presumptions, including any quantitative standards used to evaluate market shares or concentration.

Comment 3: Agencies should not make enforcement decisions to prevent or remedy a merger solely on the basis of market shares and concentration. Thus, agencies should not automatically reach a final conclusion that a merger is likely to be anticompetitive because the merger increases concentration above a certain level or reduces the number of remaining firms below a certain level. A detailed analysis of other market factors and of theories of unilateral and/or coordinated effects should always be required before definitive conclusions are drawn regarding the likely competitive effects of a merger.

V.   Entry & Expansion

A.   The assessment of firm entry and/or expansion by existing competitors should be an integral part of the analysis of whether a merger is likely to harm competition significantly (e.g., the merged firm could raise prices or reduce output, quality, or innovation).

WORKING GROUP COMMENTS
Original Comments (April 2008)

Comment 1: Entry, or the threat of entry from potential competitors or from customers turning to in-house supply, can be an important competitive constraint on the conduct of the merged firm. If the merged firm is subject to competitive constraints from the threat of market entry (e.g., if barriers to entry are low and entry is likely to be profitable at premerger prices), the merger is unlikely to have anticompetitive effects.

Comment 2: The ability of rival firms to expand capacity in a timely manner, or use existing spare capacity or switch capacity from one use to another, can also constitute an important competitive constraint on the merged firm's conduct (these shorter term supply-side responses can also be assessed in the context of market definition). Many of the factors that are used to assess entry are relevant to the analysis of expansion, including competitor expansion plans, barriers to expansion, and the profitability of expansion.

Comment 3: Competition agencies should consider whether entry and/or expansion would deter or offset the likely anticompetitive effects of a merger. Competition agencies should focus on entry and/or expansion that would occur as a result of the post-merger competitive situation as well as entry and expansion that is likely to take place independent of the merger.

B.   In assessing whether entry and/or expansion would effectively constrain the merged entity, competition agencies should consider whether entry and/or expansion would be: (a) likely; (b) timely; and, (c) sufficient in nature, scale and scope.

WORKING GROUP COMMENTS
Original Comments (April 2008)

Comment 1: For entry and/or expansion to be likely, it should be profitable for competitors of the merged entity to expand output and/or for potential entrants to enter the market in response to an attempt by the merged entity to profit from the potential reduction in competition brought about by the merger (e.g., a post-merger price increase). In assessing the *likelihood* of entry, competition agencies should also consider establishing, if possible, the history of entry into and/or exit from the relevant market by using available evidence including information on firms that have recently entered or exited the market, information about past and expected market growth, evidence of planned entry and/or expansion, direct observation of the costs, risks and benefits associated with entry and information from firms identified as potential entrants.

Comment 2: In assessing the *likelihood* of entry and/or expansion, competition agencies should consider the existence and significance of barriers to entry and expansion to the relevant market (i.e., the advantages enjoyed by incumbent firms over the potential entrants that may prevent or delay new firms from entering the market). When assessing ease of entry, agencies should focus on whether potential entrants would consider entry to be profitable in light of factors including but not limited to:

- economies of scope and/or scale, the availability of a scarce resource that is an essential input, technical capability or intellectual property rights;

- the reputation of incumbent firms, incumbent firms' investment in excessive capacity, or the duration, termination and renewal provisions in existing contracts;

- government regulations that might, for example, limit the number of market participants or impose substantial regulatory approval costs; and,

- sunk costs that could not be recovered if the entrant left the market including machinery that might be site specific or R & D that has not yet resulted in any marketable invention or innovation.

Comment 3: In assessing whether entry and/or expansion is timely, competition agencies should consider whether entry and/or expansion would take place within a reasonable period of time after the merger (many jurisdictions consider that entry must have a competitive impact within two years to have a sufficiently disciplining effect). The appropriate time horizon may vary according to the characteristics of the relevant market.

Comment 4: For entry and/or expansion to be sufficient, competition agencies should consider whether entry and/or expansion would be:

- sufficient in scale to compete effectively with the merged entity;

- able to counteract any specific anti-competitive effects resulting from the merger; and,

- able to counteract any localized effects of the merger (e.g., in markets differentiated by geographic areas or customer categories).

IV. Competitive Effects Analysis in Horizontal Merger Review: Overview

A.   The goal of competitive effects analysis in the review of horizontal mergers is to assess whether a merger is likely to harm competition significantly by creating or enhancing the merged firm's ability or incentives to exercise market power, either unilaterally or in coordination with rivals.

WORKING GROUP COMMENTS
Original Comments (June 2009)

Comment 1: Agencies should conduct competitive effects analysis in merger review to identify those mergers likely to harm competition significantly by creating or enhancing market power. When exercised by sellers, market power is the ability profitably to raise price above competitive levels for a significant period of time, and/or to lessen competition on parameters other than price, such as quality, service, or innovation. In some cases, market power may be exercised by buyers. In such cases, market power is the ability profitably to reduce the price paid to suppliers below competitive levels for a significant period of time, which may in some cases lead to an anticompetitive reduction in supplier output.

Comment 2: Agencies generally should conduct competitive effects analysis within the context of properly defined product and geographic markets. However, market definition is not an end in itself but is a tool to assist in determining whether a merger will create or enhance market power. In some cases, evidence of competitive effects, such as price effects following a consummated merger under investigation or a prior merger in the industry, may inform the analysis of the appropriate relevant markets.

Comment 3: Agencies engaged in competitive effects analysis should conduct a forward-looking inquiry focusing on a comparison of the anticipated state of competition in the relevant market(s) with and without the merger. An agency's assessment of competition without the merger (sometimes called the "counterfactual") should be informed not only by the existing conditions of competition, but also by any significant changes in the state of competition likely to occur without the merger.

Comment 4: While changes in market share or market concentration are useful indicators of potential competitive concerns, competitive effects analysis involves a comprehensive assessment of market conditions, and provides agencies with a more reliable means to assess potential harm to competition than changes in market share or market concentration alone.

B. In conducting competitive effects analysis, agencies should consider whether a merger likely will result in anticompetitive unilateral or coordinated effects. These two theories of competitive harm provide the analytical frameworks for determining whether a horizontal merger may be expected to harm competition significantly.

WORKING GROUP COMMENTS
Original Comments (June 2009)

Comment 1: Unilateral effects, also known as non-coordinated effects, arise when, as a result of a merger, it is likely that the merged firm, without any coordination with non-merger rivals, will be able profitably to exercise market power to a materially greater degree than would have been possible for either of the merged firms before the merger.

Comment 2: Coordinated effects arise when, as a result of a merger, it is likely that firms remaining in the market after the merger will be able to coordinate (either tacitly or explicitly) their behavior or strengthen existing coordination in order to exercise market power.

Comment 3: Unilateral effects and coordinated effects are broad analytical frameworks designed to encompass the full range of anticompetitive effects that may result from horizontal mergers. While anticompetitive effects of a merger within a particular market are often best characterized as either unilateral or coordinated, a merger may result in both unilateral and coordinated effects.

C. The analysis of competitive effects under either the unilateral or coordinated effects framework should be

clearly grounded in both sound economics and the facts of the particular case.

WORKING GROUP COMMENTS
Original Comments (June 2009)

Comment 1: Economic theories and models are useful in analyzing competitive effects under both unilateral and coordinated effects frameworks, but only to the extent that the theory or model used to assess the likely competitive effects of a merger is based on sound and robust economic principles and fits the factual conditions of the market to which it is applied.

Comment 2: Competitive effects analysis depends heavily on the specific facts of each case. In conducting competitive effects analysis, agencies should refine their theories or models of likely competitive harm in light of the available qualitative and quantitative evidence. Qualitative evidence often comes from documents or first-hand observations of the industry by customers or other market participants. Quantitative evidence is often derived from statistical analysis of price, quantity, or other data related to, among other things, prior market events (sometimes called "natural experiments") involving incumbent responses to prior events such as entry or exit by rivals. Competitive effects analysis should be flexible enough to adapt over time to evolving markets, business practices, and economic learning.

V.   Unilateral Effects

A.   In analyzing the potential for a horizontal merger to result in anticompetitive unilateral effects, agencies should assess whether the merger is likely to harm competition significantly by creating or enhancing the merged firm's ability or incentives to exercise market power independently.

WORKING GROUP COMMENTS
Original Comments (June 2009)

Comment 1: Horizontal mergers eliminate any competitive constraint that the merging parties formerly exerted upon one another. In the majority of mergers, this has no significant adverse effect on competition because there are other sufficient competitive constraints on the merged entity. In some cases, however, the elimination of competition between the merging parties in itself may create or enhance the ability of the merged firm independently to exercise market power, depending on market conditions, including the existence and effectiveness of other competitive constraints.

Comment 2: Agencies conducting unilateral effects analysis should look not only at market shares and market concentration, but should also examine the specific features of the market that affect the merged firm's ability to exercise market power. While market shares are a useful indicator of the potential for the merged firm to exercise unilateral market power, market shares alone may overstate or understate the potential for a merger to result in anticompetitive unilateral effects. Competitive constraints may preclude the exercise of market power even by firms with high market shares. On the other hand, even small changes in market share in some circumstances may increase the ability or incentives of a firm to exercise market power.

B.   In conducting unilateral effects analysis, agencies should apply the economic theory or model that best fits the characteristics of the market(s) at issue.

WORKING GROUP COMMENTS
Original Comments (June 2009)

Comment 1: Mergers may increase the likelihood of the exercise of unilateral market power in a variety of settings. There are a number of unilateral effects theories and models in the economic literature that address competitive effects in specific factual settings. While the specific model or theory used will vary depending on the characteristics of the market, all are designed to assess whether there is any material increase in unilateral market power as a result of the merger. Common theories and models include, but are not limited to:

- *Merger to monopoly*: A merger that would combine the only two rivals in a properly defined market raises a high risk of significant anticompetitive unilateral effects. In examining a merger combining the only two rivals in a relevant market, agencies should assess whether any competitive constraints exist, such as ease of entry, that would preclude the unilateral exercise of market power by the merged firm.

- *Merger of competitors in differentiated product markets*: A merger that would combine competing suppliers of differentiated products may raise the potential for significant anticompetitive unilateral effects if a sufficient proportion of consumers view the products combined by the merger as their first and second choices (or closest substitutes). Commonly used sources of evidence on the degree of substitutability among differentiated products include marketing surveys, analysis of purchasing patterns, cross-price elasticities, and information contained in normal course of business documents from market participants. Agencies should assess whether the merger would allow the merged firm profitably to increase price on one or more products after the merger, or whether sufficient customers would switch to products of other competitors so as to render such a price increase unprofitable for the merged firm. Agencies should also consider whether rival sellers likely would replace any loss of competition by repositioning or extending their product lines to compete more closely with the merged firm.

- *Merger of competitors in undifferentiated product markets*: In examining a merger that would combine competing suppliers of undifferentiated products in markets in which firms are distinguished primarily by capacity, agencies should consider whether the merged firm would find it profitable to raise price by reducing output below the level that would have prevailed absent the merger. The exercise of market power in such markets is likely only if competitors of the merged firm likely would not respond to the price increase and output reduction by the merged firm with increases in their own outputs sufficient in the aggregate to make the unilateral action of the merged firm unprofitable. This may occur if non-merging firms face binding capacity constraints that could not be economically relaxed in a timely manner, or if existing excess capacity is significantly more costly to operate than capacity currently in use. In such cases, competitors may find it more profitable to raise price than expand output, resulting in additional anticompetitive unilateral effects.

- *Merger of rivals in bidding or auction markets*: A merger that would combine rival bidders in bidding or auction markets may raise the potential for significant anticompetitive unilateral effects. There are a variety of models in the economic literature addressing a wide array of bidding and auction formats involving both differentiated and undifferentiated products. For example, some models focus on whether the merger would combine the two lowest-cost or otherwise closest competitors. Other models focus on whether the merger would result in a competitively significant reduction in the number of bidders. Agencies should determine the appropriate model depending upon the circumstances of the market, and each bid or auction market should be analyzed on its own facts.

Comment 2: Merger simulation and other formal economic modeling can be useful tools in unilateral effects analysis. In order to be useful, the particular model used should be based on sound and robust economic principles, fit the facts of the market, and suitable data must exist to calibrate the model. The fit of a model should be based on the totality of the evidence.

C. In conducting unilateral effects analysis, agencies should assess the competitive constraints and other factors relevant to the ability of the merged firm to exercise market power in the relevant market(s).

WORKING GROUP COMMENTS
Original Comments (June 2009)

Comment 1: In assessing the impact of a merger on the merged firm's ability to exercise market power, agencies should draw on all available evidence, especially evidence created in the ordinary course of business. Common sources of evidence include documents, information, quantitative evidence, and economic analyses from the merging parties, customers, competitors, and other third parties; statements, representations, and testimony from representatives of the merging parties and other industry participants; and generally available industry studies, reports, and market data.

Comment 2: Agencies should assess whether competitive constraints or other market conditions that will remain in the market following the merger are adequate to prevent the creation or enhancement of unilateral market power. Factors that are often relevant in assessing the likelihood of a unilateral exercise of market power as a result of a merger include, but are not limited to:

- *Availability and Responsiveness of Alternative Suppliers*: If alternative suppliers (offering adequate substitutes and with sufficient available capacity) will remain post-merger, and a significant number of customers are willing and able to turn to these alternative suppliers in the event of an anticompetitive increase in price, the threat of losing such customers may be enough to deter the exercise of market power by the merged firm.

- *Entry, Repositioning, or Expansion*: The prospect of entry by new competitors, or expansion or repositioning by existing competitors, may be sufficient in time, scope, and likelihood to deter or defeat any attempt by the merged firm to exercise market power.[1] In some cases, however, a merger may lessen the potential for entry, expansion or repositioning to act as a competitive constraint against the exercise of market power.

- *Buyer Power*: In some circumstances, customers may have the incentive and ability to defeat the exercise of market power through their bargaining strength against the seller because of their size, commercial significance to the seller, or ability to switch to alternative sources of supply. Customers also may have the ability to encourage or sponsor competitive entry or expansion, or to produce the relevant product themselves. In such cases, even firms with very high market share may not be in a position to exercise market power post-merger. To prevent significant anticompetitive effects, however, buyer power must constrain the exercise of market power in the market and not merely protect certain individual customers.

- *Efficiencies*: Agencies should carefully assess any substantiated claims by the merging parties that a merger will generate efficiencies sufficient to prevent or mitigate anticompetitive unilateral effects from the merger. For instance, cost reductions may reduce a merged firm's incentive to raise price. Efficiencies may also result in benefits in the form of new or improved products, even when price is not immediately and directly affected. Agencies should consider the impact of substantiated efficiencies that are unlikely to be achieved in the absence of the merger on the merged firm's ability and incentives to compete, and whether such efficiencies may preserve or intensify competition, thereby benefiting consumers.

---

[1]   Recommended Practice for Merger Analysis III addresses the analysis of entry and expansion.

VI. Coordinated Effects

A.   In analyzing the potential for a horizontal merger to result in coordinated effects, agencies should assess whether the merger increases the likelihood that firms in the market will successfully coordinate their behaviour or strengthen existing coordination in a manner that harms competition significantly.

WORKING GROUP COMMENTS
Original Comments (June 2009)

Comment 1: To identify those mergers that materially enhance the likelihood of coordination or strengthen existing coordination, agencies should: (a) assess whether market conditions are conducive to coordination in the relevant market(s) affected by the merger; and (b) analyse specifically whether and how the merger would affect market conditions and firms' ability or incentives that would make coordination more likely post merger.

Comment 2: The fact that a market has conditions that are conducive to coordination in itself is not sufficient to conclude that a merger is likely to further or enhance coordination. Agencies should also be able to determine whether the merger will make coordination easier or more likely, considering the specific features of the market that affect the merged firm's ability and incentives to exercise market power in coordination with rivals.

Comment 3: Changes in market concentration and market share are relevant, but not determinative, factors in assessing whether a merger is likely to further or enhance coordinated interaction. Agencies should focus on whether the merger will materially alter firms' ability or incentives to achieve and sustain coordination. An examination of the role each competitor plays in the competitive dynamics of the market may help to determine how the merger is likely to impact the likelihood of coordination post-merger.

B.   In conducting coordinated effects analysis, agencies should assess whether the conditions that are generally necessary for successful coordination are present: (a) the ability to identify terms of coordination, (b) the ability to detect deviations from the terms of coordination, and (c) the ability to punish deviations that would undermine the coordinated interaction.

WORKING GROUP COMMENTS
Original Comments (June 2009)

Comment 1: Coordinated behaviour can take many forms: it may be tacit or explicit and may or may not be lawful in itself. In some markets, firms may coordinate their behaviour on prices in order to keep them above the competitive level. In other markets, firms' coordination may aim at limiting production or the amount of new capacity brought to the market. Firms may also coordinate by dividing the market, for instance by geographic area or other customer characteristics, or by allocating contracts in bidding markets.

Comment 2: In order to coordinate, firms need to achieve an understanding as to how to do so. This need not involve explicit agreements among competitors, or any communication between them, nor need it involve all firms or perfect coordination between firms. Agencies should assess whether it is likely that participants could achieve terms of coordination that would be sufficiently successful to result in significant harm to competition. When assessing market conditions conducive to reaching terms of coordination, important factors include, but are not limited to:

- The number of firms in a market, since it is easier to coordinate among a few players than among many;

- The existence of frequent and regular orders, which make it easier to coordinate and to detect deviations from the terms of coordination;

- The homogeneity of the products, since it is easier to coordinate on terms such as price when competing products are substantially the same;

- The homogeneity of the firms, especially in terms of symmetry of market shares, similarity of cost structures, levels of vertical integration, and the impact that such homogeneity may have on their ability or incentives to coordinate;

- The degree of transparency of important information that could provide a focal for coordination, such as information concerning prices, output, capacity, customers served, territories served, discounts, new product introductions, etc.;

- Cross-shareholdings and other links that may make it easier for competitors to exchange information on

terms of coordination, and may reduce their incentives
to compete; and,

- Other market conditions: for instance, it is easier to
  coordinate on price when demand and supply
  conditions are relatively stable than when they are
  frequently changing (e.g., because of the ease of entry
  by new firms or rapid, significant product innovations).

Comment 3: Firms may be able to identify terms of coordination even
in markets with complex product characteristics or terms of trade.
For instance, in a market with many differentiated products, firms
may still be able to coordinate on prices by establishing simple
pricing rules that reduce the complexity of coordinating on a large
number of prices or to coordinate on terms other than prices.
Moreover, coordination may not necessarily be achieved on all
dimensions of competition.

Comment 4: Although coordination may be in the collective interest
of participants, it is often in a firm's individual interest to deviate
from the terms of coordination in order to take advantage of the profit
opportunity created when other firms raise their prices or otherwise
coordinate their behaviour. For coordination to be maintained,
participants must have the ability to detect and respond to deviations
from the terms of coordination. Agencies should assess the extent to
which firms would have the ability to monitor the important terms of
coordination and to detect deviations from the terms of coordination
in a timely manner. When assessing the likelihood and timeliness of
detection of deviations from the coordinated behaviour, important
factors include, but are not limited to:

- The degree of transparency of important information
  necessary to verify compliance by other firms with the
  terms of coordination, such as information concerning
  other firms' pricing, output levels, or individual
  transactions. For instance, if orders for the relevant
  products are regular both in terms of frequency and
  size, it may be difficult for a firm to deviate (by
  expanding its output) without being detected. Also, if
  there is little fluctuation in demand or costs, deviations
  may be easier to detect. On the other hand, if orders for
  the relevant products are infrequent and large, firms
  may have a greater incentive to deviate to secure
  orders and the threat of later punishment may not
  serve as an effective deterrent.

- The extent to which the homogeneity or heterogeneity
  of the products and firms may make monitoring of

compliance with the terms of coordination and detection of deviations more or less difficult.

Comment 5: In order to deter deviations from the terms of coordination, firms must have the ability to punish deviations in a manner that will ensure that coordinating firms find it more profitable to adhere to the terms of coordination than to deviate, given the cost of reprisal. Punishment may take many forms, including temporary abandonment of the terms of coordination by other firms in the market. In assessing whether there will be a sufficiently credible and severe punishment when a deviation by one of the firms is detected, important factors include, but are not limited to:

- The effectiveness of the deterrent mechanism itself: e.g., the threat of expanding output to punish a deviating firm may not be credible or effective if coordinating firms have no or little excess capacity;

- The speed with which the deterrent mechanism can be implemented, given that reprisal that manifests itself after some significant time lag is less likely to be sufficient to offset the benefits from deviating; and,

- the costs of implementing the deterrent mechanism compared to the long-term benefits of coordination.

Other factors, such as the presence of the same firms in several markets (sometimes called "multi-market contacts"), may also be of relevance in determining the likelihood of sufficiently credible and severe punishment.

C. In conducting coordinated effects analysis, agencies should assess the extent to which existing competitive constraints and other factors would likely deter or disrupt effective coordination. In making this assessment, agencies should consider all available evidence, including the pre-merger market conditions that may constrain or facilitate successful coordination, and the impact of the merger on these conditions.

WORKING GROUP COMMENTS
Original Comments (June 2009)

Comment 1: Agencies should assess whether competitive constraints or other market conditions that will remain in the market following the merger are adequate to prevent the creation or enhancement of coordinated interaction. Factors that are often relevant in making this assessment include, but are not limited to:

- *Past Coordination/Behaviour of Firms*: In assessing
  the likelihood of coordinated effects, agencies should
  take into account information on the pre-merger
  characteristics of the markets concerned, including the
  past behaviour of firms. Evidence of past coordination
  is important and may serve as strong evidence that all
  three conditions for successful coordination are present
  if the relevant market characteristics have not
  changed appreciably or are not likely to do so in the
  near future.

- *Entry or Expansion*: Agencies should also consider the
  actions of competitors not expected to participate in the
  coordination ("non-coordinating competitors") and
  potential competitors, which may be sufficient in time,
  scope, and likelihood to jeopardise the outcome
  expected from coordination. [2] For instance, the
  existence of non-coordinating competitors with the
  ability to expand capacity to take sales from
  coordinating firms may deter or disrupt coordination.
  Agencies should therefore consider the existence and
  significance of barriers to entry and expansion into the
  relevant market(s) since low barriers to entry and
  expansion may render successful coordination unlikely
  or impossible.

- *Maverick Firm*: Coordination may also be difficult to
  sustain in the presence of a maverick firm—a firm with
  a different competitive strategy and a greater economic
  incentive than its rivals to deviate from the terms of
  coordination. Particular care is needed in mergers
  involving the acquisition of a maverick firm because in
  some circumstances those mergers may eliminate a
  significant constraint to effective coordination and
  make coordinated interaction more likely, more
  successful, or more complete.

- *Buyer Power*: Agencies should consider whether the
  actions or characteristics of customers affect the
  likelihood of successful coordination. In some
  circumstances, buyers may be able to undermine
  coordinated behaviour, for example by sponsoring
  entry or expansion. Where large buyers likely would

---

[2] Recommended Practice for Merger Analysis III addresses the analysis of entry and expansion.

engage in long-term contracting, so that sales covered by such contracts would be large relative to a firm's total output, firms may have a greater incentive to deviate from the terms of coordination.

- *Efficiencies*: Agencies should carefully assess any substantiated claims by the merging parties that a merger will generate efficiencies sufficient to prevent or mitigate coordinated effects from the merger. For instance, cost reductions may enhance a merged firm's incentives to lower prices, thus reducing incentives to coordinate. Efficiencies may also result in benefits in the form of a new or improved product that could undermine coordination. Agencies should consider the impact of substantiated efficiencies that are unlikely to be achieved in the absence of the merger on the merged firm's incentives to coordinate.

Comment 2: In assessing market conditions conducive to coordination, competition authorities should bear in mind that no single factor or group of factors is always determinative.

VII. Assessment of Potential Efficiencies

A. The assessment of potential efficiencies should be part of a competition agency's overall analytical framework for merger review. In specific cases where the merging parties assert that a merger is unlikely to harm competition significantly because of expected efficiencies, agencies should carefully assess appropriate efficiency claims.

Comment 1: Mergers can produce significant efficiencies for the merged firm and such efficiencies can be important business motivation for a merger. Merger efficiencies can include cost savings in production or distribution, more intensive use of existing capacity, economies of scale or scope, increased innovation leading to new or improved products, increased network size or product quality, among others. Some of these efficiencies (innovation, combination of complementary assets, etc.) may bring synergies in a potentially continuous basis, thus considerably enhancing the potential performance of the merged entity.

Comment 2: Mergers can produce efficiencies that may counteract potential anti-competitive effects. To counteract likely anticompetitive harm, efficiencies need to increase rivalry by enhancing the ability and economic incentive of the merged firm to compete. Efficiencies can have such impact if they lower costs and there is sufficient competitive pressure remaining. The benefits of some merger efficiencies can be passed on to consumers, for example, in lower prices or gains in innovation that lead to new or improved products.

Comment 3: In order to determine the impact of a merger that potentially harms competition, agencies should take into account substantiated and likely efficiencies put forward by the parties.

Agencies should not challenge a proposed merger if the demonstrated efficiencies likely would be passed through to consumers and likely would counteract the anticompetitive effects in any relevant market(s) that otherwise would be likely to result from the merger. Efficiency claims should be assessed in light of all other evidence. Efficiencies are most likely to impact merger analysis when the likely adverse competitive effects, absent the efficiencies, are not large.

Comment 4: In most cases, a merger will not raise competition concerns because there are sufficient competitive constraints in the market to prevent significant harm regardless of whether the merger will enable efficiencies. When a merger does not raise competition concerns, the assessment of efficiencies is not necessary.

Comment 5: Efficiencies can be important to merger remedy design. Where feasible, merger remedies should eliminate the anti-competitive effects of a merger in the relevant market without unnecessarily sacrificing substantiated efficiencies in other markets or aspects of the transaction.

Comment 6: Agencies should provide transparency with respect to their approach to evaluating potential efficiencies in merger control, including the weight the agency is likely to place on efficiency claims, the types of efficiencies that are likely to be taken into account, and any evidentiary requirements for substantiating efficiencies. Such guidance may be provided, for example, through public merger guidelines and other statements explaining merger analysis, as well as through decisions in specific cases in which efficiency claims are raised by the parties.

B. In assessing claims that a merger will not harm competition significantly because it will produce efficiencies, agencies should carefully review whether the claimed efficiencies are (a) merger specific, (b) sufficient enough to counteract the potential harm of the proposed merger, and (c) properly substantiated.

Merger Specificity

Comment 1: Agencies should credit only those efficiencies that are merger specific. Merger-specific efficiencies are those that are of direct consequence of the merger, unlikely to be accomplished in the absence of the merger, and cannot be achieved by less anticompetitive alternatives. In many cases, efficiencies can be achieved without the proposed merger. Efficiencies that are achievable, for instance, via internal growth, modernizing equipment, or adoption of industry best practices are not merger specific. In assessing whether efficiencies can be achieved by alternatives other than the merger, only practical business alternatives should be considered.

Sufficiency

Comment 2: Agencies should evaluate whether the claimed efficiencies are sufficient to counteract the merger's potential anticompetitive harm in the relevant market(s), e.g., by likely enhancing the merged firm's ability and incentive to lower prices or otherwise compete.

Comment 3: In many jurisdictions, this sufficiency requirement includes a showing that a sufficient share of the benefits expected to be realised from the efficiencies is likely to be passed on to consumers (or customers), usually in the form of lower prices or increased output. Efficiencies that reduce variable or marginal costs are more likely to be passed on to customers in the form of lower prices and thus more likely to be relevant to the assessment than those that reduce fixed costs. Cost reductions due to anticompetitive reductions in input prices, innovation, output, or service should not be considered. When dynamic efficiencies are important, they may benefit consumers by resulting in either improved or new products stemming from higher R&D investment or new combinations of understanding, experience or technologies.

Comment 4: Where reasonably possible, efficiencies and resulting benefits should be quantified. Efficiency claims should be assessed net of the costs to achieve the expected efficiencies. While the quantification of claimed efficiencies is often among the most speculative elements of merger review, it can better inform identifiable benefits to consumers and a comparison of the efficiencies with the likely harm to competition.

Substantiation

Comment 5: Merger-specific efficiency gains are difficult to assess and verify both for merging parties and for competition agencies. Agencies should advise merging parties to submit efficiency claims very early in the process as their verification by reasonable means typically requires a significant amount of time and resources. The merging parties typically have the best knowledge about the likely efficiencies that a merger may create as the information about the claimed efficiencies is normally solely in their possession. Therefore, the merging parties should be required to present evidence regarding the type, likelihood, size, and timing of any claimed efficiencies, including how they would be achieved, how they would enhance the firm's ability and incentive to compete, and why they are merger specific. Efficiency gains are often claimed by merging parties but not frequently supported with convincing evidence.

Comment 6: To verify efficiency claims, agencies typically review internal data and documents from the merging firms to determine how realistic the claims are. Evidence that agencies consider in evaluating efficiency claims typically includes internal documents that were used by management to decide on the merger, company statements about the expected efficiencies, business plans on how the company plans to achieve the efficiencies, examples of past efficiencies and any studies on the type and size of expected efficiency gains. Proof that similar efficiencies were achieved in the past from similar actions can be among the most convincing evidence in evaluating efficiency claims. In evaluating the information submitted to substantiate efficiency claims and any conclusions, agencies should assess the accuracy of the parties' data and information, as well as the analytical methods and assumptions used.

Comment 7: The greater the likely adverse effects on competition, the greater the need to demonstrate clear, significant, and verifiable efficiencies and their impact on competition and consumers. When the potential adverse competitive effects of a merger are likely to be substantial, significant verifiable efficiencies that are likely to benefit consumers would be necessary to prevent the merger from being anticompetitive. Likewise, the more uncertain and modest the likely harm to competition, the greater potential role for claimed efficiencies to outweigh the harm.

Comment 8: The stronger the evidence to substantiate the efficiency claims, the more confidence an agency is likely to have in relying on the claims as part of its analysis. Efficiency claims that are vague, speculative, and cannot be verified by reasonable means should not be credited.

Comment 9: The time horizon for claimed efficiencies can be an important consideration in evaluating efficiencies in light of potential anti-competitive harm. Efficiencies should have a timely impact on the merged firm's ability and incentives to compete. The more time projected for the efficiencies to be realised, the more uncertainty and difficulty there is with respect to predicting their effects.

Possible addition to A, comment 3, for consideration and comment:

The evaluation of efficiencies commonly is part of an agency's competitive assessment, focusing on whether the claimed efficiencies counteract the harm in the market in which the lessening of competition occurs. In a few jurisdictions, efficiencies also are considered after a merger is determined to be anticompetitive, as a separate assessment of the offsetting customer benefits of a merger.

[Parts VIII and IX, on entry and expansion and the failing firm defense, are omitted]

XI. Remedies

A. **A remedy should address the identified competitive harm arising from the proposed transaction.**

WORKING GROUP COMMENTS
(2017)

Comment 1: The object of a remedy should be to maintain or restore competition otherwise lost due to the merger. A remedy should be considered only if the agency has a sound basis to believe that the proposed transaction, if implemented, would contravene the applicable merger review law. The remedy should adequately address the potential competitive harm identified, but should not have the object of improving upon premerger competition. Tailoring the remedy to the competitive harm allows competition agencies to require the least intrusive remedy and permit, if possible, the realization of the merger's benefits, without compromising effectiveness.

Comment 2: There are instances in which only an outright prohibition can adequately address the competitive concerns. The merging parties should be permitted, however, to propose alternative resolutions that permit the transaction to proceed with appropriate modifications, conditions, and/or obligations that maintain or restore competition otherwise likely to be lost due to the proposed transaction, consistent with the applicable merger review law. Before pursuing or adopting an outright prohibition, agencies should consider such alternative resolutions. In addition, the agency may take the initiative to propose alternative resolutions.

Comment 3: The proposal, discussion, and adoption of remedies should be conducted in a manner consistent with other

Recommended Practices, particularly those on Conduct of Merger Investigations, Procedural Fairness, Transparency, and Interagency Coordination and informed by the Merger Remedies Guide and the Practical Guide on International Cooperation.

B.   The merger review system should provide a transparent framework for the proposal, discussion, and adoption of remedies.

WORKING GROUP COMMENTS
(2017)

Comment 1: Information on the jurisdiction's procedures for proposing, discussing, evaluating, and adopting remedies should be readily available to those involved in merger review proceedings. Such information may include, as applicable, when, how and to whom remedies should be proposed, the types of remedies that the agency generally prefers and in which instances, and any standard terms or implementation provisions the remedy would be expected to include.

Comment 2: In the event the competition agency identifies competitive concerns, the agency should provide the merging parties with timely and substantiated information on those concerns so the parties can consider and propose remedies to address those concerns in due time prior to the final enforcement decision. Merger review procedures should provide means to ensure that competition agencies have adequate time to discuss suitable remedies with the merging parties, evaluate the proposed remedies, and consult appropriate third parties on the effectiveness of the remedies.

C.   Procedures and practices should be established to ensure that remedies are effective and easily administrable.

WORKING GROUP COMMENTS
(2017)

Comment 1: Remedies should be effective in maintaining or restoring competition otherwise lost due to the proposed transaction and be easily administrable. Remedies should not require significant administrative intervention by the agency after the transaction is consummated.

Comment 2: Remedies can take two basic forms: (a) structural remedies, which help to maintain or restore the pre-merger market structure (such as commitments to divest assets), and (b) non-structural remedies, which involve modifications or constraints on the future conduct of the merged entity (such as commitments with respect to certain contractual clauses). Certain remedies, such as commitments involving licensing of intellectual property rights or access to facilities, may be characterized as structural or non-structural, depending on the circumstances. An effective package of remedies adopted with respect to a proposed transaction may consist of structural and/or non-structural components, including short-term transitional arrangements that support a structural remedy.

Comment 3: Structural remedies are generally preferred over non-structural remedies because they directly maintain or restore the competitive structure of the market that would be otherwise lost due to the proposed transaction, have a durable impact, are easier to administer and do not require medium or long-term monitoring to ensure compliance. Structural remedies can take several forms. The preferred structural remedy is typically the divestiture of an ongoing, stand-alone business unit, including the sale of all the infrastructure, components, and human resources necessary for the divested business to compete immediately after the remedy is implemented. The divestiture of less than an existing business carries more risk, and requires more agency scrutiny, but may constitute an effective remedy if, taking into account resources already owned and operated by a potential buyer, the divested assets are sufficient to allow the buyer to compete successfully in the relevant market. While short-term assistance from the merging parties can be necessary to transition assets to an independent buyer, remedies should avoid creating ongoing relationships and entanglements between the merged entity and the purchaser of divested assets that may impede competition.

Comment 4: Where structural remedies are either not possible or not appropriate to address the competitive harm, or where structural remedies may undermine significant efficiency benefits, a non-structural remedy may be appropriate to address the competition concerns. Non-structural remedies that facilitate or protect competition (such as reducing switching costs and opening up tender processes) are generally more effective than those that aim to control prices or output levels (such as price controls, service level agreements, and supply commitments). In crafting non-structural remedies, competition agencies should consider whether ongoing monitoring of the remedy is feasible and be wary of high implementation costs associated with monitoring, terms that restrain potentially pro-competitive conduct, and terms that are vulnerable to circumvention and manipulation. Competition agencies should consider other alternatives before imposing price controls as remedies, as price controls can distort market forces and harm competition, require a great deal of market insight that is not readily

available, and will likely require regulatory oversight and
intervention to implement and maintain.

Comment 5: The remedy's effectiveness may depend on the identity
of the prospective purchaser of the assets to be divested, particularly
where less than an ongoing business unit is being divested. For a
remedy to be effective, it should enable the prospective purchaser to
be a viable and long-term competitor in the market in which the
competitive harm was identified. Competition agencies should
evaluate prospective purchasers for their financial strength,
managerial expertise and operational capabilities, as well as for their
independence and intention to compete with the merged firm in the
affected market after divestitures. The agency should retain the
authority and have appropriate procedures to approve a prospective
purchaser.

Comment 6: When competition agencies have concerns about the
availability of a suitable purchaser or viability of the proposed
remedy, they should consider requiring approval of a pre-identified
buyer of the divested assets before the merger is consummated. Pre-
identified buyers should also be considered when there are concerns
about a lengthy divestiture process resulting in deterioration of the
divested assets.

Comment 7: Market testing, either a formal or informal process by
which competition agencies obtain views and comments from third-
party customers, suppliers, and/or competitors, should be encouraged
when it helps to determine if the proposed remedy will adequately
address competitive concerns. Third party submissions or comments
should be evaluated for self-interest or any motives that might
attempt to influence the agencies' views.

Comment 8: Timing is a critical factor in determining whether a
merger remedy is effective. Remedies should be implemented in a
prompt and timely manner. Remedies should have a specified end
date or termination provision.

**D. Remedies should provide appropriate means to
ensure implementation, monitoring of compliance,
and enforcement of the remedy.**

*WORKING GROUP COMMENTS
(2017)*

Comment 1: Jurisdictions may have different terminology or
mechanisms for formalizing and enforcing remedies. Regardless of
the terminology used ("remedy order" or other), a formal and written
form of imposing remedies should identify, provide notice, and bind
the entities subject to its terms. The terms should be sufficiently clear

and precise to provide the parties adequate guidance in implementing the remedy, in particular with respect to the scope of any assets to be divested and any obligations regarding the ongoing conduct of the parties. The remedy order should also include provisions which will enable the competition agency to investigate compliance and ensure the order is fully implemented.

Comment 2: As part of a structural remedy, a competition agency should require the merging parties to maintain and preserve the assets pending divestiture to ensure that there is no deterioration of the assets' competitive strength. Such requirements or "hold separate" measures can help to ensure the independence and viability of divested assets by maintaining their value and goodwill, protecting sensitive information, encouraging employees to remain with the entity until divestiture, and otherwise ensuring the divested assets are not allowed to deteriorate. In some cases, a competition agency may wish to appoint a hold separate manager who can oversee implementation of hold separate provisions.

Comment 3: In a remedy order, it may be appropriate to include terms permitting the competition agency to select one or more trustees who are independent of the parties and can oversee the divestiture process or the conduct of the merging parties over the duration of a non-structural remedy. Monitoring trustees can help to oversee implementation of remedies and provide regular reports or updates to the competition agency. A divestiture trustee may take over the divestiture process from the merging parties if they fail to sell the divested assets within the required time period.

Trustees should be independent of the merging firms, have appropriate qualifications for the role, and should not be subject to conflicts of interest. The scope and limits of the trustee's responsibilities and authority should be clearly set out in a mandate provided by the competition agency, which should also state that the trustee cannot accept instructions or be dismissed by the merging firms. Nevertheless, the parties can be required to compensate the trustee.

Comment 4: The competition agency should have the means to investigate compliance with the remedy order, including the ability to inspect and copy records, conduct reviews, and to require periodic or one-time reporting obligations by the parties and/or the trustee(s) on the implementation of the remedy. The ultimate decision regarding compliance with the remedy order should rest with the agency or court, and not with the trustee.

Comment 5: Competition agencies are unable to control or predict every factor capable of impacting the implementation of remedies.

Significant and permanent changes in market conditions may impact the effectiveness of a remedy, especially in cases where a non-structural remedy continues over a long duration. Review or revision clauses, or other procedures which would permit remedies to be removed or modified upon demonstration of specified objectives or criteria, may provide flexibility to address unanticipated factors. Modifications can range from extensions of implementation deadlines to remedy substitutions or waivers to implement commitments.

Comment 6: A party's failure to comply with the terms of a remedy order should either be enforceable by the competition agency directly or through the courts. In some jurisdictions, the merger clearance may automatically lapse. To discourage non-compliance, the potential penalties should be clearly articulated. In the event of deliberate non-compliance with a remedy order by the merging parties, competition agencies should contemplate available options within their legal framework to ensure that the remedy order is properly implemented. If non-compliance results from the remedy order being impossible to implement, competition authorities can consider whether modifications or alternative remedies may be effective to address the relevant competition concerns.

2. Public Interest Defenses and Concerns

Many newer antitrust jurisdictions, and especially developing countries, allow public interest justifications for anticompetitive mergers. If many jurisdictions allow public interest justifications, why do the ICN recommended practices propose that antitrust merger analysis be confined to significant harm to competition?

a. The Public's Interest Beyond Competition and Consumer Welfare

A major design question is whether the public interest justifications, when allowed, are applied by the competition authorities themselves or by a minister after being presented with the competition analysis. The latter model (discretion of the minister) has been adopted in the UK and Germany. The former model is the one adopted in South Africa. This model has been defended by the former Chair of the South African Competition Tribunal as likely to result in greater appreciation of the competition concerns and more likely to probe whether expectations for achieving the public interest objectives are realistic. David Lewis, *The Political Economy of Antitrust*, 2001 FORDHAM CORPORATE LAW INSTITUTE, Chap. 24 (B. Hawk ed. 2002).

In South Africa a merger may be stopped or allowed on purely public interest grounds, regardless whether the merger is procompetitive or anticompetitive. Competition Act, South Africa, 1998, Section 12A. Empowering the previously discriminated-against majority (black South Africans) is a major public interest concern that pervades virtually all positive law. It is frequently put forward as a justification in merger cases, but almost never is seen as pointing towards a different result from competition concerns.

In dealing with public interest justifications, one must first try to understand the public interest standard.

The South Africa Competition Law prohibits mergers likely to substantially prevent or lessen competition, except that the Commission and Tribunal must also examine the transaction's impact on the public interest and it may allow or disallow a merger on public interest grounds whether or not the merger is anticompetitive. The statute says:

> When determining whether a merger can or cannot be justified on public interest grounds, the Competition Commission or the Competition Tribunal must consider the effect that the merger will have on—
>
> a) a particular industrial sector or region;
>
> b) employment;
>
> c) the ability of small business, or firms controlled or owned by historically disadvantaged persons, to become competitive; and
>
> d) the ability of national industries to compete in international markets. § 12 A(3).

In the large merger between Shell South Africa (Pty) Ltd. and Tepco Petroleum (Pty) Ltd., Competition Tribunal, Republic of South Africa, case 66/LM/Oct01, Feb. 22, 2002. Thebe Investment Corporation, a black empowerment investment holding company established to use economic opportunities to benefit previously disadvantaged people and communities, owned Tepco, an employer of 38 people, 80% of whom were historically disadvantaged. Tepco owned 14 gas stations country-wide, and was failing. Thebe proposed to sell Tepco to Shell South Africa, and at the same time acquire 17.5% to 25% of Shell South Africa Marketing. Shell South Africa Marketing expected to maintain Tepco brand as a separate brand for the foreseeable future, to develop it in the market as long as it should remain profitable, and to retain Tepco's management, which was predominantly black.

The South African oil industry had adopted a charter on empowering historically disadvantaged South Africans, aiming to bring about their 25% ownership and control within 10 years. Shell's overriding reasons for purchasing Tepco was to lay the foundation for involvement of previously disadvantaged South Africans.

The Competition Commission vetted the transaction, found that it would not harm competition, and recommended that the Tribunal approve the transaction subject to three conditions designed to further the urgent South African goal of black empowerment: 1) that Tepco continue to exist jointly controlled by Thebe and Shell S.A., 2) that Tepco be maintained as a viable brand, and 3) that any agreement between the parties be submitted to the Commission for approval.

The Tribunal agreed with the Commission that the transaction would not harm competition and proceeded to examine the "public interest" conditions:

First Condition—*Tepco continue to exist in the market jointly controlled/owned by Thebe and Shell South Africa*

[42] The difficulty with the condition is that it amounts to restructuring the deal in a form that neither of the merging parties wants. Tepco is no longer viable as a self-standing company. It appears that its difficulties are, to some significant extent, structural. That is to say, it appears that a small company isolated in a low return segment of the oil industry's value chain has precious little chance of sustainable growth. The Commission's condition is no solution to this problem. Adding Shell as a shareholder will not cure Tepco's ills nor is it likely that Shell would agree to a condition that kept the companies separate operationally. Empowerment is not furthered by obliging firms controlled by historically disadvantaged persons to continue to exist on a life support machine.

Second Condition—*That the Tepco brand be maintained as a viable brand in the market place*

[43] We assume firstly that this remedy is not self-standing and must be coupled to first condition. If that is the case then it suffers from the same defects as the first condition viz. the prolonging of a non-viable option. The parties have not said they will discontinue the Tepco brand. At our hearing Mr. Shoniwe the Tepco Managing-Director confirmed this. However they want SSA to have the freedom to make this judgment call themselves. There is no public interest served by imposing on them the compulsory continuation of a brand name.

[44] If our first assumption is wrong and this is indeed a self-standing condition then we cannot understand what ill this remedy is designed to cure. Post-merger Tepco will be owned and controlled by Shell SA Marketing. Thebe, the erstwhile controlling shareholder of Tepco, will have a minority share in Shell SA Marketing. Why then propose measures ostensibly designed to protect the competitive position of Tepco, a company no longer controlled by historically disadvantaged persons? If Tepco, in its pre-merger form, was entering into an anti-competitive agreement with Shell, the Commission may, in terms of Section 10(3)(b)(ii), have been entitled to consider and grant an exemption on the grounds that the anti-competitive agreement promoted the ability of a firm owned by historically disadvantaged persons to become competitive.* But once Tepco's ownership has changed hands there can be no earthly reason for protecting its competitive position—it is manifestly no longer owned or controlled by historically disadvantaged persons. * * *

[49] The Commission may protest that it has no wish to prevent the transaction. However, it must be recognized that the imposition of a condition on the purchaser will come with a price and Thebe, precisely the firm owned and controlled by historically disadvantaged persons, will pay that price. We would however go further and insist that even if Tepco had been a company in perfect health, the Commission should be extremely careful when, in the name of supporting historically disadvantaged investors, it intervenes in a commercial decision by such an investor.

[50] Consider the following eminently plausible scenario: Thebe, in its commercial wisdom, may have decided to consolidate and expand its interests in the leisure and tourism industry. In order to do this it may have elected to dispose of its assets in the oil industry. White owned and controlled firms obviously do this with impunity—it represents a significant and perfectly respectable mode of financing business expansion. The Commission may believe that its proposed condition only constrains the acquiring firm. On the contrary its condition constrains the seller, the target firm, to sell its assets only to a purchaser who will accept these conditions, or, what is the same

---

    * Or, post-merger, we may well face the situation where the merged firm, wishing to make an anticompetitive acquisition, argues for the transaction on the ground that it will promote the competitiveness of a firm with a substantial HDP shareholding. This would be a more credible avenue for invoking the public interest clause of the merger evaluation process and may well provide a sterner test for the competition authorities in its task of balancing competition and public interest. At this stage the competition authorities may well conclude that a 25% HDP interest does not sustain a case for approving an anti-competitive transaction whereas more fulsom HDP ownership and management involvement might.

thing, it is constrained to offer its assets at a discount because the assets are accompanied by conditions specifying the post-transaction utilization of these assets.

[51] To constrain the capital-raising options of firms owned by historically disadvantaged persons in this way not only condemns these firms to the margins of the economy and the margins of those sectors in which it believes it is best able to make a significant mark, it also lays the Commission open to a charge of paternalism. The Commission's role is to promote and protect competition and a specified public interest. It is not to second-guess the commercial decisions of precisely that element of the public that it is enjoined to defend, particularly where no threat to competition is entailed.

The Competition Tribunal returned to the public interest question in a controversial case involving the US mega-retailer Wal-Mart. In 2012, the case came before the Competition Appeal Court.

WAL-MART STORES, INC. & MASSMART HOLDINGS LIMITED

Competition Appeal Court of South Africa, Case No: 110/CAC/Jul11 (March 2012)

[On 31 May, 2011 the South African Competition Tribunal conditionally approved an acquisition by Wal-Mart of a controlling interest in Massmart, a leading South African retailer. The Tribunal found that the merger raised no competition concerns. It did find that the merger raised public interest concerns—particularly the potential loss of jobs and of opportunities for local suppliers. To alleviate these concerns, the merging parties agreed to certain commitments: (1) no non-voluntary layoffs for two years; (2) employment preferences for 503 previously laid off employees; (3) to honor existing collective bargaining agreements; and (4) committing 100 million South African Rands (about $7 million) aimed at the development of South African suppliers. Despite these commitments, various entities challenged the Tribunal's approval decision, including a number of labor unions, the Minister of Economic Development, the Minister of Trade and Industry and the Minister of Agriculture, Forestry and Fisheries ("the Ministers"), and the South African Small Medium and Micro Enterprises Forum. The Competition Appeal Court ultimately upheld the Tribunal's decision to allow the merger, but with some conditions.]

The appeal

[91] SACCAWU based the foundation of its appeal upon a criticism of the normative approach adopted by the Tribunal to the application of

the Act. Thus, it contends that the approach adopted by the Tribunal and further contended for by the merging parties ignored the express language of the Act. It argues that the South African competition regime is concerned with economic or market power, its creation, extension, distribution and (ab)use, and that the entry of a firm with the scale of operations and consequent economic power of Wal-Mart into the South African economy will disrupt the competitive equilibrium and processes in the retail sector, as well as alter competition for suppliers in the retail supply chain. SACCAWU therefore contends that the merging parties' uncritical adoption of the perspective of a consumer welfare standard ignores its explicit rejection by the Act. SACCAWU suggests that s 12 A enjoins the competition authorities to take account of factors which do not play a role in terms of the consumer welfare approach to competition policy. In this connection, reference was made to David Lewis *Global Competition: Law Makers and Globalisation* (2011) and the perspective which extends beyond that of a narrow consumer welfare standard as contended for by Eleanor Fox *Poverty and Markets* (March 2009). In citing these authorities, we did not take SACCAWU to be arguing in favour of a total welfare standard which would take account only of consumer and producer surplus, but rather that the Act supported a more nuanced test than that of a consumer welfare standard.* * *

[98] Viewed holistically, there is merit in the argument that the Act should be read in terms of an economic perspective that extends beyond a standard consumer welfare approach. By virtue of an embrace of the goals of a free market and effective competition together with an incorporation of uniquely South African elements, including the need to address our exclusionary past, which need is reflected expressly in the preamble together with s 2 of the Act, the legislature imposed ambitious goals upon the competition authorities created in terms of the Act. Within the context of the present dispute, this ambition is further captured in s 12 A which mandates an enquiry into substantial public interest grounds.* * *

[104] Much of the debate [between the parties' economists], turned on the question, which was considered to be of extreme importance to the merger by the Tribunal, namely can Wal-Mart post-merger source goods from overseas and in particular Asia more cheaply than can Massmart and if so will it? This question was deemed to hold the key to the determination of whether the potential losses which flowed from the merger, particularly when analysed in terms of factors set out in s 12 A (3) would outweigh the proclaimed consumer advantages of the merger. The Tribunal complained about an absence of more precise evidence, commenting, however, that 'it is

highly probable that if Massmart was procuring at the prices near to those of Wal-Mart, this exercise—entirely within the knowledge of the merging parties—would have been done. Is it likely that the two firms did not at sometime over their lengthy contact, explore this possibility? Hence the Tribunal appeared sceptical of the claim that no change to procurement patterns would take place.

However, in its view,

> "The problem is that the concern raised in relation to local procurement/imports is also associated with important benefits for consumers. A possible loss of jobs in manufacturing of an uncertain extent must be weighed up against consumer interests in lower prices and job creation at Massmart. Since the evidence is that the likely consumers who will benefit most from the lower prices associated with the merger are low income consumers and those consumers without any means of support of their own, thus the poorest of South Africans, the public interest in lower prices is no less compelling."

105 The determination of the trade-off between consumer benefits and job losses caused by increased importation of goods presently obtained in South Africa, was bedevilled by the lack of precise evidence. * * *

115 The evidence in this case thus becomes crucial as to the proper judicial engagement with the range of enquires. As is apparent from observations made earlier in this judgment, the intervening parties, admittedly, had some difficulty in obtaining the comprehensive picture which would have included the merging parties' proposals with regard to the ratio between domestic procurement and imports. This is somewhat surprising as it could have been expected that Wal-Mart had developed a series of business models in order to test the extent to which the considerable investment in Massmart would prove to be profitable. In turn, these ratios could then have been expected to have been employed to further examine the arguments about shifts towards imports.

116 Nonetheless, even if all of this information had been made available, it would not have gainsaid the conclusion, based on uncontested evidence, that prices will be reduced to the benefit of consumers as a result of the merger. The legitimate criticism about insufficient evidence notwithstanding, it is clear from the record as a whole that consumer benefits will flow from this merger.

117 It does not appear to be disputed either that there is the potential for small and medium sized South African suppliers to gain benefit

from the presence of Wal-Mart and its unique access to global value supply chains.

118 These positive factors would need to be weighed against any losses which will be experienced by small and medium sized businesses, as well as the consequences for employment, when the transaction is viewed holistically. But, as we have noted, in dealing with a standard that seeks to balance consumer and other forms of societal welfare as set out in the Act, it is highly unlikely that, even with further information as sought by the Ministers, a set of calculations could have been produced which would ultimately have justified the conclusion based on such a standard, that the merger should not have been approved. The available evidence, together with inferences that could reasonably be drawn, particularly from uncontested evidence, supports this conclusion. * * *

Employment rights

122 SACCAWU sought the intervention of this court in order to protect its members against the adverse effects of what it termed 'the Wal-Mart model' on employment levels, particularly terms and conditions of employment and the organisational rights of workers within the merged firm. It conceded that the conditions imposed by the Tribunal, to which reference has already been made, had gone some way towards achieving the protection of workers. However, Mr Kennedy contended that more was required to protect the union structurally against what he termed 'Wal-Mart's anti-union stance'.

123 SACCAWU contended that there was compelling evidence relating to Wal-Mart's practice and policies concerning workers; in particular empirical evidence of the adverse impact of Wal-Mart's employment practices and policies and wages and other terms and conditions of employment. In its view, Wal-Mart had ruthlessly pursued a labour relations strategy which was designed to prevent the unionisation of its workers. It had done so successfully that 1.3 million out of 2.1 million of its workers in the United States of America were not unionised. This had resulted in wage levels of Wal-Mart employees being 12.4% less than for workers employed by other retailers. According to SACCAWU, the merging parties, in their evidence before the Tribunal, had provided no firm and enforceable commitments regarding labour and employment issues but merely required the Tribunal to accept their 'bold denials or say-so' that 'Wal-Mart's global reputation for poor labour relations' would not be imported into South Africa through the merger. * * *

[After reviewing a lengthy body of conflicting evidence on Wal-Mart's effect on labor conditions, the court held that such questions should be left to labor law rather than competition law]: In summary, it is not the role of competition law to provide legal protections to potential disputes of interest which stand to be resolved by the exercise of collective power. To the extent that the merging parties would seek to erode union or employee rights guaranteed under existing law, these will be protected by the labour courts, which are set up to deal with disputes of rights.

The Tribunal's order

[The court turned finally to the sufficiency of the commitment to invest in local suppliers. It found that the concern about Wal-Mart turning to global supply chains was insufficient to block the merger. But that did not end the court's remedial analysis].

164 In summary, the concern that Wal-Mart's coordinated global purchasing operation and superior infrastructure for exploiting global value chains will result in the importation of consumer goods, thereby harming domestic producers, which harm will exceed the benefits of cheaper products for local consumers, cannot, on the basis of the available evidence, particularly that of the intervening parties, justify the prohibition of the merger. But that does not lead to the conclusion that the Act justifies a blanket approval. The solution to the possible threats of greater imports and therefore detrimental consequences for local manufacturers is not, in our view, to impose a domestic content requirement. The Tribunal has shown the difficulties which such a proposal would create. Further, a blanket procurement quota can give rise to distortions both between the merged firm and other large firms in the market and in respect of manipulation of the product mix in order to circumvent the designated procurement levels. It may also facilitate forms of price collusion. For these reasons, the Tribunal's rejection of the proposals for import restrictions cannot be disturbed on appeal.

165 The problem however with the existing conditions as approved by the Tribunal is that they reflect an offer made by the merging parties which was accepted by the Tribunal, without sufficient interrogation as to precisely how the programme would be implemented and the consequences for dealing with the potential difficulties which may be encountered by local manufacturers, the effects on employment and the ability of small and medium sized businesses to operate within a competitive global environment, as outlined in this judgment. * * *

168 To this end therefore, a variation of the proposal put up by the merging parties is justified. The merging parties suggested that the programme could benefit from the advice given by a committee which would comprise representatives of trade unions business and in particular small, medium size enterprises together with government. Before accepting this vague condition set out by the Tribunal without

any significant considerations of the benefits that it might achieve, it would be preferable if a committee comprising of an expert chosen by SACCAWU, another by Wal-Mart and a third by government be invited to produce a report within three months of the delivery of this judgment which would then allow this court to develop an investment remedy which is both rational, justifiable in terms of the evidence provided, as well as in terms of the challenges with which the South African economy is confronted as a result of this merger and the legitimate concerns which follow from the provisions of s 12 A (1) read with (3), in particular the future of small and medium sized producers.

[169] The parties would in turn, be entitled to place further affidavits before this court, following upon the report, in order to assist the Court in framing the precise nature of this particular condition. There is, of course, the option of referring the matter back to the Tribunal which could hold further hearings and gather evidence before reformulating this condition. We are cognisant of the time already taken to resolve the disputes concerning this merger and the need to bring this matter to finality as expeditiously as possible.

[170] For these reasons, a dialogic model in which this court can engage with the parties to resolve the outstanding disputes is, in our view, suitable for adjudication in these kind of matters and thus justifies an order that the court benefit from expert advice, further responses from the parties, all of which must be made available in the shortest possible time.

Contrast the South African Wal-Mart decision to the following US case. Was the federal court right to hold that Puerto Rico's Attorney General acted unconstitutionally in seeking to impose restrictions on a merger based on their effects on local jobs and supply opportunities?

WAL-MART STORES, INC. v. RODRIGUEZ

238 F.Supp.2d 395 (D.P.R. 2002)

(The opinion was vacated as part of a settlement; it is not precedent)

Wal-Mart sought to buy Supermercados Amigo, a supermarket chain in Puerto Rico. The parties notified both the federal and commonwealth antitrust authorities. The FTC approved the acquisition subject to divestiture of four stores at locations where there were competitive overlaps. Meanwhile, local interests were pressuring the Puerto Rico Department of Justice and Anabelle

Rodriguez, Secretary of Justice, to stop the merger under the Puerto Rico Anti-Monopoly Act, or at least to protect the public interest in jobs and local sales. Rodriguez believed that she was at liberty to negotiate for concessions on these points for the good of the people of the Commonwealth of Puerto Rico. "[T]he protection and preservation of existing jobs, as well as the creation of new ones, [was] the highest priority of the current administration." Rodriguez demanded that Wal-Mart "will not reduce or suspend its current volume of local agricultural and/or food products" and that Wal-Mart guarantee the maintenance of the current work force. Wal-Mart was willing to commit to buy as much locally as "it could" and submitted evidence that its local purchases were increasing; and it was willing even to maintain the *level* of its current workforce, but not to retain all existing employees. When the negotiations faltered, Rodriguez (for Puerto Rico) sued to enjoin the "monopolistic" merger.

In turn, Wal-Mart sued Rodriguez to block her from prohibiting the merger. The court granted Wal-Mart a preliminary injunction on grounds that Rodriguez had evidenced a pattern of bad faith in the negotiations and that the imposition of the conditions guaranteeing jobs and local purchases violated the Commerce Clause and Equal Protection Clause of the US Constitution.

In the course of its analysis, the court noted these effects of the "public policy" clauses:

Labor

> The controversy in the language of the agreements with regards to [the] labor issue can be best summarized as follows: while the PRDOJ wanted to get Wal-Mart to agree not to alter the current labor force, that is, the employees that are currently working at the Amigo stores, Wal-Mart was willing to agree to maintain the current number of employees, leaving open the possibility that current employees could be terminated as long as their positions were not eliminated. But despite their lack of intention to downsize their current work force, Plaintiffs could not agree to maintain the current employees and forego the possibility of ever letting go of anyone who currently works at Amigo. Wal-Mart anticipated that just like in any other acquisition, there was a possibility that the integration process would reveal deficiencies in the labor force that would need to be remedied. Moreover, no layoffs in the stores were anticipated, but Wal-Mart could not make the same commitment with regards to positions in their administrative and home offices. The phenomenon of

attrition, over which they have no control, was also raised as a concern for Wal-Mart. Finally, as with the levels of purchase condition, Wal-Mart would be at a disadvantage with competitors if forced to maintain the current labor work force.

Buy-local

. . . Defendant suggested in her various press releases that the people of Puerto Rico would be negatively affected by the merger of Wal-Mart and Amigo since there was no guarantee that they would buy the same level of merchandise and agricultural goods from local suppliers and distributors as Amigo had in the past. But Wal-Mart understood that these requests were not only unfair but contrary to the interest of the people of Puerto Rico. Knowledge of imposed quotas on Wal-Mart would limit its bargaining power with suppliers, who would end up selling goods at higher prices in light of the quotas, and that increment would have to be passed on to consumers, of course, the people of Puerto Rico. * * *

. . . In both its effect and purpose, the requirement differentiates between local Puerto Rico growers and out-of-state producers by mandating a quota of local products to be purchased annually. This differential treatment favors the interests of Puerto Rico growers, who are given a guaranteed market for the products sheltered from the usual perils of the market, while shutting out out-of-state growers from the potentially lucrative business relationship with Wal-Mart. Regardless of the quality of their products, the consistency of their supply, or the prices they offer, local growers would have a guaranteed and insurmountable advantage over out-of-state growers. This, in part, violates Wal-Mart's right to engage in interstate commerce, which is now reduced to "exclusivity contracts" with local growers, despite the myriad alternatives in interstate commerce.

In the face of this direct and discriminatory interference with interstate commerce, the Secretary of Justice offers no legitimate purpose. As has been suggested throughout this opinion, she invokes the public policy of the administration she currently works with as her source of authority that allows her to make these demands from Plaintiffs during their negotiations. She stated in a press release that "the public policy is directed at protecting the necessary balance that should exist between Puerto Rican and foreign capital and the benefits that it entails for the consumers." Whether or not Wal-Mart *should* attempt to strike that balance is not for this Court nor any other to determine for as long as it engages as a free market participant within the boundaries of the law, it is to make its own business decisions without governmental interference. But confronted with facially discriminatory remarks such as this one, we can and do determine that the Secretary is engaging in state protectionism prohibited by the federal constitution.

———

Many jurisdictions, prominently including developing countries, settle merger cases with consent orders that preserve factories, preserve jobs, or preserve brands. For example, the Competition and Tariff Commission of Zimbabwe vetted the acquisition of Portland Holdings Ltd. (Porthold), Zimbabwe's largest of only three cement manufacturers, by Pretoria Cement Company (PCC), a South African company. The number two producer had recently been acquired by Lafarge of France. It was suspected that PCC planned to close the to-be-acquired Zimbabwean plant and to supply the Zimbabwean market from South Africa. The Zimbabwean Commission welcomed the acquisition as a check against Lafarge's power. It approved the transaction on condition that PCC agree "to maintain Porthold's cement plant as a going concern and to continue producing cement in Zimbabwe." Alexander J. Kububa, *Anti-Competitive Practices and Their Adverse Effects on Consumer Welfare: The Zimbabwean Experience, in* THE EFFECTS OF ANTI-COMPETITIVE BUSINESS PRACTICES ON DEVELOPING COUNTRIES AND THEIR DEVELOPMENT PROSPECTS (H. Qaqaya and G. Lipimile eds., UNCTAD 2008), pp. 73,107. What is the probable effect on competition or efficiency of the order to continue operations of the Zimbabwean plant? Does it depend in part on whether PCC's reasons for its plan were anticompetitive; e.g., to close down a competitor?

China, one of the newest yet most visible antitrust jurisdictions, exercised its merger enforcement powers to block the proposed acquisition by Coca Cola of Huiyuan, a major maker and seller of juices. Huiyuan is a leading brand in China. MOFCOM, the Ministry of Commerce, which has charge of mergers, prohibited the merger on "competition grounds": that Coca Cola would leverage its power in the carbonated soft drink market, raise entry barriers, and cause "negative influences" on competition in the juice market in China. (MOFCOM, March 2009) To critics, the facts did not seem to reveal harm to competition that could hurt consumers. Some observers speculated that perhaps MOFCOM wished to preserve for China ownership of a leading brand, or to hold back inroads by a large Western multinational.

The financial crisis of 2008–09 threatened the viability of banks (whose failure, it was feared, would have a domino effect, undermining whole economies), and of auto producers, among others. US, European, and other jurisdictions sponsored mergers and bailouts and took government stakes in the supported businesses. In the UK, HBOS was in crisis. The UK government engineered a rescue by Lloyds, in the form of a merger. The Office of Fair Trading determined that the proposed merger would be anticompetitive, and that the failing firm defense would not be available in that case. The Secretary of State, however, decided that the public interest in "maintaining the stability of the UK financial system" outweighed the harm to competition, and the UK passed legislation to allow threat to the financial system to justify an anticompetitive merger. See Harshita Mathur, *UK Merger Control in Times of Financial Crisis: Rebutting the Justifications for Lloyds—HBOS*, Concurrences N° 4–2009, *www.concurrences.com*.

Consider the range of non-competition concerns that inform merger cases. Comment on the wisdom of incorporating the non-competition factors into merger review; on the wisdom of the institutional design (e.g., who decides), and on how likely it is that the specified public interests will be furthered by the merger law. Contrariwise, consider the legitimacy of the competition law if public interest considerations are out of bounds.

b.   National Interest, National Champions and Merger Policy

Beyond the public interest in mergers, often expressed in terms of labor effects or distributive concerns, mergers sometimes raise questions of national interest. A national government may believe that a merger creates a dominant domestic company—a "national champion"—that will strengthen the government's own global position, or it may be concerned that a merger of foreign companies may adversely affect national interests. Although such considerations undoubtedly sometimes motivate competition policy decisions, should they?

US caselaw generally holds that there is no place in antitrust law for consideration of any public interest other than competition itself. Efficiency and technological progressiveness are deemed to be part of competition. The failing firm defense to mergers might be an exception; but it is usually rationalized as part of competition/market power analysis.

Boeing/McDonnell Douglas

Boeing was the largest manufacturer of commercial jet aircraft in the world, accounting for about 64% of world market sales. Its only competitors were McDonnell Douglas (its acquisition target), which accounted for about 5% of the market, and Airbus Industrie, with about 30%. Airbus was a consortium of manufacturers in Britain, France, Germany and Spain. Those countries had helped to finance Airbus.

Boeing and McDonnell Douglas were US companies and had no production assets in Europe, although they regularly made sales there. McDonnell Douglas also produced military jets, and its technology portfolio included patents from research and development undertaken with US government financing. In the commercial jet market, McDonnell Douglas had failed to invest in important new-generation developments and was facing financial and competitive difficulties. Its market share was withering. Boeing, meanwhile, had recently concluded 20-year exclusive supply agreements with three big American airlines—Delta, American, and Continental. The exclusive supply agreements represented about 11% of all world purchases of big commercial jets.

Commercial jet airplanes are very complex and sell in the range of $32 million to $171 million each. An order from an airline is typically worth billions of dollars. In view of the fact that each sale to an airline is so significant, Airbus and Boeing were fierce competitors for sales around the world.

Boeing and McDonnell Douglas filed premerger notifications in the United States and in the European Union. EC Competition Commissioner Karel Van Miert immediately expressed concerns about the merger and the exclusive agreements. On the US side, the Federal Trade Commission opened an investigation. The European Commission and the FTC made notifications to one another under the 1991 cooperation agreement (see Chapter 9, infra), and the European and American officials shared their perspectives. They sharply disagreed on the analysis of anticompetitive effects.

Early on, politicians entered the fray, with Europeans declaring that the merger was blatantly anticompetitive and seriously harmful to competition and to Airbus, and Americans declaring that the merger was good for the American economy. Laura D'Andrea Tyson, former head of the Council of Economic Advisors, was quoted in the Washington Post (May 4, 1997, p. H6) as saying that this merger was good for America "even if consumers of airplane seats are somewhat worse off." Commissioner Van Miert threatened that, if the merger should be consummated without EC approval, the European Commission would impose prohibitive fines on Boeing and might seize Boeing planes flying into Europe.

On July 1, 1997, the US FTC issued a statement announcing the closing of its investigation.

MATTER OF THE BOEING COMPANY/McDONNELL DOUGLAS CORPORATION

U.S. Federal Trade Commission, Statement
[FTC File No. 971–0051, available at *https://www.ftc.gov/public-statements/1997/ 07/statement-chairman-robert-pitofsky-commissioners-janet-d-steiger-roscoe-b*]

After an extensive and exhaustive investigation, the Federal Trade Commission has decided to close the investigation of The Boeing Company's proposed acquisition of McDonnell Douglas Corporation. For reasons discussed below, we have concluded that the acquisition would not substantially lessen competition or tend to create a monopoly in either defense or commercial aircraft markets.

There has been speculation in the press and elsewhere that the United States antitrust authorities might allow this transaction to go forward—particularly the portion of the transaction dealing with the manufacture of commercial aircraft—because aircraft manufacturing occurs in a global market, and the United States, in order to compete in that market, needs a single powerful firm to serve as its "national champion." A powerful United States firm is all the more important, the argument proceeds, because that firm's success contributes much to improving the United States' balance of trade and to providing jobs for U.S. workers.

The national champion argument does not explain today's decision. Our task as enforcers, conferred in clear terms by Congress in enacting the antitrust statutes, is to ensure the vitality of the free market by preventing private actions that may substantially lessen competition or tend to create a monopoly. In the Boeing-McDonnell Douglas matter, the Commission's task was to review a merger between two direct competitors.

We do not have the discretion to authorize anticompetitive but "good" mergers because they may be thought to advance the United States' trade interests. If that were thought to be a wise approach, only Congress could implement it. In any event, the "national champion" argument is almost certainly a delusion. In reality, the best way to boost the United States' exports, address concerns about the balance of trade, and create jobs is to require United States' firms to compete vigorously at home and abroad. Judge Learned Hand put the matter well a half century ago in describing the reasons for the commitment in the United States to the protection of the free market:

"Many people believe that possession of unchallenged economic power deadens initiative, discourages thrift and depresses energy; that immunity from competition is a narcotic, and rivalry is a stimulant, to industrial progress; that the spur of constant stress is necessary to counteract inevitable disposition to let well enough alone." [citing *United States v. Alcoa*, 148 F.2d 416, 427 (2d Cir. 1945)]

On its face, the proposed merger appears to raise serious antitrust concerns. The transaction involves the acquisition by Boeing, a company that accounts for roughly 60% of the sales of large commercial aircraft, of a non-failing direct competitor in a market in which there is only one other significant rival, Airbus Industrie, and extremely high barriers to entry. The merger would also combine two firms in the US defense industry that develop fighter aircraft and other defense products. Nevertheless, for reasons we will now discuss, we do not find that this merger will substantially lessen competition in any relevant market. * * *

With respect to the commercial aircraft sector, our decision not to challenge the proposed merger was a result of evidence that (1) McDonnell Douglas, looking to the future, no longer constitutes a meaningful competitive force in the commercial aircraft market and (2) there is no economically plausible strategy that McDonnell Douglas could follow, either as a stand-alone concern or as part of another concern, that would change that grim prospect.

The evidence collected during the staff investigation, including the virtually unanimous testimony of forty airlines that staff interviewed, revealed that McDonnell Douglas's commercial aircraft division, Douglas Aircraft Company, can no longer exert a competitive influence in the worldwide market for commercial aircraft. Over the past several decades, McDonnell Douglas has not invested at nearly the rate of its competitors in new product lines, production facilities, company infrastructure, or research and development. As a result, Douglas Aircraft's product line is not only very limited, but lacks the state of the art technology and performance characteristics that Boeing and Airbus have developed. Moreover, Douglas Aircraft's line of aircraft do not have common features such as cockpit design or engine type, and thus cannot generate valuable efficiencies in interchangeable spare parts and pilot training that an airline may obtain from a family of aircraft, such as Boeing's 737 family or Airbus's A–320 family.

In short, the staff investigation revealed that the failure to improve the technology and efficiency of its commercial aircraft products has lead to a deterioration of Douglas Aircraft's product line to the point that the vast majority of airlines will no longer consider purchasing Douglas aircraft and that the company is no longer in a position to influence significantly the competitive dynamics of the commercial aircraft market.

Our decision not to challenge the proposed merger does not reflect a conclusion that McDonnell Douglas is a failing company or that Douglas Aircraft is a failing division. Nor does our decision not to challenge the proposed merger reflect a conclusion that Douglas Aircraft could maintain competitively significant sales, but has simply decided to redeploy or retire its assets. While McDonnell Douglas's prospects for future commercial aircraft sales are virtually non-existent, its commercial aircraft production assets are likely to remain in the market for the near future as a result of a modest backlog of aircraft orders. As a result, it is unlikely that the aircraft division would have been liquidated quickly. Moreover, the failing company defense comes into play only where the Commission first finds that the transaction is likely to be anticompetitive. Here, the absence of any prospect of significant commercial sales, combined with a dismal financial forecast, indicate that Douglas Aircraft is no longer an effective competitor, and there is no prospect that position could be reversed. * * *

While the merger seems to pose no threat to the competitive landscape in either the commercial aircraft or in various defense markets, we find the twenty year exclusive contracts Boeing recently entered with three major airlines potentially troubling. Boeing is the largest player in the global commercial aircraft market and though the contracts now foreclose only about 11% of that market, the airlines involved are prestigious. They represent a sizeable portion of airlines that can serve as "launch" customers for aircraft manufacturers, that is, airlines that can place orders large enough and have sufficient market prestige to serve as the first customer for a new airplane. We intend to monitor the potential anticompetitive effects of these, and any future, long term exclusive contracts.

———————

Immediately after the FTC closed its investigation, the Clinton Administration began to take an active political role in defending the merger to Europe. Key White House officials, including the President of the United States, argued to key European officials, including the President of the European Commission, that the merger was not anticompetitive, that it was important to employment and to the defense interests of the United States (the military assets of McDonnell Douglas would be best preserved in the hands of Boeing), and that the United States was "considering how to retaliate against Europe if it makes good on its threat to try and undermine the merger of [the] US aerospace giants. . . ." The Washington Post, July 17, 1997, p. C1. Reportedly, the Administration officials were considering imposing tariffs on European planes, limiting flights between the United States and France (the most adamant objector to the merger), and filing a protest with the World Trade Organization in view of European subsidies to Airbus.

On July 30, 1997, the Commission issued its decision in the matter of Boeing/McDonnell Douglas. It found that the merger would increase Boeing's dominance but backed away from a plan to prohibit the merger, and imposed significant conditions.

Glencore/Xstrata

On 16 April 2013 the Ministry of Commerce of the People's Republic of China (MOFCOM) granted conditional approval to the acquisition by Glencore International plc. (Glencore) of all of the remaining shares of Xstrata plc. (Xstrata), in which Glencore already held a minority equity interest. MOFCOM's assessment focused on the markets for copper concentrate, zinc concentrate and lead concentrate—in particular copper concentrate—where Glencore and Xstrata had overlapping production. Although the merged entity held a relatively limited market share of China's copper concentrate market (17.8% of China's imports in 2011), MOFCOM imposed both structural and behavioral conditions on the merger, including the extraterritorial divestiture of the $5.7 billion Las Bambas copper mine in Peru.

MOFCOM explicitly acknowledged that its decision was based on the strategic importance of copper to China:

> China is the world's major importing country for copper concentrate, with China's present demand accounting for about 50% of the total global demand. China's imports of copper concentrate in 2011 accounted for 68.5% of total domestic supply, and the trend shows an upward trajectory. In 2011, Glencore's and Xstrata's exports of copper concentrate to China accounted for 13.3% and 4.5% respectively of China's total imports, or 17.8% on a combined basis. The Chinese market is a major market for the undertakings concerned in the concentration. In 2011, Glencore and Xstrata sold respectively 53.7% and 17% of their copper concentrate supplies to the Chinese market.

The Chinese decision stood out among the major jurisdictions reviewing the merger. Both the Australian Competition and Consumer Commission and the US Department of Justice cleared the deal unconditionally in 2012. The European Commission focused on the markets for the production and trading of zinc (ultimately requiring the divestment of Glencore's minority stake in the world's largest zinc smelter, Nyrstar), but found no concerns as to copper. The South African Competition Tribunal gave clearance with conditions in January 2013, but its concerns did not relate to competition considerations but rather to public interest issues involving employment.

Was it right for MOFCOM to base its competition assessment on China's unique interest as a leading copper importer and the wider effects on China's economy?

c.   *Executive and Legislative Measures That Trump Antitrust*

Statements extolling the "purity" of US antitrust do not prove that US competition *policy* is pure. Political pressures make themselves felt in one way or another. Examples include the failure of Chinese CNOOC's bid for UNOCAL because of US Congressional opposition; the US government-driven big bank and big auto mergers; the "buy American" conditionality of the bailouts often accompanying the government-sponsored mergers; and the large US government stakes taken in bailout beneficiaries. See, e.g., Bruce Lyons, *Competition Policy, Bailouts and the Economic Crisis*, Working Paper 09–4, Centre for Competition Policy, ISSN 1745–9648. See also Chapter 6, The State, points E. and F.

As of this writing, President Trump's antitrust policy remains to be discovered, but early signs suggest that he may wield his stick to extract economic and employment concessions from parties wishing to merge. For example, in January 2017, the President-elect met with executives from the German chemical company Bayer and the agriculture company Monsanto at a time when their proposed $66 billion merger was pending antitrust review. According to media reports, Bayer and Monsanto made a number of economic commitments, although the parties denied that these were specifically linked to antitrust review of the merger: $8 billion in new R&D spending in the US, retention of 100 percent of Monsanto's US workforce; creation of 3,000 new US high-tech jobs, and keeping Monsanto's headquarters in St. Louis. *Bayer, Monsanto tout jobs, investment pledge to Trump, but analysts question how much is new,*

CNBC (Jan 17, 2017) *http://www.cnbc.com/2017/01/17/bayers-pledge-to-trump-has-some-analysts-scratching-their-heads.html.*

Is it appropriate for governments to use their prosecutorial discretion to negotiate for better deals for their citizens when parties propose to merge? Does such horse trading corrupt the ostensible objectivity of competition law?

D. COOPERATION AND CONFLICT

1. Convergence on Pre-Merger Notification and Process

By year 2000 there were some 50 premerger notification regimes around the world. (As of this writing, that number is approaching 100). Parties planning a multijurisdictional merger had to know the rules of all regimes, many of which were not transparent. Some regimes required pre-merger notification and accompanying large filing fees even when the merger had no significant nexus with the jurisdiction and it could not possibly have harmed competition in the jurisdiction. Jurisdictions required filings based on different triggering events, and many requested different information in different formats. The business community's felt need to rationalize the merger process was a major impetus to the formation of the International Competition Network.

The ICN has proved to be a productive forum for coordination and convergence on pre-merger notification and process. One of the first working groups formed in the ICN was the Merger Working Group. Beginning with the first annual ICN conference in 2002, guiding principles and recommended practices were proposed and adopted; additional recommended practices are continually added, and steps are taken to publicize and track their implementation. See *www.internationalcompetitionnetwork.org.* For a description and assessment of the ICN, See Eleanor Fox, *Linked-In: Antitrust and the Virtues of a Virtual Network*, 43 International Lawyer 151 (2009).

2. Cooperation in Vetting Mergers of Common Interest

Jurisdictions cooperate, often intensely, in vetting mergers of common interest. In a 2013 OECD study, 21 agencies reported international cooperation with other agencies and the number of cases for which those agencies reported cooperating with other international agencies rose from approximately 90 in 2007 to 120 in 2011. Organization for Economic Co-operation and Development Competition Committee, Report on the OECD/ICN Survey on International Enforcement Co-operation (Feb. 12, 2013), *available at http://search.oecd.org/officialdocuments/publicdisplaydocument pdf/?cote=DAF/COMP/WP3%282013%292&docLanguage=En.*

Chapter 9, on Global Governance, contains further information on the procedures jurisdictions follow to engage in cooperative merger assessment, including measures employed to protect the confidentiality of information collected during the review process.

3. Conflict

As more countries become active in merger regulation, conflicts among the decisions of competition authorities are bound to increase. Some well-known conflicts involved the mergers of Boeing/McDonnell Douglas and General Electric/Honeywell. We begin with those cases, and then turn to the conflicts surrounding the merger of Gencor/Lonhro, which involved the jurisdictions of South Africa and the European Union, and Eurotunnel's acquisition of SeaFrance, which French competition authorities approved but the UK Supreme Court ultimately prohibited.

See the outlines of the *Boeing* case earlier in this chapter. GE/Honeywell was the first merger cleared by the United States and prohibited by the European Union.

General Electric/Honeywell

General Electric was the largest of the three leading manufacturers of engines for large commercial jet aircraft, the other two being Rolls Royce and Pratt & Whitney. Honeywell was the leading supplier of certain avionic and non-avionic equipment used in jet aircraft, and competed with Thales and Rockwell Collins (in avionics) and Hamilton Sundstrand (in non-avionics). Honeywell was the dominant maker of engine starters for jet engines, which was a necessary input. It, as well as GE, manufactured jet engines for certain large regional jet aircraft and corporate jet aircraft, and small marine gas turbines. GE had a financial subsidiary, GE Capital, which provided financial assistance to airframe manufacturers in the form of platform program development, and it had a leasing subsidiary, GECAS, which was the world's largest buyer of airplanes, representing nearly 10 percent of all purchases of new commercial jet aircraft. GECAS had a policy of buying only airplanes that were fitted with GE engines, and GE Capital had bailed out at least one major airline, which returned the favor with an exclusive purchase order of GE jet engines.

The US authorities cleared the merger subject to a spin-off of some overlapping jet engine assets. The European Commission found more serious problems and eventually issued a decision. COMP/M 2220, Commission Decision 2004/134/EC. The Commission found that GE was a dominant firm in the markets for jet engines for large commercial aircraft and large regional aircraft, and that the acquisition, through leveraging, bundling, and strategic behavior, would enhance GE's dominance and confer dominance on Honeywell in certain avionic and non-avionic products. It also found anticompetitive horizontal overlaps, but the more significant parts of the case were conglomerate. The finding of anticompetitive conglomerate effects was based on the prediction that GE would offer package and bundled deals and use its leverage to shift market share away from competitors until their business was no longer profitable and they abandoned competition with Honeywell.

When the Commission enjoined the merger, American officials denounced the decision. Treasury Secretary Paul O'Neil called the European Commission "the closest thing you can find to an autocratic organization that can successfully impose their will on things that one would think are outside their scope of attention."[3] US Justice Department officials announced that the decision protected competitors, not competition, and implied that the European Commission was less than proficient in economics. If the merged firm offered bundles at low prices, this was competition; let the competitors compete.

GE appealed to the European Court of First Instance. The Court upheld the decision of the European Commission, but only on grounds of residual horizontal engine overlaps. The Commission had not sufficiently proved that the merged firm would use leverage. Case T–210/01, [2005] ECR II–5575. By the time the Court judgment came down four-and-a-half years after the Commission decision, the tensions had dissipated. See Eleanor Fox, *GE/Honeywell: The U.S. Merger that Europe Stopped—A Story of the Politics of Convergence*, supra p. 321.

Gencor/Lonrho

Two South African platinum and rhodium mining companies proposed to merge, combining Implats, a subsidiary of Gencor, having about 17% of world market sales, and LPD (a subsidiary of the UK firm, Lonrho, which had a principal sales office in Belgium), having about 15% of sales. The combined firm would have 32% of sales. The leading firm, Anglo American ("Amplats"), had about 43% of sales. Together the two remaining South African firms would hold about 89% of world reserves. Russia, through its firm Almaz, had a 22% share of sales and 10% of reserves. North American producers accounted for 5% of sales and had 1% reserves; and recycling firms

---

[3]   Tom Brown, Update 2—U.S. Treasury Chief Slaps at Europe Over GE Deal, Reuters, June 27, 2001.

accounted for 6% of sales. Russia was expected to dispose of its stocks in two years.

The South African Competition Board vetted the merger and found no competition problem. The European Commission vetted the merger and was concerned that, when the Russian stocks were depleted in a couple of years, Gencor/LPD (Lonrho) and Anglo American, the world market leader, would jointly exercise dominant market power (collective dominance).

While examining the proposed merger, the Competition Directorate of the European Commission invited comment from the South African authorities. The South African Deputy Minister of Foreign Affairs officially submitted his government's observations to the Commission. He stated in a letter to the European Commission that the South African Government favored the consolidation. As to competitive effects, the Minister noted that the two remaining platinum firms in South Africa were now more equally matched, and he conveyed the South African view that the market would work better with two equally matched competitors than under market domination by Anglo American. The Minister did not contest the intervention of the European Community. However, he wrote: "Having regard to the importance of mineral resources to the South African economy," South Africa favored allowing the consolidation and attacking any collusion between Anglo American and Gencor/LPD if and when it arose. (judgment, para. 3)

The European Commission proceeded to find that the merger would create a dominant duopoly and was therefore incompatible with the common market, and it prohibited it. Gencor appealed.

Gencor argued on appeal not only that the merger was procompetitive but that the Community had no jurisdiction since the merger involved economic activities conducted within the territory of a non-member country and had been approved by authorities of that country. Gencor contended that the European Merger Regulation applied only to concentrations carried out within the European Community. It based its construction on the language of the Merger Regulation (especially recitals), the Treaty articles on which the Regulation was based, and the international law principle of territoriality. Gencor addressed the one important extraterritorial European Court of Justice authority, *Wood Pulp*, [1988] ECR 5193, see Chapter 8 infra, wherein the Court had asserted jurisdiction over an offshore cartel designedly raising prices in Europe. Gencor distinguished *Wood Pulp* on grounds that the wood pulp cartel was implemented in Europe. Gencor said: While the high prices [of wood pulp] were agreed to offshore, the conspiracy to raise prices was implemented by selling at the conspiratorial prices into the Community. By contrast, the platinum merger was implemented in South Africa and "is thus primarily relevant to the industrial and competition policy of that non-member country." (para. 56)

The Court of First Instance rejected Gencor's construction of the Merger Regulation. *Gencor Ltd. v. Commission*, Case T–102/96, [1999] ECR II–753. The court said:

> According to *Wood pulp*, the criterion as to the implementation of an agreement is satisfied by mere sale within the Community, irrespective of the location of the sources of supply and the production plant. It is not disputed that Gencor and Lonrho carried out sales in the Community before the concentration and would have continued to do so thereafter. (para. 87)

The CFI proceeded to assess the legitimacy of jurisdiction under international law. Noting that the transaction entailed the merger of the firms' marketing operations throughout the world, including the Community, it said:

> Application of the Regulation is justified under public international law when it is foreseeable that a proposed concentration will have an immediate and substantial effect in the Community. (para. 90)

The CFI concluded that the merger's effect in the Community would be immediate, substantial and foreseeable. It construed "immediate" to include "medium term"—after Russian platinum stocks were exhausted and thus after a force that could be disruptive of Anglo and Gencor's duopoly behavior would have been removed. It concluded that an *abuse* (a price rise resulting from collective behavior) need not be immediate; it is enough that a transaction causes a lasting structural alteration, making abusive behavior economically rational.

As to substantiality of the effect, Gencor claimed that the merging parties' sales and market shares in Europe were too small to cause a substantial effect and that the merging parties' greater sales elsewhere—Japan and the United States—undermined "substantiality." The court rejected this claim. It said:

> The fact that, in a world market, other parts of the world are affected by the concentration cannot prevent the Community from exercising its control over a concentration which substantially affects competition within the common market by creating a dominant position.

Likewise, the court rejected the claim that the exercise of jurisdiction violated an international principle of non-interference, if there is such a principle, or the principle of proportionality. The court said that there was no conflict between the laws of the two jurisdictions and therefore no interference because South Africa did not require the firms to do what the European Community required them not to do. Nor was it shown how the completion of the merger would enhance South Africa's vital economic or commercial interests.

Moreover, as the European Commission had argued, the merger was like an export cartel. Only a small amount of platinum was sold in South Africa. South Africa stood to gain more by exploiting the world than it stood to lose by exploiting its own consumers.

Thus, the court held, it had jurisdiction.

South Africa did not further resist Europe's decision.

Eurotunnel/SeaFrance

SeaFrance, provided ferry service across the English Channel, went into liquidation in 2012 following years of heavy losses. The French Commercial Court overseeing the liquidation process received bids for SeaFrance and ultimately chose Eurotunnel's bid, finding that it offered the best outcome for creditors and was the only bid that would preserve the employment of former SeaFrance employees.

The French Autorité de la Concurrence and the UK Office of Fair Trading both opened investigations into the acquisition. By the end of 2012, the French authority had cleared the deal, but the OFT referred the matter to the UK Competition Commission, worried about a lessening of competition in the provision of short-sea cross-Channel transport services. In June of 2013, the Competition Commission issued a decision finding the acquisition unlawful and prohibiting Eurotunnel from operating ferry services at the port of Dover.

While agreeing on market definition and the potential for anticompetitive effects in the cross-Channel transport services market, the French and UK authorities differed in several important respects. The UK authority believed that, absent the acquisition by Eurotunnel, SeaFrance would have been acquired by another buyer whose acquisition would have been competitively preferable. The French authority found such possibilities too speculative to entertain. Additionally, the UK authority found that, given the existence of excess capacity in the market, the acquisition would likely lead to the exit of another rival—DFDS/LD—from Dover-

Calais route, at least in the short term. By contrast, the French authority found that the existence of excess authority would constrain price increases.

What accounts for the difference in analysis of the two national authorities? Commentators have pointed out several distinctions in the statutory and procedural dimensions of merger review on the two sides of the Channel. The UK merger guidelines specifically call for a consideration of counterfactual scenarios in assessing whether a merger substantially lessens competition, whereas the French guidelines contain no analogous provision. Further, the Competition Commission's in-depth investigation following the referral from the OFT allowed it to uncover some troubling references in Eurotunnel documents, to the effect that Eurotunnel's motivation for the acquisition was to prevent DFDS/ LD from acquiring SeaFrance's vessels at a low cost and driving down prices. The French authority did not have access to these documents when it made its decision. *See* Matt Evans & Marguerite Lavedan, *Eurotunnel/SeaFrance: Unbridgeable gap over the Channel?*, *http://www.jonesday.com/ eurotunnelseafrance-unbridgeable-gap-over-the-channel-mlex-ab-extra-07-02-2013/*.

In 2015, the UK Supreme Court upheld the finding of illegality. *Société Coopérative de Production SeaFrance SA (Respondent) v. The Competition and Markets Authority*, [2015] UKSC 75.

4. Resolution of Conflict

The forces of global competition combined with a high level of cooperation seem constantly to push towards convergence of substantive law and analysis, and to make it less likely that another *Boeing/McDonnell Douglas* or *GE/Honeywell* will occur. But still, conflicts arise. Not every nation applies the same mode of analysis or adopts the same platform or presumptions at the same time. When Oracle, the largest proprietary database company, proposed to take over Sun Microsystems, a leading open-source database company, the transaction was cleared by the US as not anticompetitive; but the European Commission proceeded with an investigation and a Statement of Objections. It expressed concern that Oracle would suppress Sun's popular open-source product, despite the insistence by both Oracle and the US Department of Justice that there were many other open-source and proprietary database companies. Ultimately, the EU cleared the acquisition with commitments from Oracle that it would maintain Sun's open-source database as a competitive force.

China, too, has asserted itself in merger clearances. Coca Cola proposed to acquire Huiyuan, the leading juice company in China and one with a strong brand name. The US and the EU approved the acquisition. China prohibited it. Likewise, the US and EU approved General Motors' acquisition of Delphi, a major automobile electronic parts supplier. China allowed but conditioned the deal.

What modus operandi should be in place for a next time when divergence on a major issue of common concern is brewing? As a beginning, the authorities of the potentially conflicting jurisdictions might adopt a protocol to confer intensively, pinpoint their differences, and attempt to resolve them. But they did this in *Boeing/McDonnell Douglas* and *GE/Honeywell*. Should there be protocols for deferring to the party with the greatest contacts and largest consumer market at least where there is a single world market or at least common competitive conditions in the different jurisdictions? Will developing countries—sometimes victims of increased buying power that is beyond the radar of developed countries—be part of the conversation?

For further discussion of conflict and its resolution, see Chapter 9, Global Governance.

Chapter 6

THE STATE

_____

A. INTRODUCTION

Thus far we have spoken of restraints of competition by private firms. But market competition can be harmed just as well, and often more severely and enduringly, by acts of the state. The state may act at all levels—from local to national—in ways that keep the forces of competition from working or that bias its results in favor of cronies, ordained winners, or other favorites. In many cases the harms to competition are mere by-products of policies that are part of a legitimate governance system, such as rent control or utility regulation. In many other cases, the acts are "rogue" acts, such as misuse of power by an official to benefit his friends. In between are state acts or measures that suppress competition excessively in view of any proper government purpose.

In many jurisdictions, such as the United States, neither the state (of the Union) nor federal bodies are covered by the antitrust laws, although local government acts may be covered. The state is presumed to act in the public interest. The boundaries between legislatures and courts are an inherent part of the checks and balances of the system, and the boundaries between states and the federal government are an inherent part of U.S. federalism. If state government exceeds its proper bounds, the citizens of the state may resist politically within the institutions of the state. And if a state exceeds its federalist bounds and harms the country, it may be called to account through the commerce clause of the Constitution for unduly burdening interstate commerce, or the federal legislature can pass preemptive legislation. The United States was not and is not a statist society. Few firms are state-owned. Business has grown on its merits (or luck, or sometimes by misuse of business power), not by state command or privilege. And the political and institutional checks are cherished. Accordingly, the issue of anticompetitive state acts and measures has not surfaced as an antitrust issue in the United States, except to the extent that the antitrust agencies advocate against excessively restrictive government measures.

A critical mass of other jurisdictions embed state offenses within their antitrust laws. Most prominently and predictably, this is done in common markets, which have functions both of policing internal market "trade" restraints (member state laws may improperly impair free movement), as well as policing business restraints. European Union law is the most mature example and is a model for other common markets and nations, and we therefore spend considerable time on this model. In addition, a number of transitional, developing and emerging economies include state restraints in their antitrust coverage, especially where an inherited "excessive state" is one of the most daunting problems they confront in moving to a functioning market system. China's Anti-Monopoly Law includes the most highly articulated prohibitions against anticompetitive abuses of power by government bodies, and antitrust enforcement in Russia and Central and Eastern European countries focuses to a significant extent on local governmental measures that block trade and competition across provincial borders. See Eleanor M. Fox and Deborah Healey, *When the State Harms Competition—The Role for Competition Law*, 79 Antitrust L.J. 769 (2014).

In the United States when we speak of state action in the context of antitrust, we refer not to condemning anticompetitive state action but, contrariwise, to allowing private anticompetitive action when firms are acting in the shadow of state command or policy. Most nations have some form of this defense, which we discuss below.

The subject of anticompetitive state restraints has gained an increasingly high profile in international antitrust fora such as the UNCTAD Competition and Consumer Branch and the International Competition Network (ICN). The ICN curriculum project has produced a training module on State Restraints, which you may want to watch. It is available at *http://www.internationalcompetition network.org/about/steering-group/outreach/icncurriculum/state% 20restraints.aspx.*

Because of the importance of European Union law in crafting the model for antitrust violations by the State, we begin with an overview of the EU model, and then we outline the coverage of the chapter.

The European context at the birth of the Treaty of Rome establishing the European Economic Community was entirely different. Parochial state restraints were the principal problem. Border barriers were high; high barriers fueled hatreds; they could undermine the project of a peaceful Europe. The principal effort of the founders of the European Community was to abolish Member State restraints that undermined free movement of goods, services, capital and people. Accordingly, Europe adopted its free-movement articles: states were enjoined not to impair free movement. See Articles 30–37, 45–66 of the Treaty on the Functioning of the European Union (TFEU). Read the selected articles in Appendix 1. It was foreseen that, when state barriers went down, the businesses within each nation would try to re-erect them (and they did try; see Chapter 2, Cartels). To protect the internal market as well as to protect the people from economic abuses, the drafters included the competition articles, now 101 and 102 of the TFEU. The drafters were also mindful of the statist tradition in most of the original six nations (France, Italy, Germany and the Benelux countries). Many state-owned firms procured their supplies only or at least preferentially from nationals; and many states conferred exclusive franchises and other privileges. The drafters knew that state firms and their privileged beneficiaries would claim exemptions from antitrust and try to continue their discriminatory operations in the manner to which they were accustomed, thus undermining the cause of market integration. Therefore they included in the Treaty Article 37—Member States must "adjust any State monopolies of a commercial character" to assure no discrimination in procurement or marketing; Article 4(3) of the Treaty on European Union (TEU)—Member States must "facilitate the achievement of the Union's tasks" and refrain from measures that could jeopardize the achievement of the Union's objectives; and Article 106 TFEU—"In the case of public undertakings, and undertakings to which Member States grant special or exclusive rights," Member States may not enact or maintain any measure contrary to the anti-discrimination (based on nationality) and competition articles; and undertakings entrusted with operation of services of general economic interest are subject to the competition rules insofar as application of those rules does not obstruct the performance of the tasks assigned to them.

Finally, the drafters were confronted with national governments that maintained their nationalism by giving large subsidies and other aids to their own firms, either creating national champions that would have state-backed muscle to outcompete businesses across the borders, or propping up firms that would otherwise close doors and jobs. The freedom of states to grant aids as they chose would also perpetuate economic nationalism and discrimination and undermine the mission of one common market. Therefore the drafters, in now Articles 107 and 108 TFEU, prohibited Member States from granting aids that may distort competition. Member States must file their intention to grant aids, which are subject to approval as specified in legislation.

Thus, the European Union centrally addresses state measures and restraints in its competition policy. It has developed a mature case law defining the contours.

As noted, Europe is not alone in pinpointing the state as a source of impairment of competition. Many developing countries face the dilemma of corrupt governments that privilege cronies in various markets, and governments that freely grant economic privileges. Moreover, some jurisdictions such as Russia and China prohibit state and local measures that restrict the free flow of goods across provincial lines. China, which has no commerce clause in its constitution and has a history of provincial roadblocks against goods from other provinces, prohibits such restraints as part of a larger section against "abuse of administrative monopoly."

This chapter presents the problem of competition and the state (which may be local, provincial, or national) in six parts. First, advocacy, which is competition *policy* to reduce state restraints. Second, state-owned enterprises' abuses of dominance. Third, abuse of dominance by state-privileged firms. Fourth, state measures and the scope of state action defenses as justification for private anticompetitive acts. Fifth, the relationship between competition law and sectoral regulation and the extent of regulatory preemption. Sixth, the status of hybrid state-and-private restraints, including a limited antitrust jurisdiction in the World Trade Organization.

Act of state, foreign sovereign immunity, and foreign sovereign compulsion were treated in Chapter 1 in our discussion of cartels, since that is the area in which these doctrines are most commonly asserted. The problems treated in this chapter involve either state acts or measures that may harm competition within the state's own community, or such state acts or measures seen within a larger polity of which the state is a part.

B. ADVOCACY

One of the most important tasks of a competition agency, especially agencies that face powerful business lobbies and institutional structures built in pre-market eras, is competition advocacy. The advocacy may be addressed both to the government and to the people. The International Competition Network has highlighted the important role of advocacy since its foundation in 2001. Influential papers and remarks have been contributed by Allan Fels of Australia, Beatriz Boza of Peru, John Fingleton of Ireland and the UK, and Bill Kovacic of the United States, who have been among the most successful advocates of pro-competition solutions to complex economic problems and whose work has been a counter to private interest lobbying. The work of ICN's Advocacy Working Group is described at *http://internationalcompetitionnetwork.org/working-groups/current/advocacy.aspx.*

Meanwhile, on the ground, competition officials of developing countries have highlighted problems and helped industries work for the benefit of the people, including by alleviation of poverty of exploited farmers. See Thulasoni Kaira, The Role of Competition Law and Policy in Alleviating Poverty—The Case of Zambia, in THE EFFECTS OF ANTI-COMPETITIVE BUSINESS PRACTICES ON DEVELOPING COUNTRIES AND THEIR DEVELOPMENT PROSPECTS, 133, 150–57 (cotton) (Qaqaya & Lipimile eds, UNCTAD 2008).

Here is one example of effective advocacy. Numerous others are continuously unfolding, as highlighted in an annual competition held by the World Bank in coordination with the ICN. We tell the story of cement in Tanzania, as relayed by Godfrey Mkocha, Director General of the Fair Competition Commission of Tanzania.

Cement is a basic commodity; a necessity for shelter and buildings. Cement markets are notoriously oligopolistic and perennially a breeding ground for cartels. In Tanzania, there are three significant cement companies: Tanzania Portland Cement, Tanga Cement, and Mbeya Cement. India and Pakistan are well positioned to ship their own higher quality, lower cost cement into Tanzania.

In 2005 the East African Community (EAC) signed a protocol classifying cement as a sensitive product, thereby warranting a protective duty of 55%, which was to be reduced to 35% by 2009. Meanwhile, a great shortage occurred, leading the EAC states to agree, in 2008, to reduce the duty to zero. Their effort succeeded; supply increased and prices fell.

But when the prices fell, the East African Cement Producers Association went into action. They lobbied the Government at the highest levels to reinstate the 35% duty. They took their case to the press, convincing reporters to sound the alarm that cheap cement imports from Pakistan and India were about to destroy thousands of jobs and undermine the Tanzanian economy. A headline in the Tanzanian Sunday Citizen read: "Cheap cement now threatens economy." (May 31, 2009) The article reported that citizens were celebrating the falling price of cement "little knowing the situation is precipitating their country's economic doom." It continued:

"This situation is bound to affect the forthcoming budget, which has already suffered from the shrink in revenue due to the global financial crisis. * * *

Cement industry is estimated to contribute about Sh30 billion as income tax only. The industry also contributes other billions to Government coffers through import duty and other taxes.

There are fears that if the imports trend will continue at the current level, the Government might lose billions in revenue from the industry."

The Fair Competition Commission quickly sent a response to the press:

The Editor,
The Citizen

The Fair Competition Commission (FCC) wishes to address the messages contained in the articles which appeared in your esteemed newspaper on 25th May, 2009 written by George Sembony, headed *Import said to be hurting Tanga firm;* and 31st May, 2009 by Sunday Citizen Reporter headed *Decision on cement duty awaits new budget* and Mnaku Mbani headed *cheap cement now threatens economy*.

FCC commends the writer's efforts to report on the views of local manufactures on cement sub-sector which is very important to Tanzania industrial development. The writer reported that there is fear among local cement manufacturers, over the influx of cement imported from giant factories in Pakistan and India, likely to kill the country's cement industry due to the fact that Tanzania cement sector cannot compete with that of India and Pakistan since the costs of production in the country are 2.5% higher due to higher power tariffs. The cement manufacturers want the duty re-introduced in order to curb what they term oversupply, marked distortion and dumping.

Reading through the article, it is evident that the challenge to ensure the public understands fundamental principles of market economy particularly competition and its eventual benefits remains enormous across the citizenry. FCC as a market support institution whose role is to promote and protect competition in trade and commerce would like to put the issues in context.

For the past one year, consumers country-wide were concerned about the rise of retail prices and the scarcity of cement in the market. An analysis of the cement sub-sector was conducted in order to establish the underlying causes or price rises and scarcity in the cement market and the following were observed to be the issues undermining consumers of the benefits that they would have otherwise enjoyed.

(i) There are only three cement producers in the country who also own cement plants in other East African countries. This situation restrained competition in the country and within the East African sub region.

(ii) Cement being a bulky product, transportation cost is a significant factor in the determination of final prices to the consumer. In Tanzania, cement factories are sparsely and unevenly located (Tanga, Mbeya and Dar es Salaam). Also, most of the cement factories lack depots in different parts of the country; as a result they have left distribution and transportation in the hands of few private businesses. The foregoing, coupled with the current weak and limited transportation network alternatives, make the final cement price higher.

(iii) The contestability of Tanzania cement market through imports of cement from the world market was limited due to the then high protection rate set for cement in the East African market; therefore the internal producers were simply taking advantage of the protection without doing anything to the high prices caused by the rising demand.

A short term solution was then sought to lower substantially the protection rate for cement in order to discipline the internal industry through competition.

Generally, the rationale for governments to protect an industry is to maintain employment and the attendant benefits in their countries. However, in the case of the cement industry which is capital intensive, such intended benefits have to be weighed against the high construction costs such a policy introduces in the economy. This situation is worse where our country is developing and therefore construction is a must and where the Government itself is using a high proportion of its budget in construction. It means the country is increasing the costs to itself and limits the growth of the downstream construction industry thus curtailing the employment benefits which the country was purporting to protect in the first place.

We wish to recall that the cement industry has registered success particularly as a result of the ever booming construction industry in the country, and the profit enjoyed by manufacturers has never lower as evidenced by the dividends paid to their investors.

The Governments of the East African Community decision eventually to reduce the suspended duty should be commended. Also the decision of the Government of Tanzania to encourage the location of new cement plants to new areas in Tanzania is a smart decision.

It is against this background that The Fair Competition Commission would like to echo the Government move to ensure that the market remains open and contestable by allowing the interplays that discipline the market and lessen the consumer's burden. If cement produced thousands of miles from Tanzania can beat the production costs of our local cement industry, then the economists should think again on what we want to protect by re-introducing the suspended duty.

>Michael Shilla
>Ag. DIRECTOR GENERAL
>FAIR COMPETITION
>COMMISSION

The Citizen printed the FCC's letter, on June 6, 2009. The Business Times Economic & Financial Weekly also printed the letter (June 5–11 edition) but with one addition: a provocative headline (provocative because the industry was still importuning the Ministry of Industry and Trade to reinstate the duty): "As Cheaper cement from India, Pakistan floods market ... Government tells local manufacturers 'NO' to protection."

The Ministry of Industry and Trade was angry with the message of the headline. It confronted the Fair Competition Commission. Why was the FCC pretending to speak for the Government? The FCC demurred; it had not spoken for the Government; it was speaking for competition, as it had the duty to do. The press, not the Commission, wrote the misleading headline: The Government says No.

Meanwhile, the FCC's procompetition arguments convinced Tanzanian President Jayaka Kikwete. Kikwete stood up for competition, not protection. In the midst of the controversy between the competition authority and the trade ministry, the President was the guest of honor at the inaugural ceremony of a new plant of Tanzania Portland Cement. He used the opportunity to announce that, indeed, the Government said no. The Government would not reinstate the protective duty.

On July 10, 2009, The Business Times Economic & Financial Weekly changed its tone. It carried a headline: "Locally manufactured cement: consumers' confidence wanes." The subhead said: "Kikwete cautions on high prices; Pakistan cement better— Experts." The article reported the experts' opinion that Pakistan produced a far higher quality cement than the Tanzanian producers, and it reported Kikwete's advice to the local producers to find the way to lower the price of cement.

Notes and Questions

The Tanzanian incident illustrates the tangled web produced when domestic competitors fight to protect their markets. Protection means less competition at home and higher prices. Protection of the domestic cement producers, in the Tanzania story, meant worse roads, neglected infrastructure, vulnerable buildings for schools and housing, and fewer jobs in these sectors, while protecting existing jobs (and profits) in the laggard domestic cement plants and removing a spur to make them better.

Competition advocacy can cover very wide ground. You may think of it as pro-market advocacy. Competition advocacy includes examination of and recommendations regarding existing and proposed legislation. In 2016, China adopted a Fair Competition Review System in Market Development, according to which all proposed legislation is examined to avoid "excessive and inappropriate intervention in the market." In Peru, the competition authority INDECOPI is charged with challenging anticompetitive regulations. The US agencies, while not having such a mandate, do extensive competition advocacy.

C. ABUSE OF DOMINANCE BY STATE-OWNED ENTERPRISE: PARADIGM CASES

Many jurisdictions that have recently adopted market systems and antitrust laws were traditionally statist economies. The state owned and operated the businesses. Others were mixed economies: a mix of state and private ownership. Yet others reserved state ownership for services and goods of critical importance, often in regulated sectors, such as electricity, utilities, and transport. A number of the state-owned entities have now been privatized, but often they retained historical privileges conferred by the state. Often the state, to maximize the revenues it would receive from the sale, sold the business with its monopoly intact, realizing a monopoly premium. The "people" did not feel the promised benefits of privatization, and sometimes felt more exploited under a market regime.

An initial question, often answered by the antitrust statute, is whether state-owned enterprises are covered by the antitrust laws and to what extent. In the European Union, the competition law applies to state-owned enterprises with an exception—SOEs are exempted to the extent necessary to fulfill mandatory duties. In China, SOEs in regulated sectors are answerable to sector regulation; the. Anti-Monopoly Law, Art. 7; but they are not exempt from the competition law

In this section we deal with antitrust laws that cover state enterprises. We ask: In the application of the law against abuse of dominance or monopolization, are state-owned enterprises different from other enterprises? Is there reason to single them out?

In general, the legal analysis of SOE conduct is not differentiated, but there are characteristics of state enterprise and often its privatized successors that make them especially likely to restrain competition in ways that will not be cured by the market. Indeed, the drafters of the European Treaty of Rome were especially aware of the many state enterprises in Europe, their unique power to exploit, their habits of preferring to do business with their own nationals, and their incentives to preserve their own domains by their access to government privilege, when they drafted (now) Article 101 TFEU (abuse of dominance), and included (now) Article 106 TFEU.

For the problem of excessive pricing by state-owned and recently privatized-firms, see the South African cases, Chapter 2, supra. This section concerns exclusionary practices.

We begin here with two ports cases—cases in which state-owned ports used their power over the facility to block or disadvantage foreign shippers or competitors. The first, *Port of Genoa*, shows how European principles of free movement, non-discrimination, non-abuse of dominance, and the Member States' duty of loyalty to carry out the single market objective, interact. The second, *Rødby*, is a more traditional antitrust case that highlights the incentive of the state facility owner to keep adjacent markets for itself. Both are precursors to a number of the cases that you will read in the sections below on State Privilege and State Responsibility.

Ports Cases

Ports and ports authorities were principally owned by states. They were literally and figuratively gateways to markets. Typically, states adopted measures to bolster their ports' powers to exclude; and exclusion of competitors and exploitation of consumers were common. The ports cases are helpful illustrations 1) factually, of problems of state ownership and exclusive privilege, and 2) legally, of the interrelationship of the several Treaty articles applied to address the problems of abuse, to promote liberalization, and to assure non-discriminatory access.

Before reading the cases, read in Appendix 1 Articles 102 TFEU (abuse of dominance), Article 106 TFEU (application of antitrust to SOEs and holders of special or exclusive rights, and obligations of Member States not to legislate to the contrary effect), and Article 4(3)

TEU (Member State's duty to facilitate the achievement of the Union's tasks and to "abstain from any measure which could jeopardize the attainment of the Union's objectives").

MERCI CONVENZIONALI PORTO DI GENOVA
v. SIDERURGICA GABRIELLI SPA
Case C–179/90, EU:C:1991: 347 (European Court of Justice 1991)

The Italian Navigation Code established an exclusive right to organize dock work for third parties, and required retention of dock work companies that employed only registered workers of Italian nationality. Carriers coming to port were not permitted to use their crew to load and unload. The organizer of dock work was generally controlled by the port authority.

Merci and Compagnia enjoyed the exclusive right to organize dock work. Siderurgica Gabrielli SpA arrived in the Port of Genoa with goods, but Merci delayed in providing unloading services and Siderurgica Gabrielli suffered damages, for which it sought compensation. The Italian court asked the ECJ whether the Italian rules violated (now) Articles 4(3) TEU, 34 TFEU (free movement of goods), 45 (free movement of workers), 102 and 106, and whether Siderurgica Gabrielli had a remedy.

Advocate General Van Gerven identified the anticompetitive and discriminatory effects inherent in the Italian law:

22 [W]e must now consider whether these abuses of a dominant position within the meaning of Article [102]—in so far as the national court regards them as established—are imposed, or facilitated, or made inevitable by the relevant national legislation. I think there can be little doubt about this. In fact, the scale of charges and other, presumably unfair, contractual conditions applied by Merci and Compagnia are made possible, if not inevitable, by the national legislation applicable and are facilitated, if not made compulsory, by the port authorities under the powers conferred on them by national legislation. The other abuses too are made possible by that legislation. But for the monopoly for the performance of dock work conferred on it by the Italian legislation, Compagnia could certainly not have afforded to abstain from using modern technology, and it is clear also that the dissimilar treatment of trading parties was possible only as a result of the monopoly granted to Merci and the complexity and lack of transparency of the scale of charges devised by the authority.

The Court ruled:

19 [I]t appears from the circumstances described by the national court and discussed before the Court of Justice that the undertakings enjoying exclusive rights in accordance with the procedures laid down by the national rules in question are, as a result, induced either to demand payment for services which have not been requested, to charge disproportionate prices, to refuse to have recourse to modern technology, which involves an increase in the cost of the operations and a prolongation of the time required for their performance, or to grant price reductions to certain consumers and at the same time to offset such reductions by an increase in the charges to other consumers.

20 In these circumstances it must be held that a Member State creates a situation contrary to Article [102] of the Treaty where it adopts rules of such a kind as those at issue before the national court, which are capable of affecting trade between Member States as in the case of the main proceedings, regard being had to the factors mentioned in . . . this judgment relating to the importance of traffic in the Port of Genoa.

21 As regards the interpretation of Article [102] of the Treaty requested by the national court, it is sufficient to recall that a national measure which has the effect of facilitating the abuse of a dominant position capable of affecting trade between Member States will generally be incompatible with that article, which prohibits quantitative restrictions on imports and all measures having equivalent effect (see Case 13/77 GB–INNO–BM v ATAB [1977] ECR 2115, paragraph 35) in so far as such a measure has the effect of making more difficult and hence of impeding imports of goods from other Member States.

22 In the main proceedings it may be seen from the national court' s findings that the unloading of the goods could have been effected at a lesser cost by the ship' s crew, so that compulsory recourse to the services of the two undertakings enjoying exclusive rights involved extra expense and was therefore capable, by reason of its effect on the prices of the goods, of affecting imports.

23 It should be emphasized in the third place that even within the framework of Article [106], the provisions of Articles [34, 45 and 102] of the Treaty have direct effect* and give rise for interested parties to

---

* Editors' note: This means that the specified Articles are positive law in the Member States. They do not need implementing legislation to become enforceable law.

rights which the national courts must protect (see in particular, as regards Article [102] of the Treaty).

24 The answer to the first question, as reformulated, should therefore be that:

> Article [106(1) TFEU], in conjunction with Articles [34, 45 and 102 TFEU], precludes rules of a Member State which confer on an undertaking established in that State the exclusive right to organize dock work and require it for that purpose to have recourse to a dock-work company formed exclusively of national workers; Articles [34, 45 and 102] of the Treaty, in conjunction with Article [106], give rise to rights for individuals which the national courts must protect.

Notes and Questions

1.   Note how the law condemns national measures as affronting competition and free movement rules intertwined. While these are common market cases, the EU competition provisions have been incorporated into many national laws. Moreover, more and more nations are now part of free trade areas and common markets, and the European jurisprudence is a model of how the competition rules integrate with the internal market free movement rules.

2.   Following the judgment, Italy revised its law to open up competition for port-handling. The Commission, however, was not satisfied. It found that local authorities systematically refused to grant operating licenses to potential competitors of long-established dock services companies. Italy, in response, issued licensees. XXVth Report on Competition Policy (1995), pp. 58–59. The Commission again found that the Italian reform was insufficient and indeed that it created new problems. It found additional infringements, by decision of 97/744, 21 October 1997.

PORT OF RØDBY

94/119/EC, Commission decision of 21 Dec. 1993, O.J. L 055
26 January 1994 at 0052

[DSB was a Danish public undertaking which operated as a department of the transport ministry. It held the exclusive right to organize railroad traffic in Denmark and the exclusive right to manage the Port of Rødby, and it operated ferry services between Denmark and neighboring countries. Stena was a Swedish shipping group which specialized in ferry services and wished to operate between Denmark and Germany (Puttgarden), which essentially links eastern Denmark with Germany and the rest of western Europe.

Stena requested permission from the Danish government to use the existing port facilities at Rødby or to build a port in the vicinity. The Danish government refused. Stena complained to the Commission.]

Abuse of dominant position

[12] The refusal to allow 'Euro-Port A/S', a subsidiary of the Swedish group [Stena] to operate from Rødby has the effect of eliminating a potential competitor on the Rødby-Puttgarden route and hence of strengthening the joint dominant position of DSB and [its partner] DB on that route.

According to the case law of the Court, an abuse within the meaning of Article [102] is committed in cases where, without any objective necessity, an undertaking holding a dominant position on a particular market reserves to itself an ancillary activity which might be carried out by another undertaking as part of its activities on a neighbouring but separate market, with the possibility of eliminating all competition from such undertaking.

Thus an undertaking that owns or manages and uses itself an essential facility, i.e. a facility or infrastructure without which its competitors are unable to offer their services to customers, and refuses to grant them access to such facility is abusing its dominant position.

Consequently, an undertaking that owns or manages an essential port facility from which it provides a maritime transport service may not, without objective justification, refuse to grant a shipowner wishing to operate on the same maritime route access to that facility without infringing Article [102].

[13] According to the case-law of the Court, Article [106] (1) prohibits Member States from placing, by law, regulation or administrative provision, public undertakings and undertakings to which they grant exclusive rights in a position in which those undertakings could not place themselves by their own conduct without infringing Article [102]. The Court added that, where the extension of the dominant position of a public undertaking or an undertaking to which the State has granted exclusive rights resulted from a State measure, such a measure constituted an infringement of Article [106], read in conjunction with Article [102] of the Treaty. . . .

Thus, for the reasons given above, any firm in the same position as DSB which refused to grant another shipping operator access to the port it controlled would be abusing a dominant position. Where, as in the present case, a Member State has refused such access and has strengthened the effects of the refusal by also refusing to authorize the construction of a new port, it constitutes a State measure in breach of Article [106], read in conjunction with Article [102].

14 The reasons given by the Danish Transport Ministry for rejecting both requests of 'Euro-Port A/S' . . . are the following:

> —the plan of 'Euro-Port A/S' . . . (Stena), to build a new terminal is not acceptable as that undertaking has allegedly 'not established that there is an unsatisfied demand for a ferry service' and it is 'most unlikely that such a demand would arise', . . .

> —'Euro-Port A/S' (Stena) could not operate from the existing port facilities as this would have the effect of preventing the companies already operating in the port from expanding their activities. * * *

> The Commission concludes . . . that:

> —there was indeed an unsatisfied demand for ferry services in May 1990 since one year later DSB and DB had expanded their services,

> —the increase in the activities of DB and DSB in 1991 confirms that the port of Rødby was not saturated.

15 The Commission also considers that there is no evidence that the existing facilities at Rødby would today be saturated or that, subject to alterations which Stena has informed the Commission it is prepared to finance, existing port capacity is unable to cope with an increase in trade.

The Commission also notes that the Swedish group (Stena) has acquired land adjacent to the port facilities of Rødby which is perfectly suitable for development as a terminal by Stena.

It therefore concludes that there are no technical constraints preventing the Stena group from sailing between Rødby and Puttgarden.

16 . . . [T]he Danish authorities . . . [stressed] that their refusals were justified under Community law. They stated that it would be impossible to allow Stena access to the existing facilities, giving technical reasons and referring for the first time, without any further

details, to obligations incumbent upon DB and DSB in the general interest.

This would appear to indicate that, in the view of the Danish authorities, the technical feasibility of access to the port is not a problem or is not the only problem and that they also have a duty to protect the public undertaking DSB from a competitor on the market for ferry services.

Nor can the Commission share the view of the Danish authorities that the alleged saturation of the existing port facilities would make pointless any attempt to introduce competition since this could not in any event lead to an increase in the number of sailings between Rødby and Puttgarden.

Even on a saturated market, an improvement in the quality of products or services offered or a reduction in prices as a result of competition is a definite advantage for consumers; this could also lead to an increase in demand which, in the present case, could be met by expanding the port. * * *

Article [106](2)

[18] The Commission considers that the application of the competition rules in the present case does not impede the particular task entrusted to the public undertaking DSB namely to organize rail services and manage the port facilities at Rødby. Therefore the exception provided for in Article [106](2) [where application would obstruct the performance of tasks assigned to them] does not apply.

Conclusion

[19] In view of the foregoing, the Commission considers that the measures referred to in paragraphs 1 and 2 constitute infringements of Article [106](1) of the Treaty, read in conjunction with Article [102].

Notes and Questions

1. Does the Commission rule out the defense of market saturation in law as well as in fact? Does it suggest why DSB denied the permission? What does the case imply about incentives, and how can the incentives be aligned with competition values?

2. In the aftermath of the *Rødby* case, the Commission became concerned that construction of a new port would be inefficient. It adopted a revised remedy "legally separating the provision of the network from the commercial services using the network." *http://www.eubusiness.*

com / topics / competition / liberalisation. Is this a superior remedy? Explain the difference.

3. How would the *Port of Genoa* problem be dealt with in the United States? In view of the synergies among the Treaty articles and the differences in US and EU competition law treatment, comment on the constitutional dimension of EU competition law.

4. How would the *Rødby* problem be dealt with under US law? Is the port an essential facility? Would the entity that both owned or managed the port and operated the ferry have a duty to license a competing ferry service? See Verizon Communications Inc. v. Law Offices of Curtis V. Trinko, 540 U.S. 398 (2004). Would insufficient demand be a defense?

5. In several important cases, the state-owned entities had tried, unsuccessfully, to use state ownership as a shield to Article 102 liability. In *British Telecom* (Italy v. Commission), the Court held that a state telecommunications monopoly abused its dominance by preventing private message-forwarding agencies from receiving and forwarding international telephone calls. Case 41/83, EU:C:1985:120. In *Telemarketing*, the Court stated that a broadcasting monopoly would abuse its dominant position by refusing to sell broadcasting time to a telemarketing firm that competed with the monopoly firm's subsidiary. Case 311/84, *Centre Belge d'Etudes de Marché-Télémarketing SA v. Compagnie Luxembourgeoise de Télédiffusion SA*, EU:C:1985:394.

6. The port cases reflect principles and problems common to a range of infrastructure industries and regulated sectors, including transport, post, telecommunications and energy. The European law that applies to restrictive state measures and to abusive action by undertakings is intertwined. In some sectors, notably energy and telecommunications, the EU undertook major liberalization projects, aided by framework directives. The objective was to *improve* conditions of competition, not just to prevent its restriction. See Neelie Kroes, *Improving Competition in European Energy Markets through Effective Unbundling*, Chapter 9 in 2007 Fordham Competition Law Institute, INTERNATIONAL ANTITRUST LAW & POLICY, p. 247 (B. Hawk ed. 2007).

D. STATE PRIVILEGE OR LICENSE; LIMITS TO EXCLUSIVITY

Many states grant to a designated enterprise exclusive rights or privileges, such as the exclusive right to run an employment service, the exclusive right to deliver the mail, or, as we saw above, the exclusive right to run a port. What are the implications for competition of these exclusive grants?

Article 106(2) of the Treaty on the Functioning of the European Union, as we have just seen, prohibits public undertakings or undertakings to which special or exclusive rights are granted from violating the antitrust provisions and the anti-discrimination provisions of the Treaty. They are subject to these articles insofar as their application does not obstruct their performance of the particular tasks assigned to them.

HÖFNER v. MACROTRON GMBH

Case C–41/90, EU:C:1991:161 (European Court of Justice 1991)

[German law, intended to achieve a high level of employment and to improve the distribution of jobs, conferred on the Bundesanstalt für Arbeit (Federal Employment Office) the exclusive right of placement; i.e. exclusivity as employment agent. The law required the Office to provide the service free of charge. Placement activities by others were punishable by fine. Messrs. Höfner and Elser contracted with Macrotron to present to Macrotron a suitable candidate for the post of sales manager, for a fee. They presented such a candidate, but Macrotron decided not to employ him and refused to pay the fee stipulated, alleging, inter alia, that the contract was void by reason of the German law. Höfner and Elser rejoined that the German law was void because it unnecessarily restrained their competition in violation of Article 106, and exclusion of their competition amounted to abuse of dominance under Article 102. The national court referred questions to the Court of Justice.]

[16] In its fourth question, the national court asks more specifically whether the monopoly of employment procurement in respect of business executives granted to a public employment agency constitutes an abuse of a dominant position within the meaning of Article [102], having regard to Article [106](2). . . .

[17] According to the appellants in the main proceedings, an agency such as the Bundesanstalt is both a public undertaking within the meaning of Article [106](1) and an undertaking entrusted with the operation of services of general economic interest within the meaning of Article [106](2) of the Treaty. The Bundesanstalt is therefore, they maintain, subject to the competition rules to the extent to which the application thereof does not obstruct the performance of the particular task assigned to it, and it does not in the present case. The appellants also claim that the action taken by the Bundesanstalt, which extended its statutory monopoly over employment procurement to activities for which the establishment of a monopoly is not in the public interest, constitutes an abuse within the meaning of Article [102] of the Treaty. They also consider that any Member State which makes such an abuse possible is in breach of Article

[106](1) and of the general principle whereby the Member States must refrain from taking any measure which could destroy the effectiveness of the Community competition rules.

[18] The Commission takes a somewhat different view. The maintenance of a monopoly on executive recruitment constitutes, in its view, an infringement of Article [106](1) read in conjunction with Article [102] of the Treaty where the grantee of the monopoly is not willing or able to carry out that task fully, according to the demand existing on the market, and provided that such conduct is liable to affect trade between Member States. * * *

[21] It must be observed, in the context of competition law, first that the concept of an undertaking encompasses every entity engaged in an economic activity, regardless of the legal status of the entity and the way in which it is financed and, secondly, that employment procurement is an economic activity.

[22] The fact that employment procurement activities are normally entrusted to public agencies cannot affect the economic nature of such activities. Employment procurement has not always been, and is not necessarily, carried out by public entities. That finding applies in particular to executive recruitment.

[23] It follows that an entity such as a public employment agency engaged in the business of employment procurement may be classified as an undertaking for the purpose of applying the Community competition rules.

[24] It must be pointed out that a public employment agency which is entrusted, under the legislation of a Member State, with the operation of services of general economic interest . . . remains subject to the competition rules pursuant to Article [106](2) of the Treaty unless and to the extent to which it is shown that their application is incompatible with the discharge of its duties.

[25] As regards the manner in which a public employment agency enjoying an exclusive right of employment procurement conducts itself in relation to executive recruitment undertaken by private recruitment consultancy companies, it must be stated that the application of Article [102] of the Treaty cannot obstruct the performance of the particular task assigned to that agency in so far as the latter is manifestly not in a position to satisfy demand in that area of the market and in fact allows its exclusive rights to be encroached on by those companies.

[26] Whilst it is true that Article [102] concerns undertakings and may be applied within the limits laid down by Article [106](2) to public undertakings or undertakings vested with exclusive rights or specific

rights, the fact nevertheless remains that the Treaty requires the Member States not to take or maintain in force measures which could destroy the effectiveness of that provision. . . . * * *

[29] . . . [T]he simple fact of creating a dominant position of that kind by granting an exclusive right within the meaning of Article [106](1) is not as such incompatible with Article [102] of the Treaty. A Member State is in breach of the prohibition contained in those two provisions only if the undertaking in question, merely by exercising the exclusive right granted to it, cannot avoid abusing its dominant position.

[30] Pursuant to Article [102](b), such an abuse may in particular consist in limiting the provision of a service, to the prejudice of those seeking to avail themselves of it.

[31] A Member State creates a situation in which the provision of a service is limited when the undertaking to which it grants an exclusive right extending to executive recruitment activities is manifestly not in a position to satisfy the demand prevailing on the market for activities of that kind and when the effective pursuit of such activities by private companies is rendered impossible by the maintenance in force of a statutory provision under which such activities are prohibited and nonobservance of that prohibition renders the contracts concerned void. * * *

[34] In view of the foregoing considerations, it must be stated in reply to the fourth question that a public employment agency engaged in employment procurement activities is subject to the prohibition contained in Article [102] of the Treaty, so long as the application of that provision does not obstruct the performance of the particular task assigned to it. A Member State which has conferred an exclusive right to carry on that activity upon the public employment agency is in breach of Article [106](1) of the Treaty where it creates a situation in which that agency cannot avoid infringing Article [102] of the Treaty. That is the case, in particular, where the following conditions are satisfied:

 —the exclusive right extends to executive recruitment activities

 —the public employment agency is manifestly incapable of satisfying demand prevailing on the market for such activities

 —the actual pursuit of those activities by private recruitment consultants is rendered impossible by the maintenance in force of a statutory provision under which such activities are prohibited and non-observance of that prohibition renders the contracts concerned void

—the activities in question may extend to the nationals or to the territory of other Member States.

Notes and Questions

1.   What is the standard for running afoul of Article 106(2) of the Treaty? How difficult will it be for Messrs. Höfner and Elser to win their argument before the national court?

2.   Note the difference between plaintiffs' proposed formulation (para. 17) and the Commission's (para. 18). Which did the Court accept? Which is the more workable? Which is the better standard, given the Community's dual interests in respecting Member State regulation in the public interest and supporting freedom of competition?

3.   Does the Court in effect require an efficiency audit of the Federal Employment Office to determine whether it manifestly cannot satisfy demand? Is the Office's ability to satisfy demand a function of the resources that the German government makes available to it? Do all dominant firms abuse their dominance by simply not providing enough goods or service (at what price level?), or is it critical that the government-granted exclusive privilege prevents anyone else from serving the market?

4.   In Case C–320/91, *Régie des Postes v. Corbeau*, EU:C:1993:198, a Belgian law—enacted before the development of courier service—gave exclusive mail delivery rights to the Belgian Post Office and prohibited private mail delivery. Mr. Corbeau set up a private mail delivery service in Liège. Corbeau collected mail from his clients and guaranteed delivery before noon the following day to all addressees within town limits. He delivered in-town mail and dispatched the out-of-town mail by post. When prosecuted, Corbeau asserted a violation of Article 106.

In answer to a question posed by the Belgian court (a procedure available under Article 267 TFEU), the European Court of Justice advised the Belgian court that an undertaking charged with the provision of universal service may not restrict competition more than necessary to achieve its public mission in view of contemporary market conditions. The Court of Justice left it to the national court to determine what was "more than necessary."

Was Corbeau skimming the cream from the Belgian Post's business? At some point, would cream-skimming compromise the economic stability of the post office and disable it from fulfilling its obligation to provide universal service? How can the national court determine how much competition is too much for the Belgian Post to fulfill its public mission?

Note the effect of the law: the holder of state-granted exclusive rights may forfeit exclusivity.

5.   There is a gap in the coverage of Articles 101, 102 and 106 of the Treaty. Member State bodies are subject to those Treaty obligations only if they carry out economic activities. Bodies that regulate the market but do not participate in it are not covered. In Case C–205/03 P, *FENIN v. Commission,* EU:C:2006:453, the Court of Justice acknowledged that the public bodies that ran the Spanish national healthcare system and provided free services funded by social security contributions and other state funding were not "undertakings," and it held that a state body that is not an undertaking does not become so in its role as purchaser of goods—here, medical goods and equipment. The purchasing activity is not "dissociable from the service subsequently provided." The holding of *FENIN* means that suppliers to state bodies carrying out public functions are not protected by Article 102 from the state body's exploitative and discriminatory purchasing conduct. Does this holding shield too much activity from the antitrust provisions? Is it sufficient protection that the state is subject to Article 18 TFEU, which prohibits the state from discriminating based on nationality?

6.   The United States Sherman Act imposes liability on "any person" who restrains trade or monopolizes. "Person" includes associations, corporations, and other entities. State and local government-owned entities may qualify as persons. See City of Lafayette v. Louisiana Power & Light Co., 435 U.S. 389 (1978). However, in *U.S. Postal Service v. Flamingo Industries (USA) Ltd.,* 540 U.S. 736 (2004), the US Supreme Court held that the U.S. Postal Service, in view of its public characteristics and responsibilities, should be treated as part of the US Government and not as a market participant; therefore it was not a "person" within the meaning of the Sherman Act.

E. STATE MEASURES

1.   State Measures—State Responsibility

State legislation is a frequent source of distortion of competition. Distortions may result from national laws on price control, sector regulation (e.g., oil, tobacco, transport), taxation, and various social and national industrial policies. But states, of course, must be empowered to take action in the public interest, meaning that some balance must be struck and the question is, what is that balance?

To what extent do EU Article 4 TEU [duty of sincere cooperation], the competition provisions, and the freedoms of movement, suggest a generous overriding of anticompetitive state legislation? The Court of Justice bowed in the direction of a broad preemption in its judgment in Case 13/77, *NV GB–INNO–BM v. Vereniging van de Kleinhandelaars in Tabak* (*INNO/ATAB*), EU:C:1977:185. A Belgian law required, for tax collection purposes, that tobacco products be sold at a price affixed to the label by the manufacturer or importer. The Court of Justice said:

> [W]hile it is true that Article [102] is directed at undertakings, nonetheless it is also true that the Treaty [now Article 4 TEU] imposes a duty on Member States not to adopt or maintain in force any measure which could deprive that provision of its effectiveness. *Id.*, para. 31.

In succeeding decades, the Court took a more modest (but still firm) view of Member State obligations. In 1993, amid concerns that the "center" had taken too much power for itself and was unduly eclipsing Member State prerogatives, the Court of Justice restruck the balance in cases involving national law with a by-product effect on free movement of goods, *Keck*, EU:C:1993:905. The shifted perspective, which would give greater regard to Member State prerogatives, bore its imprint in a trio of contemporaneous competition cases.

In this trio, the Court held: A Member State infringes Articles TEU4/TFEU101 if it "requires or favors the adoption of agreements, decisions or concerted practices contrary to Article [101], or reinforces such effects, or deprives its own legislation of its official character by delegating economic responsibility to private traders" (quoting from *INNO/ATAB*). *Ohra Schadeverzekeringen NV v. Netherlands* (*Ohra*), Case C–245/91, EU:1993:887; *W. Meng v. Germany* (*Meng*), Case C–2/91, EU:C:1993:885; *Gebrüder Reiff GmbH & Co. KG v. Bundesanstalt für den Güterfernverkehr* (*Reiff*), Case C–185/91, EU:C:1993:886. The cases exonerated Member State measures that had anticompetitive effects; namely, national law that forbade insurance agents from granting rebates, and national law that entrusted trucking tariffs to boards that included individuals recommended by the truckers, where the board members were obliged to act in the public interest and the Minister of Transport could intervene to set the tariff.

The question remained, how broadly or narrowly would the Court construe its mandate that the State must not undermine the effectiveness of Articles 101 and 102.

CONSORZIO INDUSTRIE FIAMMIFERI
(*ITALIAN MATCHES*)
(responsibility of the state)
Case C–198/01, EU:C:2003:430 (European Court of Justice, 2003)

[In *Consorzio Industrie Fiammiferi* (*Italian matches*), Case C–198/01, EU:C:2003:8055, Italy, by an 80 year-old Royal Decree, organized a match cartel. Italy required the Italian match producers to join a consortium. The minister set the price for matches, and the consortium of competitors was required to allocate quotas. Government officials had the duty to oversee the quotas. A German match producer complained to the Italian Antitrust Authority that it was having difficulty entering the Italian market. Swedish producers later complained that they were denied a fair quota and could sell only to the Italian match consortium. The Italian Antitrust Authority opened proceedings. It found Treaty violations both by Italy and the Italian producers. An Italian Tribunal referred questions to the Court of Justice. Here is the response of the Court regarding Italy's responsibility.]

45 . . . [A]lthough Articles [101 and 102 TFEU] are, in themselves, concerned solely with the conduct of undertakings and not with laws or regulations emanating from Member States, those articles, read in conjunction with Article [4 TEU], which lays down a duty to cooperate, none the less require the Member States not to introduce or maintain in force measures, even of a legislative or regulatory nature, which may render ineffective the competition rules applicable to undertakings.

46 The Court has held in particular that Articles [4 TEU and 101 TFEU] are infringed where a Member State requires or favours the adoption of agreements, decisions or concerted practices contrary to Article [101 TFEU] or reinforces their effects, or where it divests its own rules of the character of legislation by delegating to private economic operators responsibility for taking decisions affecting the economic sphere.

47 Moreover, since the Treaty of Maastricht entered into force, the . . . Treaty has expressly provided that in the context of their economic policy the activities of the Member States must observe the principle of an open market economy with free competition. . . .

48 It is appropriate to bear in mind, second, that in accordance with settled case-law the primacy of Community law requires any provision of national law which contravenes a Community rule to be disapplied, regardless of whether it was adopted before or after that rule.

[49] The duty to disapply national legislation which contravenes Community law applies not only to national courts but also to all organs of the State, including administrative authorities, which entails, if the circumstances so require, the obligation to take all appropriate measures to enable Community law to be fully applied.

[50] Since a national competition authority such as the Authority is responsible for ensuring, *inter alia*, that Article [101 TFEU] is observed and that provision, in conjunction with Article [4 TEU], imposes a duty on Member States to refrain from introducing measures contrary to the Community competition rules, those rules would be rendered less effective if, in the course of an investigation under Article [101 TFEU] into the conduct of undertakings, the authority were not able to declare a national measure contrary to the combined provisions of Articles [4 TEU] and [101 TFEU] and if, consequently, it failed to disapply it.

[51] In that regard, it is of little significance that, where undertakings are required by national legislation to engage in anti-competitive conduct, they cannot also be held accountable for infringement of Articles [101 and 102 TFEU]. Member States' obligations under Articles 3(1)(g) EC,* [4 TEU, 101 TFEU and 102 TFEU], which are distinct from those to which undertakings are subject under Articles [101 and 102 TFEU], none the less continue to exist and therefore the national competition authority remains duty-bound to disapply the national measure at issue.

In the following case, legislation itself—which would have extended a postal monopoly to an adjacent market that had been developed by private firms, was impugned. By adopting the legislation, the Slovak Republic infringed the Treaty.

SLOVAKIAN POSTAL LEGISLATION RELATING TO HYBRID MAIL SERVICES
Commission Decision of 7 Oct. 2008, Case COMP/39.562,
O J C322 (17 Dec. 2008, p. 10)

[The Postal Act of the Slovak Republic (2004) reserved to the government entity, Slovenská Pošta, the sole right and the duty to provide universal service for delivery of all collected mail. Hybrid mail (electronically transmitted to the service provider and printed, put into an envelope, and delivered by the provider) was not covered

---

* Editors' Note: Article 3(1)(g) of the EC Treaty identified "undistorted competition" as an activity of the Community. The Treaty of Lisbon removed this provision and put a substitute into a protocol. The protocol states that the Treaty on European Union "includes a system ensuring that competition is not distorted . . . ."

by the reservation. Slovak Telecom issued a call for tenders for sending its invoices by hybrid mail. Triggered by this event, two private companies answered the tender and entered the market for receipt, conversion and delivery of hybrid mail. They delivered hybrid mail within their areas, which covered about three-fourths of the Slovak population, and used the network of Slovenská Pošta for the rest. Three years later, with the state post office unhappy with the competition, the Slovak Parliament enacted an amendment to the Postal Act extending the state reservation to hybrid mail.

The European Commission brought proceedings alleging that the announcement breached (now) Article 106 in conjunction with Article 102. Slovenská Pošta argued in justification that the extension was necessary to maintain the provision of a service of general economic interest. It submitted studies on the cost of universal service, and projected losses in the future if it were not assured of a monopoly of the hybrid mail. The European Commission found the cost figures and projections unreliable and unrealistic. It found a violation. The General Court affirmed.]

3. COMMISSION ANALYSIS

3.1. Applicability of Article [106](1) of the Treaty

[85] Article [106](1) reads as follows: *"In the case of public undertakings and undertakings to which Member States grant special or exclusive rights, Member States shall neither enact nor maintain in force any measure contrary to the rules contained in this Treaty, in particular to those rules provided for in Article [18] and Articles [101] to [109]."*
* * *

[87] The Postal Act reserves to Slovenská Pošta the right to distribute certain postal items, as defined in Article 7 of the Act. Slovenská Pošta thus also enjoys exclusive rights within the meaning of Article [106] (1).

[88] The Amendment constitutes a State measure within the meaning of Article [106](1) of the . . . Treaty as do the enforcement measures by the Slovak authorities against an alleged breach of the reserved area. The Postal Regulatory Office, notwithstanding the fact that it might enjoy independence with regard to the central government and administration of the Slovak Republic, is a public body under Slovak law, invested with public powers and is as such, as regards the application of the Treaty rules, to be regarded as bound by the rules incumbent on the Member States. Enforcement activities of the Postal Regulatory Office are state measures which must conform to the rules of the . . . Treaty.

* * *

3.1.3. *Dominant Position on the market for traditional mail services*

113 According to constant case law, an undertaking holding a statutory monopoly on a substantial part of the common market is considered to occupy a dominant position within the meaning of Article [102] of the Treaty. Slovakia is a substantial part of the common market within which, as demonstrated earlier, Slovenská Pošta has been granted an exclusive statutory licence to provide basic postal services.

3.1.4. *Infringement of Article [106](1) in conjunction with Article [102] of the Treaty*

114 In its 1998 Postal Notice, the Commission set out its approach as regards the respect of competition rules in the postal sector. The Notice stresses that "... *the Commission will ensure that monopoly power is not used for extending a protected dominant position into liberalized activities.*" The Notice further clarifies that "... *the use, without objective justification, of a dominant position on one market to obtain market power on related or neighboring markets which are distinct from the former, at the risk of eliminating competition on those markets*" would be contrary to Articles [106] in conjunction with Article [102]. More particularly, the use of a dominant position to extend the monopoly from the reserved market to a previously liberalized market would be "... *incompatible with the Treaty provisions, in the absence of specific justification, if the functioning of services in the general economic interest was not previously endangered. The Commission considers that it would be appropriate for Member States to inform the Commission of any extension of special or exclusive rights and of the justification therefore.*"

115 The Commission has come to the conclusion that the State measure at stake infringes Article [106](1) in conjunction with Article [102] of the Treaty in two ways:

3.1.4.1. *Extension of Slovenská Pošta's exclusive right*

116 According to the Court of Justice of the European Communities, an abuse within the meaning of Article [102] is committed where, without any objective justification, an undertaking holding a dominant position on a particular market reserves to itself other ancillary activities in neighbouring but distinct markets, although these activities could also be carried out by another undertaking as part of its activities on this neighbouring but separate market. With regard to Article [106](1) in conjunction with Article [102], it is settled case law that the extension by means of a measure adopted by the State, of a monopoly into a neighbouring and competitive

market, without any objective justification, is prohibited as such by Article [106](1) in conjunction with Article [102].

[117] . . . . The state measure in question . . . reserves a part of the value chain of the hybrid mail service (the distribution of such items) to the incumbent postal operator Slovenská Pošta, while it was liberalised before that state measure.

[118] In their replies to the letter of formal notice as well as in subsequent submissions, the Slovak authorities and Slovenská Pošta argued that the legislative changes did not amount to an extension of Slovenská Pošta's exclusive right to the activity of distributing hybrid mail items since this activity already fell within the reserved area before the Amendment. In their view, the purpose of the new law was merely to *"eliminate the possibility of incorrect interpretation of the postal service act"* and to *"confirm and maintain"* the current legal situation.

[119] The Commission has carefully considered the arguments put forward by the Slovak government and Slovenská Pošta in support of their contention that the delivery of hybrid mail items was always part of the reserved area and that therefore the Amendment merely provides further clarification to the matter. For the reasons set out below, the Commission maintains its conclusion set out in the letter of formal notice that the delivery of hybrid mail items was an activity open to competition prior to the adoption of the state measure in question.

* * *

[148] Consequently, the Commission considers that before the entry into force of the Amendment, hybrid mail delivery services were *de iure* and *de facto* open to competition in Slovakia. Thus, the Amendment extended the exclusive rights of Slovenská Pošta to the activity of distributing items of hybrid mail, an activity which, before the Amendment, was open to competition.

3.1.4.2. Limitation of the output to the end-user

[149] It is settled case law that *"an abuse may in particular consist in limiting the provision of a service, to the prejudice of those seeking to avail themselves of it. A Member State creates a situation in which the provision of a service is limited when the undertaking to which it grants an exclusive right . . . is manifestly not in a position to satisfy the demand prevailing on the market for activities of that kind and*

when the effective pursuit of such activities by private companies is rendered impossible . . . ".[33]

[150] To the extent that only private operators are able to offer additional services such as tracking services and seven day a week delivery together with their offer of hybrid mail services, the reservation of hybrid mail delivery would deprive customers of these services. These extra services, in particular track-and-trace services, appear to be one of the main criteria used by customers to select postal service providers. As has been explained above, hybrid mail is a particularly attractive form of postal services for customers such as banks, insurance and telecommunications companies which have regular invoices to send to end-users. For such customers of postal service operators, additional services such as track-and-trace are of particular importance as they allow them to avoid bad credit and to have precise information on whether a particular postal item has been distributed to the end user. Such information is valuable for companies sending invoices. In its reply to the letter of facts, whilst Slovenská Pošta contests the "other" additional services alleged by SMS, it does not contest that the track and trace services offered to Slovak Telekom by SMS are value-added services.

[151] Slovenská Pošta is currently not offering such additional services for items of hybrid mail correspondence. In fact, insofar as the private competitors have to rely on the distribution network of Slovenská Pošta, they are themselves not able to offer their customers such services. After the reservation of the delivery of hybrid mail services, these additional services as offered by the private competitors (such as track-and-trace service and seven days a week delivery) will thus no longer be available to customers.

* * *

3.1.6.   Conclusion

[158] On the basis of the above, the Commission considers that the Slovak Republic has infringed Article [106](1) in conjunction with Article [102].

3.2. No justification under Article [106](2) of the Treaty

[159] Under Article [106](2) of the Treaty, *"undertakings entrusted with the operation of services of general economic interest [. . .] shall be subject to [Treaty rules], in particular the rules on competition, in so far as the application of such rules does not obstruct the performance, in law or in fact of the particular task assigned to them. The*

---

[33]   Case C–41/90 *Höfner and Elser*, [1991] ECR p. I-1979.

development of trade must not be affected to such an extent as would be contrary to the interests of the Community".

3.2.1. Burden of proof

160 As the Court held in a number of cases, it is incumbent on a Member State which invokes Article [106](2), as a derogation from the fundamental rules of the Treaty, to show that the conditions for application of that provision are fulfilled.

* * *

3.2.2. No obstruction of the universal service in case hybrid mail remains open to competition

165 Even though there is a presumption of *prima facie* justification under Article [106](2) for services covered by the reserved area as defined in the Postal Directive . . ., this is different if a service was already liberalised and if the functioning of the public service was not previously endangered. In such a case the extension of the monopoly in the previously liberalised activity would be incompatible, in the absence of a specific justification. . . .

166 Article 7 of the Postal Directive only allows such reservation *"to the extent necessary to ensure the maintenance of universal service"*. In *International Mail Spain*39, the Court held that Member States may extend the postal monopoly if they *"establish that, in the absence of such a reservation, achievement of that universal service would be precluded, or that reservation is necessary to enable that service to be carried out under economically acceptable conditions"*.

167 In light of this jurisprudence, the Member State has to demonstrate that, without the requested extension or reservation, the achievement of the universal service would be either precluded or could at least not be carried out under economically acceptable conditions. The Commission considers that the Slovak government has not met this standard.

* * *

3.2.3. Extension of the monopoly is not necessary to ensure the quality of postal service provided by Slovenská Pošta's competitors

195 The Slovak Authorities further submit that the *status quo "might impair the quality of the postal services provided in Slovakia"*. They argue that alternative postal operators have destroyed postal items: *"After 1 April 2008 it has been demonstrated that certain items of mail*

---

39   Case C–162/06, *International Mail Spain*, [2007] ECR p. I-9911.

*up to 50g have been distributed by alternative operators; some cases
have been documented by the police. The mail items concerned were
found in rubbish bins and did not bear the logo of Slovenská Pošta
a.s., i.e. they were not distributed by means of the distribution network
of Slovenská Pošta".*

196 The Commission cannot accept this line of argument. First, under
competitive conditions postal service providers have an obvious
incentive to ensure that mail items entrusted to them are delivered
to the recipients. Contracts are concluded accordingly. In particular,
postal operators commit themselves to achieve certain quality
targets. If they do not reach these targets and do not satisfy their
customers, they risk losing these customers to competitors featuring
a higher quality performance.

197 Moreover, Article 9 of the Postal Directive allows Member States
to condition the granting of authorisations to certain requirements in
terms of quality, availability and performance of the postal services.
To the extent that competitive forces are not sufficient to prevent
postal items ending up in rubbish bins, this authorisation regime
constitutes a much less intrusive and more flexible tool to ensure
high quality standards. Against this background, the Commission
considers that it is disproportionate to extend Slovenská Pošta's
monopoly on the grounds that alternative postal operators have in
some instances provided a service of bad quality. * * *

3.2.4.   Conclusion

199 On the basis of the above, the Slovak government and Slovenská
Pošta have failed to prove that the extension of the postal monopoly
to hybrid mail services was necessary for the universal service to be
provided under economically acceptable conditions.

Slovakia and its Post Office were enraged by the Commission's
decision, refused to comply, and filed an appeal (which they lost). A
local headline declared: "Slovakia to EC: 'The State is no Chicken to
be Plucked.'" ePostal News, Dec. 1, 2008. The Commission ordered
Slovakia to implement its order. It advised the competitors that they
were free to compete. See Commission press release, 29 Oct. 2009,
IP/09/1632. The General Court affirmed, in the judgment above, and
appeal of the General Court. judgment is pending. Slovenská Pošta
v. Commission, Case T–556/08, EU:T:2015:189.

DEI v. COMMISSION

(Greek lignite)

Case C–553/12P, EU:C:2014:2083 (European Court of Justice 2014)

[In Dimosia Epicheirisi Ilektrismou AE (DEI) v. Commission (Greek lignite), Greece granted its state-owned enterprise quasi-exclusive rights to deposits of lignite, the cheapest and most attractive source of electric energy, after the liberalization of the electricity market. The Commission found that this grant protected DEI's dominant position on the downstream market for the wholesale sale of electricity, creating inequality of opportunities between economic operators, in violation of Articles 102/106(1). The General Court annulled the decision on grounds that the Commission had not shown "that privileged access to lignite was capable of creating a situation in which, by the mere exercise of its exploitation rights, [DEI] could have been able to commit abuses of a dominant position on the wholesale electricity market or was led to commit such abuses on that market." para. 92. The Court of Justice annulled the General Court judgment, holding that it was not necessary for the Commission to demonstrate an abuse to which the measure could have led; it was sufficient that the challenged act created inequality of opportunity between economic operators and thus distorted competition. Thus:]

41 . . . [A] Member State is in breach of the prohibitions laid down by Article [106(1)] in conjunction with Article [102] if it adopts any law, regulation or administrative provision that creates a situation in which a public undertaking or an undertaking on which it has conferred special or exclusive rights, merely by exercising the preferential rights conferred upon it, is led to abuse its dominant position or when those rights are liable to create a situation in which that undertaking is led to commit such abuses. In that respect, it is not necessary that any abuse should actually occur. * * *

43 It is clear from the Court's case-law that a system of undistorted competition, such as that provided for by the Treaty, can be guaranteed only if equality of opportunity is secured as between the various economic operators.

44 It follows that if inequality of opportunity between economic operators, and thus distorted competition, is the result of a State measure, such a measure constitutes an infringement of Article [106(1)] read together with Article [102]. * * *

46 It follows from the matters addressed in paragraphs 41 to 45 above that, as the Advocate General states in point 55 of his Opinion, infringement of Article 86(1) EC in conjunction with Article 82 EC

may be established irrespective of whether any abuse actually exists. All that is necessary is for the Commission to identify a potential or actual anti-competitive consequence liable to result from the State measure at issue. Such an infringement may thus be established where the State measures at issue affect the structure of the market by creating unequal conditions of competition between companies, by allowing the public undertaking or the undertaking which was granted special or exclusive rights to maintain (for example by hindering new entrants to the market), strengthen or extend its dominant position over another market, thereby restricting competition, without it being necessary to prove the existence of actual abuse.

47 In those circumstances, it follows that, contrary to the General Court's analysis . . . , it is sufficient to show that that potential or actual anti-competitive consequence is liable to result from the State measure at issue; it is not necessary to identify an abuse other than that which results from the situation brought about by the State measure at issue. It also follows that the General Court erred in law in holding that the Commission, by finding that DEI, a former monopolistic undertaking, continued to maintain a dominant position on the wholesale electricity market by virtue of the advantage conferred upon it by its privileged access to lignite and that that situation created inequality of opportunity on that market between the applicant and other undertakings, had neither identified nor established to a sufficient legal standard the abuse to which . . . the State measure in question had led or could have led DEI.

———————

Is this holding dramatic, in its limitation on Member States' power to grant privileges to their state-owned firms even if the SOE might do nothing to abuse dominance? The grant of such special privileges is sometimes referred to as a breach of the notional norm of competitive neutrality. Some jurisdictions such as Australia implement the norm as part of a regulatory process to determine whether legislation may give the state or state-owned entities unnecessary advantages.

———————

Notes and Questions

1.   Article 37 of the TFEU requires that Member States must "adjust any State monopolies of a commercial character so as to ensure that no discrimination regarding conditions under which goods are procured and marketed exists between nationals of Member States."

Sweden maintained an alcohol monopoly for sales at retail, and provided a procedure for the grant of licenses to import, export, produce, and sell at wholesale. Mr. Franzen, without a license, imported wine from Denmark and sold it in Sweden. When he was prosecuted, he argued that the Swedish monopoly was itself illegal under Articles 34 and 37 and also that the system of licensing was illegal. The Court of Justice did not endorse the idea that monopolies are inconsistent with Article 37 of the Treaty. Merely, monopolies must be so organized and operated so as to exclude discrimination between nationals and non-nationals so that goods from other Member States are not put at a disadvantage. Case C–189/95, *Franzen*, EU:C:1997:504, paras. 39–41.

2.   If monopolies are permissible under Article 37, can they be made impermissible under Article 106? Can they be made impermissible only if they constitute a new monopolization? Was Slovakia's only mistake that it had not anticipated and thus reserved hybrid mail delivery from the start? If it had reserved this function from the start, what would have been the Commission's and (would-be) competitors' claims, and how likely would they have been to prevail?

Regulation of the Professions

In some jurisdictions, professions are exempt from the competition laws. In other jurisdictions they get special treatment, especially when the state restrains their competition. In Chapter 3, we saw that jurisdictions have widely varying perspectives on how to address anticompetitive restraints by members of learned professions. The following case regards an Italian law restraining the price competition of lawyers.

CIPOLLA V. FAZARI AND MACRINO v. MELONI
Joined cases C–94/04 and C–202/04, EU:C:2006:758
(European Court of Justice 2006)

[Pursuant to a 73-year old Italian law, Italy adopted maximum and minimum fee schedules for lawyers, from which there could be no derogation except in narrow circumstances. The schedules were based on a draft prepared by the National Lawyers' Council—a body of lawyers.

In connection with three fee disputes, an Italian court referred questions regarding the validity of the Italian law to the Court of Justice. First the Court held that the procedure did not encourage or require agreements or abuses contrary to Articles 4 TEU/101 TFEU or 102 TFEU.]

[58] The prohibition of derogation, by agreement, from the minimum fees set by a scale such as that laid down by the Italian legislation is liable to render access to the Italian legal services market more

difficult for lawyers established in a Member State other than the Italian Republic and therefore is likely to restrict the exercise of their activities providing services in that Member State. That prohibition therefore amounts to a restriction within the meaning of Article [56 TFEU].

59 That prohibition deprives lawyers established in a Member State other than the Italian Republic of the possibility, by requesting fees lower than those set by the scale, of competing more effectively with lawyers established on a stable basis in the Member State concerned and who therefore have greater opportunities for winning clients than lawyers established abroad.

60 Likewise, the prohibition thus laid down limits the choice of service recipients in Italy, because they cannot resort to the services of lawyers established in other Member States who would offer their services in Italy at a lower rate than the minimum fees set by the scale.

61 However, such a prohibition may be justified where it serves overriding requirements relating to the public interest, is suitable for securing the attainment of the objective which it pursues and does not go beyond what is necessary in order to attain it.

62 In order to justify the restriction on freedom to provide services which stems from the prohibition at issue, the Italian Government submits that excessive competition between lawyers might lead to price competition which would result in a deterioration in the quality of the services provided to the detriment of consumers, in particular as individuals in need of quality advice in court proceedings.

63 According to the Commission, no causal link has been established between the setting of minimum levels of fees and a high qualitative standard of professional services provided by lawyers. In actual fact, quasi-legislative measures such as, inter alia, rules on access to the legal profession, disciplinary rules serving to ensure compliance with professional ethics and rules on civil liability have, by maintaining a high qualitative standard for the services provided by such professionals which those measures guarantee, a direct relationship of cause and effect with the protection of lawyers' clients and the proper working of the administration of justice.

64 In that respect, it must be pointed out that, first, the protection of consumers, in particular recipients of the legal services provided by persons concerned in the administration of justice and, secondly, the safeguarding of the proper administration of justice, are objectives to be included among those which may be regarded as overriding requirements relating to the public interest capable of justifying a

restriction on freedom to provide services . . ., on condition, first, that the national measure at issue in the main proceedings is suitable for securing the attainment of the objective pursued and, secondly, it does not go beyond what is necessary in order to attain that objective.

[65] It is a matter for the national court to decide whether, in the main proceedings, the restriction on freedom to provide services introduced by that national legislation fulfils those conditions. For that purpose, it is for that court to take account of the factors set out in the following paragraphs.

[66] Thus, it must be determined, in particular, whether there is a correlation between the level of fees and the quality of the services provided by lawyers and whether, in particular, the setting of such minimum fees constitutes an appropriate measure for attaining the objectives pursued, namely the protection of consumers and the proper administration of justice.

[67] Although it is true that a scale imposing minimum fees cannot prevent members of the profession from offering services of mediocre quality, it is conceivable that such a scale does serve to prevent lawyers, in a context such as that of the Italian market which, as indicated in the decision making the reference, is characterised by an extremely large number of lawyers who are enrolled and practising, from being encouraged to compete against each other by possibly offering services at a discount, with the risk of deterioration in the quality of the services provided.

[68] Account must also be taken of the specific features both of the market in question, as noted in the preceding paragraph, and the services in question and, in particular, of the fact that, in the field of lawyers' services, there is usually an asymmetry of information between "client-consumers" and lawyers. Lawyers display a high level of technical knowledge which consumers may not have and the latter therefore find it difficult to judge the quality of the services provided to them.

[69] However, the national court will have to determine whether professional rules in respect of lawyers, in particular rules relating to organisation, qualifications, professional ethics, supervision and liability, suffice in themselves to attain the objectives of the protection of consumers and the proper administration of justice.

* * *

Notes and Questions

1.   Doesn't the Italian law facilitate an anticompetitive agreement among lawyers on minimum fees? What is the best argument that state

measures setting minimum lawyer fees harm free movement *and* consumers and should be caught at least presumptively by Articles 4 TEU/101 TFEU?

Note the Commission's argument that enforced price floors do not correlate with higher quality services. Note also that, in most jurisdictions, competitors have a right to combine to procure government action (the right to lobby)—a point relevant to Private Responsibility (the question of liability of the lawyers) below.

The main question of this section is the responsibility of the state not to solicit a minimum fee schedule from the lawyers and not to adopt such a schedule.

2.   How will the national court determine whether the law "actually serves the objectives of the protection of consumers and the proper administration of justice" and whether the restrictions are "disproportionate in light of those objectives?" Would a bright line (e.g., states may not adopt minimum fee schedules) have been superior? Did the Court miss two good opportunities for declaring the lawyers' fee schedules anticompetitive and inconsistent with the Treaties: Articles 4/101, and Article 56? In the aftermath of the case, Italy concluded that minimum lawyer fees are not in the public interest, and it abolished them.

3.   The US Constitution protects free speech. Under First Amendment protections as incorporated in the Fourteenth Amendment, states of the United States may not prevent lawyers' truthful price-advertising of routine legal services. Bates v. State Bar of Arizona, 433 U.S. 350 (1977). But states may regulate lawyers and other professionals in the public interest. *Id.* For example, states may limit the number of lawyers in their state by requiring that they pass state bar examinations. See Hoover v. Ronwin, 466 U.S. 558 (1984).

In general, states of the United States *may* restrain competition unless they impose an undue burden on interstate commerce. Parker v. Brown, 317 U.S. 341 (1943). US law does not have an Article 4 TFEU or Article 106. The question in the United States centers almost entirely on whether private actors can hide behind an order or policy of the state; that is, whether they have a state action defense.

Can a state of the United States, through its courts, order lawyers to adhere to a minimum fee schedule as long as "the state" sets or supervises the fee level?

2.   Private Responsibility and the State Action Defense

Private actors may disown responsibility on grounds that the anticompetitive act was not theirs; it was the act of the state.

Students of US law will know the progeny of *Parker v. Brown*, delineating when private actors who engage in anticompetitive acts can successfully attribute their acts to the state and accordingly be sheltered by the state action defense. In short, the state must have a clearly articulated and affirmatively expressed policy to replace competition, and the private anticompetitive conduct must be actively supervised by the state. California Retail Liquor Dealers Association v. Midcal Aluminum, Inc., 445 U.S. 97 (1980). Also recall the Cartel chapter, above, including the foreign sovereign compulsion defense interposed by the Chinese vitamin cartelists. The European Union has a substantial body of law corresponding to the US state action defense.

COMMISSION AND FRANCE v. LADBROKE RACING LTD.

Cases C–359/95 P and C–379/95 P, EU:C:1997:531
(European Court of Justice 1997)

[French law created Pari Mutuel Urbain (PMU) as a joint service of the authorized racing companies to manage their rights in off-track betting, and it granted PMU exclusive rights to run off-track betting on horse races held in France and horse race betting organized in France. French law prohibited anyone other than PMU to place or accept bets on horse races.

Ladbroke Racing Ltd., an operator of off-track betting, filed with the Commission a complaint against France under Article 106, and a complaint against the ten main racing companies in France and PMU under Articles 101 and 102.

Before taking a position on the Article 106 claim, which included allegations of illegal state aid, the Commission rejected the allegations of violation of Articles 101 and 102 on grounds that those articles did not apply. The General Court reversed. The Court of Justice upheld the Commission.]

[33] Articles [101] and [102] of the Treaty apply only to anti-competitive conduct engaged in by undertakings on their own initiative. If anti-competitive conduct is required of undertakings by national legislation or if the latter creates a legal framework which itself eliminates any possibility of competitive activity on their part, Articles [101] and [102] do not apply. In such a situation, the restriction of competition is not attributable, as those provisions implicitly require, to the autonomous conduct of the undertakings.

[34] Articles [101] and [102] may apply, however, if it is found that the national legislation does not preclude undertakings from engaging in

autonomous conduct which prevents, restricts or distorts competition. * * *

CONSORZIO INDUSTRIE FIAMMIFERI
(*ITALIAN MATCHES*)
(responsibility of producers; see supra for responsibility of the state)
Case C–198/01, EU:C:2003:430 (European Court of Justice, 2003)

[*Consorzio Industrie Fiammiferi* (*Italian matches*) (see facts *supra*) concerned a state-sponsored match cartel. Italian law required the Italian match producers to join a consortium and to set sellers' quotas. A minister set the prices, the match producers set the quotas, and government officials had the duty to oversee the quotas. The Italian Antitrust Authority brought proceedings. It observed that the producers had the autonomy to set the quotas in the most anticompetitive way, and they did so by substantially keeping the Germans and the Swedes out of the market. The Authority held, and the Court confirmed, that the Italian match producers violated the competition law to the extent that they took autonomous action, and (as we saw above) that the Italian law offended the Treaty and had to be disapplied. The consortium contested the decision in the Italian Administrative Tribunal, and the Tribunal referred questions to the Court of Justice.]

[42] [The CIF (the consortium) argues] . . . that is inconceivable that the undertakings should be obliged not to apply the Italian legislation when faced with mandatory national rules. * * *

The first question * * *

[52] As regards . . . the penalties which may be imposed on the undertakings concerned, it is appropriate to draw a two-fold distinction by reference to whether or not the national legislation precludes undertakings from engaging in autonomous conduct which might prevent, restrict or distort competition and, if it does, by reference to whether the facts at issue pre-dated or post-dated the national competition authority's decision to disapply the relevant national legislation.

[53] First, if a national law precludes undertakings from engaging in autonomous conduct which prevents, restricts or distorts competition, it must be found that, if the general Community-law principle of legal certainty is not to be violated, the duty of national competition authorities to disapply such an anti-competitive law cannot expose the undertakings concerned to any penalties, either criminal or administrative, in respect of past conduct where the conduct was required by the law concerned.

⁵⁴ The decision to disapply the law concerned does not alter the fact that the law set the framework for the undertakings' past conduct. The law thus continues to constitute, for the period prior to the decision to disapply it, a justification which shields the undertakings concerned from all the consequences of an infringement of Articles [101 and 102 TFEU] and does so vis-à-vis both public authorities and other economic operators.

⁵⁵ As regards penalising the future conduct of undertakings which, prior to that time, were required by a national law to engage in anti-competitive conduct, it should be pointed out that, once the national competition authority's decision finding an infringement of Article [101 TFEU] and disapplying such an anti-competitive national law becomes definitive in their regard, the decision becomes binding on the undertakings concerned. From that time onwards the undertakings can no longer claim that they are obliged by that law to act in breach of the Community competition rules. Their future conduct is therefore liable to be penalised.

⁵⁶ Second, if a national law merely encourages, or makes it easier for undertakings to engage in autonomous anti-competitive conduct, those undertakings remain subject to Articles [101 and 102 TFEU] and may incur penalties, including in respect of conduct prior to the decision to disapply that national law.

⁵⁷ It must none the less be made clear that, although such a situation cannot lead to acceptance of practices which are likely further to exacerbate the adverse effects on competition, it nevertheless means that when the level of the penalty is set the conduct of the undertakings concerned may be assessed in the light of the national legal framework, which is a mitigating factor.

⁵⁸ In light of the foregoing considerations, the answer to be given to the first question referred for a preliminary ruling is that, where undertakings engage in conduct contrary to Article [101(1) TFEU] and where that conduct is required or facilitated by national legislation which legitimises or reinforces the effects of the conduct, specifically with regard to price-fixing or market-sharing arrangements, a national competition authority, one of whose responsibilities is to ensure that Article [101 TFEU] is observed:

  —has a duty to disapply the national legislation;

  —may not impose penalties in respect of past conduct on the undertakings concerned when the conduct was required by the national legislation;

  —may impose penalties on the undertakings concerned in respect of conduct subsequent to the decision to disapply the national legislation, once the decision has become definitive in their regard;

—may impose penalties on the undertakings concerned in respect of past conduct where the conduct was merely facilitated or encouraged by the national legislation, whilst taking due account of the specific features of the legislative framework in which the undertakings acted.

The second question

59 By its second question, the referring court wishes to know whether national legislation, under which competence to fix the retail selling prices of a product is delegated to a ministry and power to allocate production between undertakings is entrusted to a consortium to which the relevant producers are obliged to belong, may be regarded, for the purposes of Article [101(1) TFEU], as preventing those undertakings from engaging in autonomous conduct which hinders, restricts or distorts competition.

60 First, it should be noted that, in the Authority's submission, the CIF was a consortium of which membership was compulsory only until 1994. Decree-Law No 331/1993 made membership optional for the undertakings.

61 In those circumstances, it is for the referring court to decide whether its second question relates solely to the period prior to entry into force of Decree-Law No 331/1993 or whether it also relates to the subsequent period. * * *

63 The CIF submits that, by requiring it to allocate quotas between the member undertakings—regardless of the rules and criteria by reference to which the quotas are set—the Italian legislature eliminated *ab initio* any opportunity which those undertakings might have had to engage in competition in order to win larger market shares.

64 It explains that Article 4 of the 1992 agreement requires match production to be allocated between member undertakings by a committee, the quota allocation committee, composed of representatives from the industry and presided over by an official from the State Monopolies Board, appointed by the Finance Minister.

65 Therefore, quite apart from the quota actually awarded to each undertaking, the quota-allocation system imposed by the legislature eliminates in principle competition between the member undertakings, which must in any event comply with the production quota allocated. Consequently, any competitive effort intended to increase production is futile.

66 In order to answer the second question, it is appropriate to consider first whether national legislation of the kind at issue in the main proceedings precludes undertakings from engaging in autonomous conduct which remains capable of preventing, restricting or distorting competition and, if it does, to go on to ascertain whether any additional restrictions for which the undertakings are blamed are actually attributable to the Member State concerned.

67 First, it should be observed that the possibility of excluding particular anti-competitive conduct from the scope of Article [101(1) TFEU] on the ground that it has been required of the undertakings in question by existing national legislation or that the legislation has precluded all scope for any competitive conduct on their part has been only partially accepted by the Court of Justice.

68 It is appropriate to observe, second, that price competition does not constitute the only effective form of competition or that to which absolute priority must in all circumstances be given.

69 Consequently, pre-determination of the sales price of matches by the Italian State does not, on its own, rule out all scope for competitive conduct. Even if limited, competition may operate through other factors.

70 Third, although the Italian legislation at issue in the main proceedings confers on the CIF, a consortium membership of which is compulsory for manufacturers, power to allocate production between the member undertakings, it does not set out either the rules or the criteria by reference to which allocation is to be carried out. In addition, . . . it seems that the CIF's commercial monopoly was abolished as early as 1983 when the prohibition on non-members of the consortium manufacturing and selling matches was lifted.

71 In those circumstances, the remaining competition between the member undertakings is liable to distortion going beyond that already brought about by the legal obligation itself.

72 In that regard, the investigation carried out by the Authority revealed a system of ongoing and *ad hoc* transfers of production quotas and agreements on exchanges of quotas between the undertakings, that is to say agreements which were not provided for by the law.

73 In addition, the Commission referred to a fixed quota of about 15% set aside for imports. In its submission, that quota was not set by national law and thus the CIF enjoyed autonomous decision-making power in that regard.

[74] The Commission also submits that the agreement concluded between the CIF and Swedish Match, which, as early as 1994, enabled Swedish Match to supply significant quantities of matches for the CIF to sell in Italy in return for Swedish Match's undertaking not to enter the Italian market directly, bears witness to the CIF's freedom of action as regards business decisions.

[75] It is for the referring court to assess whether there are any grounds for such assertions.

[76] Fourth and finally, the documents before the Court do not show that decisions of the CIF such as those mentioned in paragraphs 70 to 74 of this judgment fall outside the scope of Article [101(1) TFEU] as a result of a measure taken by a public authority.

[77] On the one hand, four of the five members of the quota-allocation committee are representatives of the manufacturers, whom nothing in the relevant national legislation prevents from acting exclusively in their own interests. The committee, which takes decision by simple majority, may adopt resolutions even if its chairman, the only person with public-interest duties, votes against them, and the committee can therefore act in accordance with the requirements of the member undertakings.

[78] Furthermore, the public authorities do not have an effective means of controlling decisions taken by the quota-allocation committee.

[79] On the other hand, the Authority's investigation showed that the task of allocating production between the member undertakings is actually carried out not by the quota-allocation committee but by the quota-compliance committee, which is composed solely of CIF members on the basis of agreements drawn up by the member undertakings.

[80] The answer to be given to the second question referred for a preliminary ruling must therefore be that it is for the referring court to assess whether national legislation such as that at issue in the main proceedings, under which competence to fix the retail selling prices of a product is delegated to a ministry and power to allocate production between undertakings is entrusted to a consortium to which the relevant producers are obliged to belong, may be regarded, for the purposes of Article [101(1) TFEU], as precluding those undertakings from engaging in autonomous conduct which remains capable of preventing, restricting or distorting competition.

Notes and Questions

1.   Since prices were set by the government official, what competition was left to harm?

2.   A major precedent preceded Case C–35/96, *Italian matches*: *Commission v. Italy (CNSD)*, EU:C:1998:303. In this case regarding customs agents, Italy had delegated to a competitors' association the legal responsibility to set the tariffs, and it required the customs agents to adhere to the tariffs their association had set. The Court of Justice held that, by this delegation and measure, Italy breached its obligations under Articles 4 TEU/101 TFEU. Italy had required the conclusion of an agreement contrary to Article 101, declined to influence its terms, and assisted in ensuring compliance. para. 55. By giving the tariffs an official character, it deterred customers from contesting the custom agents' prices. Moreover, the competitors' association violated Article 101. It set the maximum and minimum prices.

3.   Comment on the scope, in Europe, for public and for private responsibility for anticompetitive acts in shadow of state policy. Compare and contrast *Parker v. Brown* and its progeny. Does Europe appropriately limit state anticompetitive action, or does it interfere too much with the sovereignty of the Member States?

4.   For a comparison of the *Italian matches* case with US law, see Eleanor Fox, *State Action in Comparative Context: What if* Parker v. Brown *were Italian*, Chap. 19 in Fordham Corp. L. Inst., INTERNATIONAL ANTITRUST LAW & POLICY (B. Hawk ed. 2004).

F. STATE AID: EU

1. Introduction

States are tempted to give money and other benefits to support local firms and to attract non-local firms. Frequently states are asked to favor one competitor, sector or region over another, often to save a failing business and to save jobs. At mid-twentieth century before adoption of the EC Treaty of Rome, extensive and undisciplined state support of industry was the norm in Europe. If trade barriers were removed but state aids flourished, Europe would never be one common market.

In order to contain state aid and provide transparency for permissible aid, the European Treaty includes (now) TFEU Articles 107–109. The United States, however, does not have state aid control.

In Europe, state aid is "any aid granted by a Member State or through state resources in any form whatsoever. . . ." Direct subsidy is the most common form of aid, but state aid also includes exemptions from fiscal or social charges, credit guarantees, credit at low interest, credit or equity investments that would not be available in the market, payment by the state of a higher price to domestic suppliers, sale by the state below the market price to domestic buyers, assumption by the state of part of an undertaking's risk, tax concessions (e.g., to encourage the takeover of an ailing firm), and virtually any other benefit conferred by the state on terms that would not be acceptable to a private investor.

Article 107(1) declares that any state aid that "distorts or threatens to distort competition by favouring certain undertakings or the production of certain goods shall, insofar as it affects trade between Member States, be incompatible with the common market." Paragraphs (2) and (3) are derogations from this general prohibition.

Paragraph (2) lists forms of aid that "shall be compatible" with the common market. Aid that shall be compatible under paragraph (2) is:

(a)   aid of a social character granted to individual consumers without discrimination as to origin of products,

(b)   damage relief in natural disasters or exceptional occurrences, and

(c)   aid to the economy of certain areas of the Federal Republic of Germany affected by the division of Germany insofar as it is required to compensate for economic disadvantages caused by that division.

Paragraph (3) specifies aid that the Commission *may* declare compatible with the common market. Frequently invoked by Member States, this section empowers the Commission to declare compatible aid in the following five categories:

(a)   "aid to promote the economic development of areas where the standard of living is abnormally low or where there is serious underemployment";

(b)   "aid to promote the execution of an important project of common European interest or to remedy a serious disturbance in the economy of a Member State";

(c)   "aid to facilitate the development of certain economic activities or of certain economic areas, where such aid does not adversely affect trading conditions to an extent contrary to the common interest";

(d)   "aid to promote cultural and heritage conservation where such aid does not affect trading conditions and competition in the Community to an extent that is contrary to the common interest"; and

(e)   other categories added by decision of the Council.

Article 108 sets forth a notification, waiting and adjudication procedure for state aids. Member States must notify to the Commission all proposed measures of state aid that may affect Member State commerce. The proposed measures must not be put into effect until clearance. The Commission may authorize the aid without conditions, authorize the aid after agreed modifications, or open formal proceedings. The Commission must give notice to concerned parties to submit their comments. See Regulation 2015/1589, laying down detailed rules for the application of Article 108 TFEU. [2015] O.J. L 248/9.

If the Commission finds that the proposed aid is not compatible with the common market or that aid is being misused, it must direct the state to abolish or alter the aid within a specified time period. If the Member State fails to comply, the Commission or an interested Member State may refer the matter to the Court of Justice. If a Member State grants illegal aid, it must recover it from the recipient.

To eliminate red tape and to concentrate on the cases that matter most, the Commission has enacted block exemption regulations that eliminate the need for notification if certain conditions are met. The General Block Exemption Regulation 651/2014 covers a wide array of state aid targets, including aid for environmental protection, risk capital, R&D and innovation, newly created small enterprises, and broadband rollout. The regulation on de minimis aid, 1407/2013, also exempts Member States from the notification requirement for small amounts of aid. Various horizontal and sector-specific rules and guidelines clarify the Commission's policy to approve different forms of aid.

There is considerable case law on what is a state aid. An investment at market rates is not state aid. The Treaty does not prevent a state from participating in the economy as long as it acts as a "market economy operator." The state can therefore be a shareholder without breaching Article 107 TFEU if the transaction is at market rate.

In its progressive privatization of Electricité de France (EDF), the former electricity monopoly, France restructured EDF's accounts. It converted a debt it was owed by EDF into equity. The transaction had fiscal consequences; EDF avoided paying a tax by incorporating the debt into capital. France argued that this was neutral from a state aid perspective; it could have requested EDF to pay the tax and later make a capital injection to the amount of the tax. In other words, France argued, it acted as a market economy operator and provided no advantage to EDF.

The Commission disagreed. It found that it was not possible to apply the market economy operator test to a fiscal operation, since taxation is the exclusive province of the state and it is not possible to compare its fiscal policy with that of a hypothetical private investor.

The Court of Justice annulled the Commission decision. EDF v. Commission, Case C–124/10 P, EU:C:2012:318. It recalled that Article 107(1) TFEU covers state aid "in any form whatsoever." The form of the measure does not matter, only its effects do. Therefore, the Commission was required to take a global view of the measures and assess their overall effects. A Member State that wishes to rely on the market economy operator principle needs to demonstrate, using evidence prepared before or at the moment of its investment decision, that it was rational for it do so as an investor. Policy considerations such as social or environmental objectives cannot be taken into account (although they might be relevant in assessment of the compatibility of the aid).

Does a privatized transport receive state aid when the state continues to cover the costs of public service obligations? Altmark Trans sought to organize public transport in a new East German länder. In *Altmark Trans GmbH, Regierungspräsidium Magdeburg*, Case C–280/00, EU:C:2003:415, the Court of Justice held that public subsidies for transportation services are not state aids, and therefore do not require notification and justification, where they constitute compensation for the discharge of public service obligations. Such subsidies fall outside of Article 107 if the following conditions are satisfied: 1) the recipient must be required to discharge clearly defined public service obligations, 2) the formula for calculating the compensation must be established beforehand in an objective and transparent matter, 3) the compensation must not exceed what is necessary to discharge the public service, and 4) either the undertaking must be chosen in a public procurement procedure or the level of compensation needed to fulfill the public service obligation must have been determined on the basis of the costs of a typical, well-run undertaking.

The Commission has issued detailed rules based on the *Altmark* principles to enable states to assess their practices and increase legal certainty. A package regarding services of general economic interest (SGEI) includes Commission communications, a decision and a regulation setting forth de minimis thresholds for the compensation of public services. It is available at *http://ec.europa.eu/competition/state_aid/legislation/sgei.html*.

Earlier, Germany decided to promote windmill energy. German law obliged all regional public electricity suppliers to buy windmill power as a portion of their energy and to pay the wind-generated electricity at a price higher than the price of other energy; and it obliged upstream electricity suppliers to pay to the regional suppliers a part of the extra costs. PreussenElektra, an upstream supplier, tried to avoid paying part of the extra costs of windmill energy on grounds that its supplementary payment to the regional supplier (Schleswag, which happened to be Preussen's own subsidiary) would constitute an illegal subsidy of wind energy. The Court rejected the argument. It ruled that Preussen Elektra's supplementary payment, although commanded by the state, was merely a private payment and did not take the mantle of German aid. *PreussenElektra*, C–379/98, EU:C:2001:160.

Why wasn't the supplementary payment in fact a subsidy? Did this interpretation bless an end run around Article 107? Could Preussen and Schleswag sue Germany for maintaining a state measure that restrained trade by putting them at a competitive disadvantage vis-à-vis Electricité de France and others in violation of Article 34 or 35 of the Treaty?

2.   State Aid Policy

State aid control is a major facet of European Community policy. It accounts for half of the enforcement activity of the Competition Directorate. Alexander Schaub, when Director General for Competition, described the system as follows:

General developments in State aid control

> . . . [T]he maintenance of a system of free and undistorted competition is one of the cornerstones of the European Union. It is undisputed that competition may be distorted by advantages given by public authorities to certain companies which compete with other companies in the Union. All efforts under the anti-trust rules to ensure that companies do not distort competition and trade within the Union would be to no avail if Member States were allowed to seek to outbid each other in offering subsidies to save firms in economic difficulties or to attract investment.

> Today, this applies more than ever. There are three major reasons for the increasing importance of State aid control:

> —First, as the Internal Market becomes a reality, the elimination of a vast number of trade barriers between Member States also progresses. This means that the more classical forms of distortion of competition by Member States have disappeared. If not properly controlled, state

aid may be used to replace the barriers to trade that have already been dismantled.

—Second, the single market in Europe and increased world-wide competition have led to widespread liberalisation of sectors where competition was or is still restricted or even excluded, such as telecommunications, postal services and energy. The consequence of this trend is obvious: introducing competition necessarily means enlarging the scope of State aid control to these sectors.

—There is a third reason for the increasing importance of State aid control: in periods of serious economic difficulties with politically unsustainable levels of unemployment, Governments—not only in the EU, but also in other regions of the world—are tempted to use aid as an instrument to combat unemployment, often merely shifting the problem to another factory, another sector, another area, another country.

The characteristics of State aid control in the EU

One might, of course, at least in theory, advocate the simple ban of State aid to achieve free and undistorted competition throughout the European Union. However, experience has shown that in some cases there are valid reasons to grant aid.

Properly controlled, the granting of aid may contribute to the development of the Community as a whole, whilst potentially harmful or protectionist effects can be eliminated.

But who would be able to carry out this task in a neutral and well-balanced way? The Treaty of Rome solved this question by entrusting the Commission with the task of ensuring a level playing field of competition throughout Europe.

This is indeed the very centre-piece of State aid control in the European Union: the Treaty of Rome not only obliges the Member States to inform the Commission of subsidies granted to enterprises. The obligation goes an important step further and makes the award of aid subject to prior approval by the Commission.

The obligation of notification prior to implementation and, more than that, the fact that the implementation of a plan to grant or alter aid is subject to approval by an independent authority, is one of three key elements which make the control of State aid in the European Union unique both in international and national law. Only the Commission may find aid compatible by applying one of the exemption clauses provided for in the Treaty. Implementing new aid without having obtained the Commission's approval is illegal.

The second element characterizing the State aid control system established by the European Union follows from the first: there are remedies against State aid decisions. Also private operators, in particular aid recipients and competitors, may seek judicial review before the European Courts.

Third, the Commission is not only entrusted with the day-to-day application of the State aid rules, but is also empowered to develop the Community's State aid control policy. Within the wide margin of discretion entrusted to it, the Commission has gradually developed policy through cases and through a variety of policy frameworks, communications and notices. Furthermore, we have established a strict and consistent policy on recovery of incompatible aid in cases where a Member State has not fulfilled its obligation to await the Commission's decision before awarding aid.

To sum up: what we have achieved during the past years is an increased notification discipline and a very high public awareness of the distortive effects of aid. In many sectors, industry is the Commission's best ally in combatting unlawfully granted aid—through complaints to the Commission and through an increasing number of cases brought to national Courts. I take this as an encouraging sign that industry widely supports a strict state aid discipline. . . .

Alexander Schaub, remarks to CIRFS General Assembly, European Competition Policy—in particular developments in policy on State aid control, Brussels, May 14, 1997.

In 2005, under Competition Commissioner Neelie Kroes, the Commission adopted a State Aid Action Plan. The plan put state aid on a more focused, economic basis. It was intended to improve competitiveness of European industry, create sustainable jobs, ensure social and regional cohesion, and improve public services—all of which were major objectives of the European Union's "Lisbon Strategy" of 2005.

* * *

The financial crisis hit Europe and most of the world in 2008. The 2008 Report on Competition Policy devoted the state aid control section to the crisis and the role of state aid policy in recovery.

REPORT ON COMPETITION POLICY (2008)
European Commission

* * *

1.4. State Aid Control

1.4.1.   Shaping the rules and policy

[32] At the beginning of 2008 the Commission's focus in the State aid field was to continue with the implementation of the State Aid Action Plan (SAAP). However, the onset of the financial and economic crisis shifted that focus and the Commission rapidly issued three Communications on the role of State aid policy in the context of the crises and the recovery process.

[33] In the context of the financial crisis, the Commission first gave initial guidance on the application of State aid rules to measures taken in relation to financial institutions, which exceptionally were based on Article [107](3)(b) of the [TFEU] which allows for aid to remedy a serious disturbance in the economy of a Member State. Subsequently, the Commission supplemented and refined its guidance with a new Communication on how Member States can recapitalise banks in the current financial crisis to ensure adequate levels of lending to the rest of the economy and stabilise financial markets, whilst avoiding excessive distortions of competition. In addition, the Commission adopted a new temporary framework providing Member States with additional possibilities to tackle the effects of the credit squeeze on the real economy. All measures are time-limited until the end of 2010, although the Commission, based on Member States' reports, will evaluate whether the measures should be maintained beyond 2010, depending on whether the crisis continues.

[34] As regards the implementation of the SAAP, the Commission adopted, as announced, a General Block Exemption Regulation (GBER) giving automatic approval for a range of aid measures and so allowing Member States to grant such aid without first notifying the Commission, provided that they fulfil all the requirements laid down in the Regulation. In the context of the Climate Change Package, the Commission adopted new guidelines on State aid for environmental protection which introduce a standard assessment for minor cases and a detailed assessment for cases that may involve

significant distortions of competition. The Commission also prolonged the Framework on State aid rules for shipbuilding for a further three years, until 31 December 2011. A new Notice on State aid in the form of guarantees sets out clear and transparent methodologies to calculate the aid element in a guarantee and provides simplified rules for SMEs, including predefined safe-harbour premiums and single premium rates for low-amount guarantees.

35 In addition, public consultations were launched on new rules relating to public service broadcasting, the possible extension until 2012 of the Cinema Communication (scheduled for adoption in January 2009), the guidance documents on the in-depth assessment of regional aid to large investment projects and on criteria for the compatibility analysis in the field of training, as well as on disadvantaged and disabled workers for State aid cases subject to individual notification.

36 The Commission also launched in 2008 a number of public consultations on procedural issues, such as a consultation on a draft Best Practice Code (BPC) on the conduct of State aid control proceedings and the draft notice on Simplified procedure (SP) for the treatment of certain types of State aid. The aim of both documents is to ensure greater transparency, predictability and efficiency of State aid procedures in line with the SAAP. The discussion with the Member States and other stakeholders regarding the BPC and SP will take place early 2009. The drafts are currently due to be adopted in the first half of 2009. The Commission also consulted on a draft Commission Notice on the enforcement of State aid law by national courts.

37 In 2008, the Commission continued its efforts to improve the enforcement and monitoring of State aid decisions. The Commission is seeking to achieve, on the basis of the recovery notice adopted in 2007, a more effective and immediate execution of recovery decisions. Information submitted by the Member States concerned shows that good progress towards recovery was made during that period. This is also reflected in the amounts of aid recovered. Of the EUR 10.3 billion of illegal and incompatible aid to be recovered under decisions adopted since 2000, some EUR 9.3 billion (i.e. 90.7% of the total amount) had actually been recovered by the end of 2008. In addition, a further EUR 2.5 billion in recovery interest had been recovered.

38 As announced in the SAAP, the Commission continued to take a strict line towards Member States that failed to effectively implement recovery decisions addressed to them. In 2008 the Commission initiated legal action under either Article [108(2) TFEU]

or Article [260(2) TFEU] for failure by Member States to comply with recovery obligations. It decided to initiate Article [108(2) TFEU] in five cases involving Italy and Slovakia, as well as decisions to proceed with Article [260(2) TFEU] in eight cases involving Italy and Spain.

[39] In the interest of increased transparency and better communication, DG Competition has published on its webpage a Vademecum on State aid rules summarizing the main rules applicable to State aid control.

1.4.2.   *Applying the rules*

[40] The update of the State aid Scoreboard in autumn 2008 shows that Member States are increasingly making use of the possibilities offered by the recently revised EU State aid rules to better target their aid. Member States awarded on average 80% of their aid to horizontal objectives in 2007, compared with around 50% in the mid-1990s, with increased spending on Research and Development (R&D) and environmental aid. In the face of the current financial crisis, coordinated action by Member States and the Commission has ensured that support schemes for the financial sector have been implemented promptly in compliance with State aid rules.

[41] Over the last 25 years, the overall level of State aid has fallen from over 2% of GDP in the 1980s to around 0.5% in 2007. Whilst highlighting the continuing trend for Member States to focus their aid on horizontal objectives, the Scoreboard nevertheless showed that, following the recent financial crisis, the share of rescue and restructuring aid is likely to increase significantly for some countries in 2008.

[42] In 2008, the Commission approved 88 notified schemes on the basis of the 2006 Community Framework for research and development and innovation; 66 of these were purely R&D schemes, nine were innovation-oriented aid schemes and 13 were mixed, pursuing both R&D and innovation objectives.

[43] In addition, an important decision was adopted in several individual cases involving the Italian aeronautic sector, following an assessment on the basis of the Community frameworks for State aid for R&D of 1996 and 1986. The decision, adopted on 11 March, covers 17 individual R&D projects in the aeronautic sector supported by the Italian authorities during the 1990s. The decision requires the immediate reimbursement of the loans for most of the individual projects, plus interest on arrears in certain cases. The beneficiaries have reimbursed around EUR 350 million within the time limit of two months laid down by the decision.

⁴⁴ In the area of risk capital financing for SMEs, the Commission approved 18 risk capital schemes under the Risk Capital Guidelines. Eleven schemes were assessed on the basis of Chapter 4 of the guidelines, since they complied with the safe harbour provisions allowing a light assessment; three schemes were assessed under Chapter 5, following a detailed assessment. In three cases the Commission considered that the scheme did not involve State aid. One scheme was partly considered as no aid and partly assessed under Chapter 4 of the Guidelines.

⁴⁵ In the field of industrial restructuring, the Commission adopted a decision requesting Romania to recover EUR 27 million unlawful aid in relation to the privatisation of Automobile Craiova, which had been sold on conditions aiming at ensuring a certain level of production and employment, accepting in exchange a lower sales price. Furthermore, following several years of investigation, the Commission concluded that the attempts of the Polish authorities to restructure the shipyards in Gdynia and Szczecin and to return them to viability had failed. As a result, the Commission required Poland to recover the illegal State aid from the shipyards through a controlled sale of the yards' assets and subsequent liquidation of the companies.

* * *

3.   State Aid in Time of Financial Crisis

The financial crisis of 2008–09 prompted the establishment of an Economic Crisis Team and the adoption of a temporary framework.   See   *http://ec.europa.eu/competition/state_aid/ overview/tackling_economic_crisis.html.* The Commission urged the Member States to contact the Economic Crisis Team regarding all state aid related measures and national recovery plans. The Commission maintains a "scoreboard" of Member State action to fight the financial crisis, and summarizes the states' plans and actions and the Commission's responses in approving or disapproving the proposed aid. *See http://ec.europa.eu/competition/state_aid/ studies_reports/studies_reports.html* under "Scoreboard, reports and studies."

Not surprisingly, the financial crisis of 2008–2009 gave rise to emergency calls for mergers and restructurings. Several Member States announced plans to pour state monies into their firms to keep them afloat. French President Sarkozy announced plans to lend Peugeot Citroen and Renault three billion euros each in exchange for a promise not to shut French plants or lay off French workers. Competition   Commissioner   Neelie   Kroes   responded   that nationalistic measures violated Community law, and, working with the Directorate General for Competition, she offered community-wide plans to speed up the vetting of emergency mergers and state-aid approvals. Sarkozy withdrew the conditionality of his plan.

In several speeches, Commissioner Neelie Kroes described problems and solutions, and called for the Member States to resist a descent into nationalism that could threaten the single market. Her successors, Joaquin Almunia and Margrethe Vestager, have consistently followed suit.

4.   State Aid and the Tax Cases

Since 2013, the European Commission has been investigating allegations of favorable tax treatment given to certain companies through tax rulings that give "advanced clarification." By mid-2016, that investigation had led to the opening of formal proceedings against The Netherlands for aid granted to Starbucks, Luxembourg for aid granted to Fiat, McDonald's and Amazon, and Belgium for operating an excess profit exemption scheme. As expressed by Commissioner Vestager, the overall concern was that Member States artificially reduce certain companies' tax base and thus their overall tax burden by means of rulings that rely on transfer prices and do not reflect economic reality. The strategy artificially reduces taxable profits.

The Commission characterizes its investigation into Member States' tax ruling practices as part of an overall plan for "fair and effective taxation" aimed at tackling tax avoidance (and, conversely, fiscal dumping). It has attracted criticism from the United States, which claims that the Commission is discriminating against American companies, depriving them of deals they have negotiated with host countries to invest in those countries; and that the Commission is challenging the deals illegitimately under the banner of state aid when it is really a matter of individual Member States' tax policy—a function reserved to the states under EU law.

Director General of DG Competition Johannes Laitenberger gave the following explanation.

STATE AID TAX CASES: SINE TIMORE AUT FAVORE

Director General Johannes Laitenberger
Competition Directorate General, European Commission
St. Gallen, 20 May 2016

* * *

. . . EU competition law has a specific feature that does not exist in other jurisdictions. It is the complementarity of antitrust and merger control, on the one hand, and of State aid control, on the other, that makes for a comprehensive system to prevent and control distortions of competition in our Single Market. So I thought that it would be of interest to open a window on this area of the Commission's competition enforcement work.

Rationale of State aid law

It would have been impossible to build a common market in post-war Europe without a confidence-building, equitable, law-based framework for the working of such a market. Setting the rules to integrate the Member States' markets was the task of lawmakers. To make sure that the rules would have their intended effect on the ground through effective enforcement, they empowered the Commission as a supranational authority. And this included enforcing the principle of competitive neutrality.

For almost 60 years now, the Commission has protected what is today the Single Market against distortive practices of private businesses, state-owned enterprises and governments alike. The EU's competition rules are ultimately based on a double rationale:

- As an agreed set of rules, they build economic peace between nations and peoples.

- As rules against anti-competitive practices, they make markets work better and enhance consumer welfare.

In all likelihood, the EU's Single Market will always be work in progress. The financial and economic crisis has clearly shown that. But without its rules, it is difficult to imagine how the EU and its Member States would have been able to tackle this and other critical developments and build and restore prosperity together.

* * *

State aid modernisation

Over the last few years, the Commission has introduced a comprehensive programme to modernise the implementation of State aid rules. Building on a more economic approach, and in line with better regulation principles, it makes it easier for EU countries to grant aid that is unproblematic from a competition point of view.

The new rules allow Member States to further economic development and address equity issues while the Commission can scrutinise more rigorously measures with a significant potential to distort the Single Market. The new rules do so by extending the block exemption possibilities in such a way that nowadays some 90% of all aid measures need no longer be notified to the Commission. There's also a comprehensively new set of compatibility rules for notified aid anchored on the same economic principles.

Just yesterday, the Commission adopted a Notice on the Notion of State aid—a key policy document that completes the State aid modernisation process. This makes today a good day to take a look at one of the workstreams in State aid control that is often in the news these days—our State aid cases on aggressive corporate tax planning practices.

In the field of taxation, the Notice consolidates the Commission's practice and the Court's jurisprudence. As such, it is meant to give guidance on broad principles of State aid control in

this field and thus can be useful to national policy makers. Against this background, let me say a few words about our approach to aggressive corporate tax planning practices that may result in selective advantages for some businesses over others.

State aid control and aggressive tax planning

A special Task Force was set up within DG Competition to look into the issue as early as 2013. This was motivated by the gradual emergence of market information suggesting that tax rulings were being exploited to grant selective advantages to certain multinational businesses. I would like to situate our work on aggressive corporate tax planning in a wider context.

Since the financial and economic crisis of 2007–2008, there has been sustained and multifaceted work on the root causes that have led to the instability and imbalances for which we're still paying the price. This is a vast agenda pursued at international, regional and national level.

Tackling tax evasion and tax avoidance is a key point in that agenda. A lot of the work done under this point is on the regulatory side. Think of the OECD's Base Erosion and Profit Shifting project. The organisation has worked on the project with G20 countries on an equal footing and over 80 more countries have been involved.

Within the EU, the Commission has put forward an Action Plan to reform corporate taxation, increase transparency and close loopholes. At the start of the year, the Anti-Tax Avoidance Package was adopted. It included—among other things—anti-abuse measures and better exchanges of information among national tax authorities. Just last month, new rules were proposed requiring multinational groups to report on profits made and taxes paid on a country by-country basis.

The underlying principle of these reforms is to have companies pay tax where they make their profits. Our work in State aid control does not substitute or replace this agenda by other means. But the Commission's special responsibility in the field of State aid control arises in this context as naturally as in others. Let me turn to how DG Competition approaches this task.

Fiscal aid is State aid

Since our aggressive corporate tax planning cases were formally opened, some commentators were surprised that the Commission would look into tax arrangements on the basis of State aid rules. I must say that they seem to have a rather short memory. Before this expert audience, the point that State aid can come in many forms—including fiscal aid—should nevertheless be obvious.

When government measures distort competition in the Single Market, it doesn't matter whether they come as direct subsidies or tax relief to certain economic operators. The European Court of Justice confirmed this principle in 1974 with its seminal judgment in Case 173/73 Italy v Commission. It's the effect that counts—and the effect is not negligible. More than one third of non-crisis State aid is granted in the form of fiscal advantages.

In plain language, State aid control of tax practices and other fiscal arrangements is old hat for the Commission. I will give you a few examples.

As far back as 1998, the Commission found that an Irish 10% corporate tax rate for the manufacturing sector was incompatible aid and ordered its phase-out. In the same year, to give guidance to national authorities, it also issued a Communication on the application of State aid rules to direct business taxation.

In 2001, then Competition Commissioner Mario Monti announced the launch of a large scale investigation into business taxation schemes involving twelve Member States. The main competition concern at the time were preferential tax arrangements—the so-called 'coordination centres'—which multinational corporations used to determine their tax bills.

The Commission later closed the most significant cases and found incompatible fiscal aid in Belgium, Germany, Spain, France, the Netherlands, Finland, the UK, Ireland, Greece, Italy and Sweden. The Member States were requested to terminate the measures. The crux of the matter was that these practices were only benefitting a selected number of multinationals and many of them were not in compliance with the arm's length principle.

The idea behind this principle is quite straightforward. The terms of commercial transactions between two companies belonging to the same group should reflect conditions observed in the market for similar transactions between independent companies.

The European Court of Justice later confirmed the Commission's approach. The arm's length principle—the Court said—was the correct yardstick the Commission could use to ensure that multinationals would be taxed in the same way as non-integrated, standalone companies.

Fiscal aid today

Commissioner Monti's initiative came in the wake of efforts to tackle harmful tax competition among EU Member States in the late 1990s. For example, in 1997 the Council of Economy and Finance Ministers adopted a Code of Conduct for direct business taxation.

As I have mentioned, the context is different today. The financial and economic crisis has drawn attention to aggressive corporate tax planning practices, in particular those benefiting multinational corporations operating as groups. Some economic operators seem to have been pushing the limits of aggressive corporate tax planning very far. In doing so, a number of them have taken advantage of so-called tax rulings and other fiscal arrangements that are available in certain EU Member States.

Allegations about these instances were, for instance, the object of public hearings in the US Senate and the UK's House of Commons. The Commission regarded the media reports and the parliamentary debates of a few years back as market information. The Commission listened and decided to look deeper into the matter.

In response to this, the Task Force mentioned earlier was set up under Vice-President Joaquín Almunia. Its task was looking into aggressive corporate tax planning practices, with an emphasis on tax rulings. The Task Force set out to collect factual evidence by studying the tax ruling practices of Member States and analysing nearly 1,000 rulings.

Given that fiscal secrecy had barred scrutiny hitherto; this has allowed the Commission to gain an unprecedented insight into this matter. While certain practices in favour of businesses relying on tax rulings have always been at odds with State aid rules, their scale had never surfaced before. If the advantages granted to selected multinationals are significant, the need to restore the level playing field has become greater.

Member States' corporate taxation law as reference system

Let me address a criticism sometimes addressed to us that our State aid cases call into question existing corporate taxation law of EU Member States.

I believe that the claim is misguided. To establish whether a tax measure raises State aid concerns, we examine whether it gives a selective advantage to one or several economic operators over others. To that end, we compare the tax treatment of the companies that benefit from them to the ordinary tax treatment reserved to companies in comparable circumstances under national law.

So, the truth is that we take ordinary corporate-tax law in each Member State as the very reference against which we assess whether the tax treatment in individual cases departed from national law or practice. Let me make this even clearer using tax rulings as an example.

In general, granting tax rulings is a normal and justified practice in so far as they provide legal certainty to taxpayers. Provided the rulings do not grant selective advantages to specific companies, but clarify individual situations in line with tax rules as applied to everybody else in comparable factual and legal situations, they do not raise issues under EU State aid law.

The Commission is not in the business of second-guessing the work of national tax authorities with regard to every single tax ruling. The Commission has subjected to deeper scrutiny those rulings where taxation did not reflect actual economic reality—in particular regarding transactions between companies that belong to the same group.

Selective advantages and competition distortions

When determining selectivity we are comparing the tax treatment of the company benefitting from a tax ruling or a special tax regime to the ordinary tax treatment of companies under national law.

The profits made by standalone companies are taxed in the jurisdiction where they are recorded according to the rules and rates that apply in that jurisdiction. In contrast, a multinational group can record its profits in different entities and across multiple jurisdictions. What happens when the multinational needs to allocate profits between the companies it controls?

These internal allocations raise no concern when taxes are paid where profits are generated. Things can become problematic when

profits are shifted from high-taxation to low-taxation jurisdictions—
or even to jurisdictions where companies are allowed to pay almost
no taxes. To be more precise, things become problematic when this is
done by agreeing inflated prices for the transfer of goods and services
between group companies that don't reflect market conditions—and
with tax rulings that confirm these agreements.

Many rulings also determine a company's tax basis as a markup on performance indicators. Often, taxable profits are calculated as
a percentage of operating expenses. In principle, this system could be
justified when the value-added of a group company is closely linked
to the type of expenses used in the calculation and when the
contribution the company makes to the overall operations of the
group is not substantial. However, concerns may arise when
indicators like these are used in a way that fails to capture the
company's actual commercial value and thus artificially reduce the
group's taxable profits.

And here the matter goes beyond the mere mis-application of
national tax law or discrimination between taxpayers. The matter
becomes a distortion of competition. Subsidies—including selective
forms of tax relief—have the potential to distort the ability of
companies to compete on the merits.

Moreover, economic activity generated on the back of such
arrangements may lack a sound economic rationale and be
unsustainable. Activity created in this fashion in one EU Member
State could come at the expense of another EU Member State which
is not in a position to offer tax advantages. Benefits granted to
selected operators can harm their rivals.

These distortions eventually translate into economic
inefficiencies and, possibly, even into macroeconomic imbalances
because activities and capital flows are displaced. Many factors
influence companies' investment and expansion decisions, such as
infrastructure, labour skills and costs, and proximity to customers.
Of course, tax rates can also be a legitimate consideration. However,
these decisions should not be driven by the possibility for specific,
selected operators to artificially lower their tax bases and effective
taxation. And there should be no financial-capacity distortion
between economic operators by allowing a few to build up war chests
thanks to untaxed profits.

Let me add that standalone companies are not the only ones that
are harmed by these practices. Large integrated companies that pay
their taxes in different countries following the arm's length principle
are also at a disadvantage.

By analysing the situations that give rise to these concerns with a view of restoring level competition conditions, the Commission therefore fulfils the classic State aid mission—that is, identifying and correcting competition distortions that are not justified. If a company has received undue advantages, State aid law specifies in which cases it should return them in order to restore competitive conditions in the markets.

The rules are clear. Here, this means recovering unpaid taxes— up to a period of ten years—and making sure that taxes are paid correctly in the future. Obviously, the rules specify that the company cannot be asked to return the money if it has legitimate expectations—that is, if the Commission has previously expressed a different view or assessment. Also, there is no recovery when the legal certainty principle can be invoked. A typical example is when the Commission takes a decision on a novel case. However—as we will see presently—neither of these conditions applied in the State aid decisions the Commission has taken so far.

Decisions taken so far

So far, formal proceedings were opened on tax arrangements in Luxembourg, the Netherlands, Ireland and Belgium between 2014 and 2015. In the meantime, following the proposals of Competition Commissioner Margrethe Vestager, the Commission has taken three decisions.

The first two came in October last year, when the Commission found that the tax rulings offered to Fiat Finance & Trade in Luxembourg and to Starbucks in the Netherlands were illegal forms of State aid. To level the playing field, each of the two groups was ordered to return an estimated €20–30 million—broadly equivalent to the tax rebates they had unduly received. Let me tell you what we have found in these cases in a nutshell.

With a tax ruling, a tax authority tells a company in advance the amount of tax it will pay given certain conditions. In principle—as I said—there is nothing wrong with tax rulings. They need not pose competition concerns. In fact, they are useful to companies, which can better predict their costs. In contrast, the rulings that were sanctioned in our decisions endorsed artificial systems that did not reflect economic reality and granted selective advantages.

In the cases of Starbucks and Fiat, the systems worked on the basis of transfer prices. These are the prices that a company within a group pays for things such as a loan or royalties to another company belonging to the same group. Once again, transfer prices are fine as long as they follow the arm's length principle. But the transfer prices of Starbucks and Fiat did not meet these requirements.

The Dutch Starbucks roaster paid a substantial royalty to another group company for coffee roasting know-how, although no other Starbucks or independent roaster in a similar situation paid such royalty. The end result was that—because of this royalty payments—Starbucks ended up paying little tax in the Netherlands.

Fiat Finance & Trade is based in Luxembourg and provides financial services, such as intra-group loans, to other Fiat Group companies. As these activities can be compared to those of a bank, the taxable profit can also be determined similarly to that of a bank. However, here the tax ruling endorsed an artificial method lowering both the capital basis and its remuneration. As a result, Fiat Finance & Trade has only paid taxes on a small portion of its actual capital at a very low remuneration that is not in line with market rate.

The decisions the Commission took last year will offer guidance to tax administrations in the EU. They must make sure that the transfer prices they accept are credible and in line with market terms.

The third and latest decision taken by the Commission is from last January and involves Belgium's so-called Excess Profit scheme, where we found a different method to reduce the tax burden. The scheme was open only to multinational groups and their actual profits were compared to a notional profit they would have made if they had been standalone companies.

The excess profit that resulted from this hypothetical comparison was not taxed. As a result, the multinationals that were part of the scheme—and only them—got tax discounts of more than 50% and in some cases of up to 90%. To bring things back to balance, the Commission ordered Belgium to recover from the more than 30 companies that had received the undue rebates an estimated €700 million in total.

Cases in the pipeline

These are the three decisions the Commission has taken. There are ongoing investigations as well, with openings so far involving Apple in Ireland, and Amazon and McDonald's in Luxembourg.

Moreover, the Task Force has been reviewing over a thousand tax rulings from the LuxLeaks files and from EU countries, which we requested a few years ago. The review reveals that the majority of rulings are not used for aggressive corporate tax planning. Most are well documented and aim at allocating profits between companies with genuine economic activities.

The rule that tax be paid where profit is made seems to be respected more often than not. So, most rulings don't seem to grant a selective advantage. But there seem to be outliers. Our ongoing review is looking for rulings that may grant individual companies terms that are not available to others in comparable circumstances. . . .

As you can see, what is sometimes depicted as an extraordinary and unprecedented initiative is in fact deeply rooted in the Commission's enforcement work. The extraordinary part are the practices the Commission has to correct—not the fact that the Commission is correcting them.

As far as the Commission is concerned, all cases are equal and none is more equal than others. Every case—regardless of its visibility—is investigated and assessed on its own merits. We try to obtain the best possible information; we look at the facts; and we reach a decision based on evidence and the law.

Our assessment is based at all times on applicable State aid rules and the jurisprudence of the European Court of Justice. Finally—and perhaps most importantly—we take great care to respect due process and the right of defence of the administrations and companies involved. There's a Latin phrase that sums up our approach: sine timore aut favore. We will continue to enforce the rules without fear or favour.

This is a message that I would like to send to the law-abiding competitors of the corporations that receive illegal aid, which end up sustaining higher costs. The message also goes to tax authorities in EU countries, which must check the final result of the arrangements they make with corporations.

But above all the message goes out to the people, who expect businesses to play by the rules—more so since each and every citizen is expected to play by the rules. In this sense, State aid rules are part of good governance. The financial and economic crisis has shaken the people's belief in economic governance. Our work can help restore that belief.

Notes and Questions

1. Article 107(1) prohibits state aid that "distorts or threatens to distort competition by favoring certain [firms or goods]. . . ." What does

"distort[ing] competition" mean? Does the phrase mean the same thing in Article 107(1) as in Article 101(1) TFEU?

2.   Do you agree that state aid normally "distorts competition"? In what sense? Does it harm competition from the viewpoint of consumers? from the viewpoint of competitors? from the vantage of protecting the competition process and the right to compete on the merits? Can state aid intensify competition? How can or should the Commission and Court deal with procompetitive effects (lower prices, more business formation) of state aid?

3.   The United States, in contrast with the EU, has no national subsidy control, except as required by the GATT/WTO, and except for prohibition of discriminatory subsidies that impose an undue burden on interstate commerce. See West Lynn Creamery v. Healy, 512 U.S. 186 (1994). US law reflects the belief that freedom of state and local governments to grant subsidies or other benefits, whether to compete for business establishment or to prop up business in financial difficulty, is a healthy form of state autonomy and competition. See *Camps Newfound/Owatonna, Inc. v. Town of Harrison*, 520 U.S. 564, 589 (1997); and see Justice Scalia, dissenting, at 605–08. Are there good reasons why Europe has state aid control and the United States does not?

4.   Firms in Europe frequently challenge a grant of state aid to their rivals, and typically they are accorded standing to do so. Thus, when Ford and Volkswagen set up a joint venture in Portugal to make multi-purpose vehicles—a new endeavor for both joint venture partners—Matra, the dominant maker of MPVs, complained that Portugal's grant of infrastructure aid to the new entrant violated Article 107 TFEU, and that the joint venture agreement itself violated Articles 101 and 102 TFEU in part because the aid distorted competition. (How would Matra argue this point?) Matra lost on the merits; both the aid and the joint venture were allowed. See Case T–17/93, Matra Hachette SA v. Commission, EU:T:1994:89.

Why would a firm challenge a grant of aid to its rival? Why, in particular, would a dominant firm challenge a grant of aid to a new entrant? Is the complainant likely to be complaining about harm to competition, about unfair advantages, or about competition itself? Would buyers of the products produced by a subsidized firm ever have an interest in challenging a state aid? Would it be accurate to view rivals' complaints about grants of state aid as complaints about unfair competition?

5.   Explain the relationship between the state aid body of law and the antitrust (Articles 101 and 102 TFEU) and merger control bodies of law. While there are many differences, Europe took advantage of the synergies of its laws in the financial crisis of 2008, using its combined

powers of subsidy control, merger control and restructuring, and doing so on an emergency basis. See Neelie Kroes, Competition Law in an Economic Crisis, Opening address at the 13th Annual Competition Conference of the International Bar Association, Fiesole, 11 September 2009 (SPEECH/09/385).

6. Are the deep tax breaks offered by certain Member States to certain multinational firms to induce investment in their countries better viewed under the lens of Member State tax policy or EU state aid policy? For developments on state aid and tax rulings, see *http://ec. europa.eu/competition/state_aid/tax_rulings/index_en.html*. See also Case T–755/15, *Luxembourg v. Commission*, pending; and Case T– 759/15, *Fiat Chrysler Finance Europe v. Commission*, pending.

7. European Commission officials take pride in what they view as a coherent and holistic competition system in Europe. Are they right to extol the virtues of the European system? Does US competition policy need more coherence? Should the US Attorney General in Charge of Antitrust have a seat at the economic-policy table? Would the US be served or disserved by a state (or federal) aid policy, requiring notification and justification of significant state, local, or federal aid to enterprises?

G. THE RELATIONSHIP BETWEEN REGULATION AND COMPETITION: US/EU

Every antitrust jurisdiction must make decisions on the relationship between sector regulation and competition law. Does regulation oust the competition law regime, or do the two regimes co-exist where co-existence is possible?

The answer can depend on a jurisdiction's system of federalism and hierarchy of laws. For example, in the United States, an exemption from antitrust law may be implied where sector regulation covers the same set of practices as those sought to be challenged under antitrust law. See Credit Suisse Securities v. Billing, 551 U.S. 264 (2007). Also see *Trinko*, supra, 540 U.S. 398 (2004), suggesting deferral of antitrust to a regulatory regime. In Europe, the perspective is quite different. In *Deutsche Telekom*, concerned with a price squeeze that the German regulator allowed and virtually ordered, the General Court said: If the firm is caught in such a bind between the regulator and EU law, the firm should go back to the regulator and request a price change that would dissipate the price squeeze. Case T–271/03, *Deutsche Telekom AG v. Commission*, EU:T:2008:101, paras. 261–271, affirmed on other grounds; the Court of Justice believed that Deutsche Telekom could cure the price squeeze without a modification of the regulator's orders. C–280/08 P, EU:C:2010:603.

The design of the two systems can produce different outcomes. In the United States, federal regulation is on a hierarchical par the antitrust system. Congress can privilege one or the other. In the EU, the antitrust system is Treaty law, and the sector regulation derives from the Member State.

Which system, US or EU, is more protective of competition? of efficiency? In which case or regime do consumers get the better deal? Does it matter whether Deutsche Telekom would lower its wholesale price or raise its retail price to avoid an illegal price squeeze?

H. CHINA: ABUSE OF ADMINISTRATIVE MONOPOLY

On the eve of adoption of China's Anti-Monopoly Law in 2008, distinguished Professor Huang Yong, a consultant to the drafters, wrote Pursuing the Second Best: The History, Momentum and Remaining Issues of China's Anti-Monopoly Law, 75 Antitrust L.J. 117 (2008). In this article Professor Huang says:

. . . . China which has a culture thousands of years old, with an ideology that is extremely conservative and even feudalistic, is a country undergoing a painful transition from command economy to market orientation. . . .

* * *

The Desire to Contain Abusive State Power

"The abuse of executive power to distort or restrict competition is a phenomenon that exists among state agencies and organizations which are authorized by the law and regulations to control public affairs, albeit to a various degree. The AML needs to tackle this problem seriously."

—*Cao Kangtai, Notes to the Draft PRC Anti-Monopoly Law*

As provided by Article 8 of the AML, the so-called administrative monopoly generally refers to abusive conduct committed by state agencies and organizations, which are authorized by the law and regulations to control public affairs, to the extent that they distort or restrict competition. Two factors account for the widespread and intractable existence of administrative monopoly in the Chinese economic system. The first is the tradition, hundreds of years old, that "state power comes first"; in other words, a tradition that state power controls every single aspect of the society's economic life. The second is the current political and economic structure, which has closely linked monopoly enterprises to the government since the 1949 revolution.

In today's China, people have agreed upon two conclusions with respect to the corrosive effects caused by intrusive State power upon economic development and even upon the political system. First, ever expanding abusive State power is the biggest threat to a functioning competitive market system; second, the problem of administrative monopoly stems from the social structure, which is beyond any single statute to resolve. The ultimate solution relies on both economic and political reform. However, for China, the process of reform can take a long time, longer than competition could afford. Therefore, a second best option would be to adopt some technical restraints against certain State powers within the AML framework, which might be an unsatisfactory but realistic approach. This is a reflection of the "doctrine of the golden mean" in the Confucian school, an equivalent to pragmatism.

* * *

Responding to its unique problem, China has a unique provision in its Anti-Monopoly Law. Chapter V prohibits abuse of administrative powers to restrict competition, known as abuse of administrative monopoly. After much debate in the drafting process, it was decided to include such a provision but not to give the antitrust authorities the power to enforce the provision directly. Under Article 51, they must identify the conduct to the superior authority of the offending body and persuade the superior authority to prohibit the conduct.

China has no commerce clause or free movement clause in its constitution, and provinces notoriously try to keep neighboring producers' goods out of their province. The law is meant to attack such artificial barriers, preferential treatment, and other discrimination. But it potentially goes much deeper.

Matters initiated by the enforcement agency National Development and Resources Commission in 2014 include: In Yunan Province the Provincial Communication Administration organized a cartel among the Yunan branches of China Mobile, China Telecom, China Unicom and China Railcom restricting refunds to customers. The NDRC reported the suspected violation to the superior authority, the National Communication Administration, and the superior authority ordered the local authority to cease the practice. The cartel members were fined.

In Shandong Province, the Department of Transport adopted policies for vehicles, including those carrying hazardous chemicals, to be monitored and required that they use a designated company for platform services and testing. The NDRC found that designating the supplier of services deprived road transport companies of freedom to choose their supplier and elevated fees. It suggested to the Shandong provincial government to order the Shangdong DOT to allow the users free choice.

In Hebei Province, the NDRC found that the Department of Transportation, the Department of Finance and the Price Bureau jointly gave local passenger transport companies a 50% discount on road tolls. The NDRC found that the discount was a subsidy giving the local firms an unfair competitive advantage over their out-of-province competitors, and requested the Hebei provincial government to withdraw the policy. See Susan Ning, China's Antimonopoly Law and Its Enforcement against State Monopolies: Achievements and Limitations, in Antitrust in Emerging and Developing Countries (Fox, First, Charbit, Ramundo eds., Concurrences Review 2016), at 9.

Meanwhile, SAIC (State Administration for Industry & Commerce, the agency in charge of non-price restraints) took action in Inner Mongolia, finding that the local Safety Supervision and Administration Bureau was responsible for an illegal division of geographic markets among fireworks wholesale companies, which the Bureau claimed would prevent accidents caused by fireworks of poor quality induced by aggressive competition. The local SAIC branch fined the wholesalers 7% of their annual revenue for the prior year, and imposed a fine of 8% on those wholesalers who, taking advantage of their monopoly, imposed unreasonable conditions on retailers.

Private parties may also sue to enforce Chapter V, and litigation is pending.

In their article, "Fair Competition Review—key step in competition policy," in King & Wood Mallesons' China Law Insight, Susan Ning, Kate Peng and Gong Ting describe China's establishment of its Fair Competition Review Mechanism for all draft laws, regulations, administrative policies, practices and instruments to ensure against (for example) state and local discriminations on entry and exit, preferential treatments including tax exemptions, and designation of who shall provide goods and services. They then outline the scope of Chapter V and show the connection between the AML enforcement, the Fair Competition Review Mechanism, and other mechanisms to attack obstructions of competition by government bodies. The authors write:

> Another latest effort made by China's top government
> to fight against administrative monopoly to elevate the

deterring effects for such potential violations is in the
NDRC's latest draft (for public consultation) guidelines on
determining the illegal gains generated from monopoly
conduct and on setting fines ("Fining Guidelines"). The
Fining Guidelines stipulate that when determining the
aggravating circumstances on setting fines, if certain
undertakings take the initiative to impel the administrative
authorities to eliminate or restrict competition through
abusing their administrative powers, the AMEAs (Anti-
Monopoly Enforcement Authorities) may deem it as
aggravating circumstance when setting fines.

b) In the context of Administrative Litigation Law * * *

Another effort was lately made to reduce the legal barrier to
prevent private individuals and enterprises from initiating
administrative litigation against administrative monopoly. The
previous Administrative Litigation Law ("ALL") makes a distinction
between "abstract administrative act" and "concrete (individualized)
administrative act." A private individual or entity can only bring to
court cases against concrete administrative acts or administrative
acts specifically issued against an individual or company. This
approach is similar to the EU's direct effect principle, which enables
a private individual or entity to bring a competition law case before
a national court. In contrast, administrative litigation against
"abstract administrative activity" (i.e., a legislative measure issued
by a government agency) was explicitly excluded by the previous
ALL. The abuses of administrative monopolies, in practice, are
usually carried out in the form of legislative or other similar
measures, and therefore are categorized as "abstract administrative
act". At such, if these measures are not concrete or addressed to
individuals, under the previous Administrative Litigation Law, no
administrative litigation could be successfully initiated. The revised
ALL, however, has removed such limitations.

c) Achievements and Limitations

There is no doubt that significant achievements were made by
the AML and the ALL to fight against administrative monopoly.
Recent intensified enforcement decisions underline the point that the
AMEAs have targeted abuses by administrative monopolies as their
enforcement priority.

There are, however, certain limitations such as the lack of direct
power to enforce Chapter V against administrative monopoly. Article
51 merely provides the AMEAs with the power to refer matters so
they can be considered by the superior authority of the infringing
body. This inherent weakness of the AML renders the law less

deterring when fight against administrative monopoly. Besides, these ex post controls over administrative monopoly are emerged on a case by case basis and therefore require a relatively long time to realize such deterring effects and thus remedy such infringements. Against such backdrop, the said Opinions bring, for the first time, a systematically ex ante control mechanism into the competition enforcement landscape in China. Such mechanism will provide a comprehensive review of all the government measures in place (or in future) by the prescribed competition standards. This review will not only remove the very roots of administrative monopoly, and also promote the awareness of all the government officials at different levels to fully recognize the importance of competition policy in a market economy.

Conclusion

The importance of market competition is increasingly well understood in China. As mentioned above, two features of China's systemic and policy environment raise issues for market competition: abuse of the administrative powers of government agencies, and policies to promote the development of particular sectors and firms. While these features exist in all modern economies, their extent in China is exceptionally large. Alongside the current enforcement of the AML and the ALL, the introduction of fair competition review, conceived by the highest level of the Chinese government, represent a significant change in the government's thinking about the role of the state and its relationship with the economy. With more resources provided to the Chinese competition authorities to fight against administrative monopoly, we are expecting a more vigorously developing China's market featured with more fair competition among market participants. In view of the above, the establishment of the fair competition review mechanism is indeed a milestone in China's efforts to fully transform into a market economy.

Available at: *http://www.chinalawinsight.com/2016/06/ articles/antitrust-international-trade/fair-competition-review-key-step-in-competition-policy/.*

Notes and Questions

1.   Comment on the Chinese law against abuse of administrative monopoly and China's project to identify and correct unnecessarily anticompetitive legislation and regulations. Are these provisions likely to make a significant contribution to China's (socialist) market economy?

2.   What will it take to make these laws successful?

3.   Are other jurisdictions that are faced with extensive state restraints likely to take lessons from China?

4.   Would   separation-of-powers   issues   counsel   against administrative monopoly law in some jurisdictions?

I.   TRADE INSTRUMENTS

1.   The WTO: Hybrid State and Private Restraints

Combinations of state and private action may pose serious anticompetitive restraints. But the private action might be shielded from challenge by state action, and the state action, even if anticompetitive and excessive, may not be proscribed. This was a problem in *Kodak/Fuji Film*.* Kodak, in its attempts to contest the Japanese film market, alleged that it was severely handicapped by the combination of Japanese state and private restraints that, cumulatively, blocked all efficient ways to get to market in Japan. Rules of the World Trade Organization provided no recourse—even if one accepts the facts as argued by Kodak.

The World Trade Organization has few antitrust rules, but it does have a set of rules applicable to telecommunications companies and the state measures that regulate them. Telecoms companies have historically been state-owned. Many were newly privatized. The modus operandi of the telecoms firms has frequently been nationalistic, undermining the promise of an open and competitive world telecommunications system. This combination of factors led to the   adoption   of   antitrust   rules   accompanying   the Telecommunications Agreement in the WTO. Only one antitrust case has   arisen   under   the   antitrust   rules   accompanying   the Telecommunications   Agreement.   The   case   demonstrates   the potential for analyzing intertwined public and private restraints as a coherent whole.

MEXICAN TELECOMS**

Telmex is the dominant telecommunications company in Mexico. It was state-owned then privatized. Telmex is regulated by COFETEL, the Mexican telecommunications regulatory agency. Telmex is also subject to the Mexican Federal Competition Law, but

---

*   Panel Report, *Japan-Measures Affecting Consumer Photographic Film and Paper*, WT/DS44/R (Mar. 31, 1998) (adopted Apr. 22, 1998). Since this was a WTO case, it was limited to Japan's trade-restraining laws or acts.

**   Based on Eleanor Fox, *Mexican Telecoms*: Modest World Antitrust, 21 Antitrust 74 (ABA Antitrust Law Section, fall 2006).

it has been notoriously successful in maneuvering around control by the Mexican Federal Competition Commission.

COFETEL regulates the sector through rulemaking. COFETEL rules conferred on Telmex the power to fix the rate to be paid by all foreign carriers (e.g., AT&T and MCI) terminating calls in Mexico. Mexico had licensed several Mexican firms (the "concessionaires") in addition to Telmex to terminate calls in Mexico. COFETEL rules required these firms to charge no less than the Telmex fee for termination, and the rules decreed a market-sharing system in support of the high price. This, according to the United States, was an anticompetitive, incumbent-protecting strategy that amounted to a cartel. It was a strategy carried out by and for the benefit of Mexican firms, and one that Mexico was bound to prevent by its WTO commitment in the General Agreement on Trade in Services (GATS), the Telecommunications Annex to the GATS, and the accompanying Reference Paper. The United States filed a claim before the WTO alleging that Mexico had failed to open its telecommunications market, as promised. The claim included an antitrust charge.[1]

Mexico was among 69 member states of the WTO that signed the GATS Annex on Telecommunications and the Reference Paper. The Reference Paper contains the antitrust obligation that lay at the center of the dispute. The Reference Paper requires signatories to maintain "appropriate measures" to prevent major suppliers "from engaging in or continuing anti-competitive practices." The relevant provisions are as follows:

(1) *Competitive safeguards*

(1.1) *Prevention of anti-competitive practices in telecommunications*

Appropriate measures shall be maintained for the purpose of preventing suppliers who, alone or together, are a major supplier from engaging in or continuing anti-competitive practices.

(1.2) *Safeguards*

The anti-competitive practices referred to in the above paragraph shall include in particular:

(a) engaging in anti-competitive cross-subsidization;

(b) using information obtained from competitors with anti-competitive results; and

---

[1] See Panel Report, Mexico—Measures Affecting Telecommunications Services, WT/DS204/R (Apr. 2, 2004) (adopted June 1, 2004), ¶¶ 7.222–.224.

(c) not making available to other services suppliers on a timely basis technical information about essential facilities and commercially relevant information which are necessary for them to provide services.

Based on this language, the WTO panel was called upon to decide a series of difficult questions: Was it an anticompetitive practice for Telmex to set an excessive termination fee and for all Mexican rivals to accede to charging no less than the fee Telmex would set? Was this behavior a contemplated "anti-competitive practice," in view of the fact that the conduct was ordered by rules of the nation's regulatory agency? Were Mexico's antitrust law and regulatory rules "appropriate measures" to prevent anticompetitive practices, obviating any violation? Indeed, were the regulatory rules procompetitive (as Mexico improbably maintained)? If they were anticompetitive, were the Mexican rules and practices a justified form of industrial policy (if so, Mexico did not fail to maintain "appropriate" measures) on the theory that the monopoly border-charge was meant to be used by the Mexican telecommunication firms to fund infrastructure in the poorest parts of Mexico and thus to enhance Mexico's economic development?

The questions for the panel were difficult in light of the wording of the main document at issue, the Reference Paper. The antitrust obligation clearly was not drafted by antitrust lawyers. Its wording and context gave fodder to Mexico's strategy of playing with the meaning of "anti-competitive." It also gave Mexico cover to claim that measures protecting Mexican carriers from being played off one another by foreign carriers, preventing new entrants from triggering a price war and preventing large carriers from undercutting new entrants, were procompetitive measures.

Construing the Reference Paper

The Meaning of "anti-competitive." Mexico argued for a narrow construction of Section 1 of the Reference Paper. It relied heavily on the three stated examples of "anti-competitive" practices in Section 1.2. The examples are: unfair low prices because of cross-subsidization, unfair use of information, and unfair withholding of information. Mexico contended that the examples demonstrated the meaning of "anti-competitive" in the Reference Paper. The word referred, said Mexico, to: "actions taken by private companies to gain an advantage over their competitors." Thus cartels were not "anti-competitive practices."

The heading *"Safeguards"* over the text of the antitrust obligations tended to support Mexico's narrow interpretation. The

GATS obliges nations to open their markets. Safeguards are protections against a surge of trade that may result from openness. The antitrust clause could be seen as a check against the inflow of unfair (e.g., low-priced) competition.

This argument did not convince the panel. Cartels, it pointed out, are the paradigmatic anticompetitive practice. The anti-cartel principle is well recognized around the world. It is well documented in the Havana Charter, the OECD Hard Core Cartel Recommendation, and the UNCTAD Set of Multilateral Rules. It is unthinkable (the panel implied) that the phrase "anti-competitive practices" does not include cartels.

State action. Mexico further argued that "anti-competitive practices" at least means no more than practices illegal under antitrust laws, and the conduct in question was ordered by COFETEL's rules. It was protected by the state action doctrine, said Mexico, and therefore was not legally an "anti-competitive practice." The European Union joined Mexico in arguing that the state action doctrine and the nature of the rules as a regulatory choice defeated the United States's case.

Again, the panel was not convinced. It said: "The Panel is aware that, pursuant to doctrines applicable under the competition laws of some Members, a firm complying with a specific legislative requirement of such a Member . . . may be immunized . . . ." But in most of these jurisdictions, domestic legislatures have the power to limit the scope of competition law. GATS commitments, by contrast, are international; they are designed to limit the regulatory powers of WTO members. A member "cannot unilaterally erode its international commitments."

The panel said that a state action defense should be particularly disfavored in an international context. The use of state power to insulate a national champion at the expense of outsiders is a discrimination of the sort that, conceptually, trade law does not tolerate. A state should not be permitted to *order* trade-harming anticompetitive conduct to evade its burden to prohibit just such conduct.

The panel might also have noted the limits to the state action defense, in both the United States and the European Union. US law holds that a state of the United States may not order price fixing and then immunize the price fixers from violating the federal antitrust laws.[2] A Member State of the European Union may not order "its" firms to fix quotas and then insulate them from EU competition law when they decline to allocate quotas to outsiders.[3] If a Mexican antitrust action had been brought against the Mexican firms, they may not have had a successful state action defense.

A "right" to industrial policy? Mexico had a third string to its bow. Regardless of a state action or immunity defense, said Mexico, the Reference Paper obligation is limited. It says only that "*appropriate* measures shall be maintained for the purpose of preventing [major] suppliers . . . from engaging in or continuing anti-competitive practices." Mexico said it maintained appropriate measures: it had an antitrust law and enforced it. Moreover, Mexico was required to take only *appropriate* measures. It was appropriate for Mexico to adopt cartel-organizing rules as a matter of regulatory sovereignty to protect and promote Mexican investment in domestic infrastructure and thereby to advance its economic development.

There are two convincing answers to Mexico's claim of right to design its own industrial policy. First, Mexico itself had undertaken in its WTO obligations not to charge an excessive termination fee. COFETEL's rules authorized private firms to do what Mexico could not do. Nations have the power to contract away the right to adopt regulation that handicaps foreign traders. Second, Mexico's regulation was clearly not likely to achieve its putative object: help the Mexican poor. Extra private profits for national firms do not translate into infrastructure investment. Moreover, lower prices of the incoming calls were good for poor Mexicans. Large numbers of the callers into Mexico are Mexicans who have come to the United States for work to support their families, and they need to be in touch with the families they left behind.[4]

---

[2]   Schwegmann Bros. v. Calvert Distillers Corp., 341 U.S. 384, 71 S.Ct. 745, 95 L.Ed. 1035 (1951).

[3]   Case C–198/01, *Italian Matches*, EU:C:2003:430.

[4]   *See* Mary Anastasia O'Grady, *Americas: A Telecom Monopoly Cripples Mexico*, WALL ST. J., Feb. 10, 2006, at A19 ("Telmex has 95% of the country's fixedline market," leading to high prices and sub-optimal use. TELMEX—through its powerful owner Carlos Slim, and successive presidents (Zedillo, Fox) who are beholden to Mr. Slim—suppresses the growth of wireless and voice-over-Internet. The Minister for Communication and Transportation, Pedro Cerisola, is a former TELMEX district manager. Cerisola "has actively engaged in protecting Telmex against competition." Not only do the poor suffer from prices that are too high, but they suffer from suppressed growth. "[T]he rest of the country suffered from [TELMEX's] favored position. In a modern age when businesses need low-priced, high-quality telecommunications to compete in a global economy, Mexican growth has borne the cost of Mr. Slim's privilege. Any genuine effort to help the poor necessarily requires more healthy competition, starting in the telecom market.").

Because Mexico's means were so unlikely to achieve its putative ends, one might suspect a different driving force behind the COFETEL rules. Perhaps the aim was to continue the privileges of a former state-owned monopoly and its legendarily powerful, politically well-connected owner, Carlos Slim. As EU policy makers often observe, it may take a supranational law to give a nation the will to say no; the will to deny advantages to a powerful player.[5]

Conclusion

Mexican Telecoms was a hard case. It was hard because it was not clear that the nations meant to limit their regulatory powers by agreeing to Section 1 of the Reference Paper. It was hard because Mexico had a credible argument at every fork in the road. (Did "anti-competitive" practice mean only unfair competition? Was there a state-action shield? Was there a national regulatory policy defense?)

But *Mexican Telecoms* was a wise decision. In this first WTO antitrust case,[6] the panel gave a victory to markets over nationalism. The panel report was a first step towards integrating trade and competition.

---

2.   **Regional Agreements**

The new generation of regional free trade agreements may include a chapter on state-owned enterprises and designated monopolies. These chapters would approximate competitive neutrality for state and state-owned enterprises and monopolies designated by the state and provide transparency as to the identities of these enterprises. The chapter negotiated for the Trans-Pacific Partnership, which is in abeyance since the US withdrawal, may be

---

[5]   See Rafael del Villar, Competition and Equity in Telecommunications, Chapter 9 in NO GROWTH WITHOUT EQUITY? INEQUALITY, INTERESTS, AND COMPETITION IN MEXICO (S. Levy and M. Walton eds. 2009), at 321. Del Villar describes how Mexico privatized Telmex while continuing its monopolistic privileges, and argues that:

> Mexico could achieve a good deal simply by complying with the provisions of the Federal Telecommunications Act and the reference paper, as well as by ensuring clear separation between the major carriers and the regulatory agency.

[6]   In a prior matter, *Kodak/Fuji Film*, the United States complained that Japan tolerated private anticompetitive restraints; but when the United States brought its case in the GATT, it challenged only Japan's trade-restraining laws. The United States lost. See Panel Report, Japan—Measures Affecting Consumer Photographic Film and Paper, WT/DS44/R (Mar. 31, 1998) (adopted Apr. 22, 1998).

a guide for such chapters in the future. Here is a relevant excerpt from the chapter in TPP:

TRANS-PACIFIC PARTNERSHIP

(2016, not adopted)

Chapter 17

State-Owned Enterprises and Designated Monopolies

(footnotes deleted)

Article 17.3: Delegated Authority

Each Party shall ensure that when its state-owned enterprises, state enterprises and designated monopolies exercise any regulatory, administrative or other governmental authority that the Party has directed or delegated to such entities to carry out, those entities act in a manner that is not inconsistent with that Party's obligations under this Agreement.

Article 17.4: Non-discriminatory Treatment and Commercial Considerations

1.   Each Party shall ensure that each of its state-owned enterprises, when engaging in commercial activities:

(a)   acts in accordance with commercial considerations in its purchase or sale of a good or service, except to fulfil any terms of its public service mandate that are not inconsistent with subparagraph (c)(ii);

(b)   in its purchase of a good or service:

(i) accords to a good or service supplied by an enterprise of another Party treatment no less favourable than it accords to a like good or a like service supplied by enterprises of the Party, of any other Party or of any non-Party; and

(ii) accords to a good or service supplied by an enterprise that is a covered investment in the Party's territory treatment no less favourable than it accords to a like good or a like service supplied by enterprises in the relevant market in the Party's territory that are investments of investors of the Party, of any other Party or of any non-Party; and

(c)   in its sale of a good or service:

(i)   accords to an enterprise of another Party treatment no less favourable than it accords to enterprises of the Party, of any other Party or of any non-Party; and

(ii) accords to an enterprise that is a covered investment in the Party's territory treatment no less favourable than it accords to enterprises in the relevant market in the Party's territory that are investments of investors of the Party, of any other Party or of any non-Party.

2.   Each Party shall ensure that each of its designated monopolies:

(a)   acts in accordance with commercial considerations in its purchase or sale of the monopoly good or service in the relevant market, except to fulfil any terms of its designation that are not inconsistent with subparagraph (b), (c) or (d);

(b)   in its purchase of the monopoly good or service:

(i)   accords to a good or service supplied by an enterprise of another Party treatment no less favourable than it accords to a like good or a like service supplied by enterprises of the Party, of any other Party or of any non-Party; and

(ii) accords to a good or service supplied by an enterprise that is a covered investment in the Party's territory treatment no less favourable than it accords to a like good or a like service supplied by enterprises in the relevant market in the Party's territory that are investments of investors of the Party, of any other Party or of any non-Party; and

(c)   in its sale of the monopoly good or service:

(i)   accords to an enterprise of another Party treatment no less favourable than it accords to enterprises of the Party, of any other Party or of any non-Party; and

(ii) accords to an enterprise that is a covered investment in the Party's territory treatment no less favourable than it accords to enterprises in the relevant market in the Party's territory that are investments of investors of the Party, of any other Party or of any non-Party; and

(d)   does not use its monopoly position to engage in, either directly or indirectly, including through its dealings with its parent, subsidiaries or other entities the Party or the designated monopoly owns, anticompetitive practices in a non-monopolised market in its territory that negatively affect trade or investment between the Parties.

3.   Paragraphs 1(b) and 1(c) and paragraphs 2(b) and 2(c) do not preclude a state-owned enterprise or designated monopoly from:

    (a)   purchasing or selling goods or services on different terms or conditions including those relating to price; or

    (b)   refusing to purchase or sell goods or services, provided that such differential treatment or refusal is undertaken in accordance with commercial considerations.

Article 17.5: Courts and Administrative Bodies

1.   Each Party shall provide its courts with jurisdiction over civil claims against an enterprise owned or controlled through ownership interests by a foreign government based on a commercial activity carried on in its territory. This shall not be construed to require a Party to provide jurisdiction over such claims if it does not provide jurisdiction over similar claims against enterprises that are not owned or controlled through ownership interests by a foreign government.

2.   Each Party shall ensure that any administrative body that the Party establishes or maintains that regulates a state-owned enterprise exercises its regulatory discretion in an impartial manner with respect to enterprises that it regulates, including enterprises that are not state-owned enterprises.

Notes and Questions

    1.   What advances are made by these provisions? How significant do you expect them to be, if they are enforced?

    2.   China was not party to the TPP negotiations, but the agreement would have been open to non-founding nations to join. Would China be likely to see the excerpted provisions as in China's interests? Would the US see China's acceptance of these provisions as good for the US?

    3.   Why is the antitrust clause (Article 17.4 2(d)) only in paragraph 2 (re designated monopolies) and not in paragraph 1 (re SOEs)? Why is the antitrust clause limited to leveraging a monopoly position into a non-monopolized market in its territory rather than

inclusive of all monopolistic restraints? Would greater coverage in each case be good for competition? a step too far for sovereignty?

4.   Does EU law, for the internal market, prohibit all conduct addressed in TPP Chapter 17? Does it go further? See sections C through H above.

J. CONCLUSION

US antitrust law disciplines private power and private restraints. Other jurisdictions, trying to create markets, face an additional challenge: the state. State restraints, including acts and measures that privilege favored firms, are serious barriers. The European Union led the way in integrating the law against undue public and private restraints. China's young antitrust law significantly targets state restraints. In virtually all jurisdictions, whether or not their law covers state restraints, the competition agencies commonly engage in advocacy against disproportionate competition-harming state and local measures. Increasingly, nations are part of free trade areas that may integrate trade and competition disciplines. The World Trade Organization is, notionally, a logical forum to integrate the disciplines on a world level, but it does so only exceptionally, as in telecoms. The challenge is left to national and regional agendas.

Chapter 7

ENFORCEMENT: SYSTEMS AND INSTITUTIONS

A. INTRODUCTION

As new jurisdictions join the antitrust community, they must not only adopt substantive antitrust rules but also create institutional apparatuses for the enforcement of antitrust law. Usually, the choice of institutional structure is heavily influenced by preexisting constitutional, statutory, administrative, cultural, and historical opportunities and constraints. A variety of institutional systems are emerging around the world. In this chapter, we cannot describe all of the different models. Rather, we introduce some of the standard institutional questions that antitrust regimes must frequently decide.

At the outset, it may be useful to take a quick look at the two most significant institutional models—those of the US and the EU. In the US, antitrust enforcement is both public and private (meaning that both governmental prosecutors and agencies and private litigants may seek to enforce the antitrust laws). On the public side, there are two separate antitrust agencies—the Department of Justice Antitrust Division and the Federal Trade Commission—with much concurrent and overlapping jurisdiction. Every state may also enforce federal antitrust law, as well as its own antitrust laws, through civil actions by the state Attorney General. The Justice Department alone can bring federal criminal enforcement actions. In order to sue civilly, it must bring injunctive actions in federal court. The Federal Trade Commission has a choice of suing in federal district court and hence subjecting itself to ordinary civil litigation rules and procedures or else bringing an administrative action within the agency. However, even when administrative actions are brought within the agency, they are essentially adversarial in nature, with administrative law judges playing the judicial role, agency prosecutorial teams playing the prosecutorial function, and the defendants entitled to a full evidentiary hearing on the record. The full Commission sits as a quasi-appellate court, reviewing administrative law judge decisions, and from Commission decisions the losing defendant may take an appeal to a federal appellate court.

Private enforcement for treble damages is authorized by statute, and in recent years has far outstripped public enforcement (at least in terms of the number of cases filed). Private enforcement can occur in state or federal court and follows ordinary civil litigation rules. Both parties theoretically have a right to demand a jury trial in damages actions, although in practice there are fewer than 10 civil antitrust jury trials a year in the federal system. Prevailing plaintiffs are entitled to automatic trebling of their damages and to collect their attorneys' fees—often in the tens of millions of dollars—from defendants. Defendants are exposed to joint and several liability and members of class actions can usually opt out of the class and pursue individual actions against the defendant.

Federal antitrust law generally does not preempt state regulatory schemes that displace competition with some other regulatory framework. So long as the state clearly and affirmatively articulates a policy to suppress competition in favor of some other objective and actively supervises the anticompetitive scheme, state law prevails over federal law.

The EU system is quite different in many respects. At a European Union level (as opposed to the institutional arrangements within each Member State), the institutions most critical to competition law and policy are the Commission, the Council, and the General Court and the Court of Justice of the European Union. The Commission acts as a collegial body for the good of the whole Community. The members are expected not to pursue national interests. The Commission is often referred to as the executive body of the European Union. It initiates legislative process by drafting legislation in the form of Council Regulation, such as merger control, Commission Regulation, such as for group exemptions for certain common forms of agreement, and Commission Notices, such as safe harbors for de minimis restraints. Also, and very importantly for competition law, the Commission has adjudicative powers. It decides competition law cases that originate with the Commission.

The Council, or Council of Ministers, is comprised of the head of state of each Member State. The constituency changes according to the subject matter at hand, so, for example, the economic ministers sit on economic matters. The Council exercises primary legislative power in the Community. Increasingly in fields other than competition law, it shares power with the European Parliament.

Competition cases may be initiated in the Competition Directorate General of the Commission (Directorate General for Competition or "DG" for short). The Commission has powers to investigate and to obtain documents. The Commission may file a

Statement of Objections, which describes the conduct involved and contains a preliminary assessment. If a compromise is reached at this point, the Commission issues a preliminary assessment with commitments by the entities involved (called "undertakings"). Otherwise, the firms involved may file written objections, submit documents, and request a hearing, which is held before a hearing examiner. The case handlers within the Competition Directorate General draft a preliminary decision. The draft is vetted by the Legal Service (lawyers' lawyers to the various directorates of the Commission and to the other institutions) and by an advisory committee of the Member State representatives. The resulting revised draft decision is submitted to and ordinarily adopted by the College of Commissioners. The firms involved or other persons with a special interest can seek annulment or modification of the decision in the General Court, which is comprised of a judge from each Member State (at present). Either party can appeal the court judgment to the highest court of the European Union, the Court of Justice ("CJEU"), which is comprised of a judge from each Member State. When an appeal is taken to the CJEU, an advocate general is assigned to the case. The advocate general—who has the standing of a judge of the Court—hears the case along with the panel of judges and writes a usually learned opinion, analyzing the facts and law and expressing his or her opinion as to the appropriate outcome. In a high percentage of cases, the Court of Justice adopts the advice of the advocate general. The judgments of both courts must be by consensus; there are no dissents.

Parties often choose to settle investigations by proposing "commitments" to resolve the Commission's investigation. The Commission will not accept proposed commitments without first "market testing" them by seeking public comment. In cartel cases, the Commission or the parties may propose a settlement—essentially, a fine level. If the parties agree on a settlement, the defendants must acknowledge upfront their participation in the cartel, the parties must make an oral or written submission acknowledging their liability and stating that they accept the Commission's statement of objections.

The Commission cannot enforce the Treaty's competition law provisions criminally, nor can private litigants file cases before the Commission. The process is strictly civil and administrative. The Commission's essential coercive power is to order fines, which may be quite large (up to 10% of the defendant corporations' annual worldwide revenue).

Competition law cases may also be initiated by national competition authorities or by private litigants, in national courts.

However, for reasons that will be discussed shortly, private antitrust litigation is far less common in Europe than in the US. If an issue of EU competition law arises in a national court and the interpretation of EU law is not clear, the national court may (and the national court of last resort must) refer the issue to the Court of Justice under Article 267 TFEU. This is called a preliminary reference. In these cases, too, an advocate general provides his or her opinion to the Court.

B. PUBLIC ENFORCEMENT MODELS AND DISTINCTIVE ISSUES

1.   Single Agency or Multiple Agencies?

The US's dual agency system (FTC and Department of Justice) has long been a curiosity. Why would you have two different federal agencies with largely concurrent and overlapping jurisdiction? Every few years some group studies this question and recommends leaving the existing system largely intact. In 2007, the bi-partisan, Congressionally appointed Antitrust Modernization Commission released an evaluative report on the entire gambit of modern US antitrust law. Among other things, the twelve members of the Commission considered whether dual federal enforcement should continue. Three of the twelve—including two former heads of the Antitrust Division—voted to recommend abolishing the FTC's antitrust enforcement authority and vesting responsibility for all antitrust enforcement with the Justice Department. But the majority recommended retaining the dual enforcement structure. With the benefit of nearly 100 years of dual-agency history, the Commissioners asserted that the real justification for continuing with dual enforcement is not any theoretical or practical advantage to having multiple agencies, but rather path dependence: "Although concentrating enforcement authority in a single agency generally would be a superior institutional structure, the significant costs and disruption of moving to a single-agency system at this point in time would likely exceed the benefits." The Commissioners noted further practical difficulties with such a switch: "there is no consensus as to which agency would preferably retain antitrust enforcement authority" and any such move "would likely be politically very difficult."

China's Anti-Monopoly law goes even further than the US and grants antitrust authority to three agencies: the National Development and Reform Commission ("NDRC") with jurisdiction over price-related offenses, the State Administration of Industry and Commerce ("SAIC") with jurisdiction over other non-merger offenses, and the Ministry of Commerce ("MOFCOM") with jurisdiction over merger review.

Nonetheless, the trend in most of emerging antitrust jurisdictions seems to be going in the opposite direction. In 2014, the United Kingdom moved from two agencies—the Office of Fair Trading and the Competition Commission—to a single agency—the Competition and Markets Authority ("CMA"). Brazil consolidated three agencies into a single independent agency: the Brazilian Antitrust Authority—CADE—in 2012. India's 2002 Anti-Monopoly Law created a single Competition Commission. In 2003, Portugal migrated from a two-agency system to a single Competition Authority (Autoridade da Concorrência) consisting of a council (Conselho) and the sole supervisor (Fiscal Único). In 2008, France consolidated its merger and general competition enforcement functions in a new competition authority, although the Economics Minister reserves significant powers to intervene in merger cases based on "industrial development, competitiveness of the undertakings concerned relative to international competition or the creation and preservation of jobs."

Is the handwriting on the wall for the US's multiple-agency system? Probably not. The Antitrust Division and FTC have been around too long and have too many constituencies in high places. Still, for younger antitrust regimes that are open to experimenting with different models, single agency models seem to be the most popular.

2. Administrative vs. Judicial Enforcement

As new antitrust jurisdictions design their own institutions, a fundamental question is whether to prefer an administrative model in which first-instance decisions are handled by a board or agency, or whether instead to make the public enforcer an executive or prosecutorial entity that brings cases before a court or tribunal. A common argument for the administrative model is that it permits competition law experts to handle the matter more efficiently and thoroughly and saves judicial review for appellate courts that can resolve any purely legal questions rather than muddling through complex and contested factual records and obtuse economic questions. On the other hand, proponents of the executive model argue that separation between the investigatory/prosecutorial and adjudicative functions advances the legitimacy of competition law enforcement and increases the quality of decision-making by sharpening the executive's preparation of its case.

Both models—and, sometimes, hybrid models—can be seen in emerging antitrust jurisdictions.

India's 2002 Competition Act creates a Competition Commission consisting of no more than ten members. The Commission has the power to investigate violations of the Act, impose injunctive remedies, and mete out monetary penalties. Article 36 of the Act gives the Commission the right to regulate its own procedures. Appeals may be taken to the National Company Law Appellate Tribunal.

As already noted, China has three separate agencies—NDRC, SAIC, and MOFCOM—that enforce the Antimonopoly Law. These agencies operate as administrative bodies with the power to investigate and issue binding decisions. Affected parties may apply for administrative review or file suit in a Chinese court to annul the administrative decision. (Seeking administrative review does not impair the right to see subsequent judicial review). In the case of merger decisions, administrative practice holds that the parties must first seek administrative review before seeking judicial review.

In contrast to the administrative approach in China and India, South Africa and Chile follow an executive/prosecutorial model. In South Africa, the Competition Commission investigates potential violations of the Competition Act and decides whether to bring a case If the investigation reveals a violation of the Act, the Commission may bring an enforcement action before the Competition Tribunal— a court. From decisions of the Tribunal, appeals can be taken to the Competition Appeal Court.

In Chile, Fiscalía Nacional Económica ("FNE") is an executive department similar to the US Justice Department's Antitrust Division. When it decides to bring a case, it sues before the Tribunal for the Defense of Free Competition (TDLC) and acts as a prosecutor in the proceedings.

3. Due Process, Procedural Fairness, and Rule of Law

Systems that rely primarily on administrative enforcement have come under increasing challenge in recent years by critics that claim that administrative processes often deprive them of procedural rights necessary to fair administration of justice and due process of law. As noted, at the European Commission, defendants are accorded certain rights of defense, including access to the file (excluding confidential documents), a right of written reply, and a hearing before an independent hearing officer. Despite these allowances, calls for reforms to provide greater checks on administrative processes have increased in recent years, particularly as European fines for violations of competition law have swelled to over 1 billion € in some cases.

In *A. Menarini Diagnostics S.R.L. v. Italy,* 43509 Eur. Ct. H.R. 08 (2011), the European Court of Human Rights ("ECtHR") held that Article 6(1) of the European Convention on Human Rights, which guarantees the right to a fair trial in criminal cases, applies in competition cases. In 2001, the *Autorità Garante della Concorrenza e del Mercato (AGCM)*, the Italian competition authority, investigated Menarini, an Italian pharmaceutical company, for price fixing and market division and imposed a € 6 million fine. Menarini brought an action before the ECtHR, arguing that although the enforcement action was classified as administrative under Italian law, it was functionally criminal under the Convention. The ECtHR agreed, holding that whether Article 6 applied could not be predicated on the designation of a particular process as administrative rather than criminal as a matter of domestic law. But despite finding Article 6 applicable, the court held the Article not infringed since the administrative decision had been reviewed by a juridical court with plenary power of review over the administrative decision.

The moral of *Menarini* remains unclear. Some commentators view the decision's precedent as significantly expanding the availability of due process arguments for European defendants charged with competition law violations. In a decision issued shortly after *Menarini, Posten Norge v. EFTA Surveillance Authority,* Case E–15/10 EFTA (April 18, 2012), the European Free Trade Area Court held that Article 6 requires that antitrust defendants be afforded a presumption of innocence. On the other hand, officials at the European Commission lauded *Menarini* as vindicating the Commission's administrative procedures, since the Italian system upheld in *Menarini* was closely predicated on EU procedure.

Questions continue to be raised concerning the adequacy of judicial review of administrative processes. Some critics have argued that the standard of judicial review is too lax. European courts have generally accorded the European Commission a broad "margin of discretion," whereby judicial review is limited "to an examination of the relevance of the facts and of the legal consequences which the Commission deduces therefrom" which limits judicial review to "verifying whether the relevant procedural rules have been complied with, whether the facts have been accurately stated and whether there has been any manifest error of assessment or a misuse of powers." *Consten and Grundig v. Commission,* Case C–56/64, EU:C:1966:41; *Remia v. Commission,* Case 42/84, EU:C:1985:327. Is such a standard of review sufficient in light of the severe consequences of an administrative finding of violation of the TFEU?

After years of criticism from some corners that the European system fails to sufficiently protect defendants' procedural rights, European institutions appear to be responding. In March of 2017, in *United Parcel Service, Inc. v. Commission*, the General Court annulled a 2013 Commission decision prohibiting UPS from acquiring TNT Express NV. The General Court held that that the Commission had violated UPS's due process rights by failing to communicate to UPS a final version of its econometric analysis—which contained substantive changes to the models discussed during the administrative procedure—and therefore had failed to give UPS an opportunity to express its views before adopting its decision. Although acknowledging the need for speed in merger review, the General Court held that at least the essential elements of the Commission's revised econometric analysis should have been communicated to UPS.

C. SPECIALIZED ANTITRUST COURTS

The US has no specialized antitrust court. When the Department of Justice sues, it must do so in the generalist Article III federal district courts. Review from FTC decisions goes to the generalist Article III federal appellate courts. Although there has occasionally been talk about the possibility of creating a specialized antitrust court, the experience with the specialized patent court (the Court of Appeals for the Federal Circuit) has been mixed and a specialized antitrust court is nowhere on the horizon.

Similarly, review from EC decisions are to the General Court and then to the CJEU, neither of which is a specialized antitrust court. The General Court and CJEU may be expected to acquire more antitrust expertise than their sister courts in the US since a higher percentage of their docket is probably competition law cases, but they are still not entirely antitrust specialists.

A number of jurisdictions, however, have experimented with specialized antitrust courts. The Canada Competition Tribunal, created in 1986, is one of the oldest specialized antitrust tribunals. The Tribunal is composed of up to six judicial members appointed from among the judges of the Canadian Federal Court and not more than eight lay members. Appeals from the Competition Tribunal are to the Federal Court of Appeal and from there to the Canadian Supreme Court. Other jurisdictions with specialized antitrust courts include the UK, China, India, and South Africa.

As the complexity of antitrust increases, perhaps we should expect that more jurisdictions will migrate toward specialized antitrust courts. One of the major issues that many developing countries face in implementing an effective antitrust system is a lack of training and economic sophistication in the judiciary. Creating an antitrust court can alleviate some of these concerns, although there may be constitutional or administrative law reasons why this may be difficult or impossible in some jurisdictions.

On the other hand, there are reasons to be skeptical that specialized antitrust courts are better than generalist courts. Generalist courts may be better at seeing the big picture of economic and social consequences of particular decisions, more deferential to agency decision-makers, and less likely to develop "tunnel vision." With the development of more specialized antitrust courts around the world, it will be interesting to compare the performance of generalist and specialized judges and see what lessons can be drawn about their comparative performance.

D. FEDERALISM AND ENFORCEMENT BY MULTIPLE SOVEREIGNS

1. Division of Authority

An issue that arises in federal or quasi-federal systems like the US, Australia, Canada, and the EU is how best to divide authority between the national (or regional) authority and the states, territories, or Member States. The US follows a model of essentially concurrent and equal authority for the federal government (whether FTC or Department of Justice) and the states to bring antitrust enforcement actions. Usually, the state Attorneys General have focused on local or regional issues whereas the Federal Government has pursued large matters of national importance.

The US system has occasionally generated some friction between the federal and state governments. The one high-profile case where some commentators perceived such friction was the *Microsoft* case. In addition to the Department of Justice, a number of states participated in the case as plaintiffs. Judge Richard Posner, who acted as a mediator in the case, complained afterwards that the state Attorneys General were an obstacle to settling the case and proposed a federal statute that would allow the Justice Department to settle cases in a way that would preempt state hold-outs. Needless to say, Judge Posner's proposal generated some controversy. The state antitrust personnel that participated in *Microsoft* have a very different view of their role in the case, viewing their own contributions as important to the development of the legal theories and the evidence and denying that there was friction between federal and state personnel.

The EU has faced its own "federalism" issues" Like the US, the EU system includes a trans-state (indeed, trans-national) authority, the European Commission, trans-state (indeed, trans-national) courts, General Court and CJEU, and national competition authorities and courts in each state. The relationships between these different institutions on a European and national level naturally create complex legal, political, and regulatory policy issues.

One of the major moves in the EU in recent years has been an effort to decentralize competition law decision making and grant increased authority and responsibility to national competition authorities and courts. This has particularly been manifested with respect to the treatment of anticompetitive agreements—what in the US would be analyzed under Section 1 of the Sherman Act and what in the EU is analyzed under Article 101 of the TFEU. Article 101 sets forth a two-stage process for assessing possible anticompetitive effects of such agreements. Article 101(1) catches agreements that prevent, restrict, or distort competition. Article 101(2) declares such agreements void. Article 101(3) states that Article 101(1) may be declared inapplicable [later translated as "an exemption may be given"] if four conditions are met. In essence, the conditions are that the agreement must be on balance procompetitive, efficient or technologically progressive, that competition must be restrained no more than necessary to fulfill these objectives, and consumers must get a fair share of these benefits.

Article 101 needed legislative implementation, and was implemented in 1962 by Regulation 17, which declared that the Commission alone could give Article 101(3) exemptions. Regulation 17 set out a structure for clearing and exempting agreements. Under this structure, if parties notified an agreement, the provision declaring the agreement void was stayed until the Commission ruled on the entitlement to the exemption.

The centralized notification/exemption system required a huge amount of paperwork and analysis, but the process was important for the young European Community. The Competition Directorate General had to get acquainted with the types of restraints business imposed, and to develop policies and rules based on the facts. By the 1990s, however, the balance had shifted. The paperwork and time and effort it took to analyze the thousands of filed agreements were extraordinary, and the workload increased geometrically with the admission of new accession states. Delays were long. The bureaucratic and reactive work drained resources, to the marginalization of major proactive work. Moreover, the structure of the system had resulted in highly rigid and regulatory rules that were out of step with increasingly well accepted modes of economic analysis.

In 2003, the Commission undertook a program of modernization and adopted Council Regulation (EC) No 1/2003. Regulation 1/2003 is printed in Appendix 3. The introduction of Regulation 1 was a dramatic event. It reflected significant procedural reform whereby powers would devolve to Member States but Member States would be obliged to carry out EU law and policy, and a new network of national authorities, combined with continuing sharing of information about all relevant national court judgments, would assure consistency and coherence.

The core of Regulation 1 was the abolition of the requirement that agreements that fall within Article 101(1) must be notified. It makes Article 101(3) directly effective, so that national competition authorities and national courts, as well as the Commission, may decide whether agreements fulfill the requirements of Article 101(3). This sharing of power lightens the Commission's workload, giving it more time to consider more serious restraints of Community-wide interest.

Regulation 1 established the following procedures, among others:

(1)   Article 3 imposes two fundamental obligations on the courts and competition authorities of the Member States, to preserve the realm of EU law. First, where national competition law is applied to agreements and abusive practices that may affect trade between Member States, Article 3(1) imposes the obligation on national authorities and courts to apply Articles 101 and/or 102 concurrently with the national law. Second, Article 3(2) obliges the competition authorities and courts of the Member States not to invoke national law to prohibit agreements or concerted practices that may affect trade between Member States but that are not prohibited by Community competition law. Member States may, however, be more aggressive than Article 102 in applying national laws against abuse of dominance.

(2)   The Commission retains the ability to deal with any case affecting trade between Member States, thereby relieving national authorities of their competence to apply EU law in a particular case. In addition, Article 10 equips the Commission with the sole power to adopt, on its own initiative and when the Community public

interest so requires, ex ante decisions finding that a particular agreement or practice does not infringe Articles 101 or 102. An exercise of Article 10 power precludes national courts and competition authorities from adopting decisions in the same case that would run counter to the Commission's decision.

(3) In order to ensure the consistent application of EU competition law throughout the Community, Regulation 1 creates mechanisms for information sharing and consultation among national competition authorities and the center through the creation of the European Competition Network (ECN)—a robust and well-functioning network that has encouraged cooperation in handling cases, facilitated case allocation, and produced soft convergence of national laws and procedures. Also, national courts are entitled to ask the Commission for its support in the application of Articles 101 and 102, and both national competition authorities and the Commission are empowered to make amicus curiae submissions before the national courts. The Commission is entitled to publish opinions on any particular novel or unresolved questions for the application of Article 101 or 102.

Read Regulation 1/2003 in Appendix 3. Consider its virtues in terms of devolution, empowerment, shared deliberation, cross-fertilization, coherence, and networking. What lessons might Regulation 1 hold for other communities of nations facing multiple and sometimes overlapping systems of law? Although the EU has now withdrawn the notification and exemption system, a large number of jurisdictions have adopted the procedural framework and substance of EU law, and a number of notification and exemption systems remain in place.

Regulation 1/2003's devolution of enforcement authority required new efforts to ensure homogenous application of Articles 101 and 102 TFEU by separate national competition authorities. As noted the ECN serves this function by creating a framework for competition authorities to exchange information and cooperate on cases. In order to ensure successful interaction at the right personnel level, the ECN has created a variety of working groups. There is a Directors' working group for the highest level decision-making, topical expertise working groups (Cartels, Chief Economists, Cooperation and Due Process, Forensic IT, and International), and sectoral working groups (Energy, Environment, Food, Pharmaceuticals, Banking and Financial Services, Sports,

Telecommunications, and Transportation). In many significant cases, national competition authorities have used these processes successfully to coordinate and strengthen their enforcement efforts. As noted in Chapter 3, for example, multiple member states took action to prevent anticompetitive restrictions in the hotel booking sector. Information about these efforts was shared through the ECN.

By most accounts, the ECN has been successful at achieving a high degree of homogeneity and cooperation among national competition authorities in the wake of 1/2003. Still, more work remains. On 22 March 2017, the Commission presented a proposal intended to empower Member States' competition authorities to be more effective enforcers. The proposal aims to ensure that when applying the same legal basis—the EU antitrust rules—national competition authorities have the appropriate enforcement tools in order to bring about a genuine common competition enforcement area. To that end, the proposal provides for minimum guarantees and standards (i.e., funding, investigatory powers, sanctioning tools, leniency programs) to empower national competition authorities to reach their full potential. As of this writing, the proposal for a Directive has been forwarded to the European Parliament and the Council for adoption.

2. Competition Law Preemption of Anticompetitive Local Regulations

One set of issues that often come up in federal systems is whether anticompetitive regulations adopted by local or national governments should be preempted by national or European competition law principles. The US and the EU have developed extensive bodies of law about when state or national laws or regulatory schemes are repugnant to federal or European competition law norms. The issues are complicated, and we will not try to deal with them substantively here. We dealt with aspects of these issues in Chapter 6 on the State.

Focusing on the institutional aspects, it may be of interest to briefly survey a model that was successfully implemented by the Australian Government between 1994 and 2007. In 1994, the Australian government launched a National Competition Policy ("NCP") in order to remedy a relative decline in Australia's economic performance. The NCP committed Australia to a national policy of competition as the key driver of economic performance. A Competition Principles Agreement of 1996 between the federal and state governments contained a "guiding legislative principle" that competition should not be restricted unless the restriction creates some net public benefit that could not be achieved in some way less restrictive of competition. This is called the competitive neutrality principle.

Acting in tandem with the states and territories, the government identified 1,800 pieces of legislation extending across a range of industries and sectors, for competition impact review. The competitive impact reviews were to be undertaken by the governments and bureaucracies of the states and territories. A federal entity—the National Competition Council ("NCC") was assigned a supervisory and consolidating function with respect to the competition impact review effort. The NCC published detailed guidelines for review of the legislation. It listed the following as examples of the types of restrictions that may restrict competition: legislatively created monopolies to provide or operate infrastructure, marketing schemes (particularly in agriculture) or special government-backed initiatives; licensing schemes which restrict entry to particular businesses such as taxi licenses and airline agreements; regulations which restrict entry to particular professions such as the medical profession; quota restrictions to preserve natural resources; regulations which specify strict technical standards for products or services; and administratively determined pricing arrangements for nominated goods and services. The guidelines called for three principal phases of review: (1) establishment of review, determining scope and structure, appointing the review team, ascertaining terms of reference, and ensuring stakeholder involvement; (2) undertaking the review, by clarifying objectives, identifying any restrictions, analyzing costs and benefits, and reviewing alternatives; and (3) implementing the review and recommendations, by promulgating changes to the legislation, ensuring adequate means to facilitate the adjustment, and making a public explanation of the changes.

During the course of the competitive impact review, the states and territories reported their findings and actions to the NCC. The NCC, in turn, consolidated and reviewed the information reported by the states and territories and transmitted the information to the Ministry of the Treasury. An important aspect of the competition review framework was that the federal government committed to make specified payments to the states and territories if they met certain benchmark goals in regulatory reform. The NCC made recommendations to the Treasury about whether the relevant goals had been met and the Treasury made final decisions about deductions from the incentive payments for unmet goals.

The NCP review and incentive payment process ended in the 2005–2006 period. Overall, however, the NCP process appears to have been a success. In February of 2005, the Australian Productivity

Commission (another independent commission) released a report largely praising the effect of the NCP. Among the Commission's findings were that the NCP contributed to the productivity surge that underpinned 13 years of consecutive economic growth and associated strong growth in household incomes, directly reduced the prices of goods and services such as electricity and milk, stimulated business innovation, customer responsiveness, and choice, and helped meet some environmental goals, including the more efficient use of water. One particular area of success was in agricultural marketing. Examples include Queensland ending its export marketing monopoly for barley; Victoria deregulating its monopoly barley marketing arrangements; Western Australia and Tasmania removing supply and marketing restrictions on eggs; Western Australia and South Australia removing entry and pricing restrictions on bulk handling; and all jurisdictions removing centralized price fixing for poultry growing services. PRODUCT COMMISSION, REVIEW OF NATIONAL COMPETITION POLICY REFORMS, PRODUCTIVITY COMMISSION INQUIRY REPORT, No. 33, February 2005 (Austl.).

The Australian example is interesting because it shows how much progress can be made to increase the competitiveness of markets in a federal system when the federal and local governments commit themselves to a reform process and the federal government doles out payments to the local governments as incentives to achieve specified goals. Instead of using a "stick" to coerce local adherence to national competition norms, Australia very successfully relied on a "carrot" approach instead. You have seen other examples in Chapter 6.

The need for national competition law to play a role in preempting anticompetitive local regulations is particularly acute in countries that are transitioning from state-owned and operated to market economies. However, there are often very significant impediments to antitrust law playing this role. For example, China's Anti-Monopoly Law (AML) prohibits abuse of "administrative powers to restrict competition." Administrative abuses include, and the law targets, measures of provincial and local governments that discriminate against and burden the flow of goods from one province or locality into another. The enforcement powers against these abuses are weak, but the competition authorities have had some modest success in rolling back abuses. The law does not exclude from its coverage state-owned enterprises, but the most important and dominant SOEs are in strategic sectors. Enterprises in strategic sectors remain under the supervision of the Chinese state and in some cases they seem as a practical matter to be immune from enforcement by the antitrust authorities.

In June 2016, China's State Council issued its *Opinions of the State Council on Establishing a Fair Competition Review System During the Development of Market-oriented Review System*. The Fair Competition Review System ("FCRS") is designed to prevent actions by state agencies that unduly distort competition. FCRS is so have three facets: (i) public education and awareness campaigns; (ii) development of implementation regulations and mechanisms; and (iii) FCRS reviews of state regulations. As of this writing, it is too early to know how far-reaching the FCRS will be in fostering more pro-competitive regulation in China, but early indications suggest that the measure could be successful in limiting governmental distortions of competition.

E. PRIVATE ENFORCEMENT

In most jurisdictions, antitrust enforcement largely means enforcement by the government—usually a competition commission or public prosecutor. In some jurisdictions, injured persons can sue for compensation only if the government first gets a judgment or order. In the US, however, enforcement has come to be as much or more a private enterprise as a governmental one. Indeed, in raw numerical terms, private lawsuits (those initiated by private plaintiffs) far outnumber public ones. In the federal courts, there are roughly 800–1000 new private lawsuits filed every year compared to fewer than 80 antitrust actions by the Department of Justice Antitrust Division and Federal Trade Commission. The incidence of case filings can be misleading, since the antitrust agencies are involved in many enforcement activities that do not result in the filing of a lawsuit and some private actions are follow-ons to government cases or strategic counterclaims in contract or intellectual property suits. Still, it is clear that private enforcement is an essential part of the US enforcement system. In recent years, almost all of the Supreme Court's antitrust decisions have involved only private parties.

Should the rest of the world follow the US example and open up their enforcement system to private litigants? It's a complicated question. The US private antitrust litigation system is part of a much larger system of private enforcement of law. Culturally, the US has tended to be individualistic, decentralized, and adversarial in its view of rights and wrongs, thus allowing many aspects of society to be governed by private litigation rather than governmental regulation. The US has far more advanced and complex systems and institutions of private litigation than do most other countries. Even if other countries wanted to follow the US model, building the necessary systems would take time.

Still, in many countries there is a growing sense that the government should not be the only antitrust enforcer and that an effective system of private enforcement is necessary for detection and deterrence and is important for compensation. Indeed, many countries have theoretically had a right of private enforcement for a long time, and the move now is to make the theoretical right a practical right.

Unlike in the US's federal system where private antitrust claims can be asserted in both state and federal court, in the EU system there is no procedural vehicle for injured parties to sue antitrust violators in a European court. Private enforcement can take place only within the courts of the Member States. European Union law requires that the Member States provide remedies for persons whose rights under EU law are violated. *See Marshall*, Case C–271/91, EU:C:1993:335. In the *Crehan* case, Case C–453/99, EU:C:2001:465, the European Court of Justice applied these principles to competition law.

However, European litigants have historically faced considerable obstacles to effect private redress for violations of the competition provisions of the TFEU. Among these are the absence of procedural rights enjoyed by US litigants. Collective redress mechanisms (such as class actions) are not generally available, contingency fee arrangements are often prohibited, discovery is unavailable or tightly controlled, and only single damages are allowed. In addition, many European jurisdictions follow the English rule on fee-shifting in which the loser pays the winner's attorney's fees. Such a rule can discourage the initiation of private litigation.

On December 5, 2014, after a ten-year period of study and political engagement, a European Council "Directive on Antitrust Damages Actions" became effective in the European Union. Compliance was required by the end of 2016. Because of the importance of the Directive, we include most of the document below.

DIRECTIVE 2014/104/EU OF THE EUROPEAN PARLIAMENT AND OF THE COUNCIL

of 26 November 2014 on certain rules governing actions for damages under national law for infringements of the competition law provisions of the Member States and of the European Union

(Text with EEA relevance)

[Preamble Omitted]

CHAPTER I

SUBJECT MATTER, SCOPE AND DEFINITIONS

Article 1

SUBJECT MATTER AND SCOPE

1.   This Directive sets out certain rules necessary to ensure that anyone who has suffered harm caused by an infringement of competition law by an undertaking or by an association of undertakings can effectively exercise the right to claim full compensation for that harm from that undertaking or association. It sets out rules fostering undistorted competition in the internal market and removing obstacles to its proper functioning, by ensuring equivalent protection throughout the Union for anyone who has suffered such harm.

2.   This Directive sets out rules coordinating the enforcement of the competition rules by competition authorities and the enforcement of those rules in damages actions before national courts.

Article 2

DEFINITIONS [OMITTED]

Article 3

RIGHT TO FULL COMPENSATION

1.   Member States shall ensure that any natural or legal person who has suffered harm caused by an infringement of competition law is able to claim and to obtain full compensation for that harm.

2.   Full compensation shall place a person who has suffered harm in the position in which that person would have been had the infringement of competition law not been committed. It shall therefore cover the right to compensation for actual loss and for loss of profit, plus the payment of interest.

3.   Full compensation under this Directive shall not lead to overcompensation, whether by means of punitive, multiple or other types of damages.

Article 4

PRINCIPLES OF EFFECTIVENESS AND EQUIVALENCE

In accordance with the principle of effectiveness, Member States shall ensure that all national rules and procedures relating to the exercise of claims for damages are designed and applied in such a way that they do not render practically impossible or excessively difficult the exercise of the Union right to full compensation for harm caused by an infringement of competition law. In accordance with the principle of equivalence, national rules and procedures relating to actions for damages resulting from infringements of Article 101 or 102 TFEU shall not be less favourable to the alleged injured parties than those governing similar actions for damages resulting from infringements of national law.

CHAPTER II

DISCLOSURE OF EVIDENCE

Article 5

DISCLOSURE OF EVIDENCE

1.   Member States shall ensure that in proceedings relating to an action for damages in the Union, upon request of a claimant who has presented a reasoned justification containing reasonably available facts and evidence sufficient to support the plausibility of its claim for damages, national courts are able to order the defendant or a third party to disclose relevant evidence which lies in their control, subject to the conditions set out in this Chapter. Member States shall ensure that national courts are able, upon request of the defendant, to order the claimant or a third party to disclose relevant evidence.

This paragraph is without prejudice to the rights and obligations of national courts under Regulation (EC) No 1206/2001.

2.   Member States shall ensure that national courts are able to order the disclosure of specified items of evidence or relevant categories of evidence circumscribed as precisely and as narrowly as possible on the basis of reasonably available facts in the reasoned justification.

3.   Member States shall ensure that national courts limit the disclosure of evidence to that which is proportionate. In determining whether any disclosure requested by a party is proportionate,

national courts shall consider the legitimate interests of all parties and third parties concerned. They shall, in particular, consider:

(a) the extent to which the claim or defence is supported by available facts and evidence justifying the request to disclose evidence;

(b) the scope and cost of disclosure, especially for any third parties concerned, including preventing non-specific searches for information which is unlikely to be of relevance for the parties in the procedure;

(c) whether the evidence the disclosure of which is sought contains confidential information, especially concerning any third parties, and what arrangements are in place for protecting such confidential information.

4. Member States shall ensure that national courts have the power to order the disclosure of evidence containing confidential information where they consider it relevant to the action for damages. Member States shall ensure that, when ordering the disclosure of such information, national courts have at their disposal effective measures to protect such information.

5. The interest of undertakings to avoid actions for damages following an infringement of competition law shall not constitute an interest that warrants protection.

6. Member States shall ensure that national courts give full effect to applicable legal professional privilege under Union or national law when ordering the disclosure of evidence.

7. Member States shall ensure that those from whom disclosure is sought are provided with an opportunity to be heard before a national court orders disclosure under this Article.

8. Without prejudice to paragraphs 4 and 7 and to Article 6, this Article shall not prevent Member States from maintaining or introducing rules which would lead to wider disclosure of evidence.

Article 6

DISCLOSURE OF EVIDENCE INCLUDED IN THE FILE OF A COMPETITION AUTHORITY

1. Member States shall ensure that, for the purpose of actions for damages, where national courts order the disclosure of evidence included in the file of a competition authority, this Article applies in addition to Article 5.

2.   This Article is without prejudice to the rules and practices on public access to documents under Regulation (EC) No 1049/2001.

3.   This Article is without prejudice to the rules and practices under Union or national law on the protection of internal documents of competition authorities and of correspondence between competition authorities.

4.   When assessing, in accordance with Article 5(3), the proportionality of an order to disclose information, national courts shall, in addition, consider the following:

   (a)   whether the request has been formulated specifically with regard to the nature, subject matter or contents of documents submitted to a competition authority or held in the file thereof, rather than by a non-specific application concerning documents submitted to a competition authority;

   (b)   whether the party requesting disclosure is doing so in relation to an action for damages before a national court; and

   (c)   in relation to paragraphs 5 and 10, or upon request of a competition authority pursuant to paragraph 11, the need to safeguard the effectiveness of the public enforcement of competition law.

5.   National courts may order the disclosure of the following categories of evidence only after a competition authority, by adopting a decision or otherwise, has closed its proceedings:

   (a)   information that was prepared by a natural or legal person specifically for the proceedings of a competition authority;

   (b)   information that the competition authority has drawn up and sent to the parties in the course of its proceedings; and

   (c)   settlement submissions that have been withdrawn.

6.   Member States shall ensure that, for the purpose of actions for damages, national courts cannot at any time order a party or a third party to disclose any of the following categories of evidence:

   (a)   leniency statements; and

   (b)   settlement submissions.

7.   A claimant may present a reasoned request that a national court access the evidence referred to in point (a) or (b) of paragraph 6 for

the sole purpose of ensuring that their contents correspond to the definitions in points (16) and (18) of Article 2. In that assessment, national courts may request assistance only from the competent competition authority. The authors of the evidence in question may also have the possibility to be heard. In no case shall the national court permit other parties or third parties access to that evidence.

8.   If only parts of the evidence requested are covered by paragraph 6, the remaining parts thereof shall, depending on the category under which they fall, be released in accordance with the relevant paragraphs of this Article.

9.   The disclosure of evidence in the file of a competition authority that does not fall into any of the categories listed in this Article may be ordered in actions for damages at any time, without prejudice to this Article.

10.   Member States shall ensure that national courts request the disclosure from a competition authority of evidence included in its file only where no party or third party is reasonably able to provide that evidence.

11.   To the extent that a competition authority is willing to state its views on the proportionality of disclosure requests, it may, acting on its own initiative, submit observations to the national court before which a disclosure order is sought.

Article 7

LIMITS ON THE USE OF EVIDENCE OBTAINED SOLELY THROUGH ACCESS TO THE FILE OF A COMPETITION AUTHORITY

1.   Member States shall ensure that evidence in the categories listed in Article 6(6) which is obtained by a natural or legal person solely through access to the file of a competition authority is either deemed to be inadmissible in actions for damages or is otherwise protected under the applicable national rules to ensure the full effect of the limits on the disclosure of evidence set out in Article 6.

2.   Member States shall ensure that, until a competition authority has closed its proceedings by adopting a decision or otherwise, evidence in the categories listed in Article 6(5) which is obtained by a natural or legal person solely through access to the file of that competition authority is either deemed to be inadmissible in actions for damages or is otherwise protected under the applicable national rules to ensure the full effect of the limits on the disclosure of evidence set out in Article 6.

3.   Member States shall ensure that evidence which is obtained by a natural or legal person solely through access to the file of a competition authority and which does not fall under paragraph 1 or 2, can be used in an action for damages only by that person or by a natural or legal person that succeeded to that person's rights, including a person that acquired that person's claim.

Article 8

PENALTIES

1.   Member States shall ensure that national courts are able effectively to impose penalties on parties, third parties and their legal representatives in the event of any of the following:

(a)   their failure or refusal to comply with the disclosure order of any national court;

(b)   their destruction of relevant evidence;

(c)   their failure or refusal to comply with the obligations imposed by a national court order protecting confidential information;

(d)   their breach of the limits on the use of evidence provided for in this Chapter.

2.   Member States shall ensure that the penalties that can be imposed by national courts are effective, proportionate and dissuasive. The penalties available to national courts shall include, with regard to the behaviour of a party to proceedings for an action for damages, the possibility to draw adverse inferences, such as presuming the relevant issue to be proven or dismissing claims and defences in whole or in part, and the possibility to order the payment of costs.

CHAPTER III

EFFECT OF NATIONAL DECISIONS, LIMITATION PERIODS, JOINT AND SEVERAL LIABILITY

Article 9

EFFECT OF NATIONAL DECISIONS

1.   Member States shall ensure that an infringement of competition law found by a final decision of a national competition authority or by a review court is deemed to be irrefutably established for the purposes of an action for damages brought before their national courts under Article 101 or 102 TFEU or under national competition law.

2.   Member States shall ensure that where a final decision referred to in paragraph 1 is taken in another Member State, that final decision may, in accordance with national law, be presented before their national courts as at least prima facie evidence that an infringement of competition law has occurred and, as appropriate, may be assessed along with any other evidence adduced by the parties.

3.   This Article is without prejudice to the rights and obligations of national courts under Article 267 TFEU.

Article 10

LIMITATION PERIODS

1.   Member States shall, in accordance with this Article, lay down rules applicable to limitation periods for bringing actions for damages. Those rules shall determine when the limitation period begins to run, the duration thereof and the circumstances under which it is interrupted or suspended.

2.   Limitation periods shall not begin to run before the infringement of competition law has ceased and the claimant knows, or can reasonably be expected to know:

   (a)   of the behaviour and the fact that it constitutes an infringement of competition law;

   (b)   of the fact that the infringement of competition law caused harm to it; and

   (c)   the identity of the infringer.

3.   Member States shall ensure that the limitation periods for bringing actions for damages are at least five years.

4.   Member States shall ensure that a limitation period is suspended or, depending on national law, interrupted, if a competition authority takes action for the purpose of the investigation or its proceedings in respect of an infringement of competition law to which the action for damages relates. The suspension shall end at the earliest one year after the infringement decision has become final or after the proceedings are otherwise terminated.

Article 11

JOINT AND SEVERAL LIABILITY

1.   Member States shall ensure that undertakings which have infringed competition law through joint behaviour are jointly and severally liable for the harm caused by the infringement of

competition law; with the effect that each of those undertakings is bound to compensate for the harm in full, and the injured party has the right to require full compensation from any of them until he has been fully compensated.

2.   By way of derogation from paragraph 1, Member States shall ensure that, without prejudice to the right of full compensation as laid down in Article 3, where the infringer is a small or medium-sized enterprise (SME) as defined in Commission Recommendation 2003/361/EC (8), the infringer is liable only to its own direct and indirect purchasers where:

(a)   its market share in the relevant market was below 5 % at any time during the infringement of competition law; and

(b)   the application of the normal rules of joint and several liability would irretrievably jeopardise its economic viability and cause its assets to lose all their value.

3.   The derogation laid down in paragraph 2 shall not apply where:

(a)   the SME has led the infringement of competition law or has coerced other undertakings to participate therein; or

(b)   the SME has previously been found to have infringed competition law.

4.   By way of derogation from paragraph 1, Member States shall ensure that an immunity recipient is jointly and severally liable as follows:

(a)   to its direct or indirect purchasers or providers; and

(b)   to other injured parties only where full compensation cannot be obtained from the other undertakings that were involved in the same infringement of competition law.

Member States shall ensure that any limitation period applicable to cases under this paragraph is reasonable and sufficient to allow injured parties to bring such actions.

5.   Member States shall ensure that an infringer may recover a contribution from any other infringer, the amount of which shall be determined in the light of their relative responsibility for the harm caused by the infringement of competition law. The amount of contribution of an infringer which has been granted immunity from fines under a leniency programme shall not exceed the amount of the harm it caused to its own direct or indirect purchasers or providers.

6.   Member States shall ensure that, to the extent the infringement of competition law caused harm to injured parties other than the direct or indirect purchasers or providers of the infringers, the amount of any contribution from an immunity recipient to other infringers shall be determined in the light of its relative responsibility for that harm.

CHAPTER IV

THE PASSING-ON OF OVERCHARGES

Article 12

PASSING-ON OF OVERCHARGES AND THE RIGHT TO FULL COMPENSATION

1.   To ensure the full effectiveness of the right to full compensation as laid down in Article 3, Member States shall ensure that, in accordance with the rules laid down in this Chapter, compensation of harm can be claimed by anyone who suffered it, irrespective of whether they are direct or indirect purchasers from an infringer, and that compensation of harm exceeding that caused by the infringement of competition law to the claimant, as well as the absence of liability of the infringer, are avoided.

2.   In order to avoid overcompensation, Member States shall lay down procedural rules appropriate to ensure that compensation for actual loss at any level of the supply chain does not exceed the overcharge harm suffered at that level.

3.   This Chapter shall be without prejudice to the right of an injured party to claim and obtain compensation for loss of profits due to a full or partial passing-on of the overcharge.

4.   Member States shall ensure that the rules laid down in this Chapter apply accordingly where the infringement of competition law relates to a supply to the infringer.

5.   Member States shall ensure that the national courts have the power to estimate, in accordance with national procedures, the share of any overcharge that was passed on.

Article 13

PASSING-ON DEFENCE

Member States shall ensure that the defendant in an action for damages can invoke as a defence against a claim for damages the fact that the claimant passed on the whole or part of the overcharge resulting from the infringement of competition law. The burden of proving that the overcharge was passed on shall be on the defendant, who may reasonably require disclosure from the claimant or from third parties.

Article 14

INDIRECT PURCHASERS

1.　Member States shall ensure that, where in an action for damages the existence of a claim for damages or the amount of compensation to be awarded depends on whether, or to what degree, an overcharge was passed on to the claimant, taking into account the commercial practice that price increases are passed on down the supply chain, the burden of proving the existence and scope of such a passing-on shall rest with the claimant, who may reasonably require disclosure from the defendant or from third parties.

2.　In the situation referred to in paragraph 1, the indirect purchaser shall be deemed to have proven that a passing-on to that indirect purchaser occurred where that indirect purchaser has shown that:

(a)　the defendant has committed an infringement of competition law;

(b)　the infringement of competition law has resulted in an overcharge for the direct purchaser of the defendant; and

(c)　the indirect purchaser has purchased the goods or services that were the object of the infringement of competition law, or has purchased goods or services derived from or containing them.

This paragraph shall not apply where the defendant can demonstrate credibly to the satisfaction of the court that the overcharge was not, or was not entirely, passed on to the indirect purchaser.

Article 15

ACTIONS FOR DAMAGES BY CLAIMANTS FROM DIFFERENT LEVELS IN THE SUPPLY CHAIN

1.　To avoid that actions for damages by claimants from different levels in the supply chain lead to a multiple liability or to an absence of liability of the infringer, Member States shall ensure that in assessing whether the burden of proof resulting from the application of Articles 13 and 14 is satisfied, national courts seized of an action for damages are able, by means available under Union or national law, to take due account of any of the following:

(a) actions for damages that are related to the same infringement of competition law, but that are brought by claimants from other levels in the supply chain;

(b) judgments resulting from actions for damages as referred to in point (a);

(c) relevant information in the public domain resulting from the public enforcement of competition law.

2. This Article shall be without prejudice to the rights and obligations of national courts under Article 30 of Regulation (EU) No 1215/2012.

Article 16

GUIDELINES FOR NATIONAL COURTS

The Commission shall issue guidelines for national courts on how to estimate the share of the overcharge which was passed on to the indirect purchaser.

CHAPTER V

QUANTIFICATION OF HARM

Article 17

QUANTIFICATION OF HARM

1. Member States shall ensure that neither the burden nor the standard of proof required for the quantification of harm renders the exercise of the right to damages practically impossible or excessively difficult. Member States shall ensure that the national courts are empowered, in accordance with national procedures, to estimate the amount of harm if it is established that a claimant suffered harm but it is practically impossible or excessively difficult precisely to quantify the harm suffered on the basis of the evidence available.

2. It shall be presumed that cartel infringements cause harm. The infringer shall have the right to rebut that presumption.

3. Member States shall ensure that, in proceedings relating to an action for damages, a national competition authority may, upon request of a national court, assist that national court with respect to the determination of the quantum of damages where that national competition authority considers such assistance to be appropriate.

CHAPTER VI

CONSENSUAL DISPUTE RESOLUTION

Article 18

SUSPENSIVE AND OTHER EFFECTS OF CONSENSUAL DISPUTE RESOLUTION

1. Member States shall ensure that the limitation period for bringing an action for damages is suspended for the duration of any consensual dispute resolution process. The suspension of the limitation period shall apply only with regard to those parties that are or that were involved or represented in the consensual dispute resolution.

2. Without prejudice to provisions of national law in matters of arbitration, Member States shall ensure that national courts seized of an action for damages may suspend their proceedings for up to two years where the parties thereto are involved in consensual dispute resolution concerning the claim covered by that action for damages.

3. A competition authority may consider compensation paid as a result of a consensual settlement and prior to its decision imposing a fine to be a mitigating factor.

Article 19

EFFECT OF CONSENSUAL SETTLEMENTS ON SUBSEQUENT ACTIONS FOR DAMAGES

1. Member States shall ensure that, following a consensual settlement, the claim of the settling injured party is reduced by the settling co-infringer's share of the harm that the infringement of competition law inflicted upon the injured party.

2. Any remaining claim of the settling injured party shall be exercised only against non-settling co-infringers. Non-settling co-infringers shall not be permitted to recover contribution for the remaining claim from the settling co-infringer.

3. By way of derogation from paragraph 2, Member States shall ensure that where the non-settling co-infringers cannot pay the damages that correspond to the remaining claim of the settling injured party, the settling injured party may exercise the remaining claim against the settling co-infringer.

The derogation referred to in the first subparagraph may be expressly excluded under the terms of the consensual settlement.

4. When determining the amount of contribution that a co-infringer may recover from any other co-infringer in accordance with

their relative responsibility for the harm caused by the infringement of competition law, national courts shall take due account of any damages paid pursuant to a prior consensual settlement involving the relevant co-infringer.

Notes and Questions

1.   Implementing the Directive requires affirmative action by each Member State to make the Directive effective in domestic law—a complicated task in some instances given the procedural and institutional differences among Member States. As of February of 2017, only fifteen Member States have communicated to the Commission that they have fully transposed the Directive. *http://ec.europa.eu/ competition/antitrust/actionsdamages/directive_en.html* (last visited June 5, 2017). The Commission anticipates that most Member States will complete the transposition process in the year 2017, but that it will have to remain in dialogue with Member States about whether their transposition fully comports with the directive.

2.   The Directive rejects US law in a number of important ways. Among others, it rejects treble or punitive damages (although it allows for prejudgment interest), allows for standing by indirect purchasers, the pass-on defense (i.e., that a particular plaintiff's damages should be reduced because that plaintiff passed on some of the monopoly overcharge to downstream purchasers), and permits a right of contribution against co-defendants. US law rejects these positions. *See Hanover Shoe, Inc. v. United Shoe Machinery Corp.*, 392 U.S. 481 (1968) (rejected pass-on defense); *Illinois Brick Co. v. Illinois*, 431 U.S. 720 (1977) (rejecting indirect purchaser standing); *Texas Indus., Inc. v. Radcliff Mat., Inc.*, 451 U.S. 630 (1981) (rejecting right of contribution). One way to understand these differences is based on the differing objectives of private enforcement in the two systems. Article 2 of the Directive places compensation of injured parties as the overriding objective of private enforcement in Europe. By contrast, US law tends to treat private litigants as "private attorneys general" who serve the public interest in deterrence. Is it possible for a private litigation system to serve both the compensation and deterrence objectives simultaneously, or must trade-off decisions be made? If so, then which objective should be prioritized?

3.   How much weight should other jurisdictions place on the American experience with private enforcement? In *Chadha v. Bayer Inc.* (2003), 63 O.R. (3d) (C.A.), leave to appeal refused [2003] S.C.C.A. No 106, the Ontario Court of Appeal stated the following: "[W]hile the decisions of the Supreme Court of the United States [particularly *Hanover Shoe* (no pass-on defense) and *Illinois Brick* (no indirect purchaser standing)] deserve serious consideration by this court, they plainly are not binding. Moreover, it appears that the two decisions relied on are based significantly upon policy considerations relating to

the enforcement of American antitrust law. These policy considerations may well differ from the values underlying Canadian competition law. One need look no further than the treble damages remedy which played a significant role in the Supreme Court decisions referred to above." On September 28, 2009, the Ontario Superior Court of Justice issued the first decision by a Canadian court in a contested case certifying a price-fixing class action on behalf of a class including indirect purchasers. In *Irving Paper Limited et al. v. Atofina Chemicals Inc.*, [2009] O.J. No. 4021. Courts in British Columbia and other Canadian provinces have refused similar requests, influenced in part by the US precedents. *See, e.g., Pro-Sys Consultants Ltd. v. Infineon Technologies AG*, 2008 BCSC 575.

4.   Is it a good idea to limit private suits to only those cases in which the government has already established liability in a private suit? Certainly, this diminishes the amount of frivolous litigation. But it also means that private enforcement will not be a robust addition to public enforcement in ferreting out wrong-doing, serving as a counterweight to politically motivated refusals to bring meritorious cases, or bringing additional resources to antitrust enforcement. In 2005, South Korea legislatively abolished its requirement that a prior suit by the Korea Fair Trade Commission (KFTC) must be brought to a successful conclusion before a private suit could be brought and is currently considering other measures to liberalize private enforcement. Private antitrust filings in Korea appear to be growing, with up to 30 cases pending in recent years. COMPETITION POLICY INTERNATIONAL, OVERVIEW OF CURRENT ANTITRUST ENFORCEMENT IN KOREA (2014), *https://www.competitionpolicy international.com/overview-of-current-antitrust-enforcement-in-korea/*.

Private Enforcement in China and Chile: A Comparative Note

Chile is one of the most active competition law jurisdictions in Latin America. As in much of the world, private antitrust has been slowly developing in Chile in recent years. *See generally* Nicolás Lewin & Franciso Borquez, *The Development of Private Enforcement Regarding Damages Actions in Chile* (CPI Antitrust Chronicle, January 2016). Private litigants seeking damages typically await a final decision in the Chilean Competition Defense Tribunal ("TDLC")—Chile's specialized antitrust court, in favor of the National Economic Prosecutor's Office ("FNE") before pressing their damages claim in a civil court as a follow-on action. However, as of this writing there is a division of authority among the lower Chilean courts as to whether a stand-alone action in civil court can be brought. Consumer associations have begun to test the possibility of stand-alone cases.

The Chilean competition statute does not provide directly for class actions, but class actions are allowed under the consumer protection act, and consumers have been allowed to use the consumer protection act to seek damages for violations of the competition act. Chilean courts have not yet resolved the possibility of the pass-on defense and direct purchaser rules, although this has been subject to intensive academic commentary and among the Chilean competition law bar.

Chile does not allow for punitive damages or damages multipliers, and attorney fee shifting is only allowed in rare cases. All defendants are jointly and severally liable and contribution is allowed. The statute of limitations for competition law violations is four years. Significantly, Chile does not recognize a right of compulsory discovery, which impairs the ability of private plaintiffs to obtain evidence to substantiate their claims if the FNE has not already established all of the relevant facts.

Despite procedural and institutional obstacles, private plaintiffs have seen some significant victories. In 2015, for example, a telecom company that was in the business of converting landline calls to cellular calls won a $20 million judgment against Telefonica, a Spanish telecommunications company, on refusal to deal, margin squeeze, and price discrimination claim. Many Chilean observers expect a significant growth in private competition law enforcement in coming years. NICOLAS LEWIN & FRANCISCO BORQUEZ, COMPETITION POLICY INTERNATIONAL, THE DEVELOPMENT OF PRIVATE ENFORCEMENT REGARDING DAMAGES ACTIONS IN CHILE (2016), *https://www.competitionpolicyinternational.com/wp-content/uploads/2016/01/Lewin.pdf.*

China, like Chile, has seen the gradual expansion of private antitrust litigation since the adoption of China's Antimonopoly Law ("AML") in 2007. Article 50 of the AML provides that "[w]here the monopolistic conduct of an undertaking has caused losses to another person, it shall bear civil liabilities according to law," hence creating a private right of action for damages.

Like Chile, China has granted jurisdiction over antitrust cases to specialized or semi-specialized courts. The Intermediate People's Courts, which are ordinarily appellate courts, hear private antitrust cases in most jurisdictions. The apparent rationale for lodging original jurisdiction in an appellate court was the complexity of antitrust cases. Also, in 2014 China established Intellectual Property Courts in Beijing, Shanghai, and Guangzhou, and those courts hear private antitrust cases in their districts.

The Civil Procedure Law permits any plaintiff with a "direct interest" in a case to sue. "Direct" here does not have the "direct injury" sense of US law—indirect purchasers apparently have standing to sue for overcharges. Class actions or group actions brought by public interest associations are in principle permitted, but to date no such actions have been brought.

Chinese law permits private standalone cases, *i.e.,* the private plaintiff need not await a successful public enforcement action. Most cases to date have been standalone proceedings. However, there remains an open question as to whether the People's Courts would permit a private case to proceed if there were an ongoing administrative investigation on the same subject. Further, a finding of liability by the administrative agency does not guarantee success in a private follow-on action. In a widely watched decision in November of 2016, *Junwei Tian v. Beijing Carrefour Shuangjing Store*, the Beijing High Court rejected a private follow-on case on grounds of insufficiency of evidence. The plaintiff purchased a tin of Abbott's infant formula in February of 2013. A few months later, China's National Development and Reform Commission ("NDRC") fined six infant formula suppliers, including Abbott, for engaging in resale price maintenance. The High Court held that the plaintiff could not rely on the NDRC decision, since the Commission had not identified the particular retailers with which Abbott had agreed to RPM. Further, the only contract between Abbott and the retailer admitted into evidence contained only non-binding pricing recommendations, which did not permit an inference of actual RPM.

Despite many obstacles, private enforcement in China is growing. The Supreme People's Court reports 70 cases filed in 2014 and 150 cases in 2015. As with Chile, we can expect the numbers to continue to rise in coming years.

F. CRIMINAL ENFORCEMENT

1. Justifications for Criminal Enforcement

Most countries treat antitrust as a civil and administrative matter and do not impose criminal penalties. The historical exception to this rule is the United States, which aggressively prosecutes cartels and imposes substantial prison sentences on the ring-leaders. Other jurisdictions have adopted criminal enforcement over the years, and more recently, the notion increasingly has gained popularity (a list of jurisdictions with criminal cartel enforcement appears at the end of Chapter 1). In Korea, the Monopoly Regulation and Fair Trade Act was revised in 2013 to facilitate increased criminal prosecutions of individuals who now face a substantial fine and three year prison sentence. In August of 2016, the Parliament of Chile adopted a new criminal provision applicable to hard-core cartels, with the possibility of imprisonment up to ten years. Similarly, in 2016 South Africa introduced individual criminal liability for "knowing acquiescence" in a cartel, with a maximum prison sentence of six months.

Why should a regime consider criminalization of cartel behavior? Consider the following succinct explanation from the Australian Competition & Consumer Commission, which added a criminal component to its cartel law in 2008: "Cartel activity will not be deterred if the potential penalties are perceived by firms and their executives to be outweighed by the potential rewards. Under Australia's existing penalty regime, there was a real danger that, at least for some of the bigger international cartels, the penalties were simply not a deterrent. Imprisonment has no such qualifications—it is a penalty for which no company or shareholder can be forced to pick up the cost."

Consider also the following 2001 statement from the Director General of the British Chambers of Commerce: "If there is a guiding principle that dictates the way we do business in the UK it is that it should be conducted fairly. Anti-competitive practices create weak markets, protect the inefficient, deprive us of choice, stifle innovation and support bad practice. They defraud consumers and break the will of those business people who work hard to pursue their ambitions— the kinds of business people who are my members. . . . It is right that managers should also face sanctions, because they can gain significantly if the companies they work for make excess profits—it feeds through into executive bonuses and share options. Those operating a cartel are engaging in theft and should face a similar sanction. . . ."

Another argument commonly made in favor of criminalizing cartel behavior is that antitrust sanctions need to be applied to individuals, and not merely to corporations, in order to achieve optimal deterrence. Although corporate fines may contribute to deterrence, corporate fines are only effective in changing managerial behavior if corporations are able adequately to police their managers, which is not always the case. Further, a corporate fine has little effect on a culpable manager who has left the corporation since the time of the violation and does not own many of the corporate defendant's shares. Hence, individual criminal liability—including jail time— may be necessary to change business culture and behavior.

Assuming that individuals are criminally prosecuted for antitrust violations, what remedies should be imposed upon convicted defendants that achieve not only general deterrence, but also ameliorate competitive conditions in the future? In recent years, there has been an increasingly vibrant conversation in white collar criminal law circles about suspension and debarment of cartel ringleaders as devices to reform corporate culture and reduce recidivism. For example, under UK law a director involved in a cartel conspiracy may be debarred from continuing to serve as a director. Proponents of debarment argue that it more effectively changes future behavior than fines; skeptics worry that it may detract from criminal fines, which have the potential of deterring violations in the first place.

Even assuming that criminal enforcement against individuals is necessary for adequate deterrence, there remains a fairness question: Is it just to impose criminal penalties for non-fraudulent, non-coercive business agreements that are still legal, or at least culturally accepted, in parts of the world? Consider this fundamental question as you read about leniency programs next.

2.   Leniency

Even beyond the basic question of whether criminal enforcement is appropriate, there is a further question about whether the methods used to "crack" cartel cases are fair. The US has long used various "leniency" tools to encourage cartel members to "rat out" their co-conspirators. The US offers two different forms of leniency. The first, complete amnesty from prosecution, is only available to cartel participants (whether corporate or individual) who are the first to come forward with information about the cartel. The requirements for obtaining amnesty are strict. In the case of a corporation, for example, the cooperator must satisfy six criteria: (1) at the time the corporation came forward, the Antitrust Division had not yet received information about the cartel; (2) the corporation, upon discovering the cartel, took prompt and effective action to terminate its part in the conspiracy; (3) the corporation reports its wrongdoing with candor and completeness and provides continuing cooperation throughout the investigation; (4) the confession is truly a corporate act; (5) where possible, the corporation makes restitution to injured parties; and (6) the corporation did not coerce another party to participate in the illegal activity and was not the leader or originator of the cartel.

If a party does not qualify for amnesty, it may still seek the additional kind of leniency—a reduction in their penalty. In the case of a corporation, this means a lower fine and in the case of an individual, usually a reduced prison sentence. Such a reduction in the fine is available in exchange for "substantial assistance" with an ongoing cartel investigation. As with the amnesty program, there is an incentive to get in earlier, since the fine reduction diminishes the later a defendant comes forward to cooperate. *See* the remarks of Scott Hammond, Chapter 1, Cartels, above.

The European Commission follows a similar amnesty program and fine reduction program, although all of the Commission's enforcement powers are civil and benefits are not reserved for the first in. The following is the Commission's description of its amnesty and leniency program:

In essence, the leniency policy offers companies involved in a cartel—which self-report and hand over evidence—either total immunity from fines or a reduction of fines which the Commission would have otherwise imposed on them. It also benefits the Commission, allowing it not only to pierce the cloak of secrecy in which cartels operate but also to obtain insider evidence of the cartel infringement. The leniency policy also has a very deterrent effect on cartel formation and it destabilizes the operation of existing cartels as it seeds distrust and suspicion among cartel members.

In order to obtain total immunity under the leniency policy, a company which participated in a cartel must be the first one to inform the Commission of an undetected cartel by providing sufficient information to allow the Commission to launch an inspection at the premises of the companies allegedly involved in the cartel. If the Commission is already in possession of enough information to launch an inspection or has already undertaken one, the company must provide evidence that enables the Commission to prove the cartel infringement. In all cases, the company must also fully cooperate with the Commission throughout its procedure, provide it with all evidence in its possession and put an end to the infringement immediately. The cooperation with the Commission implies that the existence and the content of the application cannot be disclosed to any other company. The company may not benefit from immunity if it took steps to coerce other undertakings to participate in the cartel.

Companies which do not qualify for immunity may benefit from a reduction of fines if they provide evidence that represents "significant added value" to that already in the Commission's possession and have terminated their participation in the cartel. Evidence is considered to be of a "significant added value" for the Commission when it reinforces its ability to prove the infringement. The first company to meet these conditions is granted 30 to 50% reduction, the second 20 to 30% and subsequent companies up to 20%.

The Commission considers that any statement submitted to it within the context of its leniency policy forms part of the Commission's file and may therefore not be disclosed or used for any other purpose than the Commission's own cartel proceedings.[33]

Corporate leniency programs have proven so effective at catching cartels (think of the familiar Prisoner's Dilemma to see why) that they have spread quickly around the world. Most jurisdictions with an anti-cartel law also offer some sort of leniency or amnesty to incentivize cartel defections and obtain necessary information to convict other participants. For example, in 2014—ten years into its modern antitrust regime—Egypt amended its competition law to add a cartel leniency provision. In the following year, 2015, Egypt was reportedly able to crack a cartel much more quickly than before— obtaining hard evidence and wrapping up the case quickly through the use of its new leniency tool. *http://globalcompetitionreview.com/ insight/the-european-middle-eastern-and-african-antitrust-review- 2017/1067875/egypt-competition-authority.*

Undoubtedly, leniency can be effective, but some critics claim that it diverts agencies from detection efforts and creates undue complexity. Further, should it bother us that two very similarly situated cartel participants receive very different legal treatment? Does leniency get in the way of other important values, such as compensation and compliance? With the widespread popularity of leniency tools leading to record fines around the world, academics and enforcers have begun increasingly to pose these questions. For a comprehensive look, see ANTI-CARTEL ENFORCEMENT IN A CONTEMPORARY AGE: LENIENCY RELIGION (Caron Beaton-Wells & Christopher Tran, eds., 2015). As you ponder this question, you may want to revisit a question lurking at the foundations of antitrust law—are the purposes of antitrust law only economic, or are they moral as well?

3.   Double Jeopardy and Extradition

In previous times, when the US was virtually alone in vigorously prosecuting cartels, US and foreign executives involved in the same price-fixing conspiracy often received vastly different treatment. The US executives might serve serious prison time while the foreign executives got off scott free. This happened because the foreign executives (unless they happen to be present in the US) were beyond the jurisdiction of the US courts and foreign governments refused to extradite to the US for antitrust violations.

---

[33]   *http://ec.europa.eu/competition/cartels/leniency/leniency.html.*

The US still had some leverage with foreign executives, since for professional reasons many of them needed to be able to travel in the US. So the prevailing practice was for the Justice Department to negotiate a plea deal that had the foreign executives paying a fine but not serving prison time.

In the last decade, this has all begun to change. In 1999, the Justice Department announced a shift in policy, stating that it would no longer allow foreign executives a free pass from jail time. Then, as other jurisdictions began shifting toward criminal enforcement themselves, they began to revisit their traditional reluctance to extradite on antitrust charges. The United Kingdom had long been the leader in resisting extradition to the US for antitrust violations, but has now come to cooperate with US extradition requests. Other countries are now joining suit. In April 2014, Romano Pisciotti, an Italian national, was extradited from Germany to the United States on charges of conspiring to rig bids, fix prices, and allocate market shares for marine hose. According to a US Justice Department press release, this marked the first successfully litigated extradition on an antitrust charge. *https://www.justice.gov/opa/pr/first-ever-extradition-antitrust-charge.*

Although extradition for antitrust offenses remains unlikely in many parts of the world, the arm of criminal justice has certainly grown longer in recent years. Consider the speech by Scott Hammond on cartel enforcement quoted in Chapter 1.

The increasing possibility that international business executives will not only be extradited to the US but also be prosecuted in another jurisdiction raises the possibility of double jeopardy—prosecution twice for the same crime. Formally, successive prosecutions by separate sovereign governments does not count as double jeopardy especially when each suit is based on effects in separate jurisdictions, but one might still worry that in a world of overlapping jurisdiction, multiple layers of criminal and civil enforcement, and aggressive amnesty and leniency programs, the potential for vastly disparate treatment of different members of the same cartel will be aggravated. And this is on top of treble damages in private enforcement actions.

At the same time, antitrust regimes around the world are increasingly cooperating not only to share information leading to the detection and successful prosecution of cartels, but also to coordinate penalties. For example, in 2008 the US Justice Department and several European competition agencies uncovered an international cartel to allocate markets, rig bids, and fix prices for marine hose (a flexible rubber hose used to transfer oil between tankers and storage facilities) that operated in the US, Europe, and Japan. As a result of coordinated prosecutions and plea deals, several defendants were sentenced to concurrent prison terms both in the US and in the UK, which meant that they only ended up serving prison time in the UK where the court imposed the longer sentence. For example, Bryan Allison of Dunlop, Oil & Marine Ltd., a marine hose manufacturer located in Grimsby, UK, was sentenced to pay a $100,000 criminal fine and serve a 24 month prison sentence in the US. However, the UK Crown Court sentenced him to serve 36 months in jail in the UK and, given the concurrent nature of the sentences, he is serving jail time in the UK only.

G. MERGER ENFORCEMENT

An important procedural issue in modern competition law enforcement is the requirement of filing notification of mergers and large acquisitions with governmental antitrust enforcers. In the US, the Hart-Scott-Rodino Act ("HSR") requires firms that meet specified dollar thresholds to file a premerger notification 30 days (or 15 days for an all-cash transaction) prior to closing their merger. The HSR filing goes to both federal antitrust agencies—Department of Justice and FTC—who then decide among themselves which will review the merger. If the 30 days expire without any further action from the government, the parties may close the transaction. However, prior to the expiration of the 30 days, the agencies can issue a "second request" for documents that extends the prohibition on closing the transaction until the parties have substantially completed the document production requested.

The practical effect of the HSR is to transform merger control from an adjudicatory process in the courts, as it was prior to HSR's adoption in 1976, into a largely administrative process where decisions on mergers and compromises over divestiture packages or conduct remedies are made internally within the agencies in a dialogue with the merging parties. Although parties do sometimes chose to comply with second requests and then litigate if the agencies sue for a preliminary injunction, parties often cannot afford the delay and uncertainty inherent in fully satisfying a second request and then waiting for the government to sue, if it's still unhappy with the merger. Hence, parties have a strong incentive to cooperate with the government in order to assuage its concerns or, failing that, to walk away from problematic mergers.

Although people often speak of HSR "clearance," HSR is not a clearance process. The statute does not affect the substance of merger legality under Section 7 of the Clayton Act, nor do the agencies formally "clear" a merger when it goes through the HSR process. Formally, the only legal requirement is that all notifiable mergers be notified and not closed until the various disclosure requirements are satisfied and the waiting period expires. Neither the government nor private parties are formally barred from suing the merging parties after the closure of a merger that the government did not challenge during the HSR review process. There have been a small number of private challenges to such mergers, some by state Attorneys General, and even some by federal agencies. Still, the practical effect of HSR has been to transform merger review into a largely public and largely administrative process in the US.

The EU also has a premerger notification requirement, but it differs from HSR in some important respects. Subject to various exceptions, parties to a "concentration" (the relevant term of art) with a Community dimension (as specified, similarly to HSR, using complex monetary thresholds) must file premerger notification forms and wait for a final decision before closing the transaction. The Commission has exclusive power, vis-à-vis the Member State authorities, to allow or disallow these transactions. The Member States have ceded authority to prevent or authorize such transactions, except when legitimate national interests such as security, plurality of media, or prudential concerns are at stake, and except in certain circumstances when a distinct State market is affected.

In some cases, a concentration even with a Community dimension threatens competition in a distinct market within one Member State. In such cases the Member State authority may ask the Commission to refer the concentration to it, and the Commission *may* grant the reference. But if the affected territory is not a substantial part of the common market, the Commission *must* grant the reference. The Commission may also investigate mergers not of Community dimension at the request of one or more Member States.

Unlike under HSR, some joint ventures—those that are created to "perform[ ] on a lasting basis all of the functions of an autonomous economic entity"—are concentrations that require notification. These joint ventures are called "full-function" joint ventures, and get the benefits of one-stop Merger Regulation if they meet the thresholds.

Despite their differences, the US and the EU share one very important feature—they both require that notification be given *before* the merger closes. Not so in all parts of the world. Some jurisdictions have adopted post-merger notification provisions where the merging parties cannot notify certain categories of merger until they have already closed. For example, South Korea requires pre-merger notification of mergers exceeding certain monetary thresholds and post-merger notification for mergers with lower monetary values. Japan had long followed a post-merger notification system, but in 2009 adopted a new pre-merger notification system for securities acquisitions exceeding the prescribed thresholds.

Premerger notification regulations must specify a number of criteria, including the types of transactions covered, the economic threshold of the transaction, the amount of filing fee, what information must be supplied with the notification, and the required nexus of the transaction to the domestic economy. Consider, for example, Brazil's 2012 introduction of a new mandatory pre-merger notification for all mergers meeting the statutory thresholds. Law No. 12 529/2011. Mergers of foreign companies are included in the statute's coverage if (1) the companies directly operate in Brazil; (2) a vertical or horizontal relationship between the parties could directly affect Brazilian commerce; or (3) the companies export goods or services to Brazil or perform any activities in Brazil. The filing fee is about $26,000 and a substantial amount of information, including a 500-word description of the transaction, corporate financial documents, all agreements involved in the merger, the parties' definition of the relevant market, a description of the business or service of the parties, the structure of demand, an assessment of monopoly purchasing power, an assessment of entry and rivalry conditions, and an assessment of oligopolistic coordination. Plenty to keep lawyers busy!

Premerger notification regimes are now the norm. The increasing number of regimes with merger notification requirements and the variety of the requirements themselves is increasing the complexity and costs of large international mergers. Merger filing fees can be in the tens or hundreds of thousands of dollars, which adds up quickly for the merging parties if exacted in scores of jurisdictions but merger filing fees have become an attractive revenue source for jurisdictions. Should we be concerned about excessive global taxation of mergers? Further, the uncoordinated nature of merger notification and review procedures and timing creates the possibility that national authorities could use their power to delay mergers to exact concessions from the merging parties that have little to do with any anticompetitive effects of a merger. Suppose, for example, that a merger could result in the closure of a plant in a particular jurisdiction or the elimination of local suppliers to the merger companies, even though the merging parties would not obtain any market power from the merger. One could imagine the national competition authority in the affected jurisdiction using its power over the merger process to hold up the merger until it had exacted a promise from the merging parties not to eliminate local jobs or suppliers.

Concerns such as these have led some commentators to call for a unified international merger notification system and the harmonization of procedures for merger review. We return to such issues in Chapter 10 when we consider the possibility of global antitrust governance. In the meantime, it may be useful to consider a list of eight guiding principles for merger review recommended by the International Competition Network ("ICN"), an international network of competition enforcement agencies:

GUIDING PRINCIPLES FOR MERGER NOTIFICATION AND REVIEW PROCEDURES

1.   Sovereignty. Jurisdictions are sovereign with respect to the application of their own laws to mergers.

2.   Transparency. In order to foster consistency, predictability, and fairness, the merger review process should be transparent with respect to the policies, practices, and procedures involved in the review, the identity of the decision-maker(s), the substantive standard of review, and the bases of any adverse enforcement decisions on the merits.

3.   Non-discrimination on the basis of nationality. In the merger review process, jurisdictions should not discriminate in the application of competition laws and regulations on the basis of nationality.

4.   Procedural fairness. Prior to a final adverse decision on the merits, merging parties should be informed of the competitive concerns that form the basis for the proposed adverse decision and the factual basis upon which such concerns are based, and should have an opportunity to express their views in relation to those concerns. Reviewing jurisdictions should provide an opportunity for review of such decisions before a separate adjudicative body. Third parties that believe they would be harmed by potential anticompetitive effects of a proposed transaction should be allowed to express their views in the course of the merger review process.

5.   Efficient, timely, and effective review. The merger review process should provide enforcement agencies with information needed to review the competitive effects of transactions and should not impose unnecessary costs on transactions. The review of transactions should be conducted, and any resulting enforcement decision should be made, within a reasonable and determinable time frame.

6.   Coordination. Jurisdictions reviewing the same transaction should engage in such coordination as would, without compromising

enforcement of domestic laws, enhance the efficiency and effectiveness of the review process and reduce transaction costs.

7.   Convergence. Jurisdictions should seek convergence of merger review processes toward agreed best practices.

8.   Protection of confidential information. The merger review process should provide for the protection of confidential information.

* * *

Understanding antitrust institutions and procedures is critical to understanding the operation of antitrust law. Two different jurisdictions may have identical-sounding substantive laws that operate very differently in practice because of the institutional mechanisms by which they are enforced. Conversely, two different jurisdictions may have very different sounding substantive rules that tend to converge in practice because they are mediated by institutions that wish to bring their national competition law into conformity with comparative or international standards. In this chapter, we have surveyed some of the chief institutional attributes of competition law systems. When studying a new country's competition law, it is always important to be aware not only of what the laws are, but *how* and *by whom* they are enforced.

Chapter 8

EXTRATERRITORIALITY AND JURISDICTION OVER OFFSHORE ACTS

A. INTRODUCTION

In this global economy, where suppliers and buyers participate in global markets and effects of cartels and mergers cross many borders, courts ponder the limits of their jurisdiction. When does the competition law of one nation reach an off-shore cartel or merger? When does it reach acts and strategies of dominant firms located abroad that affect the nation's market?

In the United States, for many years these questions were identified as questions of "subject matter jurisdiction"—Does the court have jurisdiction over the subject matter of the claim? Today the US procedural terminology may be "reach of the law," for the question is not jurisdictional for purposes of when the issue must be resolved and which party has the burden of proof.[1] We are not concerned here with the procedural aspects and will use the two terms interchangeably.

"Extraterritorial" may in some sense be an obsolete or not-quite-descriptive term. Each nation has an interest in controlling activity that harms competition in its borders and in its commerce. Suppose a price-fixing cartel in Asia of a product solely or mostly demanded in the US. To the United States, the effects are territorial. The practical question is, Can US institutions reach the offenders?[2] Suppose now a price-fixing cartel in Asia that affects the whole world. There is then a question of harm in the global commons and who may and should regulate the global commons. And suppose, third, the Asia-based cartel is desired and supported by the home government of the price-fixers to advance its industrial policy, or the home government claims the activity is not a cartel at all. We then have

---

[1]   Morrison v. National Australia Bank, 561 U.S. 247 (2010).

[2]   One procedural issue is personal jurisdiction: Do the actors have sufficient contacts in the United States, so that they can be "found" in the United States, and can they and will they in fact be reached by US process bringing them before US courts. We do not cover these questions.

questions of competing interests of sovereign nations and how to resolve them in the absence of supra-national law. Supra-national law would be a logical solution, all things being equal. But all things are not equal and there is virtually no supra-national law of antitrust. See Chapter 9, Global Governance.

The US has a larger, more developed body of case law on subject matter jurisdiction than any other nation or community. Since the 1940s, US courts have had "effects" jurisdiction; that is, if foreigners act abroad, with the intent to affect US commerce, and they cause a direct effect on US commerce, the US courts have subject matter jurisdiction and the Sherman Act applies. *United States v. Aluminum Co. of America*, 148 F.2d 416 (2d Cir. 1945) ("Alcoa"). US courts may not, however, require foreign firms acting in their home territory to do what their home governments forbid, or to abstain from doing what the home government requires, for such an order would interfere impermissibly with the sovereignty of the foreign state. See *United States v. Watchmakers of Switzerland Info. Center*, 1963 (CCH) Trade Cas. ¶ 70,600 (S.D.N.Y. 1962); 1965 (CCH) Trade Cas. ¶ 71,352 (S.D.N.Y. 1965) (judgment revised to apply only to conduct that operated outside of Switzerland).

In the 1960s and 1970s, applications of the *Alcoa* doctrine were subject to criticism by various nations, especially Great Britain, whose nationals were sued for treble damages in US courts as members of world cartels that had targeted American buyers. Cases against Rio Tinto Zinc and its co-conspirators in a world-wide uranium cartel targeted at Westinghouse (the big user of enriched uranium in electricity generators) and at the US in general caused an outcry by the British. The uranium cartel cases, along with proceedings against a shipping conference, led to Britain's enactment of a blocking and clawback statute, the British Protecting of Trading Interests Act, 1980, ch. 11. The blocking provisions blocked the production of UK-based documents for purposes of foreign litigation. The clawback provisions allowed a British firm to recover (to "claw back") in Great Britain penal damages paid pursuant to a foreign judgment. Hence, two-thirds of treble damages awards could be retrieved. Various other nations, including France, Germany, Australia, and Canada, also adopted blocking or clawback statutes. See Restatement (Third) of Foreign Relations Law of the United States § 442, Reporters' Note No. 4 (1987).

In response to the criticism and to threats of retaliation by trading partners, some US courts developed balancing principles, on the theory that courts either lack jurisdiction or should refrain from exercising jurisdiction if foreign nations' and foreign nationals' interests in non-application of US law outweigh the US interests in enforcement. *Timberlane Lumber Co. v. Bank of America*, 549 F.2d 597 (9th Cir. 1976); *Mannington Mills, Inc. v. Congoleum Corp.*, 595 F.2d 1287 (3d Cir. 1979). However, at least one other American court observed that a court cannot balance incommensurables (i.e., American interests in antitrust enforcement cannot be balanced against British interests against it), and the court declared that it had concurrent jurisdiction with UK courts over a conspiracy among American, British, and other airlines allegedly designed to destroy maverick Freddie Laker's no-frills "sky train" that featured low-cost flights between London and New York. *Laker Airways Ltd. v. Sabena, Belgian World Airlines*, 731 F.2d 909 (D.C. Cir. 1984).

In 1982, the US Congress, responding especially to concerns of American business that US antitrust law was following them into foreign markets and also to give more certainty to foreign trading partners, adopted the Foreign Trade Antitrust Improvements Act ("FTAIA"). The FTAIA clarified or cut back the reach of the Sherman Act in matters involving foreign commerce, principally to protect US sellers from Sherman Act challenges for their activity abroad. Thus export cartels that hurt only foreigners are clearly not covered by the Sherman Act. Second, import commerce is clearly still covered by the Sherman Act under pre-existing rules, for the FTAIA explicitly does not apply to it. Otherwise, however, the statute is convoluted. This did not matter much for nearly two decades, during which the questions that arose were principally whether claimed harm was only abroad and therefore not covered by the Sherman Act. Then, in the late 1990s and early 2000s, a dramatic new construction was claimed for a clause in the FTAIA that would cut back the Sherman Act considerably, and this construction won. The Supreme Court case declaring the new construction is *Empagran*, which we cover below. To prepare for this material, we set forth the important language of the FTAIA, to which we shall return to.

As to all other [all non-import] commerce with foreign nations, the FTAIA provides that the Sherman Act shall not apply unless:

(1) such conduct has a direct, substantial and reasonably foreseeable effect—

(A) on [domestic] trade or commerce . . . or

(B) on export trade or commerce . . . [and]

(2) such effect gives rise to a claim under [the Sherman Act] other than this section.

The cases that follow provide fuller explanations of the effects test for establishing jurisdiction, comity limitations, and the meaning of the FTAIA. In part B we study three foundational cases among others—the EU's *Wood Pulp* judgment and the US's *Hartford Fire* and *Empagran* decisions, and then turn to a modern series of cases involving input cartels abroad, assembly of the inputs into finished devices abroad, and then sale of the finished product into the regulating jurisdiction.

B. THE EFFECTS TEST AND COMITY CONCERNS

In Chapter 1, particularly in the Chinese *Vitamin C* cartel case, we saw that comity concerns may play a role in cartel cases in the form of defenses and their equivalents even when the effect on US commerce is direct, substantial, and foreseeable. You may wish to revisit *Vitamin C* (Chapter 1.F.2. supra) now. The following cases are principally about the effects test and reach of the law. We begin with the *Wood Pulp* case of the EU, which previously had resisted adopting an effects test.

Å. ÅHLSTRÖM OSAKEYHTIÖ v. COMMISSION (*WOOD PULP*)

(jurisdiction)(for proof of agreement, see Chapter 1)
Cases C–89, 104, 114, 116–117, 125–129/85, ECLI:EU:C:1988:447
(European Court of Justice, 1988)

[The Commission brought proceedings against 41 wood pulp producers from the United States, Canada, and Finland and two of their trade associations for allegedly making concerted price announcements and fixing prices. The Commission found infringements and imposed fines. The firms sued for annulment both for lack of agreement and lack of jurisdiction. The jurisdictional issue came before the Court first. The Court found jurisdiction, but later found that there was insufficient evidence to infer agreement. In the portions of the opinion that appear below, the court established the existence of jurisdiction over conduct that occurred outside the territorial boundaries of the European Union.]

[3] [T]he Commission set out the grounds which in its view justify the Community's jurisdiction to apply Article [101] of the Treaty to the concertation in question. It stated first that all the addressees of the decision were either exporting directly to purchasers within the Community or were doing business within the Community through branches, subsidiaries, agencies or other establishments in the Community. It further pointed out that the concertation applied to the vast majority of the sales of those undertakings to and in the Community. Finally it stated that two-thirds of total shipments and 60 per cent of consumption of the product in question in the Community had been affected by such concertation. The Commission

concluded that 'the effect of the agreements and practices on prices announced and/or charged to customers and on resale of pulp within the EEC was therefore not only substantial but intended, and was the primary and direct result of the agreements and practices'. * * *

[6] All the applicants which have made submissions regarding jurisdiction maintain first of all that by applying the competition rules of the Treaty to them the Commission has misconstrued the territorial scope of Article [101]. They note that in its judgment of 14 July 1972 (Case 48/69, *ICI v. EC*: [1972] ECR 619) the Court did not adopt the 'effects doctrine' but emphasized that the case involved conduct restricting competition within the Common Market because of the activities of subsidiaries which could be imputed to the parent companies. The applicants add that even if there is a basis in Community law for applying Article [101] to them, the action of applying the rule interpreted in that way would be contrary to public international law which precludes any claim by the Community to regulate conduct restricting competition adopted outside the territory of the Community merely by reason of the economic repercussions which that conduct produces within the Community.

[7] The applicants which are members of the KEA further submit that the application of Community competition rules to them is contrary to public international law in so far as it is in breach of the principle of non-interference. They maintain that in this case the application of Article [101] harmed the interest of the United States in promoting exports by United States undertakings as recognized in the Webb-Pomerene Act of 1918 under which export associations, like the KEA, are exempt from United States antitrust laws.

[8] Certain Canadian applicants also maintain that by imposing fines on them and making reduction of those fines conditional on the producers giving undertakings as to their future conduct the Commission has infringed Canada's sovereignty and thus breached the principle of international comity. * * *

Incorrect assessment of the territorial scope of Article [101] of the Treaty and incompatibility of the decision with public international law

(a) The individual undertakings

[11] In so far as the submission concerning the infringement of Article [101] of the Treaty itself is concerned, it should be recalled that that provision prohibits all agreements between undertakings and concerted practices which may affect trade between member-States and which have as their object or effect the restriction of competition within the Common Market are prohibited.

[12] It should be noted that the main sources of supply of wood pulp are outside the Community, in Canada, the United States, Sweden and Finland and that the market therefore has global dimensions. Where wood pulp producers established in those countries sell directly to purchasers established in the Community and engage in price competition in order to win orders from those customers, that constitutes competition within the Common Market.

[13] It follows that where those producers concert on the prices to be charged to their customers in the Community and put that concertation into effect by selling at prices which are actually co-ordinated, they are taking part in concertation which has the object and effect of restricting competition within the Common Market within the meaning of Article [101] of the Treaty.

[14] Accordingly, it must be concluded that by applying the competition rules in the Treaty in the circumstances of this case to undertakings whose registered offices are situated outside the Community, the Commission has not made an incorrect assessment of the territorial scope of Article [101].

[15] The applicants have submitted that the decision is incompatible with public international law on the grounds that the application of the competition rules in this case was founded exclusively on the economic repercussions within the Common Market of conduct restricting competition which was adopted outside the Community.

[16] It should be observed that an infringement of Article [101], such as the conclusion of an agreement which has had the effect of restricting competition within the Common Market, consists of conduct made up of two elements, the formation of the agreement, decision or concerted practice and the implementation thereof. If the applicability of prohibitions laid down under competition law were made to depend on the place where the agreement, decision or concerted practice was formed, the result would obviously be to give undertakings an easy means of evading those prohibitions. The decisive factor is therefore the place where it is implemented.

[17] The producers in this case implemented their pricing agreement within the Common Market. It is immaterial in that respect whether or not they had recourse to subsidiaries, agents, sub-agents, or branches within the Community in order to make their contacts with purchasers within the Community.

[18] Accordingly the Community's jurisdiction to apply its competition rules to such conduct is covered by the territoriality principle as universally recognized in public international law.

[19] As regards the argument based on the Infringement of the principle of non-interference, it should be pointed out that the applicants who are members of KEA have referred to a rule according to which where two States have jurisdiction to lay down and enforce rules and the effect of those rules is that a person finds himself subject to contradictory orders as to the conduct he must adopt, each State is obliged to exercise its jurisdiction with moderation. The applicants have concluded that by disregarding that rule in applying its competition rules the Community has infringed the principle of non-interference.

[20] There is no need to enquire into the existence in international law of such a rule since it suffices to observe that the conditions for its application are in any event not satisfied. There is not, in this case, any contradiction between the conduct required by the United States and that required by the Community since the Webb-Pomerene Act merely exempts the conclusion of export cartels from the application of United States antitrust laws but does not require such cartels to be concluded.

[21] It should further be pointed out that the United States authorities raised no objections regarding any conflict of jurisdiction when consulted by the Commission pursuant to the OECD Council Recommendation of 25 October 1979 concerning Co-operation between member Countries on Restrictive Business Practices affecting International Trade.

[22] As regards the argument relating to disregard of international comity, it suffices to observe that it amounts to calling in question the Community's jurisdiction to apply its competition rules to conduct such as that found to exist in this case and that, as such, that argument has already been rejected.

[23] Accordingly it must be concluded that the Commission's decision is not contrary to Article [101] of the Treaty or to the rules of public international law relied on by the applicants.

(b) KEA

[24] According to its Articles of Association, KEA is a non-profit-making association whose purpose is the promotion of the commercial interests of its members in the exportation of their products and it serves primarily as a clearing-house for its members for information regarding their export markets. KEA does not itself engage in manufacture, selling or distribution.

[25] It should further be pointed out that within KEA a number of groups have been formed, including the Pulp Group, to cover the different sectors of the pulp and paper industry. Under Article I of

the By-Laws of KEA, undertakings may only join KEA by becoming a member of one of those groups. Article II of the By-Laws provides that the groups enjoy full independence in the management of their affairs.

[26] It should lastly be noted that according to a policy statement adopted by the Pulp Group, . . . the members of the group may conclude price agreements at meetings which they hold from time to time provided that each member is informed in advance that prices will be discussed and that the meeting is quorate. The unanimous agreement of the members present is also binding on members who are absent when the decision is adopted.

[27] It is apparent from the foregoing that KEA's price recommendations cannot be distinguished from the pricing agreements concluded by undertakings which are members of the Pulp Group and that KEA has not played a separate role in the implementation of those agreements.

[28] In those circumstances the decision should be declared void in so far as it concerns KEA.

Notes and Questions

1.   *Wood Pulp* established a form of effects jurisdiction for Europe. The basis for jurisdiction was later to be applied to off-shore mergers that were sufficiently linked to Europe to allow a conclusion that the merger was implemented in Europe, as we saw in Chapter 6 on Mergers: *Gencor/Lonrho*. Later, in *Intel*, Case C–413/14P, 6 Sept. 2017, the Court of Justice of the EU endorsed the "qualified effects" doctrine, allowing jurisdiction when it is foreseeable that the off-shore conduct will have an immediate and substantial effect in the European Economic Area. Does this make the EU test substantially the same as the US test?

2.   Why did the EU dismiss KEA? Would there be any advantages to including the trade association that was the forum for the cartel?

3.   Not long after *Wood Pulp*, the US Supreme Court also decided a major case on point.

HARTFORD FIRE INS. CO. v. CALIFORNIA
509 U.S. 764 (1993)

[Lloyds of London reinsurers had allegedly collaborated with US insurers and also among themselves in London to limit reinsurance in the US market. Their agreements not to supply certain high risk coverage, and therefore to "boycott" the forums that included such coverage, were specifically directed at the US market. When sued, the British reinsurers moved to dismiss, arguing that comity required dismissal. In the passage that follows, the Supreme Court rejected the British reinsurers' argument.]

JUSTICE SOUTER: * * *

Finally, we take up the question presented, whether certain claims against the London reinsurers should have been dismissed as improper applications of the Sherman Act to foreign conduct. The Fifth Claim for Relief in the California Complaint alleges a violation of § 1 of the Sherman Act by certain London reinsurers who conspired to coerce primary insurers in the United States to offer CGL coverage on a claims-made basis, thereby making "occurrence CGL coverage . . . unavailable in the State of California for many risks." The Sixth Claim for Relief in the California Complaint alleges that the London reinsurers violated § 1 by a conspiracy to limit coverage of pollution risks in North America, thereby rendering "pollution liability coverage . . . almost entirely unavailable for the vast majority of casualty insurance purchasers in the State of California." The Eighth Claim for Relief in the California Complaint alleges a further § 1 violation by the London reinsurers who, along with domestic retrocessional reinsurers, conspired to limit coverage of seepage, pollution, and property contamination risks in North America, thereby eliminating such coverage in the State of California.

At the outset, we note that the District Court undoubtedly had jurisdiction of these Sherman Act claims, as the London reinsurers apparently concede. . . . Although the proposition was perhaps not always free from doubt, see *American Banana Co. v. United Fruit Co.*, 213 US 347 (1909), it is well established by now that the Sherman Act applies to foreign conduct that was meant to produce and did in fact produce some substantial effect in the United States. See *Matsushita Elec. Industrial Co. v. Zenith Radio Corp.*, 475 US 574, 582, n. 6 (1986); *United States v. Aluminum Co. of America*, 148 F.2d 416, 444 (CA2 1945) (L. Hand, J.); Restatement (Third) of Foreign Relations Law of the United States § 415, and Reporters' Note 3 (1987) (hereinafter Restatement (Third) Foreign Relations Law); 1 P. Areeda & D. Turner, Antitrust Law ¶ 236 (1978). . . . Such is the conduct alleged here: that the London reinsurers engaged in unlawful conspiracies to affect the market for insurance in the United States and that their conduct in fact produced substantial effect.

According to the London reinsurers, the District Court should have declined to exercise such jurisdiction under the principle of international comity. The Court of Appeals agreed that courts should look to that principle in deciding whether to exercise jurisdiction under the Sherman Act. This availed the London reinsurers nothing, however. To be sure, the Court of Appeals believed that "application of [American] antitrust laws to the London reinsurance market 'would lead to significant conflict with English law and policy,' " and that "[s]uch a conflict, unless outweighed by other factors, would by itself be reason to decline exercise of jurisdiction." But other factors, in the court's view, including the London reinsurers' express purpose to affect United States commerce and the substantial nature of the effect produced, outweighed the supposed conflict and required the exercise of jurisdiction in this litigation.

When it enacted the FTAIA, Congress expressed no view on the question whether a court with Sherman Act jurisdiction should ever decline to exercise such jurisdiction on grounds of international comity. See H.R.Rep. No. 97–686, p. 13 (1982) ("If a court determines that the requirements for subject matter jurisdiction are met, [the FTAIA] would have no effect on the court['s] ability to employ notions of comity . . . or otherwise to take account of the international character of the transaction") (citing *Timberlane*). We need not decide that question here, however, for even assuming that in a proper case a court may decline to exercise Sherman Act jurisdiction over foreign conduct (or, as Justice Scalia would put it, may conclude by the employment of comity analysis in the first instance that there is no jurisdiction), international comity would not counsel against exercising jurisdiction in the circumstances alleged here.

The only substantial question in this litigation is whether "there is in fact a true conflict between domestic and foreign law." *Société Nationale Industrielle Aérospatiale v. United States Dist. Court for Southern Dist. of Iowa,* 482 US 522, 555 (1987) (Blackmun, J., concurring in part and dissenting in part). The London reinsurers contend that applying the Act to their conduct would conflict significantly with British law, and the British Government, appearing before us as *amicus curiae,* concurs. They assert that Parliament has established a comprehensive regulatory regime over the London reinsurance market and that the conduct alleged here was perfectly consistent with British law and policy. But this is not to state a conflict. "[T]he fact that conduct is lawful in the state in which it took place will not, of itself, bar application of the United States antitrust laws," even where the foreign state has a strong policy to permit or encourage such conduct. Restatement (Third) Foreign Relations Law § 415, Comment *j;* see *Continental Ore Co., supra,* 370 US, at 706–707. No conflict exists, for these purposes, "where a person subject to regulation by two states can comply with the laws of both." Restatement (Third) Foreign Relations Law § 403, Comment *e.* Since the London reinsurers do not argue that British law requires them to act in some fashion prohibited by the law of the

United States, or claim that their compliance with the laws of both countries is otherwise impossible, we see no conflict with British law. See Restatement (Third) Foreign Relations Law § 403, Comment *e,* § 415, Comment *j.* We have no need in this litigation to address other considerations that might inform a decision to refrain from the exercise of jurisdiction on grounds of international comity.

* * *

JUSTICE SCALIA, dissenting in part, joined by JUSTICES O'CONNOR, KENNEDY, and THOMAS:

Petitioners, various British corporations and other British subjects, argue that certain of the claims against them constitute an inappropriate extraterritorial application of the Sherman Act. It is important to distinguish two distinct questions raised by this petition: whether the District Court had jurisdiction, and whether the Sherman Act reaches the extraterritorial conduct alleged here. On the first question, I believe that the District Court had subject-matter jurisdiction over the Sherman Act claims against all the defendants (personal jurisdiction is not contested). Respondents asserted nonfrivolous claims under the Sherman Act, and 28 U.S.C. § 1331 vests district courts with subject-matter jurisdiction over cases "arising under" federal statutes.

The second question—the extraterritorial reach of the Sherman Act—has nothing to do with the jurisdiction of the courts. It is a question of substantive law turning on whether, in enacting the Sherman Act, Congress asserted regulatory power over the challenged conduct. If a plaintiff fails to prevail on this issue, the court does not dismiss the claim for want of subject-matter jurisdiction—want of power to adjudicate; rather, it decides the claim, ruling on the merits that the plaintiff has failed to state a cause of action under the relevant statute.

There is, however, a type of "jurisdiction" relevant to determining the extraterritorial reach of a statute; it is known as "legislative jurisdiction," "jurisdiction to prescribe." This refers to "the authority of a state to make its law applicable to persons or activities," and is quite a separate matter from "jurisdiction to adjudicate." There is no doubt, of course, that Congress possesses legislative jurisdiction over the acts alleged in this complaint. But the question in this litigation is whether, and to what extent, Congress *has* exercised that undoubted legislative jurisdiction in enacting the Sherman Act.

Two canons of statutory construction are relevant in this inquiry. The first is the "longstanding principle of American law 'that legislation of Congress, unless a contrary intent appears, is meant to apply only within the territorial jurisdiction of the United States.' " ... The Sherman Act contains ... "boilerplate language," [coverage of foreign commerce] and if the question were not governed by precedent, it would be worth considering whether that presumption controls the outcome here. We have, however, found the presumption to be overcome with respect to our antitrust laws; it is now well established that the Sherman Act applies extraterritorially.

But if the presumption against extraterritoriality has been overcome or is otherwise inapplicable, a second canon of statutory construction becomes relevant: "[A]n act of congress ought never to be construed to violate the law of nations if any other possible construction remains." *Murray v. Schooner Charming Betsy,* 2 Cranch 64 (1804) (Marshall, C.J.). This canon ... is relevant to determining the substantive reach of a statute because "the law of nations," or customary international law, includes limitations on a nation's exercise of its jurisdiction to prescribe. See Restatement (Third) §§ 401–416. Though it clearly has constitutional authority to do so, Congress is generally presumed not to have exceeded those customary international-law limits on jurisdiction to prescribe.

Consistent with that presumption, this and other courts have frequently recognized that, even where the presumption against extraterritoriality does not apply, statutes should not be interpreted to regulate foreign persons or conduct if that regulation would conflict with principles of international law.

* * *

... [T]he principle was expressed in *United States v. Aluminum Co. of America,* 148 F.2d 416 (CA2 1945), the decision that established the extraterritorial reach of the Sherman Act. In his opinion for the court, Judge Learned Hand cautioned "we are not to read general words, such as those in [the Sherman] Act, without regard to the limitations customarily observed by nations upon the exercise of their powers; limitations which generally correspond to those fixed by the 'Conflict of Laws.' " *Id.,* at 443.

More recent lower court precedent has also tempered the extraterritorial application of the Sherman Act with considerations of "international comity.". . . . The "comity" they refer to is not the comity of courts, whereby judges decline to exercise jurisdiction over matters more appropriately adjudged elsewhere, but rather what might be termed "prescriptive comity": the respect sovereign nations afford each other by limiting the reach of their laws. That comity is exercised by legislatures when they enact laws, and courts assume it has been exercised when they come to interpreting the scope of laws their legislatures have enacted. It is a traditional component of choice-of-law theory. Comity in this sense includes the choice-of-law principles that, "in the absence of contrary congressional direction," are assumed to be incorporated into our substantive laws having extraterritorial reach. Considering comity in this way is just part of determining whether the Sherman Act prohibits the conduct at issue.

In sum, the practice of using international law to limit the extraterritorial reach of statutes is firmly established in our jurisprudence. In proceeding to apply that practice to the present cases, I shall rely on the Restatement (Third) for the relevant principles of international law.

Under the Restatement, a nation having some "basis" for jurisdiction to prescribe law should nonetheless refrain from exercising that jurisdiction "with respect to a person or activity having connections with another state when the exercise of such jurisdiction is unreasonable." Restatement (Third) § 403(1). The "reasonableness" inquiry turns on a number of factors including, but not limited to: "the extent to which the activity takes place within the territory [of the regulating state]," id., § 403(2)(a); "the connections, such as nationality, residence, or economic activity, between the regulating state and the person principally responsible for the activity to be regulated," id., § 403(2)(b); "the character of the activity to be regulated, the importance of regulation to the regulating state, the extent to which other states regulate such activities, and the degree to which the desirability of such regulation is generally accepted," id., § 403(2)(c); "the extent to which another state may have an interest in regulating the activity," id., § 403(2)(g); and "the likelihood of conflict with regulation by another state," id., § 403(2)(h). Rarely would these factors point more clearly against application of United States law. The activity relevant to the counts at issue here took place primarily in the United Kingdom, and the defendants in these counts are British corporations and British subjects having their principal place of business or residence outside the United States. Great Britain has established a comprehensive regulatory scheme governing the London reinsurance markets, and clearly has a heavy "interest in regulating the activity," id., § 403(2)(g). Finally, § 2(b) of the McCarran-Ferguson Act allows state regulatory statutes to override the Sherman Act in the insurance field, subject only to the narrow "boycott" exception set forth in § 3(b)—suggesting that "the importance of regulation to the [United States]," Restatement (Third) § 403(2)(c), is slight. Considering these factors, I think it unimaginable that an assertion of legislative jurisdiction by the United States would be considered reasonable, and therefore it is inappropriate to assume, in the absence of statutory indication to the contrary, that Congress has made such an assertion. * * *

I would reverse the judgment of the Court of Appeals on this issue, and remand to the District Court with instructions to dismiss for failure to state a claim on the three counts at issue.

Notes and Questions

We have included substantial excerpts from Justice Scalia's dissent because of the extent to which Justice Scalia's perspective has gained greater currency. How does Scalia's dissent differ from the opinion of the Court? Consider in particular what is a "true conflict?"

After *Hartford Fire* and for much of the next decade, US courts asserted antitrust jurisdiction broadly as usual. But then, in the wake of the worldwide vitamins cartel, defendants—foreign price-fixers—pressed their plea for a construction of the FTAIA that was to have large implications for the future of private damage actions against foreign actors.

During the 1990s, a global vitamins cartel—self-styled "Vitamins, Inc."—fixed the prices of vitamins sold around the world. The conspirators included multinational corporations located in Belgium, France, Germany, Japan, the Netherlands, Switzerland, and the US (US subsidiaries of Japanese firms). Total sales affected by the cartel have been estimated at $34 billion. Primarily as the result of enforcement actions of the US Justice Department, the cartel was cracked in the late 1990s. Competition authorities in Australia, Canada, the EU, Japan, and South Korea also imposed penalties. Then the private class actions were filed, all in the US, with its plaintiff-friendly incentives of class actions, broad discovery, contingent lawyer fees, cost rules, and treble damages. One class comprised solely non-US plaintiffs, who hailed from Australia, Ecuador, Panama, and Ukraine. By the time this litigation reached the US Supreme Court, the legal dispute had crystallized into a single question: Does a US court have jurisdiction over the claims of a foreign purchaser—*i.e.*, one who purchased in a foreign country—from a global cartel that also fixed prices in the US? Seven foreign governments (Germany, Belgium, Canada, Japan, Great Britain and Northern Ireland, Ireland, and the Netherlands) submitted four amicus curiae briefs, all of them urging the Court to adopt a rule restrictive of the rights of foreigners to sue in US courts for antitrust damages. The various national governments made different kinds of arguments. The British, for example, argued that the UK was trying to build its own private enforcement system and that allowing British purchasers to sue in US courts would undermine that effort; and the Japanese argued that excessive damages awards could bankrupt Japanese companies. We print below excerpts from three of numerous amicus briefs.

AMICUS BRIEF OF CERTAIN PROFESSORS IN SUPPORT OF PLAINTIFFS IN F. HOFFMANN-LA ROCHE LTD. v. EMPAGRAN S.A.

Brief of Professors Darren Bush, John M. Connor,
John J. Flynn, Shubha Ghosh, Warren Grimes,
Joseph E. Harrington, Jr., Norman Hawker,
Robert Lande, William G. Shepherd
and Steven Semeraro

The past decade has witnessed nothing less than an explosion in the discovery of private international cartels with global price-fixing ambitions. This brief presents two major economic arguments in support of the decision below. First, in the context of international price-fixing conspiracies conduct relating to "wholly foreign" purchases necessarily affects domestic commerce. This is because international cartels must prevent international geographic arbitrage in order to succeed in controlling prices in any targeted national market.

Second, this brief assembles empirical evidence that, in the absence of affirmance of the judgment below, the global aspirations of contemporary cartels offer an insuperable challenge to a core aim of the antitrust laws: Deterrence. The broad geographic harm generated by the scores of modern global price-fixing conspiracies has overwhelmed the ability of corporate antitrust sanctions to provide enough financial disincentives to discourage the formation of similar cartels in the future. These sanctions have been inadequate to deter cartel formation because the probability of being caught by one or more of the world's antitrust authorities remains well below 100% and because the *expected* illegal monopoly profits made worldwide are more than sufficient to compensate would-be conspirators for their *expected* liabilities in jurisdictions with effective antitrust laws and enforcement. Permitting foreign buyers who purchased the products of international cartels abroad to pursue civil antitrust damages actions in U.S. courts is necessary to produce the level of damages needed to protect the U.S. economy and its consumers from future cartel injuries. Affirmance will also enhance the probability of discovery of clandestine cartels by multiplying the number of jurisdictions in which private parties have an incentive to investigate collusive behavior. * * *

[T]he international vitamin cartel generated the largest total of antitrust fines and penalties in history, which are calculated to be between $4.4 and $5.6 billion. But the cartel's monopoly profits in all areas of the world were $9 to $13 billion. Thus, the criminal and civil justice systems of the globe produced fines and damages that amounted to only about half of this cartel's illegal profits. These sanctions are much less than the amount needed to discourage future cartel formation. One of the best ways to discourage cartels is to increase the expected costs in the event the participants are caught, in order that the expected penalties exceed the expected benefits. As a practical matter, this deterrence benefit to the United States' consumers and its economy—something surely intended by Congress—is likely to be achieved only if federal law is construed to give injured foreign customers like Respondents the power to sue in the courts of the United States under American antitrust laws. * * *

[If the United States market were not included in the cartel, arbitrage would undermine the cartel and could even destroy it.]

To summarize, the average price effects of the vitamins cartel appear to be lowest for buyers in the United States, averaging somewhere in the 20% to 35% range. Canada and Europe were higher, roughly in the 30% to 40% range. The rest of the world came closer to European levels than to U.S. levels. Applying these price effects to the affected sales mentioned in the previous section implies that global injuries were between $9 and $13 billion, of which 15% accrued in the United States, 1% in Canada, 26% in the EU, and 58% in the rest of the world. * * *

[T]he maximum financial antitrust liability that would face global cartels in the absence of affirmance here would be, *de jure*, the sum of (1) five to six times the harm generated in the United States, (2) approximately single U.S. damages in the European Union, and (3) negligible fines or penalties elsewhere. As noted above, the injuries caused by global cartels spread beyond North America and Western Europe. Therefore, as a proportion of the monopoly profits garnered worldwide, the theoretical upper limit of lawful antitrust liability would be limited to approximately double global damages. *De facto* the application of fines and private suits to global cartels has resulted in total monetary sanctions that have been less than double actual global damages in all cases and less than single damages on average. In the end, then, even international cartels that are uncovered and prosecuted tend to be profitable. As explained below, such sanctions offer woefully suboptimal deterrence, but under the reading of the Sherman Act adopted below, deterrence might approach optimal levels. * * *

The fact that so many companies engage in repeated violations of U.S. and EU competition laws is symptomatic of deeply rooted business behavior. The roots of price-fixing conduct lie in the structures of markets. Common to all discovered cartels is "small numbers" (a high degree of industrial concentration of ownership among sellers) coupled with a high degree of control of the market by members of the cartel. Similarly, cartels are more effective when buyers are many and none purchase large shares of the cartelized product. A third nearly universal feature of markets with cartel activity is that the products are standardized commodities with few or no substitutes even when a cartel raises its price to a level well above normal. Storable products that are cheaply transported long distances make better candidates for internationally collusive schemes than perishable items. * * *

There are two major reasons why it is rational for firms contemplating global price fixing to proceed. First, *actual* cartel profits have historically exceeded the financial penalties meted out by the world's courts and commissions. It is reasonable to suppose that *future expectations* about the benefit/cost ratio of international price fixing will be tempered by historical experience. As this brief has demonstrated, the total collusive overcharges imposed by the vitamins cartel greatly exceeded the global fines and penalties extracted from the cartelists. This result follows from the leniency policies of the most active anticartel authorities, from the difficulties of plaintiffs in U.S. civil suits in achieving double or even single damages, from the absence of civil suits abroad, and from the near absence of any kind of enforcement outside North America and the EU. The facts regarding anticartel sanctions presented above support a similar conclusion in the case of other global cartels uncovered since 1990.

Second, global cartelists have reason to expect that their secret price fixing will probably remain hidden. The probability of being apprehended by one or more of the world's antitrust authorities is not known with certainty, but it is certainly less than 100%. The most reliable sources assert that the probability of any kind of private cartel being caught before the agreement is dissolved for other reasons is in the range of 10% to 33%. It is true that most of these estimates date from periods before the full force of today's U.S. criminal sanctions and leniency inducements were felt. Nevertheless, there is little reason to believe that the true probability of detection is outside this range. * * *

Modern international cartels with global reach present a knotty challenge to current antitrust enforcement practices.

Cartels that sell internationally tradable commodities and that aim to fix prices in two or more regions with different national currencies cannot control currency exchange rates. As a consequence, private international cartels must prevent geographic arbitrage through frequent realignment of national prices if their control over price is to succeed. The vitamins cartels and scores of the largest cartels uncovered by antitrust authorities since 1990 embody these characteristics, and direct evidence exists that cartel managers in fact were aware that unchecked arbitrage would undermine their scheme. Therefore, the purchases of wholly foreign buyers play an integral role in creating the antitrust injury incurred by wholly domestic direct purchasers.

Even under ideal prosecutorial outcomes, in the absence of affirmance of the decision below, the global reach of modern cartels insures that the monetary payouts of guilty international cartelists cannot succeed in disgorging all the illegal cartel profits. That is, the imposition of maximum government fines combined with fully successful civil suits in North America will inevitably result in amounts less than single global damages. It would therefore be utterly rational for would-be cartelist to form or join an international price-fixing conspiracy. Only if treble damages are available to wholly foreign buyers might the balance tip: if plaintiffs like Respondents are successful in American courts, the monetary penalties imposed on prosecuted members of cartels could, at least in theory, in most cases exceed the monopoly profits. Cartel formation will be discouraged.

Even assuming prosecutorial conditions will resemble recent historical patterns of punishment, a judgment of affirmance will greatly improve international cartel deterrence and will lead it to approach optimal deterrence. The precise degree of deterrence will depend on the perceived probability that international cartels will be detected, investigated, and convicted. It is widely believed that the probability of detecting clandestine cartels is less than one-third. The degree of deterrence will also depend on the proportion of the price-fixing overcharges awarded to plaintiffs in civil suits, which on average has been less than 100% and in individual cases never exceeds double damages. If these estimates are correct and conditions remain unchanged, permitting wholly foreign buyers to seek redress for antitrust injury in U.S. courts, will mean that typical would-be cartelists will face, if not an optimal level of deterrence, the likelihood of a much smaller degree of underdeterrence than exists today.

AMICUS BRIEF OF GERMANY AND BELGIUM
IN SUPPORT OF DEFENDANTS

The court of appeals' decision incorrectly interprets the FTAIA in a manner that will do grave harm to the antitrust enforcement efforts of the international community. The court's interpretation drastically expands the extraterritorial reach of the United States' antitrust laws to situations in which the conduct and the alleged anticompetitive effects suffered by foreign plaintiffs occur only in foreign countries. Yet, in those situations, other nations have a significant interest in the transaction and its effects and have jurisdiction to regulate or prohibit that conduct. The court's holding thus directly conflicts with the well-established principle that United States statutes are to be construed to avoid conflict with other nations' laws and to avoid unreasonableness in the exercise of U.S. courts' jurisdiction.

The court of appeals' expansive interpretation of the United States' antitrust laws will permit foreign civil litigants to use United States lawsuits to circumvent the choices made by foreign governments about the most appropriate remedies available for anticompetitive behavior. The court's interpretation of the FTAIA also threatens to undermine international antitrust cooperation and enforcement, contrary to the "underlying policies of deterrence" upon which the court relied. For example, foreign governments use leniency programs similar to the one utilized by the Department of Justice ("DOJ") to obtain information about violations; they then use that information to deter other abuses. Yet private suits, such as respondents', create strong disincentives for companies to participate in such programs because to do so increases the risk that the information they disclose to governments will subject them to private civil liability and treble damages.

* * *

. . . [T]he theory and application of the competition laws of Belgium, Germany, the EU, and the U.S. differ in important ways. For example, in the U.S., agency practice and courts decide whether certain agreements restraining competition are illegal by applying a "rule of reason" analysis. By contrast, German law provides for a very broad-reaching prohibition of agreements between competitors, with enumerated exceptions. So, too, for the Belgian regime, which prohibits cartels under the Belgian Act, and then provides for exemptions . . .

Sometimes those varying approaches may result in different decisions as to the method of enforcement or whether a prohibition is appropriate at all. And, irrespective of whether a different outcome may result under the various systems, U.S. law should not trump Germany's and Belgium's sovereign rights to make their own choices about how to structure and apply their competition laws in determining liability and imposing remedies.

For this reason, permitting suits such as respondents' encroaches directly on contrary sovereign choices made by other countries. German, Belgian, and European laws treat the vitamin case as a hard-core cartel that cannot be subject to an individual exemption. Germany, Belgium, and other EU Member States should be given the freedom to impose different remedies than those that would be imposed under the U.S. system. And the EC has, in fact, already imposed considerable fines on account of the vitamin cartel's effects in Germany and other EU Member States.

[I]t is especially intrusive on other nations' interests that the court of appeals' decision opens the door to private foreign plaintiffs who seek treble damages, as opposed to opening the door simply for DOJ enforcement. Private plaintiffs rarely exercise the type of self-restraint or demonstrate the requisite sensitivity to the concerns of foreign governments that mark actions brought by the United States government. . . .

In analyzing the deterrence effects of its extension of United States antitrust laws to foreign plaintiffs, the court of appeals failed to consider the detrimental impact an expansive application of U.S. law would have on the cooperation that is vital to international investigation and prosecution of cartels and enforcement of judgments. The investigation and prosecution of global conspiracies in restraint of trade often depends upon the cooperation and coordination of countries where the offenders might be domiciled or located. For that reason, the United States has entered into cooperative treaties or agreements with other nations . . . Left unchecked, the court of appeals' decision threatens to undermine those efforts. * * *

Historically, other nations have bristled at extraterritorial applications of United States antitrust laws. These concerns have resulted in foreign governments taking a number of measures to counter what they perceive to be an illegitimate encroachment into their sovereignty. Such encroachments by U.S. courts invariably will alter the relationships between nations. The effectiveness of international treaties is threatened when other nations conclude that the U.S. has overreached in the application of its domestic laws to foreign conduct.

German officials already have expressed concern about the court of appeals' expansive application of U.S. jurisdiction in this case. In a recent lecture given at an antitrust conference in Bonn and attended by United States and EU officials, former German Economic Minister (and recent chief German negotiator of the German-U.S. forced labor settlement) Otto Graf Lambsdorff commented on the *Empagran* decision. Mr. Lambsdorff opined that "American antitrust laws were created to protect the American consumer and not to regulate the competitive conditions in foreign countries," and he observed that "[a] German court—as well as every other European—would obviously deny jurisdiction" were the roles reversed, because "[a]ny other decision would rightly provoke protest by both US companies and the US government."

One consequence of foreign disapproval with U.S. encroachments on other nation-states' antitrust enforcement efforts will be a refusal to enforce judgments obtained in U.S. lawsuits. . . .

These and other international reactions to the extraterritorial application of U.S. law should make apparent the high stakes of this case.

AMICUS BRIEF OF UK, IRELAND, AND THE NETHERLANDS IN SUPPORT OF DEFENDANTS

The decision below would permit United States courts to hear private claims by foreign plaintiffs seeking redress for antitrust injuries allegedly suffered by them in Australia, Ecuador, Panama and Ukraine from sales of vitamins there and in other foreign countries by foreign sellers. These injuries do not arise from any contacts or relationships with plaintiffs in the United States. The argument that treble damages for foreign injuries can be recovered in a United States court because the conduct at issue also resulted in injuries to *other* parties who made purchases in the United States is a complete *non sequitur*. These unrelated injuries were the basis for other private actions in United States courts and have been fully compensated. In addition, such a rule potentially would permit virtually any significant commercial transaction to be the basis for private United States treble damage claims, usurping the enforcement systems of other countries to United States private actions.

This decision would provide substantial encouragement for widespread forum shopping, might impede competition law enforcement programs in the United Kingdom, Ireland and the Netherlands as well as the European Community, and would undermine respect for national sovereignty. The court of appeals' ruling has the potential for generating needless friction between foreign and United States legal systems and could lead to less, not more, cooperation and coordination of competition laws by all nations. It would wrongly expand the extraterritorial reach of the United States antitrust laws beyond this Court's or, to our knowledge, any foreign court's exercise of jurisdiction. International law principles recognize that a nation may prescribe laws and adjudicate claims beyond its own territory only where its assertion of jurisdiction does not infringe the rights of other nations to determine the law applicable to conduct within their own territories. * * *

Effective antitrust enforcement in an increasingly global economy depends on close governmental cooperation and coordination as well as respect for the decisions of other nations. Neither commercial transactions nor anticompetitive behavior by private firms is constrained by national boundaries. Antitrust enforcement officials thus place a high priority on closely knit international investigations. * * *

Price fixing and other cartels are elusive targets despite cooperation and coordination among national or regional enforcement authorities. Cartels can generate enormous profits; they operate in secret because they are illegal; and severe penalties make voluntary disclosure by members of the cartel risky and perilous. These problems are compounded when the cartel operates in international commerce because evidence of the cartel is difficult to gather; procedures differ among countries; and the participants are scattered among several jurisdictions.

Prior to the 1990's traditional tactics such as plea bargains had only limited success because cartels were not condemned by all countries and enforcement practices varied widely among countries. In addition, potential whistle-blowers were unwilling to reveal themselves without formal assurances of protection.

To counteract this failure, competition enforcement authorities have developed leniency programs and cooperated on collecting evidence, offering amnesty and prosecuting cartels operating across borders. . . . The development of amnesty programs has grown, and the authorities in the United Kingdom, Ireland, the Netherlands and EC as well as other countries have adopted specific programs. Typically, the leniency applicant can receive total or substantial immunity from criminal and civil antitrust penalties if it is the first to come forward with credible or material evidence of a cartel before the enforcement authority has knowledge of the cartel or has begun an investigation. The terms vary as each country assesses the proper mix of incentives and penalties. These programs are a deliberate effort to balance interests of disclosure, deterrence and punishment.

* * *

The international convergence of amnesty programs has become effective because it is "much easier and far more attractive for companies to simultaneously seek and obtain leniency in the United States, Europe, Canada, and in other jurisdictions where the applicants have exposure." The Governments, however, are concerned about any policy or action that would make the programs less attractive to whistle-blowers. Competition authorities in the United Kingdom, Ireland and the Netherlands have all concluded that the proposed expansion of United States jurisdiction over private treble damages claims could have an adverse effect on international cartel enforcement. Enforcement officials from Germany and the United States agree. The issue here is that participants in leniency programs receive no immunity from private damage actions. The expansion of United States jurisdiction and the accompanying availability of private treble damages may discourage potential whistle-blowers from providing evidence. When coming forward to expose secret agreements, they may be required to pay much greater damages than if the cartel otherwise would have not have been detected. If these forecasts are borne out by experience, cartel detection and deterrence will be diminished and consumer welfare will not be served. * * *

No other country has adopted the United States' unique "bounty hunter" approach that permits a private plaintiff to "recover threefold the damages by him sustained, and the cost of suit, including a reasonable attorney's fee." The rules governing United States treble damage actions strongly favor private antitrust plaintiffs. They provide for generous class action certifications, broad discovery rules, virtually irrebuttable presumptions of liability based on successful government actions, jury trials, subsidized contingency fee arrangements, asymmetrical rules on payment of attorneys' fees, and no contribution among defendants. The parliaments of the United Kingdom, Ireland and the Netherlands all recently enacted statutes allowing private actions for competition law violations, but have chosen to do so on a more limited basis.

Expanding the jurisdiction of this generous United States private claim system could skew enforcement and increase international business risks. It makes United States courts the forum of choice without regard to whose laws are applied, where the injuries occurred or even if there is any connection to the court except the ability to get *in personam* jurisdiction over the defendants. Lord Denning best captured these anomalies when he observed: "As a moth is drawn to the light, so is a litigant drawn to the United States. If he can only get his case into their courts, he stands to win a fortune." *Smith Kline & French Labs Ltd. v. Bloch,* [1983] 1 W.L.R. 730 (C.A. 1982). Enlarging the prescriptive jurisdiction of the United States to provide a US antitrust remedy to foreign buyers with no cognizable US nexus will attract even more litigants and will increase the number of private antitrust claims filed in United States courts. There is no apparent justification for such a shift. While additional penalties could marginally increase deterrence, in this circumstance where international public enforcement is diminished, the likely effect may be to lessen overall detection. * * *

Today, private antitrust actions authorized in the United Kingdom, Ireland and the Netherlands apply to a range of competition offenses and generally provide for only single damages. The "loser pays" rule for attorneys fees applies in each country and competition law claims are heard either by judges or by administrative tribunals unlikely to be swayed by emotional appeals common to United States treble damages jury trials. . . . The absence of multiple damages and the different attorney fee authority in the United Kingdom, Ireland and the Netherlands are not simple oversights.

Other amicus briefs focused on statutory construction as well as deterrence. For example, it was argued on behalf of the plaintiffs that the FTAIA did not withdraw jurisdiction over the subject matter of this action, which was the international vitamins cartel; and that the FTAIA conditions for reach of the Sherman Act were satisfied, for the cartel had a direct, substantial, and reasonably foreseeable effect on US commerce and *that effect gave rise to a claim under Section 1 of the Sherman Act.* The brief argued that the relation of the foreign plaintiffs to the US violation was a question of their standing, not a question of subject matter jurisdiction (or reach of US law). Amicus Brief of Harry First and Eleanor Fox. Defendants and other amici argued for a different construction, which the Court adopted, as we see below.

F. HOFFMANN-LA ROCHE LTD. v. EMPAGRAN S.A.
542 U.S. 155 (2004)

JUSTICE BREYER:

The Foreign Trade Antitrust Improvements Act of 1982 (FTAIA) excludes from the Sherman Act's reach much anticompetitive conduct that causes only foreign injury. It does so by setting forth a general rule stating that the Sherman Act "shall not apply to conduct involving trade or commerce . . . with foreign nations." 15 U.S.C. § 6a.

It then creates exceptions to the general rule, applicable where (roughly speaking) that conduct significantly harms imports, domestic commerce, or American exporters.

We here focus upon anticompetitive price-fixing activity that is in significant part foreign, that causes some domestic antitrust injury, and that independently causes separate foreign injury. We ask two questions about the price-fixing conduct and the foreign injury that it causes. First, does that conduct fall within the FTAIA's general rule excluding the Sherman Act's application? That is to say, does the price-fixing activity constitute "conduct involving trade or commerce . . . with foreign nations"? We conclude that it does.

Second, we ask whether the conduct nonetheless falls within a domestic-injury exception to the general rule, an exception that applies (and makes the Sherman Act nonetheless applicable) where the conduct (1) has a "direct, substantial, and reasonably foreseeable effect" on domestic commerce, and (2) "such effect gives rise to a [Sherman Act] claim." §§ 6a(1)(A), (2). We conclude that the exception does not apply where the plaintiff's claim rests solely on the independent foreign harm.

To clarify: The issue before us concerns (1) significant foreign anticompetitive conduct with (2) an adverse domestic effect and (3) an independent foreign effect giving rise to the claim. In more concrete terms, this case involves vitamin sellers around the world that agreed to fix prices, leading to higher vitamin prices in the United States and independently leading to higher vitamin prices in other countries such as Ecuador. We conclude that, in this scenario, a purchaser in the United States could bring a Sherman Act claim under the FTAIA based on domestic injury, but a purchaser in Ecuador could not bring a Sherman Act claim based on foreign harm.

I.

The plaintiffs in this case originally filed a class-action suit on behalf of foreign and domestic purchasers of vitamins under, inter alia, § 1 of the Sherman Act, 26 Stat. 209, as amended, 15 U.S.C. § 1, and §§ 4 and 16 of the Clayton Act, 38 Stat. 731, 737, as amended, 15 U.S.C. §§ 15, 26. Their complaint alleged that petitioners, foreign and domestic vitamin manufacturers and distributors, had engaged in a price-fixing conspiracy, raising the price of vitamin products to customers in the United States and to customers in foreign countries.

As relevant here, petitioners moved to dismiss the suit as to the foreign purchasers (the respondents here), five foreign vitamin distributors located in Ukraine, Australia, Ecuador, and Panama, each of which bought vitamins from petitioners for delivery outside the United States. Respondents have never asserted that they purchased any vitamins in the United States or in transactions in United States commerce, and the question presented assumes that the relevant "transactions occurr[ed] entirely outside US commerce." The District Court dismissed their claims. It applied the FTAIA and found none of the exceptions applicable. Thereafter, the domestic purchasers transferred their claims to another pending suit and did not take part in the subsequent appeal.

A divided panel of the Court of Appeals reversed. The panel concluded that the FTAIA's general exclusionary rule applied to the case, but that its domestic-injury exception also applied. It basically read the plaintiffs' complaint to allege that the vitamin manufacturers' price-fixing conspiracy (1) had "a direct, substantial, and reasonably foreseeable effect" on ordinary domestic trade or commerce, i.e., the conspiracy brought about higher domestic vitamin prices, and (2) "such effect" gave "rise to a [Sherman Act] claim," i.e., an injured domestic customer could have brought a Sherman Act suit, 15 U.S.C. §§ 6a(1), (2). Those allegations, the court held, are sufficient to meet the exception's requirements.

The court assumed that the foreign effect, i.e., higher prices in Ukraine, Panama, Australia, and Ecuador, was independent of the domestic effect, i.e., higher domestic prices. But it concluded that, in light of the FTAIA's text, legislative history, and the policy goal of deterring harmful price-fixing activity, this lack of connection does not matter.

We granted certiorari to resolve a split among the Courts of Appeals about the exception's application. . . .

II.

The FTAIA seeks to make clear to American exporters (and to firms doing business abroad) that the Sherman Act does not prevent them from entering into business arrangements (say, joint-selling arrangements), however anticompetitive, as long as those arrangements adversely affect only foreign markets. It does so by removing from the Sherman Act's reach, (1) export activities and (2) other commercial activities taking place abroad, unless those activities adversely affect domestic commerce, imports to the United States, or exporting activities of one engaged in such activities within the United States.

The FTAIA says:

"Sections 1 to 7 of this title [the Sherman Act] shall not apply to conduct involving trade or commerce (other than import trade or import commerce) with foreign nations unless—

"(1) such conduct has a direct, substantial, and reasonably foreseeable effect—

"(A) on trade or commerce which is not trade or commerce with foreign nations [i.e., domestic trade or commerce], or on import trade or import commerce with foreign nations; or

"(B) on export trade or export commerce with foreign nations, of a person engaged in such trade or commerce in the United States [i.e., on an American export competitor]; and

"(2) such effect gives rise to a claim under the provisions of sections 1 to 7 of this title, other than this section.

"If sections 1 to 7 of this title apply to such conduct only because of the operation of paragraph (1)(B), then sections 1 to 7 of this title shall apply to such conduct only for injury to export business in the United States." 15 U.S.C. § 6a.

This technical language initially lays down a general rule placing all (nonimport) activity involving foreign commerce outside the Sherman Act's reach. It then brings such conduct back within the Sherman Act's reach provided that the conduct both (1) sufficiently affects American commerce, i.e., it has a "direct, substantial, and reasonably foreseeable effect" on American domestic, import, or (certain) export commerce, and (2) has an effect of a kind that antitrust law considers harmful, i.e., the "effect" must "giv[e] rise to a [Sherman Act] claim." §§ 6a(1), (2).

We ask here how this language applies to price-fixing activity that is in significant part foreign, that has the requisite domestic effect, and that also has independent foreign effects giving rise to the plaintiff's claim.

* * *

IV.

We turn now to the basic question presented, that of the exception's application. Because the underlying antitrust action is complex, potentially raising questions not directly at issue here, we reemphasize that we base our decision upon the following: The price-fixing conduct significantly and adversely affects both customers outside the United States and customers within the United States, but the adverse foreign effect is independent of any adverse domestic effect. In these circumstances, we find that the FTAIA exception does not apply (and thus the Sherman Act does not apply) for two main reasons.

First, this Court ordinarily construes ambiguous statutes to avoid unreasonable interference with the sovereign authority of other nations. . . . This rule of construction reflects principles of customary international law-law that (we must assume) Congress ordinarily seeks to follow. See Restatement (Third) of Foreign Relations Law of the United States §§ 403(1), 403(2) (1986) (hereinafter Restatement) (limiting the unreasonable exercise of prescriptive jurisdiction with respect to a person or activity having connections with another State); . . . *Hartford Fire Ins. Co. v. California*, 509 US 764, 817 (1993) (Scalia, J., dissenting) (identifying rule of construction as derived from the principle of " 'prescriptive comity' ").

This rule of statutory construction cautions courts to assume that legislators take account of the legitimate sovereign interests of other nations when they write American laws. It thereby helps the potentially conflicting laws of different nations work together in harmony-a harmony particularly needed in today's highly interdependent commercial world.

No one denies that America's antitrust laws, when applied to foreign conduct, can interfere with a foreign nation's ability independently to regulate its own commercial affairs. But our courts have long held that application of our antitrust laws to foreign anticompetitive conduct is nonetheless reasonable, and hence consistent with principles of prescriptive comity, insofar as they reflect a legislative effort to redress domestic antitrust injury that foreign anticompetitive conduct has caused. See *United States v. Aluminum Co. of America*, 148 F.2d 416, 443–444 (C.A.2 1945) (L.Hand, J.) . . . .

But why is it reasonable to apply those laws to foreign conduct insofar as that conduct causes independent foreign harm and that foreign harm alone gives rise to the plaintiff's claim? Like the former case, application of those laws creates a serious risk of interference with a foreign nation's ability independently to regulate its own commercial affairs. But, unlike the former case, the justification for that interference seems insubstantial. See Restatement § 403(2) (determining reasonableness on basis of such factors as connections with regulating nation, harm to that nation's interests, extent to which other nations regulate, and the potential for conflict). Why should American law supplant, for example, Canada's or Great Britain's or Japan's own determination about how best to protect

Canadian or British or Japanese customers from anticompetitive conduct engaged in significant part by Canadian or British or Japanese or other foreign companies?

We recognize that principles of comity provide Congress greater leeway when it seeks to control through legislation the actions of American companies, see Restatement § 402; and some of the anticompetitive price-fixing conduct alleged here took place in America. But the higher foreign prices of which the foreign plaintiffs here complain are not the consequence of any domestic anticompetitive conduct that Congress sought to forbid, for Congress did not seek to forbid any such conduct insofar as it is here relevant, i.e., insofar as it is intertwined with foreign conduct that causes independent foreign harm. Rather Congress sought to release domestic (and foreign) anticompetitive conduct from Sherman Act constraints when that conduct causes foreign harm. Congress, of course, did make an exception where that conduct also causes domestic harm. See House Report, at 13 (concerns about American firms' participation in international cartels addressed through "domestic injury" exception). But any independent domestic harm the foreign conduct causes here has, by definition, little or nothing to do with the matter.

We thus repeat the basic question: Why is it reasonable to apply this law to conduct that is significantly foreign insofar as that conduct causes independent foreign harm and that foreign harm alone gives rise to the plaintiff's claim? We can find no good answer to the question.

The Areeda and Hovenkamp treatise [1978] notes that under the Court of Appeals' interpretation of the statute

> "a Malaysian customer could . . . maintain an action under United States law in a United States court against its own Malaysian supplier, another cartel member, simply by noting that unnamed third parties injured [in the United States] by the American [cartel member's] conduct would also have a cause of action. Effectively, the United States courts would provide worldwide subject matter jurisdiction to any foreign suitor wishing to sue its own local supplier, but unhappy with its own sovereign's provisions for private antitrust enforcement, provided that a different plaintiff had a cause of action against a different firm for injuries that were within US [other-than-import] commerce. It does not seem excessively rigid to infer that Congress would not have intended that result."

We agree with the comment. We can find no convincing justification for the extension of the Sherman Act's scope that it describes.

Respondents reply that many nations have adopted antitrust laws similar to our own, to the point where the practical likelihood of interference with the relevant interests of other nations is minimal. Leaving price fixing to the side, however, this Court has found to the contrary. See, e.g., *Hartford Fire*, 509 US, at 797–799 (noting that the alleged conduct in the London reinsurance market, while illegal under United States antitrust laws, was assumed to be perfectly consistent with British law and policy). * * *

Regardless, even where nations agree about primary conduct, say, price fixing, they disagree dramatically about appropriate remedies. The application, for example, of American private treble-damages remedies to anticompetitive conduct taking place abroad has generated considerable controversy. And several foreign nations have filed briefs here arguing that to apply our remedies would unjustifiably permit their citizens to bypass their own less generous remedial schemes, thereby upsetting a balance of competing considerations that their own domestic antitrust laws embody. E.g., Brief for Government of Federal Republic of Germany et al. as Amici Curiae 2 (setting forth German interest "in seeing that German companies are not subject to the extraterritorial reach of the United States' antitrust laws by private foreign plaintiffs-whose injuries were sustained in transactions entirely outside United States commerce-seeking treble damages in private lawsuits against German companies"); Brief for Government of Canada as Amicus Curiae 14 ("treble damages remedy would supersede" Canada's "national policy decision"); Brief for Government of Japan as Amicus Curiae 10 (finding "particularly troublesome" the potential "interfere[nce] with Japanese governmental regulation of the Japanese market").

These briefs add that a decision permitting independently injured foreign plaintiffs to pursue private treble-damages remedies would undermine foreign nations' own antitrust enforcement policies by diminishing foreign firms' incentive to cooperate with antitrust authorities in return for prosecutorial amnesty. * * *

Respondents alternatively argue that comity does not demand an interpretation of the FTAIA that would exclude independent foreign injury cases across the board. Rather, courts can take (and sometimes have taken) account of comity considerations case by case, abstaining where comity considerations so dictate.

In our view, however, this approach is too complex to prove workable. The Sherman Act covers many different kinds of anticompetitive agreements. Courts would have to examine how foreign law, compared with American law, treats not only price fixing but also, say, information-sharing agreements, patent-licensing price conditions, territorial product resale limitations, and various forms of joint venture, in respect to both primary conduct and remedy. The legally and economically technical nature of that enterprise means lengthier proceedings, appeals, and more proceedings-to the point where procedural costs and delays could themselves threaten interference with a foreign nation's ability to maintain the integrity of its own antitrust enforcement system. Even in this relatively simple price-fixing case, for example, competing briefs tell us (1) that potential treble-damages liability would help enforce widespread anti-price-fixing norms (through added deterrence) and (2) the opposite, namely, that such liability would hinder antitrust enforcement (by reducing incentives to enter amnesty programs). How could a court seriously interested in resolving so empirical a matter-a matter potentially related to impact on foreign interests-do so simply and expeditiously?

We conclude that principles of prescriptive comity counsel against the Court of Appeals' interpretation of the FTAIA. Where foreign anticompetitive conduct plays a significant role and where foreign injury is independent of domestic effects, Congress might have hoped that America's antitrust laws, so fundamental a component of our own economic system, would commend themselves to other nations as well. But, if America's antitrust policies could not win their own way in the international marketplace for such ideas, Congress, we must assume, would not have tried to impose them, in an act of legal imperialism, through legislative fiat.

Second, the FTAIA's language and history suggest that Congress designed the FTAIA to clarify, perhaps to limit, but not to expand in any significant way, the Sherman Act's scope as applied to foreign commerce. And we have found no significant indication that at the time Congress wrote this statute courts would have thought the Sherman Act applicable in these circumstances.

* * *

The upshot is that no pre-1982 case provides significant authority for application of the Sherman Act in the circumstances we here assume. Indeed, a leading contemporaneous lower court case contains language suggesting the contrary. See *Timberlane Lumber Co. v. Bank of America N.T. & S.A.*, 549 F.2d 597, 613 (C.A.9 1976) (insisting that the foreign conduct's domestic effect be "sufficiently large to present a cognizable injury to the plaintiffs" . . . .

Taken together, these two sets of considerations, the one derived from comity and the other reflecting history, convince us that Congress would not have intended the FTAIA's exception to bring independently caused foreign injury within the Sherman Act's reach.

* * *

V.

Finally, respondents point to policy considerations, namely, that application of the Sherman Act in present circumstances will (through increased deterrence) help protect Americans against foreign-caused anticompetitive injury. Petitioners, however, have made important experience-backed arguments (based upon amnesty-seeking incentives) to the contrary. We cannot say whether, on balance, respondents' side of this empirically based argument or the enforcement agencies' side is correct. But we can say that the answer to the dispute is neither clear enough, nor of such likely empirical significance, that it could overcome the considerations we have previously discussed and change our conclusion.

For these reasons, we conclude that petitioners' reading of the statute's language is correct. That reading furthers the statute's basic purposes, it properly reflects considerations of comity, and it is consistent with Sherman Act history.

VI.

We have assumed that the anticompetitive conduct here independently caused foreign injury; that is, the conduct's domestic effects did not help to bring about that foreign injury. Respondents argue, in the alternative, that the foreign injury was not independent. Rather, they say, the anticompetitive conduct's domestic effects were linked to that foreign harm. Respondents contend that, because vitamins are fungible and readily transportable, without an adverse domestic effect (i.e., higher prices in the United States), the sellers could not have maintained their international price-fixing arrangement and respondents would not have suffered their foreign injury. They add that this "but for" condition is sufficient to bring the price-fixing conduct within the scope of the FTAIA's exception.

The Court of Appeals, however, did not address this argument, and, for that reason, neither shall we. Respondents remain free to ask the Court of Appeals to consider the claim. The Court of Appeals may determine whether respondents properly preserved the argument, and, if so, it may consider it and decide the related claim.

For these reasons, the judgment of the Court of Appeals is vacated, and the case is remanded for further proceedings consistent with this opinion.

Notes and Questions

1.   Did the Court properly construe FTAIA subparagraph (2) to require that the US effect gives rise to *the plaintiff's claim* rather than, as the statute says, "gives rise to a claim under the provisions of [the Sherman Act] other than this section"? Note that the Court made the most restrictive construction possible. Under principles of interpretation it may choose a construction only where the statutory language is ambiguous, and a question was whether the statutory language—"gives rise to a [Sherman Act] claim"—was ambiguous at all.

2.   Note that the Court assumed that the cartel's US effects had nothing to do with the effects that harmed plaintiffs. Thus the Court assumed a wholly foreign cartel that hurt only foreign plaintiffs. Such cartel injury would not be covered by the Sherman Act with or without the FTAIA.

3.   The assumption was proved wrong on remand. To determine whether plaintiffs' harms were sufficiently connected to the US effects, the lower Court announced a rule of proximate cause—Did the US effects proximately cause plaintiffs' injury? The court answered No and dismissed the case. 417 F.3d 1267, 1271 (D.C. Cir. 2005).

4.   Would all foreign nations prefer that the US be disqualified as a forum for hosting their citizens' claims for harms from a world cartel? Might Ecuador—which did not yet have an antitrust law—have been happy to let their citizens recover damages in US courts?

5.   *Empagran* has also been invoked to limit the scope of the conduct that an American plaintiff suing an American defendant can challenge under the Sherman Act. In *Advanced Micro Devices, Inc. v. Intel Corporation*, 452 F.Supp.2d 555 (D.Del.2006), AMD argued that there was a single global market for microprocessors and that Intel's anticompetitive conduct around the world "neutered" AMD both in Europe and in the US. Nevertheless, the court ruled that AMD could not assert a monopolization claim regarding AMD's sale of microprocessors manufactured in Germany and sold to foreign customers, even though it could assert a monopolization claim as to microprocessors sold in the US. Does this approach balkanize individual litigations and require different parts of the same case to be litigated in different jurisdictions?

C. POST-EMPAGRAN: OFFSHORE ACTS AND DIRECTNESS; INPUT CARTELS WITH ASSEMBLY ABROAD

Post-*Empagran*, three important issues have arisen and are still in play. The first is whether directness means immediately direct (a tight and narrow interpretation) or reasonably direct; proximate. Does the first sale abroad break the chain? The second is whether in any case an offshore price-fix of inputs which are assembled into the finished product abroad before reaching the US (or the regulating country) are per se indirect and beyond reach. The third is whether statutory reach is or should be different for public and private actions.

The US agencies' address these issues in Guidelines § 3.2, printed below.

US AGENCIES' ANTITRUST GUIDELINES FOR INTERNATIONAL ENFORCEMENT AND COOPERATION (2017)

* * *

3.2   CONDUCT INVOLVING NON-IMPORT FOREIGN COMMERCE

The FTAIA initially places conduct involving non-import foreign commerce, which   means U.S. export commerce and wholly foreign commerce, outside the reach of the   Sherman Act and FTC Act.[90] What is commonly referred to as the FTAIA's "effects exception"[91] brings such conduct back within the reach of the Acts if the conduct has   a direct, substantial, and reasonably foreseeable effect on commerce within the   United States, U.S. import commerce, or the export commerce of a U.S. exporter,   and that effect gives rise to a claim.

Whether an alleged effect on such commerce is direct, substantial, and reasonably   foreseeable is a question of fact. An effect on commerce is "direct" if there is a reasonably proximate causal nexus, that is, if the effect is proximately caused by   the alleged anticompetitive conduct.[93] In other words, an effect is direct if, in the

---

[90]   F. Hoffmann-La Roche Ltd. v. Empagran S.A., 542 U.S. 155, 162–63 (2004).

[91]   See, e.g., Animal Sci. Prods., Inc. v. China Minmetals Corp., 654 F.3d 462, 471 (3d Cir. 2011). * * *

[93]   See Minn-Chem, 683 F.3d at 857; Lotes Co. v. Hon Hai Precision Indus. Co., 753 F.3d 395, 409–13 (2d Cir. 2014). Although one court of appeals has held that an effect on U.S. commerce is "direct" for purposes of Section 6a only if it follows "as an

natural or ordinary course of events, the alleged anticompetitive conduct would produce an effect on commerce. The substantiality requirement does not provide a minimum pecuniary threshold, nor does it require that the effects be quantified. Finally, the "reasonable foreseeability" requirement is an objective test, requiring that the effect be foreseeable to "a reasonable person making practical business judgments."[95]

Illustrative Example C

Situation: Corporation 1 and Corporation 2 have factories in Country Alpha where they manufacture Component X, a piece of high-tech hardware used in electronic products. Corporation 1 and Corporation 2 agree to raise prices for Component X sold to finished product integrators. These integrators have factories in Country Beta where they incorporate Component X into finished electronic products sold in the United States.

Discussion: Assuming Corporation 1 and Corporation 2 do not sell Component X in or for delivery to the United States, their conspiracy to fix the prices of Component X is conduct involving wholly foreign commerce, that is, commerce between Countries Alpha and Beta, and thus would not fall within the FTAIA's import commerce exclusion.

The conduct would still fall within the reach of the Sherman Act if it has a (1) direct, (2) substantial, and (3) reasonably foreseeable effect on U.S. import commerce in finished electronic products that incorporate Component X.

Assessing the conduct's effects can be a fact-intensive inquiry. Here the Agencies would collect and analyze evidence to determine whether the price fixing of the component had an effect on U.S. import commerce. If it does, the Agencies would further analyze the evidence and collect additional evidence, as necessary, to determine: (1) whether the price fixing was the proximate cause of that effect, (2) whether the effect was substantial, and (3) whether that effect

---

immediate consequence" of the defendant's activity, *United States v. LSL Biotechs.*, 379 F.3d 672, 680 (9th Cir. 2004), the proximate cause standard is more consistent with the language of the statute. As the Seventh Circuit explained "[s]uperimposing the idea of immediate consequence on top of the full [integrated] phrase ['direct, substantial, and reasonably foreseeable'] results in a stricter test than the complete text of the statute can bear" and "comes close to ignoring the fact that straightforward import commerce has already been excluded from FTAIA's coverage." *Minn-Chem*, 683 F.3d at 857. Nevertheless, any difference between these two tests is unlikely to yield different results in the vast majority of cases.* * *

[95] *Animal Sci.*, 654 F.3d at 471.

was a result of the price fixing that was foreseeable to a reasonable person making practical business judgments.

The fact that the price-fixed component was first sold to integrators in Country Beta, where it was incorporated into finished electronic products which were then sold in, or for delivery to, the United States would not render indirect an effect on import commerce in those products. Nor would the fact that the finished products were sold around the world or that Corporation 1 and Corporation 2 were unaware or indifferent to whether the finished products were sold in the United States render insubstantial or not reasonably foreseeable the effect on import commerce. In this context, substantiality is not a question of proportion. So long as the effect on import commerce is substantial, it does not matter if that effect is smaller than the conduct's effect outside the United States. Reasonable foreseeability is an objective standard, which asks not whether the conspirators actually foresaw the effect, but rather whether a reasonable person would foresee the effect on import commerce.

The relative size of Component X as a cost component of the finished electronic products may be relevant to determining whether the price-fixing conduct has the requisite effect, but it is not dispositive. For example, Component X may account for a large portion of the cost of the finished product, but competition from substitutes for the finished electronic products that do not incorporate Component X makes it unlikely that a price increase on Component X will affect import commerce in the finished products. Conversely, Component X may account for a small fraction of the cost of the finished product but the finished electronic product pricing is closely tied to input costs due to market conditions or contractual arrangements, or for other reasons. Thus, any price increase on Component X could, as a practical matter, have the requisite effect on import commerce in the finished electronic product.

Evidence that the conspirators actually expected their conduct to cause an effect on import commerce in the finished products would help to show that a direct, substantial, and reasonably foreseeable effect existed. Such evidence might include Corporation 1 and Corporation 2's contacts with purchasers in the United States, including negotiations regarding Component X pricing, as well as Corporation 1 and Corporation 2's discussing market conditions and tracking sales of the finished products in the United States. But the presence or absence of such evidence would not fundamentally alter the Agencies' analysis.[96]

Illustrative Example D

Situation: Company 1 and Company 2 are located in Country Alpha, where they extract Mineral X. Company 3 is located in the United States, where it extracts Mineral X. Company 3 is able to meet the entire U.S. demand for Mineral X and does so. Company 1 and Company 2 supply the rest of the world with Mineral X, but not the United States. By mutual agreement, Company 1 and Company 2 reduce their sales of Mineral X, significantly driving up the price of Mineral X outside the United States. Because of the increased price for Mineral X outside the United States, Company 3 begins to export much of the U.S. supply of Mineral X. No other firms replace Company 3's diverted sales, and the price of Mineral X rises inside the United States.

Discussion: Company 1 and Company 2's conspiracy to reduce their sales of Mineral X outside the United States is conduct involving wholly foreign commerce. Such conduct would fall within the reach of the Sherman Act if it has a direct, substantial, and reasonably foreseeable effect on U.S. interstate commerce in Mineral X. Here, the conspiracy had the effect of raising prices on interstate sales of Mineral X. That effect appears to be direct, substantial, and reasonably foreseeable.[97]

The FTAIA's effects exception also requires that the effect on commerce within the United States, U.S. import commerce, or the export commerce of a U.S. exporter "gives rise to" a claim under the antitrust laws. In a damages action brought under the antitrust laws, this provision requires that the effect on U.S. commerce be an adverse one and that the effect proximately cause the plaintiff's antitrust injury. It is therefore appropriate for courts to distinguish among damages claims based upon the underlying transaction that forms the basis of the injury to ensure that each claim redresses injury consistent with the requirements of the antitrust laws,

---

[96] *See generally Hsiung*, 778 F.3d at 756–60 (affirming Sherman Act convictions on alternate ground that evidence that price fixing of components sold abroad had a direct effect on U.S. import commerce in finished products containing price-fixed components satisfied Section 6a's effects exception).

[97] *Cf.* H.R. REP. NO. 97–686, at 13 (1982) ("For example, if a domestic export cartel were so strong as to have a 'spillover' effect on commerce within this country— by creating a world-wide shortage or artificially inflated world-wide price that had the effect of raising domestic prices—the cartel's conduct would fall within the reach of our antitrust laws. Such an impact would, at least over time, meet the test of a direct, substantial and reasonably foreseeable effect on domestic commerce."). * * *

including the FTAIA. For example, when anticompetitive conduct affects commerce around the world, a plaintiff whose antitrust injury arises from that conduct's effect on U.S. import commerce may recover damages for that injury, but a plaintiff that suffers a foreign injury that is independent of, and not proximately caused by, the conduct's effect on U.S. commerce cannot recover damages under the U.S. antitrust laws.

Similarly, when the United States is a plaintiff seeking damages under Section 4A of the Clayton Act for injury to its business or property, the United States must establish that the alleged conduct's effect on U.S. commerce proximately caused the injury to the United States' business or property. Civil actions for equitable relief brought by the Agencies or criminal enforcement actions brought by the Department, on behalf of the United States, do not seek to redress a pecuniary injury to the government. Instead, such actions are brought by the sovereign to enjoin or prosecute a violation of its laws. In such cases, a direct, substantial, and reasonably foreseeable effect on U.S. commerce would give rise to the sovereign's claim.[100]

Thus, as a result of the effects exception's "gives rise to" provision, the Sherman Act can apply and not apply to the same conduct, depending upon the circumstances, including the plaintiff bringing the claim, the nature of the claim, and the injury underlying the claim.[101]

Notes and Questions

1. The Guidelines are a statement of how the agencies plan to interpret and enforce the law. Are there any areas in which you think

---

[100] The Department's Antitrust Corporate Leniency Policy requires applicants to make restitution to the victims of their offense. . . . Consistent with the Supreme Court's and courts of appeals' interpretation of the "gives rise to" provision that damages for violations of the Sherman Act are not available for foreign injuries independent of and not proximately caused by any adverse effect on U.S. commerce, the Department construes the leniency policy to not require restitution to victims whose antitrust injuries are independent of and not proximately caused by an adverse effect on (i) trade or commerce within the United States, (ii) import trade or commerce, or (iii) the export trade or commerce of a person engaged in such trade or commerce in the United States, which effect was proximately caused by the anticompetitive activity being reported.

[101] *Empagran*, 542 U.S. at 174; *see also Motorola Mobility LLC v. AU Optronics Corp.*, 775 F.3d 816, 820, 825 (7th Cir. 2014) (noting that the FTAIA "would not block the Department of Justice from seeking criminal or injunctive remedies" for price fixing that had the requisite effect on U.S. commerce, while holding private plaintiff could not recover damages because the injury did not arise from that effect).

the Guidelines' interpretation would give the agencies too broad a reach, either in view of the FTAIA or good policy?

2.   Note that there is a split of circuits on whether "direct" is a literal and narrow or flexible and relative term. This issue came up in the case of the Canadian/Russian potash cartel. The cartel members drastically decreased their output in lockstep. They negotiated prices in China, India and Brazil and used those prices as benchmarks for sales that would be made to US customers. The US was the biggest market after China. The Court of Appeals for the Seventh Circuit said that the US sales were within the reach of the Sherman Act. Minn-Chem, Inc. v. Agrium, Inc., 683 F.3d 845 (7th Cir. 2012). However, in United States v. LSL Biotechs., 379 F.3d 672 (9th Cir. 2004), the Ninth Circuit held that "direct" means "follows as an immediate consequence," and it dismissed a case by the US government challenging a restrictive clause that kept the most important potential competitor—an Israeli researcher of fresh market tomato seeds—out of the North American market for long-shelf-life tomato seeds for five years after termination of the joint venture. The chain of causation was, however, attenuated for the Israeli firm had not yet developed such a seed.

3.   Illustrative Example D postulates a price cartel abroad [in Mineral X] that raises prices of Mineral X abroad. This produces an export opportunity for the sole US producer of Mineral X. The US producer diverts US supply to meet the export opportunity, and the diversion causes US prices of Mineral X to rise. Can and should the US Department of Justice prosecute the foreign price fixers?

———————

Some of the most interesting current questions flow from two input cartels—liquid crystal display (LCD) panels and cathode ray tubes (CRT).

The LCD panels are the main component of thin flat screens used in TVs, computer monitors, electronic notebooks, and smart phones. The panels were made by Samsung, AU Optronics, and four Korea or Taiwanese firms. They fixed the prices of the panels through scores of meetings, mainly in hotels in Taiwan, over the course of five years. The final products were sold throughout the world, including in the EU, US, and Brazil. An executive of AU Optronics was sentenced to prison in the United States.

In the EU, cartel member InnoLux, a vertically integrated company, had sold the price-fixed panels to its subsidiaries outside of the European Economic Area. The foreign subsidiaries had incorporated the panels into the finished products that they—the subsidiaries—sold in the EEA. InnnoLux claimed that its price fix was not "implemented in" the EEA, and that counting the finished product sales as a basis for its fine exceeded the EU's territorial jurisdiction in the application of Article 101. It made the following legal and policy arguments to the Court:

[40] InnoLux also submits that the General Court disregards the test in the judgment in Ahlström Osakeyhtiö [*Wood* Pulp] when it states . . . that sales of finished products incorporating LCD panels are 'harmful to competition within the EEA.' Those sales of finished products are not made on the EEA market concerned by the infringement. By definition, those sales cannot therefore restrict competition on that market. It is not sufficient to identify 'sales having a link with the EEA' in order to establish jurisdiction of the European Union under the test set out in Ahlström Osakeyhtiö. What must, however, be shown is the existence of sales in the EEA of the goods concerned by the infringement, namely LCD panels.

[41] In the fourth place, InnoLux submits that it is contrary to . . . Commercial Solvents to take the view that internal deliveries of LCD panels to manufacturing facilities in the EEA, as in Samsung's case, are not sales in the EEA when the finished products into which the LCD panels are incorporated are sold outside the EEA. The view that an internal sale of LCD panels within the EEA restricts competition within the EEA only when the finished product into which the LCD panel is incorporated is sold in the EEA is misconceived.

[42] In the fifth place, InnoLux submits that the test used by the Commission and the General Court to identify the place of internal deliveries gives rise to a risk of concurrent penalties and jurisdictional conflict with other competition authorities, in that it may lead to the self-same transaction being subject to a finding of infringement and sanctioned by multiple competition authorities worldwide. Consequently, in the present case, if the Commission imposes a fine in relation to a transaction concerning a component delivered outside the EEA on the ground that a finished product in which that component has been incorporated was sold in the EEA, the self-same transaction may be sanctioned both outside and inside the EEA.

The Court disagreed. It noted that the value of the finished products was taken into account in the fine only to the extent of the value of the LCD panels. It held:

[57] It follows that the General Court was fully entitled to hold, . . . that when a vertically-integrated undertaking incorporates the goods in respect of which the infringement was committed into the finished products in its production units situated outside the EEA, the sale by that undertaking of those finished products in the EEA to independent third parties is liable to affect competition on the

market for those products and, therefore, such an infringement may be considered to have had repercussions in the EEA, even if the market for the finished products in question constitutes a separate market from that concerned by the infringement . . . . * * *

[62] It should also be pointed out that excluding those sales would have the effect of artificially minimizing the economic significance of the infringement committed by a particular undertaking, since the mere fact such sales genuinely affected by the cartel in the EEA are excluded from being taken into account would lead to the imposition of a fine which bore no actual relation to the scope of application of that cartel in that territory . . . .

Case C–231/14P, *InnoLux v. Commission*, EU:C:2015:451.

Another question of territorial reach is pending before the European Court of Justice in *Intel v. Commission*, C–413/14P. One episode of this complex Article 102 case involves communications from Intel salespeople in the US with Lenovo, a major Chinese manufacturer of laptops and a user of Intel's computer chips. The conversation was to the following effect: Do not buy AMD's new chip. I will pay you to break your contract with AMD. Lenovo broke its contract with AMD, continued to use Intel's chip in its laptops, and sold the finished products in the EEA and the rest of the world. Does Article 102 extend to the Intel/Lenovo episode? If the conversations were between a dominant European producer and a Chinese manufacturer, leading to price rises in the US market, would the Sherman Act apply? (Revisit your answer after you read *Motorola Mobility*, below.)

Japan dealt with extraterritoriality in connection with the TV cathode ray tube cartel. The cartel members were CRT manufacturers located in Malaysia, Indonesia and Thailand. Their parent companies sold the price-fixed cathode ray tubes to Southeast Asian subsidiaries of a Japanese TV manufacturer and distributor. The Japanese manufacturer/distributor directly negotiated some of the terms of the purchase on behalf of its Southeast Asian subsidiaries. The TV sets were sold internationally, including into Japan. The JFTC fined the foreign price fixers. This was the first time that it fined foreign price fixers. *http://www.jftc.go.jp/en/press releases/yearly-2009/oct/individual-000037.html.*

US treatment of the input cartel problem surfaced most dramatically in the twin cases of *United States v. AU Optronics* (criminal prosecution) and *Motorola Mobility v. AU Optronics* (private damage action). In the criminal case, a Korean executive who engaged in price-fixing the LDC panels in Korea and Taiwan defended in the US courts that price-fixing of the panels, which were sold to the Chinese subsidiaries of Motorola Mobility for incorporation into smartphones and then sold to Motorola Mobility-US (and elsewhere), was too indirect and beyond reach of the US law. The Korean executive's defense did not succeed; he was convicted. *United States v. Hsiung*, 758 F.3d 1074 (9th Cir. 2014).

The defendants had better luck in the civil case. Their case came before the Court of Appeals for the Seventh Circuit on plaintiff's appeal from a grant of partial summary judgment to defendants. The court, by Judge Posner, held that the harm from the LCD cartel to Motorola Mobility was too indirect and moreover, applying FTAIA paragraph 2, the effect in the US did not give rise to Motorola Mobility's claim. As to directness, the court said (in what is now a vacated opinion):

> . . . But what is missing from Motorola's case is a "direct" effect. The effect is indirect—or "remote," the term used in MinnChem, Inc. v. Agrium, Inc., to denote the kind of effect that the statutory requirement of directness excludes.

> The alleged price fixers are not selling the panels in the United States. They are selling them abroad to foreign companies (the Motorola subsidiaries) that incorporate them into products that are then exported to the United States for resale by the parent. The effect of component price fixing on the price of the product of which it is a component is indirect, compared to the situation in Minn-Chem, where "foreign sellers allegedly created a cartel, took steps outside the United States to drive the price up of a product that is wanted in the United States, and then (after succeeding in doing so) sold that product to U.S. customers." 863 F.3d at 860. It is closer to the situation in which we said the foreign trade act would block liability under the Sherman Act: the "situation in which action in a foreign country filters through many layers and finally causes a few ripples in the United States." Id.

When Motorola sought rehearing en banc, the Department of Justice, endorsed by the Departments of State and Commerce, supported Motorola's motion. The Justice Department was apparently alarmed that the ruling on (indirect) effect would undermine its criminal prosecutions. The Seventh Circuit granted rehearing but not en banc and the case was returned to Judge Posner and the same panel. Perhaps not wanting or intending to interfere with the government litigation, Judge Posner and the panel vacated the earlier opinion, noted that this case was harder than *Minn Chem* but that the effect was not a mere ripple effect after passing through many layers, and assumed arguendo that the requirement that the US effect be "direct, substantial and reasonably foreseeable" was satisfied.

Applying FTAIA paragraph (2), Judge Posner proceeded to find that the effect of the LDC cartel on domestic commerce did not give rise to Motorola's claim. "[T]he cartel-engendered price increase in the components and in the price of cellphones that incorporated them occurred entirely in foreign commerce." He proceeded to elaborate on the inappropriateness of Motorola Mobility's action, stating that it was barred by *Illinois Brick* (Motorola Mobility was not a direct purchaser) and rightly so, he thought, because of the difficulty of estimating damages if any, and that Motorola Mobility had chosen China as the forum for contesting price-fixing to the Chinese subsidiaries and had to live with that choice.

As for the DOJ's brief in support of plaintiff, Judge Posner said: "Motorola has lost its best friend." The DOJ no longer wanted reversal of partial summary judgment against Motorola Mobility but merely a disclaimer that such a ruling against Motorola would not interfere with the government's criminal and injunctive remedies against the foreign cartelists. Judge Posner obliged. 775 F.3d 816 (7th Cir. 2015).

Notes and Questions

1.   Why didn't the effect of the cartel in the United States give rise to Motorola Mobility's claim? If the effect of the cartel in the United States was first and foremost on Motorola Mobility itself, shouldn't we fairly conflate the effect in the US and the effect on Motorola Mobility (the plaintiff's claim)? Didn't the FTAIA mean to weed out claims that were not real antitrust claims and antitrust claims that were solely foreign? If that is correct, isn't Motorola Mobility directly in the center of the antitrust wrong (as long as it was injured by the price fixing) and therefore deserving of the antitrust right to sue? This is exactly not an *Empagran* case, where foreign plaintiffs were injured in foreign markets by goods that never came into the United States.

2.   If the effect of the cartel on domestic commerce did not give rise to Motorola Mobility's claim because the claim arose solely in foreign commerce, why didn't the federal government's claim also arise solely in foreign commerce? The criminal defendant so argued. Both Motorola and the criminal defendant sought certiorari, but cert was denied.

3.   Has the court (under the guidance of *Empagran)* now turned standing issues into reach-of-law issues? Was this a good idea? Is there a possible drawback in terms of under-deterrence and victims' loss of

rights of compensation? Do you expect the Chinese manufacturers who bought the price-fixed panels to sue and recover for their losses in China, Korea, or Taiwan?

4.   In the EU, there is no *Illinois Brick*; thus, no indirect purchaser defense. Nor is there an FTAIA. Also the European Court has shown willingness to treat a firm and its manufacturing subsidiaries as a single vertically integrated entity. If Motorola Mobility were a European firm domiciled in a Member State, transforming the LCD panels into smart phones through its Chinese subsidiaries, could it recover its losses by suit in the courts of its Member State for damages under TFEU Article 101?

5.   Mergers too, and famously, have extraterritorial effects. Large multinational mergers tend to affect the world. Scores of jurisdictions may require pre-merger filings for the same mergers, and competition authorities of several countries may clear the merger with inconsistent remedies. Occasionally, one country prohibits a merger that the other jurisdictions allow. Today, many nations' competition authorities coordinate intensely on mergers of common concern. Still, divergences occur. You have met these issues in Chapter 5.

6.   As we have seen, conduct may harm competition in many nations. All of those nations have a stake in enforcement against offending acts. Ideally application by any one nation would not handicap procompetitive acts, or over-handicap even offensive acts. Coordination works to some extent (see Chapter 10), but not entirely. Do we need a world norm on proper and improper extraterritorial reach? What would be a wise norm? Should the norm of appropriate reach of the law differ according to whether the substantive law is convergent? For example, should there be more flexibility for outreach against hard core cartels that have no state support, which are condemned virtually everywhere, and more restraint in condemning abuses of dominance where the substantive rule is contested, the conduct is legal where done, and the harms are less direct?

D. OTHER FRONTIERS OF ANTITRUST JURISDICTION

1.   Alien Tort Claims Act and Customary International Law

Before the FTAIA's limits became a palpable constraint on foreign plaintiffs' actions, plaintiffs' lawyers attempted to open new frontiers for US antitrust, but they failed. In *Kruman v. Christie's Intern.*, 129 F.Supp.2d 620 (S.D.N.Y. 2001), plaintiffs sought to invoke the Alien Tort Claim Act as a basis for federal court jurisdiction over claims by foreign purchasers and sellers in the London art auction houses Christie's and Sotheby's. The Court was not persuaded. It said:

The Alien Tort Claims Act confers jurisdiction on district courts to hear "any civil action by an alien for a tort only, committed in violation of the law of nations or a treaty of the United States." Plaintiffs maintain that "a broad consensus has developed that certain basic anticompetitive activities, such as . . . price-fixing . . . [are] condemned worldwide" and thus "have risen to the level of customary international law . . . ." Accordingly, they argue, this Court has subject matter jurisdiction over the second count on the theory that defendants' actions were torts "committed in violation of the law of nations."

Plaintiffs' position, which only recently was rejected in the *Microsoft* case, borders on the frivolous. Customary international law, sometimes referred to as the law of nations, consists of those rules that "command the 'general assent of civilized nations.'" There is no substantial support for the proposition that there is an international consensus proscribing price fixing that fairly might be characterized as customary international law, much less an international consensus that price fixing gives rise to tort claims on behalf of victims. In consequence, it is unnecessary even to consider whether, as defendants maintain, violations of the law of nations require state action.

In view of subsequent rulings on the scope of the Alien Torts Claims Act, it is clear that antitrust plaintiffs cannot invoke the Act for conduct beyond the reach of the FTAIA. In Kiobel v. Royal Dutch Petroleum Co., 133 S. Ct. 1659 (2013), the Supreme Court held that the Alien Torts Claims Act does not apply extraterritorially. It does not apply to violations—even heinous civil rights violations— occurring abroad.

2. Trying to Outflank *Empagran*

a. *EU Claims in US Courts*

Another argument that US plaintiffs' lawyers occasionally assert, now that the rule against private cartels is accepted around the world, is that US courts should accept jurisdiction over antitrust claims arising under the laws of another country, and should apply the foreign law. There is nothing in principle that bars a US court from doing this. As long as the court has subject matter jurisdiction over the case (for example, because of the diverse nationality of the parties in a federal case) and personal jurisdiction over the parties (in view of their contacts with the US), a US court can do so. It can, for example, entertain a contract case involving paper sales in

Sweden and arising under Swedish law. If that's true of a contract case, why not of an antitrust case?

Some US judges have allowed such claims to be tested. For example, in a 2003 decision in *Multi-Juice v. Snapple Beverage Corp.*, No. 02 Civ. 4635, 2003 WL 1961636 (S.D.N.Y. Apr. 25, 2003), a federal judge in New York entertained a case alleging antitrust violations under the law of Greece and the EU. Although the court dismissed the complaint for failing to state a claim, it did so after applying ordinary US procedural rules to the adjudication of the motion to dismiss. The judge considered the elements of the various Greek and EU antitrust claims alleged and ruled that the plaintiff had not properly alleged them. As to the EU claim the court held:

> [A] prerequisite for a claim pursuant to Article [102] of the Treaty . . . is that the company alleged of a violation must hold a dominant position in the common market or a substantial part thereof. In this case, Plaintiffs assert that both Snapple and Mistic "enjoyed a dominant position within the Republic of Greece [and] throughout the European common market in the market for Premium Alterative Beverages." Nonetheless, several other allegations in the Complaint contradict this general assertion and state that, at the time of the agreement, Snapple sales were minimal as a result of prior harm inflicted on the company's reputation by Quaker, specifically: "Multi-Juice had to reestablish the reputation of the Snapple product in Greece because Quaker had destroyed the reputation of the Snapple name among Greek vendors" and "Multi-Juice had to work very hard to convince stores to put the Snapple brand back on the store shelves." In the face of these contrary allegations and the Complaint's failure to state what market share was held by either Snapple or Mistic, and Plaintiff's admission at oral argument that they do not have any studies to support an allegation of dominance, a more specific allegation regarding market dominance is necessary to permit these claims to continue.

Not all US judges have been willing to consider the merits of foreign antitrust claims. Under the doctrine of *forum non conveniens*, a court may dismiss a claim on the ground that it would be better to have it adjudicated elsewhere. In a 2001 decision in the same federal court that decided *Multi-Juice*, another judge (in re *Information Resources v. Dun & Bradstreet*, 127 F.Supp. 2d 411 (S.D.N.Y. 2000), declined to exercise jurisdiction over claims arising under the European Treaty:

[A] district court may decline to exercise supplemental jurisdiction over otherwise cognizable claims which raise novel or complex issues of State law, even if they are so related to claims in the action that they form part of the same case or controversy. Passing the point that the "State" involved is the European Economic Community, the United Kingdom, France, Germany, Italy, the Netherlands or Spain (or all of them), the novel and complex issues presented by Article [102 TFEU] (to which the United States is not a party) counsel against exercising supplemental jurisdiction over its application to the subsidiaries' claims.

Normally the subsidiary's claims under Article [102] would be brought in its national court, which would apply its own substantive and procedural rules and remedies in giving effect to the Treaty, and would have the option of seeking an opinion from the European Court of Justice on questions of European Community law. This court does not have that option; it would have to decide what European Community law would be, *de novo*. European countries' laws are neither uniform nor individually fully developed with respect to issues arising under the Treaty (*e.g.* statutes of limitation, degree of injunctive relief, awards of attorney's fees and expenses), and expert testimony might be required concerning the law of each jurisdiction. * * *

Although [Article 102 of the TFEU] is "roughly analogous" to the Sherman Act, its application to the subsidiaries' claims in six separate European markets would present sufficiently novel and complex issues of foreign law to persuade this court to decline to exercise supplemental jurisdiction, even if the Article [102] claims are otherwise cognizable.

The court also declined to apply EU competition law In re *Air Cargo Shipping Services Antitrust Litigation*, No. MD 06–1775, 2008 WL 5958061, at *30 (E.D.N.Y. Sept. 26, 2008), stating: "[T]he EU claims do not belong in United States courts. First, the choice by the EU plaintiffs, who are largely foreign, of the United States as a forum deserves comparatively less deference. Second, there are adequate alternative forums, outside the United States, where they can bring their EU claims. And third, the totality of the circumstances indicates that a foreign forum 'will be most convenient and will best serve the ends of justice.' The plaintiffs' EU claims should be dismissed on the grounds of *forum non conveniens*."

b.   German Claims in British Courts

As US courts grow increasingly inhospitable to claims by foreign plaintiffs, there may be increasing opportunities to test the willingness of other national courts to entertain claims by foreign purchasers. In 2003, the British Queen's Bench Division held that German vitamins purchasers were entitled to sue for damages in British courts, invoking Article 101 TFEU as the basis for the cartel's liability. *Provimi, Ltd. v. Aventis Animal Nutrition SA,* [2003] EWHC 961 (Comm) (Eng).

Why wouldn't German buyers simply sue in Germany? Plaintiffs may be drawn to British courts for some of the same reasons that they are drawn to US courts. British courts generally allow more liberal discovery rights than continental courts and have fully adversary proceedings. Further, the British Competition Appeal Tribunal is a specialized competition law body that litigants may prefer to generalist courts.

Will expanded private enforcement rights in the EU (see Chapter 9) mean more home-grown litigation in the Member States or more forum shopping by European plaintiffs eager to find the most receptive forum? If the US experience is predictive, there may be a good deal of forum shopping. Would it be beneficial for European nations to adopt some version of *Empagran* requiring plaintiffs even from another Member State to sue in the courts of their own country? Or is the fact that they are suing under a common substantive law sufficient to alleviate the concerns expressed in *Empagran*?

E.   CONCLUSION

Since so many acts and transactions occur beyond the borders of the nations they harm, nations are struggling with questions of the reach of their law. Should it be fair game for all nations' laws to reach offshore acts that harm them? Would a world vision to protect the global competition commons demand no less? Or do sovereign interests, combined with concerns of double counting, incoherent cumulative remedies, substantive disagreements, and procedural differences, counsel significant limits? The questions are playing out in the courts and the agencies of the world.

Chapter 9

GLOBAL GOVERNANCE

A. INTRODUCTION

For more than half a century we have debated the wisdom of an international antitrust regime. At the close of World War II, the free nations of the world began negotiating a global trading system to control transnational restrictive business practices. The Havana Charter, negotiated in 1947 to 1948, would have required nations to take measures against transborder business practices such as price-fixing, market divisions, and restraints limiting market access and fostering monopolistic conduct. The Havana Charter was never adopted, but was the precursor to the General Agreement on Tariffs and Trade.

Also in the 1940s, in the wake of world cartels that harmed America in its war effort, the United States pioneered the effects doctrine to protect itself from offshore cartels. *United States v. Aluminum Co. of America ("Alcoa")*, 148 F.2d 416 (2d Cir. 1945). Although resisted for years, effects jurisdiction is now well accepted in the world. See *Wood Pulp*, EU:C:1998:447 (European Court of Justice 1998) and see generally Chapter 8.

Effects jurisdiction is unilateral. It protects nations' citizens even in the absence of world cooperation or an international framework. This chapter is about the next step: community rather than unilateralism. It is about cooperation, convergence, and a possible international framework.

This chapter explores cooperative and integrative modalities for acts and transactions whose effects cross borders. It covers cooperation, including agreement on principles, guidelines, and bilateral cooperation agreements; proceeds to more integrative solutions through free trade areas and common markets, and concludes (even as it begins) with world norms and aspirations to solve problems at a higher level.

All elements and modalities, from the local to the global, are woven together at various times and in various regions, so we do not divide them sharply in our organization of this chapter.

As you will see as we document the journey, ambitions for a world regime began early on, in the 1940s. Concerns for sovereignty dictated caution and defeated the earliest world initiative. Extraterritorial jurisdiction filled the slack in some measure but also triggered conflicts and generated the need for comity if not convergence. Globalization exposed the limits of national law and led to renewed global vision. Then once again, sovereignty concerns and national interests overwhelmed cosmopolitan thinking, and it has produced robust efforts, which continue today, to nurture roots-up voluntary solutions, most prominently through the vehicle of the International Competition Network.

B. THE UNCTAD SET OF PRINCIPLES: VOLUNTARY RULES FOR THE WORLD

We revert to the 1960s at a time when certain world norms on competition and business restraints seemed possible and necessary. The 1960s were years of expansion of antitrust law in the United States and also in Europe. They were also years of the growth of the multinational firm. Developing countries saw themselves as targets of multinational firms. They triggered talks under the aegis of the United States Conference on Trade and Development (UNCTAD) with the hope to establish common rules against MNEs' restrictive business practices. (Most of the practices complained of were then illegal per se under US antitrust law but US antitrust law was subsequently relaxed to require an effects analysis for all but cartels.). The industrialized countries, the developing countries, and the communist block were the three negotiating groups. The nations reached agreement at the end of the 1970s and, in 1980, UNCTAD promulgated the Set of Multilaterally Agreed Principles and Rules for the Control of Restrictive Business Practices (RBPs), also known as the UNCTAD Set of Principles. The United States signed the UNCTAD Set of Principles—but not before bargaining for and procuring the provisions it really wanted: state-owned enterprises were covered; transfer pricing within one firm, whereby a subsidiary got a more favorable price than an outsider, was not included as an RBP, and all RBPs could be justified as reasonable. The Set applied to all business actors, not just multinational enterprises; and the Set was voluntary, not mandatory; there were no sanctions for its breach.

The UNCTAD Set remains the only multilaterally agreed (albeit voluntary) set of antitrust principles in the world. It has been reaffirmed every five years.

It was negotiated at a time when the developing countries saw the newly powerful and expanding multinational enterprises as feared and often predatory economic actors that would devastate their local industries, and as you will see the developing countries bargained for sympathetic treatment. We wish to highlight the substantive principles and rules agreed upon (point D of the Set, below).

Here are excerpts from the UNCTAD Set:

THE SET OF MULTILATERALLY AGREED EQUITABLE PRINCIPLES FOR THE CONTROL OF RESTRICTIVE BUSINESS PRACTICES
(excerpts, UNCTAD 1980)

* * *

A. Objectives

Taking into account the interests of all countries, particularly those of developing countries, the Set of Multilaterally Agreed Equitable Principles and Rules are framed in order to achieve the following objectives:

1.   To ensure that restrictive business practices do not impede or negate the realization of benefits that should arise from the liberalization of tariff and non-tariff barriers affecting world trade, particularly those affecting the trade and development of developing countries;

2.   To attain greater efficiency in international trade and development, particularly that of developing countries, in accordance with national aims of economic and social development and existing economic structures, such as through:

(a)   The creation, encouragement and protection of competition;

(b)   Control of the concentration of capital and/or economic power;

(c)   Encouragement of innovation;

3.   To protect and promote social welfare in general and, in particular, the interests of consumers in both developed and developing countries;

4.   To eliminate the disadvantages to trade and development which may result from the restrictive business practices of transnational corporations or other enterprises, and thus help to maximize benefits to international trade and particularly the trade and development of developing countries;

5.   To provide a Set of Multilaterally Agreed Equitable Principles and Rules for the control of restrictive business practices for adoption at the international level and thereby to facilitate the adoption and strengthening of laws and policies in this area at the national and regional levels.

* * *

C. Multilaterally agreed equitable principles for the control of restrictive business practices

In line with the objectives set forth, the following principles are to apply:

(i) *General principles*

1.   Appropriate action should be taken in a mutually reinforcing manner at national, regional and international levels to eliminate, or effectively deal with, restrictive business practices, including those of transnational corporations, adversely affecting international trade, particularly that of developing countries and the economic development of these countries.

2.   Collaboration between Governments at bilateral and multilateral levels should be established and, where such collaboration has been established, it should be improved to facilitate the control of restrictive business practices.

3.   Appropriate mechanisms should be devised at the international level and/or the use of existing international machinery improved to facilitate exchange and dissemination of information among Governments with respect to restrictive business practices.

4.   Appropriate means should be devised to facilitate the holding of multilateral consultations with regard to policy issues relating to the control of restrictive business practices.

5.   The provisions of the Set of Principles and Rules should not be construed as justifying conduct by enterprises which is unlawful under applicable national or regional legislation.

* * *

(iii) *Preferential or differential treatment for developing countries*

7.   In order to ensure the equitable application of the Set of Principles and Rules, States, particularly developed countries, should take into account in their control of restrictive business practices the development, financial and trade needs of developing

countries, in particular of the least developed countries, for the purposes especially of developing countries in:

(a) Promoting the establishment or development of domestic industries and the economic development of other sectors of the economy, and

(b) Encouraging their economic development through regional or global arrangements among developing countries.

* * *

D. Principles and Rules for enterprises, including transnational corporations

1. Enterprises should conform to the restrictive business practices laws, and the provisions concerning restrictive business practices in other laws, of the countries in which they operate, and, in the event of proceedings under these laws, should be subject to the competence of the courts and relevant administrative bodies therein.

2. Enterprises should consult and co-operate with competent authorities of countries directly affected in controlling restrictive business practices adversely affecting the interests of those countries. In this regard, enterprises should also provide information, in particular details of restrictive arrangements, required for this purpose, including that which may be located in foreign countries, to the extent that in the latter event such production or disclosure is not prevented by applicable law or established public policy. Whenever the provision of information is on a voluntary basis, its provisions should be in accordance with safeguards normally applicable in this field.

3. Enterprises, except when dealing with each other in the context of an economic entity wherein they are under common control, including through ownership, or otherwise not able to act independently of each other, engaged on the market in rival or potentially rival activities, should refrain from practices such as the following when, through formal, informal, written or unwritten agreements or arrangements, they limit access to markets or otherwise unduly restrain competition, having or being likely to have adverse effects on international trade, particularly that of developing countries, and on the economic development of these countries:

(a) Agreements fixing prices, including as to exports and imports;

(b) Collusive tendering;

(*c*)   Market or customer allocation arrangements;

(*d*)   Allocation by quota as to sales and production;

(*e*)   Collective action to enforce arrangements, e.g. by concerted refusals to deal;

(*f*)   Concerted refusal of supplies to potential importers;

(*g*)   Collective denial of access to an arrangement, or association, which is crucial to competition.

4.   Enterprises should refrain from the following acts or behavior in a relevant market when, through an abuse* or acquisition and abuse of a dominant position of market power, they limit access to markets or otherwise unduly restrain competition, having or being likely to have adverse effects on international trade, particularly that of developing countries, and on the economic development of these countries:

(*a*)   Predatory behavior towards competitors, such as using below cost pricing to eliminate competitors;

(*b*)   Discriminatory (i.e. unjustifiably differentiated) pricing or terms or conditions in the supply or purchase of goods and services, including by means of the use of pricing policies in transactions between affiliated enterprises which overcharge or undercharge for goods or services purchased or supplied as compared with prices for similar or comparable transactions outside the affiliated enterprises;

---

*   Whether acts or behavior are abusive or not should be examined in terms of their purpose and effects in the actual situation, in particular with reference to whether they limit access to markets or otherwise unduly restrain competition, having or being likely to have adverse effects on international trade, particularly that of developing countries, and on the economic development of these countries, and to whether they are:

(*a*) Appropriate in the light of the organizational, managerial and legal relationship among the enterprises concerned, such as in the context of relations within an economic entity and not having restrictive effects outside the related enterprises;

(*b*) Appropriate in light of special conditions of economic circumstances in the relevant market such as exceptional conditions of supply and demand or the size of the market;

(*c*) Of types which are usually treated as acceptable under pertinent national or regional laws and regulations for the control of restrictive business practices;

(*d*) Consistent with the purposes and objectives of these principles and rules.

(*c*) Mergers, takeovers, joint ventures or other acquisitions of control, whether of a horizontal, vertical or a conglomerate nature;

(*d*) Fixing the prices at which goods exported can be resold in importing countries;

(*e*) Restrictions on the importation of goods which have been legitimately marked abroad with a trademark identical with or similar to the trademark protected as to identical or similar goods in the importing country where the trademarks in question are of the same origin, i.e. belong to the same owner or are used by enterprises between which there is economic, organizational, managerial or legal interdependence and where the purpose of such restrictions is to maintain artificially high prices;

(*f*) When not for ensuring the achievement of legitimate business purposes, such as quality, safety, adequate distribution or service:

> (i) Partial or complete refusals to deal on the enterprise's customary commercial terms;

> (ii) Making the supply of particular goods or services dependent upon the acceptance of restrictions on the distribution or manufacture of competing or other goods;

> (iii) Imposing restrictions concerning where, or to whom, or in what form or quantities, goods supplied or other goods may be resold or exported;

> (iv) Making the supply of particular goods or services dependent upon the purchase of other goods or services from the supplier or his designee

* * *

F. International measures

Collaboration at the international level should aim at eliminating or effectively dealing with restrictive business practices, including those of transnational corporations, through strengthening and improving controls over restrictive business practices adversely affecting international trade, particularly that of developing countries, and the economic development of these countries. In this regard, action should include:

1.   Work aimed at achieving common approaches in national policies relating to restrictive business practices compatible with the Set of Principles and Rules.

2.   Communication annually to the Secretary-General of UNCTAD of appropriate information on steps taken by States and regional groupings to meet their commitment to the Set of Principles and Rules, and information on the adoption, development and application of legislation, regulations and policies concerning restrictive business practices.

3.   Continued publication annually by UNCTAD of a report on developments in restrictive business practices legislation and on restrictive business practices adversely affecting international trade, particularly the trade and development of developing countries, based upon publicly available information and as far as possible other information, particularly on the basis of requests addressed to all member States or provided at their own initiative and, where appropriate, to the United Nations Center on Transnational Corporations and other competent international organizations.

4.   Consultations:

(*a*)   Where a State, particularly of a developing country, believes that a consultation with another State or States is appropriate in regard to an issue concerning control of restrictive business practices, it may request a consultation with those States with a view to finding a mutually acceptable solution. When a consultation is to be held, the States involved may request the Secretary-General of UNCTAD to provide mutually agreed conference facilities for such a consultation;

(*b*)   States should accord full consideration to requests for consultations and, up on agreement as to the subject of and the procedures for such a consultation, the consultation should take place at an appropriate time;

(*c*)   If the States involved so agree, a joint report on the consultations and their results should be prepared by the States involved and, if they so wish, with the assistance of the UNCTAD secretariat, and be made available to the Secretary-General of UNCTAD for inclusion in the annual report on restrictive business practices.

* * *

Notes and Questions

1.   Consider the equitable principles in part C and the rules and principles in part D. Does the Set give too much preference and deference to developing countries, or too little?

2.   If you were called upon to modernize the Set, how would you change it?

3.   UNCTAD has prepared a Model Law on Competition based on the Set, along with commentaries which it continually updates. These can be found at *http://unctad.org/en/Pages/DITC/Competition Law/The-Model-Law-on-Competition.aspx.*

The UNCTAD Set and the Model Law on Competition are actively used for reference by developing and younger jurisdictions but not usually by mature jurisdictions such as the US or EU. What differences do you detect between the US and EU models and the UNCTAD model?

C. COOPERATION

Coherence in international antitrust law and practice requires not only relatively common rules and principles but also cooperation in understanding them and identifying differences, and cooperation in enforcement and application. Facilitating international cooperation is a key mission of the ICN, and has been a major goal as well for the OECD and the UNCTAD. ICN launched a major project on international cooperation in 2012, explaining in a steering group paper:

ICN Steering Group
International Enforcement Cooperation Project

(March 2012)

* * *

The Need for International Enforcement Cooperation

Businesses around the world work in a globalized way. This applies not only to large multinational corporations with production, services and/or sales in many different jurisdictions around the globe, but also to smaller firms that, even if based in only one or two or a few different jurisdictions, have business relations with firms in other jurisdictions. The interconnection and globalization of the world's economies are here to stay. There may be debate about how quickly this interconnection and globalization will increase, what the effect of the economic downturn will be over the mid and longer term, and which economies will prosper most. But no one doubts that interconnection and globalization are, and will continue to be, key features of our economies and business relations and that they will increasingly impact agency enforcement, consumers, and economies worldwide.

Historically, international enforcement cooperation has tended to be practiced on a bilateral basis and by only a few jurisdictions or groups of jurisdictions (e.g., the ECN [the European Competition Network]) around the world. This is changing. The last few years have witnessed international enforcement cooperation involving agencies from six continents demonstrating that cooperation is now a global phenomenon. The consensus is that this trend will continue to develop over the years to come, driven by the continued globalization of business and commerce and the need for efficient and effective enforcement by agencies. International enforcement cooperation helps to avoid inconsistencies in remedies and outcomes of enforcement actions, and it also helps businesses reduce their costs of compliance. The general experience thus far is that the more international enforcement cooperation increases, the more complex it becomes in practice as agencies with different legal powers, experiences, traditions and cultures seek to work closely together. Finding the tools and the ways to take these objectives forward will require open dialogue, respect and trust of all the participants involved.

* * *

Under the aegis of this initiative, ICN adopted Guidance on Investigative Process, available at *http://www.international competitionnetwork.org/uploads/library/doc1031.pdf* and the ICN Practical Guide to International Enforcement Cooperation in Mergers, available at *http://www.internationalcompetitionnetwork. org/uploads/library/doc1031.pdf.*

The guidance focuses on the tools available, transparency, engagement, information sharing and confidentiality, and for mergers, making the contact, aligning timetables, and cooperation in substantive assessment and remedies.

The US and the EU have been leaders in facilitating and implementing cooperation. The US Antitrust Guidelines for International Enforcement and Cooperation (2017) provide guidance on the principles that will guide the US agencies. Thus:

US Antitrust Guidelines
for International Enforcement and Cooperation

(2017) (footnotes omitted)

* * *

5. International Cooperation

Effective enforcement of the U.S. antitrust laws in a global economy benefits from cooperation with foreign authorities. The Agencies are committed to cooperating with foreign authorities on both policy and investigative matters. This cooperation contributes to convergence on substantive enforcement standards that seek to advance consumer welfare, based on sound economics, procedural fairness, transparency, and non-discriminatory treatment of parties. The Agencies' international policy work and case cooperation are closely connected. As noted above, consistent approaches to competition law, policy, and procedures across jurisdictions facilitate case cooperation among competition authorities. Moreover, through case cooperation, the Agencies and cooperating authorities often raise important substantive and procedural issues as they arise in practice, which can lead to greater convergence in substantive analysis and procedures. In keeping with these Guidelines' focus on international enforcement and practice, this Chapter focuses on investigations and case cooperation.

International case cooperation helps agencies investigating a particular matter to identify issues of common interest, gain a better understanding of relevant facts, and achieve consistent outcomes. Cooperation can yield better results for competition and promote efficiency for both cooperating agencies and subjects of an investigation. It can improve substantive analyses and procedures, and ensure that investigations and remedies are as consistent and predictable as possible, which improves outcomes, and reduces uncertainty and expense to firms doing business across borders. When either Agency reviews a case that raises possible competitive concerns in jurisdictions outside of the United States, it may consult with the relevant foreign authorities about the matter and coordinate and cooperate with those authorities conducting parallel investigations. As described in greater detail throughout this chapter, cooperation can include a broad range of practices, from initiating informal discussions and informing cooperating authorities of the different stages of their investigations, to engaging in detailed discussions of substantive issues, exchanging information, conducting interviews at which two or more agencies may be present, and coordinating remedy design and implementation, as relevant and appropriate.

5.1 Investigations and Cooperation

Increasingly, the Agencies' investigations involve conduct, entities, individuals, and information located outside the United States. The Agencies employ a combination of their own investigative tools and cooperation with foreign authorities in investigating and seeking appropriate remedies in certain international matters.

5.1.1 Investigative Tools

When practical and consistent with enforcement objectives, the Agencies may request that parties and third parties voluntarily: provide documents; submit to interviews; or provide other information related to an investigation. These requests may seek documents or information located outside the United States. The Agencies also may use compulsory measures to obtain documents and information. Specifically, the Agencies may compel production of documents or information via civil investigative demand ("CID") or subpoena. U.S. law provides authority for such compulsory measures directed to persons over whom the courts have personal jurisdiction. The Agencies may compel the production of documents or information, including documents or information located outside the United States, when the documents or information sought are within the "possession, custody, or control" of an individual or entity subject to the jurisdiction of the United States and are not protected by the attorney-client privilege or the work-product doctrine.

When one of the Agencies investigates a transaction notified under the HSR Act, it may issue a request for additional documents or information, typically called a "Second Request." Compliance with a Second Request requires production of all responsive documents and information, no matter where located.

Conflicts can arise where foreign statutes purport to prevent individuals or entities from disclosing documents or information for use in U.S. proceedings. The mere existence of such statutes, however, does not excuse noncompliance with a request for documents or information from one of the Agencies.

Because unilaterally collecting documents or information from individuals or entities located abroad can adversely affect law enforcement relationships with foreign countries, the Agencies use compulsory measures after carefully considering the importance of the documents or information to the investigation or prosecution and the availability of other means to obtain them. When such compulsory measures are warranted, the Agencies may seek to work with the foreign authority involved as appropriate.

5.1.2   Confidentiality

The Agencies' enforcement activities benefit greatly from access to sensitive, nonpublic information from businesses and consumers. The Agencies recognize the importance of protecting the confidentiality of sensitive, nonpublic information received from parties and foreign authorities. The Agencies protect the confidentiality of all such information received, be it from businesses or consumers located domestically or abroad, or from foreign authorities, under applicable provisions of U.S. law.

Several statutes require the Agencies to treat as confidential certain information obtained in the course of an investigation. The HSR Act prohibits the Agencies from disclosing information obtained pursuant to the act, including the fact that the parties filed notice of a proposed transaction and confidential business information provided in a filing or in response to a document or information request. The FTC Act restricts disclosure of information that the Commission receives pursuant to compulsory process, or produced voluntarily in lieu of process, in a law enforcement investigation. The FTC Act also prohibits the Commission from making public any trade secret or any commercial or financial information it obtains that is privileged or confidential, except in limited circumstances. The Antitrust Civil Process Act prohibits the Department from disclosing documents or testimony obtained pursuant to a CID without the consent of the person that produced the materials, except in limited circumstances. Other federal laws also require the Agencies to treat specific types of information as confidential, without regard to the manner in which the information is obtained. For example, laws governing privacy, national security information, and trade secrets require that the Agencies treat certain information as confidential.

There are certain, discrete circumstances in which the Agencies may disclose a person's confidential information for a specific use. The HSR Act, the FTC Act, and the Antitrust Civil Process Act do not bar the Agencies' use of a person's confidential information in judicial and administrative proceedings. However, the Federal Rules of Civil Procedure and FTC Rules of Practice include procedures to protect confidential information used in judicial proceedings or FTC administrative proceedings.

The Agencies also are subject to the Freedom of Information Act ("FOIA"), which provides the public with a right of access to certain agency records. This statute, however, contains several exemptions that protect information provided to the Agencies. It permits the

Agencies to withhold certain categories of documents from requesters, including information protected by statute (such as the HSR Act or FTC Act), "commercial or financial information obtained from a person [that is] privileged or confidential," inter- or intra-agency memoranda or letters that would be routinely privileged in civil discovery, and "files the disclosure of which would constitute a clearly unwarranted invasion of personal privacy." In addition, an exemption from FOIA's disclosure regime applies to certain information compiled for law enforcement purposes, including when disclosure could interfere with enforcement proceedings or disclose the identity of a confidential source.

5.1.3   Legal Bases for Cooperation

The Agencies' authority to cooperate with foreign authorities is inherent in their ability to act in furtherance of their mandates. The Department and FTC, therefore, each has the discretion to cooperate, including when it furthers its enforcement interests. Cooperation can be facilitated by bilateral and multilateral arrangements. The Agencies have also developed best practices and guidance documents on cooperation for specific types of investigations. These arrangements and guidance documents can serve as a catalyst for cooperation and provide useful guidance to coordinate and facilitate enforcement activities. They are not necessary for cooperation to take place, and the Agencies may cooperate with relevant foreign authorities in the absence of any formal arrangement. These bilateral and multilateral arrangements do not change the signatories' laws, including laws concerning the treatment of confidential information.

The IAEAA authorizes the Agencies to enter into antitrust-specific mutual assistance agreements with foreign authorities that allow the Agencies to share evidence relating to antitrust violations already in their possession and provide each other with investigatory assistance in obtaining evidence, subject to certain limitations. As noted in Section 2.6, the IAEAA does not apply to materials submitted pursuant to the HSR Act.

5.1.4   Types of Information Exchanged
and Waivers of Confidentiality

If a transaction or conduct under antitrust investigation in the United States is also being investigated by a foreign authority, the Department or the Commission may contact the authority. The Agencies may share with these foreign authorities relevant publicly available information. Similarly, it remains in the Agencies' discretion whether to share with cooperating foreign authorities agency non-public information, which is information that the Agencies are not statutorily prohibited from disclosing, but that the

Agencies normally treat as non-public and withhold from public disclosure. Examples of agency non-public information include the existence of an open investigation and the Agencies' staff views as to the merits of a case, market definition, competitive effects, substantive theories of harm, and remedies. Before exchanging agency non-public information, the Agencies will have reached an understanding that the foreign authority will maintain the information in confidence and in accordance with that authority's laws and rules. This may be through bilateral or multilateral cooperation agreements or arrangements, or other means.

While confidentiality obligations generally prohibit the Agencies from disclosing to foreign authorities confidential information submitted by a person, that person can enable the Agencies to engage in more meaningful cooperation with foreign authorities by granting the Agencies a waiver of confidentiality as to information that may be otherwise protected from disclosure. The Agencies issued a joint model waiver of confidentiality for use in civil matters, which serves to streamline the waiver process and published explanatory materials that provide further details on waivers of confidentiality, applicable confidentiality rules, and the process for providing a waiver of confidentiality.

A waiver identifies the terms under which a person agrees to waive statutory confidentiality protections vis-à-vis the agency that originally received the person's confidential information. A waiver also describes an agency's policy regarding how it will treat the information it receives from another agency pursuant to a waiver, although it is not an agreement signed by the agency. Waivers are limited in scope to a specific, named matter and designate the agencies that may share the waiving person's confidential information. Waivers generally allow the cooperating authorities to share documents, statements, data, and other information.

Waivers enable deeper communication, cooperation, and coordination among competition authorities concurrently reviewing a matter. They can lead to more effective, efficient investigations and better-informed, more consistent enforcement decisions based on the Agencies' increased ability to share information.

The Agencies will protect information received from a foreign authority pursuant to a waiver under applicable provisions of U.S. law. The Agencies will not seek information that is privileged under U.S. law from foreign authorities through waivers or other cooperative activities.

Similarly, the Agencies will provide information to foreign authorities pursuant to a waiver when they have reached an understanding with the recipient agency that it will maintain the confidentiality of such information consistent with its laws and rules. Generally, a person that has waived the confidentiality of its information as to one of the Agencies also will provide a separate waiver of confidentiality to the relevant foreign authority, based on the waiving person's understanding of the foreign authority's confidentiality protections.

The Agencies may request a waiver of confidentiality, but the decision whether to provide one rests solely with the producing person. Refusal to provide a waiver will not prejudice the outcome of an investigation, though, in some cases, the absence of a waiver may have practical effects such as increasing the risk of inconsistent outcomes between jurisdictions. Further, declining to grant a waiver will not preclude the Agencies from sharing publicly available or agency non-public information with foreign authorities.

Illustrative Example G

Situation: Corporation 1 and Corporation 2 each manufacture Product X and Product Y. Corporation 1 and Corporation 2 enter into an agreement to merge. The proposed merger meets the threshold for premerger notification in the United States under the HSR Act and the thresholds for premerger notification in several other jurisdictions. Corporation 1 and Corporation 2 inform the U.S. Agency reviewing the merger as well as reviewing foreign authorities that the merger will be notified or reviewed in multiple jurisdictions. Pre-notification consultations and pre-merger filings are timed to facilitate communication and cooperation among reviewing authorities at key decision-making stages of their respective investigations.

Discussion: After learning that the merger will be notified or reviewed in more than one jurisdiction, the U.S. Agency contacts the foreign reviewing authorities to discuss review timetables and assess the potential for cooperation. The extent of cooperation with each foreign authority reviewing the matter will vary depending on factors including the depth of that authority's investigation, the competitive conditions in that authority's jurisdiction, and the scope of potential remedies likely to be considered. The U.S. Agency requests a waiver of confidentiality from Corporation 1 and Corporation 2 to allow for the exchange of confidential information with the reviewing authorities in Countries Alpha, Beta, and Gamma, given the nature of the competitive concerns raised by the merger in these jurisdictions. Corporation 1 and Corporation 2 voluntarily grant these waivers, as well as the waivers of confidentiality requested by each of these reviewing authorities. The U.S. Agency cooperates with

the reviewing authorities in Countries Delta and Epsilon on the basis
of publicly available and agency non-public information, without
exchanging confidential business information.

As reviews of the merger proceed, the U.S. Agency and the other
reviewing authorities arrange communications between and among
themselves as appropriate to their investigations. The U.S. Agency
and authorities of Alpha, Beta, and Gamma each arrange regular,
bilateral calls and, in some instances, certain of these agencies
conduct interviews together, facilitated by waivers. These reviewing
agencies, as well as the reviewing authorities of Delta and Epsilon,
also conduct status calls, based on publicly available and agency non-
public information to update each other on the timing of reviews and
theories of harm. The reviewing authorities of Delta and Epsilon
identify that the merger's effects in their jurisdictions are likely to be
insignificant, and that they will close their investigations
accordingly.

5.1.5 Remedies

The Agencies seek remedies that effectively address harm or
threatened harm to U.S. commerce and consumers, while attempting
to avoid conflicts with remedies contemplated by their foreign
counterparts. An Agency will seek a remedy that includes conduct or
assets outside the United States only to the extent that including
them is needed to effectively redress harm or threatened harm to
U.S. commerce and consumers and is consistent with the Agency's
international comity analysis.

When multiple authorities are investigating the same
transaction or same conduct, the Agencies may cooperate with other
authorities, to the extent permitted under U.S. law, to facilitate
obtaining effective and non-conflicting remedies. Cooperation also
may facilitate the development of a proposed remedies package that
comprehensively addresses the concerns of multiple authorities. In
some circumstances, cooperation may result in one authority closing
an investigation without remedies after taking another authority's
remedies into account.

Illustrative Example H

Situation: After investigating the merger as outlined in
Illustrative Example G, the U.S. Agency finds that the merger is
likely to substantially lessen competition in the U.S. market for
Product X, and therefore that the merger would violate Section 7 of
the Clayton Act. The U.S. Agency determines that these competitive
concerns likely can be addressed through a divestiture of Corporation
1's assets related to Product X. Countries Alpha, Beta, and Gamma

also find that the merger will harm competition in their markets for Product X, and Country Gamma has additional concerns about a reduction of competition in Gamma's market for Product Y.

Discussion: The U.S. Agency and the authorities in Alpha, Beta, and Gamma discuss, among themselves and with Corporation 1 and Corporation 2, a proposed remedy for the competitive concerns regarding Product X, in an effort to identify a package of assets for divesture that addresses the reviewing agencies' competitive concerns.

In this instance, the U.S. Agency and the foreign reviewing authorities agree that the same divestiture remedy for Product X will effectively address the competitive concerns in their respective jurisdictions. Corporation 1 and Corporation 2 enter into a consent decree in the United States that includes divestiture of specified assets of Corporation 1's related to Product X, and the authority in Alpha seeks the same divestiture remedy to ensure enforceability of the remedy in its jurisdiction. Country Beta concludes that the remedies secured in the United States and in Country Alpha are sufficient to address its competitive concerns and closes its investigation. Country Gamma seeks a remedy identical to that entered into in the United States and Country Alpha regarding Product X, coupled with an additional remedy to address the competitive harm in its jurisdiction regarding Product Y.

5.2 Special Considerations in Criminal Investigations

Among the Department's top priorities is the criminal investigation and prosecution of international price-fixing cartels. Because these cartels often involve foreign located defendants, witnesses, and evidence, antitrust enforcement in this context can present not only an investigatory challenge but also a special need for international cooperation and coordination. Mutual Legal Assistance Treaties ("MLATs") are an important basis for international cooperation in the Department's criminal antitrust enforcement. MLATs are used often in criminal investigations to gather evidence located outside the United States. Parties to these agreements have agreed to assist one another in criminal law enforcement matters. The specific provisions of MLATs vary, but they generally provide for assistance in obtaining evidence and in serving documents in one jurisdiction at the request of the other.

The Department also coordinates with foreign authorities when they are conducting cartel investigations parallel with the Department's own. The Department sometimes shares information to coordinate investigative steps. For example, to minimize the risk of document destruction, the Department and foreign authorities can time dawn raids and searches to coincide in multiple jurisdictions. And the Department and foreign authorities may also coordinate on logistical aspects of their parallel investigations to help minimize overlapping and inconsistent demands placed on cooperating individuals and firms. The Department recognizes that such coordination has the benefit of decreasing the costs to cooperators and increasing the pace of the investigations and is committed to engaging in such coordination where practicable.

The Department's ability to share information with foreign authorities is not unlimited, however. An essential component in the investigation and enforcement of the criminal antitrust laws is the grand jury, which is subject to the grand jury secrecy rule. Through its subpoenas, a grand jury can "compel the production of evidence or the testimony of witnesses as it considers appropriate, and its operation generally is unrestrained by the technical procedural and evidentiary rules governing the conduct of criminal trials." The Department is prohibited, however, from disclosing matters occurring before the grand jury absent an applicable exception. This prohibition cannot be waived by a subject of the investigation, a grand jury witness, or a recipient of a grand jury subpoena. The prohibition, however, does not apply to these persons and therefore does not generally prohibit disclosures by them.

In addition, a criminal investigation can gather information through the assistance of an applicant under the Department's Corporate and Individual Leniency Policies for antitrust crimes. To qualify for leniency under those policies, the applicant is required, among other things, to report the wrongdoing with candor and completeness and provide full, continuing, and complete cooperation. That required cooperation includes the production of all documents, information, or other materials in the applicant's possession, custody, or control, wherever located, that are requested by the Department in connection with the criminal antitrust investigation and are not protected by the attorney-client privilege or the workproduct doctrine.

Notes and Questions

1. Comment on the extent of cooperation between the US agencies and their counterparts in other jurisdictions. What might be the next step in enhanced cooperation?

2. Is agency cooperation likely to advance the cause of efficiency in enforcement throughout the world? How? Is it likely to advance other goals? Convergence of law and analysis? Fairness in treatment (due process)?

3.   Note the considerable attention, and deferential attention, given to parties' claims of confidentiality. Why is it important for authorities to respect these claims, despite the greater ease in enforcement if documents are shared? Business firms often very generously claim confidentiality. What happens or should happen if firms over-claim confidentiality of documents particularly key to an enforcement?

4.   What is the rule of restraint that the agencies impose on themselves in seeking remedies? (See § 5.1.5.) Revisit also the comity section of the Guidelines, § 4.1 (see Chapter 8, supra). Can you derive from these self-restraints notional world norms to reconcile conflicting sovereign interests? If all competition authorities of the world followed these norms, would problems of conflict be solved? Would the norms affect deterrence?

5.   The Guidelines are about agency-to-agency cooperation. They do not tell courts what to do. What is the significance of the fact that the courts are outside of the purview of the Guidelines? Are there aspects of the Guidelines that the courts could and should apply to themselves?

Bilateral cooperation agreements

The US Guidelines refer to and cite the numerous bilateral cooperation agreements and best practices agreements to which the US is a party. These include agreements with China, India, Canada, Brazil, Mexico, Japan, and many others. The EU is party to even more such agreements. These agreements are generally about sharing information and avoiding conflicts. To give you an idea of the coverage of such agreements, we include excerpts from the US/EU agreements of 1991 and 1998. Together, they establish notions of both negative and positive comity. Negative or traditional comity involves deferring to a trading partner when the first party's enforcement would adversely affect the important interests of the other party. Positive comity involves situations in which both parties have an interest in the antitrust enforcement but one is better placed to bring the proceedings than the other. The first party may request and await the better-placed party's investigation and enforcement before taking action itself.

Here are excerpts from the US/EU 1991 and 1998 agreements. The second agreement further elaborates on positive comity, but excludes mergers from its scope.

US/EU ANTITRUST COOPERATION
AGREEMENT OF 1991

* * *

Article II
NOTIFICATION

1.   Each Party shall notify the other whenever its competition authorities become aware that their enforcement activities may affect important interests of the other Party.

2.   Enforcement activities as to which notification ordinarily will be appropriate include those that:

a)   Are relevant to enforcement activities of the other Party;

b)   Involve anticompetitive activities (other than a merger or acquisition) carried out in significant part in the other Party's territory;

c)   Involve a merger or acquisition in which one or more of the parties to the transaction, or a company controlling one or more of the parties to the transaction, is a company incorporated or organized under the laws of the other Party or one of its states or member states;

d)   Involve conduct believed to have been required, encouraged or approved by the other Party; or

e)   Involve remedies that would, in significant respects, require or prohibit conduct in the other Party's territory.

3.   With respect to mergers or acquisitions required by law to be reported to the competition authorities, notification under this Article shall be made:

a)   In the case of the Government of the United States of America,

(i)   not later than the time its competition authorities request, pursuant to 15 U.S.C. § 18a(e), additional information or documentary material concerning the proposed transaction,

(ii)   when its competition authorities decide to file a complaint challenging the transaction, and

(iii) where this is possible, far enough in advance of the entry of a consent decree to enable the other Party's views to be taken into account; and

b)   In the case of the Commission of the European Communities,

(i)   when notice of the transaction is published in the Official Journal, pursuant to Article 4(3) of Council Regulation no. 4064/89, or when notice of the transaction is received under Article 66 of the ECSC Treaty and a prior authorization from the Commission is required under that provision,

(ii)   when its competition authorities decide to initiate proceedings with respect to the proposed transaction, pursuant to Article 6(1)(c) of Council Regulation no. 4064/89, and

(iii)   far enough in advance of the adoption of a decision in the case to enable the other Party's views to be taken into account.

4.   With respect to other matters, notification shall ordinarily be provided at the stage in an investigation when it becomes evident that notifiable circumstances are present, and in any event far enough in advance of

a)   the issuance of a statement of objections in the case of the Commission of the European Communities, or a complaint or indictment in the case of the Government of the United States of America, and

b)   the adoption of a decision or settlement in the case of the Commission of the European Communities, or the entry of a consent decree in the case of the Government of the United States of America, to enable the other Party's views to be taken into account.

5.   Each Party shall also notify the other whenever its competition authorities intervene or otherwise participate in a regulatory or judicial proceeding that does not arise from its enforcement activities, if the issues addressed in the intervention or participation may affect the other Party's important interests. Notification under this paragraph shall apply only to

a)   regulatory or judicial proceedings that are public,

b)   intervention or participation that is public and pursuant to formal procedures, and

c)   in the case of regulatory proceedings in the United States, only proceedings before federal agencies.

Notification shall be made at the time of the intervention or participation or as soon thereafter as possible.

6.   Notifications under this Article shall include sufficient information to permit an initial evaluation by the recipient Party of any effects on its interests.

Article III
EXCHANGE OF INFORMATION

1.   The Parties agree that it is in their common interest to share information that will (a) facilitate effective application of their respective competition laws, or (b) promote better understanding by them of economic conditions and theories relevant to their competition authorities' enforcement activities and interventions or participation of the kind described in Article II, paragraph 5.

2.   In furtherance of this common interest, appropriate officials from the competition authorities of each Party shall meet at least twice each year, unless otherwise agreed, to

> a)   exchange information on their current enforcement activities and priorities, (b) exchange information on economic sectors of common interest, (c) discuss policy changes which they are considering, and (d) discuss other matters of mutual interest relating to the application of competition laws.

3.   Each Party will provide the other Party with any significant information that comes to the attention of its competition authorities about anticompetitive activities that its competition authorities believe is relevant to, or may warrant, enforcement activity by the other Party's competition authorities.

4.   Upon receiving a request from the other Party, and within the limits of Articles VIII and IX, a Party will provide to the requesting Party such information within its possession as the requesting Party may describe that is relevant to an enforcement activity being considered or conducted by the requesting Party's competition authorities.

Article IV
COOPERATION AND COORDINATION IN
ENFORCEMENT ACTIVITIES

1.   The competition authorities of each Party will render assistance to the competition authorities of the other Party in their enforcement activities, to the extent compatible with the assisting Party's laws and important interests, and within its reasonably available resources.

2.   In cases where both Parties have an interest in pursuing enforcement activities with regard to related situations, they may agree that it is in their mutual interest to coordinate their enforcement activities. In considering whether particular enforcement activities should be coordinated, the Parties shall take account of the following factors, among others:

a)   the opportunity to make more efficient use of their resources devoted to the enforcement activities;

b)   the relative abilities of the Parties' competition authorities to obtain information necessary to conduct the enforcement activities;

c)   the effect of such coordination on the ability of both Parties to achieve the objectives of their enforcement activities; and

d)   the possibility of reducing costs incurred by persons subject to the enforcement activities.

3.   In any coordination arrangement, each Party shall conduct its enforcement activities expeditiously and, insofar as possible, consistently with the enforcement objectives of the other Party.

4.   Subject to appropriate notice to the other Party, the competition authorities of either Party may limit or terminate their participation in a coordination arrangement and pursue their enforcement activities independently.

Article V
COOPERATION REGARDING ANTICOMPETITIVE ACTIVITIES IN THE TERRITORY OF ONE PARTY THAT ADVERSELY AFFECT THE INTERESTS OF THE OTHER PARTY

1.   The Parties note that anticompetitive activities may occur within the territory of one Party that, in addition to violating that Party's competition laws, adversely affect important interests of the other Party. The Parties agree that it is in both their interests to address anticompetitive activities of this nature.

2.   If a Party believes that anticompetitive activities carried out on the territory of the other Party are adversely affecting its important interests, the first Party may notify the other Party and may request that the other Party's competition authorities initiate appropriate enforcement activities. The notification shall be as specific as possible about the nature of the anticompetitive activities and their effects on the interests of the notifying Party, and shall include an offer of such further information and other cooperation as the notifying Party is able to provide.

3. Upon receipt of a notification under paragraph 2, and after such other discussion between the Parties as may be appropriate and useful in the circumstances, the competition authorities of the notified Party will consider whether or not to initiate enforcement activities, or to expand ongoing enforcement activities, with respect to the anticompetitive activities identified in the notification. The notified Party will advise the notifying Party of its decision. If enforcement activities are initiated, the notified Party will advise the notifying Party of their outcome and, to the extent possible, of significant interim developments.

4. Nothing in this Article limits the discretion of the notified Party under its competition laws and enforcement policies as to whether or not to undertake enforcement activities with respect to the notified anticompetitive activities, or precludes the notifying Party from undertaking enforcement activities with respect to such anticompetitive activities.

Article VI
AVOIDANCE OF CONFLICTS OVER ENFORCEMENT ACTIVITIES

Within the framework of its own laws and to the extent compatible with its important interests, each Party will seek, at all stages in its enforcement activities, to take into account the important interests of the other Party. Each Party shall consider important interests of the other Party in decisions as to whether or not to initiate an investigation or proceeding, the scope of an investigation or proceeding, the nature of the remedies or penalties sought, and in other ways, as appropriate. In considering one another's important interests in the course of their enforcement activities, the Parties will take account of, but will not be limited to, the following principles:

1. While an important interest of a Party may exist in the absence of official involvement by the Party with the activity in question, it is recognized that such interests would normally be reflected in antecedent laws, decisions or statements of policy by its competent authorities.

2. A Party's important interests may be affected at any stage of enforcement activity by the other Party. The Parties recognize, however, that as a general matter the potential for adverse impact on one Party's important interests arising from enforcement activity by the other Party is less at the investigative stage and greater at the stage at which conduct is prohibited or penalized, or at which other forms of remedial orders are imposed.

3. Where it appears that one Party's enforcement activities may adversely affect important interests of the other Party, the Parties

will consider the following factors, in addition to any other factors that appear relevant in the circumstances, in seeking an appropriate accommodation of the competing interests:

a)	the relative significance to the anticompetitive activities involved of conduct within the enforcing Party's territory as compared to conduct within the other Party's territory;

b)	the presence or absence of a purpose on the part of those engaged in the anticompetitive activities to affect consumers, suppliers, or competitors within the enforcing Party's territory;

c)	the relative significance of the effects of the anticompetitive activities on the enforcing Party's interests as compared to the effects on the other Party's interests;

d)	the existence or absence of reasonable expectations that would be furthered or defeated by the enforcement activities;

e)	the degree of conflict or consistency between the enforcement activities and the other Party's laws or articulated economic policies; and

f)	the extent to which enforcement activities of the other Party with respect to the same persons, including judgments or undertakings resulting from such activities, may be affected.

Article VII
CONSULTATION

[Parties shall consult on request.]

* * *

Article VIII
CONFIDENTIALITY OF INFORMATION

* * *

The 1991 cooperation agreement was an advance over the earlier agreements in criminal matters (MLATs), which merely require each party to notify the other party when an action is being brought that might affect the other's important interests and suggest refraining from suit in appropriate cases. The 1998 agreement further articulates positive comity. Here are excerpts.

US/EU ANTITRUST COOPERATION AGREEMENT OF 1998 . . . ON THE APPLICATION OF POSITIVE COMITY PRINCIPLES IN THE ENFORCEMENT OF THEIR COMPETITION LAWS

* * *

Article I
SCOPE AND PURPOSE OF THIS AGREEMENT

1.   This Agreement applies where a Party satisfies the other that there is reason to believe that the following circumstances are present:

a.   Anticompetitive activities are occurring in whole or in substantial part in the territory of one of the Parties and are adversely affecting the interests of the other Party; and

b.   The activities in question are impermissible under the competition laws of the Party in the territory of which the activities are occurring.

2.   The purposes of this Agreement are to:

a.   Help ensure that trade and investment flows between the Parties and competition and consumer welfare within the territories of the Parties are not impeded by anticompetitive activities for which the competition laws of one or both Parties can provide a remedy, and

b.   Establish cooperative procedures to achieve the most effective and efficient enforcement of competition law, whereby the competition authorities of each Party will normally avoid allocating enforcement resources to dealing with anticompetitive activities that occur principally in and are directed principally towards the other Party's territory, where the competition authorities of the other Party are able and prepared to examine and take effective sanctions under their law to deal with those activities.

* * *

Article III
POSITIVE COMITY

The competition authorities of a Requesting Party may request the competition authorities of a Requested Party to investigate and, if warranted, to remedy anticompetitive activities in accordance with the Requested Party's competition laws. Such a request may be made regardless of whether the activities also violate the Requesting Party's competition laws, and regardless of whether the competition authorities of the Requesting Party have commenced or contemplate taking enforcement activities under their own competition laws.

Article IV
DEFERRAL OR SUSPENSION OF INVESTIGATIONS IN RELIANCE ON ENFORCEMENT ACTIVITY BY THE REQUESTED PARTY

1.   The competition authorities of the Parties may agree that the competition authorities of the Requesting Party will defer or suspend pending or contemplated enforcement activities during the pendency of enforcement activities of the Requested Party.

2.   The competition authorities of a Requesting Party will normally defer or suspend their own enforcement activities in favor of enforcement activities by the competition authorities of the Requested Party when the following conditions are satisfied:

   a.   The anticompetitive activities at issue:

   i.   do not have a direct, substantial and reasonably foreseeable impact on consumers in the Requesting Party's territory, or

   ii.   where the anticompetitive activities do have such an impact on the Requesting Party's consumers, they occur principally in and are directed principally towards the other Party's territory;

   b.   The adverse effects on the interests of the Requesting Party can be and are likely to be fully and adequately investigated and, as appropriate, eliminated or adequately remedied pursuant to the laws, procedures, and available remedies of the Requested Party. The Parties recognize that it may be appropriate to pursue separate enforcement activities where anticompetitive activities affecting both territories justify the imposition of penalties within both jurisdictions; and

   c.   The competition authorities of the Requested Party agree that in conducting their own enforcement activities, they will:

   i.   devote adequate resources to investigate the anticompetitive activities and, where appropriate, promptly pursue adequate enforcement activities;

   ii.   use their best efforts to pursue all reasonably available sources of information, including such sources of information as may be suggested by the competition authorities of the Requesting Party;

iii. inform the competition authorities of the Requesting Party, on request or at reasonable intervals, of the status of their enforcement activities and intentions, and where appropriate provide to the competition authorities of the Requesting Party relevant confidential information if consent has been obtained from the source concerned. The use and disclosure of such information shall be governed by Article V;

iv. promptly notify the competition authorities of the Requesting Party of any change in their intentions with respect to investigation or enforcement;

v. use their best efforts to complete their investigation and to obtain a remedy or initiate proceedings within six months, or such other time as agreed to by the competition authorities of the Parties, of the deferral or suspension of enforcement activities by the competition authorities of the Requesting Party;

vi. fully inform the competition authorities of the Requesting Party of the results of their investigation, and take into account the views of the competition authorities of the Requesting Party, prior to any settlement, initiation of proceedings, adoption of remedies, or termination of the investigation; and

vii. comply with any reasonable request that may be made by the competition authorities of the Requesting Party.

When the above conditions are satisfied, a Requesting Party which chooses not to defer or suspend its enforcement activities shall inform the competition authorities of the Requested Party of its reasons.

3. The competition authorities of the Requesting Party may defer or suspend their own enforcement activities if fewer than all of the conditions set out in paragraph 2 are satisfied.

4. Nothing in this Agreement precludes the competition authorities of a Requesting Party that choose to defer or suspend independent enforcement activities from later initiating or reinstituting such activities. In such circumstances, the competition authorities of the Requesting Party will promptly inform the competition authorities of the Requested Party of their intentions

and reasons. If the competition authorities of the Requested Party continue with their own investigation, the competition authorities of the two Parties shall, where appropriate, coordinate their respective investigations under the criteria and procedures of Article IV of the 1991 Agreement.

Article V
CONFIDENTIALITY AND USE OF INFORMATION

* * *

Article VI
RELATIONSHIP TO THE 1991 AGREEMENT

This Agreement shall supplement and be interpreted consistently with the 1991 Agreement, which remains fully in force.

* * *

Notes and Questions

Before the effective date of the 1998 agreement, in the case of alleged discriminatory treatment of an American computer airline reservation system by Amadeus, a European airline computer reservation system, the US Justice Department referred the matter to the European Commission under the 1991 agreement. Despite infrequency of formal use, the cooperation agreements and many other interactions discussed below have fostered a mood and spirit of cooperation, and the antitrust authorities of the world are in fact deeply cooperative and mutually supportive.

D. REGIONAL COOPERATION AND INTEGRATION

1.   Introduction

We have spoken thus far of coordination and cooperation, which can ease conflicts and, when convergence results, create a more familiar and consistent playing field. But we have not spoken of a higher level antitrust law or the integration of trade and competition regimes. These possible objectives can be fulfilled in free trade areas and common markets. The European Union has led the way, with the most successful common market in the world. It creates a higher level competition law for the member nations while also fostering development of the member nations' own competition laws, and it integrates trade (state restraints) and competition in the internal market. There are many other free trade areas and common markets in the world. None are so integrative as the EU, but many use or aspire to use the opportunity and environment to enhance the smooth enforcement of competition law. Clusters of nations have adopted free trade agreements (FTAs) with various degrees of success in anchoring their competition laws.

2.   Australia-New Zealand Closer Economic Relations

One of the most successful longstanding cooperations is that between Australia and New Zealand. A protocol in the Australia New Zealand Closer Economic Relations Trade Agreement (ANZCERTA) provided for abolition of the anti-dumping laws between the two countries and extension of competition laws to trade in goods affecting trans-Tasman trade. Pursuant thereto, in 1990, both Australia and New Zealand amended their competition laws to prohibit misuse of market power in trans-Tasman trade and to provide for trans-Tasman jurisdiction. In particular, a person who has a dominant position in Australia, New Zealand, or Australia and New Zealand must not take advantage of that power to restrict entry or prevent or deter competition. In addition, the competition commission of each jurisdiction may use its discovery powers in the other country, and the two countries agree to give mutual assistance in investigations. See New Zealand Commerce Act 1986 as amended, section 36A; Australian Trade Practices Act 1974 as amended, section 46A.

3.   The North American Free Trade Agreement

The North American Free Trade Agreement (1994) is an example of a free trade agreement with promise for adopting a regional competition law. This did not happen, in part because of the asymmetries of the countries. But the three parties, the US, Canada and Mexico, have nonetheless cooperated on competition enforcement in deep and successful ways outside of NAFTA, through bilateral cooperation agreements, nurturing personal relations, and devotion to the task and opportunity to cooperate.

NAFTA includes competition provisions in Chapter 15. Article 1505 provides that "[e]ach Party shall adopt or maintain measures to proscribe anticompetitive business conduct and take appropriate action with respect thereto, recognizing that such measures will enhance the fulfillment of the objectives of [the] Agreement." The same provision provides for cooperation and coordination between Members' competition authorities in issues of competition and enforcement policy. Issues covered by Article 1501 are not subject to arbitration (the authorized dispute settlement) under the NAFTA.

Article 1502 of NAFTA recognizes that the parties have the right to designate monopolies. The provision states that, whenever monopolies may affect the interests of other Members, the country establishing the monopoly should provide prior notification to the other Members wherever possible, and should "introduce at the time of the designation such conditions on the operation of the monopoly as will minimize or eliminate any nullification or impairment of benefits" established by the agreement.

The same provision establishes rules regarding application of measures to private or public monopolies designated by the government of any member. These include the guarantee that the designated monopoly will not engage in "anticompetitive practices in a non-monopolized market in its territory that adversely affect an investment of an investor of another party, including through the discriminatory provision of the monopoly good or service, cross subsidization or predatory conduct." Art. 1502(3). One proceeding has arisen under this section—a claim by United Parcel Service of America against Canada Post, a state-owned company, for anticompetitive cross-subsidies and price predation. The case was dismissed as not arbitrable; that is, not subject to dispute resolution under NAFTA.[1]

Article 1503 allows parties to maintain or establish state monopolies. But "each Party shall ensure that any state enterprise that it maintains or establishes accords non-discriminatory treatment in the sale of its goods or services to investments in the Party's territory of investors of another Party."

In Article 1504, NAFTA established a Working Group on Trade and Competition, "to report, and to make recommendations on further work as appropriate, to the Commission within five years of the date of entry into force of this Agreement on relevant issues concerning the relationship between competition laws and policies and trade in the free trade area." The working group, compromising officials of the three nations, met a number of times but it did not file a report and did not make recommendations. The working group could not reach agreement, even on subjects as basic as treatment of export cartels from one NAFTA country into another. Accordingly, there is no common US-Canada-Mexico antitrust regime or framework; although the competition authorities of all three nations frequently and even intensively consult and coordinate under bilateral agreements. See Antitrust Law Section, American Bar

---

[1]   United States Parcel Service of America, Inc. v. Government of Canada, Award on Jurisdiction (NAFTA Arbitration Tribunal, November 22, 2002), *available at www.dfait-maeci.gc.ca/tna-nac/parcel-en.asp.* See Robert Schuman, Competition Dimension of NAFTA and the European Union: Semi-common Competition Policy, Uncommon Rules, and no Common Institutions. Jean Monet/Robert Schuman Paper Series, Vol. 6. No. 18, October 2006, Miami, Florida, pp. 8–9, *available at http://www 6.miami.edu/eucenter/EULaw_LongPaper_06.pdf.*

Association, Task Force Report on the Competition Dimensions of NAFTA (1994), proposing a competition regime for NAFTA including eventual repeal of the export cartel exemptions, ratcheting back antidumping laws, and limiting state action immunity within the free trade area. *https://books.google.com/books/about/Report_of_the_Task_Force_of_the_ABA_Sect.html?id=mt_9CDyvv2gC.*

Thus, the NAFTA agreement provided a credible structure for integrated competition law, but no progress on it was made.

4.   Trans-Pacific Partnership

The unratified Trans-Pacific Partnership agreement, now all but defunct for lack of support in a new nationalistic era, is an example of a (would-be) mega-regional agreement. Its competition chapter (Chapter 16) might be regarded as state-of-the-art for competition chapters in free trade agreements. It is not an integrated competition law for the (12) collaborating nations but rather a mandate for members to have and maintain a national competition law "with the objective of promoting economic efficiency and consumer welfare." The nations would undertake to ensure procedural fairness (due process) and to provide private rights of action, and to cooperate. Adjacent Chapter 17 is a state-of-the-art provision requiring state-owned enterprises to act in accordance with commercial considerations and not to engage in anticompetitive practices.

5.   Southeast Asia

The 10 southeast Asian countries established the ASEAN Community on the last day of 2015. They aim at an integrated single market and full regional integration. ASEAN includes the ASEAN Economic Community, with Blueprint 2025 to accomplish integration and create a level playing field. ASEAN does not contemplate a central competition law but rather functioning national competition laws of each of the member states, with harmonization and cooperation. The harmonization and integration objectives pose challenges in view of "the ASEAN way"—recognition of the autonomy of each nation to design its own competition law, which may include the industrial policy and SOE privileges of each.

6.   Developing Countries and Small Jurisdictions

Developing countries and small jurisdictions may have additional reasons to form FTAs with competition competences. They may lack size and resources to run effective competition agencies. Collaborating with neighbors can enhance their effectiveness. Collaborating with neighbors at relatively equal levels of development can eliminate a fear of being exploited and can produce a community of common interests. Several such FTAs are in Latin America and Africa.

COMESA—the Common Market for Eastern and Southern Africa—is the largest common market in Africa. It has been a customs union since 2008 and is in the process of building its competition competence, of which the merger control is the most advanced. Negotiations are in process for a Tripartite FTA, which would comprise COMESA, SADC (Southern Africa Development Community), and EAC (East African Community), which have overlapping membership. It is not presently contemplated that the Tripartite FTA will become a common market.

West Africa also has common markets and indeed overlapping ones. The West African Economic and Monetary Union (WAEMU) comprises principally the French-speaking countries. WAEMU preempts all antitrust enforcement by its member states; even enforcement against restraints entirely within the state's own borders. This preemption has crippled the growing competition law enforcement of Senegal, which was in the process of positioning itself as a credible enforcer.

The Economic Community of West African States (ECOWAS) comprises 15 West African states, including the very large nation of Nigeria and many much smaller, weaker states. French and English are both official languages, and both heritages inform the law. Thus, some members have common law traditions; some, civil law. The language and cultural divides are among its many challenges.

The ECOWAS competition authority is designed to deal with regional issues. Domestic matters are left to the member states. ECOWAS "Community Competition Rules" on agreements, abuse of dominance, public enterprises, and state aids are modeled after the corresponding provisions of the European Union.

WAEMU and ECOWAS overlap in membership.

In Africa, the East African Community—comprising Burundi, Kenya, Rwanda, Tanzania and Uganda—is a customs union and is in early stages of establishing the EAC Competition Authority. The EACCA will have jurisdiction over all conduct and transaction with cross-border effects within the community. The countries are geographically close and have strong links in common ports and transportation systems. While there are many challenges including institutional and resource needs and asymmetry of the nations, increasing trade flows among the countries suggest opportunities for cartels and mergers to undermine liberalization, giving impetus to the establishment of the community competition authority.

There are yet other common markets in Africa.

7.   Latin America

Latin American countries have several overlapping RTAs. These include the Andean Community, which is modeled after the European Union and has aspirations to become a Latin American common market. The competition rules of the Andean Community forbid anticompetitive practices that may affect trade among the member states. The Secretary General of the community may impose sanctions for violations. Member states without competition laws (Bolivia and until 2009 Ecuador) can apply the Andean rules to restraints within their own jurisdictions until the nations adopt their own laws.

In the Andean Community, ideological differences of the nations, among other factors, create a challenge. The press in Peru reported that, "according to Foreign Minister José Antonio Garcia Belaunde, the Andean Community of Nations (CAN) should forget about having a common market due to the ideological differences on development models among its members. . . . He expressed [the view] that countries such as Colombia, Chile, and Peru see free trade agreements as a basic vehicle for economic development, while Venezuela [no longer a member], Ecuador, and Bolivia see them as imperialistic domination forms." World News Connection (Newswire), May 5, 2009.

Mercosur is the Common Market of the Southern Cone. Its members are Brazil, Argentina, Paraguay and Uruguay. Chile, Bolivia, Colombia, Ecuador and Peru are associate members, with Bolivia being considered for full membership. Venezuela also is an applicant for full membership. This is the largest trading group in South America. Mercosur aspires to integrate all of South America in a trading bloc. But Mercosur suffers many internal divisions including disputes on political economy—the importance, or the dangers, of free markets. In contrast to the Andean Community, Mercosur's competition policy functions largely, although not entirely, at national level. Pursuant to the Fortaleza Protocol signed in December 1996, the members are required to adopt national competition laws, set up competition authorities, and deal with restraints at national level. If a matter has Mercosur implications, the member state is charged with referring the national ruling to the Mercosur institutions. If Mercosur orders sanctions, the national authorities are tasked with enforcing them.

The Fortaleza Protocol, however, requires the approval of each member's legislature. The protocol has not yet been ratified by all member states.

CARICOM, the free trade area of the Caribbean Community, comprises a number of small and isolated states. It set up a promising Anti-Monopoly Commission in 2008, also modeled after the European single market. The CARICOM Commission is empowered to operate both on community level and within its member states, as long as there are cross-border effects. CARICOM has 15 member states, 13 of which are participating in the single market. Only Barbados, Guyana, and Jamaica have operational competition laws.

* * *

Despite challenges, RTAs and other regional cooperation may be seen as a constructive path for robust competition enforcement in small and developing countries. See generally COMPETITION PROVISIONS IN REGIONAL TRADE AGREEMENTS: HOW TO ASSURE DEVELOPMENT GAINS (Philippe Brusick, Ana María Alvarez, and Lucian Cernat eds., UNCTAD 2005).

* * *

What are the lessons of the NAFTA competition initiative? that a trade context may complicate the effort to obtain common competition rules? that wide disparities in economic development of members may complicate the effort to obtain common trade-and-competition rules? It is often observed that the success of the European effort may have derived from the over-powering common incentive: peace in Europe.

8.   Other Regional Cooperations: Examples

a.   *Asia Pacific Economic Cooperation (APEC)*

The Asia-Pacific Economic Cooperation (APEC) is a "forum for facilitating economic growth, cooperation, trade and investment in the Asia-Pacific region." APEC operates under a non-binding commitment basis. Its purpose is "to create greater prosperity for the people of the region by promoting balanced, inclusive, sustainable, innovative and secure growth and by accelerating regional economic integration." *https://www.apec.org/About-Us/About-APEC.*

In 1999, the APEC Ministers adopted the APEC Principles to enhance Competition and Regulatory Reform. They recognize the importance of developing competition principles "to support the strengthening of markets to ensure and sustain growth in the region and [to]. . . provide a framework that links all aspects of economic policy that affect the functioning of markets." Among them are the principles of non-discrimination, comprehensiveness, transparency, and accountability. *https://www.apec.org/Meeting-Papers/Leaders-Declarations/1999/1999_aelm/attachment_apec.aspx.*

Under the principles, APEC Members agree to: "make efforts to identify and review anticompetitive regulations or measures; ensure that measures to achieve desired objectives are adopted and/or maintained with the minimum distortion to competition; address anti-competitive behavior by implementing competition policy to protect the competitive process; consider issues of timing and sequencing involved in introducing competition mechanisms and reform measures, taking into account the circumstances of individual economies." Members also agree "to take practical steps to: promote consistent application of policies and rules; eliminate unnecessary rules and regulatory procedures; and improve the transparency of policy objectives and the way rules are administered."

The competition group is now called the Competition Policy and Law Group. It meets periodically to share experience, build capacity, and help improve competition enforcement across the region.

b.   The BRICS Countries

"BRICS" is an acronym referring to the five nations with (at the time) the most rapidly growing GPD and stock market capitalization: Brazil, Russia, India, China, and South Africa. The BRICS countries meet bi-annually, crafting agendas to advance common principles and attack common problems.

The BRICS countries' competition authorities signed a Memorandum of Understanding for closer cooperation in 2016. They publish an annual newsletter, and hold bi-annual competition conferences. They share information and seek to learn from one another on common challenges of institutional design, awareness of the law, the growth of global value chains, integrity of agriculture and food systems, and relationship of inclusiveness goals to competition, among others.

c.   Other Collaborations

Other roots-up collaborations are regional. They enable neighboring countries to meet common challenges through cross-fertilization and cooperation. The African Competition Forum, launched in 2012, comprises 41 of 54 African countries. It aims to spur adoption of competition laws by those nations still without them, to help build capacities of new authorities, to support advocacy, and to assist in implementing competition reforms. A subgroup undertook an ambitious common research project, studying three sectors—cement, sugar and poultry—in each of five nations— Botswana, Kenya, Namibia, South Africa and Tanzania, and comparing the data. The studies identify important linkages between trade and competition, agricultural regulatory policy, and firm behavior. They point to where competition is obstructed and provide data useful both in enforcement policy and advocacy. The research and analysis of it is compiled in Simon Roberts, ed., COMPETITION IN AFRICA (2016).

In Asia, the 10 southeastern Asian countries have formed ASEAN, a free trade agreement with common internal market trade policy but no common competition policy, as noted. The group aspires to regional integration. The ASEAN Experts Group on Competition (AWGC) is charged with facilitating convergence and cooperation among the ASEAN competition authorities in enforcing their national competition laws. The group has issued substantive guidelines. The task of the Experts is especially challenging in light of the sentiment of the region to let each country decide upon its own path, including its own industrial policy—the "ASEAN way."

The Latin American competition enforcers announced a new strategic alliance in 2017. Mexico, Brazil, Argentina and Chile, with invitations extended to Colombia and Peru, undertook the new alliance to focus on behavior and cartels with cross-border effects. They plan to develop joint strategic action, discuss potential new cases, and formulate agendas to tackle common competition problems in the region. They already work closely together on multinational mergers.

E. THE EUROPEAN INITIATIVE AND THE DEBATE ON A COMPETITION AGREEMENT IN THE WTO

We return to the 1990s and the debate regarding the wisdom and the possible architecture of a world system of competition law.

The 1990s were a rich decade for international antitrust. In 1994, European Competition Commissioner Karel van Miert appointed a Committee of Wise Men to think progressively about how antitrust should be organized in the global era. The Committee's deliberations resulted in the van Miert Report of 1995. See Competition Policy in the New Trade Order: Strengthening International Cooperation and Rules: Report of the Group of Experts, *http://aei.pitt.edu/4112/1/4112.pdf*. The Report suggests an international regime within the World Trade Organization, which would begin with building blocks of cooperation and aid to new antitrust regimes, proceed to incorporate values of transparency and non-discrimination, and eventually include the main substantive principles of antitrust. The van Miert Report was a target for criticism by American officials and some others. In response to the criticism, the European officials streamlined the recommendations, eliminating dispute settlement except for claims of failing to adopt and enforce a competition law, and eliminating substantive coverage except for hard core cartels.

We include below a paper by then European Commissioner van Miert arguing the case for an international competition initiative, and a paper by then US antitrust chief Joel Klein critiquing the proposal. The papers make abundant reference to the *Boeing McDonnell Douglas* merger, regarding which US and EU authorities had pointedly disagreed. The conflict was seen to some as a wake-up call for a coherent system of antitrust for the world. It was a wake-up call but, as it turned out, not for world antitrust but for learning from and about one another, and voluntary convergence.

INTERNATIONAL COOPERATION IN THE FIELD OF COMPETITION: A VIEW FROM THE EC*

Karel van Miert, Commissioner for Competition,
European Commission (1997)

I.   INTRODUCTION

. . . Nowadays cooperation between competition authorities in different parts of the world is a necessity. In the past antitrust enforcers have been able to prosper in the splendid isolation of their respective jurisdictions. This time has come to an end.

. . . What I would like to point to is the impact of globalization on the policies carried out by governments. Firms with multinational activities are forced to adapt to the emerging world markets. Decisions taken by industry headquarters can change the competitive environment overnight. Strategic moves by major players are felt all over the world and have consequences for the final consumer, for business partners, competitors and employees. Competition concerns raised by their conduct or by their transactions transcend national borders.

Take for instance international cartels, export cartels, mergers on a world scale and abuses of dominance on several major markets.

---

* Chapter 2 in 1997 FORDHAM CORPORATE LAW INSTITUTE (B. Hawk ed. 1998), reprinted with permission of Juris Publishing, Inc., Huntington, New York, USA, *www.jurispub.com*.

Firms involved are subject to different competition rules with different criteria for taking decisions, different procedures and different time limits. Action in some countries against anticompetitive practices may be less rigorous than in others. This may have foreclosure effects in some markets and result in trade friction. Trade disputes undermine the positive results of efforts deployed in multilateral fora to open up international trade. Furthermore, antitrust authorities may lack the necessary instruments to deal with practices that affect competition on their territory but are organized in third countries. Finally, remedies adopted by an antitrust agency in order to ensure competition within its jurisdiction may seem legitimate, but may sometimes adversely affect the interests of another country. They may also directly conflict with remedies adopted in the same case by another authority.

To overcome these difficulties we need to take into consideration each other's concerns and, to the fullest extent possible, devise remedies compatible with one another's and coherent throughout the relevant market. Failing to do so gives private parties the opportunity to pit antitrust enforcers against each other. We risk also treating companies in an inefficient manner or making them suffer fragmentary and incoherent solutions imposed upon them by antitrust authorities ignoring each other.

So clearly we must cooperate.

But what is the best way for us Europeans to go about it? Should we cooperate within a multilateral framework, like for instance within the WTO or the OECD? Or through a network of bilateral agreements like the one we have concluded with the United States? What are the advantages and pitfalls of each approach?

You will agree with me that by opting for bilateral instruments we can probably push cooperation further and more quickly among partners with converging substantive rules and similar attitudes vis-à-vis key competition issues. The question is how much further are we able or willing to go. Are so called first generation agreements, which only allow for consultations and comity, enough? Do we need to go further and envisage for instance the exchange of confidential information or the possibility to carry out enforcement activities on behalf of each other? * * *

I will consider a number of different types of international cooperation. I will not deal with the most conspicuously successful mechanism for cooperation, so successful that we now think of it as a domestic arrangement: the European Union itself!

II. MULTILATERAL OR BILATERAL FRAMEWORK FOR COOPERATION?

The main advantage of multilateral cooperation frameworks is their tendency to achieve convergence among the largest number of countries involved. Experience, for instance, from GATT negotiation rounds points in this direction. General Agreements set up common substantive rules. Members agree—to give an example—on which subsidies are acceptable and which are not. Is this approach a valid one for antitrust? Can we achieve something concrete in the short and medium term?

A. WTO—The Working Group on Trade and Competition

The "Wise Men Group," which I set up in 1994, made some interesting proposals for a multilateral framework of competition rules.[36] Its recommendation for a fully fledged international instrument, including adequate enforcement structures, a core of common principles and a positive comity provision [a harmed nation relies on enforcement in a better-placed jurisdiction] remains far-sighted and valid in my opinion. The same applies to the proposed dispute settlement mechanism. I must make clear though that this mechanism should not aim at reviewing individual decisions by antitrust authorities. It should be used to settle disputes between Members on their compliance with agreed rules and principles.

You will further recall that the EU, on a proposal by the Commission,[37] suggested last year to address these problems in the WTO. The mandate handed to the Working Group on Trade and Competition set up last December by the Singapore Conference is one of limited scope. The Group is examining "issues . . . relating to the interaction between trade and competition policy, including anticompetitive practices, in order to identify any areas that may merit further consideration in the WTO framework."[38]

This Working Group is by no means a forum for negotiations. It may not even pre-judge whether negotiations will be undertaken. The Group will consider whether it is worthwhile to pursue this attempt to increase international consciousness of the importance of competition policy and of international cooperation in this field. It

---

[36] Comm'n, Competition Policy in the New Trade Order: Strengthening International Cooperation and Rules, COM (95) 359 final.

[37] Comm'n, Communication to the Council: Towards an International Framework of Competition Rules, COM (96) 284 final.

[38] World Trade Organization, Singapore Ministerial Declaration (Dec. 13, 1996), reprinted in 36 I. L. M. 218.

will be for the WTO's General Council to decide how to proceed further.

It seems that early indications from the Group's work in Geneva are encouraging. We will play a full part in persuading the Member States of the WTO of the merits of competition policy and the need to meet the challenges of global markets. For the time being, there are strong differences of view. On one side we find those (like the United States) who view with a certain amount of apprehension the excessive intrusion of an international body into the area of antitrust policy enforcement. On the other we have those (like some Asian countries) who might be tempted to use this new forum to question the legitimacy of trade defense instruments.

I remain confident that our arguments in favor of international action on trade and competition will win the day. And, as I said, early signs give me reason to be hopeful in this regard.

B. OECD—The Recommendation

Another multilateral forum for antitrust is offered by the OECD [which compromises the developed countries]. It has already given the antitrust community a "first generation" instrument for cooperation in the form of a Recommendation, issued in 1986 and last revised in 1995.[39] It establishes a basic framework for cooperation between antitrust authorities in member countries. Certainly, compared to the WTO, the OECD presents fewer convergence problems by far. Members have more or less similar basic antitrust statutes and defend broadly the same ideology on most major issues.

The European Commission cooperates with all members of the OECD. However, our cooperation activities under the OECD instrument are considerably less intensive and less case-oriented than the cooperation we practice with the United States under a bilateral instrument. This is in part explained by the fact that the United States is a major trading partner. We both have to deal with an important number of cases affecting both markets. This in turn generates the need for custom-made bilateral cooperation agreements providing for clear rights and obligations for both parties. Such agreements appear to work better for the type of close cooperation I am about to describe in detail.

---

[39] OECD, Revised Recommendation of the Council Concerning Co-operation Between Member Countries on Anticompetitive Practices Affecting International Trade, OECD Doc. C (95) 130 final.

III. BILATERAL COOPERATION

A. EU/US Cooperation: The 1991 Agreement

As you know, our relations with the United States are governed by the bilateral agreement of 1991.[40] I will not go into details on the provisions of this agreement. They have been presented and discussed in this room often enough in recent years. I would rather like to give you an update on how the agreement works in practice, its good points and its limitations.

The exchange of *basic information*, in the form of notification or in less formal ways, is the clearest obligation stemming from the agreement. The agreement provides for an alert system whereby each party notifies its partner when it deals with cases that may affect important interests of the latter. Successive notifications may occur in the same case: for example, in a merger case we notify at the outset of the case, then, when appropriate, when the Commission decides to initiate proceedings and, eventually, "far enough in advance . . . to enable the other Party's views to be taken into account[ ]" before a final decision is adopted.[41] This part of the agreement works well and is, I would think, beneficial for both parties.

Provisions on *coordination of enforcement activities* are also very important. In all cases of mutual interest it has become the norm to establish contacts at the outset in order to exchange views and, when appropriate, to coordinate enforcement activities. The respective approaches on the definition of relevant markets are very often central to the discussions. We will often exchange views on possible remedies in order to ensure that they do not conflict. Cooperation may also, in certain cases, help to clarify a point of foreign law relevant to the interpretation of an agreement or to the effectiveness of a remedy. Factual elements relevant to the case are also exchanged within the limits of legal constraints on the protection of confidential information. Cooperation under this heading has recently involved a successful synchronization of investigations and searches. This is designed to make fact-finding action more effective. It also helps prevent companies suspected of cartel activity from destroying evidence located in the territory of the agency investigating the same

---

[40] Agreement Between the Government of the United States of America and the Commission of the European Communities Regarding the Application of Their Competition Laws (Sept. 23,1991), reprinted in 4 Trade Reg. Rep. (CCH) ¶ 13,504 (1991); GI Antitrust & Trade Reg. Rep. (BNA) 382–85 (Sept. 26,1991); O.J. L 95/45 (1991), corrected by O.J. L 131/38 (1995). [hereinafter 1991 EU/US Agreement].

[41] Id.

conduct after its counterpart on the other side of the Atlantic has acted.

Until very recently the *provisions on traditional and positive comity* have not been formally activated, although they may have been a source of inspiration in daily cooperation. We are, for instance, within the realm of traditional comity when we cooperate in a certain case to bring our respective positions and remedies closer to each other in order to avoid creating a harmful effect to the market of the partner. We may draw the attention of the partner to our concerns in a certain case. This may open a new trail for his investigation and lead to a final result taking our interests into consideration in a more appropriate way.

Activation of the positive comity provision was felt appropriate in a recent case. The U.S. authorities requested the Commission to investigate specific allegations of discrimination regarding the operation of a computerized reservation system (Amadeus) set up by Lufthansa, Air France and Iberia. The Commission is currently investigating the case in close cooperation with the U.S. Department of Justice ("DOJ").

B. Boeing

Another noteworthy case is *Boeing*.[42] The Boeing/McDonnell Douglas merger is one of these rare cases, that—if nothing else—demonstrate how appropriate the "case by case" approach is for antitrust. * * *

However, *Boeing* illustrates the natural limits of this type of bilateral cooperation. Procedures of notification and consultation and the principles of comity and positive comity allow us to bring our respective approaches closer in cases of common interest (and we have had some of them recently), but there exist no mechanisms for resolving conflicts in cases of substantial divergence of analysis. A multilateral (for instance, within the WTO) or bilateral arbitration mechanism that would allow us to go beyond the limitations of Community interest or national U.S. interest is inconceivable under current circumstances. I even wonder whether this should be pursued as a goal in the longer term. We must therefore admit that

---

[42] Boeing/McDonnell Douglas, O.J. L 336/16 (1997) (Comm'n). [Eds. note: the US FTC closed the investigation, thus clearing the merger. The EU found various harms to competition. Ultimately it resolved the case by clearing the merger with significant conditions.]
* * *

we can profitably cooperate in the majority of cases and admit that there are infrequent situations where our approaches diverge.

Our decision to challenge this merger, and the remedies we required before authorizing it, were unexceptional. * * *

. . . In *Nippon Paper* the *U.S.* authorities went beyond what we did in *Boeing*.[45] They challenged a cartel between companies that do not sell directly in the U.S. market.[46] Under similar circumstances we would probably have done the same. It is clear that if anticompetitive conduct originating outside the European Community or a transaction between companies incorporated in third countries is implemented within the Union and affects prices or consumers in Europe, we intend, like the United States, to apply our law to the fullest extent.[47]

As regards the *substance* of the case, we certainly felt entitled to express concern in the face of a merger with a post-merger HHI reaching nearly 6000 points and an HHI increase of more than 700 points. According to the U.S. Guidelines, such mergers[48] presumptively enhance market power and the Government is "likely to challenge."[49] For us this merger could jeopardize the competitive process creating an incumbent with enough market power to stifle competition and foreclose potential entry. It was argued that Douglas Aircraft ("DAC") was no longer a real force in the market for new aircraft on a stand-alone basis. However, integrated into the Boeing group, DAC represented a significant factor in the market. So we did not focus our analysis on a "distressed company" concept taking into account the pre-merger situation of DAC and its difficulty to continue competing. We took a dynamic view of what DAC could bring to the commercial strength of Boeing: access to an important fleet in service, additional capacity and, not least, enhanced possibility to offer exclusive deals. The bottom line was for us more a question of whether a dominant firm like Boeing should be allowed to enhance

---

[45]   United States v. Nippon Paper Industries Co., Ltd., 109 F.3d 1 (1st Cir. 1997, cert. denied., 522 U.S. 1044 (1998).

[46]   Id. The defendants (Nippon Paper Industries and others) were selling the product (fax paper) in Japan to unaffiliated trading houses on condition that the latter charge specified (inflated) prices for the product when they resold it in North America.

[47]   See In re WoodPulp Cartel: Å. Åhlström Osakeyhtiö and Others v. Comm'n, Joined Cases C–89/85,104/85,114/85,116–117/85 & 125–129/85, 1988 E.C.R. 5193 (C.J).

[48]   Mergers resulting with an HHI number of more than 2600 points (highly concentrated markets) and an HHI increase of over 100 points compared to the pre-merger situation.

[49]   U.S. Dep't of Justice & Federal Trade Commission, Horizontal Merger Guidelines (1992), reprinted in 4 Trade Reg. Rep. (CCH) ¶ 13,104.

its dominance by acquiring a competitor, than whether Douglas Aircraft could keep its head out of the water in the medium term. * * *

As regards the *nature of the remedies* in *Boeing*, I must say that the situation was rather unusual. After the merger only two players were left in the market for large commercial aircraft. Airbus had no interest in buying DAC. No other companies were interested in entering the market through acquisition of DAC. Therefore the classical remedy, divestiture of DAC, was not available. Putting DAC in the hands of an independent trustee with a mandate to sell would have given rise to a tendering procedure without any chance of success. Personally I think that a "divestiture" of this sort could not satisfy our competition concerns. And under the circumstances (no serious purchaser in view) it would have been harsh for DAC employees. Furthermore, we had to consider the difficult problem of spill-over effects from defense and space activities. In such a situation the Commission accepted a package of commitments. Some are structural and some are behavioral in nature.

We complied fully with the comity principle that we believe to be an established part of international law and know to be part of the EU/US Agreement of 1991 on cooperation in competition matters.[53] Comity is not, contrary to what a learned judge held recently in the United States, a mere "aspiration;" it is a rule that governs our international relations.[54] In *Boeing* we took full account of the important interests of the United States, which its Government represented to us, in the way in which we dealt with military aspects of the case and relevant features of the civilian aspects too. Also, I must reject the suggestion that European competition policy is somehow more concerned with competitors than competition. Our overriding objective is to promote consumer welfare by protecting the competitive process. This means that we will resist attempts to dominate our markets by merger or takeover, whoever the protagonists may be, wherever they may be headquartered and however powerful their friends may be. Our law is not a football to be kicked around by special interest groups. National champions are for sport, not economies. In Europe the consumer is the champion.

* * *

---

[53] 1991 EU/US Agreement, supra note 6.
[54] Nippon Paper Industries, 109 F.3d at 24.

V.   CONCLUSION

. . . I hope I have been able to convince you that international cooperation in the area of antitrust is probably the best solution to the problems created by globalization and certainly deserves more attention and contributions from all sides. Frankly, we have no choice. We are condemned to succeed, to find new ways to live and work together.

ANTICIPATING THE MILLENNIUM: INTERNATIONAL ANTITRUST ENFORCEMENT AT THE END OF THE TWENTIETH CENTURY*

Joel I. Klein, Assistant Attorney General, Antitrust Division,
U.S. Department of Justice (1997)

* * *

III.   INTERNATIONAL COOPERATION AND COORDINATION AND THE WTO

* * *

. . . [I]t is neither surprising nor objectionable that different national competition authorities could reach different results on a given merger, which may well have different competitive effects in different product or geographic markets in different countries. We have worked with other countries' antitrust agencies in numerous cases where our results differed from theirs in some way. What was unusual about *Boeing* is that the FTC and the EU reached different results in analyzing the same market: the worldwide market for large commercial aircraft. The point I want to make here is that however difficult this matter was for both U.S. and EU antitrust enforcers, our discussions would have been far more difficult had we not already established a strong relationship based on common antitrust enforcement interests.

. . . [T]he *Boeing* experience has made officials—including, at least on this side of the Atlantic, officials outside the antitrust agencies—keenly aware that, as much as we have in common, there remain important differences between U.S. and European antitrust law and enforcement philosophies. If we antitrust enforcers fail to manage these differences through effective cooperation and

---

  *   Editors' note: Chapter 1 in 1997 FORDHAM CORPORATE LAW INSTITUTE (B. Hawk ed. 1998), reprinted with permission of Juris Publishing, Inc., Huntington, New York, USA, *www.jurispub.com*.

coordination mechanisms, there will be a greatly increased risk that particular antitrust disputes will become politicized, with the obvious adverse effects on sound and predictable antitrust enforcement. For my part, continuing to build a two-way relationship of understanding and trust with the European Commission is crucial to sound U.S. antitrust enforcement policy; indeed, as Commissioner van Miert has indicated elsewhere, Antitrust Division and DG-IV staff recently have been exchanging ideas on the proposed *American Airlines/British Airways* transaction, which is of obvious interest to both agencies.

The mention of differences between U.S. and EU law and policy brings me to another subject of current interest bearing on cooperation and coordination: the recent creation of a WTO working group on trade and competition policy. I have discussed this development in several speeches over the past year, so I will give you the short version today, and briefly explain why the United States takes a cautious approach to this WTO exercise.

In response to a proposal by the EU and other WTO members to initiate a work program on trade and competition in the WTO, last December's WTO Ministerial Declaration in Singapore included an agreement to "establish a working group to study issues raised by Members relating to the interaction between trade and competition policy, including anti-competitive practices, in order to identify any areas that may merit further consideration in the WTO framework."[74] After two years, the WTO General Council will determine how (or whether) the work of the group should proceed; as the Singapore Declaration stated, "[i]t is clearly understood that future negotiations, if any, regarding multilateral disciplines in th[is] area, will take place only after an explicit consensus decision is taken among WTO members regarding such negotiations."[75] At this point, the new working group, under the expert leadership of Frederic Jenny of France, has met twice and is focusing on educating the many WTO members on basic competition law concepts.

I have serious reservations about expanding the current WTO exercise to encompass negotiations on some sort of competition rules, although I know that Commissioner van Miert has thought deeply about this issue and supports WTO negotiations in this area. As should be absolutely clear by now, the United States places a very high value on the practical law enforcement value of developing

---

[74] World Trade Organization, Singapore Ministerial Declaration (Dec. 13, 1996), reprinted in 36 I. L. M. 218.

[75] Id.

bilateral mutual assistance agreements and other cooperative efforts among antitrust agencies. I would hate to see our energy and attention diverted from these practical efforts at improving enforcement, particularly against international cartels, diminished by an unwieldy and theoretical WTO exercise. Indeed, a premature effort to negotiate rules at the WTO is fraught with risk; as Dan Tarullo, Assistant to the President for International Economic Policy, explained "a world competition code is not a good idea."[76]

First, as the *Boeing* case illustrates so graphically, it would be very hard to reach agreement in the WTO on sound competition rules, which depend so much on the strict application of neutral legal and economic principles. If the United States and the EU diverge substantially in their views of important merger enforcement rules (and on related monopolization/abuse of dominance rules), imagine how difficult it would be for the 120-odd members of the WTO, roughly one-half of which do not have competition laws, to sort these issues out in a principled way. Second, precisely because it would be so difficult to do so, what one could expect instead would be a lowest-common-denominator outcome in the development of WTO competition rules; that is, any WTO standards could end up legitimizing weak and ineffective rules that certainly would not serve the goals either of trade liberalization or antitrust enforcement. Finally, although a universal commitment to the adoption and enforcement of competition laws and cooperation in antitrust enforcement, are worthy goals, I believe that they go beyond core WTO concerns. How would the WTO even identify, much less remedy, violations of any multilateral competition obligations? I strongly suspect that nearly all of the world's 70-odd competition laws (accounting for nearly all important trading nations) would likely meet the requirements of any minimum substantive rules the WTO could adopt. So what is the point? On the other hand, if WTO dispute settlement were extended to individual decisions taken by national competition authorities—setting aside the question of how the WTO would acquire the (often disputed) evidence required for a proper competition analysis—this would interfere with national sovereignty concerning prosecutorial discretion and judicial decision-making, and could involve WTO panels in inappropriate reviews of witness credibility and highly confidential business information. For all these reasons, in my view the WTO working group should encourage participation by competition experts from around the world, foster among Members a common understanding of the

---

[76] Daniel Tarullo, Wrong Lesson From Boeing: Personal View, Financial Times (London), Aug. 13, 1997, at 12.

relationship of competition matters to the WTO framework and remain neutral regarding any conclusions that may be reached at the end of the group's two-year life. That is the course it has taken so far.

* * *

V.   CONCLUSION

As we approach the millennium, we need to build on the practical experience of the last few years to improve our ability to work with our foreign counterparts to do a better job of combatting anticompetitive behavior on a global scale. I am committed to doing so, through formal cooperation agreements and informal cooperation coordination, through positive comity referrals and through use of the enforcement tools that Congress has given us. I suspect that the coming   years   will   bring   occasional   controversies   and misunderstandings as we find our way from broad theory to case-specific practice, but I am convinced that these challenges will be far outweighed by the benefits from the growth of sound antitrust enforcement, and of antitrust cooperation, throughout the world. And I am absolutely sure that as international antitrust enforcers, we will—in the words of Benjamin Franklin—either hang together or hang separately.

In the debate on an international competition regime, who has the better view? van Miert or Klein? What are the best points of each argument? Is an international regime, or at least an international framework, inevitable? or fanciful?

As noted, Europe simplified its proposal for a world agreement in view of critical comments, both from the United States and from developing countries. The simplified proposal called for only one substantive issue—cartels—to be included in the negotiation of an antitrust agreement; and it scaled back dispute resolution, which would be available only in the case of a party's violating a clear undertaking such as the undertaking to have and maintain a world anti-cartel law. The outlines of this simplified proposal, to which the United States agreed or at least did not object, was placed on the provisional agenda for the then upcoming trade round, the Doha Development Round.

F.   THE DOHA DECLARATION

Trading nations of the world engage in rounds of negotiations to lower trading barriers. By the turn of the century it was clear that the benefits of the past rounds, in terms of growth and economic welfare, were great, but the gains were divided quite unequally; they disproportionately benefited the developed world. The countries resolved that the next round would try to reduce the barriers that mattered most to the developing world. Thus, the Doha Development Round.

Here are the competition provisions that were on the agenda at the ministerial meeting in Doha, Qatar, in November 2001.

DOHA MINISTERIAL DECLARATION
November 14, 2001

Interaction between trade and competition policy

23 Recognizing the case for a multilateral framework to enhance the contribution of competition policy to international trade and development, and the need for enhanced technical assistance and capacity-building in this area as referred to in paragraph 24, we agree that negotiations will take place after the Fifth Session of the Ministerial Conference on the basis of a decision to be taken, by explicit consensus, at that session on modalities of negotiations.

24 We recognize the needs of developing and least-developed countries for enhanced support for technical assistance and capacity building in this area, including policy analysis and development so that they may better evaluate the implications of closer multilateral cooperation for their development policies and objectives, and human and institutional development. To this end, we shall work in cooperation with other relevant intergovernmental organizations, including UNCTAD, and through appropriate regional and bilateral channels, to provide strengthened and adequately resourced assistance to respond to these needs.

25 In the period until the Fifth Session, further work in the Working Group on the Interaction between Trade and Competition Policy will focus on the clarification of: core principles, including transparency, non-discrimination and procedural fairness, and provisions on hardcore cartels; modalities for voluntary cooperation; and support for progressive reinforcement of competition institutions in developing countries through capacity building. Full account shall be taken of the needs of developing and least-developed country participants and appropriate flexibility provided to address them.

* * *

Comment on the competition provisions of the Doha agenda. Were they a wise start for an international competition regime or framework?

Negotiations were due to begin at the 2003 Cancun ministerial conference. At Cancun, negotiations on the central trade issue of agricultural subsidies got off to a difficult start. Agricultural subsidies of the developed world make it nearly impossible for many farmers in the developing world to make even a subsistence living doing what they can do most efficiently and at lower cost than Americans or Europeans. The United States and the EU failed to come forward with a proposal to sufficiently reduce the subsidies. In order to save the trade talks (which have now all but failed), less central issues were jettisoned from the agenda. The sacrificed issues included competition, which in 2004 was formally dropped from the agenda of the Doha round. Developing countries were in general not unhappy with the removal of the competition issue, for they feared a Trojan horse from the developed countries, whom they believed had taken advantage of them in the past. Nor was the United States unhappy with the result, for American officials in general maintained the view that a "top-down" antitrust would be too bureaucratic, would settle for lowest-common-denominator rules, and would end up handicapping efficient Western firms in order to protect competitors in developing and other countries.

We circle back, now, to three events or benchmarks that were concurrently evolving: 1) in 1998, the OECD Hard Core Cartel Recommendation; 2) in 2000, the ICPAC Report and its recommendations, leading to 3) in 2001, the formation of the International Competition Network, known as ICN, which is the most vital forum for cross-fertilization and convergence.

G. THE OECD HARD CORE CARTEL RECOMMENDATION

In the late 1990s, as debate on an international competition regime in the WTO intensified, American officials had another idea. Their idea was concrete, focused, grass roots, and entirely voluntary: a proposal in the Organization for Economic Cooperation and Development that jurisdictions should proscribe cartels. Why cartels? Cartels were unambiguously harmful conduct. The many other practices that would potentially be proscribed in a WTO regime—such as abuse of dominance—might in fact be efficient practices, and a world rule threatened to chill the robust competition of American firms. Why the OECD? It was an organization of developed countries only and it had no powers of rule-making or dispute resolution. The proposal, somewhat watered down, became the OECD Hard Core Cartel Recommendation of 1998. Here it is.

Recommendation of the OECD Council Concerning Effective Action Against Hard Core Cartels (1998)

The OECD Council has adopted a number of non-binding Recommendations on competition law and policy. In addition, the Competition Committee has adopted Best Practices. OECD Recommendations and Best Practices are often catalysts for major change by governments.

Hard core cartels are the most egregious violations of competition law. They injure consumers in many countries by raising prices and restricting supply, thus making goods and services completely unavailable to some purchasers and unnecessarily expensive for others.

Effective action against hard core cartels is particularly important from an international perspective—because their distortion of world trade creates market power, waste, and inefficiency in countries whose markets would otherwise be competitive—and particularly dependent upon co-operation—because they generally operate in secret, and relevant evidence may be located in many different countries.

This Council Recommendation recommends to member countries to ensure that their competition laws effectively halt and deter hard core cartels by providing for effective sanctions and adequate enforcement procedures and institutions to detect and remedy hard core cartels.

Non member countries are invited to associate themselves with this Recommendation and to implement it.

Council Recommendation of the Council Concerning Effective Action Against Hard Core Cartels

25 March 1998, C(98)35/FINAL

THE COUNCIL,

Having regard to Article 5 b) of the Convention on the Organization for Economic Co-operation and Development of 14th December 1960;

Having regard to previous Council Recommendations' recognition that "effective application of competition policy plays a vital role in promoting world trade by ensuring dynamic national markets and encouraging the lowering or reducing of entry barriers to imports"

[C(86)65(Final)]; and that "anticompetitive practices may constitute an obstacle to the achievement of economic growth, trade expansion, and other economic goals of Member countries" [C(95)130/FINAL];
* * *

Considering that hard core cartels are the most egregious violations of competition law and that they injure consumers in many countries by raising prices and restricting supply, thus making goods and services completely unavailable to some purchasers and unnecessarily expensive for others; and

Considering that effective action against hard core cartels is particularly important from an international perspective—because their distortion of world trade creates market power, waste, and inefficiency in countries whose markets would otherwise be competitive—and particularly dependent upon co-operation— because they generally operate in secret, and relevant evidence may be located in many different countries;

I.   RECOMMENDS as follows to Governments of Member countries:

A.   CONVERGENCE AND EFFECTIVENESS OF LAWS PROHIBITING HARD CORE CARTELS

C(98)35/FINAL

1.   Member countries should ensure that their competition laws effectively halt and deter hard core cartels. In particular, their laws should provide for:

a)   effective sanctions, of a kind and at a level adequate to deter firms and individuals from participating in such cartels; and b) enforcement procedures and institutions with powers adequate to detect and remedy hard core cartels, including powers to obtain documents and information and to impose penalties for non-compliance.

2.   For purposes of this Recommendation:

a)   a "hard core cartel" is an anticompetitive agreement, anticompetitive concerted practice, or anticompetitive arrangement by competitors to fix prices, make rigged bids (collusive tenders), establish output restrictions or quotas, or share or divide markets by allocating customers, suppliers, territories, or lines of commerce; b) the hard core cartel category does not include agreements, concerted practices, or arrangements that (i) are reasonably related to the lawful realisation of cost-reducing or output-enhancing efficiencies, (ii) are excluded directly or indirectly from the coverage of a Member country's own laws, or (iii) are authorized in accordance with those laws.

However, all exclusions and authorizations of what would otherwise be hard core cartels should be transparent and should be reviewed periodically to assess whether they are both necessary and no broader than necessary to achieve their overriding policy objectives.

After the issuance of this Recommendation, Members should provide the Organization annual notice of any new or extended exclusion or category of authorization.

B.   INTERNATIONAL CO-OPERATION AND COMITY IN ENFORCING LAWS PROHIBITING HARD CORE CARTELS

1.   Member countries have a common interest in preventing hard core cartels and should co-operate with each other in enforcing their laws against such cartels. In this connection, they should seek ways in which co-operation might be improved by positive comity principles applicable to requests that another country remedy anticompetitive conduct that adversely affects both countries, and should conduct their own enforcement activities in accordance with principles of comity when they affect other countries' important interests.

2.   Co-operation between or among Member countries in dealing with hard core cartels should take into account the following principles:

a)   the common interest in preventing hard core cartels generally warrants co-operation to the extent that such co-operation would be consistent with a requested country's laws, regulations, and important interests;

b)   to the extent consistent with their own laws, regulations, and important interests, and subject to effective safeguards to protect commercially sensitive and other confidential information, Member countries' mutual interest in preventing hard core cartels warrants cooperation that might include sharing documents and information in their possession with foreign competition authorities and gathering documents and information on behalf of foreign competition authorities on a voluntary basis and when necessary through use of compulsory process;

c)   a Member country may decline to comply with a request for assistance, or limit or condition its co-operation on the ground that it considers compliance with the request to be not in accordance with its laws or regulations or to be inconsistent with its important interests or on any other grounds, including its competition authority's resource constraints or the absence of a mutual interest in the investigation or proceeding in question;

d)   Member countries should agree to engage in consultations over issues relating to cooperation. In order to establish a framework for their co-operation in dealing with hard core cartels, Member countries are encouraged to consider entering into bilateral or multilateral agreements or other instruments consistent with these principles.

3.   Member countries are encouraged to review all obstacles to their effective co-operation in the enforcement of laws against hard core cartels and to consider actions, including national legislation and/or bilateral or multilateral agreements or other instruments, by which they could eliminate or reduce those obstacles in a manner consistent with their important interests.

4.   The co-operation contemplated by this Recommendation is without prejudice to any other cooperation that may occur in accordance with prior Recommendations of the Council, pursuant to any applicable bilateral or multilateral agreements to which Member countries may be parties, or otherwise.

II.   INSTRUCTS the Competition Law and Policy Committee:

1.   to maintain a record of such exclusions and authorizations as are notified to the Organization (pursuant to Paragraph I. A 2b);

2.   to serve, at the request of the Member countries involved, as a forum for consultations on the application of the Recommendation; and

3.   to review Member countries' experience in implementing this Recommendation and report to the Council within two years on any further action needed to improve co-operation in the enforcement of competition law prohibitions of hard core cartels.

III. INVITES non-Member countries to associate themselves with this Recommendation and to implement it.

* * *

While voluntary and imperfect, the Hard Core Cartel Recommendation has helped to create and reinforce a rule against cartels as a world norm.

Note that, by definition, "hard core cartel" does not include any cartels that the law exempts or does not cover. This means that, in general, export cartels are not covered. Is exemption of export cartels inconsistent with a more nearly seamless world system?

Consider the weaknesses of the Recommendation. If it should be revised (but still remain voluntary), would you strengthen it? How?

H. THE US INTERNATIONAL COMPETITION POLICY ADVISORY COMMITTEE (ICPAC)

In 1998, President Clinton's Attorney General Janet Reno and Assistant Attorney General Joel Klein convened the International Competition Policy Advisory Committee (ICPAC) to consider what new tools and concepts would be needed to address the emerging competition issues of the global economy. In particular, the Committee was asked to study multijurisdictional merger review, enforcement cooperation in international cartels, and the interface between trade and competition issues. In 2000, the Committee submitted its Report. Among other things, the Committee observed that there was no satisfactory home in which the competition authorities could meet (alone and not with trade officials) to discuss and perhaps resolve world competition issues. The Report proposed that the competition authorities of the world establish a virtual competition network. One year later, this proposed "virtual" body—with no land address, no secretariat, and no trade officials—was to become the International Competition Network (ICN). The ICN is now, perhaps along with the competition policy committee of the OECD, the most important forum and force for sharing knowledge and perspective, and for convergence.

In addition, ICPAC made many recommendations for cooperative work among antitrust authorities of the world. For example, ICPAC proposed multi-jurisdictional work-sharing in merger review. The Report says:

> The Advisory Committee views the creation of a nearly seamless multijurisdictional merger review system as the ultimate goal of all of these efforts toward expanded cooperation and coordination.[1]

Cooperation at the merger remedy stage was singled out for its importance. ICPAC suggested:

> In some cases it may be feasible to have only *one jurisdiction negotiate remedies with the merging parties*

---

[1]   ICPAC Report, p. 76. The Report is available at *www.usdoj.gov/atr/icpac/icpac.htm*.

that will address the concerns of both that jurisdiction and other interested jurisdictions. In other words, the reviewing jurisdictions would identify the remedies necessary to address their competitive concerns, and the jurisdiction best positioned to negotiate and obtain the desired remedies would do so. An approach of this kind, for example, was successfully employed by the United States and the EU in the Halliburton/Dresser transaction. There, rather than negotiating separate undertakings with the merging parties, the EC relied on the provisions of a U.S. consent decree to satisfy its concerns regarding a perceived global problem in drilling fluids.[2]

ICPAC also underlined the importance of work-sharing at the review stage. It said:

> In appropriate cases, it may be beneficial to limit the number of jurisdictions conducting independent second-stage reviews of a proposed transaction. Where the concerns of one country are likely to be the same as and subsumed by the concerns of a more distinctly affected investigating jurisdiction, it may be appropriate for the first company to refrain from independent investigation.

* * *

> One way to safeguard against the possibility that the proceeding agency may reach a different result on the merits or a remedy different from the one the other jurisdictions might have reached, while at the same time gaining efficiency in the process and other potential benefits is to ensure sufficient participation in the process by the other jurisdictions. One jurisdiction could coordinate the investigation of a proposed transaction, take into account the views of each interested jurisdiction, and recommend remedies to address the concerns of all interested jurisdictions.

> Under this advanced work-sharing arrangement, *the coordinating agency would* perform a centralized information gathering function following initial notification by the merging parties to all reviewing agencies. The coordinating agency would then assess the competitive effects of the proposed transaction in all relevant product and geographic markets. Each interested jurisdiction would

---

[2]   *Id.*, p. 77, noting use of this approach also in Federal Mogul/T & N.

be invited to submit comments to the coordinating jurisdiction regarding its particular concerns. The assessment of the coordinating agency would be binding on the coordinating agency but could either serve as a recommendation to other interested jurisdictions (with a presumption in favor of accepting the recommendation) or be binding on those jurisdictions as well. . . .[3]

ICPAC considered yet more advanced work-sharing as a vision for the future. It described this as follows:

The Advisory Committee also considered whether an even higher level of work sharing might be possible after more procedural and substantive convergence among merger review regimes has occurred. At this advanced level of work sharing, the coordinating agency would be required to accept the mantle of *parens patriae* for world competition.

Accordingly, it would endeavor to evaluate procompetitive and anticompetitive effects of a proposed transaction on a global scale, taking into account all of the merger's costs and benefits to competition, not only the net effects within its borders. This approach arguably is superior to an approach in which each jurisdiction analyzes the effects of a proposed transaction within its own borders and ignores the harms or the benefits that the transaction may generate elsewhere. Multimarket assessment would position the coordinating jurisdiction to account for what had previously been viewed as externalities, thereby enabling it to assess the net effects of the proposed transaction (under a neutral welfare standard) on a global scale. The coordinating jurisdiction could then design remedies to address the concerns of all interested jurisdictions.[4]

One member further proposed an opt-in clearing house for pre-merger filings.

I. THE INTERNATIONAL COMPETITION NETWORK (ICN)

The International Competition Network was founded in 2001. It was intended to fill a gap that could not be filled by the OECD, UNCTAD, or the WTO. The OECD is an organization of developed

---

[3]   *Id.*, pp. 78, 80 (footnote omitted).
[4]   *Id.*, p. 81.

countries. The UNCTAD is an organization devoted to developing countries. The WTO is a trade organization; and the competition authorities take a back seat to the trade representative. Moreover, the WTO jurisdictions negotiate trade rules which are then subject to dispute resolution. The competition authorities needed a "room" of their own.

They wanted and needed an organization without rule-making or administrative or adjudicatory power, creating an informal and sharing environment conducive to solving actual problems and to converging law "on the ground." ICN has passed its 16th anniversary. It now has more than 130 members. It has generated an immense and immensely useful work product. It hosts annual conferences. It convenes working groups of volunteers—including non-governmental advisors—from numerous jurisdictions, whose work ranges from coordination of jurisdictions' rules on pre-merger process to informal technical assistance, to attempts to understand the abuse of dominance laws of all of the members and to tease out the common principles on which recommended practices or guidelines can be built.

Spend time on the web site of the ICN, *www.international competitionnetwork.org.* Comment on the scope and usefulness of its work.

The ICN is generally regarded as a notable success. Successful in doing what? Is it doing all that needs to be done to make the international competition law system a coherent one? Has it alleviated the need for an antitrust regime in the WTO? Is there an unmet need for rationalizing law on export cartels or for integrating trade and competition (which thus far have been beyond the mandate of the ICN)? Is there a need for a stronger appreciation of the voices of developing countries? Given the ICN and the other existing and emerging competition institutions, what should be the next steps for advancing the coherence, effectiveness, suitability, and legitimacy of competition law and policy in the family of antitrust nations and in the world?

J. A WAY FORWARD?

Here is an assessment of the problems that remain in the absence of an international competition agreement, and possibilities for moving forward.

ANTITRUST WITHOUT BORDERS: FROM
ROOTS TO CODES TO NETWORKS

Eleanor Fox (2015, revised 2017)
footnotes omitted; available at *http://e15initiative.org/publications/antitrust-
without-borders-from-roots-to-codes-to-networks/*

* * *

A WORLD REGIME?

Few fora are devoted to "world antitrust" in contemporary times. But, not long ago, the subject held center stage in conversation on the future of antitrust.

The 1990s was the decade of reflection and debate about a world competition regime. The idea was generated principally by the EU, whose officials understand, probably more than others, the cosmopolitan virtues of "community," including the juncture of free movement and free competition. In 1995, a European committee of Wise Men proposed an international competition system, with a home in the WTO. The system would have started with building blocks of transparency, nondiscrimination, and due process; cooperation; and assistance to developing economies. It would eventually have included a framework for substantive rules—against cartels, abuse of dominance, and the other commonly condemned restraints, as applied to cross-borders effects. It would have offered dispute resolution. The committee's concept was adopted in substantial part by the EU. After criticism especially from the US, the EU watered down its recommendations and proposed a modest form of international competition law that would have encompassed the first-stage building blocks of nondiscrimination, due process, cooperation, and assistance. It would have incorporated only one substantive rule—a rule against hard-core cartels. It would have eliminated dispute resolution except for failure to fulfil clear obligations; e.g., failure to adopt a law against cartels. This more modest proposal was provisionally placed on the agenda of the WTO Doha Development trade round. The antitrust program was, however, jettisoned from the trade agenda after failure of initial trade negotiations (on agricultural subsidies) at the Cancun meeting in 2003. Developing countries were not convinced that international competition rules would be good for them; WTO antitrust might be another Trojan horse, as many regarded the agreement on Trade-Related Aspects of Intellectual Property Rights (TRIPS). The US was not convinced that international competition rules would hold any benefit that it could not achieve on its own, and feared that antitrust at the bargaining table would produce a watering down of good law and create an unaccountable bureaucracy.

Meanwhile, international cooperation was steadily improving, in part through the new, grass-roots-up ICN; and the threat of serious case-specific conflicts was alleviated by the organically occurring soft convergence. If there was a movement for a comprehensive higher-up law of competition in the 1990s and early 2000s, it seemed to have receded in the face of the networking wave of the "new world order" informed as it has been by the spirit of the rule of subsidiarity: What can be done just as well or better at a lower level should be done at the lower level.

WHERE TO GO FROM HERE

It seems clear that cooperation has worked to lessen tensions and to produce more coherence, and it should be continued and deepened. Cooperation, along with intensive cross-fertilization, has alleviated conflicts and has helped to construct a more nearly seamless world. Merger enforcement has improved. Cartel enforcement has improved. For developing countries, cooperation has helped to transfer useful knowledge, and, anchoring agencies in the culture of competition, it has helped agencies stave off protectionism, parochialism, and excessive regulation.

Still, big tasks remain. Cooperation and soft convergence solve only some of the major antitrust problems of the world.

In contemplating problems and solutions, we have been enlightened by the conversations of the last three decades: the contemplation of the need for international antitrust; the debate regarding models; the failure to embrace the antitrust measures on the Doha agenda; the birth and blossoming of the ICN, which itself has spurred heightened performance of the OECD and the UNCTAD; the surge and appreciation of networking; and the imprint of the subsidiary principle.

I have listed below nine problems, some overlapping, and I ask in each case what can be solved on a horizontal (national or nation-to-nation) level, and what remains to be resolved through higher law or modalities.

THE PROBLEM OF GAPS

In important respects, the laws stop at the nations' shores, and they are riddled with exemptions and non-coverage, often in response to vested interests. The biggest, most obvious gap involves export cartels and world cartels particularly impacting outsiders. In part, this gap persists because of the practical disenfranchisement of victim jurisdictions that lack resources and information and are vulnerable. The second biggest, most obvious gap is anticompetitive state action or involvement, including state blessing of cartels and monopolistic abuses that predominantly or significantly hurt foreigners. This gap persists because of the still Westphalian deference to the state as sovereign.

Solutions may need to come at a higher level, for the same reason that nations fail to muster the constituencies necessary to eliminate quotas and reduce tariffs without reciprocal agreements with trading partners. The agreement called for is a "flanking" agreement to perfect nations' promises, already in the WTO, not to sponsor or encourage import or export cartels.

Other efforts can come at a grass-roots level. The OECD Hard Core cartel recommendation urges signatory nations to re-examine periodically their exemptions from a "no cartel" rule and to eliminate unnecessary exemptions. This process is vital to world competition in matters affecting trade and investment. The beginnings of a framework for a multinational agreement can be built ground up, starting with guidelines, principles or best practices; possibly in the OECD or the ICN if the ICN should expand its purview from "antitrust all the time."

THE PROBLEM OF OVERLAPS

A number of jurisdictions' antitrust laws may apply to the same conduct or transactions, and treatment may be inconsistent, conflicting, or over regulatory; remedies may be pile-up remedies.

In addressing overlap problems, the antitrust authorities of the world have made much progress through informal cooperation, with and without bi-lateral agreements. A very high level of cooperation and coordination has been attained, within limits of confidentiality obligations that prevent the sharing of information. The high levels of cooperation are visible in vetting transnational mergers and investigating cartels. Still, occasionally, outcomes in jurisdictions differ, because of differences in legal principles, different appreciation of the appropriate application of the same legal principles, or different factual contexts.

A higher level solution is generally not needed. An intensified level of cross-border communications by officials engaging with the particular facts of the particular case is normally the best solution. Over-regulatory pile-on remedies can be avoided by a second jurisdiction's seriously regarding the remedies ordered by a first jurisdiction and attempting to make its remedies consistent and not duplicative. Such an obligation of sympathetic consideration could be written into cooperation agreements and could also be developed as an international best practice in the context of the ICN.

There remains to be developed a principle for bridging ad hoc conflicts, such as those that occurred in the merger cases of Boeing/McDonnell Douglas and GE/Honeywell. The ICN is an ideal forum for working out a recommended or best practice. For example, where a second jurisdiction anticipates taking a course of action that conflicts with a first jurisdiction, a consensus principle might require that the second jurisdiction sympathetically consider the analysis, reasoning, and remedies of the first jurisdiction and exercise restraint in condemning an approved transaction or unduly burdening a conditioned transaction, with a view to enhancing the economic welfare in the world.

THE PROBLEM OF MYOPIC OR BOUNDED CONCERN, OR DISREGARD

Nations deal with their problems. They are normally indifferent to harms abroad launched by their firms. They feel free to ignore negative externalities abroad. This is the "not my problem" problem: Let the victim nation protect itself, and if it does not have the resources or practical power to induce outsiders to obey the law, so be it.

This problem is integral with the problem of gaps, treated above. Indeed, it provides one explanation for gaps. The cartel externality problem has a natural home in the WTO, as discussed above. As for mergers and monopolies—to the extent they have effects at home as well as abroad—the problems are more likely to evidence themselves as overlaps, and to this extent, are amenable to a horizontal solution. But, this is not always the case. The big cement merger now being consummated (Holcim/Lafarge) principally hurts small developing economies; and mergers, agreements, and conduct may create buying power that hurts poor commodity producers (e.g. of cocoa beans), while the developed world is oblivious.

THE PROBLEM OF PAROCHIALISM: "HAPPY TO HURT YOU AND AGGRANDISE ME"

Parochialism and vested interest lobbies provide another reason for gaps and selfish concern. Parochialism, when it exists, adds invidiousness to the restraint and underscores the importance of a common solution. Parochialism could, for example, be identified and condemned by an ICN principle. Indeed, discrimination based on nationality is already condemned by ICN merger principles.

THE PROBLEM OF LACK OF "VISION FROM THE TOP"

In many cases, problems are truly global and integral. This is the case, for example, for transnational mergers where markets transcend borders. Productive efficiencies at home may not inure to consumers or the market at large.

A make-do solution could come at a horizontal level. The solution requires flexibility of law and remedies beyond state bounds. For example, as suggested by the US advisory committee, the IGAD Climate Prediction and Applications Centre (ICPAC), the forum having the most contacts might take on the project of analyzing the whole merger, its benefits, and its harms, wherever they fall. It might host interventions by other complaining jurisdictions and grant relief copious enough to cure problems worldwide as if the world were in its nation. Best or recommended practices could be worked out in the ICN. The necessary flexible extension of law and process would need to be legislated by national legislators—not an easy task under today's norms; but, norms might change if one is forced to confront the fact that the alternative is either disarray or centralized international antitrust.

THE PROBLEM OF "ANTITRUST AS AN ISLAND," ISOLATED FROM THE MAINLAND OF POLITICAL ECONOMY

Antitrust is not an island unto itself. It is deeply interrelated with trade; foreign investment; the free movement of goods, services, and capital; the law of intellectual property; sectoral regulation; and the wide variety of proposed and actual industrial policies.

This is a problem in search of articulation, as witnessed by the coming of age of antitrust in China; the pressures on antitrust in the wake of the financial crisis; the voices of the developing countries in the negotiations at the Doha trade round (distribution and equity matter); and the United Nations (UN) project to alleviate poverty and promote inclusive sustainable development.

There is room for constructive work and debate on appropriate and inappropriate industrial policy. Because the debate sits on charged territory, serious debate is often suppressed. Work should be done at the WTO to narrow the bounds of permissible antidumping laws and subsidies in view of their distortion of international trade and particular harm to developing countries. Work should also be done at a horizontal networking level, perhaps at the ICN. To begin, a working group can ask, in the context of financial crisis: what general principles define protective measures that may be helpful to a nation and those measures unlikely to be helpful? What national measures are likely to be helpful to world welfare, and how can they be coordinated to that end; which are harmful to world welfare and how could and should they be discouraged?

THE PROBLEM OF INVENTING 130 WHEELS
WHEN ONE WILL DO (BETTER)

This is the problem of unnecessary and costly duplication. An example is premerger notification. Some 80 jurisdictions require premerger notification, filing and waiting to complete covered mergers. Large multinational mergers must normally comply with the rules and processes of each.

The ICN has addressed this problem. It has adopted recommended practices concerning, for example, the earliest date on which filing is permitted, so that firms can coordinate their filings and the required nexus with the jurisdiction, so that nations do not reach out unduly to grasp and tax mergers that threaten them no harm. More work needs to be done. There is a need for a common clearing house option for merger filings, so that one document filed in one place can provide all the necessary preliminary information. This can be done horizontally—by agreement among the jurisdictions. The ICN can be the forum for working out the details.

THE SPECIAL PROBLEMS OF DEVELOPING
AND TRANSITIONAL COUNTRIES

The special problems are three fold. First, developing countries and emerging regimes are often unable to protect themselves from offshore acts and transactions that harm them. They do not have the resources, information, and practical power. Therefore, they are especially vulnerable; even though many are on a fast upward learning curve and deserve to be commended and admired Second, the substantive rules of law most suitable for them are often different from the rules of law most suitable for developed economies with well-functioning markets, little statism, qualitatively less corruption, mature antitrust systems, and large expert staffs; yet, when international standards are formulated, they commonly replicate those of the developed countries. Third, and related to both points above, the developing countries and emerging antitrust jurisdictions need help; they need a transfer of knowledge and knowhow useful to their own contexts.

The third problem identified above is best handled on a horizontal level and is under control, although still in need of more thinking and action. Technical assistance is delivered generally by more developed countries to less developed ones. The EU, Germany, South Africa, Italy, the US, other nations, and groups working with donors, such as International Development Research Centre, have been generous providers of technical assistance. Peer reviews by the OECD and the UNCTAD have been extremely helpful. A working group of the ICN arranges for informal exchange of advice, pairing givers and receivers, who conduct their work through telephone and the Internet. All these projects and arrangements can be deepened. On-the-ground technical assistance can be better coordinated. The problem of homecountry bias in advice-giving can be addressed through awareness and consciousness raising, but not through higher law.

The first problem—vulnerability—has been treated in part above. If altruism will not move national policy, a better appreciation of the local good as a function of the common good might help. The better situated nations could use their national legislative powers to require their nationals to account for all harms they cause by consensus violations (e.g., hard-core cartels), and at least to expand their rules of discovery, so that violators within their borders and the evidentiary trails they leave can be explored at the scene of the wrongful acts.

The vulnerability problem means that developing countries with poor legal systems are not only unlikely to deter incoming cartels, but also are unlikely to provide a system that will compensate their citizens, even while victims abroad get considerable recoveries. This is both unfair and inefficient. The US has stepped back from the plate by its holding in *Empagran*, and other countries are not likely to come to their aid. This means either the developing countries must accelerate their economic and institutional progress and capability in some substantial way to help themselves—perhaps through regional free-trade groupings, which can give them critical mass (but this is a slow and uncertain process), or a world or transnational system or resource must be developed, or the problem will remain unattended. For example, a specialized group might be charged with analyzing data on proven cartels, such as the vitamins, lysine, or air fuel; with identifying who was over charged by how much; and with administering a fund for pay-outs.

THE PROBLEM OF DIFFERENTIAL LAW

The remaining problem is the problem of differential law and the likelihood that developed countries' law will be the international standard even when it is not the best standard for developing countries, both because developed countries have the expertise and power to "sell" their standard and because developing countries may not have the expert staffs and advisors to develop and successfully advocate the standards that are best for them, even as a dual-track alternative. This problem can be partially addressed by regional groupings, by more learning, and by greater awareness. In any event, it is a problem suitable for horizontal solution. It cannot be solved, and indeed could be undermined, by a detailed version of top-down antitrust.

CONCLUSION

The lack of traction thus far of world antitrust in the WTO, the rise of networking, and the common sense attraction of subsidiarity have focused our thinking on lower-level solutions to world problems. Today, we are searching for horizontal solutions. We are less hopeful and less trustful that comprehensive higher law will solve real problems. At the same time, our intellectual travels over the past two decades have helped to identify the situations in which only higher-level solutions will do. Problems that may be fully resistant to lower-level solutions are outward-oriented harm (export/world cartels) and the trade-restrictive state action that supports it. For this problem, we need flanking principles in the WTO. Other desirable multilateral solutions, such as a common clearing house option for merger filings, multilateralization of cooperation agreements, and a center for data analysis of identified world cartels, can be addressed at the networking level. At least, the development of models can begin at the grass-roots level. The idea of a Doha Dome [international framework] over a roots-up garden* was a good idea at the last turn of the century and is a good idea today (despite the virtual failure of the Doha trade round). The roots and their offshoots could grow under a common canopy of open and free competition not distorted by cronyism, parochialism, and artificial borders. The dome is sure to be no more concrete than a virtual roof over our heads. It can guide us toward a coherent framework. It cannot protect us from the rain and sleet; but it probably never would have done so, even in the headier days of the vision of one-world antitrust in the WTO.

Notes and Questions

1. Comment on this view of a global mission for international antitrust. Should aspirations go further, in the direction of the more holistic vision of the (EU) Wise Men, working up to a complete antitrust framework? Or should we aspire to a more integrated trade and competition policy with opportunities for dispute resolution? *See* Eduardo Perez Motta, Competition Policy and Trade in the Global

------

* See Eleanor Fox. "International Antitrust and the Doha Dome," 43 Va. J. Int'l 911 (2003). The "Doha Dome" was the skeletal framework suggested by the Doha trade agenda: non-discrimination, due process, cooperation, assistance, and an obligation of nations to adopt and maintain a rule against cartels. See text at notes 25–26 supra therein.

Economy: Towards an Integrated Approach, synthesizing policy options proposed by the E15 expert group of the World Economic Forum and the International Centre for Trade and Sustainable Development, *http://e 15initiative.org/publications/competition-policy-trade-global-economy-towards-integrated-approach/*? Or should policy makers be more modest, especially in this increasingly nationalistic world? Should we recognize the lack of support for a WTO prohibition of export cartels and for implementing any other cosmopolitan vision, and concentrate exclusively on roots-up voluntary cooperation and convergence as illuminated in the US Antitrust Guidelines for International Enforcement and Cooperation (2017) point 5? *See https://www.justice. gov/atr/internationalguidelines/download* and the video module of the International Competition Network on international cooperation, forthcoming, *http://www.internationalcompetitionnetwork.org/ about/steering-group/outreach/icncurriculum.aspx.*

2. What factors, perspective, and practical considerations motivate your choice?

APPENDICES

Table of Appendices

Appendix 1

EUROPEAN UNION

TREATY ON EUROPEAN UNION

(1992, as amended by Treaty of Lisbon, effective December 1, 2009)

TITLE I

* * *

Article 4

* * *

3. Pursuant to the principle of sincere cooperation, the Union and the Member States shall, in full mutual respect, assist each other in carrying out tasks which flow from the Treaties.

The Member States shall take any appropriate measure, general or particular, to ensure fulfilment of the obligations arising out of the Treaties or resulting from the acts of the institutions of the Union.

The Member States shall facilitate the achievement of the Union's tasks and refrain from any measure which could jeopardise the attainment of the Union's objectives.

* * *

TREATY ON THE FUNCTIONING OF THE EUROPEAN UNION

(1957, as amended and renamed by Treaty of Lisbon, effective as of December 1, 2009)

PART ONE

PRINCIPLES

Article 1

1. This Treaty organises the functioning of the Union and determines the areas of, delimitation of, and arrangements for exercising its competences.

2. This Treaty and the Treaty on European Union constitute the Treaties on which the Union is founded. These two Treaties, which have the same legal value, shall be referred to as 'the Treaties'.

TITLE I

CATEGORIES AND AREAS OF UNION COMPETENCE

Article 2

1.　When the Treaties confer on the Union exclusive competence in a specific area, only the Union may legislate and adopt legally binding acts, the Member States being able to do so themselves only if so empowered by the Union or for the implementation of Union acts.

2.　When the Treaties confer on the Union a competence shared with the Member States in a specific area, the Union and the Member States may legislate and adopt legally binding acts in that area. The Member States shall exercise their competence to the extent that the Union has not exercised its competence. The Member States shall again exercise their competence to the extent that the Union has decided to cease exercising its competence.

3.　The Member States shall coordinate their economic and employment policies within arrangements as determined by this Treaty, which the Union shall have competence to provide.

4.　The Union shall have competence, in accordance with the provisions of the Treaty on European Union, to define and implement a common foreign and security policy, including the progressive framing of a common defence policy.

5.　In certain areas and under the conditions laid down in the Treaties, the Union shall have competence to carry out actions to support, coordinate or supplement the actions of the Member States, without thereby superseding their competence in these areas. Legally binding acts of the Union adopted on the basis of the provisions of the Treaties relating to these areas shall not entail harmonisation of Member States' laws or regulations.

6.　The scope of and arrangements for exercising the Union's competences shall be determined by the provisions of the Treaties relating to each area.

Article 3

1.　The Union shall have exclusive competence in the following areas:

(a)　customs union;

(b)　the establishing of the competition rules necessary for the functioning of the internal market;

(c)　monetary policy for the Member States whose currency is the euro;

(d)　the conservation of marine biological resources under the common fisheries policy;

(e)　common commercial policy.

2.　The Union shall also have exclusive competence for the conclusion of an international agreement when its conclusion is provided for in a legislative act of the Union or is necessary to enable the Union to exercise its internal competence, or in so far as its conclusion may affect common rules or alter their scope.

Article 4

1.　The Union shall share competence with the Member States where the Treaties confer on it a competence which does not relate to the areas referred to in Articles 3 and 6.

2.　Shared competence between the Union and the Member States applies in the following principal areas:

(a)　internal market;

(b)　social policy, for the aspects defined in this Treaty;

(c)　economic, social and territorial cohesion;

(d)　agriculture and fisheries, excluding the conservation of marine biological resources;

(e)　environment;

(f)　consumer protection;

(g)　transport;

(h)　trans-European networks;

(i)　energy;

(j)　area of freedom, security and justice;

(k)　common safety concerns in public health matters, for the aspects defined in this Treaty.

3.　In the areas of research, technological development and space, the Union shall have competence to carry out activities, in particular to define and implement programmes; however, the exercise of that competence shall not result in Member States being prevented from exercising theirs.

4.　In the areas of development cooperation and humanitarian aid, the Union shall have competence to carry out activities and conduct a common policy; however, the exercise of that competence shall not result in Member States being prevented from exercising theirs.

* * *

PART THREE

UNION POLICIES AND INTERNAL ACTIONS

* * *

TITLE II

FREE MOVEMENT OF GOODS

Article 28

1.   The Union shall comprise a customs union which shall cover all trade in goods and which shall involve the prohibition between Member States of customs duties on imports and exports and of all charges having equivalent effect, and the adoption of a common customs tariff in their relations with third countries.

2.   The provisions of Article 30 and of Chapter 2 of this Title shall apply to products originating in Member States and to products coming from third countries which are in free circulation in Member States.

* * *

CHAPTER 1

THE CUSTOMS UNION

Article 30

Customs duties on imports and exports and charges having equivalent effect shall be prohibited between Member States. This prohibition shall also apply to customs duties of a fiscal nature.

* * *

CHAPTER 3

PROHIBITION OF QUANTITATIVE RESTRICTIONS BETWEEN MEMBER STATES

Article 34

Quantitative restrictions on imports and all measures having equivalent effect shall be prohibited between Member States.

Article 35

Quantitative restrictions on exports, and all measures having equivalent effect, shall be prohibited between Member States.

Article 36

The provisions of Articles 34 and 35 shall not preclude prohibitions or restrictions on imports, exports or goods in transit justified on grounds of public morality, public policy or public security; the protection of health and life of humans, animals or plants; the protection of national treasures possessing artistic, historic or archaeological value; or the protection of industrial and commercial property. Such prohibitions or restrictions shall not, however, constitute a means of arbitrary discrimination or a disguised restriction on trade between Member States.

Article 37

1.   Member States shall adjust any State monopolies of a commercial character so as to ensure that no discrimination regarding the conditions under which goods are procured and marketed exists between nationals of Member States.

The provisions of this Article shall apply to any body through which a Member State, in law or in fact, either directly or indirectly supervises, determines or appreciably influences imports or exports between Member States. These provisions shall likewise apply to monopolies delegated by the State to others.

2.   Member States shall refrain from introducing any new measure which is contrary to the principles laid down in paragraph 1 or which restricts the scope of the articles dealing with the prohibition of customs duties and quantitative restrictions between Member States.

3.   If a State monopoly of a commercial character has rules which are designed to make it easier to dispose of agricultural products or obtain for them the best return, steps should be taken in applying the rules contained in this Article to ensure equivalent safeguards for the employment and standard of living of the producers concerned.

* * *

TITLE IV

FREE MOVEMENT OF PERSONS, SERVICES AND CAPITAL

CHAPTER 1

WORKERS

Article 45

1.　Freedom of movement for workers shall be secured within the Union.

2.　Such freedom of movement shall entail the abolition of any discrimination based on nationality between workers of the Member States as regards employment, remuneration and other conditions of work and employment.

3.　It shall entail the right, subject to limitations justified on grounds of public policy, public security or public health:

(a)　to accept offers of employment actually made;

(b)　to move freely within the territory of Member States for this purpose;

(c)　to stay in a Member State for the purpose of employment in accordance with the provisions governing the employment of nationals of that State laid down by law, regulation or administrative action;

(d)　to remain in the territory of a Member State after having been employed in that State, subject to conditions which shall be embodied in regulations to be drawn up by the Commission.

4.　The provisions of this Article shall not apply to employment in the public service.

* * *

CHAPTER 2

RIGHT OF ESTABLISHMENT

Article 49

Within the framework of the provisions set out below, restrictions on the freedom of establishment of nationals of a Member State in the territory of another Member State shall be prohibited. Such prohibition shall also apply to restrictions on the setting-up of agencies, branches or subsidiaries by nationals of any Member State established in the territory of any Member State.

Freedom of establishment shall include the right to take up and pursue activities as self-employed persons and to set up and manage undertakings, in particular companies or firms . . . , under the conditions laid down for its own nationals by the law of the country where such establishment is effected, subject to the provisions of the Chapter relating to capital.

* * *

Article 52

1.   The provisions of this Chapter and measures taken in pursuance thereof shall not prejudice the applicability of provisions laid down by law, regulation or administrative action providing for special treatment for foreign nationals on grounds of public policy, public security or public health.

2.   The European Parliament and the Council shall, acting in accordance with the ordinary legislative procedure, issue directives for the coordination of the abovementioned provisions.

* * *

CHAPTER 3

SERVICES

Article 56

Within the framework of the provisions set out below, restrictions on freedom to provide services within the Union shall be prohibited in respect of nationals of Member States who are established in a Member State other than that of the person for whom the services are intended.

The European Parliament and the Council, acting in accordance with the ordinary legislative procedure, may extend the provisions of the Chapter to nationals of a third country who provide services and who are established within the Union.

* * *

Article 61

As long as restrictions on freedom to provide services have not been abolished, each Member State shall apply such restrictions without distinction on grounds of nationality or residence to all persons providing services. . . .

* * *

TITLE VII

COMMON RULES ON COMPETITION, TAXATION AND APPROXIMATION OF LAWS

CHAPTER 1

RULES ON COMPETITION

SECTION 1

RULES APPLYING TO UNDERTAKINGS

Article 101

1.   The following shall be prohibited as incompatible with the internal market: all agreements between undertakings, decisions by associations of undertakings and concerted practices which may affect trade between Member States and which have as their object or effect the prevention, restriction or distortion of competition within the internal market, and in particular those which:

(a)   directly or indirectly fix purchase or selling prices or any other trading conditions;

(b)   limit or control production, markets, technical development, or investment;

(c)   share markets or sources of supply;

(d)   apply dissimilar conditions to equivalent transactions with other trading parties, thereby placing them at a competitive disadvantage;

(e)   make the conclusion of contracts subject to acceptance by the other parties of supplementary obligations which, by their nature or according to commercial usage, have no connection with the subject of such contracts.

2.   Any agreements or decisions prohibited pursuant to this Article shall be automatically void.

3.   The provisions of paragraph 1 may, however, be declared inapplicable in the case of:

—any agreement or category of agreements between undertakings,

—any decision or category of decisions by associations of undertakings,

—any concerted practice or category of concerted practices,

which contributes to improving the production or distribution of goods or to promoting technical or economic progress, while allowing consumers a fair share of the resulting benefit, and which does not:

(a) impose on the undertakings concerned restrictions which are not indispensable to the attainment of these objectives;

(b) afford such undertakings the possibility of eliminating competition in respect of a substantial part of the products in question.

Article 102

Any abuse by one or more undertakings of a dominant position within the internal market or in a substantial part of it shall be prohibited as incompatible with the internal market in so far as it may affect trade between Member States.

Such abuse may, in particular, consist in:

(a) directly or indirectly imposing unfair purchase or selling prices or other unfair trading conditions;

(b) limiting production, markets or technical development to the prejudice of consumers;

(c) applying dissimilar conditions to equivalent transactions with other trading parties, thereby placing them at a competitive disadvantage;

(d) making the conclusion of contracts subject to acceptance by the other parties of supplementary obligations which, by their nature or according to commercial usage, have no connection with the subject of such contracts.

* * *

Article 106

1. In the case of public undertakings and undertakings to which Member States grant special or exclusive rights, Member States shall neither enact nor maintain in force any measure contrary to the rules contained in the Treaties, in particular to those rules provided for in Article 18 [prohibiting discrimination based on nationality] and Articles 101 to 109.

2. Undertakings entrusted with the operation of services of general economic interest or having the character of a revenue-producing monopoly shall be subject to the rules contained in the Treaties, in particular to the rules on competition, in so far as the

application of such rules does not obstruct the performance, in law or in fact, of the particular tasks assigned to them. The development of trade must not be affected to such an extent as would be contrary to the interests of the Union.

3. The Commission shall ensure the application of the provisions of this Article and shall, where necessary, address appropriate directives or decisions to Member States.

SECTION 2

AIDS GRANTED BY STATES

Article 107

1. Save as otherwise provided in the Treaties, any aid granted by a Member State or through State resources in any form whatsoever which distorts or threatens to distort competition by favouring certain undertakings or the production of certain goods shall, in so far as it affects trade between Member States, be incompatible with the internal market.

2. The following shall be compatible with the internal market:

(a) aid having a social character, granted to individual consumers, provided that such aid is granted without discrimination related to the origin of the products concerned;

(b) aid to make good the damage caused by natural disasters or exceptional occurrences;

(c) aid granted to the economy of certain areas of the Federal Republic of Germany affected by the division of Germany, in so far as such aid is required in order to compensate for the economic disadvantages caused by that division. Five years after the entry into force of the Treaty of Lisbon, the Council, acting on a proposal from the Commission, may adopt a decision repealing this point.

3. The following may be considered to be compatible with the internal market:

(a) aid to promote the economic development of areas where the standard of living is abnormally low or where there is serious underemployment, and of the regions referred to in Article 349, in view of their structural, economic and social situation;

(b)   aid to promote the execution of an important project of common European interest or to remedy a serious disturbance in the economy of a Member State;

(c)   aid to facilitate the development of certain economic activities or of certain economic areas, where such aid does not adversely affect trading conditions to an extent contrary to the common interest;

(d)   aid to promote culture and heritage conservation where such aid does not affect trading conditions and competition in the Union to an extent that is contrary to the common interest;

(e)   such other categories of aid as may be specified by decision of the Council on a proposal from the Commission.

Article 108

1.   The Commission shall, in cooperation with Member States, keep under constant review all systems of aid existing in those States. It shall propose to the latter any appropriate measures required by the progressive development or by the functioning of the internal market.

2.   If, after giving notice to the parties concerned to submit their comments, the Commission finds that aid granted by a State or through State resources is not compatible with the internal market having regard to Article 107, or that such aid is being misused, it shall decide that the State concerned shall abolish or alter such aid within a period of time to be determined by the Commission.

If the State concerned does not comply with this decision within the prescribed time, the Commission or any other interested State may, in derogation from the provisions of Articles 258 and 259, refer the matter to the Court of Justice of the European Union direct.

On application by a Member State, the Council may, acting unanimously, decide that aid which that State is granting or intends to grant shall be considered to be compatible with the internal market, in derogation from the provisions of Article 107 or from the regulations provided for in Article 109, if such a decision is justified by exceptional circumstances. If, as regards the aid in question, the Commission has already initiated the procedure provided for in the first subparagraph of this paragraph, the fact that the State concerned has made its application to the Council shall have the effect of suspending that procedure until the Council has made its attitude known.

If, however, the Council has not made its attitude known within three months of the said application being made, the Commission shall give its decision on the case.

3.   The Commission shall be informed, in sufficient time to enable it to submit its comments, of any plans to grant or alter aid. If it considers that any such plan is not compatible with the internal market having regard to Article 107, it shall without delay initiate the procedure provided for in paragraph 2. The Member State concerned shall not put its proposed measures into effect until this procedure has resulted in a final decision.

4.   The Commission may adopt regulations relating to the categories of State aid that the Council has, pursuant to Article 109, determined may be exempted from the procedure provided for by paragraph 3 of this Article.

Article 109

The Council, on a proposal from the Commission and after consulting the European Parliament, may make any appropriate regulations for the application of Articles 107 and 108 and may in particular determine the conditions in which Article 108(3) shall apply and the categories of aid exempted from this procedure.

* * *

PART SEVEN

GENERAL AND FINAL PROVISIONS

* * *

Article 352

1.   If action by the Union should prove necessary, within the framework of the policies defined in the Treaties, to attain one of the objectives set out in the Treaties, and the Treaties have not provided the necessary powers, the Council, acting unanimously on a proposal from the Commission and after obtaining the consent of the European Parliament, shall adopt the appropriate measures. Where the measures in question are adopted by the Council in accordance with a special legislative procedure, it shall also act unanimously on a proposal from the Commission and after obtaining the consent of the European Parliament.

2.   Using the procedure for monitoring the subsidiarity principle referred to in Article 5(3) of the Treaty on European Union, the Commission shall draw national Parliaments' attention to proposals based on this Article.

3.   Measures based on this Article shall not entail harmonisation of Member States' laws or regulations in cases where the Treaties exclude such harmonisation.

4.   This Article cannot serve as a basis for attaining objectives pertaining to the common foreign and security policy and any acts adopted pursuant to this Article shall respect the limits set out in Article 40, second paragraph, of the Treaty on European Union.

* * *

PROTOCOL (NO 27)

ON THE INTERNAL MARKET AND COMPETITION

THE HIGH CONTRACTING PARTIES,

CONSIDERING that the internal market as set out in Article 3 of the Treaty on European Union includes a system ensuring that competition is not distorted,

HAVE AGREED that:

To this end, the Union shall, if necessary, take action under the provision of the Treaties, including under Article 352 of the Treaty on the Functioning of the European Union.

This protocol shall be annexed to the Treaty on European Union and to the Treaty on the Functioning of the European Union.

Appendix 2

EUROPEAN UNION COUNCIL REGULATION NO. 1/2003

OF 16 DECEMBER 2002 ON THE IMPLEMENTATION OF THE RULES ON COMPETITION, ARTICLES 81 AND 82 OF THE TREATY

O. J. L1/1 (4 Jan. 2003)

[This regulation references the article numbers of the Treaty establishing the European Community (TEC). These articles have been renumbered. Article 81 TEC is now Article 101 of the Treaty on Functioning of the European Union (TFEU). Article 82 TEC is now Article 102 TFEU. Article 83 TEC is now Article 103 TFEU.]

THE COUNCIL OF THE EUROPEAN UNION,

Having regard to the Treaty establishing the European Community, and in particular Article 83 thereof,

Having regard to the proposal from the Commission,

Having regard to the opinion of the European Parliament,

Having regard to the opinion of the European Economic and Social Committee,

Whereas:

(1) In order to establish a system which ensures that competition in the common market is not distorted, Articles 81 and 82 of the Treaty must be applied effectively and uniformly in the Community. Council Regulation No 17 of 6 February 1962, First Regulation implementing Articles 81 and 82 of the Treaty, has allowed a Community competition policy to develop that has helped to disseminate a competition culture within the Community. In the light of experience, however, that Regulation should now be replaced by legislation designed to meet the challenges of an integrated market and a future enlargement of the Community.

(2) In particular, there is a need to rethink the arrangements for applying the exception from the prohibition on agreements, which

restrict competition, laid down in Article 81(3) of the Treaty. Under Article 83(2)(b) of the Treaty, account must be taken in this regard of the need to ensure effective supervision, on the one hand, and to simplify administration to the greatest possible extent, on the other.

(3) The centralised scheme set up by Regulation No 17 no longer secures a balance between those two objectives. It hampers application of the Community competition rules by the courts and competition authorities of the Member States, and the system of notification it involves prevents the Commission from concentrating its resources on curbing the most serious infringements. It also imposes considerable costs on undertakings.

(4) The present system should therefore be replaced by a directly applicable exception system in which the competition authorities and courts of the Member States have the power to apply not only Article 81(1) and Article 82 of the Treaty, which have direct applicability by virtue of the case-law of the Court of Justice of the European Communities, but also Article 81(3) of the Treaty.

(5) In order to ensure an effective enforcement of the Community competition rules and at the same time the respect of fundamental rights of defence, this Regulation should regulate the burden of proof under Articles 81 and 82 of the Treaty. It should be for the party or the authority alleging an infringement of Article 81(1) and Article 82 of the Treaty to prove the existence thereof to the required legal standard. It should be for the undertaking or association of undertakings invoking the benefit of a defence against a finding of an infringement to demonstrate to the required legal standard that the conditions for applying such defence are satisfied. This Regulation affects neither national rules on the standard of proof nor obligations of competition authorities and courts of the Member States to ascertain the relevant facts of a case, provided that such rules and obligations are compatible with general principles of Community law.

(6) In order to ensure that the Community competition rules are applied effectively, the competition authorities of the Member States should be associated more closely with their application. To this end, they should be empowered to apply Community law.

(7) National courts have an essential part to play in applying the Community competition rules. When deciding disputes between private individuals, they protect the subjective rights under Community law, for example by awarding damages to the victims of infringements. The role of the national courts here complements that of the competition authorities of the Member States. They should therefore be allowed to apply Articles 81 and 82 of the Treaty in full.

(8) In order to ensure the effective enforcement of the Community competition rules and the proper functioning of the cooperation mechanisms contained in this Regulation, it is necessary to oblige the competition authorities and courts of the Member States to also apply Articles 81 and 82 of the Treaty where they apply national competition law to agreements and practices which may affect trade between Member States. In order to create a level playing field for agreements, decisions by associations of undertakings and concerted practices within the internal market, it is also necessary to determine pursuant to Article 83(2)(e) of the Treaty the relationship between national laws and Community competition law. To that effect it is necessary to provide that the application of national competition laws to agreements, decisions or concerted practices within the meaning of Article 81(1) of the Treaty may not lead to the prohibition of such agreements, decisions and concerted practices if they are not also prohibited under Community competition law. The notions of agreements, decisions and concerted practices are autonomous concepts of Community competition law covering the coordination of behaviour of undertakings on the market as interpreted by the Community Courts. Member States should not under this Regulation be precluded from adopting and applying on their territory stricter national competition laws which prohibit or impose sanctions on unilateral conduct engaged in by undertakings. These stricter national laws may include provisions which prohibit or impose sanctions on abusive behaviour toward economically dependent undertakings. Furthermore, this Regulation does not apply to national laws which impose criminal sanctions on natural persons except to the extent that such sanctions are the means whereby competition rules applying to undertakings are enforced.

(9) Articles 81 and 82 of the Treaty have as their objective the protection of competition on the market. This Regulation, which is adopted for the implementation of these Treaty provisions, does not preclude Member States from implementing on their territory national legislation, which protects other legitimate interests provided that such legislation is compatible with general principles and other provisions of Community law. In so far as such national legislation pursues predominantly an objective different from that of protecting competition on the market, the competition authorities and courts of the Member States may apply such legislation on their territory. Accordingly, Member States may under this Regulation implement on their territory national legislation that prohibits or imposes sanctions on acts of unfair trading practice, be they unilateral or contractual. Such legislation pursues a specific objective, irrespective of the actual or presumed effects of such acts on competition on the market. This is particularly the case of

legislation which prohibits undertakings from imposing on their trading partners, obtaining or attempting to obtain from them terms and conditions that are unjustified, disproportionate or without consideration.

(10) Regulations such as 19/65/EEC, (EEC) No 2821/71, (EEC) No 3976/87, (EEC) No 1534/91, or (EEC) No 479/92 empower the Commission to apply Article 81(3) of the Treaty by Regulation to certain categories of agreements, decisions by associations of undertakings and concerted practices. In the areas defined by such Regulations, the Commission has adopted and may continue to adopt so called "block" exemption Regulations by which it declares Article 81(1) of the Treaty inapplicable to categories of agreements, decisions and concerted practices. Where agreements, decisions and concerted practices to which such Regulations apply nonetheless have effects that are incompatible with Article 81(3) of the Treaty, the Commission and the competition authorities of the Member States should have the power to withdraw in a particular case the benefit of the block exemption Regulation.

(11) For it to ensure that the provisions of the Treaty are applied, the Commission should be able to address decisions to undertakings or associations of undertakings for the purpose of bringing to an end infringements of Articles 81 and 82 of the Treaty. Provided there is a legitimate interest in doing so, the Commission should also be able to adopt decisions which find that an infringement has been committed in the past even if it does not impose a fine. This Regulation should also make explicit provision for the Commission's power to adopt decisions ordering interim measures, which has been acknowledged by the Court of Justice.

(12) This Regulation should make explicit provision for the Commission's power to impose any remedy, whether behavioural or structural, which is necessary to bring the infringement effectively to an end, having regard to the principle of proportionality. Structural remedies should only be imposed either where there is no equally effective behavioural remedy or where any equally effective behavioural remedy would be more burdensome for the undertaking concerned than the structural remedy. Changes to the structure of an undertaking as it existed before the infringement was committed would only be proportionate where there is a substantial risk of a lasting or repeated infringement that derives from the very structure of the undertaking.

(13) Where, in the course of proceedings which might lead to an agreement or practice being prohibited, undertakings offer the Commission commitments such as to meet its concerns, the

Commission should be able to adopt decisions which make those commitments binding on the undertakings concerned. Commitment decisions should find that there are no longer grounds for action by the Commission without concluding whether or not there has been or still is an infringement. Commitment decisions are without prejudice to the powers of competition authorities and courts of the Member States to make such a finding and decide upon the case. Commitment decisions are not appropriate in cases where the Commission intends to impose a fine.

(14) In exceptional cases where the public interest of the Community so requires, it may also be expedient for the Commission to adopt a decision of a declaratory nature finding that the prohibition in Article 81 or Article 82 of the Treaty does not apply, with a view to clarifying the law and ensuring its consistent application throughout the Community, in particular with regard to new types of agreements or practices that have not been settled in the existing case-law and administrative practice.

(15) The Commission and the competition authorities of the Member States should form together a network of public authorities applying the Community competition rules in close cooperation. For that purpose it is necessary to set up arrangements for information and consultation. Further modalities for the cooperation within the network will be laid down and revised by the Commission, in close cooperation with the Member States.

(16) Notwithstanding any national provision to the contrary, the exchange of information and the use of such information in evidence should be allowed between the members of the network even where the information is confidential. This information may be used for the application of Articles 81 and 82 of the Treaty as well as for the parallel application of national competition law, provided that the latter application relates to the same case and does not lead to a different outcome. When the information exchanged is used by the receiving authority to impose sanctions on undertakings, there should be no other limit to the use of the information than the obligation to use it for the purpose for which it was collected given the fact that the sanctions imposed on undertakings are of the same type in all systems. The rights of defence enjoyed by undertakings in the various systems can be considered as sufficiently equivalent. However, as regards natural persons, they may be subject to substantially different types of sanctions across the various systems. Where that is the case, it is necessary to ensure that information can only be used if it has been collected in a way which respects the same level of protection of the rights of defence of natural persons as provided for under the national rules of the receiving authority.

(17) If the competition rules are to be applied consistently and, at the same time, the network is to be managed in the best possible way, it is essential to retain the rule that the competition authorities of the Member States are automatically relieved of their competence if the Commission initiates its own proceedings. Where a competition authority of a Member State is already acting on a case and the Commission intends to initiate proceedings, it should endeavour to do so as soon as possible. Before initiating proceedings, the Commission should consult the national authority concerned.

(18) To ensure that cases are dealt with by the most appropriate authorities within the network, a general provision should be laid down allowing a competition authority to suspend or close a case on the ground that another authority is dealing with it or has already dealt with it, the objective being that each case should be handled by a single authority. This provision should not prevent the Commission from rejecting a complaint for lack of Community interest, as the case-law of the Court of Justice has acknowledged it may do, even if no other competition authority has indicated its intention of dealing with the case.

(19) The Advisory Committee on Restrictive Practices and Dominant Positions set up by Regulation No 17 has functioned in a very satisfactory manner. It will fit well into the new system of decentralised application. It is necessary, therefore, to build upon the rules laid down by Regulation No 17, while improving the effectiveness of the organisational arrangements. To this end, it would be expedient to allow opinions to be delivered by written procedure. The Advisory Committee should also be able to act as a forum for discussing cases that are being handled by the competition authorities of the Member States, so as to help safeguard the consistent application of the Community competition rules.

(20) The Advisory Committee should be composed of representatives of the competition authorities of the Member States. For meetings in which general issues are being discussed, Member States should be able to appoint an additional representative. This is without prejudice to members of the Committee being assisted by other experts from the Member States.

(21) Consistency in the application of the competition rules also requires that arrangements be established for cooperation between the courts of the Member States and the Commission. This is relevant for all courts of the Member States that apply Articles 81 and 82 of the Treaty, whether applying these rules in lawsuits between private parties, acting as public enforcers or as review courts. In particular, national courts should be able to ask the

Commission for information or for its opinion on points concerning the application of Community competition law. The Commission and the competition authorities of the Member States should also be able to submit written or oral observations to courts called upon to apply Article 81 or Article 82 of the Treaty. These observations should be submitted within the framework of national procedural rules and practices including those safeguarding the rights of the parties. Steps should therefore be taken to ensure that the Commission and the competition authorities of the Member States are kept sufficiently well informed of proceedings before national courts.

(22) In order to ensure compliance with the principles of legal certainty and the uniform application of the Community competition rules in a system of parallel powers, conflicting decisions must be avoided. It is therefore necessary to clarify, in accordance with the case-law of the Court of Justice, the effects of Commission decisions and proceedings on courts and competition authorities of the Member States. Commitment decisions adopted by the Commission do not affect the power of the courts and the competition authorities of the Member States to apply Articles 81 and 82 of the Treaty.

(23) The Commission should be empowered throughout the Community to require such information to be supplied as is necessary to detect any agreement, decision or concerted practice prohibited by Article 81 of the Treaty or any abuse of a dominant position prohibited by Article 82 of the Treaty. When complying with a decision of the Commission, undertakings cannot be forced to admit that they have committed an infringement, but they are in any event obliged to answer factual questions and to provide documents, even if this information may be used to establish against them or against another undertaking the existence of an infringement.

(24) The Commission should also be empowered to undertake such inspections as are necessary to detect any agreement, decision or concerted practice prohibited by Article 81 of the Treaty or any abuse of a dominant position prohibited by Article 82 of the Treaty. The competition authorities of the Member States should cooperate actively in the exercise of these powers.

(25) The detection of infringements of the competition rules is growing ever more difficult, and, in order to protect competition effectively, the Commission's powers of investigation need to be supplemented. The Commission should in particular be empowered to interview any persons who may be in possession of useful information and to record the statements made. In the course of an inspection, officials authorised by the Commission should be empowered to affix seals for the period of time necessary for the

inspection. Seals should normally not be affixed for more than 72 hours. Officials authorised by the Commission should also be empowered to ask for any information relevant to the subject matter and purpose of the inspection.

(26) Experience has shown that there are cases where business records are kept in the homes of directors or other people working for an undertaking. In order to safeguard the effectiveness of inspections, therefore, officials and other persons authorised by the Commission should be empowered to enter any premises where business records may be kept, including private homes. However, the exercise of this latter power should be subject to the authorisation of the judicial authority.

(27) Without prejudice to the case-law of the Court of Justice, it is useful to set out the scope of the control that the national judicial authority may carry out when it authorises, as foreseen by national law including as a precautionary measure, assistance from law enforcement authorities in order to overcome possible opposition on the part of the undertaking or the execution of the decision to carry out inspections in non-business premises. It results from the case-law that the national judicial authority may in particular ask the Commission for further information which it needs to carry out its control and in the absence of which it could refuse the authorisation. The case-law also confirms the competence of the national courts to control the application of national rules governing the implementation of coercive measures.

(28) In order to help the competition authorities of the Member States to apply Articles 81 and 82 of the Treaty effectively, it is expedient to enable them to assist one another by carrying out inspections and other fact-finding measures.

(29) Compliance with Articles 81 and 82 of the Treaty and the fulfilment of the obligations imposed on undertakings and associations of undertakings under this Regulation should be enforceable by means of fines and periodic penalty payments. To that end, appropriate levels of fine should also be laid down for infringements of the procedural rules.

(30) In order to ensure effective recovery of fines imposed on associations of undertakings for infringements that they have committed, it is necessary to lay down the conditions on which the Commission may require payment of the fine from the members of the association where the association is not solvent. In doing so, the Commission should have regard to the relative size of the undertakings belonging to the association and in particular to the situation of small and medium-sized enterprises. Payment of the fine

by one or several members of an association is without prejudice to rules of national law that provide for recovery of the amount paid from other members of the association.

(31) The rules on periods of limitation for the imposition of fines and periodic penalty payments were laid down in Council Regulation (EEC) No 2988/74, which also concerns penalties in the field of transport. In a system of parallel powers, the acts, which may interrupt a limitation period, should include procedural steps taken independently by the competition authority of a Member State. To clarify the legal framework, Regulation (EEC) No 2988/74 should therefore be amended to prevent it applying to matters covered by this Regulation, and this Regulation should include provisions on periods of limitation.

(32) The undertakings concerned should be accorded the right to be heard by the Commission, third parties whose interests may be affected by a decision should be given the opportunity of submitting their observations beforehand, and the decisions taken should be widely publicised. While ensuring the rights of defence of the undertakings concerned, in particular, the right of access to the file, it is essential that business secrets be protected. The confidentiality of information exchanged in the network should likewise be safeguarded.

(33) Since all decisions taken by the Commission under this Regulation are subject to review by the Court of Justice in accordance with the Treaty, the Court of Justice should, in accordance with Article 229 thereof be given unlimited jurisdiction in respect of decisions by which the Commission imposes fines or periodic penalty payments.

(34) The principles laid down in Articles 81 and 82 of the Treaty, as they have been applied by Regulation No 17, have given a central role to the Community bodies. This central role should be retained, whilst associating the Member States more closely with the application of the Community competition rules. In accordance with the principles of subsidiarity and proportionality as set out in Article 5 of the Treaty, this Regulation does not go beyond what is necessary in order to achieve its objective, which is to allow the Community competition rules to be applied effectively.

(35) In order to attain a proper enforcement of Community competition law, Member States should designate and empower authorities to apply Articles 81 and 82 of the Treaty as public enforcers. They should be able to designate administrative as well as judicial authorities to carry out the various functions conferred upon competition authorities in this Regulation. This Regulation

recognises the wide variation which exists in the public enforcement systems of Member States. The effects of Article 11(6) of this Regulation should apply to all competition authorities. As an exception to this general rule, where a prosecuting authority brings a case before a separate judicial authority, Article 11(6) should apply to the prosecuting authority subject to the conditions in Article 35(4) of this Regulation. Where these conditions are not fulfilled, the general rule should apply. In any case, Article 11(6) should not apply to courts insofar as they are acting as review courts.

(36) As the case-law has made it clear that the competition rules apply to transport, that sector should be made subject to the procedural provisions of this Regulation. Council Regulation No 141 of 26 November 1962 exempting transport from the application of Regulation No 17 should therefore be repealed and Regulations (EEC) No 1017/68, (EEC) No 4056/86 and (EEC) No 3975/87 should be amended in order to delete the specific procedural provisions they contain.

(37) This Regulation respects the fundamental rights and observes the principles recognised in particular by the Charter of Fundamental Rights of the European Union. Accordingly, this Regulation should be interpreted and applied with respect to those rights and principles.

(38) Legal certainty for undertakings operating under the Community competition rules contributes to the promotion of innovation and investment. Where cases give rise to genuine uncertainty because they present novel or unresolved questions for the application of these rules, individual undertakings may wish to seek informal guidance from the Commission. This Regulation is without prejudice to the ability of the Commission to issue such informal guidance,

HAS ADOPTED THIS REGULATION:

CHAPTER I

PRINCIPLES

Article 1

APPLICATION OF ARTICLES 81 AND 82 OF THE TREATY

1.   Agreements, decisions and concerted practices caught by Article 81(1) of the Treaty which do not satisfy the conditions of Article 81(3) of the Treaty shall be prohibited, no prior decision to that effect being required.

2.   Agreements, decisions and concerted practices caught by Article 81(1) of the Treaty which satisfy the conditions of Article 81(3) of the Treaty shall not be prohibited, no prior decision to that effect being required.

3.   The abuse of a dominant position referred to in Article 82 of the Treaty shall be prohibited, no prior decision to that effect being required.

Article 2

BURDEN OF PROOF

In any national or Community proceedings for the application of Articles 81 and 82 of the Treaty, the burden of proving an infringement of Article 81(1) or of Article 82 of the Treaty shall rest on the party or the authority alleging the infringement. The undertaking or association of undertakings claiming the benefit of Article 81(3) of the Treaty shall bear the burden of proving that the conditions of that paragraph are fulfilled.

Article 3

RELATIONSHIP BETWEEN ARTICLES 81 AND 82 OF THE TREATY AND NATIONAL COMPETITION LAWS

1.   Where the competition authorities of the Member States or national courts apply national competition law to agreements, decisions by associations of undertakings or concerted practices within the meaning of Article 81(1) of the Treaty which may affect trade between Member States within the meaning of that provision, they shall also apply Article 81 of the Treaty to such agreements, decisions or concerted practices. Where the competition authorities of the Member States or national courts apply national competition law to any abuse prohibited by Article 82 of the Treaty, they shall also apply Article 82 of the Treaty.

2.   The application of national competition law may not lead to the prohibition of agreements, decisions by associations of undertakings or concerted practices which may affect trade between Member States but which do not restrict competition within the meaning of Article 81(1) of the Treaty, or which fulfil the conditions of Article 81(3) of the Treaty or which are covered by a Regulation for the application of Article 81(3) of the Treaty. Member States shall not under this Regulation be precluded from adopting and applying on their territory stricter national laws which prohibit or sanction unilateral conduct engaged in by undertakings.

3.   Without prejudice to general principles and other provisions of Community law, paragraphs 1 and 2 do not apply when

the competition authorities and the courts of the Member States apply national merger control laws nor do they preclude the application of provisions of national law that predominantly pursue an objective different from that pursued by Articles 81 and 82 of the Treaty.

CHAPTER II

POWERS

Article 4

POWERS OF THE COMMISSION

For the purpose of applying Articles 81 and 82 of the Treaty, the Commission shall have the powers provided for by this Regulation.

Article 5

POWERS OF THE COMPETITION AUTHORITIES OF THE MEMBER STATES

The competition authorities of the Member States shall have the power to apply Articles 81 and 82 of the Treaty in individual cases. For this purpose, acting on their own initiative or on a complaint, they may take the following decisions:

—requiring that an infringement be brought to an end,

—ordering interim measures,

—accepting commitments,

—imposing fines, periodic penalty payments or any other penalty provided for in their national law.

Where on the basis of the information in their possession the conditions for prohibition are not met they may likewise decide that there are no grounds for action on their part.

Article 6

POWERS OF THE NATIONAL COURTS

National courts shall have the power to apply Articles 81 and 82 of the Treaty.

CHAPTER III

COMMISSION DECISIONS

Article 7

FINDING AND TERMINATION OF INFRINGEMENT

1.   Where the Commission, acting on a complaint or on its own initiative, finds that there is an infringement of Article 81 or of Article 82 of the Treaty, it may by decision require the undertakings and associations of undertakings concerned to bring such infringement to an end. For this purpose, it may impose on them any behavioural or structural remedies which are proportionate to the infringement committed and necessary to bring the infringement effectively to an end. Structural remedies can only be imposed either where there is no equally effective behavioural remedy or where any equally effective behavioural remedy would be more burdensome for the undertaking concerned than the structural remedy. If the Commission has a legitimate interest in doing so, it may also find that an infringement has been committed in the past.

2.   Those entitled to lodge a complaint for the purposes of paragraph 1 are natural or legal persons who can show a legitimate interest and Member States.

Article 8

INTERIM MEASURES

1.   In cases of urgency due to the risk of serious and irreparable damage to competition, the Commission, acting on its own initiative may by decision, on the basis of a prima facie finding of infringement, order interim measures.

2.   A decision under paragraph 1 shall apply for a specified period of time and may be renewed in so far this is necessary and appropriate.

Article 9

COMMITMENTS

1.   Where the Commission intends to adopt a decision requiring that an infringement be brought to an end and the undertakings concerned offer commitments to meet the concerns expressed to them by the Commission in its preliminary assessment, the Commission may by decision make those commitments binding on the undertakings. Such a decision may be adopted for a specified period and shall conclude that there are no longer grounds for action by the Commission.

2.   The Commission may, upon request or on its own initiative, reopen the proceedings:

(a)   where there has been a material change in any of the facts on which the decision was based;

(b)   where the undertakings concerned act contrary to their commitments; or

(c)   where the decision was based on incomplete, incorrect or misleading information provided by the parties.

Article 10

FINDING OF INAPPLICABILITY

Where the Community public interest relating to the application of Articles 81 and 82 of the Treaty so requires, the Commission, acting on its own initiative, may by decision find that Article 81 of the Treaty is not applicable to an agreement, a decision by an association of undertakings or a concerted practice, either because the conditions of Article 81(1) of the Treaty are not fulfilled, or because the conditions of Article 81(3) of the Treaty are satisfied.

The Commission may likewise make such a finding with reference to Article 82 of the Treaty.

CHAPTER IV

COOPERATION

Article 11

COOPERATION BETWEEN THE COMMISSION AND THE COMPETITION AUTHORITIES OF THE MEMBER STATES

1.   The Commission and the competition authorities of the Member States shall apply the Community competition rules in close cooperation.

2.   The Commission shall transmit to the competition authorities of the Member States copies of the most important documents it has collected with a view to applying Articles 7, 8, 9, 10 and Article 29(1). At the request of the competition authority of a Member State, the Commission shall provide it with a copy of other existing documents necessary for the assessment of the case.

3.   The competition authorities of the Member States shall, when acting under Article 81 or Article 82 of the Treaty, inform the Commission in writing before or without delay after commencing the first formal investigative measure. This information may also be

made available to the competition authorities of the other Member States.

4.   No later than 30 days before the adoption of a decision requiring that an infringement be brought to an end, accepting commitments or withdrawing the benefit of a block exemption Regulation, the competition authorities of the Member States shall inform the Commission. To that effect, they shall provide the Commission with a summary of the case, the envisaged decision or, in the absence thereof, any other document indicating the proposed course of action. This information may also be made available to the competition authorities of the other Member States. At the request of the Commission, the acting competition authority shall make available to the Commission other documents it holds which are necessary for the assessment of the case. The information supplied to the Commission may be made available to the competition authorities of the other Member States. National competition authorities may also exchange between themselves information necessary for the assessment of a case that they are dealing with under Article 81 or Article 82 of the Treaty.

5.   The competition authorities of the Member States may consult the Commission on any case involving the application of Community law.

6.   The initiation by the Commission of proceedings for the adoption of a decision under Chapter III shall relieve the competition authorities of the Member States of their competence to apply Articles 81 and 82 of the Treaty. If a competition authority of a Member State is already acting on a case, the Commission shall only initiate proceedings after consulting with that national competition authority.

Article 12

EXCHANGE OF INFORMATION

1.   For the purpose of applying Articles 81 and 82 of the Treaty the Commission and the competition authorities of the Member States shall have the power to provide one another with and use in evidence any matter of fact or of law, including confidential information.

2.   Information exchanged shall only be used in evidence for the purpose of applying Article 81 or Article 82 of the Treaty and in respect of the subject-matter for which it was collected by the transmitting authority. However, where national competition law is applied in the same case and in parallel to Community competition law and does not lead to a different outcome, information exchanged

under this Article may also be used for the application of national competition law.

3.   Information exchanged pursuant to paragraph 1 can only be used in evidence to impose sanctions on natural persons where:

—the law of the transmitting authority foresees sanctions of a similar kind in relation to an infringement of Article 81 or Article 82 of the Treaty or, in the absence thereof,

—the information has been collected in a way which respects the same level of protection of the rights of defence of natural persons as provided for under the national rules of the receiving authority. However, in this case, the information exchanged cannot be used by the receiving authority to impose custodial sanctions.

Article 13

SUSPENSION OR TERMINATION OF PROCEEDINGS

1.   Where competition authorities of two or more Member States have received a complaint or are acting on their own initiative under Article 81 or Article 82 of the Treaty against the same agreement, decision of an association or practice, the fact that one authority is dealing with the case shall be sufficient grounds for the others to suspend the proceedings before them or to reject the complaint. The Commission may likewise reject a complaint on the ground that a competition authority of a Member State is dealing with the case.

2.   Where a competition authority of a Member State or the Commission has received a complaint against an agreement, decision of an association or practice which has already been dealt with by another competition authority, it may reject it.

Article 14

ADVISORY COMMITTEE

1.   The Commission shall consult an Advisory Committee on Restrictive Practices and Dominant Positions prior to the taking of any decision under Articles 7, 8, 9, 10, 23, Article 24(2) and Article 29(1).

2.   For the discussion of individual cases, the Advisory Committee shall be composed of representatives of the competition authorities of the Member States. For meetings in which issues other than individual cases are being discussed, an additional Member State representative competent in competition matters may be

appointed. Representatives may, if unable to attend, be replaced by other representatives.

3.   The consultation may take place at a meeting convened and chaired by the Commission, held not earlier than 14 days after dispatch of the notice convening it, together with a summary of the case, an indication of the most important documents and a preliminary draft decision. In respect of decisions pursuant to Article 8, the meeting may be held seven days after the dispatch of the operative part of a draft decision. Where the Commission dispatches a notice convening the meeting which gives a shorter period of notice than those specified above, the meeting may take place on the proposed date in the absence of an objection by any Member State. The Advisory Committee shall deliver a written opinion on the Commission's preliminary draft decision. It may deliver an opinion even if some members are absent and are not represented. At the request of one or several members, the positions stated in the opinion shall be reasoned.

4.   Consultation may also take place by written procedure. However, if any Member State so requests, the Commission shall convene a meeting. In case of written procedure, the Commission shall determine a time-limit of not less than 14 days within which the Member States are to put forward their observations for circulation to all other Member States. In case of decisions to be taken pursuant to Article 8, the time-limit of 14 days is replaced by seven days. Where the Commission determines a time-limit for the written procedure which is shorter than those specified above, the proposed time-limit shall be applicable in the absence of an objection by any Member State.

5.   The Commission shall take the utmost account of the opinion delivered by the Advisory Committee. It shall inform the Committee of the manner in which its opinion has been taken into account.

6.   Where the Advisory Committee delivers a written opinion, this opinion shall be appended to the draft decision. If the Advisory Committee recommends publication of the opinion, the Commission shall carry out such publication taking into account the legitimate interest of undertakings in the protection of their business secrets.

7.   At the request of a competition authority of a Member State, the Commission shall include on the agenda of the Advisory Committee cases that are being dealt with by a competition authority of a Member State under Article 81 or Article 82 of the Treaty. The Commission may also do so on its own initiative. In either case, the Commission shall inform the competition authority concerned.

A request may in particular be made by a competition authority of a Member State in respect of a case where the Commission intends to initiate proceedings with the effect of Article 11(6).

The Advisory Committee shall not issue opinions on cases dealt with by competition authorities of the Member States. The Advisory Committee may also discuss general issues of Community competition law.

Article 15

COOPERATION WITH NATIONAL COURTS

1.   In proceedings for the application of Article 81 or Article 82 of the Treaty, courts of the Member States may ask the Commission to transmit to them information in its possession or its opinion on questions concerning the application of the Community competition rules.

2.   Member States shall forward to the Commission a copy of any written judgment of national courts deciding on the application of Article 81 or Article 82 of the Treaty. Such copy shall be forwarded without delay after the full written judgment is notified to the parties.

3.   Competition authorities of the Member States, acting on their own initiative, may submit written observations to the national courts of their Member State on issues relating to the application of Article 81 or Article 82 of the Treaty. With the permission of the court in question, they may also submit oral observations to the national courts of their Member State. Where the coherent application of Article 81 or Article 82 of the Treaty so requires, the Commission, acting on its own initiative, may submit written observations to courts of the Member States. With the permission of the court in question, it may also make oral observations.

For the purpose of the preparation of their observations only, the competition authorities of the Member States and the Commission may request the relevant court of the Member State to transmit or ensure the transmission to them of any documents necessary for the assessment of the case.

4.   This Article is without prejudice to wider powers to make observations before courts conferred on competition authorities of the Member States under the law of their Member State.

Article 16

UNIFORM APPLICATION OF COMMUNITY COMPETITION LAW

1. When national courts rule on agreements, decisions or practices under Article 81 or Article 82 of the Treaty which are already the subject of a Commission decision, they cannot take decisions running counter to the decision adopted by the Commission. They must also avoid giving decisions which would conflict with a decision contemplated by the Commission in proceedings it has initiated. To that effect, the national court may assess whether it is necessary to stay its proceedings. This obligation is without prejudice to the rights and obligations under Article 234 of the Treaty.

2. When competition authorities of the Member States rule on agreements, decisions or practices under Article 81 or Article 82 of the Treaty which are already the subject of a Commission decision, they cannot take decisions which would run counter to the decision adopted by the Commission.

CHAPTER V

POWERS OF INVESTIGATION

Article 17

INVESTIGATIONS INTO SECTORS OF THE ECONOMY AND INTO TYPES OF AGREEMENTS

1. Where the trend of trade between Member States, the rigidity of prices or other circumstances suggest that competition may be restricted or distorted within the common market, the Commission may conduct its inquiry into a particular sector of the economy or into a particular type of agreements across various sectors. In the course of that inquiry, the Commission may request the undertakings or associations of undertakings concerned to supply the information necessary for giving effect to Articles 81 and 82 of the Treaty and may carry out any inspections necessary for that purpose.

The Commission may in particular request the undertakings or associations of undertakings concerned to communicate to it all agreements, decisions and concerted practices.

The Commission may publish a report on the results of its inquiry into particular sectors of the economy or particular types of agreements across various sectors and invite comments from interested parties.

2.   Articles 14, 18, 19, 20, 22, 23 and 24 shall apply mutatis mutandis.

Article 18

REQUESTS FOR INFORMATION

1.   In order to carry out the duties assigned to it by this Regulation, the Commission may, by simple request or by decision, require undertakings and associations of undertakings to provide all necessary information.

2.   When sending a simple request for information to an undertaking or association of undertakings, the Commission shall state the legal basis and the purpose of the request, specify what information is required and fix the time-limit within which the information is to be provided, and the penalties provided for in Article 23 for supplying incorrect or misleading information.

3.   Where the Commission requires undertakings and associations of undertakings to supply information by decision, it shall state the legal basis and the purpose of the request, specify what information is required and fix the time-limit within which it is to be provided. It shall also indicate the penalties provided for in Article 23 and indicate or impose the penalties provided for in Article 24. It shall further indicate the right to have the decision reviewed by the Court of Justice.

4.   The owners of the undertakings or their representatives and, in the case of legal persons, companies or firms, or associations having no legal personality, the persons authorised to represent them by law or by their constitution shall supply the information requested on behalf of the undertaking or the association of undertakings concerned. Lawyers duly authorised to act may supply the information on behalf of their clients. The latter shall remain fully responsible if the information supplied is incomplete, incorrect or misleading.

5.   The Commission shall without delay forward a copy of the simple request or of the decision to the competition authority of the Member State in whose territory the seat of the undertaking or association of undertakings is situated and the competition authority of the Member State whose territory is affected.

6.   At the request of the Commission the governments and competition authorities of the Member States shall provide the Commission with all necessary information to carry out the duties assigned to it by this Regulation.

Article 19

POWER TO TAKE STATEMENTS

1. In order to carry out the duties assigned to it by this Regulation, the Commission may interview any natural or legal person who consents to be interviewed for the purpose of collecting information relating to the subject-matter of an investigation.

2. Where an interview pursuant to paragraph 1 is conducted in the premises of an undertaking, the Commission shall inform the competition authority of the Member State in whose territory the interview takes place. If so requested by the competition authority of that Member State, its officials may assist the officials and other accompanying persons authorised by the Commission to conduct the interview.

Article 20

THE COMMISSION'S POWERS OF INSPECTION

1. In order to carry out the duties assigned to it by this Regulation, the Commission may conduct all necessary inspections of undertakings and associations of undertakings.

2. The officials and other accompanying persons authorised by the Commission to conduct an inspection are empowered:

(a) to enter any premises, land and means of transport of undertakings and associations of undertakings;

(b) to examine the books and other records related to the business, irrespective of the medium on which they are stored;

(c) to take or obtain in any form copies of or extracts from such books or records;

(d) to seal any business premises and books or records for the period and to the extent necessary for the inspection;

(e) to ask any representative or member of staff of the undertaking or association of undertakings for explanations on facts or documents relating to the subject-matter and purpose of the inspection and to record the answers.

3. The officials and other accompanying persons authorised by the Commission to conduct an inspection shall exercise their powers upon production of a written authorisation specifying the subject matter and purpose of the inspection and the penalties provided for in Article 23 in case the production of the required books or other

records related to the business is incomplete or where the answers to questions asked under paragraph 2 of the present Article are incorrect or misleading. In good time before the inspection, the Commission shall give notice of the inspection to the competition authority of the Member State in whose territory it is to be conducted.

4.   Undertakings and associations of undertakings are required to submit to inspections ordered by decision of the Commission. The decision shall specify the subject matter and purpose of the inspection, appoint the date on which it is to begin and indicate the penalties provided for in Articles 23 and 24 and the right to have the decision reviewed by the Court of Justice. The Commission shall take such decisions after consulting the competition authority of the Member State in whose territory the inspection is to be conducted.

5.   Officials of as well as those authorised or appointed by the competition authority of the Member State in whose territory the inspection is to be conducted shall, at the request of that authority or of the Commission, actively assist the officials and other accompanying persons authorised by the Commission. To this end, they shall enjoy the powers specified in paragraph 2.

6.   Where the officials and other accompanying persons authorised by the Commission find that an undertaking opposes an inspection ordered pursuant to this Article, the Member State concerned shall afford them the necessary assistance, requesting where appropriate the assistance of the police or of an equivalent enforcement authority, so as to enable them to conduct their inspection.

7.   If the assistance provided for in paragraph 6 requires authorisation from a judicial authority according to national rules, such authorisation shall be applied for. Such authorisation may also be applied for as a precautionary measure.

8.   Where authorisation as referred to in paragraph 7 is applied for, the national judicial authority shall control that the Commission decision is authentic and that the coercive measures envisaged are neither arbitrary nor excessive having regard to the subject matter of the inspection. In its control of the proportionality of the coercive measures, the national judicial authority may ask the Commission, directly or through the Member State competition authority, for detailed explanations in particular on the grounds the Commission has for suspecting infringement of Articles 81 and 82 of the Treaty, as well as on the seriousness of the suspected infringement and on the nature of the involvement of the undertaking concerned. However, the national judicial authority may

not call into question the necessity for the inspection nor demand that it be provided with the information in the Commission's file. The lawfulness of the Commission decision shall be subject to review only by the Court of Justice.

Article 21

INSPECTION OF OTHER PREMISES

1. If a reasonable suspicion exists that books or other records related to the business and to the subject-matter of the inspection, which may be relevant to prove a serious violation of Article 81 or Article 82 of the Treaty, are being kept in any other premises, land and means of transport, including the homes of directors, managers and other members of staff of the undertakings and associations of undertakings concerned, the Commission can by decision order an inspection to be conducted in such other premises, land and means of transport.

2. The decision shall specify the subject matter and purpose of the inspection, appoint the date on which it is to begin and indicate the right to have the decision reviewed by the Court of Justice. It shall in particular state the reasons that have led the Commission to conclude that a suspicion in the sense of paragraph 1 exists. The Commission shall take such decisions after consulting the competition authority of the Member State in whose territory the inspection is to be conducted.

3. A decision adopted pursuant to paragraph 1 cannot be executed without prior authorisation from the national judicial authority of the Member State concerned. The national judicial authority shall control that the Commission decision is authentic and that the coercive measures envisaged are neither arbitrary nor excessive having regard in particular to the seriousness of the suspected infringement, to the importance of the evidence sought, to the involvement of the undertaking concerned and to the reasonable likelihood that business books and records relating to the subject matter of the inspection are kept in the premises for which the authorisation is requested. The national judicial authority may ask the Commission, directly or through the Member State competition authority, for detailed explanations on those elements which are necessary to allow its control of the proportionality of the coercive measures envisaged.

However, the national judicial authority may not call into question the necessity for the inspection nor demand that it be provided with information in the Commission's file. The lawfulness of the Commission decision shall be subject to review only by the Court of Justice.

4.   The officials and other accompanying persons authorised by the Commission to conduct an inspection ordered in accordance with paragraph 1 of this Article shall have the powers set out in Article 20(2)(a), (b) and (c). Article 20(5) and (6) shall apply mutatis mutandis.

Article 22

INVESTIGATIONS BY COMPETITION AUTHORITIES OF MEMBER STATES

1.   The competition authority of a Member State may in its own territory carry out any inspection or other fact-finding measure under its national law on behalf and for the account of the competition authority of another Member State in order to establish whether there has been an infringement of Article 81 or Article 82 of the Treaty. Any exchange and use of the information collected shall be carried out in accordance with Article 12.

2.   At the request of the Commission, the competition authorities of the Member States shall undertake the inspections which the Commission considers to be necessary under Article 20(1) or which it has ordered by decision pursuant to Article 20(4). The officials of the competition authorities of the Member States who are responsible for conducting these inspections as well as those authorised or appointed by them shall exercise their powers in accordance with their national law.

If so requested by the Commission or by the competition authority of the Member State in whose territory the inspection is to be conducted, officials and other accompanying persons authorised by the Commission may assist the officials of the authority concerned.

CHAPTER VI

PENALTIES

Article 23

FINES

1.   The Commission may by decision impose on undertakings and associations of undertakings fines not exceeding 1% of the total turnover in the preceding business year where, intentionally or negligently:

(a) they supply incorrect or misleading information in response to a request made pursuant to Article 17 or Article 18(2);

(b) in response to a request made by decision adopted pursuant to Article 17 or Article 18(3), they supply incorrect, incomplete or misleading information or do not supply information within the required time-limit;

(c) they produce the required books or other records related to the business in incomplete form during inspections under Article 20 or refuse to submit to inspections ordered by a decision adopted pursuant to Article 20(4);

(d) in response to a question asked in accordance with Article 20(2)(e),

—they give an incorrect or misleading answer,

—they fail to rectify within a time-limit set by the Commission an incorrect, incomplete or misleading answer given by a member of staff, or

—they fail or refuse to provide a complete answer on facts relating to the subject-matter and purpose of an inspection ordered by a decision adopted pursuant to Article 20(4);

(e) seals affixed in accordance with Article 20(2)(d) by officials or other accompanying persons authorised by the Commission have been broken.

2. The Commission may by decision impose fines on undertakings and associations of undertakings where, either intentionally or negligently:

(a) they infringe Article 81 or Article 82 of the Treaty; or

(b) they contravene a decision ordering interim measures under Article 8; or

(c) they fail to comply with a commitment made binding by a decision pursuant to Article 9.

For each undertaking and association of undertakings participating in the infringement, the fine shall not exceed 10% of its total turnover in the preceding business year.

Where the infringement of an association relates to the activities of its members, the fine shall not exceed 10% of the sum of the total turnover of each member active on the market affected by the infringement of the association.

3.   In fixing the amount of the fine, regard shall be had both to the gravity and to the duration of the infringement.

4.   When a fine is imposed on an association of undertakings taking account of the turnover of its members and the association is not solvent, the association is obliged to call for contributions from its members to cover the amount of the fine.

Where such contributions have not been made to the association within a time-limit fixed by the Commission, the Commission may require payment of the fine directly by any of the undertakings whose representatives were members of the decision-making bodies concerned of the association.

After the Commission has required payment under the second subparagraph, where necessary to ensure full payment of the fine, the Commission may require payment of the balance by any of the members of the association which were active on the market on which the infringement occurred.

However, the Commission shall not require payment under the second or the third subparagraph from undertakings which show that they have not implemented the infringing decision of the association and either were not aware of its existence or have actively distanced themselves from it before the Commission started investigating the case.

The financial liability of each undertaking in respect of the payment of the fine shall not exceed 10% of its total turnover in the preceding business year.

5.   Decisions taken pursuant to paragraphs 1 and 2 shall not be of a criminal law nature.

Article 24

PERIODIC PENALTY PAYMENTS

1.   The Commission may, by decision, impose on undertakings or associations of undertakings periodic penalty payments not exceeding 5% of the average daily turnover in the preceding business year per day and calculated from the date appointed by the decision, in order to compel them:

(a)   to put an end to an infringement of Article 81 or Article 82 of the Treaty, in accordance with a decision taken pursuant to Article 7;

(b)   to comply with a decision ordering interim measures taken pursuant to Article 8;

(c) to comply with a commitment made binding by a decision pursuant to Article 9;

(d) to supply complete and correct information which it has requested by decision taken pursuant to Article 17 or Article 18(3);

(e) to submit to an inspection which it has ordered by decision taken pursuant to Article 20(4).

2. Where the undertakings or associations of undertakings have satisfied the obligation which the periodic penalty payment was intended to enforce, the Commission may fix the definitive amount of the periodic penalty payment at a figure lower than that which would arise under the original decision. Article 23(4) shall apply correspondingly.

CHAPTER VII

LIMITATION PERIODS

Article 25

LIMITATION PERIODS FOR THE IMPOSITION OF PENALTIES

1. The powers conferred on the Commission by Articles 23 and 24 shall be subject to the following limitation periods:

(a) three years in the case of infringements of provisions concerning requests for information or the conduct of inspections;

(b) five years in the case of all other infringements.

2. Time shall begin to run on the day on which the infringement is committed. However, in the case of continuing or repeated infringements, time shall begin to run on the day on which the infringement ceases.

3. Any action taken by the Commission or by the competition authority of a Member State for the purpose of the investigation or proceedings in respect of an infringement shall interrupt the limitation period for the imposition of fines or periodic penalty payments. The limitation period shall be interrupted with effect from the date on which the action is notified to at least one undertaking or association of undertakings which has participated in the infringement. Actions which interrupt the running of the period shall include in particular the following:

(a) written requests for information by the Commission or by the competition authority of a Member State;

(b)   written authorisations to conduct inspections issued to its officials by the Commission or by the competition authority of a Member State;

(c)   the initiation of proceedings by the Commission or by the competition authority of a Member State;

(d)   notification of the statement of objections of the Commission or of the competition authority of a Member State.

4.   The interruption of the limitation period shall apply for all the undertakings or associations of undertakings which have participated in the infringement.

5.   Each interruption shall start time running afresh. However, the limitation period shall expire at the latest on the day on which a period equal to twice the limitation period has elapsed without the Commission having imposed a fine or a periodic penalty payment. That period shall be extended by the time during which limitation is suspended pursuant to paragraph 6.

6.   The limitation period for the imposition of fines or periodic penalty payments shall be suspended for as long as the decision of the Commission is the subject of proceedings pending before the Court of Justice.

Article 26

LIMITATION PERIOD FOR THE ENFORCEMENT OF PENALTIES

1.   The power of the Commission to enforce decisions taken pursuant to Articles 23 and 24 shall be subject to a limitation period of five years.

2.   Time shall begin to run on the day on which the decision becomes final.

3.   The limitation period for the enforcement of penalties shall be interrupted:

(a)   by notification of a decision varying the original amount of the fine or periodic penalty payment or refusing an application for variation;

(b)   by any action of the Commission or of a Member State, acting at the request of the Commission, designed to enforce payment of the fine or periodic penalty payment.

4.   Each interruption shall start time running afresh.

5.   The limitation period for the enforcement of penalties shall be suspended for so long as:

(a)   time to pay is allowed;

(b)   enforcement of payment is suspended pursuant to a decision of the Court of Justice.

CHAPTER VIII

HEARINGS AND PROFESSIONAL SECRECY

Article 27

HEARING OF THE PARTIES, COMPLAINANTS AND OTHERS

1.   Before taking decisions as provided for in Articles 7, 8, 23 and Article 24(2), the Commission shall give the undertakings or associations of undertakings which are the subject of the proceedings conducted by the Commission the opportunity of being heard on the matters to which the Commission has taken objection. The Commission shall base its decisions only on objections on which the parties concerned have been able to comment. Complainants shall be associated closely with the proceedings.

2.   The rights of defence of the parties concerned shall be fully respected in the proceedings. They shall be entitled to have access to the Commission's file, subject to the legitimate interest of undertakings in the protection of their business secrets. The right of access to the file shall not extend to confidential information and internal documents of the Commission or the competition authorities of the Member States. In particular, the right of access shall not extend to correspondence between the Commission and the competition authorities of the Member States, or between the latter, including documents drawn up pursuant to Articles 11 and 14. Nothing in this paragraph shall prevent the Commission from disclosing and using information necessary to prove an infringement.

3.   If the Commission considers it necessary, it may also hear other natural or legal persons. Applications to be heard on the part of such persons shall, where they show a sufficient interest, be granted. The competition authorities of the Member States may also ask the Commission to hear other natural or legal persons.

4.   Where the Commission intends to adopt a decision pursuant to Article 9 or Article 10, it shall publish a concise summary of the case and the main content of the commitments or of the proposed course of action. Interested third parties may submit their observations within a time limit which is fixed by the Commission in

its publication and which may not be less than one month. Publication shall have regard to the legitimate interest of undertakings in the protection of their business secrets.

Article 28

PROFESSIONAL SECRECY

1.   Without prejudice to Articles 12 and 15, information collected pursuant to Articles 17 to 22 shall be used only for the purpose for which it was acquired.

2.   Without prejudice to the exchange and to the use of information foreseen in Articles 11, 12, 14, 15 and 27, the Commission and the competition authorities of the Member States, their officials, servants and other persons working under the supervision of these authorities as well as officials and civil servants of other authorities of the Member States shall not disclose information acquired or exchanged by them pursuant to this Regulation and of the kind covered by the obligation of professional secrecy. This obligation also applies to all representatives and experts of Member States attending meetings of the Advisory Committee pursuant to Article 14.

CHAPTER IX

EXEMPTION REGULATIONS

Article 29

WITHDRAWAL IN INDIVIDUAL CASES

1.   Where the Commission, empowered by a Council Regulation, such as Regulations 19/65/EEC, (EEC) No 2821/71, (EEC) No 3976/87, (EEC) No 1534/91 or (EEC) No 479/92, to apply Article 81(3) of the Treaty by regulation, has declared Article 81(1) of the Treaty inapplicable to certain categories of agreements, decisions by associations of undertakings or concerted practices, it may, acting on its own initiative or on a complaint, withdraw the benefit of such an exemption Regulation when it finds that in any particular case an agreement, decision or concerted practice to which the exemption Regulation applies has certain effects which are incompatible with Article 81(3) of the Treaty.

2.   Where, in any particular case, agreements, decisions by associations of undertakings or concerted practices to which a Commission Regulation referred to in paragraph 1 applies have effects which are incompatible with Article 81(3) of the Treaty in the territory of a Member State, or in a part thereof, which has all the characteristics of a distinct geographic market, the competition

authority of that Member State may withdraw the benefit of the Regulation in question in respect of that territory.

CHAPTER X

GENERAL PROVISIONS

Article 30

PUBLICATION OF DECISIONS

1.   The Commission shall publish the decisions, which it takes pursuant to Articles 7 to 10, 23 and 24.

2.   The publication shall state the names of the parties and the main content of the decision, including any penalties imposed. It shall have regard to the legitimate interest of undertakings in the protection of their business secrets.

Article 31

REVIEW BY THE COURT OF JUSTICE

The Court of Justice shall have unlimited jurisdiction to review decisions whereby the Commission has fixed a fine or periodic penalty payment. It may cancel, reduce or increase the fine or periodic penalty payment imposed.

Article 32

EXCLUSIONS

This Regulation shall not apply to:

(a) international tramp vessel services as defined in Article 1(3)(a) of Regulation (EEC) No 4056/86;

(b) a maritime transport service that takes place exclusively between ports in one and the same Member State as foreseen in Article 1(2) of Regulation (EEC) No 4056/86;

(c) air transport between Community airports and third countries.

* * *

Article 44

REPORT ON THE APPLICATION OF
THE PRESENT REGULATION

Five years from the date of application of this Regulation, the Commission shall report to the European Parliament and the Council on the functioning of this Regulation, in particular on the application of Article 11(6) and Article 17.

On the basis of this report, the Commission shall assess whether it is appropriate to propose to the Council a revision of this Regulation.

Article 45

ENTRY INTO FORCE

This Regulation shall enter into force on the 20th day following that of its publication in the Official Journal of the European Communities.

It shall apply from 1 May 2004.

This Regulation shall be binding in its entirety and directly applicable in all Member States.

Done at Brussels, 16 December 2002.

[footnotes omitted]

Appendix 3

UNITED STATES STATUTES

THE SHERMAN ANTITRUST ACT
(1890 as amended)

§ 1. Trusts and combinations in restraint of trade illegal

Every contract, combination in the form of trust or otherwise, or conspiracy, in restraint of trade or commerce among the several States, or with foreign nations, is declared to be illegal. Every person who shall make any contract or engage in any combination or conspiracy hereby declared to be illegal shall be deemed guilty of a felony, and, on conviction thereof, shall be punished by fine not exceeding $100,000,000 if a corporation, or, if any other person, $1,000,000, or by imprisonment not exceeding 10 years, or by both said punishments, in the discretion of the court.

§ 2. Monopolizing trade illegal

Every person who shall monopolize, or attempt to monopolize, or combine or conspire with any other person or persons, to monopolize any part of the trade or commerce among the several States, or with foreign nations, shall be deemed guilty of a felony, and, on conviction thereof, shall be punished by fine not exceeding $100,000,000 if a corporation, or, if any other person, $1,000,000, or by imprisonment not exceeding 10 years, or by both said punishments, in the discretion of the court.

* * *

§ 7. Conduct involving trade or commerce with foreign nations

FOREIGN TRADE ANTITRUST IMPROVEMENTS ACT OF 1982, TITLE IV

This Act shall not apply to conduct involving trade or commerce (other than import trade or import commerce) with foreign nations unless—

(1) such conduct has a direct, substantial, and reasonably foreseeable effect—

(A) on trade or commerce which is not trade or commerce with foreign nations, or on import trade or import commerce with foreign nations; or

(B) on export trade or export commerce with foreign nations, of a person engaged in such trade or commerce in the United States; and

(2) such effect gives rise to a claim under the provisions of sections 1 to 7 of this Act, other than this section.

If this Act applies to such conduct only because of the operation of paragraph (1)(B), then this Act shall apply to such conduct only for injury to export business in the United States.

THE CLAYTON ACT

(1914 as amended, principally in 1936 and 1950)

§ 3. Sale or lease on condition not to use goods of competitor

It shall be unlawful for any person engaged in commerce, in the course of such commerce, to lease or make a sale or contract for sale of goods, wares, merchandise, machinery, supplies, or other commodities, whether patented or unpatented, for use, consumption, or resale within the United States or any Territory thereof or the District of Columbia or any insular possession or other place under the jurisdiction of the United States, or fix a price charged therefor, or discount from, or rebate upon, such price, on the condition, agreement, or understanding that the lessee or purchaser thereof shall not use or deal in the goods, wares, merchandise, machinery, supplies, or other commodities of a competitor or competitors of the lessor or seller, where the effect of such lease, sale, or contract for sale or such condition, agreement, or understanding may be to substantially lessen competition or tend to create a monopoly in any line of commerce.

* * *

§ 4. Suits by persons injured

(a) Amount of recovery; prejudgment interest

Except as provided in subsection (b) of this section, any person who shall be injured in his business or property by reason of anything forbidden in the antitrust laws may sue therefor in any district court of the United States in the district in which the defendant resides or is found or has an agent, without respect to the amount in controversy, and shall recover threefold the damages by him sustained, and the cost of suit, including a reasonable attorney's fee.

The court may award under this section, pursuant to a motion by such person promptly made, simple interest on actual damages for the period beginning on the date of service of such person's pleading setting forth a claim under the antitrust laws and ending on the date of judgment, or for any shorter period therein, if the court finds that the award of such interest for such period is just in the circumstances. In determining whether an award of interest under this section for any period is just in the circumstances, the court shall consider only—

1) whether such person or the opposing party, or either party's representative, made motions or asserted claims or defenses so lacking in merit as to show that such party or representative acted intentionally for delay, or otherwise acted in bad faith;

2) whether, in the course of the action involved, such person or the opposing party, or either party's representative, violated any applicable rule, statute, or court order providing for sanctions for dilatory behavior or otherwise providing for expeditious proceedings; and

3) whether such person or the opposing party, or either party's representative, engaged in conduct primarily for the purpose of delaying the litigation or increasing the cost thereof.

(b) Amount of damages payable to foreign states and instrumentalities of foreign states

1) Except as provided in paragraph (2), any person who is a foreign state may not recover under subsection (a) of this section an amount in excess of the actual damages sustained by it and the cost of suit, including a reasonable attorney's fee.

2) Paragraph (1) shall not apply to a foreign state if—

A) such foreign state would be denied, under section 1605 (a)(2) of title 28, immunity in a case in which the action is based upon a commercial activity, or an act, that is the subject matter of its claim under this section;

B) such foreign state waives all defenses based upon or arising out of its status as a foreign state, to any claims brought against it in the same action;

C) such foreign state engages primarily in commercial activities; and

D) such foreign state does not function, with respect to the commercial activity, or the act, that is the subject matter of its claim under this section as a procurement entity for itself or for another foreign state.

* * *

§ 4A. Suits by United States; amount of recovery; prejudgment interest

Whenever the United States is hereafter injured in its business or property by reason of anything forbidden in the antitrust laws it may sue therefor in the United States district court for the district in which the defendant resides or is found or has an agent, without respect to the amount in controversy, and shall recover threefold the damages by it sustained and the cost of suit. The court may award under this section, pursuant to a motion by the United States promptly made, simple interest on actual damages for the period beginning on the date of service of the pleading of the United States setting forth a claim under the antitrust laws and ending on the date of judgment, or for any shorter period therein, if the court finds that the award of such interest for such period is just in the circumstances. In determining whether an award of interest under this section for any period is just in the circumstances, the court shall consider only—

(1) whether the United States or the opposing party, or either party's representative, made motions or asserted claims or defenses so lacking in merit as to show that such party or representative acted intentionally for delay or otherwise acted in bad faith;

(2) whether, in the course of the action involved, the United States or the opposing party, or either party's representative, violated any applicable rule, statute, or court order providing for sanctions for dilatory behavior or otherwise providing for expeditious proceedings;

(3) whether the United States or the opposing party, or either party's representative, engaged in conduct primarily for the purpose of delaying the litigation or increasing the cost thereof; and

(4) whether the award of such interest is necessary to compensate the United States adequately for the injury sustained by the United States.

* * *

§ 4C.　Actions by state attorneys general

(a) Parens patriae; monetary relief; damages; prejudgment interest

(1) Any attorney general of a State may bring a civil action in the name of such State, as parens patriae on behalf of natural persons residing in such State, in any district court of the United States having jurisdiction of the defendant, to secure monetary relief as provided in this section for injury sustained by such natural persons to their property by reason of any violation of sections 1 to 7 of this title. The court shall exclude from the amount of monetary relief awarded in such action any amount of monetary relief

(A) which duplicates amounts which have been awarded for the same injury, or

(B) which is properly allocable to

(i) natural persons who have excluded their claims pursuant to subsection (b)(2) of this section, and

(ii) any business entity.

(2) The court shall award the State as monetary relief threefold the total damage sustained as described in paragraph (1) of this subsection, and the cost of suit, including a reasonable attorney's fee. The court may award under this paragraph, pursuant to a motion by such State promptly made, simple interest on the total damage for the period beginning on the date of service of such State's pleading setting forth a claim under the antitrust laws and ending on the date of judgment, or for any shorter period therein, if the court finds that the award of such interest for such period is just in the circumstances. In determining whether an award of interest under this paragraph for any period is just in the circumstances, the court shall consider only—

(A) whether such State or the opposing party, or either party's representative, made motions or asserted claims or defenses so lacking in merit as to show that such party or representative acted intentionally for delay or otherwise acted in bad faith;

(B) whether, in the course of the action involved, such State or the opposing party, or either party's representative, violated any applicable rule, statute, or court order providing for sanctions for dilatory behavior or other wise providing for expeditious proceedings; and

(C) whether such State or the opposing party, or either party's representative, engaged in conduct primarily for the purpose of delaying the litigation or increasing the cost thereof.

(b)   Notice; exclusion election; final judgment

(1)   In any action brought under subsection (a)(1) of this section, the State attorney general shall, at such times, in such manner, and with such content as the court may direct, cause notice thereof to be given by publication. If the court finds that notice given solely by publication would deny due process of law to any person or persons, the court may direct further notice to such person or persons according to the circumstances of the case.

(2)   Any person on whose behalf an action is brought under subsection (a)(1) of this section may elect to exclude from adjudication the portion of the State claim for monetary relief attributable to him by filing notice of such election with the court within such time as specified in the notice given pursuant to paragraph (1) of this subsection.

(3)   The final judgment in an action under subsection (a)(1) of this section shall be res judicata as to any claim under section 15 of this title by any person on behalf of whom such action was brought and who fails to give such notice within the period specified in the notice given pursuant to paragraph (1) of this subsection.

(c)   Dismissal or compromise of action

An action under subsection (a)(1) of this section shall not be dismissed or compromised without the approval of the court, and notice of any proposed dismissal or compromise shall be given in such manner as the court directs.

(d) Attorneys' fees

In any action under subsection (a) of this section—

> (1) the amount of the plaintiffs' attorney's fee, if any, shall be determined by the court; and

> (2) the court may, in its discretion, award a reasonable attorney's fee to a prevailing defendant upon a finding that the State attorney general has acted in bad faith, vexatiously, wantonly, or for oppressive reasons.

* * *

§ 7. Acquisition by one corporation of stock of another

No person engaged in commerce or in any activity affecting commerce shall acquire, directly or indirectly, the whole or any part of the stock or other share capital and no person subject to the jurisdiction of the Federal Trade Commission shall acquire the whole or any part of the assets of another person engaged also in commerce or in any activity affecting commerce, where in any line of commerce or in any activity affecting commerce in any section of the country, the effect of such acquisition may be substantially to lessen competition, or to tend to create a monopoly.

No person shall acquire, directly or indirectly, the whole or any part of the stock or other share capital and no person subject to the jurisdiction of the Federal Trade Commission shall acquire the whole or any part of the assets of one or more persons engaged in commerce or in any activity affecting commerce, where in any line of commerce or in any activity affecting commerce in any section of the country, the effect of such acquisition, of such stocks or assets, or of the use of such stock by the voting or granting of proxies or otherwise, may be substantially to lessen competition, or to tend to create a monopoly.

* * *

§ 7A. [Hart-Scott-Rodino premerger notification and reporting omitted]

* * *

WEBB-POMERENE ACT (EXPORT TRADE ACT)
(1918 as amended)

§ 1. Terms defined

The words "export trade" wherever used in this Act mean solely trade or commerce in goods, wares, or merchandise exported, or in the course of being exported from the United States or any Territory thereof to any foreign nation; but the words "export trade" shall not be deemed to include the production, manufacture, or selling for consumption or for resale, within the United States or any Territory thereof, of such goods, wares, or merchandise, or any act in the course of such production, manufacture, or selling for consumption or for resale.

The words "trade within the United States" wherever used in this Act mean trade or commerce among the several States or in any Territory of the United States, or in the District of Columbia, or between any such Territory and another, or between any such Territory or Territories and any State or States or the District of Columbia, or between the District of Columbia and any State or States.

The word "association" wherever used in this subchapter means any corporation or combination, by contract or otherwise, of two or more persons, partnerships, or corporations.

§ 2. Export trade and antitrust legislation

Nothing contained in the Sherman Act shall be construed as declaring to be illegal an association entered into for the sole purpose of engaging in export trade and actually engaged solely in such export trade, or an agreement made or act done in the course of export trade by such association, provided such association, agreement, or act is not in restraint of trade within the United States, and is not in restraint of the export trade of any domestic competitor of such association: Provided, That such association does not, either in the United States or elsewhere, enter into any agreement, understanding, or conspiracy, or do any act which artificially or intentionally enhances or depresses prices within the United States of commodities of the class exported by such association, or which substantially lessens competition within the United States or otherwise restrains trade therein.

* * *

§ 4. Unfair methods of competition in export trade

The prohibition against "unfair methods of competition" and the remedies provided for enforcing said prohibition contained in the Federal Trade Commission Act shall be construed as extending to unfair methods of competition used in export trade against competitors engaged in export trade, even though the acts constituting such unfair methods are done without the territorial jurisdiction of the United States.

§ 5. Information required; powers of Federal Trade Commission

Every association which engages solely in export trade, within thirty days after its creation, shall file with the Federal Trade Commission a verified written statement setting forth the location of its offices or places of business and the names and addresses of all its officers and of all its stockholders or members, and if a corporation, a copy of its certificate or articles of incorporation and bylaws, and if unincorporated, a copy of its articles or contract of association, and on the 1st day of January of each year every association engaged solely in export trade shall make a like statement of the location of its offices or places of business and the names and addresses of all its officers and of all its stockholders or members and of all amendments to and changes in its articles or certificate of incorporation or in its articles or contract of association. It shall also furnish to the Commission such information as the Commission may require as to its organization business, conduct, practices, management, and relation to other associations, corporations, partnerships, and individuals. Any association which shall fail so to do shall not have the benefit of the provisions of section two and section three of this Act, and it shall also forfeit to the United States the sum of $100 for each and every day of the continuance of such failure, which forfeiture shall be payable into the Treasury of the United States, and shall be recoverable in a civil suit in the name of the United States brought in the district where the association has its principal office, or in any district in which it shall do business. It shall be the duty of the various United States attorneys, under the direction of the Attorney General of the United States, to prosecute for the recovery of the forfeiture. The costs and expenses of such prosecution shall be paid out of the appropriation for the expenses of the courts of the United States.

Whenever the Federal Trade Commission shall have reason to believe that an association or any agreement made or act done by such association is in restraint of trade within the United States or in restraint of the export trade of any domestic competitor of such association, or that an association either in the United States or elsewhere has entered into any agreement, understanding, or conspiracy, or done any act which artificially or intentionally enhances or depresses prices within the United States of commodities of the class exported by such association, or which substantially lessens competition within the United States or otherwise restrains trade therein, it shall summon such association, its officers, and agents to appear before it, and thereafter conduct an investigation into the alleged violations of law. Upon investigation, if it shall conclude that the law has been violated, it may make to such association recommendations for the readjustment of its business, in order that it may thereafter maintain its organization and management and conduct its business in accordance with law. If such association fails to comply with the recommendations of the Federal Trade Commission, said Commission shall refer its findings and recommendations to the Attorney General of the United States for such action thereon as he may deem proper.

For the purpose of enforcing these provisions the Federal Trade Commission shall have all the powers, so far as applicable, given it in the Federal Trade Commission Act.

EXPORT TRADING COMPANY ACT OF 1982

An act to encourage exports by facilitating the formation and operation of export trading companies, export trade associations, and the expansion of export trade services generally.

TITLE I—GENERAL PROVISIONS

SHORT TITLE

Sec. 101. This title may be cited as the "Export Trading Company Act of 1982".

FINDINGS; DECLARATION OF PURPOSE

Sec. 102. (a) The Congress finds that—

(1) United States exports are responsible for creating and maintaining one out of every nine manufacturing jobs in the United States and for generating one out of every seven dollars of total United States goods produced;

(2) the rapidly growing service-related industries are vital to the well-being of the United States economy inasmuch as they create jobs for seven out of every ten Americans, provide 65 per centum of the Nation's gross national product, and offer the greatest potential for significantly increased industrial trade involving finished products;

(3) trade deficits contribute to the decline of the dollar on international currency markets and have an inflationary impact on the United States economy;

(4) tens of thousands of small-and medium-sized United States businesses produce exportable goods or services but do not engage in exporting;

(5) although the United States is the world's leading agricultural exporting nation, many farm products are not marketed as widely

and effectively abroad as they could be through export trading companies;

(6)   export trade services in the United States are fragmented into a multitude of separate functions, and companies attempting to offer export trade services lack financial leverage to reach a significant number of potential United States exporters;

(7)   the United States needs well-developed export trade intermediaries which can achieve economies of scale and acquire expertise enabling them to export goods and services profitably, at low per unit cost to producers;

(8)   the development of export trading companies in the United States has been hampered by business attitudes and by government regulations;

(9)   those activities of State and local governmental authorities which initiate, facilitate, or expand exports of goods and services can be an important source for expansion of total United States exports, as well as for experimentation in the development of innovative export programs keyed to local, State, and regional economic needs;

(10) if United States trading companies are to be successful in promoting United States exports and in competing with foreign trading companies, they should be able to draw on the resources, expertise, and knowledge of the United States banking system, both in the United States and abroad; and

(11) the Department of Commerce is responsible for the development and promotion of United States exports, and especially for facilitating the export of finished products by United States manufacturers.

(b)   It is the purpose of this Act to increase United States exports of products and services by encouraging more efficient provisions of export trade services to United States producers and suppliers, in particular by establishing an office within the Department of Commerce to promote the formation of export trade associations and export trading companies, by permitting bank holding companies, bankers' banks, and Edge Act corporations and agreement corporations that are subsidiaries of bank holding companies to invest in export trading companies, by reducing restrictions on trade finance provided by financial institutions, and by modifying the application of the antitrust laws to certain export trade.

* * *

TITLE III—EXPORT TRADE
CERTIFICATES OF REVIEW

EXPORT TRADE PROMOTION DUTIES OF
SECRETARY OF COMMERCE

SEC. 301.   To promote and encourage export of trade, the Secretary may issue certificates of review and advise and assist any person with respect to applying for certificates of review.

APPLICATION FOR ISSUANCE OF
CERTIFICATE OF REVIEW

SEC. 302.   (a) To apply for a certificate of review, a person shall submit to the Secretary a written application which—

(1)   specifies conduct limited to export trade, and

(2)   is in a form and contains any information, including information pertaining to the overall market in which the applicant operates, required by rule or regulation promulgated under section 310.

(b)(1)   Within ten days after an application submitted under subsection (a) is received by the Secretary, the Secretary shall publish in the Federal Register a notice that announces that an application for a certificate of review has been submitted, identifies each person submitting the application, and describes the conduct for which the application is submitted.

(2)   Not later than seven days after an application submitted under subsection (a) is received by the Secretary, the Secretary shall transmit to the Attorney General—

(A)   a copy of the application—

(B)   any information submitted to the Secretary in connection with the application, and

(C)   any other relevant information (as determined by the Secretary) in the possession of the Secretary, including information regarding the market share of the applicant in the line of commerce to which the conduct specified in the application relates.

ISSUANCE OF CERTIFICATE

SEC. 303.   (a) A certificate of review shall be issued to any applicant that establishes that its specified export trade, export trade activities, and methods of operation will—

(1) result in neither a substantial lessening of competition or restraint of trade within the United States nor a substantial restraint of the export trade of any competitor of the applicant,

(2) not unreasonably enhance, stabilize, or depress, prices within the United States of the goods, wares, merchandise, or services of the class exported by the applicant,

(3) not constitute unfair methods of competition against competitors engaged in the export of goods, wares, merchandise or services of the class exported by the applicant, and

(4) not include any act that may reasonably be expected to result in the sale for consumption or resale within the United States of the goods, wares, merchandise, or services exported by the applicant.

(b) Within ninety days after the Secretary receives an application for a certificate of review, the Secretary shall determine whether the applicant's export trade, export trade activities, and methods of operation meet the standards of subsection (a). If the Secretary, with the concurrence of the Attorney General, determines that such standards are met, the Secretary shall issue to the applicant a certificate of review. The certificate of review shall specify—

(1) the export trade, export trade activities, and methods of operation to which the certificate applies,

(2) the persons to whom the certificate of review is issued, and

(3) any terms and conditions the Secretary or the Attorney General deems necessary to assure compliance with the standards of subsection (a)

(c) If the applicant indicates a special need for prompt disposition, the Secretary and the Attorney General may expedite action on the application, except that no certificate of review may be issued within thirty days of publication of notice in the Federal Register under section 302(b)(1).

(d)(1) If the Secretary denies in whole or in part an application for a certificate, he shall notify the applicant of his determination and the reasons for it.

(2) An applicant may, within thirty days of receipt of notification that the application has been denied in whole or in part, request the Secretary to reconsider the determination. The Secretary, with the concurrence of the Attorney General, shall notify the applicant of the determination upon reconsideration within thirty days of receipt of the request.

(e) If the Secretary denies an application for the issuance of a certificate of review and thereafter receives from the applicant a request for the return of documents submitted by the applicant in connection with the application for the certificate, the Secretary and the Attorney General shall return to the applicant, not later than thirty days after receipt of the request, the documents and all copies of the documents available to the Secretary and the Attorney General, except to the extent that the information contained in a document has been made available to the public.

(f) A certificate shall be void ab initio with respect to any export trade, export trade activities, or methods of operation for which a certificate was procured by fraud.

REPORTING REQUIREMENT; AMENDMENT OF CERTIFICATE; REVOCATION OF CERTIFICATE

SEC. 304.   (a)(1) Any applicant who receives a certificate of review—

(A) shall promptly report to the Secretary any change relevant to the matter specified in the certificate, and

(B) may submit to the Secretary an application to amend the certificate to reflect the effect of the change on the conduct specified in the certificate.

(2) An application for an amendment to a certificate of review shall be treated as an application for the issuance of a certificate. The effective date of an amendment shall be the date on which the application for the amendment is submitted to the Secretary.

(b)(1)   If the Secretary or the Attorney General has reason to believe that the export trade, export trade activities, or methods of operation of a person holding a certificate of review no longer comply with the standards of section 303(a), the Secretary shall request such information from such persons as the Secretary or the Attorney General deems necessary to resolve the matter of compliance. Failure to comply with such request shall be grounds for revocation of the certificate under paragraph (2).

(2) If the Secretary or the Attorney General determines that the export trade activities, or methods of operation of a person holding a certificate no longer comply with the standards of section 303 (a), or that such person has failed to comply with a request made under paragraph (1), the Secretary shall give written notice of the determination to such person. The notice shall include a statement of the circumstances underlying, and the reasons in support of, the determination. In the 60-day period beginning 30 days after the

notice is given, the Secretary shall revoke the certificate or modify it as the Secretary or the Attorney General deems necessary to cause the certificate to apply only to the export trade, export trade activities, or methods of operation which are in compliance with the standards of section 303(a).

(3) For purposes of carrying out this subsection, the Attorney General, and the Assistant Attorney General in charge of the antitrust division of the Department of Justice, may conduct investigations in the same manner as the Attorney General and the Assistant Attorney General conduct investigations under section 3 of the Antitrust Civil Process Act, except that no civil investigative demand may be issued to a person to whom a certificate of review is issued if such a person is the target of such investigation.

JUDICIAL REVIEW; ADMISSIBILITY

SEC.305.   (a) If the Secretary grants or denies, in whole or in part, an application for a certificate of review or for an amendment to a certificate, or revokes or modifies a certificate pursuant to section 304(b), any person aggrieved by such determination may, within 30 days of the determination, bring an action in any appropriate district court of the United States to set aside the determination on the ground that such determination is erroneous.

(b)   Except as provided in subsection (a), no action by the Secretary or the Attorney General pursuant to this title shall be subject to judicial review.

(c)   If the Secretary denies, in whole or in part, an application for a certificate of review or for an amendment to a certificate, or revokes or amends a certificate, neither the negative determination nor the statement of reasons therefor shall be admissible in evidence, in any administrative or judicial proceeding, in support of any claim under the antitrust laws.

PROTECTION CONFERRED BY CERTIFICATE OF REVIEW

SEC. 306.   (a) Except as provided in subsection (b), no criminal or civil action may be brought under the antitrust laws against a person to whom a certificate of review is issued which is based on conduct which is specified in, and complies with the terms of, a certificate issued under section 303 which certificate was in effect when the conduct occurred.

(b)(1)   Any person who has been injured as a result of conduct engaged in under a certificate of review may bring a civil action for injunctive relief, actual damages, the loss of interest on actual damages, and the cost of the suit (including a reasonable attorney's fee) for the failure to comply with the standards of section 303(a). Any action commenced under this title shall proceed as if it were an action commenced under section 4 or section 16 of the Clayton Act, except that the standards of section 303(a) of this title and the remedies provided in this paragraph shall be the exclusive standards and remedies applicable to such action.

(2) Any action brought under paragraph (1), there shall be filed within two years of the date the plaintiff has notice of the failure to comply with the standards of section 303(a) but in any event within four years after the accuse of action accrues.

(3) In any action brought under paragraph (1), there shall be a presumption that conduct which is specified in and complies with a certificate of review does comply with the standards of section 303 (a).

(4) In any action brought under paragraph (1), if the court finds that the conduct does comply with the standards of section 303(a), the court shall award to the person against whom the claim is brought the cost of suit attributable to defending against the claim (including a reasonable attorney's fee).

(5) The Attorney General may file suit pursuant to section 15 of the Clayton Act (15 U.S.C.25) to enjoin conduct threatening clear and irreparable harm to the national interest.

* * *

Editors' note: Title IV of the Export Trading Company Act is the Foreign Antitrust Improvements Act of 1982, which amends the Sherman and Federal Trade Commission Acts. The amendment to the Sherman Act is Section 7 of the Sherman Act, supra.

Index

References are to Pages